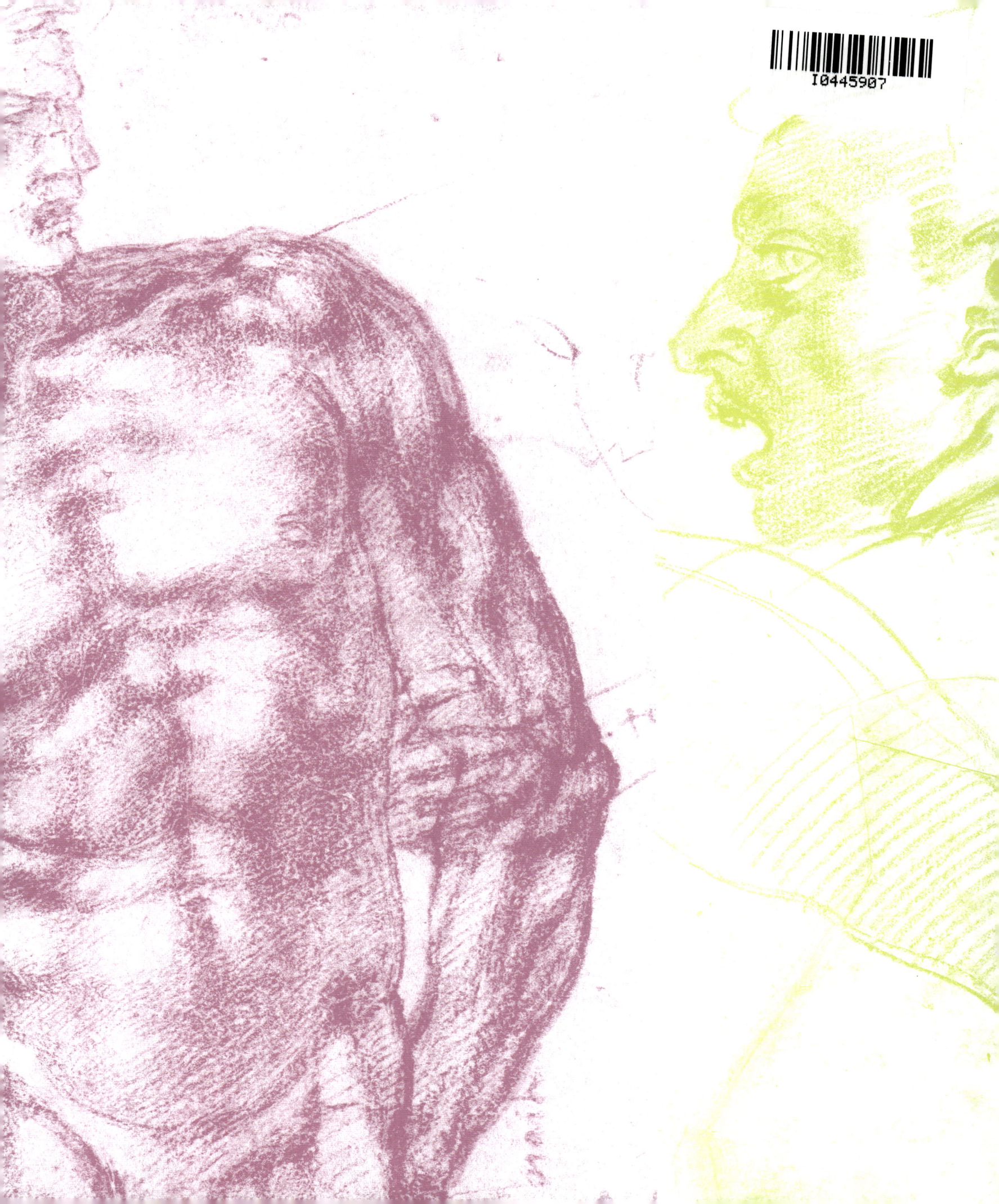

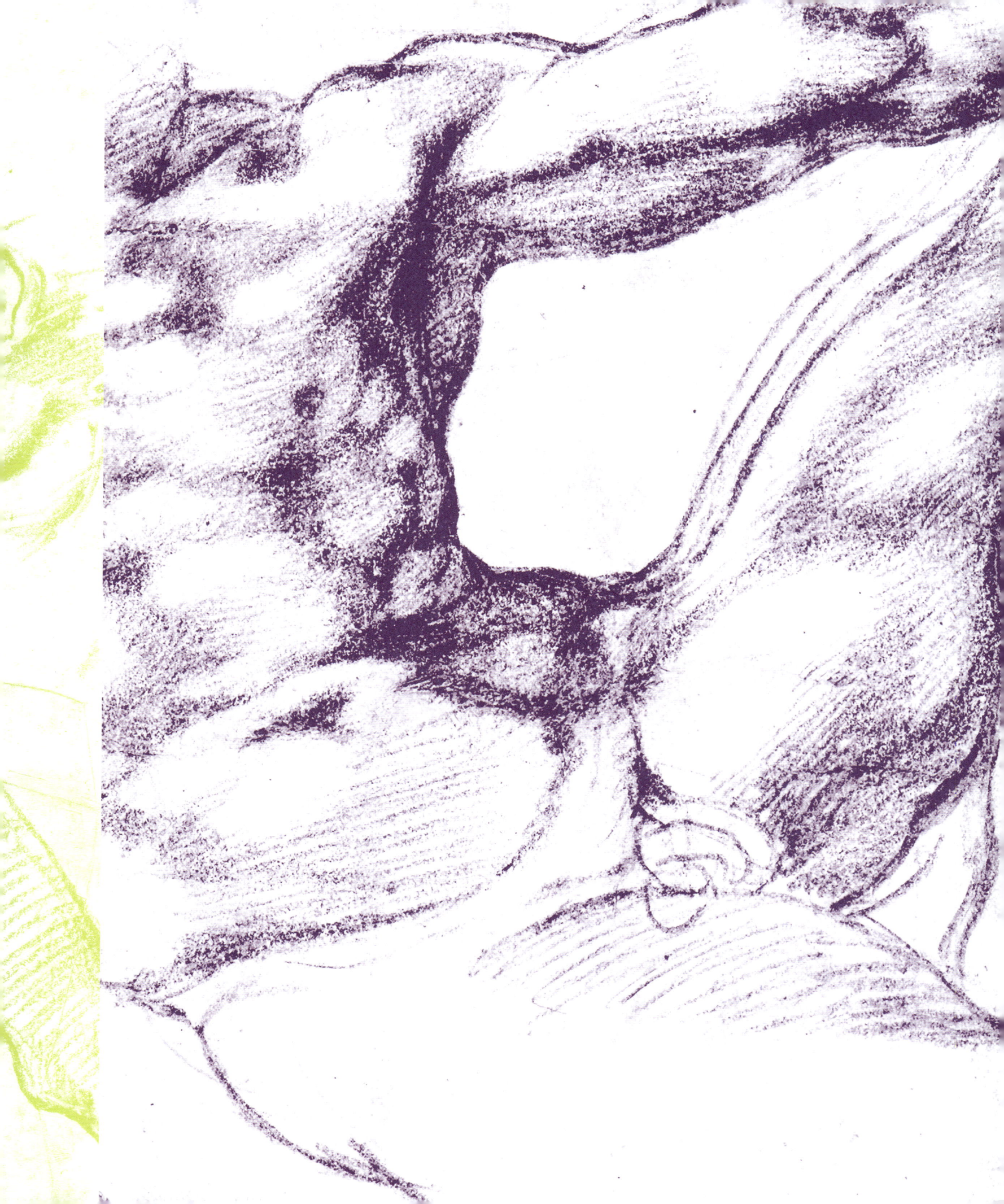

Michelangelo and Men

The Male Body in the Life and Work of Michelangelo

HANNIBAL

TEYLERS MUSEUM

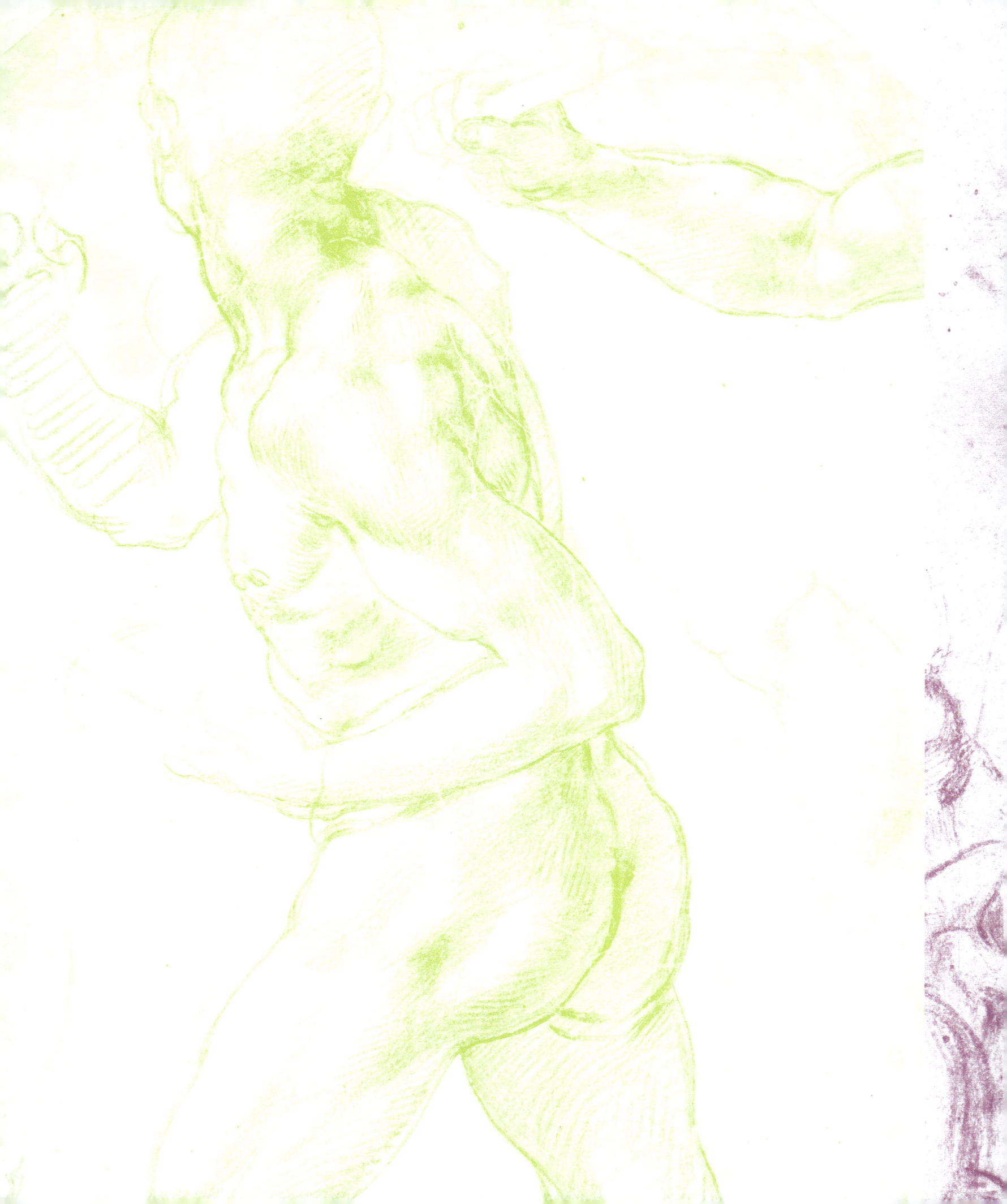

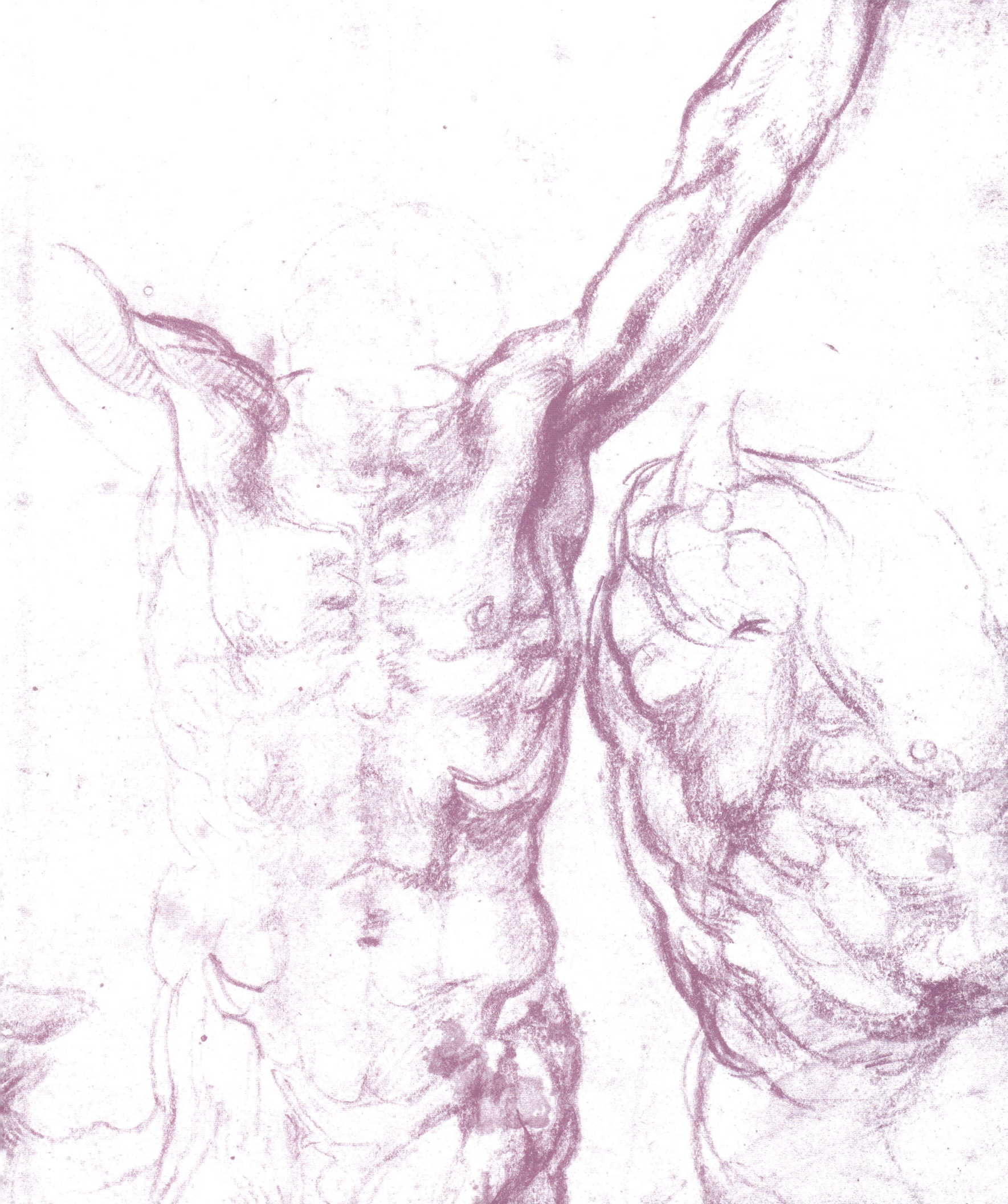

Preface   p. 11
Concise Timeline   p. 14
Introduction. Michelangelo's Men   p. 17
    Klazina Botke, Terry van Druten and Martin Gayford

Love

'Masculine Love'. Michelangelo and Boys   p. 35
    Michael Rocke
Poems and Letters. How Michelangelo Wrote the   p. 49
Unseeable and Drew the Unsayable
    Raymond Carlson

Body

Michelangelo and Antiquity. Ongoing Training   p. 73
    Martin Gayford
Baccio's Balls. Michelangelo and the Ideal Model   p. 99
    Terry van Druten
Michelangelo and the Anatomy of the Artist   p. 123
    Eric Boot

Mind

Michelangelo, Neoplatonism and the Idealised Body   p. 153
    Marieke van den Doel
Michelangelo and the Divine Body. Between Crucifixion and   p. 173
Resurrection
    Jennifer Sliwka

Connection

Michelangelo's *Battle of Cascina*. Its Context and   p. 203
Development
    Paul Joannides   p. 233
Friend and Enemy. The Men in Michelangelo's Life
    Klazina Botke

Notes   p. 250
Catalogue of Exhibited Works   p. 265
Bibliography   p. 271
Index   p. 279
Explanatory Notes   p. 281
About the Authors   p. 282
Acknowledgements   p. 282
Photo Credits   p. 283
Colophon   p. 284

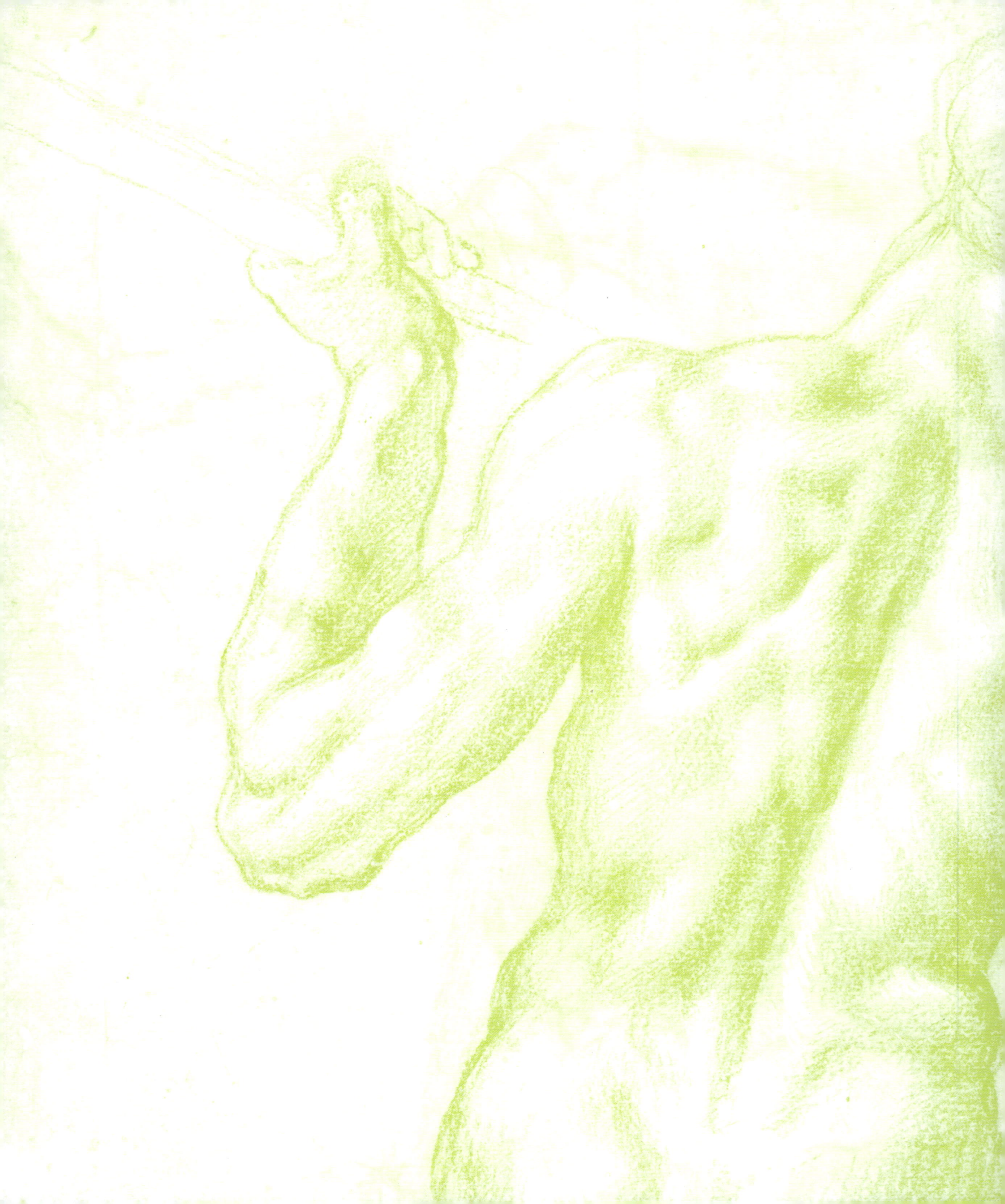

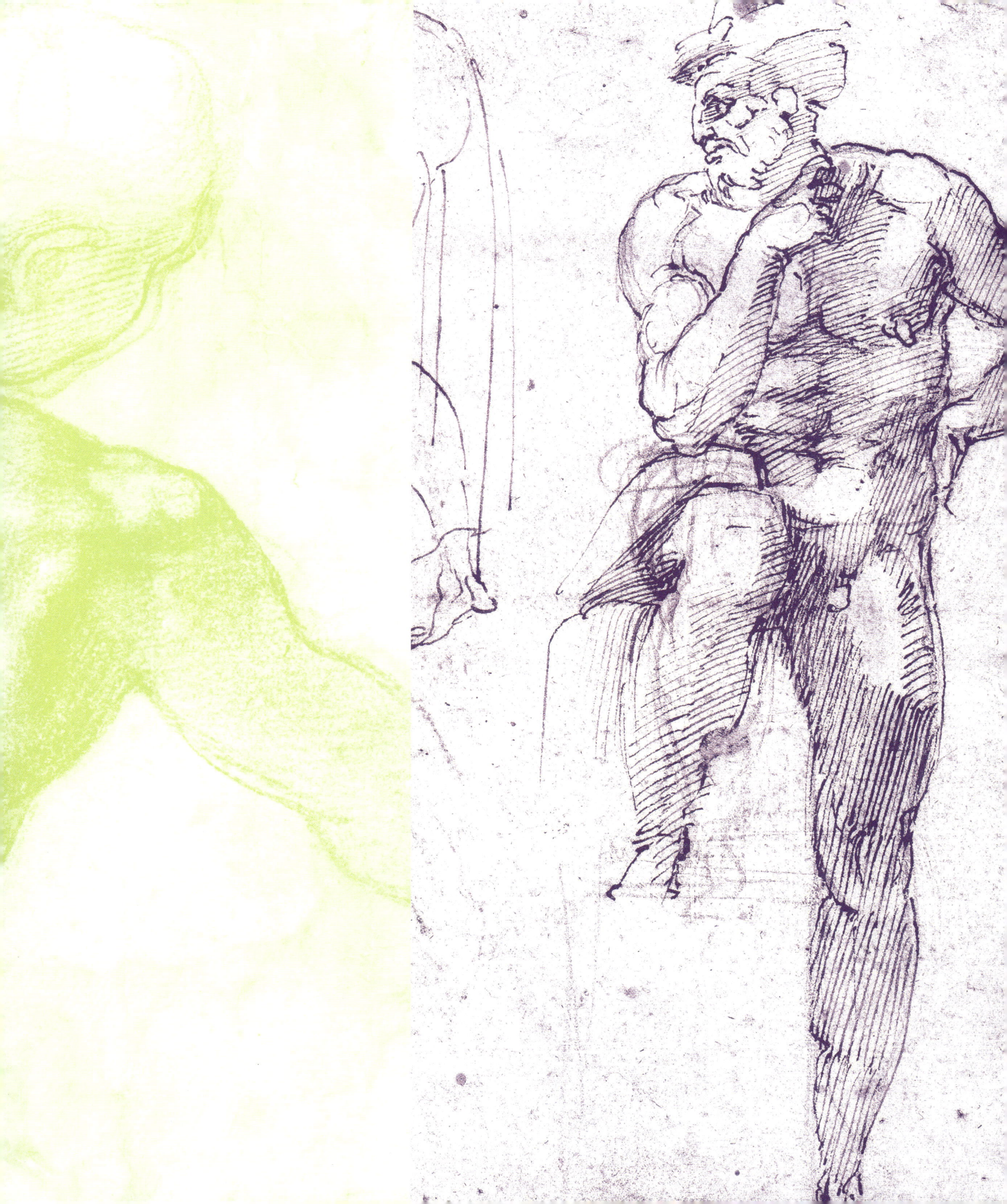

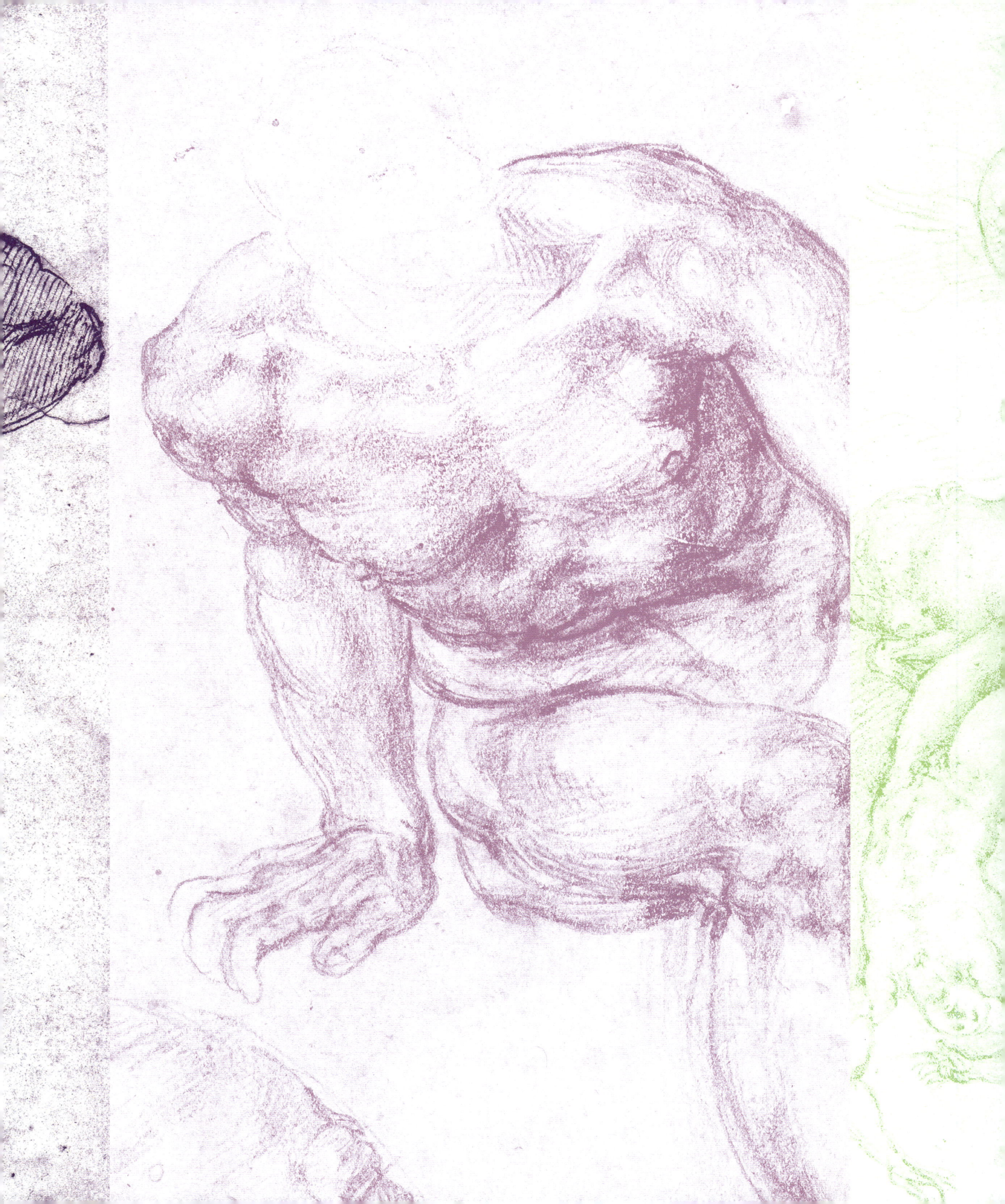

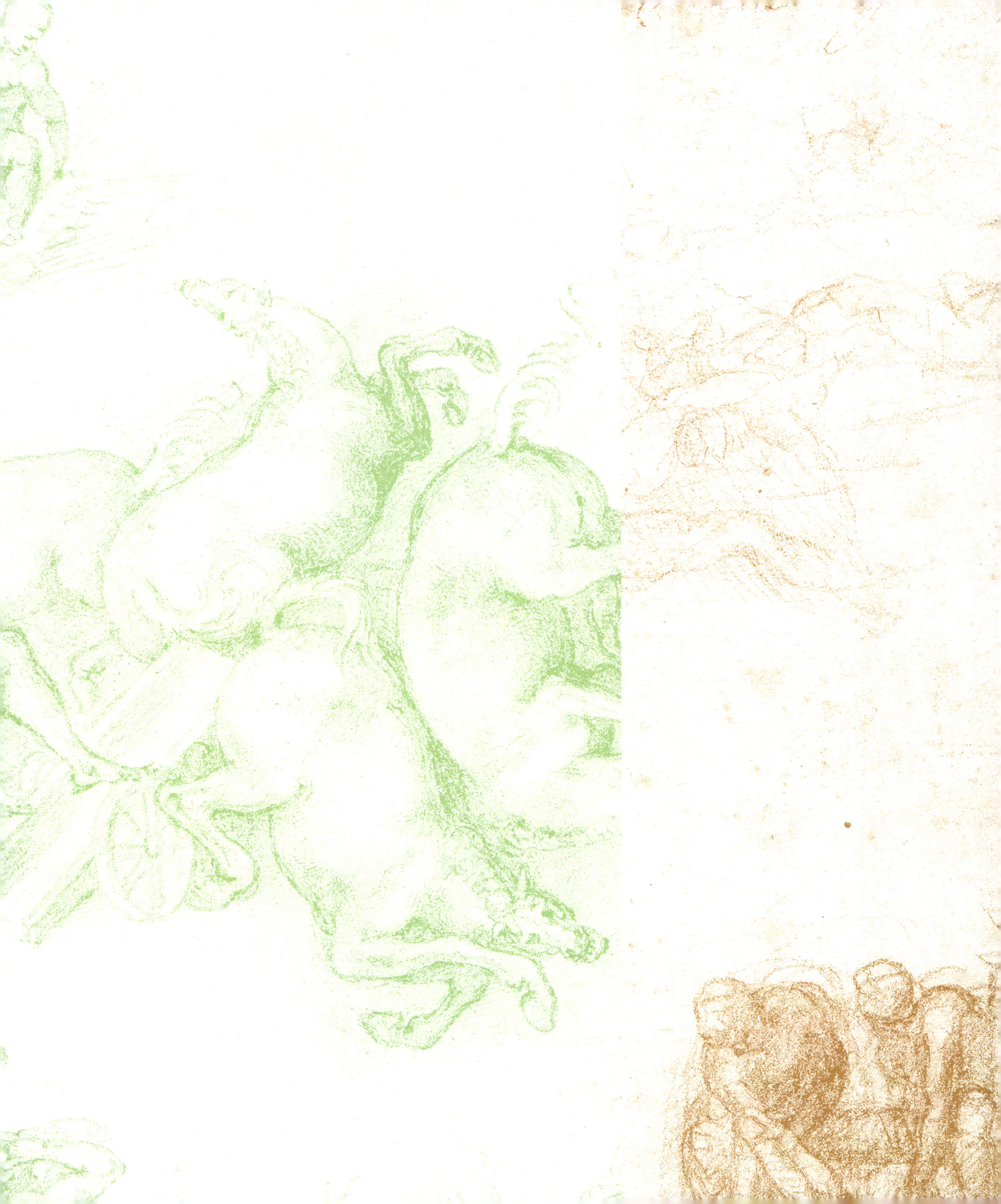

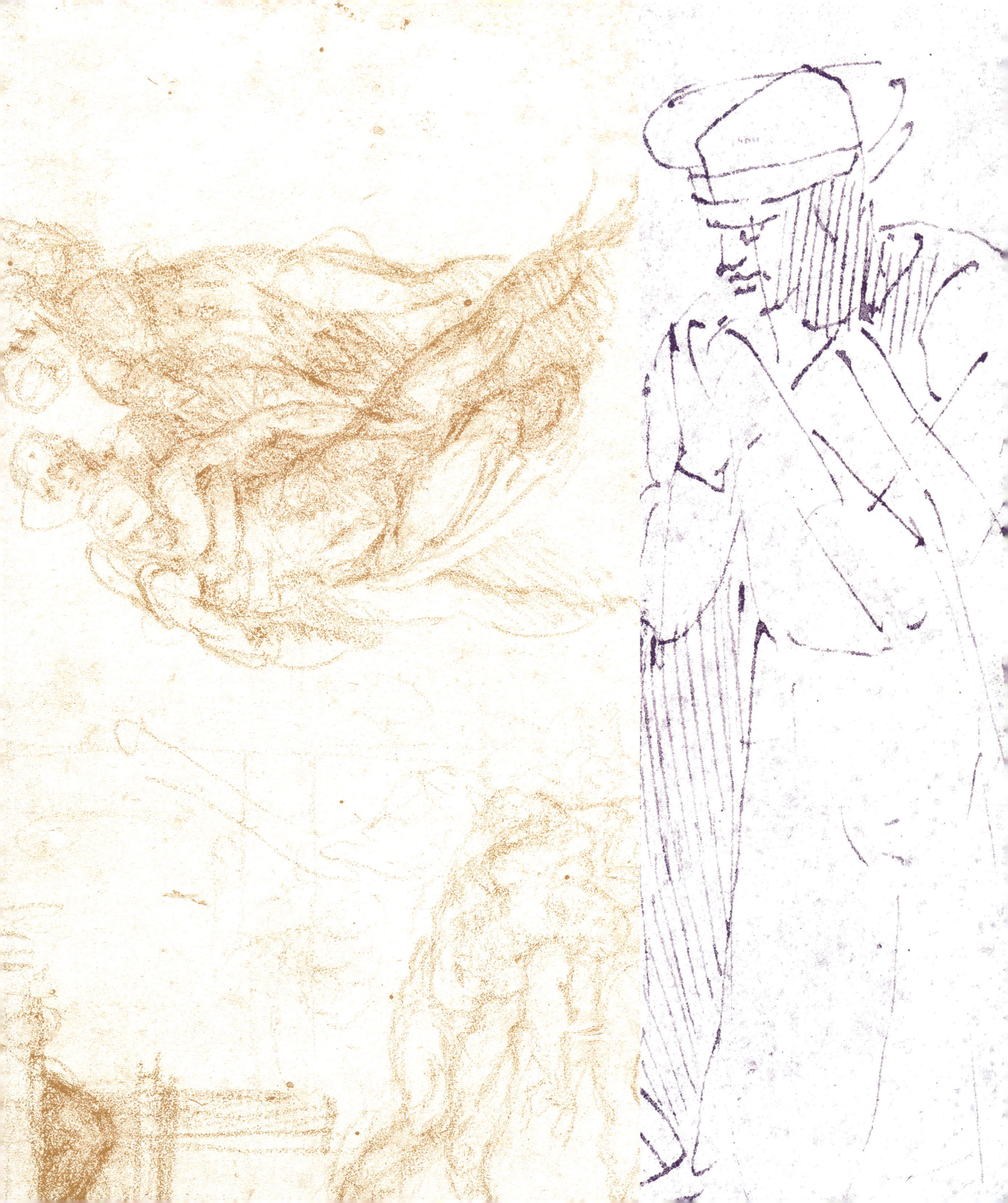

Preface

Marc de Beyer
Director, Teylers Museum

In 1790, Teylers Museum acquired one of the greatest treasures in the institution's history. Some 1,700 drawings and several hundred prints were bought from the heirs of Roman nobleman Livio Odescalchi for a total of 10,000 guilders. A substantial proportion of the drawings had previously belonged to the celebrated art collection of Christina, former Queen of Sweden, and included sheets by the greatest Italian artists, such as Raphael, Bernini and Michelangelo. So at a stroke, the recently established museum purchased a large corpus of drawings that has inspired generations to this day.

There has been no end to that inspiration. In this book, and the exhibition it accompanies, we examine for the first time the central place occupied by the male physique in Michelangelo's work and life. Few representations of a man's body are as entrenched in the collective memory as his *David* or *The Creation of Adam*, and few have had a greater influence on the history of Western art. The heroic, frequently naked male figure is a recurring motif in Michelangelo's oeuvre: the *ignudi* (nudes) on the Sistine Chapel ceiling, the dead Christ on Mary's lap in St Peter's Basilica, or the dying and rebellious captives in the Louvre. The masculine body is omnipresent in his art, even when he was drawing, painting or sculpting women.

The authors who have contributed to this book explore the artistic and personal characteristics of the male bodies in Michelangelo's art: the place occupied by models and anatomy in his oeuvre, the examples he found in the art of his own time and that of classical antiquity, and the social context in which he created his work. They also examine theoretical and theological aspects, such as Neoplatonic ideas concerning the male body as the highest ideal of perfection and beauty.

Men did not just play a central role in Michelangelo's art, however, but in his personal life too. There can be little doubt as to the artist's preference for (often younger) men. At the same time, he was a deeply religious man, which might have triggered an inner struggle for himself, and certainly for those who came after him. It is no coincidence that allusions to men in Michelangelo's love poems were altered shortly after his death to refer to women.

Each era poses questions of its own. While Michelangelo's preferences long remained taboo and unmentionable, it is now possible to address this subject in depth. This fresh perspective on Michelangelo's men is more than welcome and represents an important new contribution to the rich corpus of literature devoted to the artist. It not only affords a better understanding of the extraordinary power of his art, it also enables us to touch on a subject that is relevant to current discussions regarding ideals of beauty, gender and sexuality.

Michelangelo lived in a society different from ours; one in which men and women moved much more in separate spheres. Possibly as a result of this, sexual relationships between men were ubiquitous – behaviour that was at once common and hidden. Michelangelo's beautifully detailed drawings for Tommaso de' Cavalieri fit this picture: they were public masterpieces and intimate declarations of his love. It is interesting to compare the place homosexuality occupies in today's society with that in Michelangelo's era. Where it is now visible, it was then hidden. What was then normal – an older man's love for a teenage boy – is now unacceptable.

What about the perception of the ideal bodies Michelangelo depicted? Highly toned bodies are the norm online today. But what actually is the ideal? What is a normal body and what is not? Did such ideals only apply during the Florentine Renaissance or in our own time as well? Is this a Western ideal or a universal one? And what does all this mean for the position of women? If physical strength equates to power, do men automatically take precedence? Are Michelangelo's masculine women an expression of misogyny or, rather, one of empowerment?

Each of these questions is hard to answer, but Michelangelo's men and the culture from which they sprang can serve as a mirror for our time. I am immensely grateful therefore to everyone who has contributed to the creation of this book and the exhibition, whether substantively, practically or financially. Thanks to the efforts of so many, we can now fully enjoy the exceptional art we have inherited from Michelangelo and which, on occasion, holds up a mirror to us.

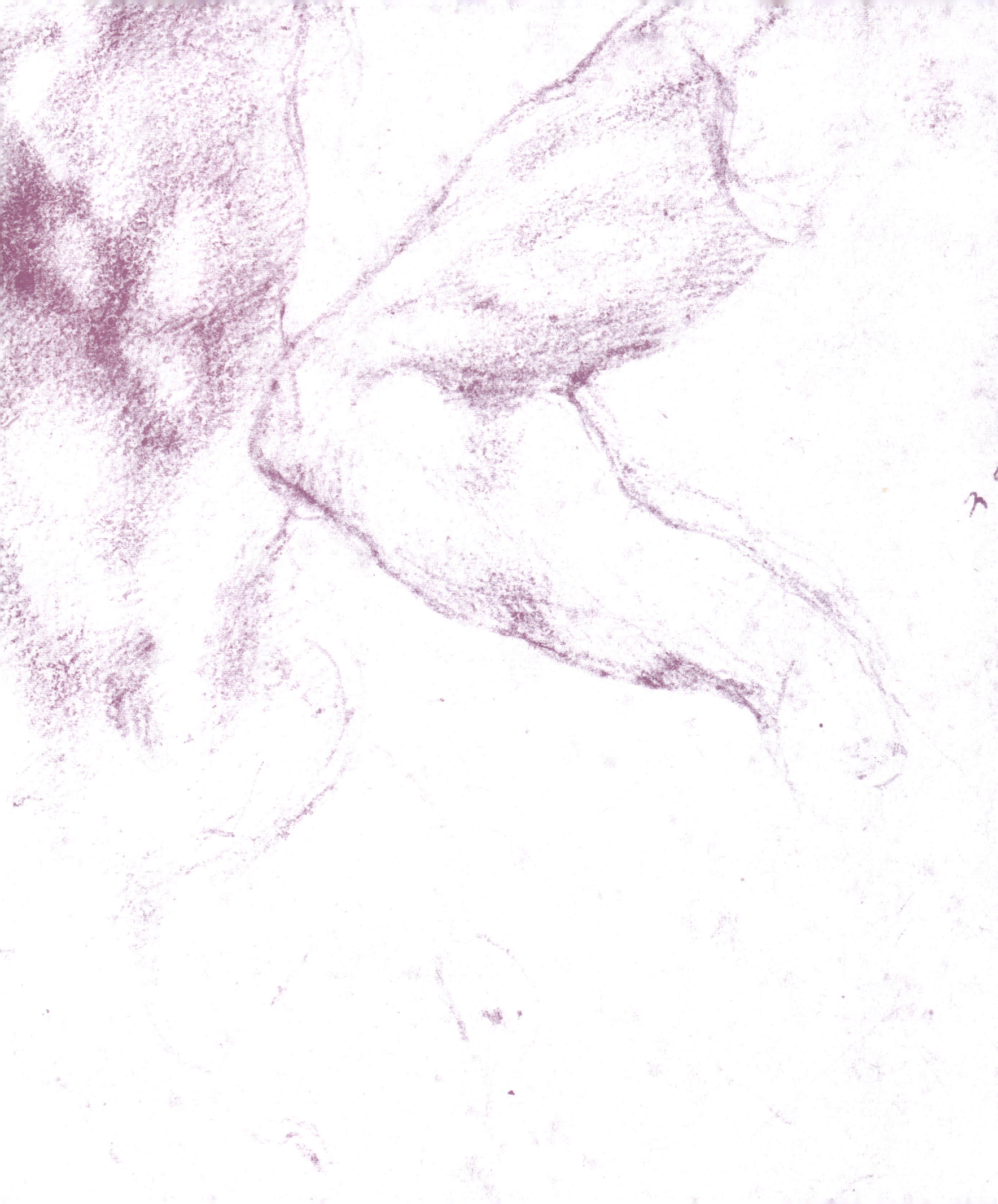

Concise Timeline

1475
Michelangelo is born on 6 March in Caprese, near Arezzo.

1487
First mention of Michelangelo as a pupil in the workshop of Domenico and Davide Ghirlandaio in Florence.

c. 1488–92
Michelangelo is taken into the household of Lorenzo de' Medici ('il Magnifico'), whose collection of antiquities he studies. It is here that he creates his first sculptures, including the *Battle of the Centaurs* (fig. 38).

1492
Lorenzo de' Medici dies and is succeeded by his son Piero.

1493
Michelangelo works for Piero de' Medici. He sculpts a marble *Hercules* (lost) and the wooden *Crucifix* for the Santo Spirito (fig. 123).

1494
The Medici are banished from Florence following the invasion of Charles VIII of France and the republic is re-established. The radical preacher Girolamo Savonarola gains significant influence. Michelangelo leaves Florence and works in Bologna on sculptures for the Arca di San Domenico.

1496–1500
Michelangelo is in Rome, where he creates works including *Bacchus* (fig. 40) and the Vatican *Pietà* (fig. 113).

1501
Michelangelo returns to Florence, where he is commissioned to sculpt the marble *David* (fig. 1).

1502
Michelangelo receives the commission for a bronze *David* (lost).

1504
The marble *David* is completed and installed in front of the Palazzo della Signoria. Michelangelo also receives the commission for the *Battle of Cascina* (fig. 133). He is working on two marble reliefs (the *Pitti Tondo* and the *Taddei Tondo*), on the *Bruges Madonna*, and probably on the *Doni Tondo* (fig. 34).

1505
Pope Julius II summons Michelangelo to Rome to design his tomb monument.

1506
Michelangelo returns to Florence without the pope's knowledge. He continues to work on the *Battle of Cascina*, among other things, but the fresco is left unfinished when Michelangelo goes to Bologna to make a bronze statue of Julius II (lost in 1511).

1508–12
Michelangelo paints the ceiling of the Sistine Chapel. The Medici return to Florence in 1512, reasserting power.

1513
Julius II dies and is succeeded by Leo X (Giovanni de' Medici). Michelangelo starts work on the *Rebellious Captive* and the *Dying Captive* (figs 33 and 86) and *Moses* (fig. 95) for Julius's tomb.

1516
Michelangelo returns to Florence, where Leo X commissions him to design a facade for San Lorenzo.

1519–20
The facade project is abandoned. Michelangelo is commissioned to design the Medici funerary chapel at San Lorenzo.

1521
Leo X dies. Michelangelo completes *The Risen Christ* for the Santa Maria Sopra Minerva in Rome.

1524
Michelangelo starts work on the sculptures for the Medici Chapel and is commissioned by Pope Clement VII to build the Laurentian Library.

1527
Rome is sacked; the Medici are once more banished from Florence. Michelangelo works for the new republic, including on the city's defences in 1529.

1530
Florence once again returns to Medici control. Michelangelo probably began work on the *Apollo-David* (fig. 44).

1531

Michelangelo completes *Leda and the Swan* (lost; fig. 22). Rather than to its commissioner, Alfonso d'Este, the painting goes to France, where King Francis I buys it.

1532

Michelangelo meets Tommaso de' Cavalieri in Rome.

1533

Michelangelo travels back and forth between Rome and Florence. He makes the presentation drawings for Tommaso and receives the commission for *The Last Judgement* (fig. 96) in November from Pope Clement VII.

1534

Michelangelo leaves Florence for good and settles in Rome.

1536–41

Michelangelo paints *The Last Judgement*. It is during these years that his friendship with Vittoria Colonna begins.

1542

Start of the frescoes in the Cappella Paolina in the Vatican (fig. 158).

1545

The tomb of Julius II is installed in the San Pietro in Vincoli in Rome.

1546

Michelangelo becomes the chief architect of St Peter's Basilica.

1547

Michelangelo starts work on a marble *Pietà* for his own tomb (fig. 120). Eight years later, he leaves the sculpture unfinished.

1550

The frescoes in the Cappella Paolina are completed. Vasari publishes the first edition of his *Lives*, in which Michelangelo is the only living artist to receive his own biography.

1552

Michelangelo begins work on his final marble sculpture, the *Rondanini Pietà* (fig. 122). The work is unfinished at the time of his death.

1553

Condivi's *Life of Michelangelo* is published.

1564

Michelangelo dies on 18 February. Daniele da Volterra and Tommaso de' Cavalieri are among those present.

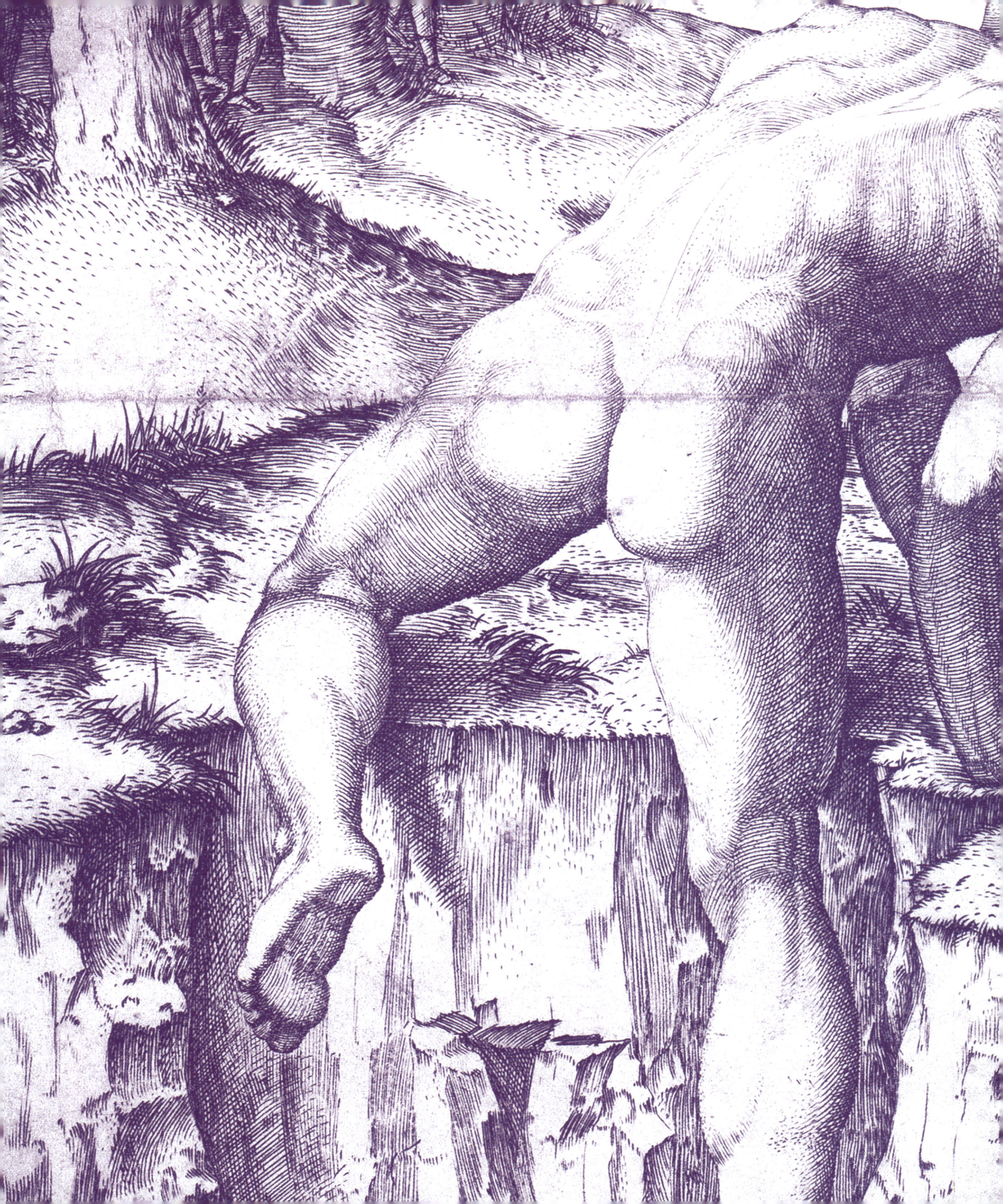

Introduction. Michelangelo's Men

Klazina Botke, Terry van Druten and Martin Gayford

Il gigante, as Michelangelo's *David* was known, is probably the most famous nude man in the history of art (fig. 1). Michelangelo was commissioned to sculpt the immense marble statue by the Opera del Duomo (the office of works at the Cathedral of Santa Maria del Fiore in Florence) in 1501, the year he returned to Florence from Rome.[1] The city he came back to was different from the one he had left several years earlier: the Medici – its long-standing de facto rulers – had been banished and the Florentine republic restored under Francesco Valori.[2] For over two years, Michelangelo worked on the marble block. When David was nearing completion, and hugely impressing the first people who saw it, a momentous decision was taken. Having originally been intended for one of the buttresses around the *tribuna* of the Santa Maria del Fiore, it was decided that *Il gigante* should instead be installed in the square in front of the Palazzo della Signoria, the seat of the republican government.[3] The biblical David – the shepherd boy who defeated the giant Goliath – had long been a symbol for Florence, a small city-state that saw itself consistently beating the greater powers around it. Michelangelo now placed the young David – grand, idealised and magisterially naked – at the centre of the city's political power. The blatant display of his penis, however, was seen as going just that bit too far,[4] and so within a month of the statue's installation, a garland of twenty-eight gilded leaves was placed over its genitals[5] – an act of censorship similar to the one that years later would befall Michelangelo's figures in *The Last Judgement* (fig. 96).

In all his majestic nudity, *David* is still as intriguing as ever. The sculpture is a spectacular culmination of the Renaissance desire to revive classical antiquity, a period at which ideal bodies were represented in the nude, yet at the same time it seems to express a new kind of self-confident masculinity within Florentine society and politics.[6] The Medici set a precedent for displaying the male nude with the installation of Donatello's bronze *David* in the garden of the Palazzo Medici around 1469 (fig. 2). When the family was banished in 1492, the statue was moved to the Palazzo della Signoria, albeit to a slightly less accessible interior space rather than the square in front. It was in this same period that Antonio Pollaiuolo made his famous engraving of nude, fighting men – a work that was widely disseminated through the medium of print (fig. 3).[7]

Masculinity of this kind seems to have been enshrined as the public ideal with the new government of Piero Soderini (who was elected *gonfaloniere* for life in 1502) and the installation of Michelangelo's *David* in 1504.[8] That same year, the artist was commissioned to paint the *Battle of Cascina* for the Salone dei Cinquecento, the large council chamber in the Palazzo della Signoria. Paul Joannides's essay in this book offers fresh insights into this unexecuted yet highly influential project for a fresco. Although Michelangelo did not get any further than the cartoon for the central part of the painting, here too the nude male body is the chief focus in the depiction of this Florentine victory (see figs 133/cat. 51 and 141/cat. 13). With their muscular, monumental, idealised and almost superhuman appearance, Michelangelo's men undeniably transformed the representation of the body in European art. Both his *David* and the expressive bodies in the *Cascina* cartoon were frequently imitated and remained the model for other artists for many years (fig. 4/cat. 49).[9]

The powerful and robust masculinity of Michelangelo's figures is frequently linked these days to his 'homosexuality' – a modern term which, as Michael Rocke demonstrates in this book, cannot be directly applied to the artist. Michelangelo's much-discussed affection for Andrea Quaratesi and Tommaso de' Cavalieri related to a love for very young men. Rocke poses an intriguing question: how can we reconcile this fascination for very muscular men's bodies that are so far removed from any adolescent physique? Michelangelo's almost hyper-virile male figures raise even more questions: what role did models, anatomical studies and examples from antiquity play in his work? How did prevailing philosophical ideas and the

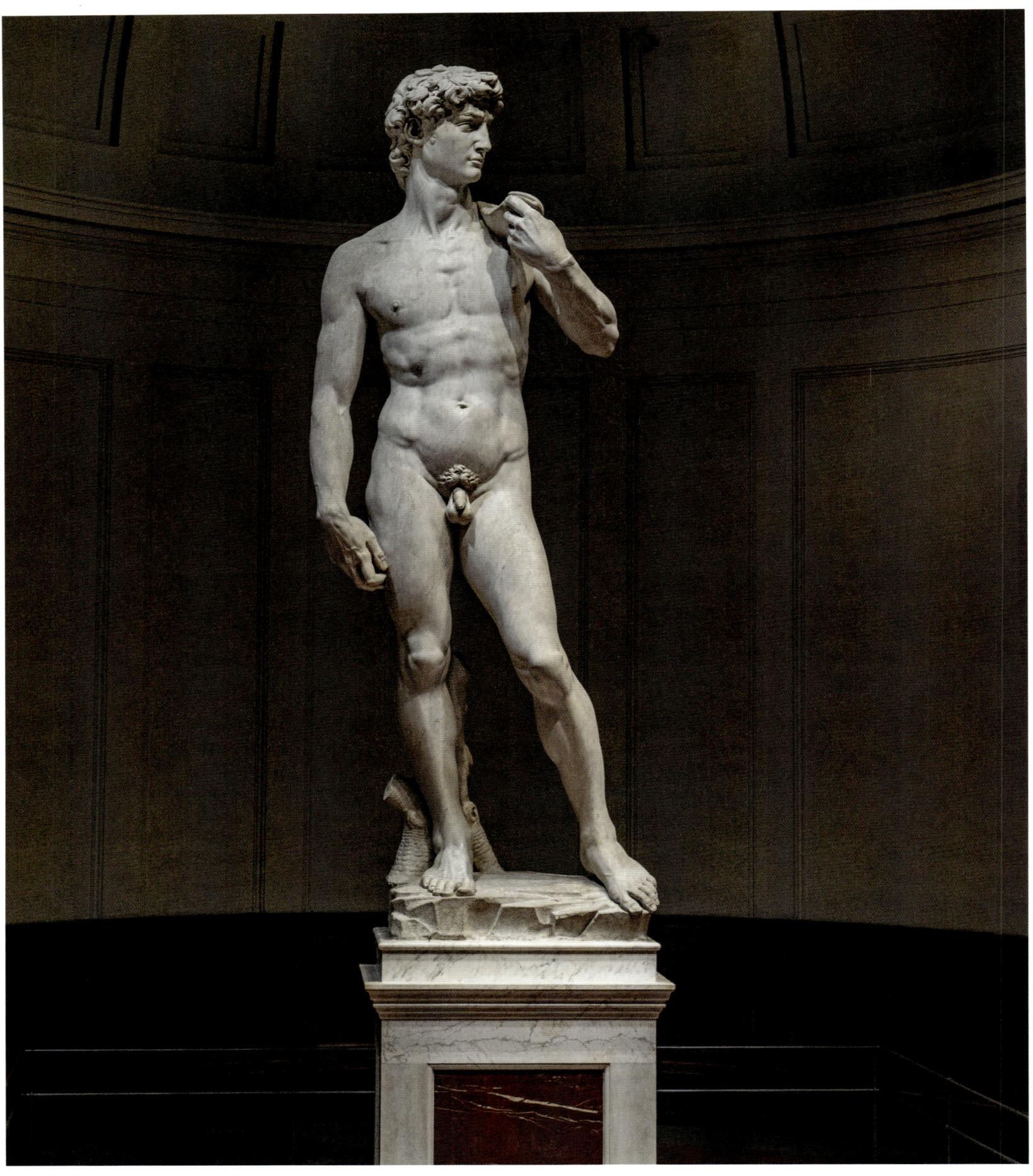

fig. 1   Michelangelo, *David*, 1501–1504. Marble, height 517 cm. Florence, Galleria dell'Accademia, inv. Sculture 1076

artist's profound religiosity influence the way he represented men? And how were his figures received by his clients and other contemporaries? Precisely who, in other words, were 'Michelangelo's men'? While this book does not pretend to answer all these questions, its nine essays nevertheless set out to achieve a better understanding of the male body in the master's oeuvre, not least by considering his relationships with and attitudes towards the actual men in his life.

Drawn Men

The human body seems to have been Michelangelo's primary interest from the outset. His earliest known pen-and-ink drawings show human figures copied from famous fresco paintings by Giotto and Masaccio. The individuals in these studies are isolated from their surroundings; the central figure is powerfully worked out while those around it are rendered more freely and loosely. The sheet in Teylers Museum in Haarlem (figs 5 and 6/cat. 9) is a good example of this. The three men with their folded hands and the two standing figures on the verso are all likely to have been taken from a narrative representation. By lifting them out of that story, Michelangelo refocused attention firmly onto their posture and movements. The same applies to a recently rediscovered sheet from the same period, the central figure of which is a young, nude man copied from Masaccio's fresco of the *Baptism of the Neophytes* in the Brancacci Chapel in Florence (fig. 51/cat. 8).[10] It is Michelangelo's earliest surviving drawing of a nude.

    Drawing formed the practical and theoretical foundation for the arts in the Florentine Renaissance and is the principal focus of this book; the Italian word *disegno* meant not only drawing, but also the intellectual ability to design. The nude – much more so than the clothed – male was a key element of this *disegno*.[11] Artists created figures by drawing living, and frequently nude, models, as Terry van Druten shows in his essay. Each fresh artistic assignment began with this practice: the (largely) unclothed body was drawn first, with clothes added to the figures at a later stage. It is striking in Michelangelo's case that many of the nude bodies remain in the final work, whether in marble, fresco or oil paint.[12]

    The renewed interest in antiquity prompted artists to look back at the ancient sculptures that were steadily being unearthed in Rome. Michelangelo too borrowed poses and forms from these historical statues, many of which had 'ideal', fixed proportions, as Martin Gayford discusses in this book. Furthermore, the artist had an exceptional knowledge of human anatomy, for the time. In his essay, Eric Boot describes Michelangelo's thorough

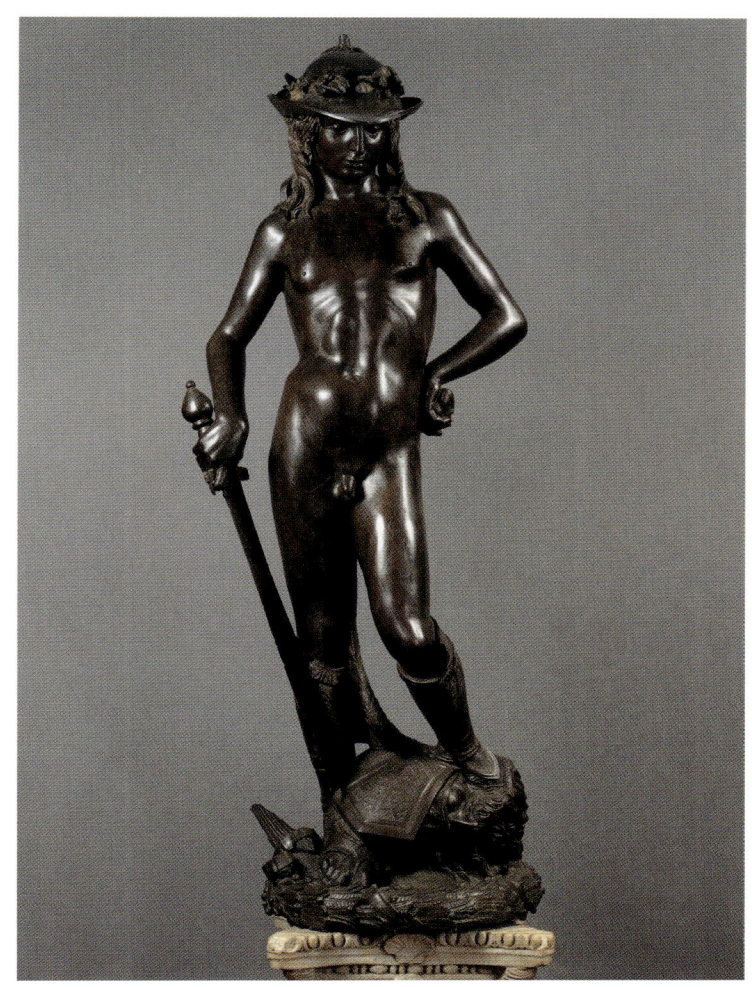

fig. 2   Donatello, *David,* c. 1435–1440. Bronze, height 158 cm. Florence, Museo Nazionale del Bargello, inv. Bronzi 95

understanding of the human body – at least, as much as he needed to be able to depict it as naturally as possible. He applied this knowledge to his pursuit of the ideal figure, ultimately enabling him to achieve a perfection that surpassed nature. His study for *Adam*, drawn from a living model and made in preparation for the fresco in the Sistine Chapel, illustrates this magnificently (fig. 7/cat. 17). The focus is on the anatomy of and the tension in the torso, and while the rotation of the upper body is undeniably strained, the body and posture seem convincingly natural. A similar effect is found in the *bozzetto* of a river god (fig. 8/cat. 33).[13] Wax models of this kind were used, among other things, to develop the pose of a sculpture – in this instance, for a work in the Medici Chapel. At the same time, the muscular anatomy, combined with the focus on the twisting of the torso, evokes the memory of ancient sculptures, a fact certainly intensified by the model's (current) lack of head or arms.

Gender Fluid

In the midst of all this masculine display, the following question inevitably arises: where are the women? They are present in Michelangelo's painted work and in his sculptures, but we only encounter them sporadically in his drawings.[14] Four small studies with copies of an antique statue of Venus depict the female body of that particular sculpture (fig. 9/cat. 27), but the drawings lack the intensity of many of Michelangelo's studies of male bodies and seem to have been primarily functional. With a practical sculptor's eye, he depicted the three-dimensional torso from four sides.[15] The studies date from the period in which he had started work on the female sculptures for the Medici tombs in the New Sacristy (Sagrestia Nuova) in Florence and might have served as inspiration.[16] A more realistic woman is found on a sheet in Teylers Museum (fig. 10/cat. 25); bent over and hoeing the soil, her posture suggests that she might have been a preliminary study for Eve after the expulsion from the Garden of Eden.[17] The figure is set down with a few flowing contour lines in pen and ink, suggesting that it was not drawn from an exist-

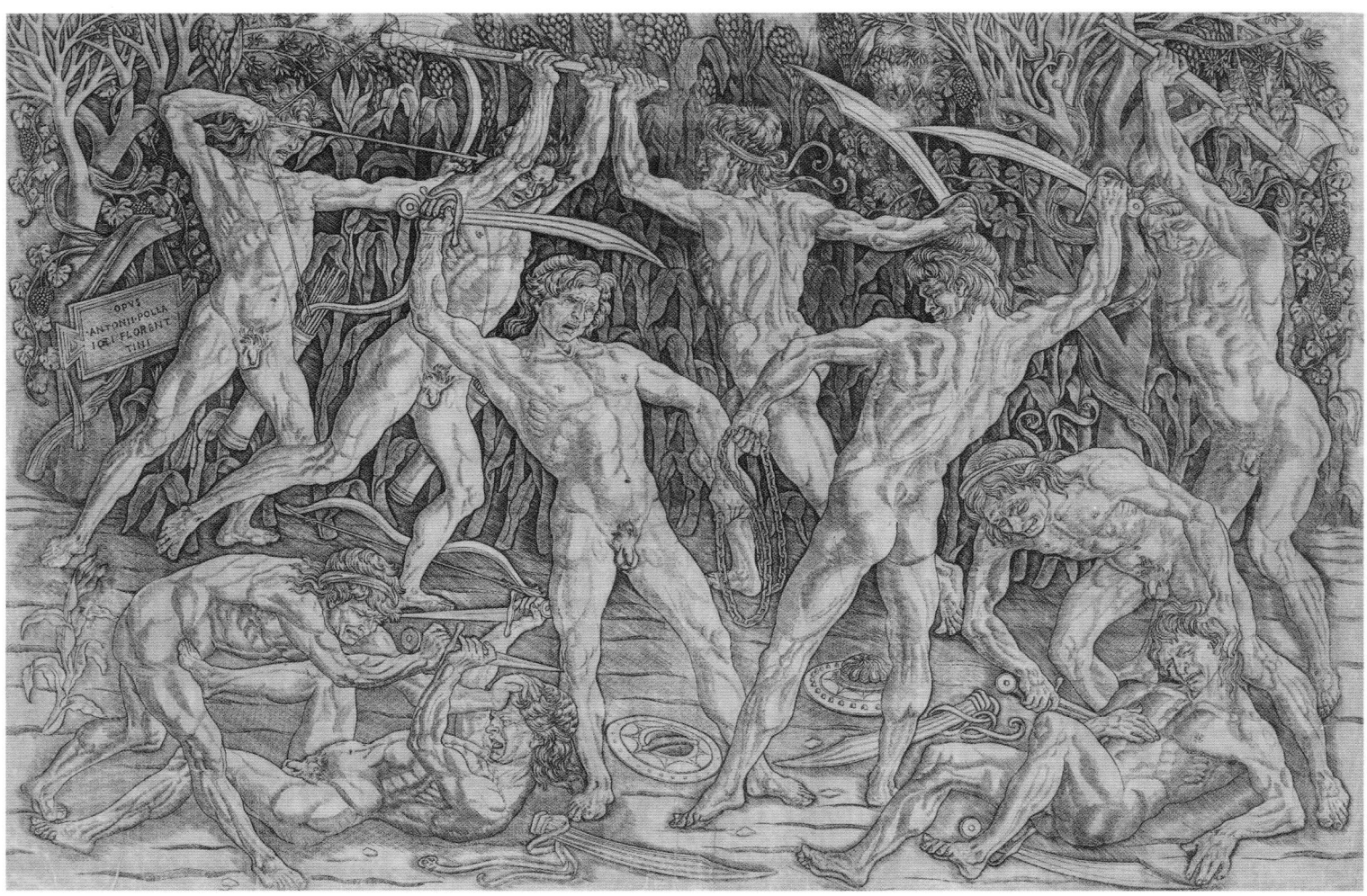

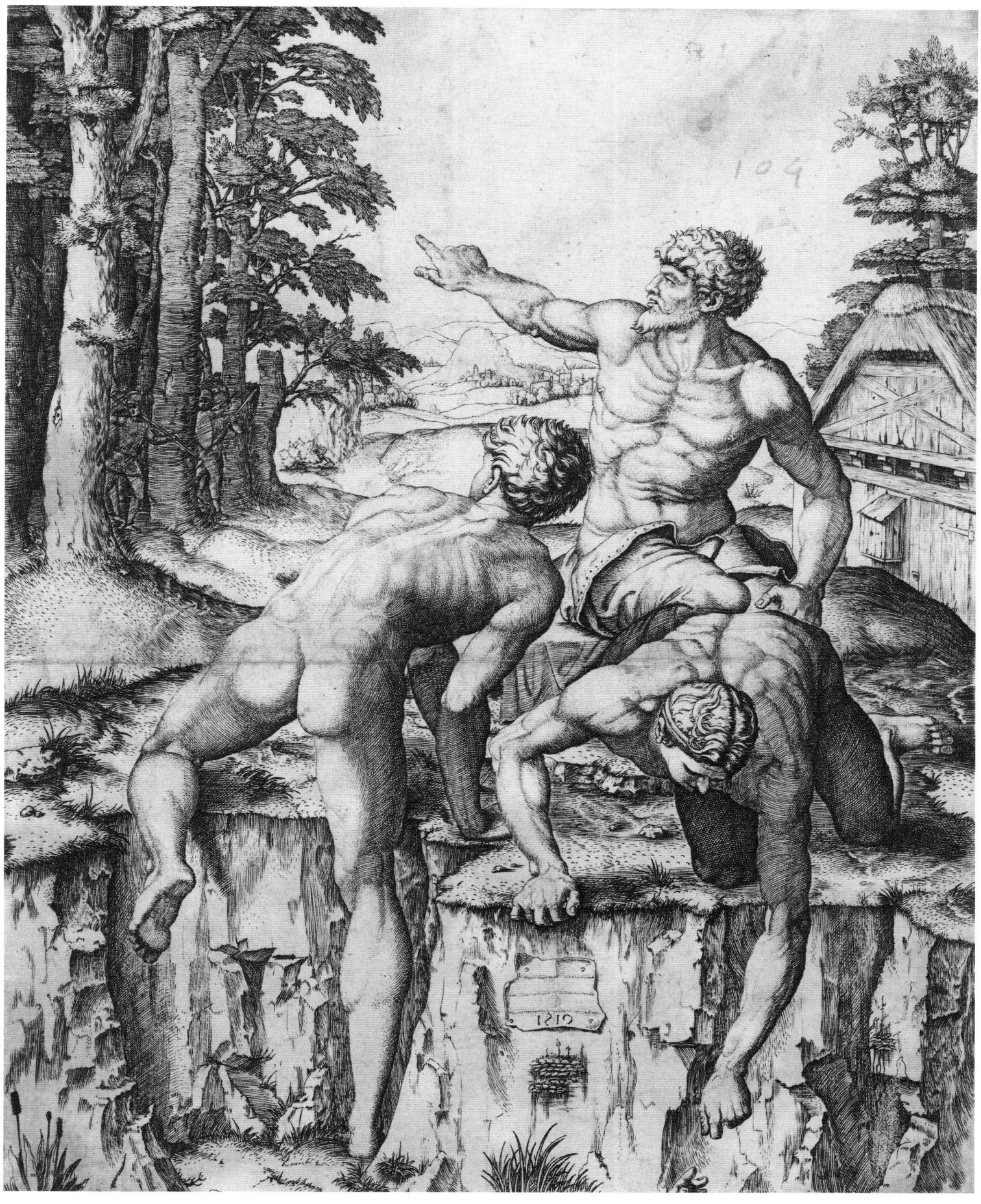

fig. 4   (cat. 49) Marcantonio Raimondi, after Michelangelo, *Bathers*, 1510. Engraving, 288 x 228 mm. Haarlem, Teylers Museum, inv. KG 00004

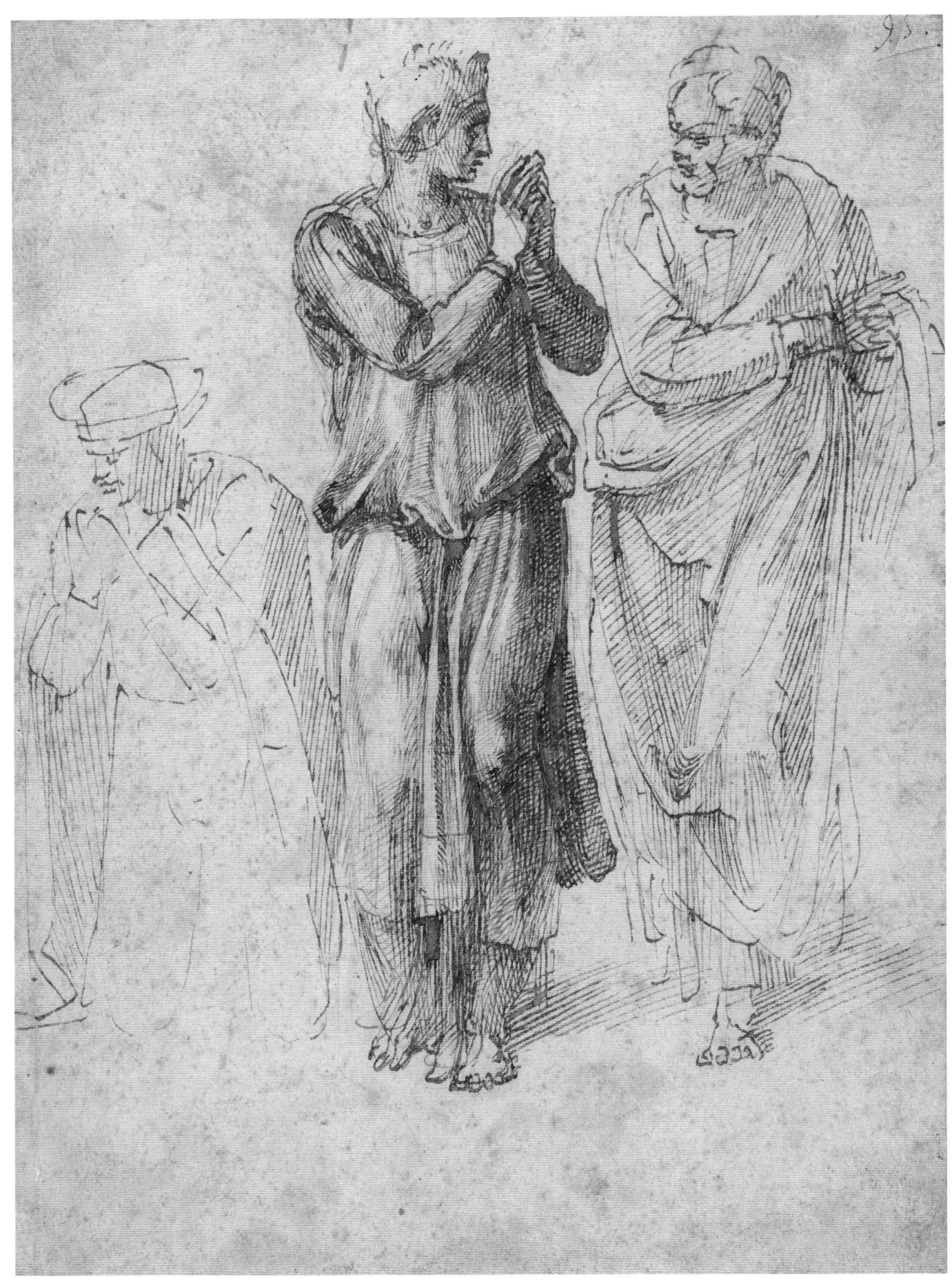

fig. 5   (cat. 9) Michelangelo, *Three Figures in Adoration*, c. 1496–1503. Pen and brown ink, black chalk, 269 x 194 mm. Haarlem, Teylers Museum, inv. A 022

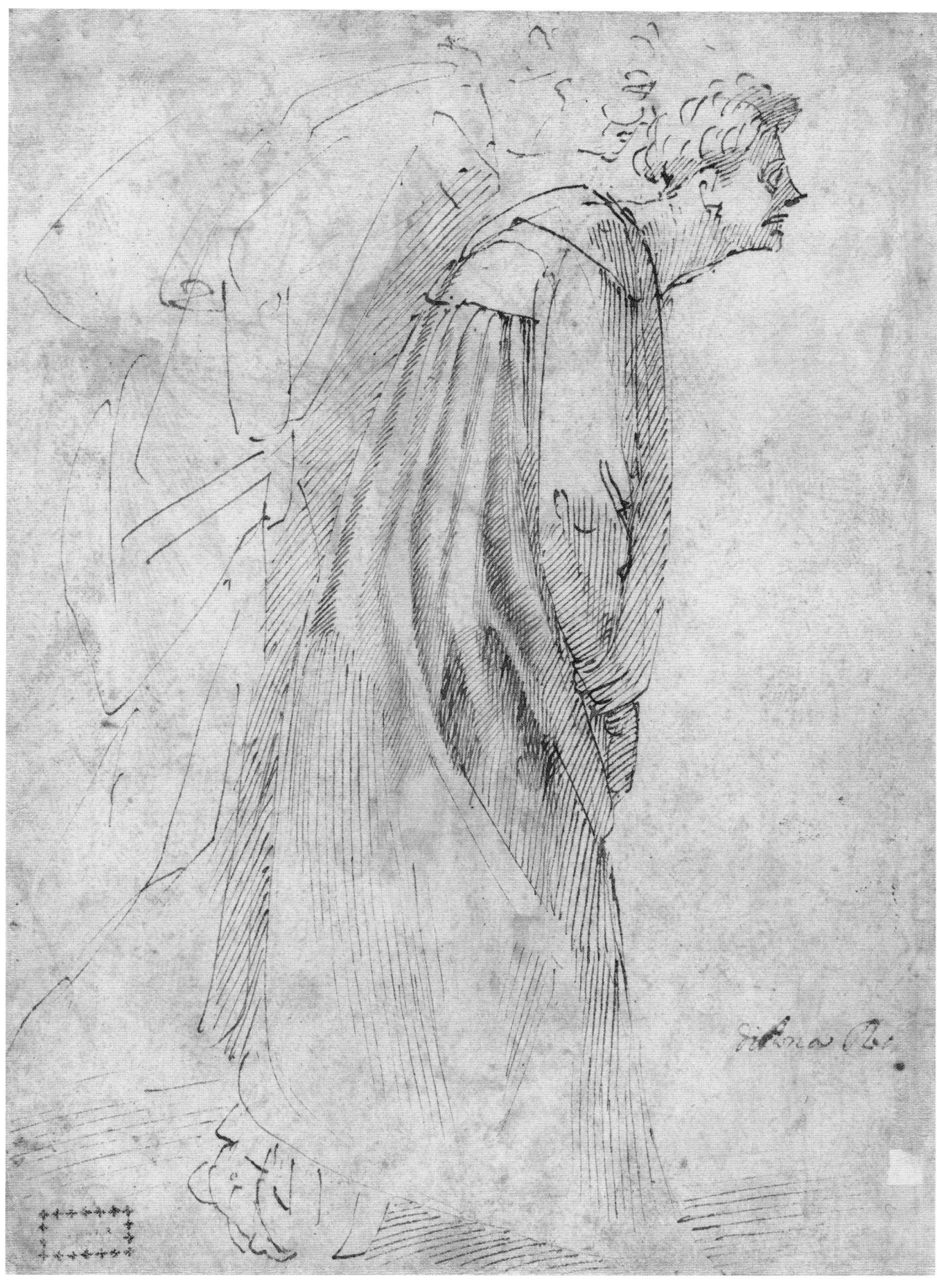

fig. 6   (cat. 9v) Michelangelo, *Two Figures, Leaning Forward*, c. 1496–1503. Pen and brown ink, 269 x 194 mm. Haarlem, Teylers Museum, inv. A 022v

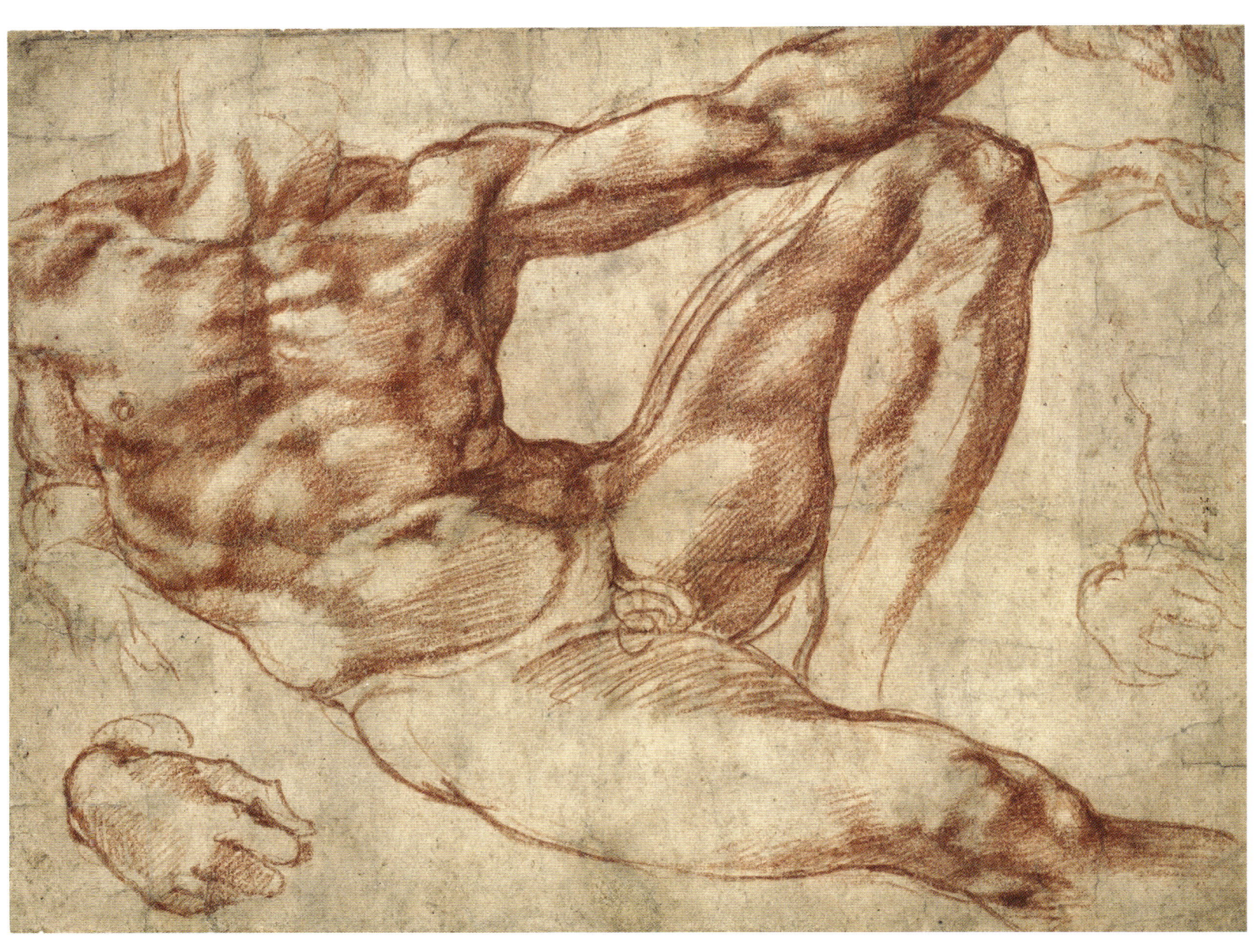

fig. 7   (cat. 17) Michelangelo, *Studies for Adam for the Sistine Chapel Ceiling*, c. 1511. Red chalk, 193 x 259 mm. London, British Museum, inv. 1926,1009.1

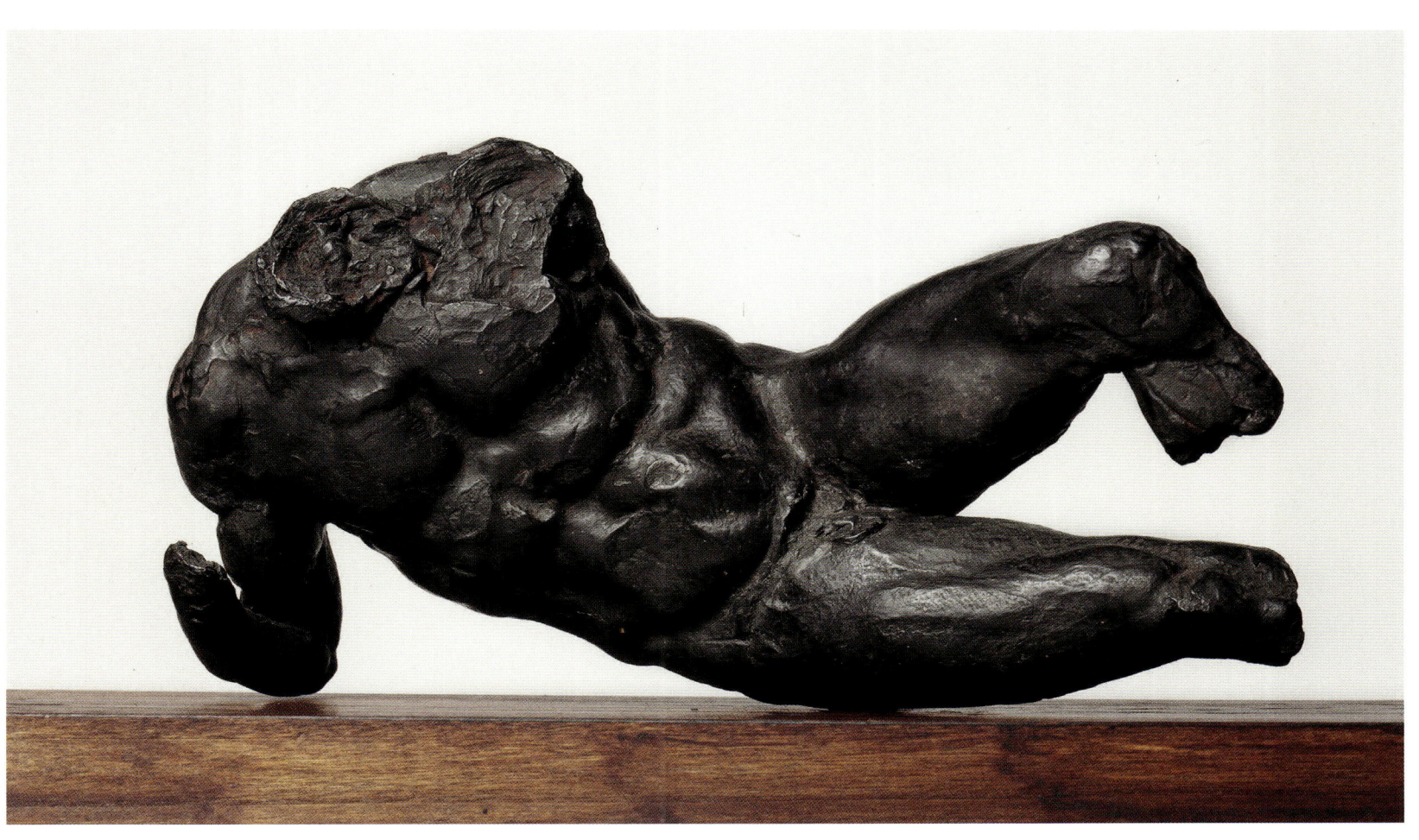

fig. 8   (cat. 33) Michelangelo, *Bozzetto of a River God*, c. 1524. Wax, length 22 cm. Florence, Casa Buonarroti, inv. 542

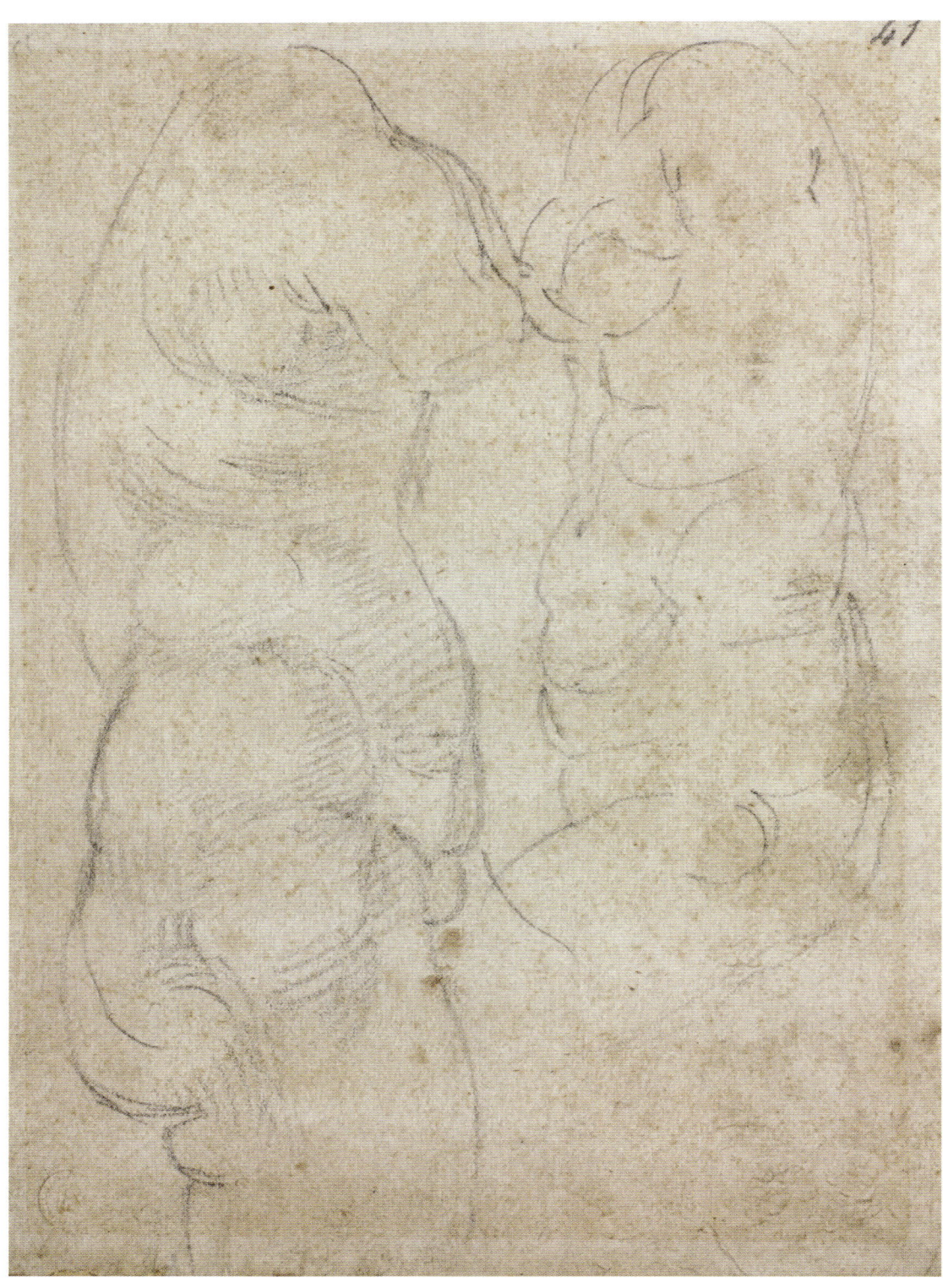

fig. 9   (cat. 27) Michelangelo, *Studies of a Classical Female Sculpture*, c. 1523–1526. Black chalk, 200 x 147 mm. Florence, Casa Buonarroti, inv. 41F

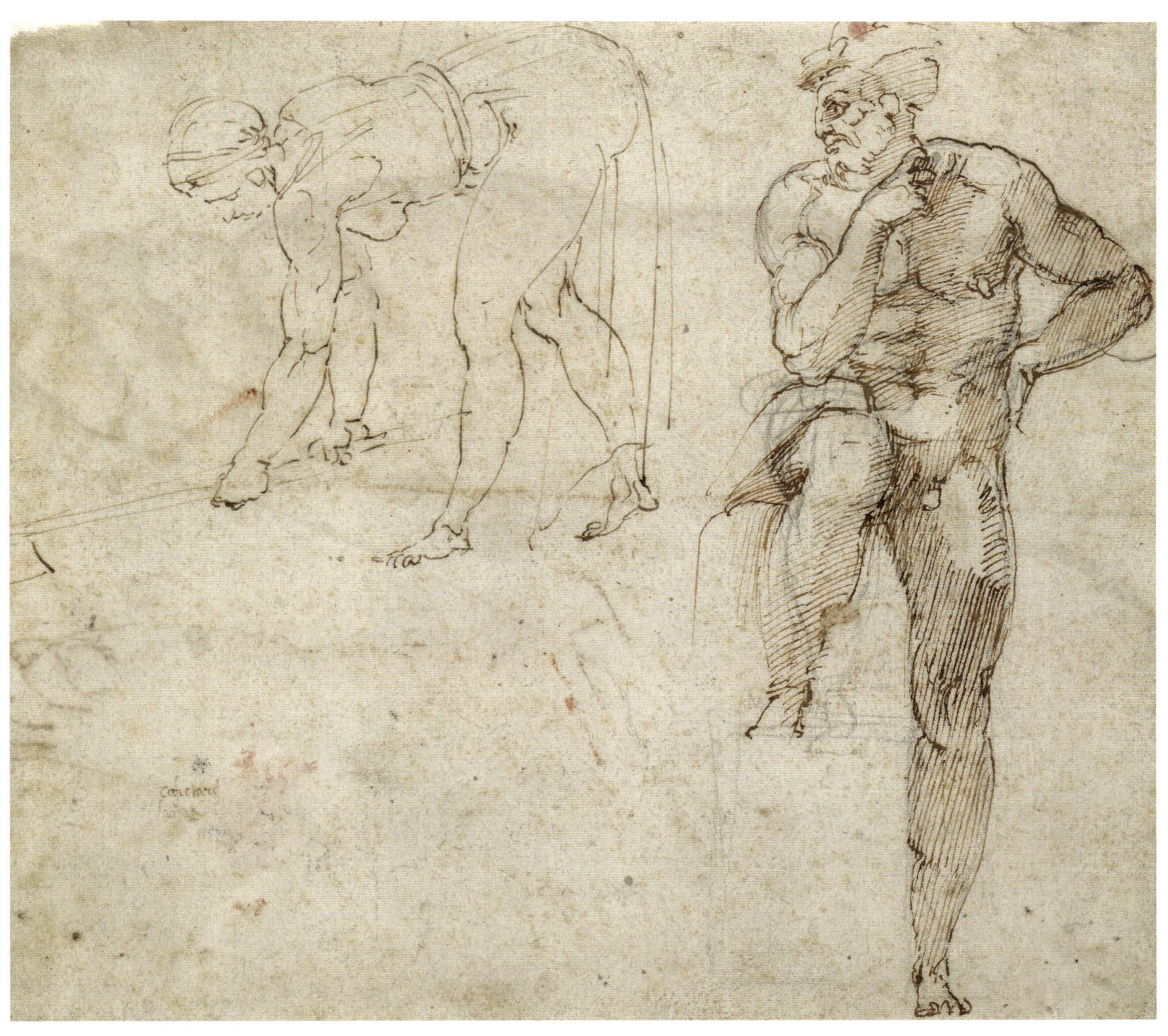

fig. 10   (cat. 25) Michelangelo, *Male Nude and Woman with a Hoe*, c. 1517–1523. Pen and brown ink, black chalk, 210 x 233 mm. Haarlem, Teylers Museum, inv. A 017

ing example or a model. This does appear to be the case, however, for the kneeling young woman, depicted on a sheet in the Louvre (fig. 11),[18] which Michael Hirst considers to be a rare example of Michelangelo working from a female model.[19] He also notes the unusual fact that the woman is depicted nude in the pose in which she later appears, fully clothed, on the left of *The Entombment*, now in London (fig. 114).

Except in Venice Italian Renaissance artists mainly worked from male models when representing female figures, and Michelangelo was no exception. Carmen Bambach has already noted that in some drawings he depicted certain body parts in less detail when he knew the figure would change gender in the final work.[20] Unlike that of his contemporaries, however, Michelangelo's final result almost always retains a visible virility. One well-known example is the Libyan sibyl on the ceiling of the Sistine Chapel (fig. 71), the preliminary study for which in red chalk, now in New York, is based on close observation of a living male model (fig. 70/cat. 16). With her powerfully muscular arms and back, and her heroic appearance, the female Sibyl in the fresco clearly preserves the anatomy of the original model.[21] Howard Hibbard has suggested that these women are an expression of Michelangelo's passion for and celebration of the male body, echoing Kenneth Clark, who believed that Michelangelo 'considered the female body inferior to the male'.[22] Another way of looking at these works, however, is to note that they fit Mary Garrard's definition of 'cross-gender images', in which stereotypical depictions of men and women are combined, so that the resulting figures transcend such characterisations. In this respect, she specifically refers to female figures with masculine 'vigor and heroic resolve'.[23]

Another place where genders merge is in the detailed studies of heads, including the magnificent face of Leda (fig. 72/cat. 37).[24] In this instance, where the male model was transformed into a woman in the final painting, what we see in the drawing is an androgynous intermediate form. A similarly gender-fluid representation is also found in some of Michelangelo's idealised heads (fig. 73/cat. 35).[25] It is striking that while this ambivalence is acknowledged by most of the literature, one gender or the other is then invariably chosen: the figure is either a man or a woman. But perhaps it is not necessary to choose. The fact that the depicted figures embody both male and female characteristics is intriguing and serves in fact to add an extra quality to the work – a quality that contributes significantly to the figures' transcendent effect. Victor Coonin has argued that their androgynous appearance might even be evidence that Michelangelo was thinking beyond the conventional binary gender division.[26] Perhaps we are more receptive to this nowadays, at a time when, in sections of our society, the traditional idea of 'man' and 'woman' is steadily shifting.

Existing Men

Michelangelo's depictions of the male nude were admired and praised in his own time, but were equally criticised and condemned, as Klazina Botke's essay demonstrates. Yet his own ideas also evolved over the course of his life, as Jennifer Sliwka explores in her essay on the depiction of Christ. Michelangelo's idealised, muscular bodies eventually gave way to a different style, in which greater prominence was afforded to emotion.[27] This was in keeping with the artist's personal development, which saw him move steadily away from the worldly and closer to the spiritual. The immense political and religious changes that occurred in the mid-sixteenth century no doubt played a part in this, as did his intense friendship with Vittoria Colonna with whom he shared the convictions of the *spirituali* – a group of influential churchmen and academics around Cardinal Reginald Pole, who believed in spiritual renewal and an inward turn in the practice of faith.

Earthly love likewise played a significant role in Michelangelo's life; his affection for men was expressed in sonnets and letters, as Raymond Carlson shows in his essay, and in his *disegni finiti* (completed drawings). Mythological themes, such as the story of Ganymede, enabled him to express his love, visually, for a number of young men (fig. 14/cat. 6). These beautifully executed drawings, some of which he presented as gifts to Gherardo Perini in the 1520s and to Cavalieri in the early 1530s, were works of art in their own right. In her essay, Marieke van den Doel shows how the Neoplatonic thinking of the philosopher Marsilio Ficino can be detected in some of these works, in which there is also a place for the physical aspects of love. These *disegni finiti,* having begun life as intensely personal gifts, quickly became widely known and highly valued images that were reproduced in large numbers (fig. 12/cat. 1). They marked the beginning of a new genre and changed the status of drawings in the early sixteenth century.

The male body almost always played the leading role throughout Michelangelo's long career. Of the six hundred or so of his drawings that have survived, most feature the male nude.[28] At the same time, the real men in his life – from patrons, popes and rulers to teachers, friends and lovers – were equally important to his art, as well as to the image we hold of him today. He achieved his near-mythical status through his work, bolstered by

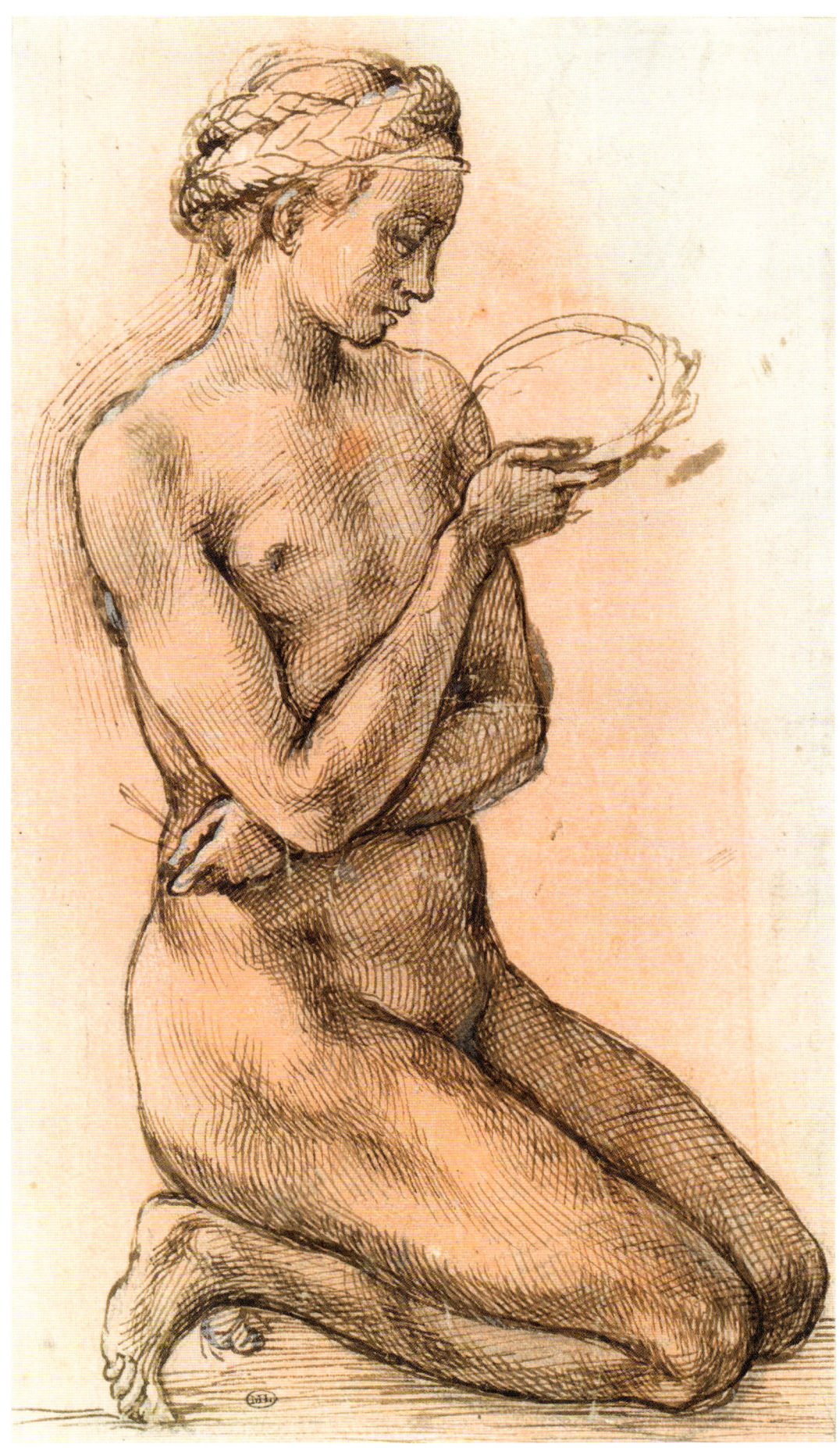

fig. 11   Michelangelo, *Study of a Female Nude*, c. 1500–1501. Black chalk, pen and ink and white heightening on pink prepared paper, 266 x 151 mm. Paris, Musée du Louvre, Département des arts graphiques, inv. 726

Giorgio Vasari's influential biography, which held him out as the greatest artist of all. Michelangelo's depiction of the male body is fixed in our collective imagination and his fame remains undiminished. He himself once commented on the subject of fame, in connection with the tomb monument in the Medici Chapel: 'Fame holds the epitaphs in position; it goes neither forward nor backward for they are dead and their work is still.'[29] In that respect, at least, we have to disagree with him. Our society's shifting perception of masculinity, beauty, gender and sexuality means that we can continually pose new questions concerning the master's work and life, and consider Michelangelo's men in a different light.

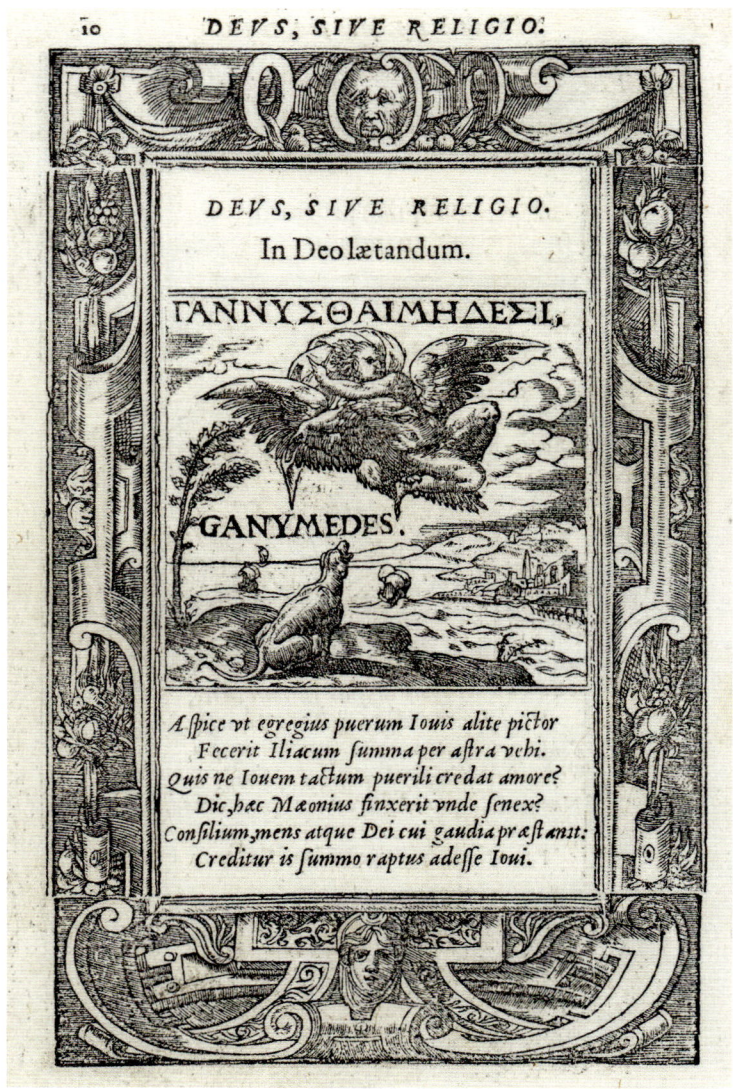

fig. 12   (cat. 1) Andrea Alciato, *Emblemata* (Guliel Rouilium, 1551), p. 10. The Hague, RKD – Netherlands Institute for Art History, inv. 201402142

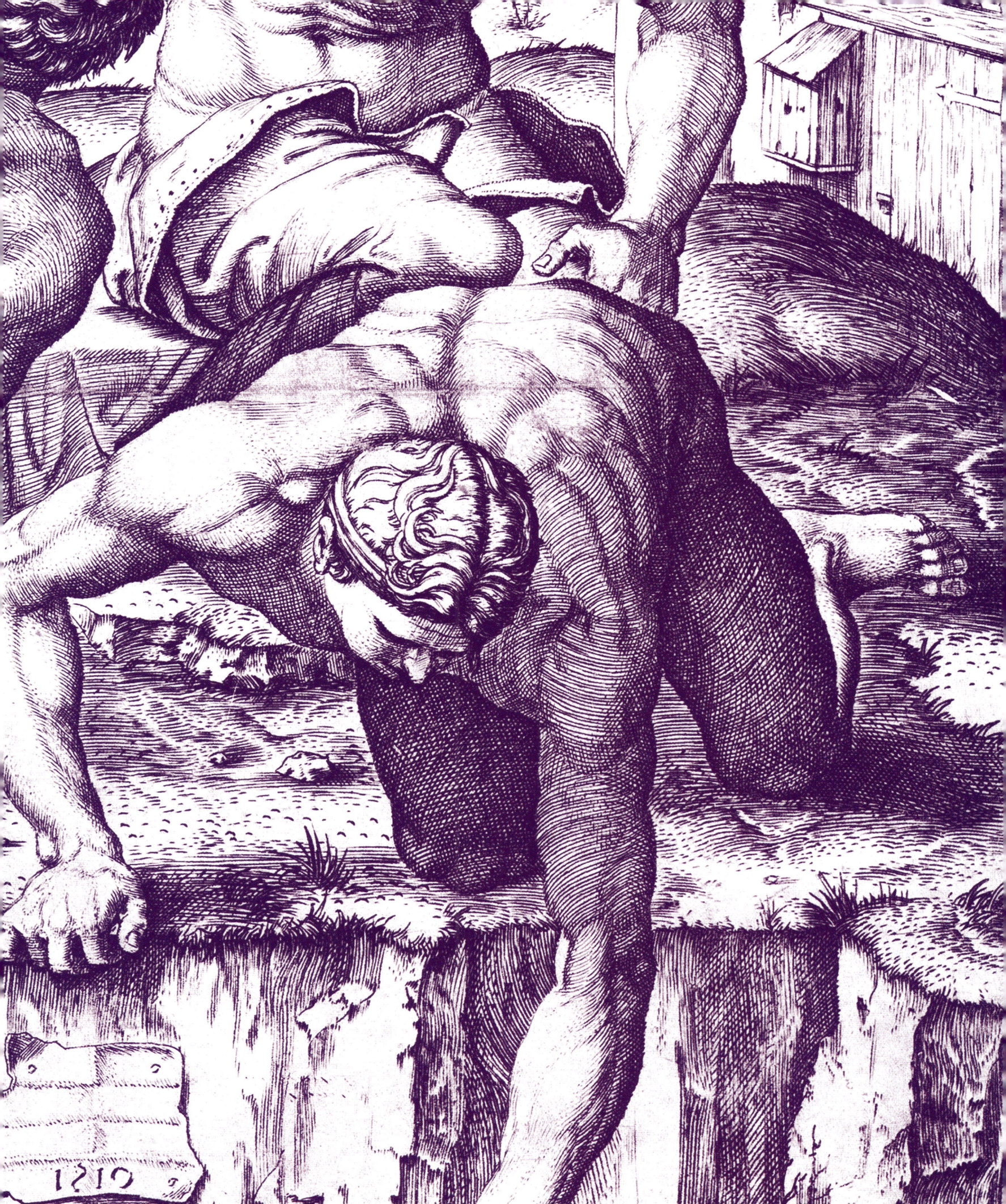

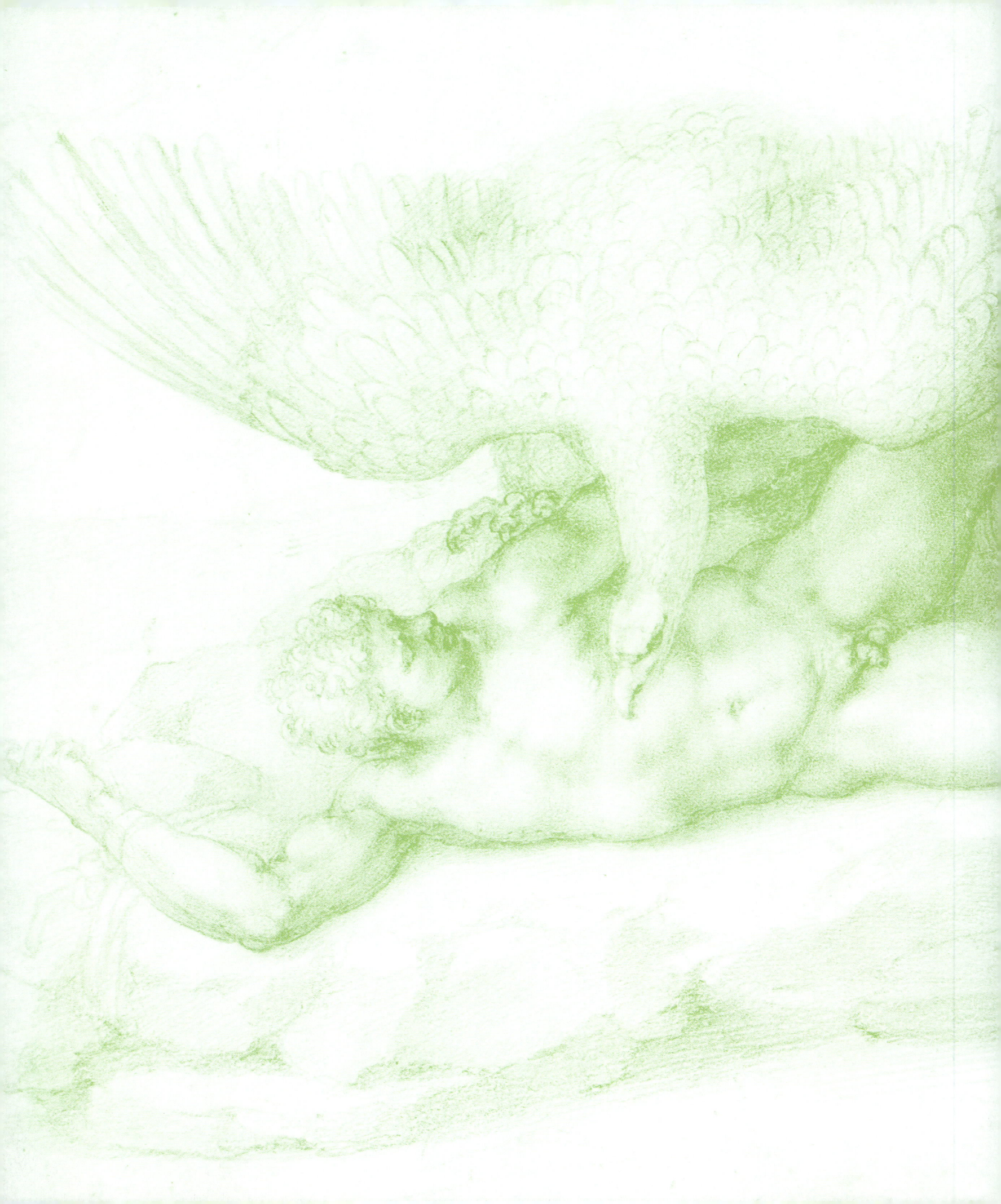

Love

"Nel voler vostro è sol la voglia mia,
i miei pensier nel vostro cor si fanno,
nel vostro fiato son le mie parole.

Come luna da sé sol par ch'io sia
ché gli occhi nostri in ciel veder non sanno
se non quel tanto che n'accende il sole."

'Within your will alone is my desire,
my thoughts are created in your heart,
and within your breath are my own words.

Alone, I seem as the moon is by itself:
for our eyes are only able to see in heaven
as much of it as the sun illuminates.'

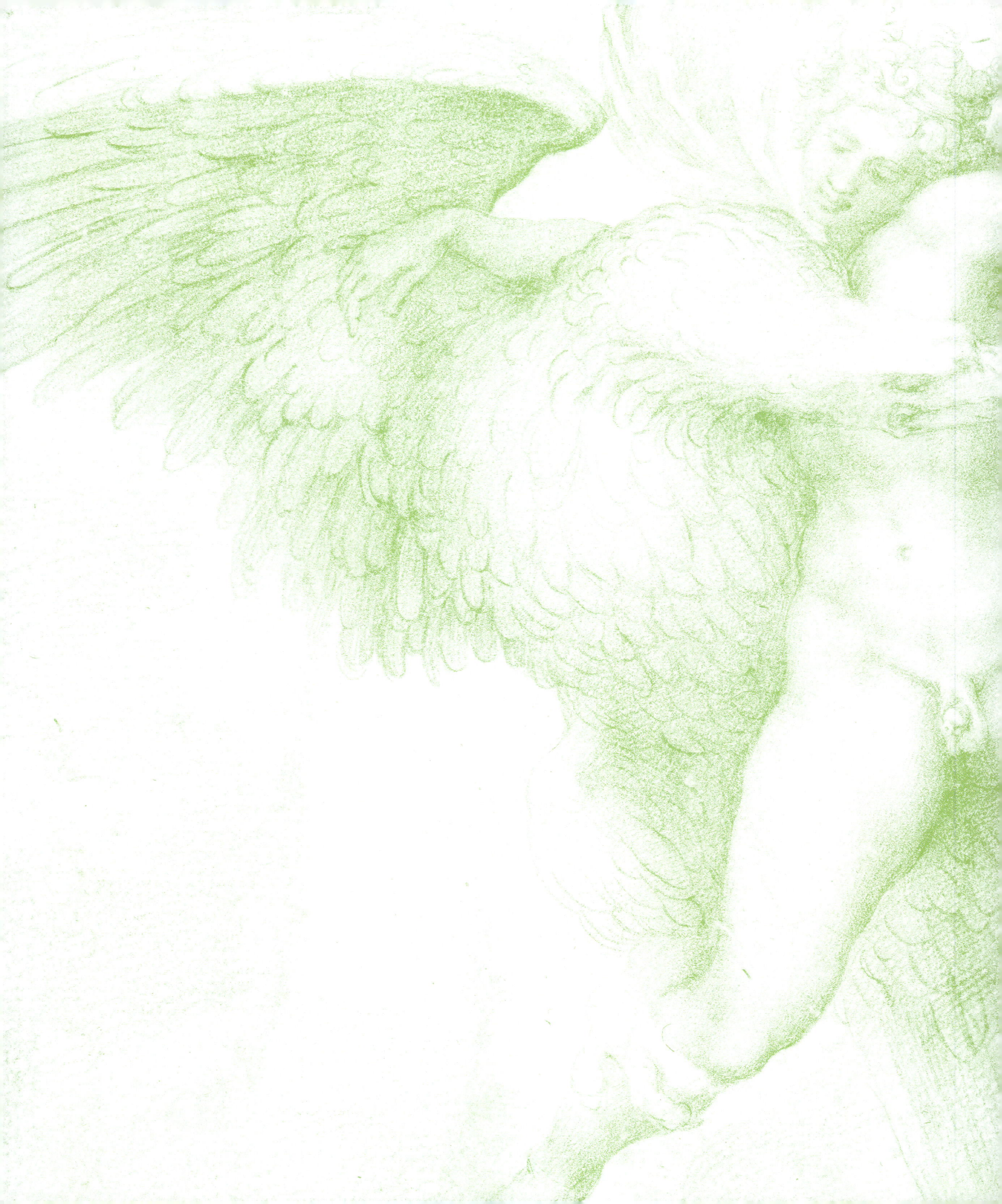

'Masculine Love'.
Michelangelo and Boys

Michael Rocke

A distinctive trait of Michelangelo's art and life was his fascination with male beauty, which in his artistic output he expressed in numerous representations of virile, often nude bodies.[1] The prominence of attractive, powerfully muscled, naked men in his drawings, paintings and sculptures, together with the homoerotic content of some of his letters and poems and his several presumed or known intense male friendships, have long fed speculation about the nature of the artist's erotic inclinations. During Michelangelo's own lifetime, some people evidently took his depictions of male nudes, or the attentions he devoted to young friends, as signs of sexual impropriety, innuendos that the artist himself and his contemporary biographers tried carefully to repudiate. Even Michelangelo's own great-nephew, his namesake known as the Younger, fretted about his great-uncle's many amorous poems whose subjects were male, admitting, while preparing the first-ever edition of his verse, that they were easily recognised expressions of what he called 'manly' or 'masculine love'. Fearing their verbatim publication would give people cause to malign his great-uncle's reputation, he chose instead to edit out any trace of troublesome 'masculine love' from his poetic oeuvre. He bowdlerised Michelangelo's incriminating verses, changing the gender of nouns and pronouns from male to female and substituting words or whole phrases when he published his fabricated version of them in 1623.[2]

In the late nineteenth century, when Cesare Guasti finally issued an edition of Michelangelo's unexpurgated poetry in 1863,[3] the artist's complete correspondence began to be published, and as the Buonarroti family archives became accessible, literary critics and historians – such as Walter Pater, John Addington Symonds and others – had more reliable sources to delve more deeply into questions regarding Michelangelo's sexual desires and identity.[4] At the same time, new scientific and scholarly investigations into same-sex sexual practices and identities were emerging, contributing to the construction of the modern figure of the 'homosexual'.[5] In his ground-breaking and popular biography of Michelangelo, published in 1893, Symonds – himself homosexual and actively involved in the new research – was the first English-language historian to discuss openly and at length the artist's relationships with young men. Though he made clear what Michelangelo's predilections were, he spoke only of his 'friendships'. He reassured readers that the artist's deep attraction towards persons of his own sex was merely idealised and spiritual, inspired by the ancient Greeks, and that no evidence existed to suggest he ever acted physically on his desires. As he noted in an appendix summing up his views:

'It is clear, I think, that Michelangelo Buonarroti was one of those exceptional, but not uncommon men, who are born with sensibilities abnormally deflected from the ordinary channel. He showed no partiality for women, and a notable enthusiasm for the beauty of young men. There is nothing in his letters, in the correspondence addressed to him, in his poetry, or in any of the numerous contemporary notices of his daily life, to raise any suspicion regarding his moral conduct.'[6]

We need not share Symonds's hypocrisy about the morality of Michelangelo's behaviour to note that there is no more hard evidence today than there was in the nineteenth century that he ever had sex with anyone, for what that is worth. There is also no evidence that he did not. The question hardly matters in the long run. Nevertheless, most scholars ever since, though with varying emphases and from different perspectives, have tended to maintain Symonds's characterisation of Michelangelo's erotic persona as a man who was profoundly inclined to love other men, and was also deeply ambivalent about his inclinations, whether he engaged with others sexually or not.[7] Over time, changing attitudes towards gender and sex have led to more widespread acceptance of the artist's same-sex affinities. As Hugo Chapman remarked sympathetically in his catalogue of the 2005–06 Teylers and British Museum exhibitions of his drawings, Michelangelo's homosexuality is by now 'almost universally acknowledged',[8] while for many today he has become a gay icon.[9]

If Michelangelo's proclivities towards other males are now generally recognised, and most of the details of his handful of presumed intimate friendships have long been known, questions remain as to how to characterise his experiences more appropriately, especially in light of more recent studies of sexual practices and conventions in his own day. Over the last few decades, historical studies of male-male sexual relationships in medieval and early modern Italy and Europe, including my own, have brought to light a mass of new evidence unavailable to earlier scholars of Michelangelo, and have fundamentally reshaped or challenged older conceptions and interpretations of the nature of pre-modern sexual behaviours and identities.[10] This essay, then, aims to situate Michelangelo and some of his loves and life experiences more firmly in a broader context of male sexual culture and masculine gender identity, especially in fifteenth- and sixteenth-century Florence, his place of birth and home for many years. It will also explore what his great-nephew understood when he censured his amorous verses with the phrase 'masculine love'. In particular, I want to question the still-common tendency to refer misleadingly to the objects of Michelangelo's amorous relationships generically as 'men', or even 'young men'. For like most men of his day and age, Michelangelo was not attracted to mature men, and not even young men, but rather to adolescents who had not yet acquired a beard, abundant body hair or other physical characteristics of full manhood.

Same-Sex Sexual Culture in Florence

Just as the vibrant artistic culture and intellectual life of Renaissance Florence shaped Michelangelo's development as an artist, so must its sexual culture – especially the prevalence and character of male-male sexual relations – have influenced him too. Born in 1475, Michelangelo spent his childhood and adolescence up to the age of nineteen in Florence and afterwards spent long periods of time there until 1534 when, at the age of fifty-nine, he moved definitively to Rome where he died thirty years later. It was in Florence that he had his formative life experiences and would have gained his culturally specific understanding of male friendships, sociability and sexuality.

In Michelangelo's home city, sexual relations between males held an unusually prominent, if ambig-

uous, place – a complex and contradictory mix of official disapproval and widespread community tolerance. As elsewhere in Europe, in Florence there were severe religious and legal proscriptions against sodomy, a term that could designate many non-reproductive sexual acts no matter which genders were involved, but in practice referred mainly to male-male sex. Like other Italian city-states between 1400 and 1600, notably Venice and Lucca, Florence also took unprecedented measures to pursue and punish sodomy. These included the creation in 1432 of a special magistracy – evocatively called the Officers of the Night – to police these illicit acts. Over their seventy years of operation, the Night Officers unearthed a remarkably large, thriving and seemingly irrepressible same-sex universe, with the numbers accused and convicted for sodomy far eclipsing those in any other place in Italy, or in Europe.[11]

The greatest concentration of sodomy prosecutions occurred in roughly the last forty years of the Quattrocento, encompassing Michelangelo's childhood and youth. From 1459 to 1502 (when the Office of the Night was eventually suppressed), as many as 15,000 boys and men were incriminated – and around 2,200 convicted – for having had sex with another male. In a city of about 40,000 people, on average some four hundred individuals came to the attention of the courts every year, and nearly fifty were convicted.[12] Sensational as these figures are, they demonstrably capture only a slice of the city's illicit sex among males. Reflecting their fellow citizens' general ambivalence, the Officers of the Night were, in effect, far from zealous and declined to pursue the vast majority of allegations, even the most credible, and they punished only a small minority.[13] Together, the sodomy they brought to light and the sexual activity they wilfully ignored suggest that in Michelangelo's Florence, male-male sexual relations, while perhaps not universal, were ubiquitous, a fairly normal occurrence in the social and sexual experience of many local boys and men.

The characteristics of male-male sexual relations in Florence, and elsewhere in this period, were quite different from what we might expect of homosexuality today, and substantially disrupt modern notions of sexual identity. Sexual encounters among males were not only common but also followed a distinctive Mediterranean pattern, rooted in notions of masculine gender identity, in which the two partners were differentiated by their ages and their roles in the sexual act.[14] Normally it was an adult man, most often in his twenties and thirties, who engaged in sex, mainly anal penetration, with an adolescent ranging in age from twelve to eighteen or at most twenty, and on average fifteen or sixteen. The objects of men's same-sex desires were thus almost always adolescents in that

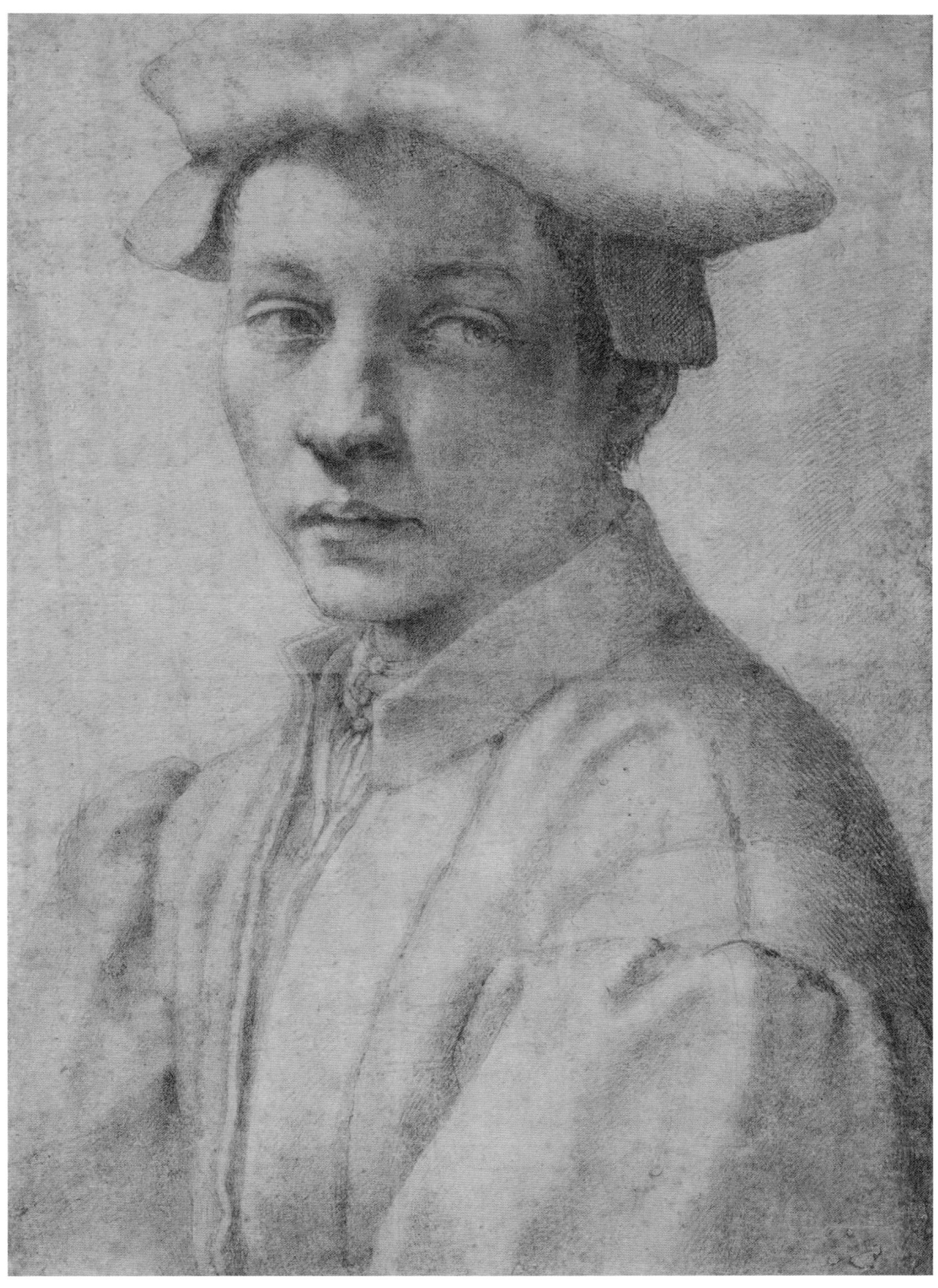

fig. 13   (cat. 36) Michelangelo, *Portrait of Andrea Quaratesi*, c. 1528–1532. Black chalk, 410 x 290 mm. London, British Museum, inv. 1895,0915.519

intermediate phase of life between the onset of puberty and the appearance of a beard and the body hair and musculature associated with fully being a man, a transitional period that for contemporary men evidently held a particular aesthetic and sexual appeal. In court records, these teenagers are regularly referred to as 'boys' ('*puer*' in Latin or '*fanciullo*' in Italian). Physically mature men, on the other hand, with very few exceptions, shunned the receptive role in sex as dishonourable and 'womanly'. Sexual relations between two adult men were very rare and highly scorned, and if discovered, were often rigorously punished.[15] Moreover, the vast majority of same-sex relations involved boys and young men up to the age of thirty-five or so – most of whom engaged in sex with other males as an occasional or temporary transgression during the long period of bachelorhood before they would typically marry. Only a comparative handful of men, mostly unmarried, are documented in sexual relations with boys well into their mature and older years.[16] As will be seen, the parallels with Michelangelo's experiences, while inconclusive as to the question of whether he engaged physically in sex or not, are striking.

From Beloved Adolescent to a Mysterious Midlife Affliction

Given the prevalence of male-male sexual relations in Florence, especially among teenagers and young men, it is unlikely that anyone growing up male there could have been oblivious to the lively illicit activity going on around him. But when Michelangelo was in his mid-teens, he found himself in circumstances that suggest he probably had more direct knowledge of it as well. In 1490, the 15-year-old budding sculptor was taken into the household of the city's *de facto* ruling family, the Medici, where he came into contact with the 'Magnificent' Lorenzo de' Medici's children, all close to his age, as well as with the brilliant circle of humanists and scholars around Lorenzo. Here it seems he was taken under the wing of Angelo Poliziano, the renowned poet and philologist and tutor to Lorenzo's sons. Poliziano was the only member of Lorenzo's circle mentioned in Ascanio Condivi's 1553 *Life of Michelagnolo Buonarroti*, surely based on information provided by the artist himself. Poliziano was credited with advising him on the subject of one of his earliest surviving works, now known as the *Battle of the Centaurs* (fig. 38). Condivi also noted that Poliziano recognised the teenager's outstanding character, helped him in his studies, and '*molto lo amava*' (loved him greatly).[17]

However one interprets this remark, it may – but not necessarily – imply that Poliziano engaged with Michelangelo sexually, though his predilections for boys of Michelangelo's age were well known through both his own writings and the insinuations of other humanists.[18] Given their close connection, intimacy cannot be excluded, but in any case, the young sculptor was likely aware of the older man's inclinations. He could scarcely have avoided knowledge of them, however, when in April 1492 Poliziano was publicly alleged, in dramatic circumstances, to have had sexual relations with a boy one year younger than Michelangelo, then seventeen. The accusation came at a critical moment for the Medici family, entourage and regime, in the days leading up to Lorenzo's death on 8 April. Spurred to action by the apocalyptic preaching of the Dominican friar Girolamo Savonarola, the government chose this tense moment to crack down on sodomy by raiding taverns, making multiple arrests and rounding up some twenty teenagers from prominent families; one of these confessed that, among many others, he had also been sodomised by Poliziano.[19] Several years later, another boy admitted Poliziano had had sexual relations with him when he was fifteen, not long before the scholar's death in September 1494.[20] Even his death was widely reputed to have been caused by a virulent disease he caught through sex with yet another beautiful boy.[21]

Young Michelangelo's reactions to these dramatic events are unknown, though one can speculate that grief over his older friend's death, or perhaps fear of some intimate revelation, figured in precipitating his sudden flight from Florence two weeks later.[22] In any case, his fond recollections of Poliziano many decades later suggest the connection between them ran deep. Scholars usually assume Michelangelo was influenced by the doctrines of Platonic love expounded by Marsilio Ficino, also in Lorenzo's circle, who encouraged virtuous lovers to contemplate the beauty of the young male beloved as a means to spiritual elevation. In this view, this intensely homoerotic but ideally sexless ethos would have been the model for the adult Michelangelo's own supposed 'spiritual' love of young friends. But Poliziano, who not only wrote about men's attraction to boys, but also plausibly enacted his desires with them in the flesh, may well have provided the teenage Michelangelo with an alternative, more carnal, model of 'masculine love'.

Whatever influence these or other early experiences had on him, nothing suggests that during his own youth Michelangelo followed the typical pattern of young Florentine men, who were more likely to engage in sex with boys while in their twenties and thirties – their footloose bachelor years – than at any other time in their lives. This impression may simply reflect the scarcity of personal evidence such as correspondence and poetry from the artist's youth. His better documented experiences more closely resemble those of the small minority of older and mostly unmarried Florentines who had sexual relations with boys at a more advanced age, for whom such intimacies were not just the occasional recreations of younger men. It was not until the 1520s and 1530s, when Michelangelo was in his later forties and fifties, that shards of evidence first emerge of friendships of a possibly amorous nature with other males – all adolescents, it turns out.

A hint in the winter of 1521/22 that he was up to some kind of dissolute behaviour, perhaps sexual, comes from several letters to him from his friend Leonardo Sellaio, who was plainly troubled. Aged forty-six, Michelangelo was then working in Florence, where he would mostly remain until 1534. In a letter to him in December, Sellaio brusquely admonished his friend 'not to go about at night, and abandon those practices that are injurious to both body and soul, so they do no harm to your soul'. Rather than some generic warning, this sounds like a reprimand for a real and potentially dangerous transgression. Three weeks later Sellaio responded happily to a now-lost missive from Michelangelo: 'Of all your news, one bit exceeds the others, and that is that you have been cured of an illness from which few recover... Persevere.' After a few weeks he reiterated his relief that 'you are free of an illness that would have damned both soul and body'.[23]

Sellaio carefully sidestepped naming the behaviour or condition he feared so threatened Michelangelo's physical and spiritual wellbeing. Scholarly speculation as to its nature has included masturbation, excessive drinking or bad company.[24] Sellaio's delicate dance around the name of Michelangelo's affliction instead calls to mind the sole vice that many Christians considered so wicked it should never be mentioned – namely, sodomy. Night-time was of course allusive of sodomy, and much sexual trafficking between men and boys occurred in the hours between sunset and the closing hour of taverns.[25] Moreover, few if any practices other than the unspeakable vice would have had the twin potential to endanger one's body, most likely through the devastating 'French pox', soon to be known as syphilis, which was often understood to be transmitted sexually;[26] and, in accordance with Catholic doctrine, condemned one's soul to eternal damnation. Whether Michelangelo was really cured of his 'ailment' remains an open question.

Michelangelo's Dearest Friends

If Sellaio's warning alluded to illicit sexual pleasures, its timing is suggestive. As Saslow has observed in his study of the artist's poetry, it was in the period between 1522 and 1524 that Michelangelo's verse took a distinctly homoerotic turn.[27] The unidentified but clearly male object of his amorous poems in these years was likely the young Florentine, Gherardo Perini. Three letters between the artist and Perini survive from early 1522, but their affectionate tone and mention of several dear friends – Michelangelo calls them 'those you know love you the most' – suggest Perini was already well established in his circle.[28] Long thought mistakenly to be in his forties when they corresponded, Perini, born in 1504, was in fact only eighteen.[29] When the two probably met he could have been as young as sixteen, and Michelangelo was twenty-eight years his senior. In his 1568 *Life of Michelangelo*, Giorgio Vasari called Perini the artist's '*amicissimo*' (dearest friend), to whom he gave several drawings as gifts, an exceptional gesture of fondness he would reserve for only a few cherished intimates.[30] On a playful drawing of a nude *putto* urinating into a vase (not among those he gave to Perini), a note in Michelangelo's hand refers to 'Perino', an affectionate nickname for the boy: 'I beg you not to make me draw this evening, because Perino isn't here.'[31] Depending on how the sentence is read, Michelangelo seems to indicate that he appreciated the boy's special company either as a diversion from the chore of drawing or as a creative inspiration for it.

A few years later, Michelangelo had a particular fondness for Andrea Quaratesi, born in November 1512, the scion of a banking family who probably studied drawing with him. Little is known about their friendship: letters between them from late 1530 to 1532 survive, but they clearly knew each other earlier. The sole extant letter to him from Michelangelo, from June 1532, includes on its reverse fragments of a poem in his hand with the suggestive phrases, '*in quel medesmo tempo ch'io vi adoro*' ('during the very time that I adore you') and '*Ben ama chi ben arde*' ('He truly loves who truly burns').[32] Textual fragments on a sheet of his drawings include Andrea's name, and the phrase '*a me m'è cho[n]solatione assai*' ('to me he [or it] is great solace').[33] The word used here, '*consolazione*', or solace, is intriguing, for not only did Florentines sometimes use it to indicate sexual relief,[34] but on an earlier occasion, Michelangelo also employed it in an explicitly sexual context referring to a boy. In that well-known anecdote, he described a father's attempt to persuade him to take his son on as an apprentice, with the brazen argument that if the artist were only to lay eyes on the handsome boy, he would not only take him into his household but would chase him into his bed; Buonarroti noted wryly that he declined

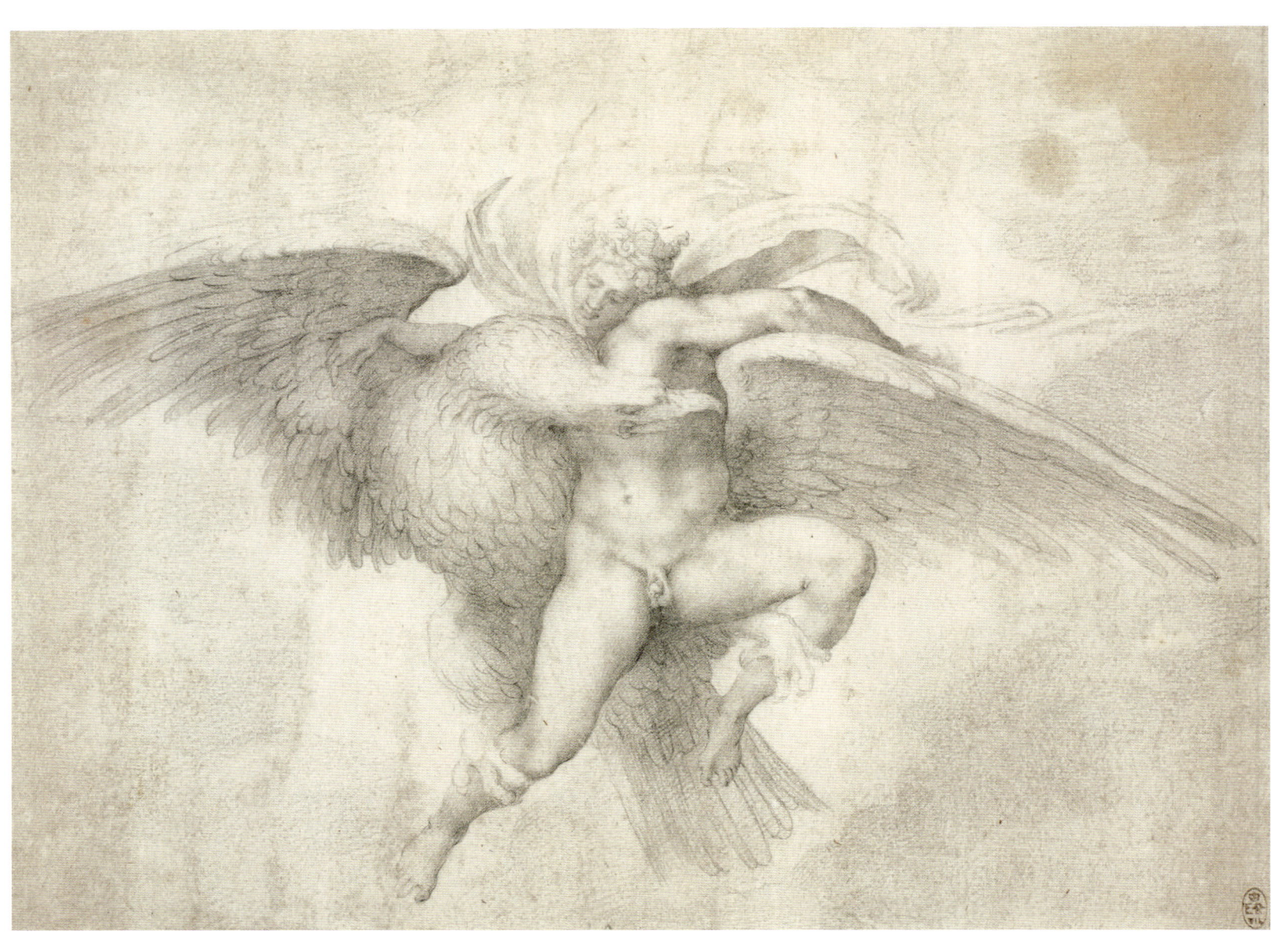

fig. 14   (cat. 6) Giulio Clovio, after Michelangelo, *Ganymede*, c. 1540. Black chalk, 192 x 260 mm. Windsor, Royal Collection Trust, inv. RCIN 913036

this *consolazione*.[35] In 1530, when Michelangelo, then aged fifty-five, may have executed his stunning portrait drawing of the ephebic Andrea Quaratesi as a gift to him – one of a handful of portraits he produced – the boy was likely no older than seventeen or eighteen (fig. 13/cat. 36).[36]

Probably in the late summer or autumn of 1532, Michelangelo, then fifty-seven, met Tommaso de' Cavalieri, the young son of a Roman nobleman and said to be exceptionally handsome and gifted, and he was soon besotted. Cavalieri became the object of the most important and ardent sentimental relationship of his lifetime, the 'open secret' that most critics assume was probably Platonic in nature and never consummated physically.[37] Michelangelo expressed his love for Cavalieri in an outpouring of amorous poems for him, and also gave him gifts of several magnificent drawings on mythological themes, most of them – especially his first gift showing the rape of the shepherd boy Ganymede by lustful Zeus in the form of an eagle (fig. 14/cat. 6) – with a high erotic charge. When the two first met, Cavalieri was most likely a teenager, not the 'young man' of twenty-three he was long thought to have been. He was born between 1512 and 1519 (the precise date remains unknown), situating him between the ages of thirteen and twenty.[38] I suspect he was sixteen or seventeen, around the same ages as Perini and Quaratesi when Michelangelo became infatuated with them, or at any rate before his beard began to appear. As he had done for Quaratesi, Michelangelo also unusually presented Cavalieri with a gift of a portrait drawing. An unidentified writer who later saw the portrait described the sitter as beardless, with beautiful eyes and other facial features, and holding a portrait or medallion in his hand.[39] The portrait was long believed lost, but a damaged drawing with this subject now in the Musée Bonnat-Helleu in Bayonne has been authoritatively attributed to Michelangelo and identified as Cavalieri's portrait (fig. 15).[40] Despite the drawing's poor condition, the slender, smooth-faced, almost delicate figure who gazes from it seems more the adolescent he almost certainly was rather than a young man.

While Michelangelo was still in the throes of his heated love for Cavalieri, before he moved to Rome in the autumn of 1534, two other Florentine boys emerge fleetingly in his correspondence in ways that strongly suggest he had been involved in intimate – and perhaps physical – relationships with them as well. Apart from their appearance here, the two remain obscure. The first instance, in the form of a letter from an otherwise unknown Simone, has received little attention despite its amorous and alluring language.[41] Simone described himself as being of '*tenera età*' (tender age) – thus certainly a boy – but despite his young years he still suffered the torments of his love for Michelangelo, then fifty-nine. Addressing Michelangelo with surprising familiarity as '*Amantissimo mio M*' (My most beloved M), and using '*tu*' rather than the respectful '*voi*', he claims he is suffering so strongly from '*le forze d'amore*' (the forces of love) that 'I know not where to turn to find my peace, if not in you. For you are the one who can give me every happiness and satisfaction.' Simone despaired he might have lost his friend, perhaps due to some ill-considered slight, but he trusted Michelangelo would forgive him 'because I want you to be my most loving friend, and I yours'. Simone then effusively offered himself – heart, soul and, it seems, body – to the much older man:

> 'Therefore, M my sweetest, gratefully receive my friendly letter, together with my heart and soul, all of which I give to you in eternity. And you can use me according to your way, because for you I'm willing to endure every passion, as long as your friendship is restored to me.'[42]

Simone's provocative final sentence is especially telling. With thinly veiled language, the boy seems to urge Michelangelo to do whatever he pleases with him, following the artist's own proclivities, and assures the much older man he is prepared to accept any suffering or desire in order to regain his affections. Whether or how Michelangelo responded is unknown.

An exchange with Febo di Poggio in late 1534–early 1535 suggests that the artist had recently had an intense connection with him too. Nothing is known about Febo beyond these two letters and some nostalgic poems Michelangelo later composed about him,[43] but these sources give the impression that he too was young and exerted a surprising fascination over the older man. The night before he left Florence never to return, Michelangelo wrote to Febo trying to patch up an apparent spat: 'though you bear great hatred towards me – I don't know why, I think not because of the love I bear towards you, but because of the talk of others, which you shouldn't believe, having put me to the test... ' Announcing his departure, he swore to Febo that he would remain at his service until the end of his life, with loyalty and love, more than any other friend.[44] Several months later, responding to another evidently lost letter, Febo reassured Michelangelo that he could never be angry with him since he considered him like a father, nor had the artist's behaviour warranted any such reaction. After reminding Michelangelo of his offer of help should he need anything, Febo then cheekily pressed him for money to buy some new clothes and to travel to a fighting match. He closed on a mildly threatening note.[45] Characterised by some scholars as a street tough, a blackmailer, or a former model on the make, Febo's easy familiarity with Michelangelo and his brazen and trivial request – unlikely his first – to my mind evoke the many teenage male hustlers, or the kept boys of older men, who animated the Florentine same-sex scene and filled the police and court records on sodomy.[46]

Unlike most of his relationships, which appear to have lasted briefly, or no more than a few years, Michelangelo and Cavalieri remained friends for over three decades. When the artist died in 1564, Cavalieri, by then long-married with children, was among the few close associates at his bedside. Michelangelo's heated passion for him after they first met in 1532, however, cooled within a few years. The drawings he made for him date only from these early years, and the torrent of love poems for Cavalieri subsided noticeably after 1534, and especially after 1536. By this time Cavalieri was maturing from boyhood into youth, when he would have lost the erotic appeal of beardless adolescent beauty that had ignited Michelangelo's desire for him so explosively, whether enacted physically or not. In this aspect, as in others, the arc of their relationship paralleled the experience of countless other same-sex lovers in their society, as the teenage partner transitioned gradually into manhood, more or less between the ages of eighteen and twenty, and thereafter became, in the blunt words of one Florentine observer in 1510, 'no longer any good to use' sexually.[47] Afterwards, the evidence hints vaguely at only one other possible love interest on the artist's part, with another stunningly beautiful but even younger boy, Cecchino Bracci, who died at the age of fifteen when Michelangelo was aged sixty-nine.[48]

Michelangelo's intense love for Tommaso de' Cavalieri was openly known among a select group of friends, and surely outside this circle too as time went on; his earlier association with Gherardo Perini must have been recalled and talked about as well.[49] Many years later, in a famous letter of 1545 castigating Michelangelo for the indecency of his nude figures in the Sistine Chapel's The Last Judgement, the poison-penned Pietro Aretino referred to both relationships. Irritated that the artist refused him the drawings he sought, he cattily noted that only certain 'Gherardi' and 'Tomai' could obtain them, referring to Perini and Cavalieri, and likely hinting at a sexual exchange.[50] While both of his early biographers felt compelled to defend Michelangelo against gossip and innuendo of this sort, his disciple Condivi was more explicit. Condivi admitted that the artist's love of the beauty of male bodies encouraged certain 'sensual men who only understand love of beauty only as something lascivious and indecent' to think and speak ill of him. He countered by likening Michelangelo to Socrates, with his impeccably pure love for the handsome young Alcibiades, who always arose from Socrates' side unsullied as if he were his own father.[51] Condivi claimed he heard his master speak often about love, but insisted he echoed only the chaste lessons from Plato, who praised the eroticised contemplation of male beauty as a means to spiritual growth, but censured love's physical expression.[52]

Elsewhere he attributed Michelangelo's good health not only to his constitution and to exercise, but also to his self-restraint both in eating habits and in 'coito' (sexual activity).[53] This last remark is intriguing in that Michelangelo, certainly the source, also later expounded on it. His reaction survives as one of many marginal glosses recorded by the artist's assistant, Tiberio Calcagni, in a copy of Condivi's Life: 'On sex. This I have always observed, and if you want to prolong your life, don't engage in sex, or at least do so as seldom as you can.'[54] His comment may mean he had always shunned sexual relations of any sort, yet his suggestive coda infers that his efforts to abstain, as he seems to admit, did not always succeed.[55]

In any case, as other scholars have emphasised, Condivi's Life, composed in close collaboration with Michelangelo, is an apologetic work that employs much self-fashioning and artful amnesia. The elderly artist, aged seventy-eight when the biography was published in 1553, was concerned about shaping the historical record and ensuring his legacy, and certain episodes from his past were best rewritten or overlooked. In this regard, it is remarkable that Condivi neglected even to mention the immediately renowned drawings that Michelangelo had made for his beloved Cavalieri. One suspects Condivi suppressed all reference to these celebrated drawings, as well as to Cavalieri himself, because Michelangelo worried about the implications both of their erotic content and of the friendship still ongoing between the two men. It was this same urge to protect Michelangelo's reputation and manage his historical legacy that would later induce his great-nephew to expurgate his verses on 'masculine love', to which we now turn.

'Masculine Love'

To justify bowdlerising his great-uncle's amorous and other verses whose subjects were male, the younger Buonarroti said he feared they might give ignorant people cause for malicious talk, because the poems were manifestly expressions of 'amor platonico virile', or 'masculine love of the Platonic species', in Symonds's translation.[56] His qualification of Michelangelo's manly love as 'Platonic' attempts to de-eroticise what he perhaps feared to be the real nature of Michelangelo's desires, before he did even more violence to them by butchering his verses.[57]

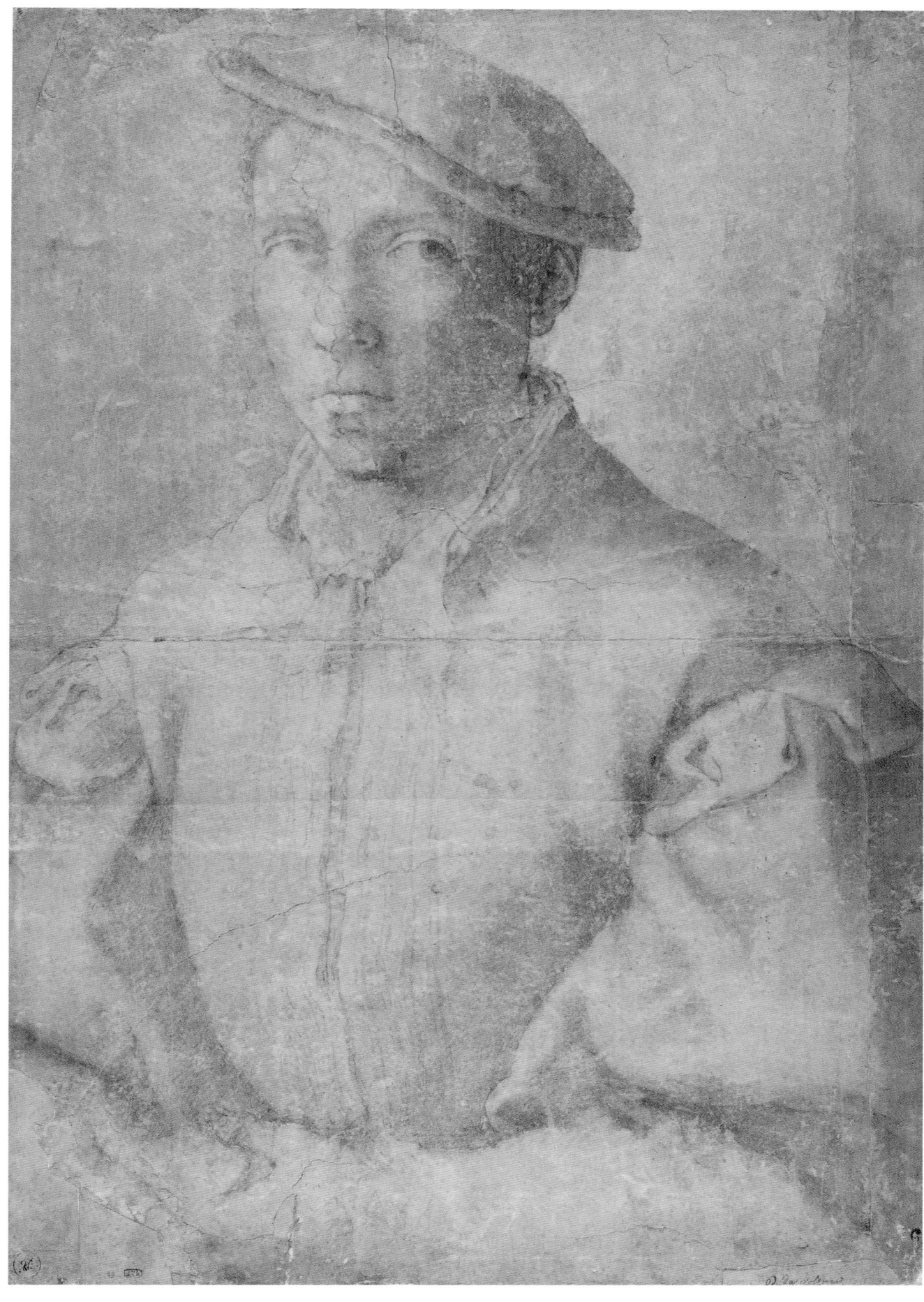

fig. 15   Attributed to Michelangelo, *Portrait of Tommaso de' Cavalieri (?)*, c. 1533–1535. Black chalk, 695 x 488 mm. Bayonne, Musée Bonnat-Helleu, inv. 595

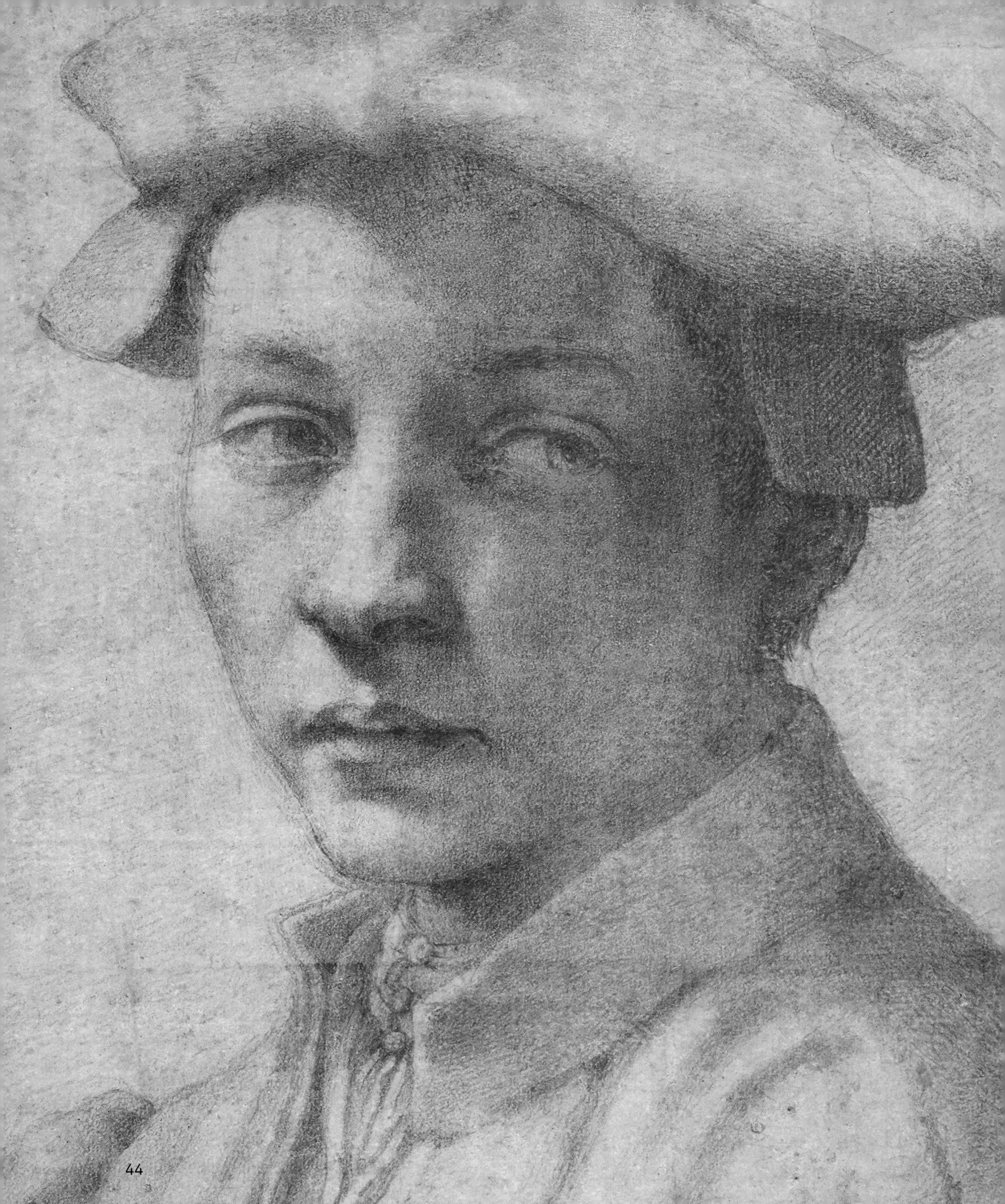

44

But what would Michelangelo the Younger have understood 'masculine love' to be? To my knowledge, Michelangelo the artist did not employ the phrase in his poems or letters, and how it became part of his great-nephew's lexicon remains unclear. In reality, use of the expression 'amore virile' or its several alternative forms – 'amor maschile', 'amore masculino', 'amor maschio' – seems not to have been very common. As far as I have been able to determine, none of these variants was part of earlier Florentine popular parlance, nor do they appear in the many hundreds of vernacular denunciations against sodomy or other sources I have seen from the fifteenth and early sixteenth centuries, or in the contemporary Italian novelle on same-sex themes. The earliest previously recorded occurrences of the expression in print in Italy seem to come from a couple of encyclopaedic works published in Latin in the 1510s, followed by only a few other vernacular literary works into the next century; from Italy it migrated to France and England, where variations have been found in a small number of works in the same period. Drawing on the example from Michelangelo the Younger and a handful of others, some historians of early modern homosexuality have argued that 'masculine love' represented a conscious and widespread affirmation in the Renaissance of a particular same-sex orientation which, in contrast to the diffuse age-differentiated model that generally prevailed in pre-modern times, embodied age-egalitarian companionate relationships, reciprocity of sexual desires and a shared sense of sexual identity. With these characteristics, 'masculine love' would supposedly have been an important precursor of modern homosexuality.[58]

In fact, several early modern Italian sources which prominently highlight 'masculine love' – and which proponents of this view have either misrepresented or ignored – point resoundingly to the opposite conclusion. In them, this expression, in whatever variant, refers not to sexual attraction between age-undifferentiated males, but specifically to the love of adult men for adolescents. Unlike the largely hostile sources cited by these other scholars, their authors are openly sympathetic or knowledgeable advocates of contemporary same-sex love, as will be seen below, so their understanding of amore masculino as occurring exclusively between men and boys carries a certain authority. While it is impossible to identify his source, Michelangelo the Younger and other early modern Italians almost certainly understood it in this way.

One example – interesting in part because it implicates another great Florentine artist and contemporary of Michelangelo, Leonardo da Vinci – comes from a curious work entitled Il libro dei sogni (The Book of Dreams), written by the Milanese painter and art theorist Gian Paolo Lomazzo around 1563 (but only published in the 1970s). In the fifth of the book's seven imagined dialogues between Leonardo and the ancient Greek sculptor and painter Phidias, the two men suddenly digress from their discussion on painting to chat about Leonardo's great love for his disciple Salai. Alluding clearly to sodomy, Leonardo admits when asked by Phidias that many times he had played 'the game from behind, the one the Florentines love so much' with young Salai because he was an extremely beautiful youngster, 'especially when he was fifteen'. He then launches into a spirited defence of the practice of men loving boys, beginning with his declaration, 'Know that masculine love is solely a work of virtue, which joins males together in various sorts of friendship, such that from out of a young age come, at a manly age, worthier and closer friends.'[59]

Except for his virtual 'outing' of Leonardo as a lover of boys, Lomazzo's apology for pederasty, including the above-cited passage, closely followed a second-century CE Greek dialogue entitled Erōtes, also known in Italian as Amori diversi (Different Loves) or in English as Affairs of the Heart, traditionally thought to be by the satirist Lucian.[60] The Erōtes is a debate between two men on the relative merits of men's love of women and their love of boys, defined as adolescents from the onset of puberty up to the age of twenty. It concludes with the judgement that men's love of boys is the preferred form of love, and not only in the chaste version espoused by certain philosophers, but above all in the physical expression of sex. Lucian's writings were widely available in Renaissance Italy, and it is likely that this dialogue was the source of the contemporary expression 'masculine love'. The Erōtes is first found in Italian translation in a manuscript collection of his dialogues dated from about 1475, and the first edition in the original Greek was printed in Florence in 1496. His works became so popular that between 1525, when they were first printed in Italian, and 1551, they appeared in seven different Italian editions and one Greek, all including the Amori diversi.[61] Literate sixteenth- and seventeenth-century Italians would thus have had ample opportunity to know this amusing dialogue on 'masculine love' that advocates men's desire for boys. It would have resonated strongly with them not only for its humour, but also because it so closely paralleled their own experience and understanding of male-male sexual relations, which typically followed this ancient Mediterranean model.

'Masculine love' is also the subject of the notorious apology for pederasty, L'Alcibiade fanciullo a scola, written by Antonio Rocco, a Venetian libertine priest and professor of philosophy, before 1630 and published in 1651/52. In this dialogue, the schoolteacher Filotimo seeks to seduce his 14-year-old pupil Alcibiade by persuading him of the sublime delights as well as the spiritual and intellectual benefits of erotic relations between men and boys. When, at a certain point, Alcibiade asks bluntly whether two mature men could not also enjoy the pleasures of sex together, Filotimo responds by roundly condemning such men as rebels against love and beasts of cruel and corrupt senses. He insists instead that '*amor maschio è fanciullo*' (masculine love means love of a boy).[62]

The various expressions denoting 'masculine love', therefore, hardly seem to herald a new sexual subjectivity in the Renaissance that embodied qualities of symmetry, reciprocity and shared sexual identity in an early model of homosexual orientation. Rather, at least in the sources discussed here, they expressed the hierarchical form of sexual relations between men and teenage boys that had prevailed in Mediterranean societies since classical times, right up to and including the early modern period. This type of erotic bond, in other words, was forged on a range of conventional social, generational, role-assuming and gendered differences rather than on mutual similarities. As Lomazzo has Leonardo express, however, these differences embedded in 'masculine love' evidently did not preclude, and may well have fostered, the establishment of long-lasting non-erotic friendships, such as that between Leonardo and Salai, or between Michelangelo and his beloved Tommaso de' Cavalieri.

Nothing presented in this essay proves that Michelangelo consummated relations with any of the boys to whom he was attracted, however passionate his engagement with them was. What the circumstantial evidence demonstrates, at least, is how closely the patterns of his experience resembled those of thousands of men around him who plausibly or verifiably acted on their sexual desires with boys. Like them, the adult Michelangelo was almost certainly not drawn erotically to other men, understood as his peers in age or masculine gender status. Rather, the objects of his attraction were males who, according to their society's canons, were not yet fully men, neither physically nor in terms of their gender. Indeed, smooth-faced juvenile males appealed sexually to physically mature men precisely because they were *not* men.

Given this historical perspective, I wonder whether the centrality of adolescents as the main focus of the same-sex desire of Quattro- and Cinquecento Italian men should not encourage us to look anew at Michelangelo's strapping, muscular male nudes. Perhaps we should reconsider the facile assumption that, as they may have for us, they must have had a clear sexual charge and meaning for Michelangelo, or for other men of his day. Those beefy, athletic men bear little resemblance to the pubescent bodies of the beardless adolescents who we now know held such strong erotic fascination for men such as Michelangelo.

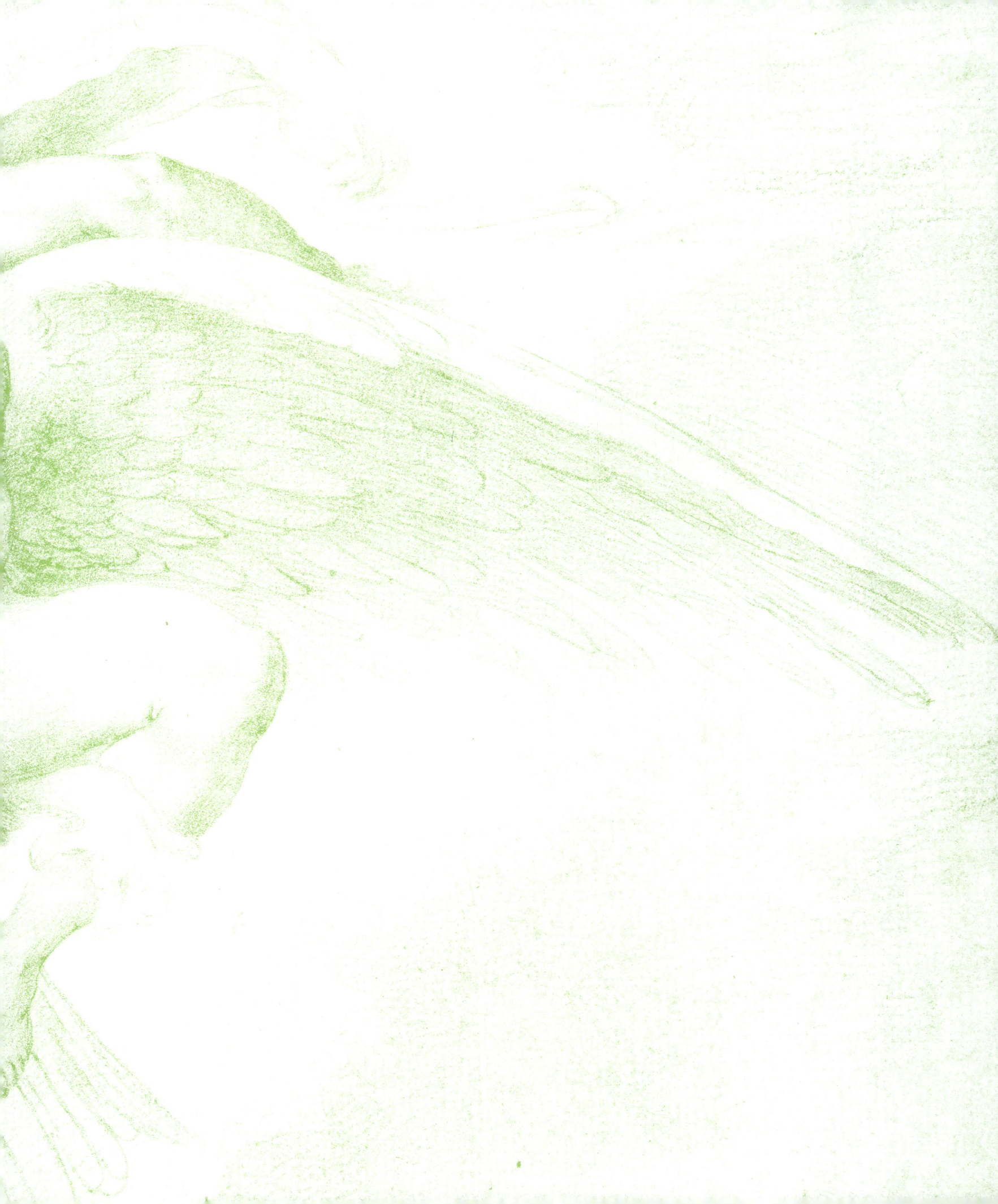

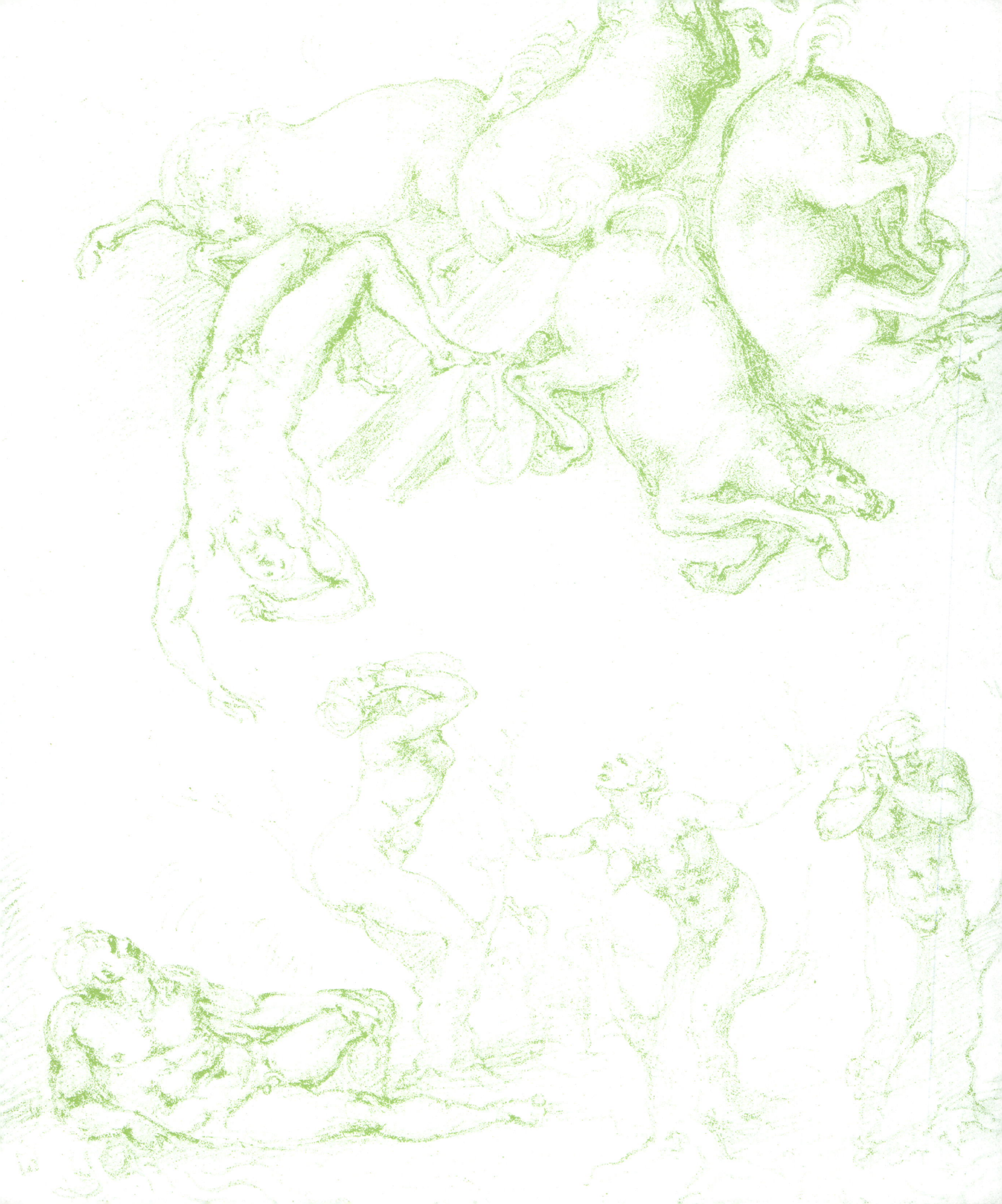

Poems and Letters.
How Michelangelo Wrote the
Unseeable and Drew the Unsayable

Raymond Carlson

The man Michelangelo loved had a beautiful body.

So announced the humanist Benedetto Varchi before a public audience on 6 March 1547. Speaking to a crowd assembled at a weekly gathering of the Accademia Fiorentina (Florentine Academy), Varchi embedded this pronouncement within his scholarly exposition of Michelangelo's poetry.[1] Towards the end of his lecture, Varchi cited two of the famed artist's sonnets after noting that Michelangelo had dedicated the first of them to Tommaso de' Cavalieri, the young Roman nobleman whom the artist had met nearly 15 years earlier.[2] About Cavalieri, Varchi added this prefatory remark: 'Beyond the incomparable beauty of his body, in Rome I already saw in him such elegant habits, excellent ingenuity and graceful manners that he much deserved – as he does still – to be increasingly loved the more one knew him.'[3]

By attesting to the unmatched beauty of Cavalieri's body, Varchi linked physical comeliness with traits expected of his noble rank: elegance, ingenuity and grace. This equivalence had established precedent. In his famed *Il Cortegiano* (Book of the Courtier) published less than two decades earlier, Baldassare Castiglione listed similar properties of a noblewoman as incitements for a courtier's virtuous love.[4] But Cavalieri was not a noblewoman. One of Michelangelo's accomplishments as a writer was to redirect an established courtly paradigm of vernacular lyric poetry toward a male rather than a female beloved. This required careful navigation of poetic forms and period norms. The sonnet cited by Varchi makes no explicit mention of Cavalieri's beauty, indicative of Michelangelo's authorial strategy to foreground his subjective experience as a narrator.[5] Indeed, the sonnet closes with Michelangelo wallowing in his amorous torment: 'naked and alone / I remain the prisoner of an armed knight', the Italian word for knight (*cavalier*) being a pun on Cavalieri's surname. By publicising this sonnet for Cavalieri, Varchi injected a biographical detail into his lecture, locating Michelangelo's creativity in a lived context.

Presented in an era when the physical enactment of same-sex eros could lead to punishments including torture, exile and death, Varchi's publicised praise of Michelangelo's amorous verses for Cavalieri can seem imprudent today.[6] But this is not how Michelangelo reacted. An intermediary sent a copy of Varchi's lecture from Florence to Michelangelo in Rome, and the famed artist responded with effusive praise, adding that he shared the text with other men.[7] He tasked the intermediary with thanking Varchi for him: 'I ask that, on my behalf, you share suitable words for him as appropriate to such love, affection, and courtesies.'[8] In Renaissance Italy, love necessitated repayment. Michelangelo's letter thereby requited Varchi's lecture about his own poetry and capacities as a lover, enacting the Neoplatonic ideals that Varchi had upheld as a guiding source of Michelangelo's verse. When Varchi's lecture was published in 1550, Michelangelo redoubled this gratitude, asking another mutual friend to thank Varchi on behalf of Cavalieri for the honours bestowed upon them both.[9]

Varchi's lecture and the responses it elicited offer a window onto the material strategies of amorous reciprocation in Michelangelo's poetry, letters and artworks. Scholars have long sought to define the emergence of love in Michelangelo's life and work through interrelated intellectual traditions and social realities.[10] Yet the writing of poems and letters held separate conventions in this period that conditioned how love was approached in each, a fact similarly true for art making. Michelangelo's poetry could not delimit each comely contour of the male body with the explicitness of his graphic line, but it could convey his personal experience in words unavailable through art. Michelangelo made his poems, drawings and letters for Cavalieri with awareness of how these three entities were exchanged together. Rather than treat such creations discretely, they should be addressed together as part of a comprehensive strategy of building an amorous relationship.

There has been a longstanding tradition of analysing Michelangelo's writings and artworks separately from one another, in part because of the sheer volume of such surviving material.[11] Over the course of his life, Michelangelo wrote over 300 extant poems, the majority of which were not published in print until centuries later.[12] Dozens among these are thought by scholars to have been addressed to young men, including Cavalieri.[13] The exact count of such poems remains uncertain, in part because Michelangelo's dedicatees are rarely named in verse, nor necessarily identified by gendered language. While in some instances Michelangelo's poems appear on the same sheets as his drawings or letter drafts (which can offer factual clues and avenues for interpretation), they are often on loose sheets with insufficient contextual details.[14] Michelangelo was a dedicated correspondent, and among the more than 1,300 surviving letters to and from him, several contain references to enclosing poems inside them and dispatching drawings alongside them.[15] The corpus of Michelangelo's drawings, while still much debated, may total over 600 sheets in collections around the world.[16]

Within the expansive array of Michelangelo's surviving letters, poems and artworks, those exchanged with Cavalieri offer invaluable detail into his most renowned relationship with another man. This rapport accrued fame not simply through Varchi's lecture but also from the set of chalk drawings Michelangelo gave to Cavalieri.[17] Citing these artworks, Giorgio Vasari wrote in his biography of Michelangelo that, of all the artist's friends, Michelangelo loved Cavalieri infinitely more than the others.[18] Of course, Michelangelo's relationships with other men were not dispassionate. Michelangelo was teaching Andrea Quaratesi, the son of a Florentine banker, how to draw, and Michelangelo produced an exceptional black-chalk portrait of him (fig. 13/cat. 36).[19] He also wrote sonnets for Febo di Poggio, about whom minimal information endures today.[20]

As the heir of a noble family who could trace patrilinear descent from the Orsini – one of the most prominent, historic Roman dynasties – Cavalieri was among Rome's elite and left an extensive record of his life.[21] Cavalieri collected a large assemblage of prints, cameos, antiquities, and objects from the New World.[22] By the time of Varchi's lecture, Cavalieri had held local civic offices in Rome and had been married to Lavinia della Valle – herself from a Roman noble family – for three years.[23] When Varchi cited Michelangelo's verses for Cavalieri at his lecture at the Accademia in 1547, he was resuscitating the creative products of an intense relationship that, by that time, had evolved into an enduring friendship.[24] How he even obtained these poems is an open question, although the most obvious answer – that Cavalieri shared some with him when they met in Rome – is entirely plausible.[25] Cavalieri likely told Varchi about the genesis of his relationship with Michelangelo, details the Florentine humanist neglected to share in his lecture but which can be partly resurrected through surviving material evidence.

Pleasure and Friendship

To establish a rapport with Cavalieri, Michelangelo apparently made the first move. In a draft of his earliest known missive to the young man, Michelangelo began by admitting that he had not received a message from him but felt compelled to write (fig. 16/cat. 42).[26] The letter proffered more than just words. Michelangelo assured Cavalieri of gratification:

'And if of my things, which I hope and promise to do, any will please you, I will call it much more accidental than right. And when I am ever able to be certain of pleasure [*piacere*], as I said, in anything for Your Lordship, I will give the present time and all that is to come for me to that.'[27]

What were the pleasing things (*cose*) that Michelangelo could provide? Cavalieri himself gives the answer in his thankful response to Michelangelo (fig. 17/cat. 5). Acknowledging that illness precluded him from seeing Michelangelo, he was grateful for items accompanying Michelangelo's letter brought by Pier Antonio Cecchini, a sculptor in Rome who acted as an intermediary: 'I will take pleasure for at least two hours each day in contemplating two of your drawings that Pier Antonio brought me, which increasingly please me the more I look at them.'[28] Cavalieri reciprocated Michelangelo's offer to provide pleasure with details of how he experienced pleasure. His offer to spend two hours over two drawings was meant to repay Michelangelo's further gift of his own time, as the fifty-seven-year-old artist had closed his letter by stressing that this resource was fleeting in his old age.[29] Cavalieri's greatest asset was his youth, which Michelangelo rewarded by volunteering what lifespan remained to him. Why?

The exchange of pleasure between Michelangelo and Cavalieri was not unidirectional. When responding to Cavalieri, Michelangelo wrote that Cavalieri's choice to receive his works, 'brought me great amazement and no less pleasure [*piacere*]'.[30] Cavalieri's letter, which Michelangelo saved, was itself a material source of satisfaction. This logic of exchange could have complemented

fig. 16   (cat. 42) Michelangelo, *Draft of a letter to Tommaso de' Cavalieri*, December 1532. Pen and brown ink, 292 x 222 mm. Florence, Casa Buonarroti, Archivio Buonarroti, V, 61

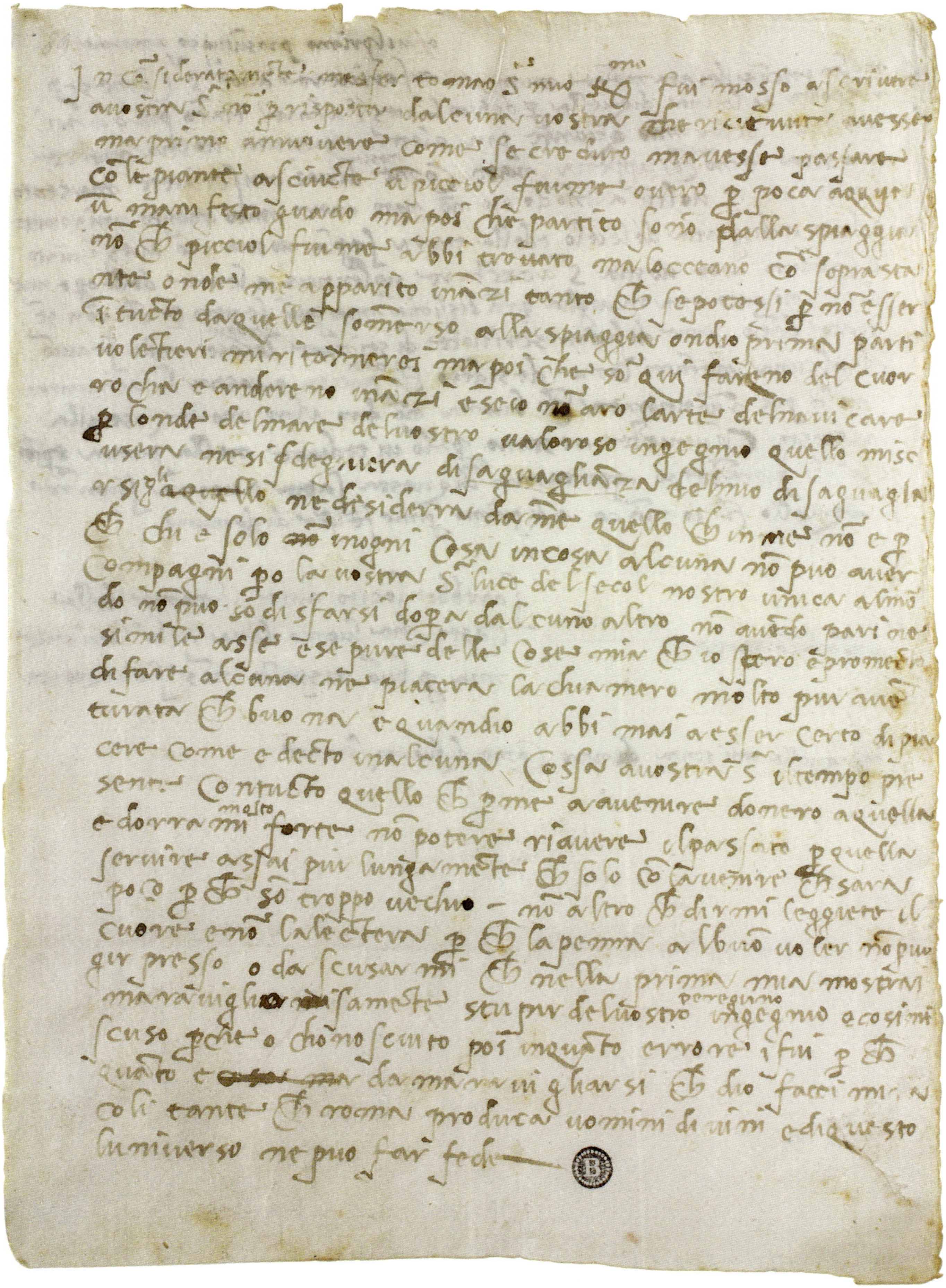

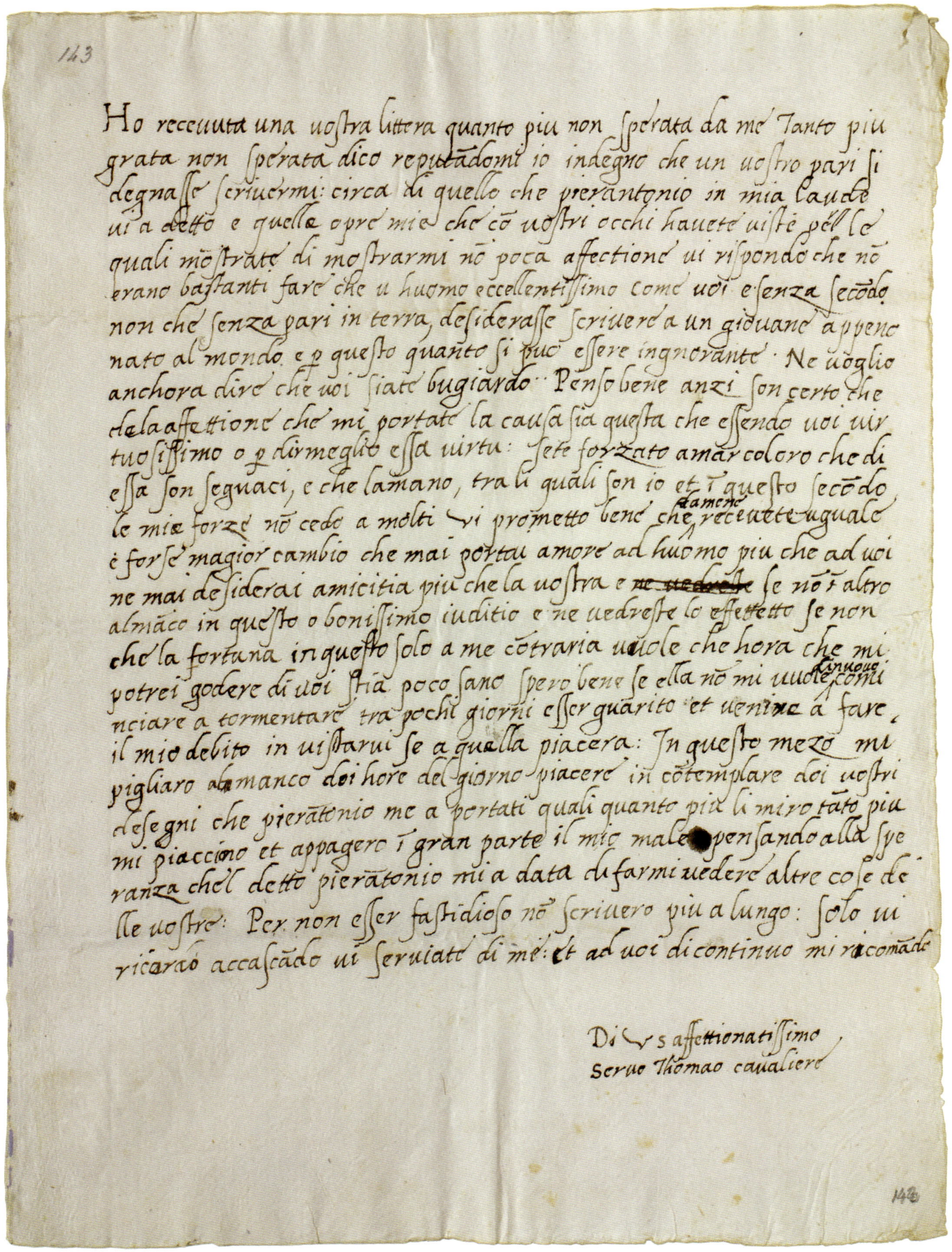

Ho receuuta una uostra littera quanto piu non sperata da me Tanto piu
grata non sperata dico reputadomi io indegno che un uostro pari si
degnasse scriuermi: circa di quello che pierantonio in mia laude
ui a detto e quelle opre mie che cō uostri occhi hauete uiste pēl le
quali mōstrate di mostrarmi nō poca affectione ui rispondo che nō
erano bastanti fare che u huomo eccellentissimo come uoi e senza secōdo
non che senza pari in terra, desiderasse scriuere a un giouane appene
nato al mondo e p questo quanto si puo essere ingnorante · Ne uoglio
anchora dire che uoi siate bugiardo · Penso bene anzi son certo che
dela affectione che mi portate la causa sia questa che essendo uoi uir
tuosissimo o p dirmeglio essa uirtu: sete forzato amar coloro che di
essa son segnaci, e che lamano, tra li quali son io et ꞇ questo secōdo
le mie forze nō cedo a molti ui prometto bene che receuete ugual mente
e forse magior cambio che mai portai amore ad huomo piu che ad uoi
ne mai desiderai amicitia piu che la uostra e ne uedrete se nō ꞇ altro
almāco in questo o bonissimo iuditio e ne uedreste lo effetto se non
che la fortuna in questo solo a me cōtraria uuole che hora che mi
potrei godere di uoi stia poco sano spero bene se ella nō mi uuole comi
nciare a tormentare tra pochi giorni esser guarito et uenire a fare
il mio debito in uisitarui se a quella piacera: In questo mezo mi
pigliaro almanco doi hore del giorno piacere in cōtemplare doi uostri
desegni che pieratonio me a portati quali quanto piu li miro ꞇato piu
mi piaccino et appagero ꞇ gran parte il mio male pensando alla spe
ranza chel detto pieratonio mi a data di farmi uedere altre cose de
lle uostre: Per non esser fastidioso nō scriuero piu a lungo: solo ui
ricarō accascādo ui seruiate di mē et ad uoi di continuo mi racomāde

Di Vs affettionatissimo
seruo Thomao caualiere

fig. 17   (cat. 5) Tommaso de' Cavalieri, *Letter to Michelangelo*, 1 January 1533. Pen and brown ink, 300 x 220 mm. Florence, Casa Buonarroti, Archivio Buonarroti, VII, 143

the erotic potential associated with the sensuous dimensions of Michelangelo's drawings of Ganymede and Tityus for Cavalieri, artworks that were mentioned in their correspondence (fig. 14/cat. 6 and fig. 18).[31] Just as Cavalieri delighted in the hours he spent looking at these drawings, Michelangelo would have revelled in making them. Vasari wrote of the enjoyment that Michelangelo derived from the time spent drawing, a commonplace that is nonetheless applicable to his lifelong impulse toward graphic elaboration.[32]

When Cavalieri received drawings from Michelangelo, he would thereby have understood the double fulfilment that the artist gained from making the work, and from knowing how Cavalieri used it. Such language of pleasure reappears in the first iteration of his drawing of *The Fall of Phaeton* for Cavalieri (fig. 19/cat. 43), at the bottom of which he wrote a note that rendered the drawing an epistle: 'Messer Tommaso, if this sketch does not please you, tell Urbino so that I have time to make you another tomorrow night, as I promised you, and if it pleases you and you wish me to finish it, return it to me'.[33] The assured immediacy of Michelangelo's response, as well as the fact that he went on to redesign the sheet multiple times, indicates his studied attunement to maximising Cavalieri's pleasure. This was a courtly *piacere* that Cavalieri would have been expected to cultivate, given his noble station, a fact underlined by Michelangelo's epistolary addresses of him – a young man several decades his junior – with the formal title 'Your Lordship'.[34] But pleasure was not an end unto itself. Poems that Michelangelo gave to Cavalieri could have offered a lesson in *how* to experience this feeling, specifically through his drawings. This possibility is distilled in one of the subsequent sonnets that Varchi cited in his original lecture, the second stanza of which reads:

> 'And if [my soul] were not made equal to God,
> it would not want more than external beauty,
> which pleases [*piace*] the eyes;
> but because such beauty is so fallacious,
> my soul transcends to the universal form.'[35]

In these verses Varchi rightly recognised a strong debt to Neoplatonism through an uplifting of Socratic love that

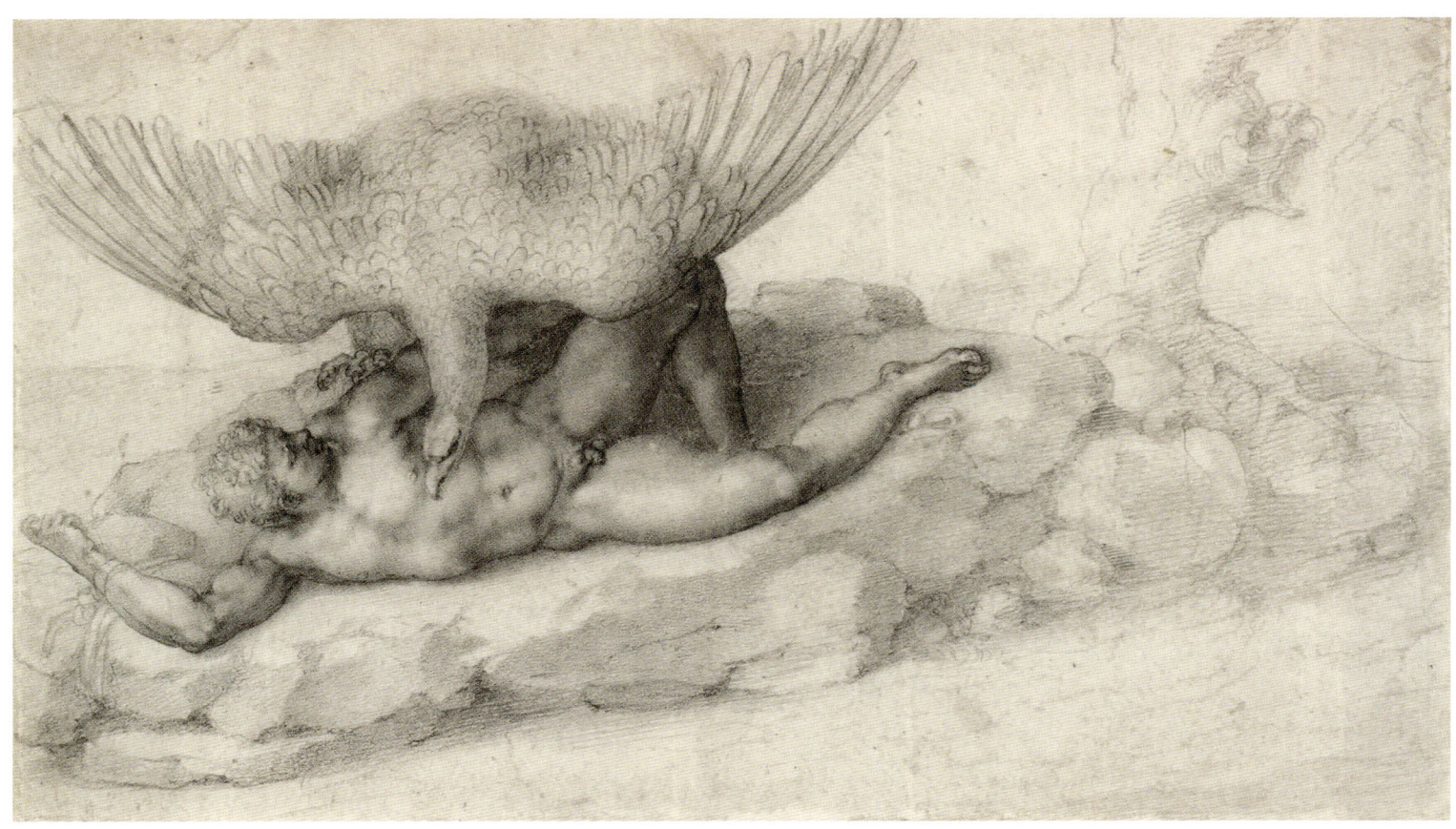

fig. 18   Michelangelo, *Tityus*, 1532. Black chalk, 190 x 330 mm. Windsor, Royal Collection Trust, inv. RCIN 912771

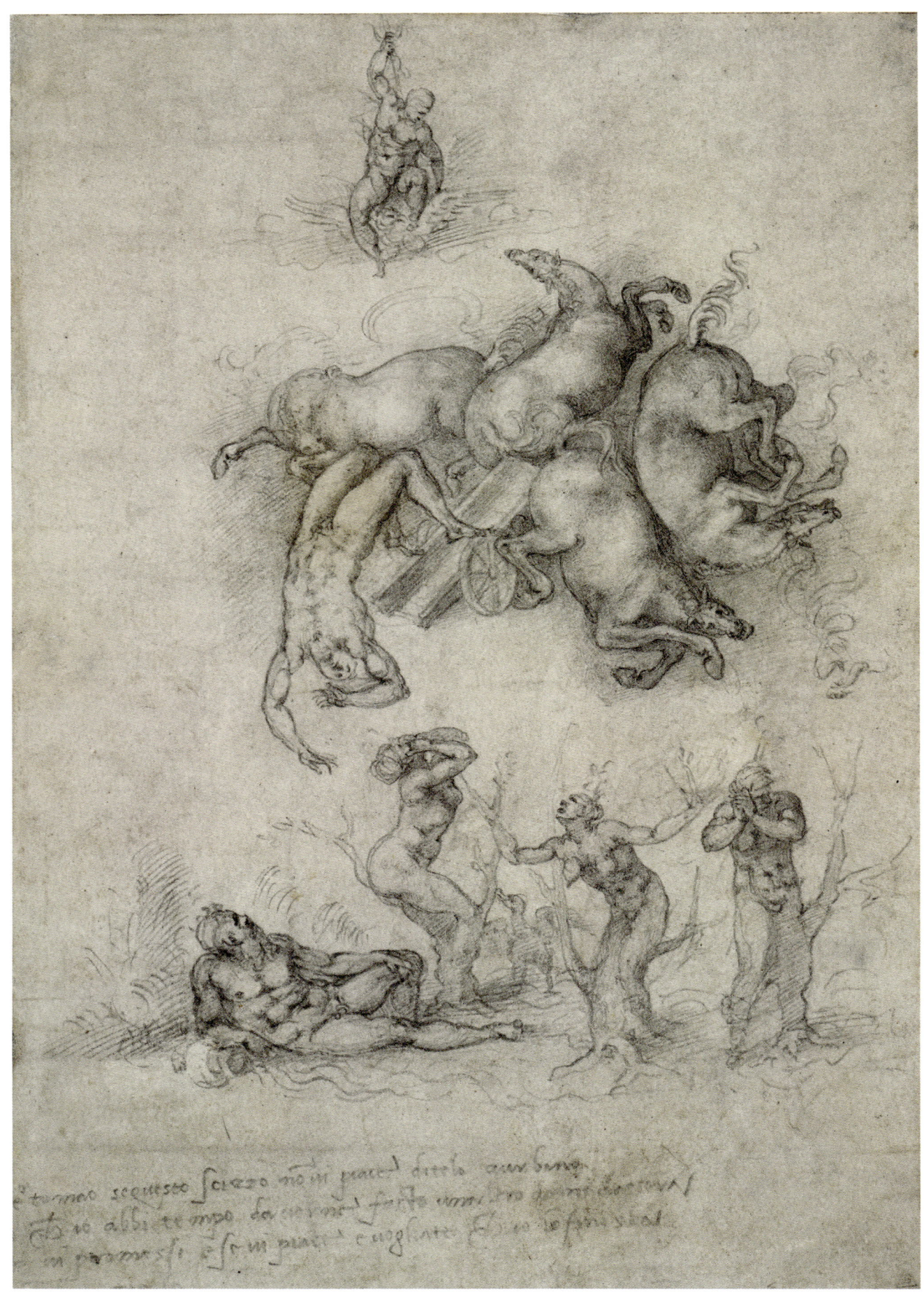

fig. 19   (cat. 43) Michelangelo, *The Fall of Phaeton*, 1533. Black chalk, 312 x 215 mm. London, British Museum, inv. 1895,0915.517

prioritises the soul's trajectory, while the risks inherent in the sensory enjoyment of beauty were a well-established feature of this philosophical tradition in Renaissance Italy.[36] One could read Michelangelo's sonnets for Cavalieri as a Neoplatonic accompaniment to his drawings.[37] But the language of this poem signals a corrective more than a parallel. The intensely erotic imagery of a drawing like Ganymede was an enticement to sensory bliss, which the poem instructed Cavalieri to redirect toward God. The final tercet of the poem celebrates this act of mitigation and the social bonds it reinforced: 'Unbridled desire pertains to sense, not love, and kills the soul; and our love makes perfect friends here, but more so after death in heaven.'[38]

Friendship was the promised outcome not only of Michelangelo's art and poetry, but also of his epistolary correspondence with Cavalieri. The young man noted in a letter to Michelangelo that he would 'never desire a friendship [*amicitia*] more than yours', while the artist later wrote that 'nothing can impede our friendship [*amicitia*]'.[39] The '*t*' in '*amicitia*' shared across such correspondence recalls the word's Latin orthography and the classical ideals of friendship that it carried.[40] This mutual choice in how Michelangelo and Cavalieri defined their friendship points to the learned form of humanist-inspired association they aspired to build. The handwriting in which Michelangelo composed both his poems and letters reflects this, as he trained himself to write in a script more closely associable with humanist erudition than mercantile tradecraft.[41] (While Michelangelo's youthful correspondence deploys a cursive *mercantesca* script, his later handwriting has a cultivated italic form.[42]) While one could regard Michelangelo and Cavalieri's epistolary correspondence as a practical requirement of a relationship conducted when the two were physically apart, it was an essential mode through which to establish *amicitia* itself. Humanist-inspired friendships enacted through letter writing had their roots in classical antiquity and were codified in the Renaissance by Petrarch, Erasmus and others.[43] Michelangelo therefore accompanied his sonnets, inspired by Petrarch's vernacular verse, with prose that also indirectly glorified Petrarch's epistles.[44] The language of Michelangelo's letters shows an awareness of the rhetorical techniques common to this genre, as well as an aspiration to honour what was fundamentally an ancient Roman literary form.[45]

The associations that Michelangelo devised between his poems, letters and drawings evaporated when they were separated. This occurred when the drawings were copied, as they were made into rock-crystal carvings and engravings almost immediately after Michelangelo gave them to Cavalieri, given the fame they quickly attained in Rome (fig. 20/cat. 2).[46] On 6 September 1533, Cavalieri wrote to Michelangelo that he tried to prevent his drawing of Tityus from falling into the hands of Cardinal Ippolito de' Medici to be carved in rock crystal.[47] This remark has often been associated with the material risks to the drawing (which indeed bears stylus marks that were surely linked to its copying).[48] There may also have been anxiety about the spread of the drawings' erotic imagery, but this was unlikely, as Vasari wrote that Cavalieri himself shared them with other artists in Rome. What may have concerned the young Roman most was such copies' disassociation from the poetry Michelangelo sent at the same time. Indeed, Cavalieri's well-known remark about the Tityus was preceded by a less well-known comment that he had received a letter from Michelangelo which revived him from a grave illness, as well as a sonnet from Michelangelo that accompanied his recovery.[49] Cavalieri's letter thereby dramatises the severance of text from image, veering midway from a meditation on the palliative power of Michelangelo's words to the forfeiture of his drawing for the cardinal's replicative purposes. The implication was that Michelangelo's letters and poems could continue to have their intended personal effect, whereas their replications would offer audiences an impoverished experience, one unmediated by prose and verse. When Vasari lavished praise on Michelangelo's drawings for Cavalieri, he notably did not accompany this with a reference to his poetry for the young man.[50] Such a disassociation may well have been intentional, given the private constellation of meanings that could emerge when the drawings and poems were analysed in tandem.

Pen and Chalk

Michelangelo's writings are profoundly multivalent, and Cavalieri would have been able to elicit many lessons from them beyond how to redirect sensory bliss towards God. Michelangelo himself said this, as he closed his first surviving letter draft to Cavalieri with the instruction: 'read the heart and not the letter, because "the pen cannot follow behind the good will"'.[51] This quoted verse is taken from a poem by Petrarch. In it, the fourteenth-century poet wrote of his frustrated inability to commune with his beloved, only to reaffirm his chosen medium of written verse: 'spoken voices were forbidden to me, / so I cried out with paper and ink'.[52] This poetic citation offered a plurality of lessons. Most importantly, the equivalence drawn by Petrarch between voice and text could cut both ways. In closing one of his other letter drafts to Cavalieri, Michelangelo signalled his awareness of what must remain unwritten: 'To keep from boring you I will stop writing more. Many things suited to this reply remain in the pen.'[53] He

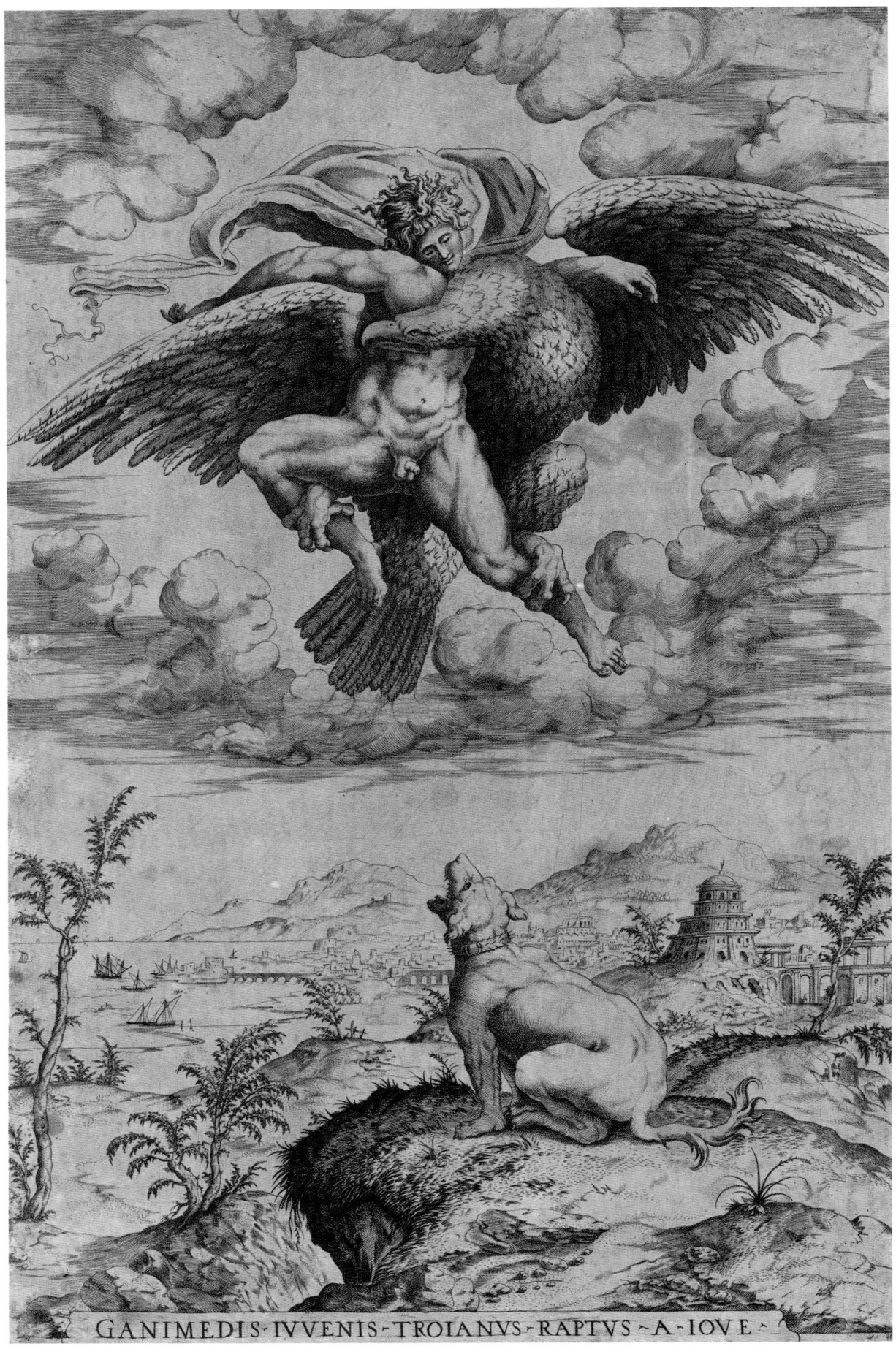

GANIMEDIS · IVVENIS · TROIANVS · RAPTVS · A · IOVE ·

fig. 20   (cat. 2) Anonymous, after Michelangelo, *Ganymede*, 1542. Engraving, 430 x 278 mm. Haarlem, Teylers Museum, inv. KG 00214

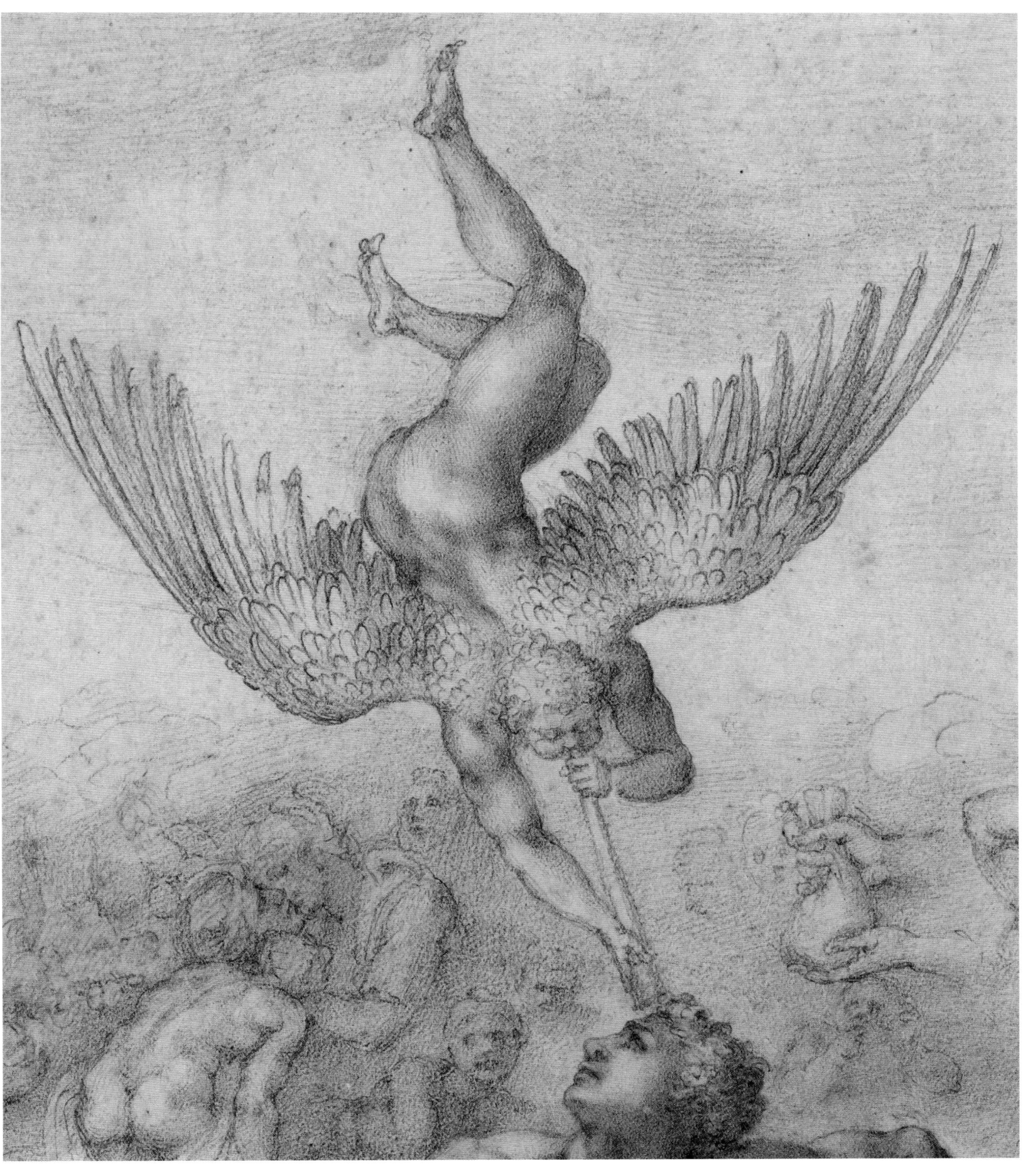

fig. 21   Michelangelo, *The Dream*, c. 1533 (detail of fig. 101/cat. 44)

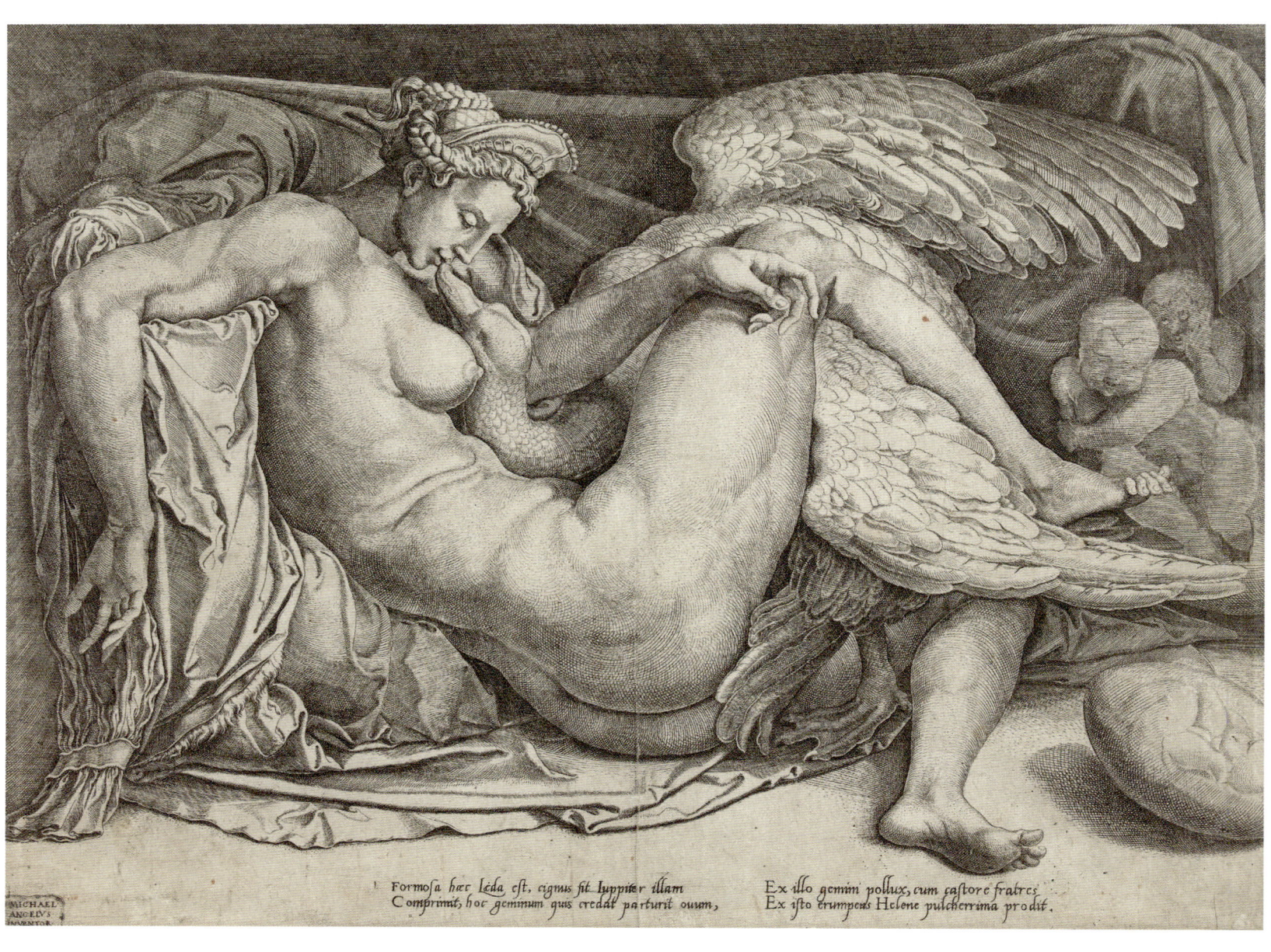

Formosa hæc Leda est, cignus sit Iuppiter illam
Comprimit, hoc geminum quis credat parturit ouum,

Ex illo gemini pollux, cum castore fratres
Ex isto erumpens Helene pulcherrima prodit.

MICHAEL
ANGELVS
INVENTOR

fig. 22   (cat. 4) Cornelis Bos, after Michelangelo, *Leda and the Swan*, 1544–1545. Engraving, 302 x 410 mm. Amsterdam, Rijksmuseum, inv. RP-P-BI-2785

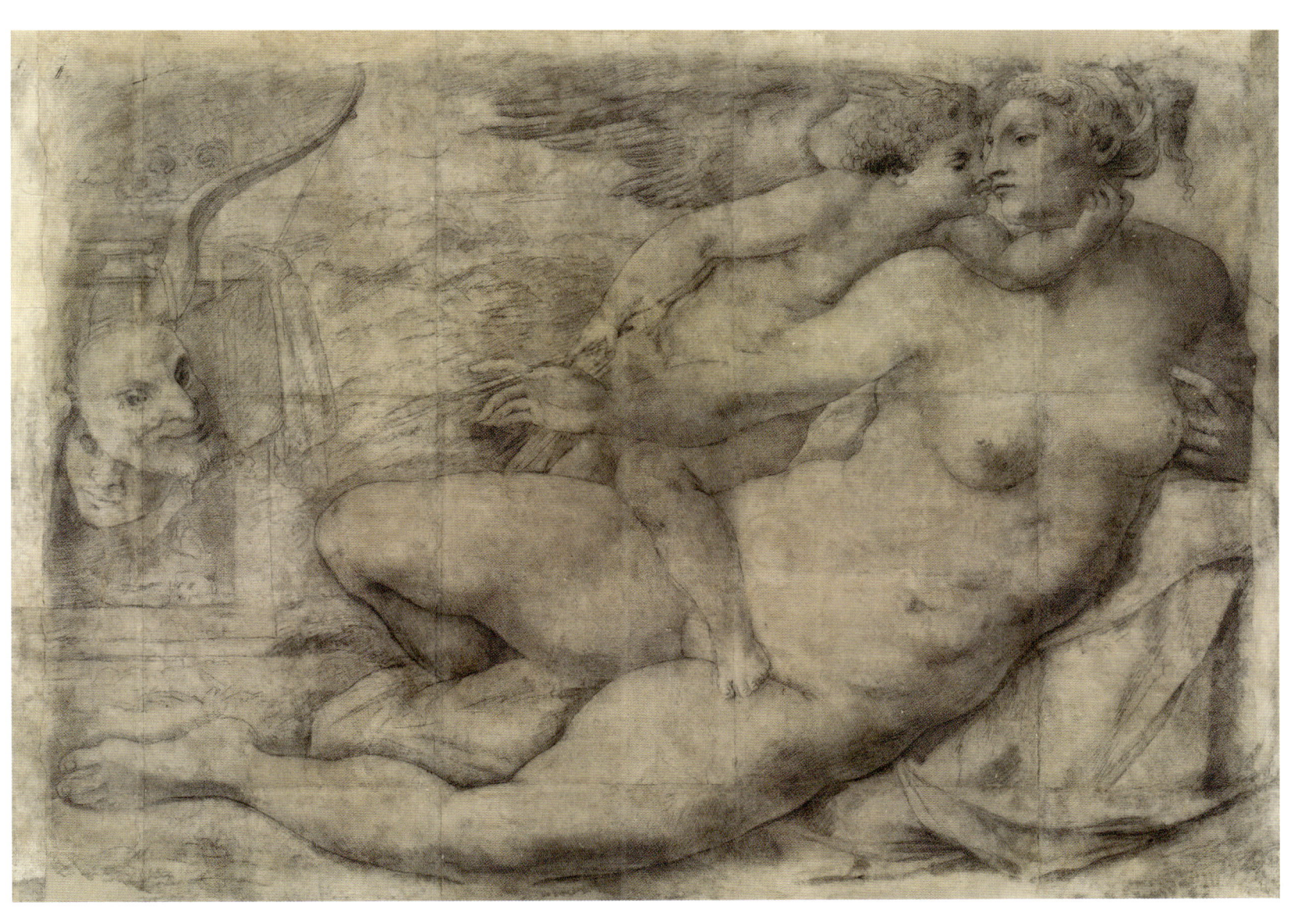

fig. 23   Attributed to Michelangelo and workshop, *Cartoon of Venus and Cupid*, c. 1531–1534. Charcoal, 128 x 183 cm. Naples, Museo Nazionale di Capodimonte, Gabinetto Disegni e Stampe, inv. 2511

then noted that the intermediary carrying the letter would relay such words to Cavalieri, adding a postscript that out of 'respect', he would not name the things he was sending the young man.[54] This epistolary lesson in the incommunicability of certain words had a direct literary association. By citing Petrarch's metapoetic reference to his writing implements in his earlier comment, Michelangelo cleverly alludes to his own status as more than a poet. Whereas Petrarch could only apply pen to paper, Michelangelo also had recourse to chalk.

Michelangelo used chalk like none before. With this friable graphic medium, Michelangelo could accomplish what pen could not. His handling of chalk has rightly been hailed as innovative in its incredibly fine technique of laying granules on the fibres of the paper. This was first observed in the mid-1980s under microscopy, and the process of making such marks — like hatching — was very time intensive because of the need to keep sharpening the chalk, not to mention modulating strokes in perfect *chiaroscuro* to delimit the body.[55] As Michelangelo was writing of sentiments inexpressible in ink, he pushed the medium of chalk to new heights in order to convey corporeal beauty that was textually ineffable.

Michelangelo used his poetry to empower Cavalieri to probe the interrelation between his labours in pen and chalk at both material and semantic levels. One sonnet of this period is particularly instructive, as Michelangelo closes with the final tercets:

'But why does it hurt more, as I see
In the eyes of this glad and single angel
My peace, my rest and my health?

Perhaps it would have been worse first
To see him, to hear him, if now equal in flight
He gives me wings [*m'impenna*] to follow his virtue
with him.'[56]

The verb *impennare* (to give wings) in the final verse vividly renders the aging narrator's flight together with his beloved, here cast as an angel. This passage could viably be glossed as a Neoplatonic representation of ascent toward the divine via virtuous love. This is wholly valid, as the verb *impennare* was a potent means of signalling such winged ascent, as earlier poets including Dante, Petrarch and Poliziano had each explored.[57] The capacity of such wings to enable the shared pursuit of virtue matches the gentlemanly trait that Cavalieri described as the source of their love:

'I am certain that the affection you have for
me is caused by this, being you most virtuous
[*virtuosissimo*], or rather to put it better this virtue,
you are forced to love those who are followers of it
and love it, of which I am one.'[58]

One could thereby view Michelangelo's drawings for Cavalieri not as visualisations of virtue so much as expressions of its pursuit.

But wings offered more than transport to virtue. When associated with the material implements of Michelangelo's correspondence, *impennare* lexically contains the implement of his writing, the pen (*penna*). In the Renaissance, pens were made of sharpened feathers, reflected in their self-same linguistic denomination as *penne*.[59] Literally meaning to create feathers, *impennare* can be read as both an artistic and poetic act. This was especially true when deployed by Michelangelo, an artist-poet. Indeed, across all his drawings for Cavalieri, a constant is Michelangelo's fixation on incorporating feathers through judiciously chosen avian subjects from Ovid.[60] If Michelangelo's poetry could stage Cavalieri as the giver of wings, the perfect way to please him would be through a profusion of physical wings that repaid hours of scrutiny (fig. 21/cat. 44). Set against tightly demarcated human flesh, such wings consist of loops of chalk that are equally liberated and deliberate. The rapidity with which Michelangelo created the contours of the wings contrasts with the subtlety of his hatching that lends them shape. Michelangelo continued to explore the visual potency of plumage in his graphic practice. His *Leda and the Swan* (fig. 22/cat. 4) and *Venus and Cupid* (fig. 23) were both destined for patrons to be inserted into larger cycles of paintings by other artists: Alfonso d'Este's *studiolo* and Bartolomeo Bettini's bedchamber.[61] But it was for a later altarpiece commission linked to Cavalieri that Michelangelo tenderly returned to details of plumage, as evident in his rendering of the wings of the holy messenger Gabriel in chalk drawings of *The Annunciation* (fig. 24).[62]

Michelangelo's correspondence and poems for Cavalieri were themselves carried by a literal angel. Bartolomeo Angelini — whose surname derives from this term — lived in Rome and was in close contact with the painter Sebastiano del Piombo, a mutual friend of both Michelangelo and Cavalieri.[63] Operating in Rome where the papal court established a node for postal exchange, Sebastiano and those around him were adept at leveraging epistolary skills for social and artistic gain.[64] Cavalieri knew Sebastiano, whose station as the keeper of the papal seals (*piombatore*) gave him access to the young man's noble ambit, and by the summer of 1533 Angelini became the intermediary between Cavalieri and Michelangelo when the artist was in Florence.[65] During Michelangelo's absence from Rome, Angelini spoke regularly in his letters of his and Cavalieri's love for him, serving to amplify and affirm the young man's amorous sentiments. As Angelini reported when sending letters addressed to Michelangelo: 'Last Saturday I sent you a letter from him [Sebastiano] with one by your Messer Tommaso, and from yours he understood how much is the affection you carry for him, and indeed, from what I saw in him, he does not love you less than you love him.'[66] The mutuality vital to the exchange of letters and poems was equally essential to love, which Angelini facilitated through such assurances.

Madrigals and Men

Michelangelo's correspondence about Cavalieri with his own epistolary intermediary grew increasingly heated. In a draft of a letter to Angelini from the summer of 1533 (fig. 25/cat. 45), Michelangelo wrote from Florence of his profound desire to be reunited in Rome with the young man.[67] He went on to express this metaphorically through the indivisibility of the body and soul. One could find continuity between such ideas and a draft of a madrigal that Michelangelo penned on the back of the same sheet (fig. 26/cat. 45v), which reads:

> 'Love holds me so,
> Nor wishes that I long for another,
> Who does not resemble you,
> Because only from your brows
> Does my health depend:
> From such hot virtue
> Which clearly reveals to the heavy soul at all times
> How much nature and heaven hide and conceal.'[68]

The importance of Cavalieri's virtue should draw further attention to Michelangelo's deployment of the epithet 'hot' (*calda*) before this term in the sixth verse. In writing the madrigal, Michelangelo clearly laboured over this term, first writing an alternative adjective ('clear' [*chiara*]) in the space directly above, then crossing it out, and finally writing two alternative verses below, eliminating

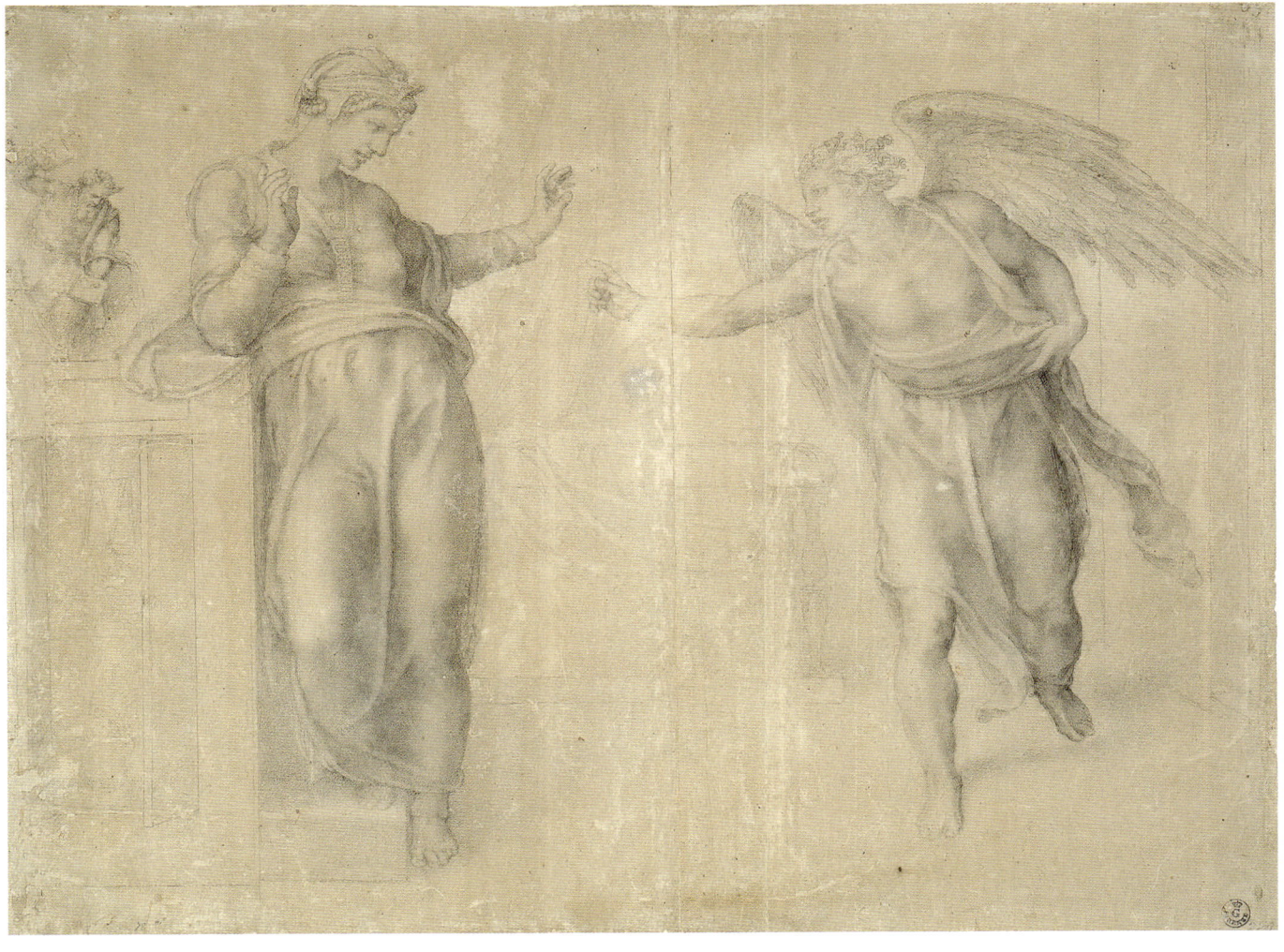

fig. 24   Michelangelo, *Annunciation*, c. 1545. Black chalk, 470 x 548 mm. Florence, Gallerie degli Uffizi, Gabinetto dei Disegni e delle Stampe, inv. 229 F

fig. 25   (cat. 45) Michelangelo, *Draft of a letter to Bartolomeo Angelini*, July–September 1533. Pen and brown ink, 290 x 218 mm. Florence, Casa Buonarroti, Archivio Buonarroti, V, 67

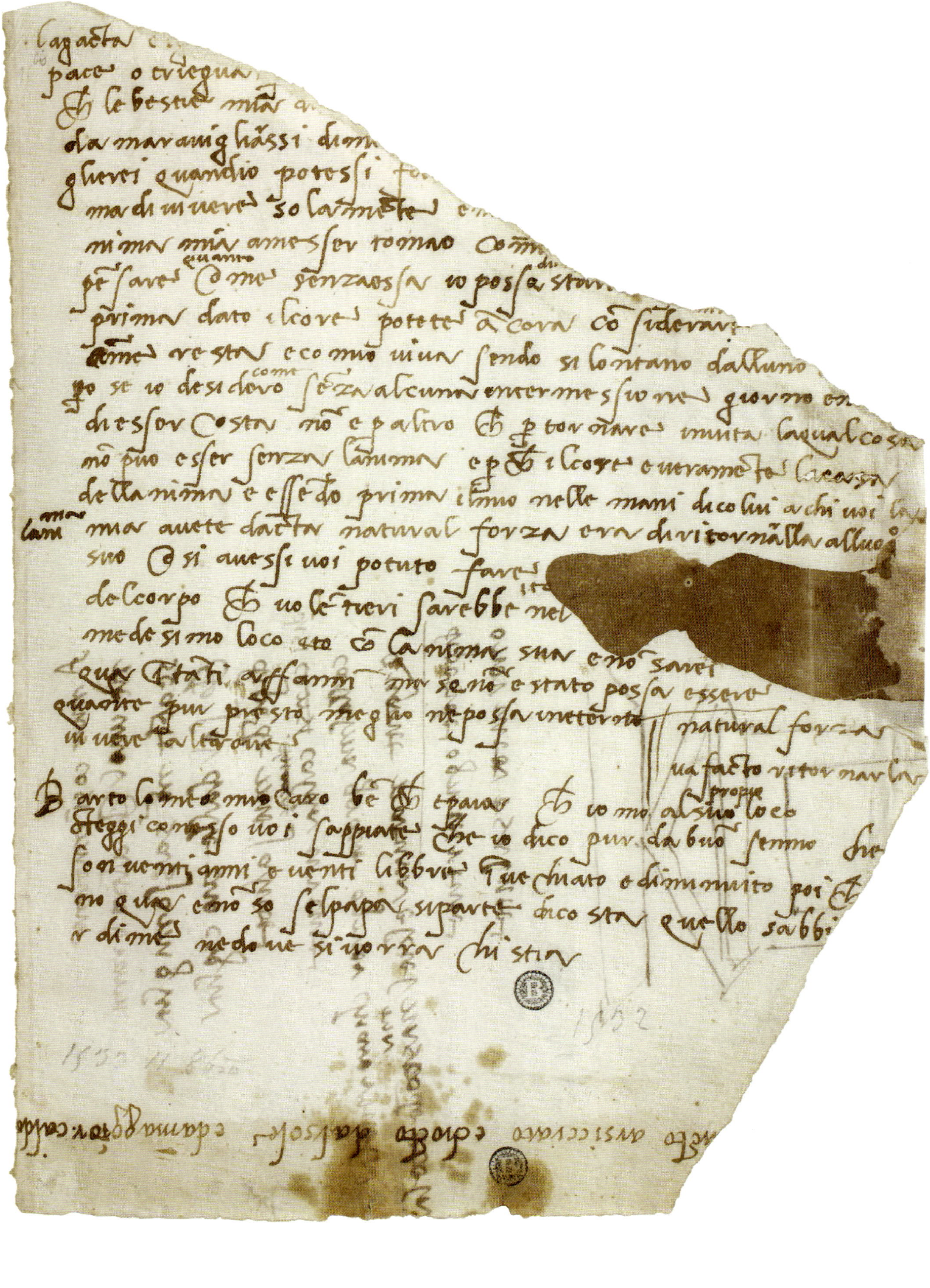

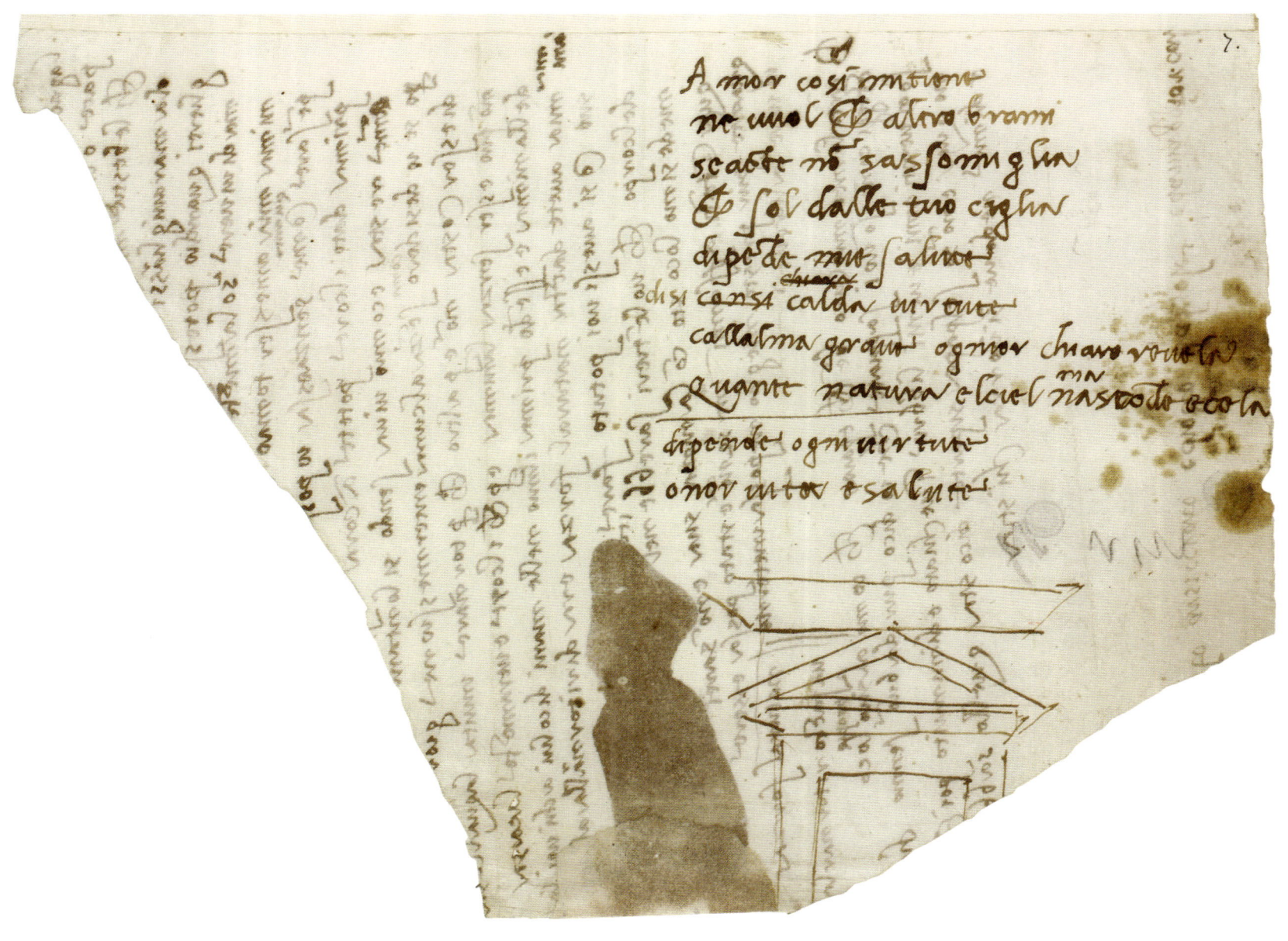

the adjective for heat and introducing instead the word 'honour'.[69] Seeking to calm the excess heat inspired by love in the first two verses, Michelangelo's textual amendments could be seen as an internal conflict about whether to temper his passionate language. Yet in constructing alternative versions of the poem adjacent to one another rather than striking them, Michelangelo was also evidently concerned with what was structurally viable in the poem, an approach commensurate with the architectural design underneath.

Michelangelo's drawing of a triangular pediment atop a window or doorframe can seem incongruous with the verses above (fig. 26/cat. 45v),[70] but it is a stark reminder that his love was enflamed because his architectural commissions in Florence kept him apart from Cavalieri in Rome. The letter draft on the opposite side of the sheet dramatises this relationship. Immediately after his lengthy exposition of his wish to return to Cavalieri, Michelangelo closed the missive by bemoaning the obligations that kept him in Florence at the behest of Pope Clement VII.[71] A massive set of endeavours at the Medici Basilica di San Lorenzo in Florence required that Michelangelo manage an expansive network of artisans and stone-labourers.[72] Two drawings in Teylers Museum suggest how, amid a project that lasted for many years, Michelangelo learnt to reconcile his joy in rendering the human form with the obligations of an architectural commission (figs 27 and 28/cat. 30; and fig. 88/cat. 29, of which the verso contains similar architectural drawings): the rectos, dated to about 1524, show bravura chalk drawings of legs for the sculpture of *Day*, while the versos in pen show a frenzied clutter of different potential architectural elements.[73] As the project became protracted during political upheaval and logistical setbacks, Michelangelo offset the weight of this burden through the lightness of his verses and winged drawings for Cavalieri.

Michelangelo's friends in Rome heard his complaints. Sebastiano del Piombo alluded jokingly in a letter to Michelangelo that he should take inspiration from his drawing for Cavalieri to decorate a cupola he was designing in the Basilica di San Lorenzo: 'It seems to me that a Ganymede would look well there, and make it the crown that appeared to St John of the Apocalypse when he was rapt in heaven.'[74] With his wryly acidic humour, Sebastiano was reminding Michelangelo that while he was at work in Florence, his architectural projects would deter him from the types of amorous art-making that most interested him, an ur subtle encouragement to come to Rome. Sebastiano was one of many in Rome who had sought to convince Michelangelo to move to the eternal city, and by 1534, Michelangelo had relocated there permanently, living in the same metropolis as him and Cavalieri. After

Michelangelo did so, almost no further correspondence between him and Cavalieri survives, presumably because its utility was obviated by their proximity.

But Michelangelo's fragmentary madrigal had a life beyond the single sheet on which it survives. Michelangelo elaborated four other madrigals with similar language, indicating how this poem was part of his expansive thinking about this type of lyric form.[75] In the same year that he and Cavalieri were corresponding most closely, Michelangelo also shared madrigals with Sebastiano del Piombo, who wrote to the famed artist that he had them set to music by the composers Costanzo Festa and Jean Conseil.[76] Sebastiano then gave copies of such musical settings to Cavalieri. In so doing, Sebastiano would have empowered Cavalieri to perform Michelangelo's madrigals or have them performed for him, as would have been customary for his noble status.[77] Petrarchan madrigals were a relatively young genre in this period, but their social utility through musical staging in household spaces made them essential for upper-class circles in Venice (where Sebastiano grew up) and in Rome (where he and Cavalieri lived).[78] Such activities could foster mixed-gender interactions, as well as distinctly homosocial gatherings within private domestic environments.[79] These musical settings facilitated the circulation of Michelangelo's poetry, and given that Festa and Conseil were both employed in the papal choir, their compositions of his verse could have been enjoyed within the walls of Vatican City and by affiliates of the papal court around Rome. It is not impossible to imagine such individuals listening to musical settings of Michelangelo's madrigals as they pored over his designs for Cavalieri, perhaps even in the young man's presence.

Restoring Connections

Years later, Michelangelo revisited the madrigal on his letter draft for Cavalieri, incorporating it into a broader collection of his poetry that he may have intended to publish.[80] Denuded of its social context and without direct reference to the gender of the poetic beloved, the madrigal could be seen to conceal his love for Cavalieri within a conventional project of assembling one's lyrics into publishable form. But just as Michelangelo revisited his figural drawings to elaborate new poses for projects throughout his life, so did he return to his poems with a comparable objective. Indeed, a sheet at Teylers Museum coalesces such approaches, as it contains Michelangelo's anatomical designs of several legs with three lines of a madrigal (fig. 29/cat. 22v).[81]

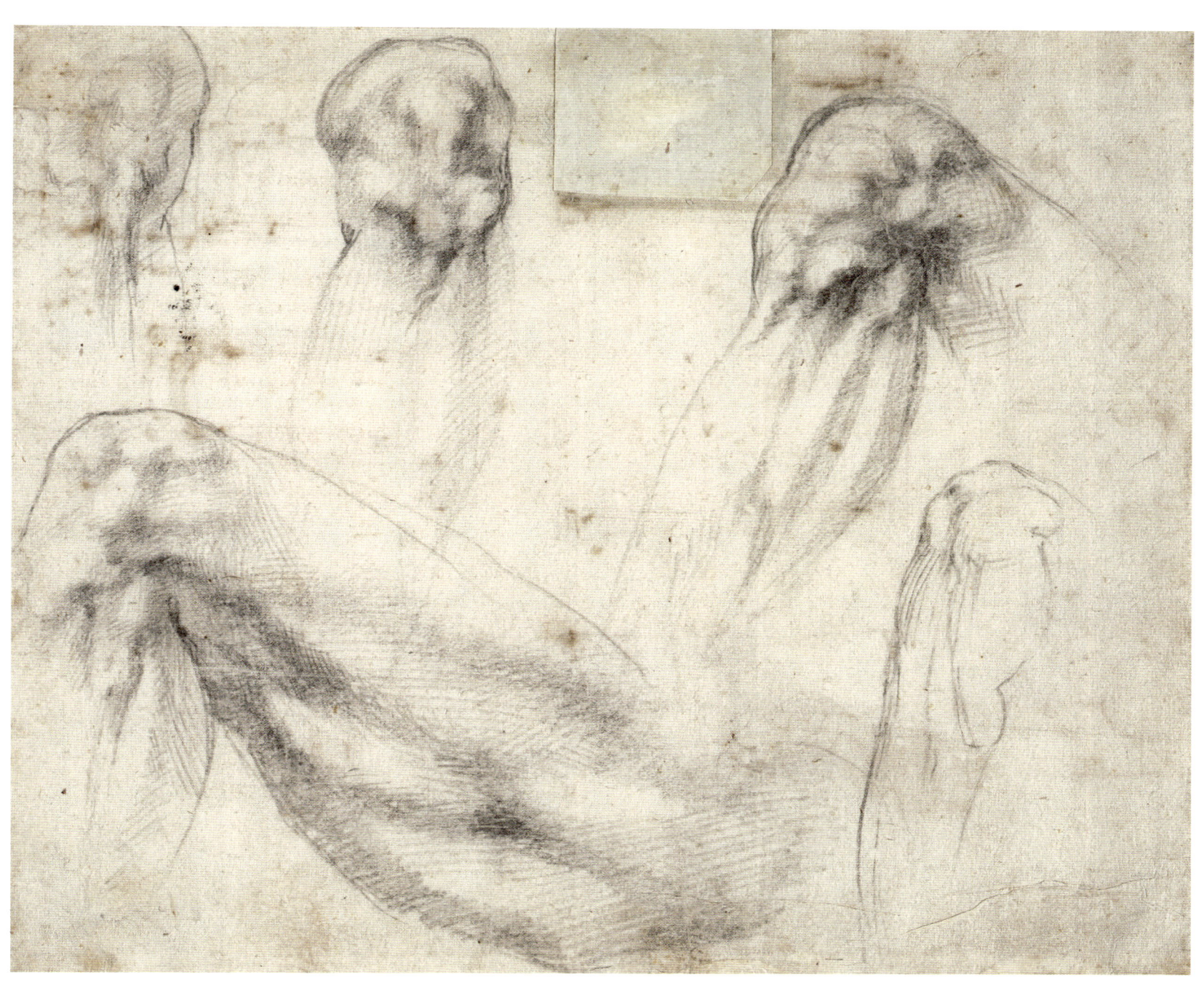

fig. 27   (cat. 30) Michelangelo, *Studies of a Left Leg and Knee for the Sculpture of* Day, 1524. Black chalk, 206 x 248 mm. Haarlem, Teylers Museum,
inv. A 033bis

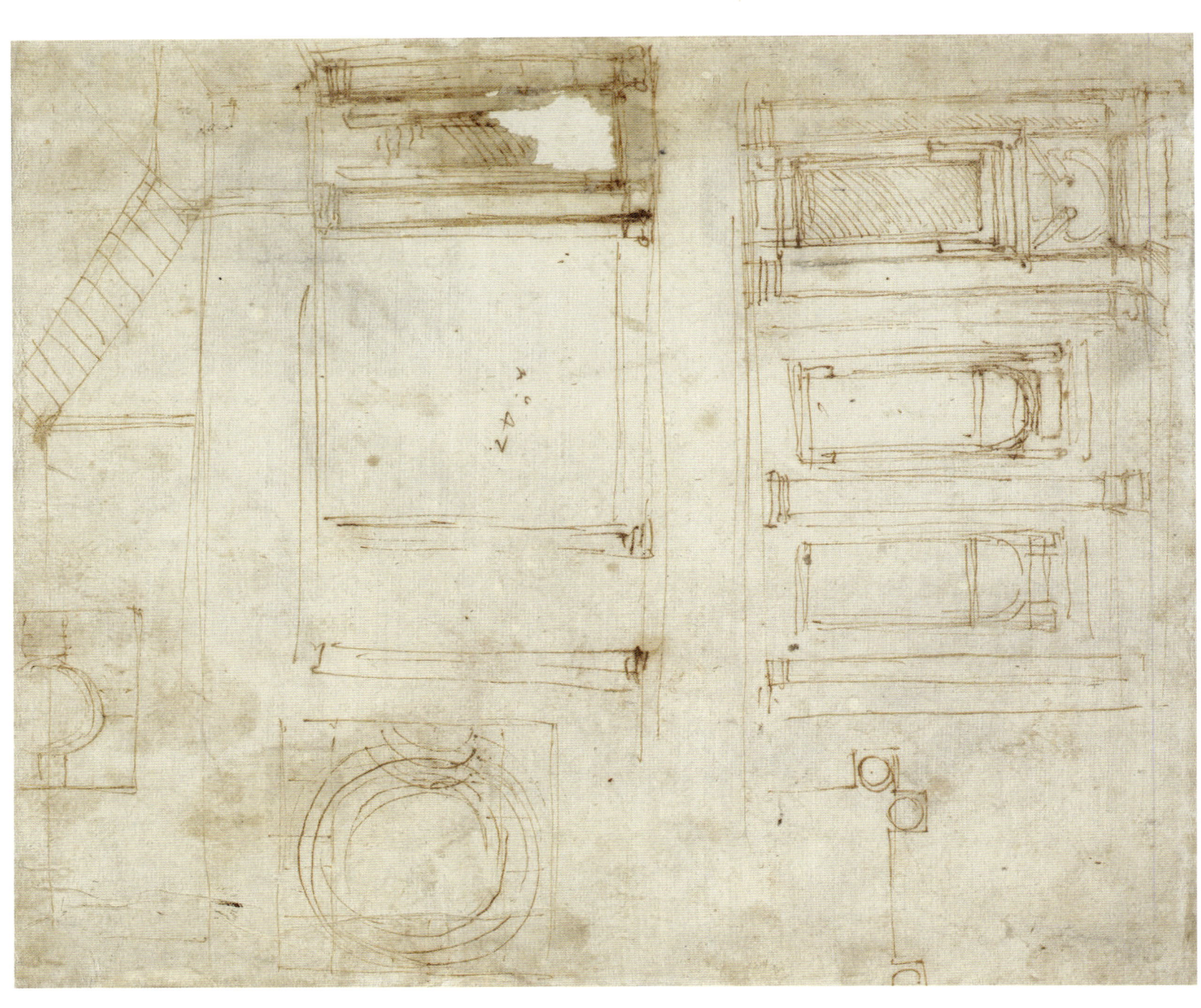

fig. 28 (cat. 30v) Michelangelo, *Studies for the Vestibule of the Laurentian Library*, 1524. Pen and brown ink, 206 x 248 mm. Haarlem, Teylers Museum, inv. A 033bisv

'Under two beautiful brows
With peace and amazement
Love has put a stop to my thoughts.'

The connective tissue between such parts of the sheet has proved challenging to restore, in part because the dating of image versus text has fluctuated wildly in scholarship, and because these verses informed another poem in Michelangelo's later life.[82] Did Michelangelo reuse a sheet with anatomical drawings to ink verses of a madrigal, or vice versa? A more productive question is how the content of Michelangelo's madrigal might reflect a wider diffusion of amorous thinking across his creative practice. The verses hinge on the same two brows (*ciglia*) mentioned in the madrigal cited above, and they likewise deploy a vocabulary of the 'marvellous' that matched his epistolary praise of Cavalieri on that same piece of paper.[83] Uniting pen and chalk, text and image, body, 'love' and 'thoughts' (*pensieri amore*, v. 3), the Teylers sheet is a compelling distillation of Michelangelo's loving approach to writing and drawing.

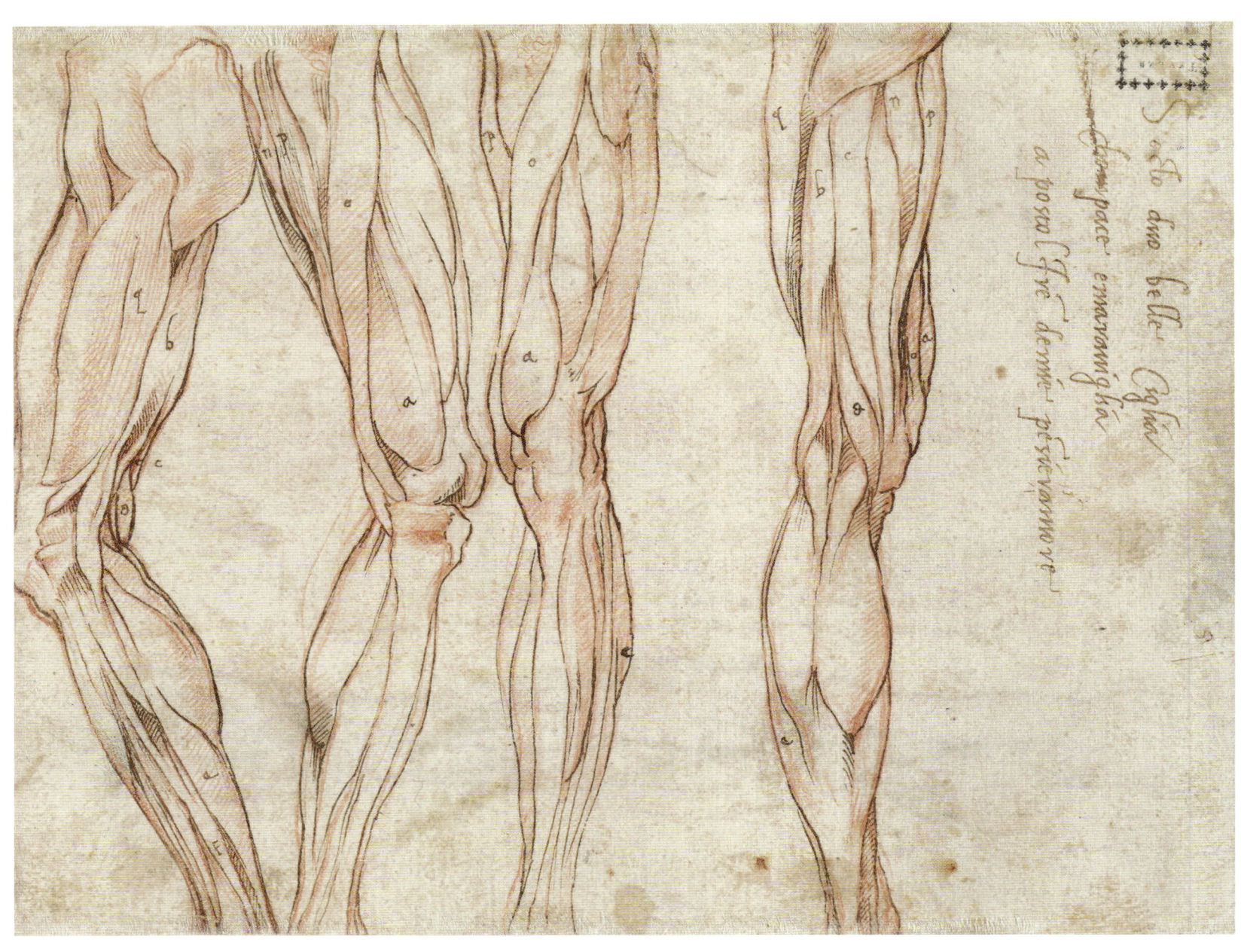

fig. 29   (cat. 22v) Michelangelo, *Anatomical Studies of a Left Leg*, c. 1515–1520. Red chalk, partly retraced with pen and brown ink, 201 x 263 mm.
Haarlem, Teylers Museum, inv. A 039v

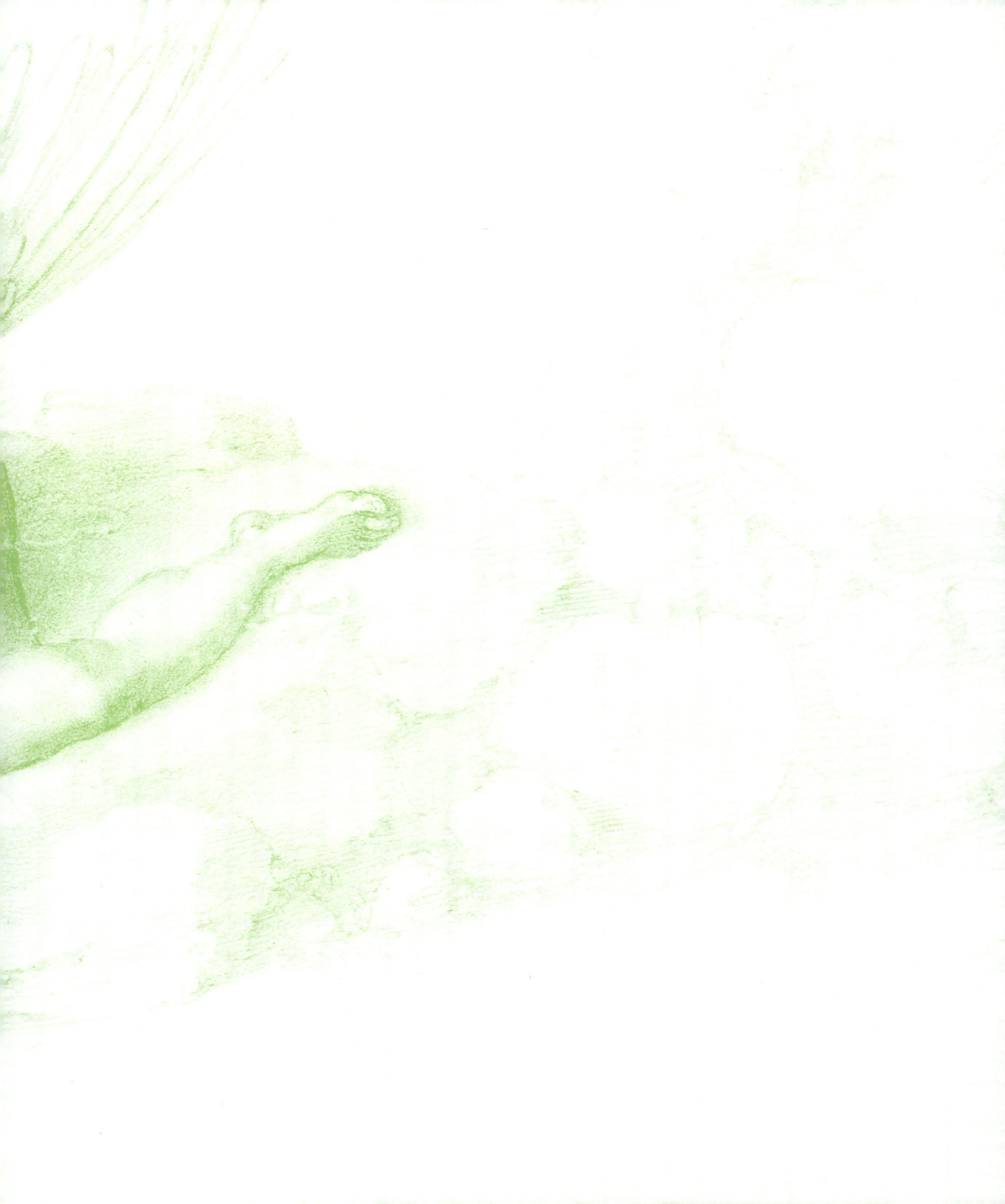

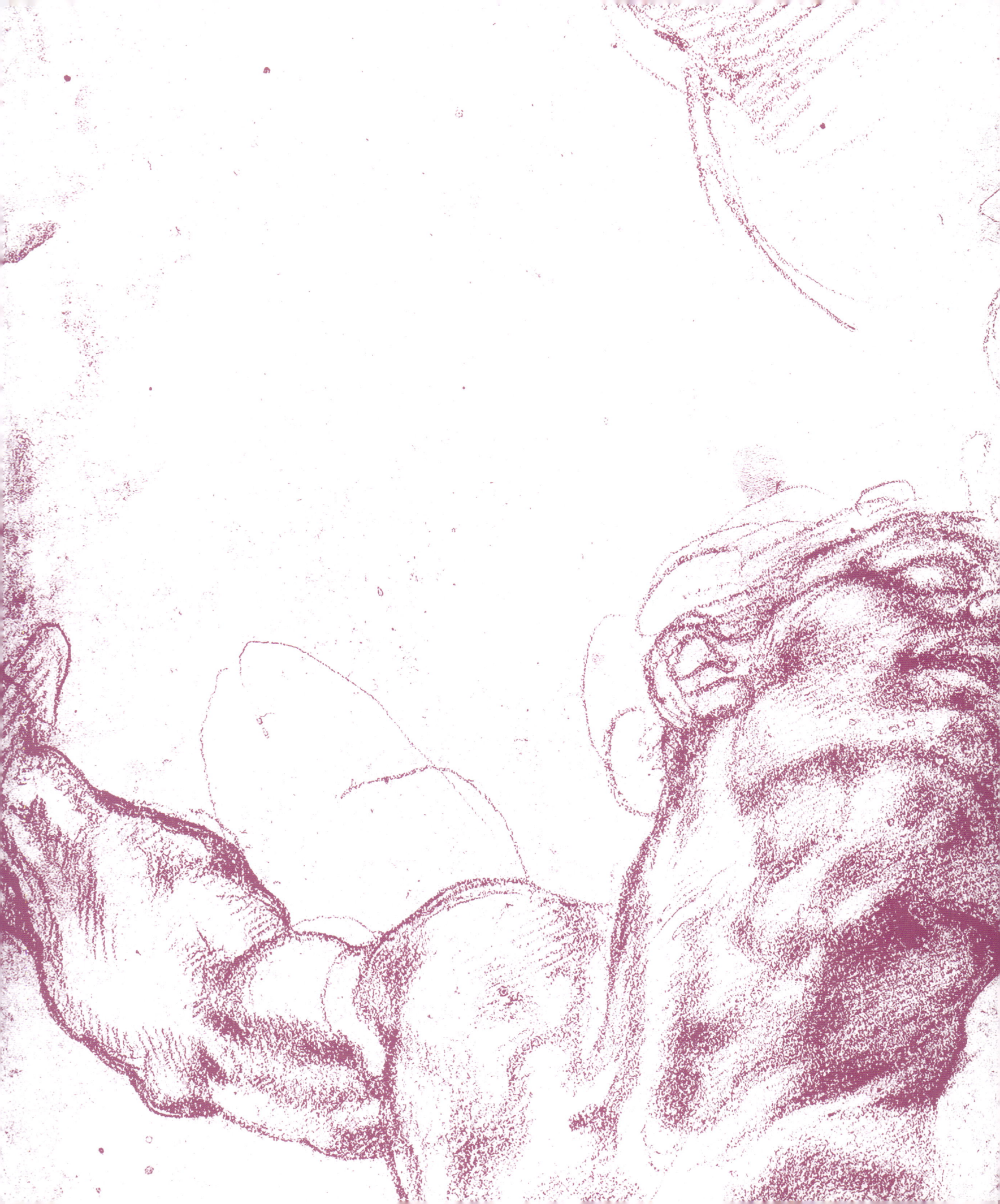

Body

"Se 'l mie rozzo martello i duri sassi
  forma d'uman aspetto or questo or quello,
  dal ministro che 'l guida, iscorge e tiello,
  prendendo il moto, va con gli altrui passi."

    'If my crude hammer shapes the hard stones
      into one human appearance or another,
      deriving its motion from the master who guides it,
      watches and holds it, it moves at another's pace.'

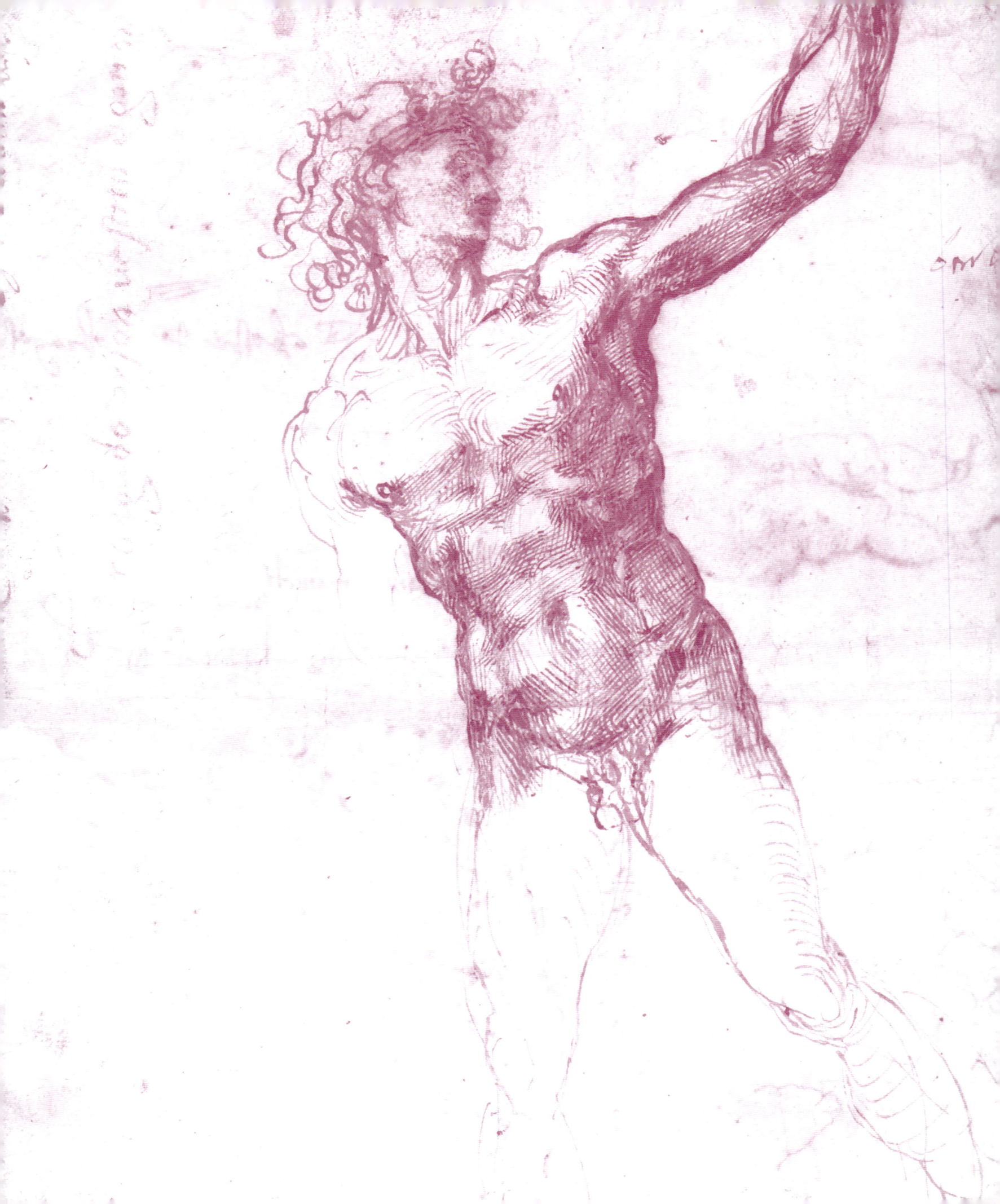

Michelangelo and Antiquity. Ongoing Training

Martin Gayford

Still Going to School

One winter's day, Cardinal Alessandro Farnese encountered the aged Michelangelo trudging through the snow towards the Colosseum. The cardinal asked the great artist, by then in old age, what he was doing in such weather; Michelangelo replied, *'Io vado ancora alla scuola per imparare'* ('I'm still going to school to learn').[1]

Since adolescence he had been immersed in the Græco-Roman past, studying and meditating on monuments of architecture such as the Colosseum, sculpture of both large and small scale, carved stones, and the scraps of information about the visual arts which were embedded in classical literature. This training set him apart from most of his contemporaries; furthermore, the high level of connoisseurship and intellectual understanding of his teachers was unique. Michelangelo himself was at pains to make this point clear for posterity.

In March 1550, he celebrated his seventy-fifth birthday. That same spring, the first edition of Vasari's *Le vite de' più eccellenti pittori, scultori, e architettori* (The Lives of the Most Excellent Painters, Sculptors and Artists) appeared, containing a long and fulsome account of his career. But Vasari's biography, flattering though it was, left out vital information, was sometimes inaccurate and emphasised points that Michelangelo did not wish to be stressed. Reading his own biography in Vasari's words might well have raised the question of how he would be remembered. Three years later, in 1553, another volume appeared: the *Vita di Michelagnolo Buonarroti* by Ascanio Condivi. The author was an assistant in Michelangelo's workshop, who had apparently taken notes of the artist's recollections, which were then put into a more polished literary form by an anonymous ghostwriter. Although somewhat garbled by this process, the result is close to a modern 'as-told-to' autobiography. One of the first points Michelangelo corrected, via his amanuensis, concerned his early schooling as an artist. Vasari stated, accurately, that Michelangelo had been apprenticed to the Florentine painter Domenico Ghirlandaio. Condivi brings this up only to deny its importance.

> 'I wanted to make mention of this, because I have been told that the son of Domenico used to attribute the divine excellence of Michelangelo in great part to the teaching of his father, who in reality gave him no assistance at all.'[2]

This passage is often regarded as an example of Michelangelo's economy with the truth – which in some respects it is. There is documentary evidence that Michelangelo was indeed apprenticed to Ghirlandaio. But the point that Condivi made, admittedly disingenuously, was different: that Ghirlandaio 'gave him no assistance at all'. That statement was not strictly accurate either. But what Michelangelo learnt from Ghirlandaio was essentially practical. In Ghirlandaio's workshop he was schooled in 'methodical and efficient techniques of painting in fresco and tempera', as Carmen Bambach put it,[3] plus other methods such as the use of cross-hatching to create form and depth in drawing.

This was an excellent grounding in the methods of Florentine art, perhaps the best he could have gained in any workshop in the city during the 1480s. The point that Condivi wanted to make, however, was that 'the divine excellence of Michelangelo' – what made him the most revered and influential artist of his age – was not the result of training by Ghirlandaio: his unique artistic development was the result of what came *after* his apprenticeship. And there Michelangelo and his mouthpiece Condivi had an important truth on their side. From the age of 15 to 19 he was quite literally living inside one of the greatest collections of antiquities of the age and learning from several of the most renowned scholars of classical literature and philosophy then living.

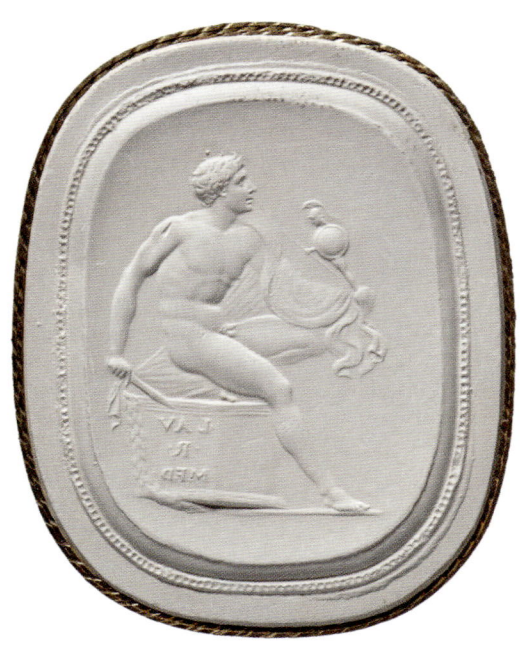

fig. 30   Roman, *Diomedes and the Palladium*,
c. 30 BCE. Chalcedony intaglio,
45 x 35 mm. Recorded in a plaster
cast in the Cades Collection, 30:
III E 283. Rome, German
Archaeological Institute

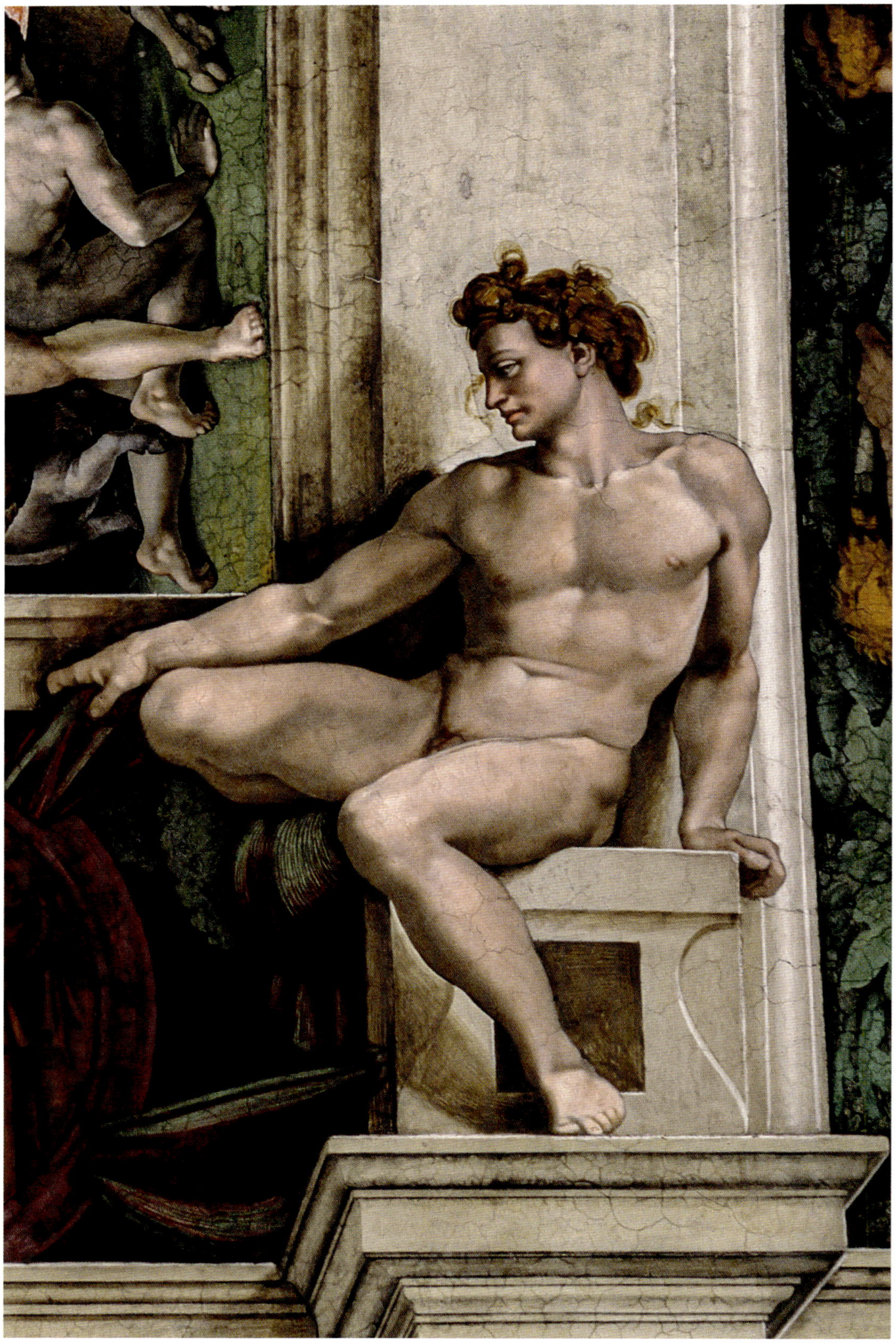

fig. 31   Michelangelo, *Ignudo above the Erythraean Sibyl*, c. 1508–1510. Fresco. Vatican City,
Ceiling of the Sistine Chapel

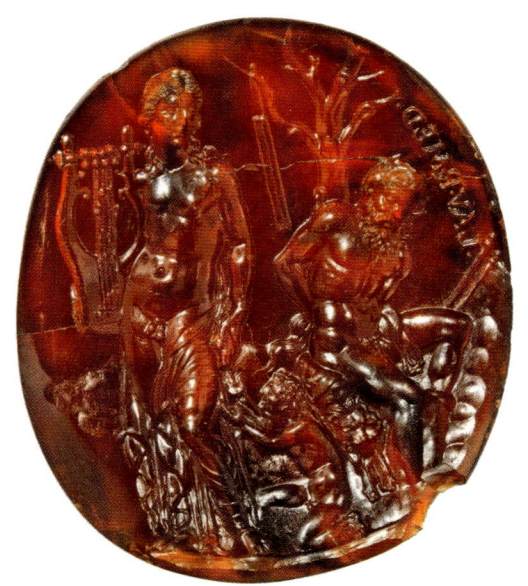

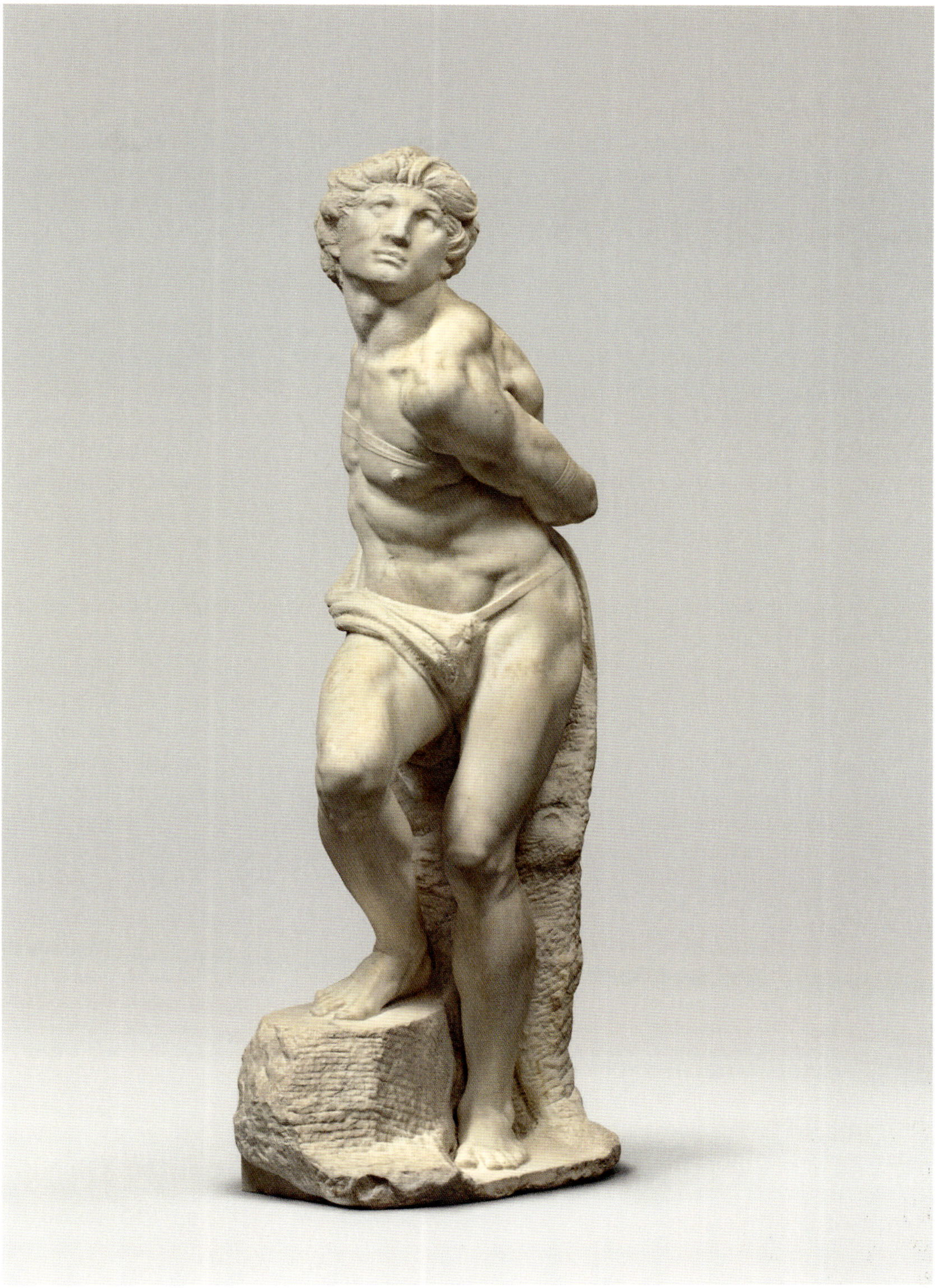

fig. 32   Roman, attributed to Dioskourides,
*Apollo, Marsyas and Olympos (the
so-called 'Sigillo di Nerone')*,
late 1st century BCE–early
1st century CE. Cornelian intaglio,
40 x 34 mm. Naples, Museo
Archeologico Nazionale, inv. 26051

fig. 33   Michelangelo, *Rebellious Captive*, c. 1513–1516. Marble, height 215 cm. Paris, Musée du Louvre,
Département des Sculptures, inv. MR 1589

Medici Collection

In his mid-teens, Michelangelo was taken into the household of Lorenzo de' Medici, the *de facto* ruler of Florence.[4] His extraordinary ability must have already been obvious, but it was the years in the inner circle of the Medici court that formed his mind and hugely ambitious conception of what art could be. Other Renaissance artists took on the role of adviser to aristocratic collectors of antiquities. Andrea Mantegna, for example, had this role at the Gonzaga court in Mantua, and the sculptor Gian Cristoforo Romano advised Isabella d'Este in the same way.[5] But only Michelangelo was trained for such a task from mid-adolescence. Consequently, his sensibility was formed by masterpieces of ancient art under the tutelage of one of the leading connoisseurs of the age – Lorenzo himself.

Nor was he Michelangelo's only distinguished mentor. Condivi described the Medici court as filled with many 'esteemed persons' in addition to Lorenzo's sons. It was home to several of the foremost scholars and intellectuals in Europe, all of whom apparently held Michelangelo 'very dear' and encouraged his 'honourable studies'. Condivi continued:

> 'But most of all this was true of the Magnifico, who many times a day had him summoned, and showed him jewels, cornelians, medals and similar things of great value, in the manner of one who knew him for a person of intelligence and of judgement.'[6]

In the past it has been debated whether Michelangelo actually spent these crucial years in the Medici household; we can now be sure the answer to that question is yes.[7] Another question has been asked less often: why should Lorenzo have taken this remarkable step?

In the Medici household, the sculptor Bertoldo di Giovanni filled a combination of roles: as custodian and curator of the sculpture-training garden, court artist and, probably, advisor on the collection of antiquities. He was a courtier as well as an artist, and on surprisingly close terms with Lorenzo himself.[8] This was to be Michelangelo's future job description; he stepped into Bertoldo's shoes when the latter died in December 1491, and he too – if Condivi is to be believed – seems to have been on remarkably intimate terms with Lorenzo. It is reasonable to deduce that from the start Michelangelo was being groomed for this role as resident curator/custodian of the collection.

Lorenzo's collection was more than a pastime; it was closely connected with his sense of himself. The sheer amount of time spent by Medici agents on seeking out acquisitions suggests it was a genuine obsession.[9]

The 'jewels, cornelians, medals and similar things' which Michelangelo was summoned to admire and discuss were kept in Lorenzo's *scriptoio* in the Palazzo Medici.[10] Several of the most prized pieces were hardstone artefacts such as cameos, which are carved in relief, and intaglios or cornelians, in which the design is cut into the stone (both might be referred to as '*gemme*' or jewels). Michelangelo spent four and a half years in contact with this array of miniature masterpieces.

After Lorenzo's death in April 1492 (according to Condivi), Michelangelo briefly returned to live with his family, perhaps because the political situation in Florence had become chaotic. Lorenzo's heir Piero took up his father's position and Vasari relates that Piero 'who had been left heir to his father Lorenzo, having long been intimate with Michelangelo, used often to send for him when he wished to buy antiques, such as cameos and other carved stones'.[11]

Given this tutelage and the years he spent contemplating the masterpieces of the Medici collection, it is not surprising that there are numerous echoes of these objects in Michelangelo's later work. Charles de Tolnay pointed out that Lorenzo's carved chalcedony of *Diomedes and the Palladium,* for example, looks like the prototype for one of the *ignudi* on the ceiling of the Sistine Chapel: the figure to the right above the Erythraean sibyl (figs 30 and 31).[12] One could go further. This lost gem might well have been the prototype for the whole tribe of Sistine *ignudi*: the muscular, naked young men arranging their limbs in complex but elegant postures.[13]

Another of the most prized items in the Medici's possession was the so-called *Sigillo di Nerone*, or 'Seal of Nero', a Roman cornelian representing Marsyas with Apollo and Olympus (fig. 32). Martha Dunkelman has pointed out that the figure of Marsyas, tied to a tree and awaiting punishment by flaying, also recalls Michelangelo's Sistine *ignudi* 'in general' – and several more specifically. She notes an even closer fit between Marsyas and the *Rebellious Captive* carved for the tomb of Pope Julius II (fig. 33). 'Both have arms held behind their backs at waist level, knees bent at unequal levels, and a bit of drapery across the upper leg.'[14] Although the *Captive* is defiant and Marsyas resigned, the resemblance is indeed close. In addition, the swaying poses of Apollo's legs and torso are a good match for the lower part of the *Dying Captive* (though not his arms) (fig. 86), and the same two figures are also echoed, with variations, by the two naked young men on the left-hand side of the *Doni Tondo* from around 1504–06 (fig. 34).[15]

The centrepiece of the Medici collection was the object now known as the *Tazza Farnese* (fig. 35).[16] This is a cup carved from four-layered sardonyx agate, a

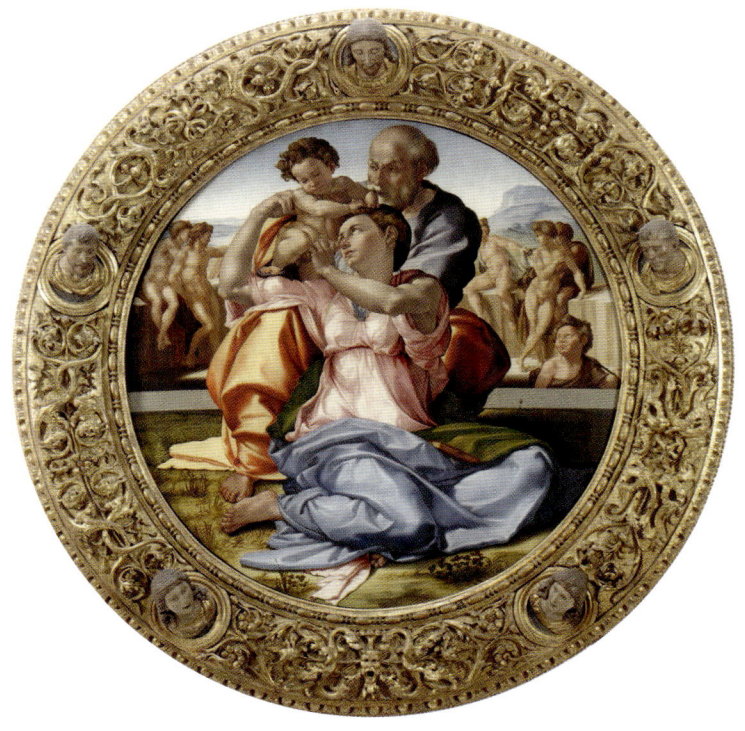

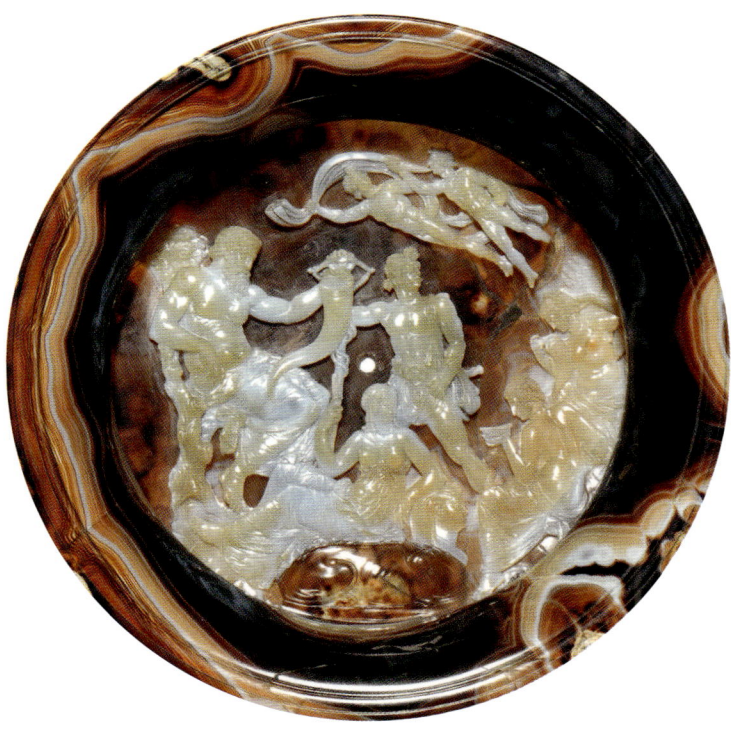

mineral which occurs naturally in multicoloured layers. It was made in ancient Alexandria, probably first or second century BCE. The artist or artists who carved it used the complex geological structure of the stone to create a sumptuously rich but also translucent effect. Dunkelman suggests Michelangelo derived the idea for God the Father in *The Creation of Adam* from the flying wind god inside this fabulous cup (fig. 36).[17]

It is as though Michelangelo's mind had been imprinted at a formative stage with beautiful ancient images such as this, and they fed his imagination for decades afterwards. Strikingly, moreover, he was impressed almost exclusively by representations of the male body – usually more or less naked, but clothed in clinging drapery in the case of more senior figures such as apostles, prophets and God the Father.

Imitation Versus Invention

In addition to having some of the responsibilities of a modern curator and teaching young artists the rudiments of classical style, Bertoldo di Giovanni was also expected to make works in the antique idiom. Of these, one of the most impressive was the bronze relief of a battle (fig. 37). This is a fairly exact reproduction of a Roman marble sarcophagus in Pisa, representing scenes from the life of a Roman military officer.[18] Bertoldo translated this scene from stone to metal, and also made it appear as if new. The sarcophagus, which still exists, is badly damaged, missing the heads of all the figures and the entire centre of the composition. These Bertoldo seamlessly replaced, making the ancient sculpture whole again. According to an inventory made in 1492, Bertoldo's relief was placed over a fireplace in a small, private room in Lorenzo's quarters.[19] Michelangelo was apparently given a similar commission to make a work based on a fragmentary antiquity, but the resulting work was both a freer interpretation of the ancient original and also much more impressive as a work of art (fig. 38). In this case, the ancient model was part of Lorenzo's collection.

Although their most prized possessions tended to be small-scale gems, the Medici were also interested in acquiring ancient marbles and bronzes. To this end, Lorenzo and his staff managed to get hold of a small, damaged piece (fig. 39). A Medici agent, Luigi da Barberino described this as:

fig. 34   Michelangelo, *Doni Tondo*, c. 1504–1506. Tempera on wood, diameter 120 cm. Florence, Gallerie degli Uffizi, inv. 1890 n. 1456

fig. 35   Hellenistic Egypt, *Tazza Farnese*, c. 2nd century BCE. Sardonyx agate, diameter 20 cm. Naples, Museo Archeologico Nazionale, inv. 27611

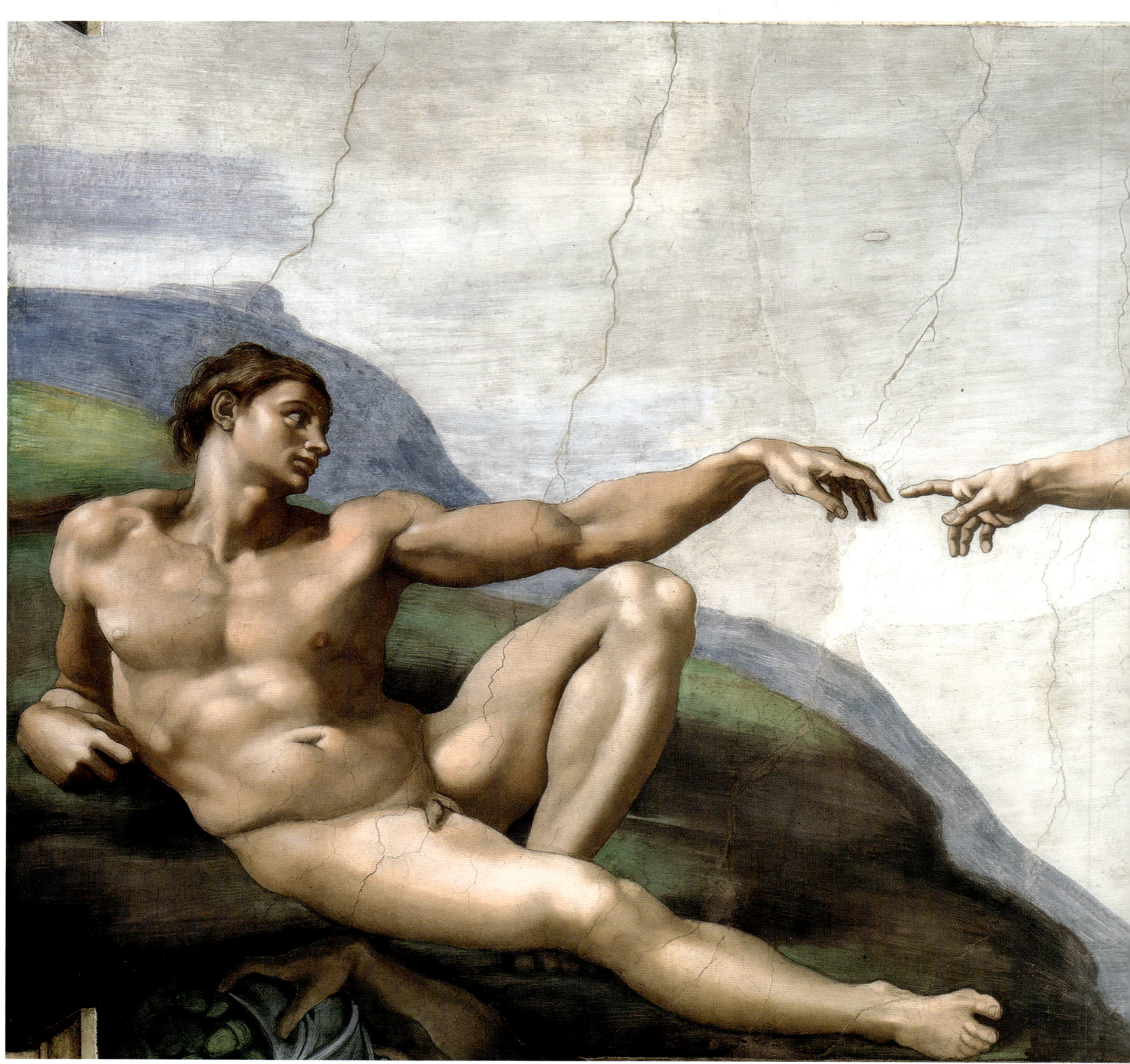

fig. 36   Michelangelo, *The Creation of Adam*, c. 1511–1512. Fresco. Vatican City, Ceiling of the Sistine Chapel

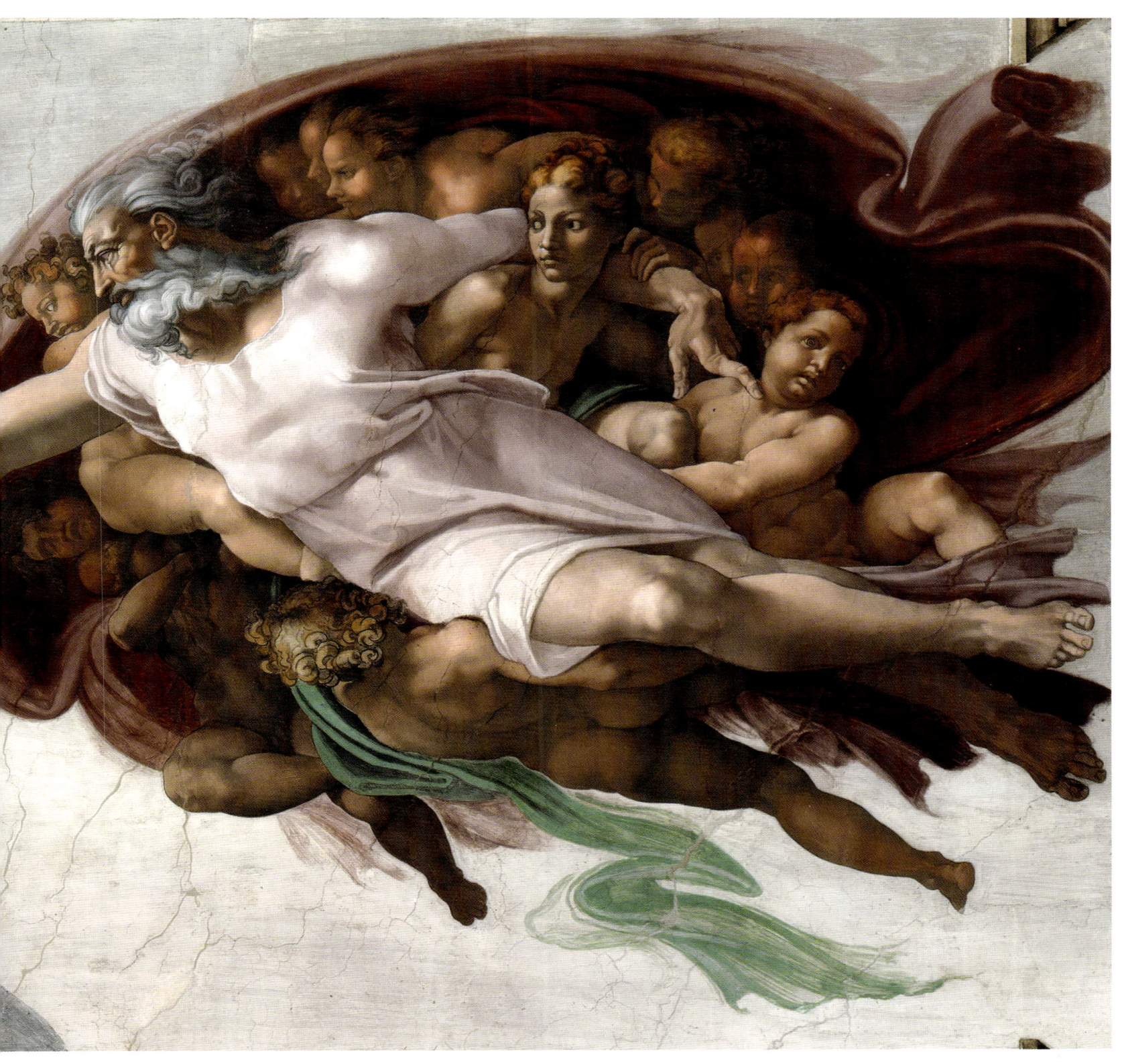

'...three beautiful fauns on a small marble base, all three bound together by a great snake... and even if one cannot hear their voices they seem to breathe, cry out, and defend themselves with wonderful gestures; that one in the middle you see almost falling down and expiring.'[20]

This battered marble group was smuggled to Florence in a crate on the back of a mule on 13 February 1489. As Fusco and Corti have demonstrated, it supplied several of the fundamental ingredients for Michelangelo's second surviving sculpture, the *Battle of the Centaurs*.[21] This relief was a commission from Lorenzo, although never delivered once his death intervened.[22] It seems likely that it was intended for a position similar to Bertoldo's bronze relief of a battle scene in Lorenzo's private quarters.[23]

The two principal figures in Michelangelo's relief – the striding full-length nude on the left and the centaur in the upper centre, with raised right arm – are based on the fauns on the left and right of the ancient group respectively. The confrontation of these two figures is the central dynamic of the relief. Around this armature Michelangelo invented a dense *mêlée* of struggling and expiring bodies, both human and equine. The *Battle of the Centaurs* was a display piece showing what this precociously brilliant adolescent could do in what was already his preferred medium of marble (as opposed to Bertoldo's bronze). It was more ambitious in conception than Bertoldo's relief, *Battle Scene*. The latter was an imaginative completion of an ancient work, whereas in his relief, Michelangelo altered the subject, changed the idiom from small scale three-dimensional to high relief, and invented a mass of new figures. Taken together, what Michelangelo made was less a copy than a brilliantly novel work in an ancient idiom, which addressed a fundamental dilemma for both Michelangelo and his patrons – the choice of whether to imitate antiquities or invent novel ones in an ancient idiom.

Michelangelo's early work veers between these two approaches. The very first of his carvings, which is described by Condivi, was of the former type: a copy of an antiquity with added details to make it look as it did when new. This was done while he was still a student in the sculpture garden before he was taken into Lorenzo's household. Apparently, one day:

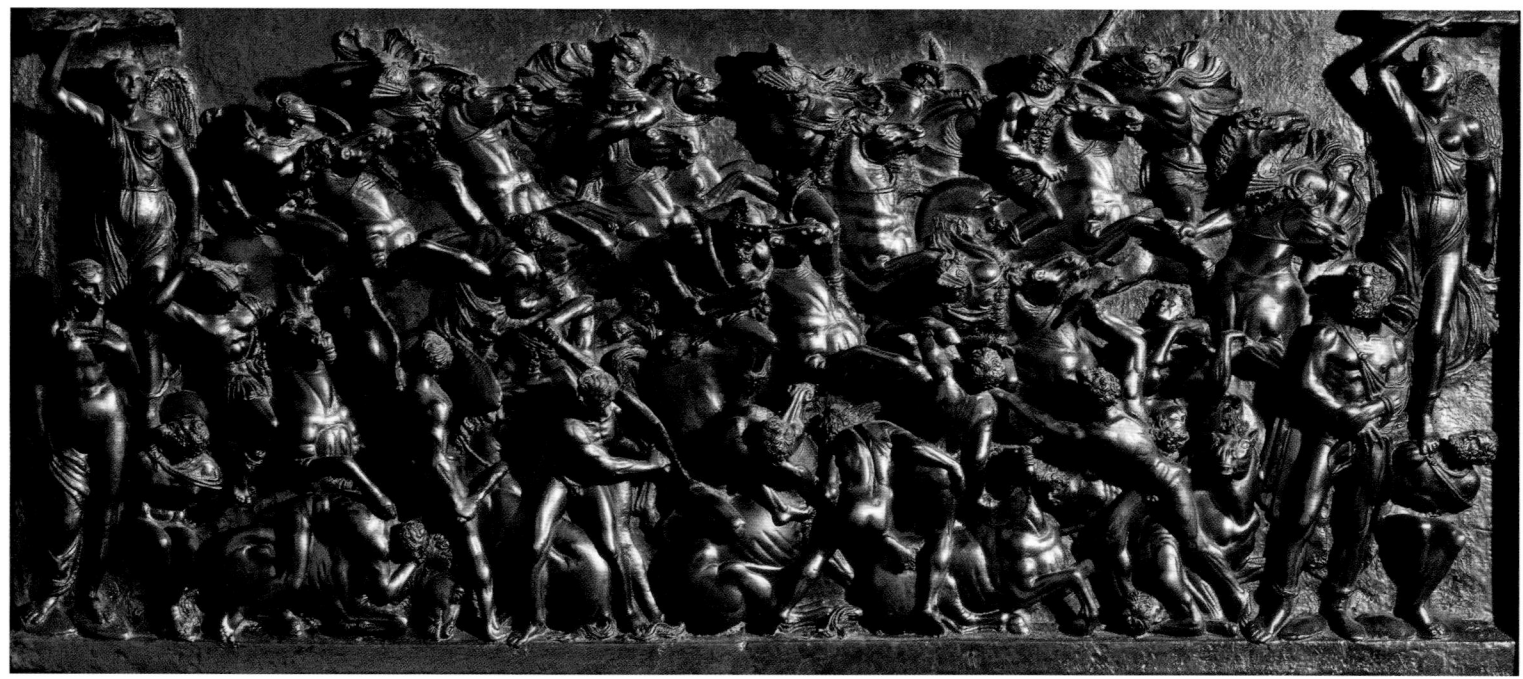

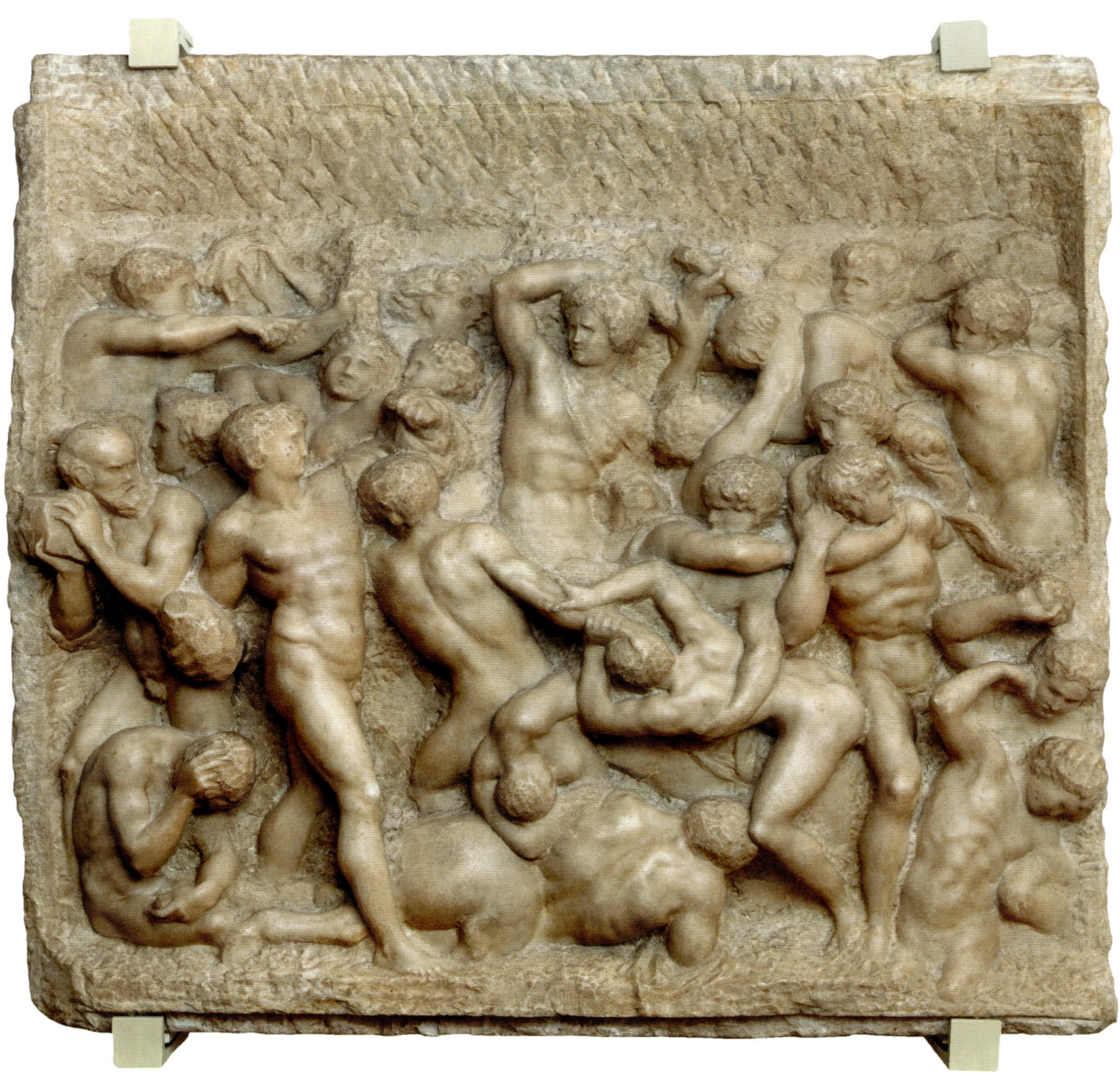

fig. 38   Michelangelo, *Battle of the Centaurs*, c. 1492. Marble, 84.5 x 90.5 cm. Florence, Casa Buonarroti, inv. 194

'...he came to consider the head of a faun, in appearance already old, with a long beard and laughing looks, although the mouth could scarcely be seen it was so ancient, nor could it be seen for what it was; but it pleased him beyond measure.'[24]

According to Condivi, it was this restoration or pastiche which first attracted Lorenzo's attention to the young artist.[25] Another carving from a few years later was clearly of the same type. By this time, however, the Medici regime had fallen from power. Short of money and without a patron, between Christmas 1495 and January 1496, Michelangelo made a free copy of an ancient Cupid in the Medici collection[26] – a piece he would have known well.

In lieu of a wealthier supporter, Michelangelo teamed up with Lorenzo di Pierfrancesco de' Medici, a cousin of the leading branch of the Medici family (now cast out of power). Lorenzo di Pierfrancesco commissioned a small work, an 'infant St John'.[27] He also, apparently, contracted a partnership with the sculptor to sell his *Sleeping Cupid* in the antique style; Lorenzo di Pierfrancesco suggested the transaction could be helped along by outright fraud, 'If you were to prepare it, so that it should appear to have been buried, I shall send it to Rome and it would pass for an antique, and you would sell it much more profitably'.[28] It is just as likely, of course, that the artificial aging of this sculpture was Michelangelo's idea – he certainly did it.

The *Sleeping Cupid* (complete with fake patina) was sold as a genuine antiquity to a wealthy cardinal, Raffaele Riario. The deal fell through, however, because the middleman, a dealer named Baldassare del Milanese, held on to most of the price of 200 ducats, letting Michelangelo have only 30. At this point, someone, quite possibly the artist, let Riario know that he had bought a modern work. His reaction was interesting. He demanded his money back,[29] but also found out who had made this Cupid and sent for him. Renaissance collectors were clearly conscious that they might be offered fakes, but they drew the line between authenticity and forgery in a different position from where we would today. Obviously, then an outstanding work in an ancient idiom – even if forged – still had value and could be enjoyed.

After the *Sleeping Cupid* was returned by Riario, it was considered by various collectors, including Isabella d'Este (who was advised not to buy it as her agent suspected it was not antique). Eventually Cesare Borgia, the pope's son, snapped it up, then gave it to the Duke of Urbino, who in turn presented it to none other than Isabella d'Este. In her inventory of 1542, it was listed as a work by Michelangelo, alongside another ancient cupid attributed to Praxiteles (which is given a slightly higher valuation).[30]

She wrote that for a modern sculpture it had 'no equal'.[31] By that time of course, a Michelangelo was a valuable item in its own right.

The first extant letter from Michelangelo is to Lorenzo di Pierfrancesco and describes a visit he paid to Cardinal Riario on 27 June 1496. He had arrived in Rome on that date for the first time in his life and immediately went to see the cardinal; the meeting went well. 'He seemed pleased to see me and immediately desired me to go and look at certain figures; this took me all day.'[32] Those 'certain figures' were undoubtedly the celebrated ancient sculptures in the cardinal's collection. The following Sunday, Michelangelo had another audience with the great man, at which it seems the cardinal challenged him to produce not another copy of an antiquity, but a work of his own in the classical idiom:

'...he asked me what I thought of the things I had seen. In reply to this I told him what I thought; and I certainly think he has many beautiful things. Then the Cardinal asked me whether I had courage enough to attempt some work of art of my own.'[33]

Michelangelo's answer was fittingly modest, but he accepted the commission. 'I replied that I could not do anything as fine, but that he should see what I could do'. Michelangelo immediately bought a block of marble and intended to begin work the following Monday, 6 July.[34] The result was *Bacchus*, a work which was – and remains – highly controversial (fig. 40).

Michelangelo went off-script in two respects. Firstly, the god's body suggests the god led a thoroughly unhealthy life. Instead of an heroically muscular physique, Bacchus is under-exercised and overweight with incipient 'man breasts', his body is covered in a layer of fat, his stomach bulging. Secondly, he is obviously drunk, reeling on his feet. The effect is part classical pastiche, part medieval personification of a vice. Where did Michelangelo get this idea? His carving is unlike most classical statues of the god, who is generally shown as a noble, nude figure identified by his attributes of grapes, vine leaves and a drinking cup. On the other hand, it recalls a passage in Pliny the Elder concerning the Greek sculptor of the 4th century BCE, Praxiteles.

Pliny described a bronze by Praxiteles of the god Dionysus (or Bacchus), accompanied by 'a figure of Drunkenness'; he also described a famous sculpture of a satyr, known by the Greek title '*Periboëtos*' meaning 'Celebrated'.[35] Pliny may have been confusing two or more works, and it seems that Michelangelo conflated the two descriptions in this passage and set about making a carving of Bacchus, drunk, attended by a beautiful child

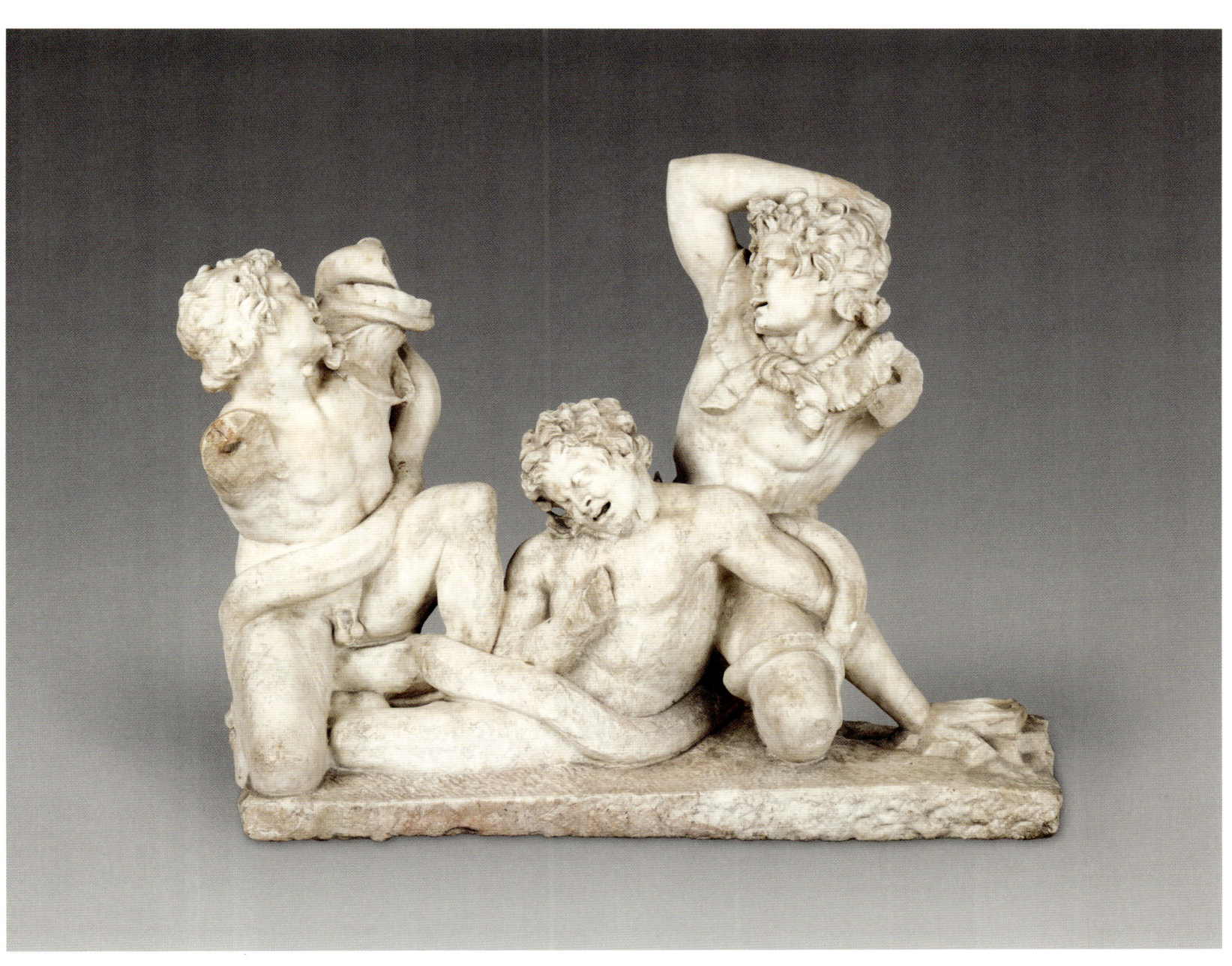

fig. 39   Roman, *Three Satyrs Fighting a Serpent*, c. 1st century CE. Marble, 64.1 x 80 cm. Private collection, on loan to the Art Institute of Chicago, inv. 190.2012

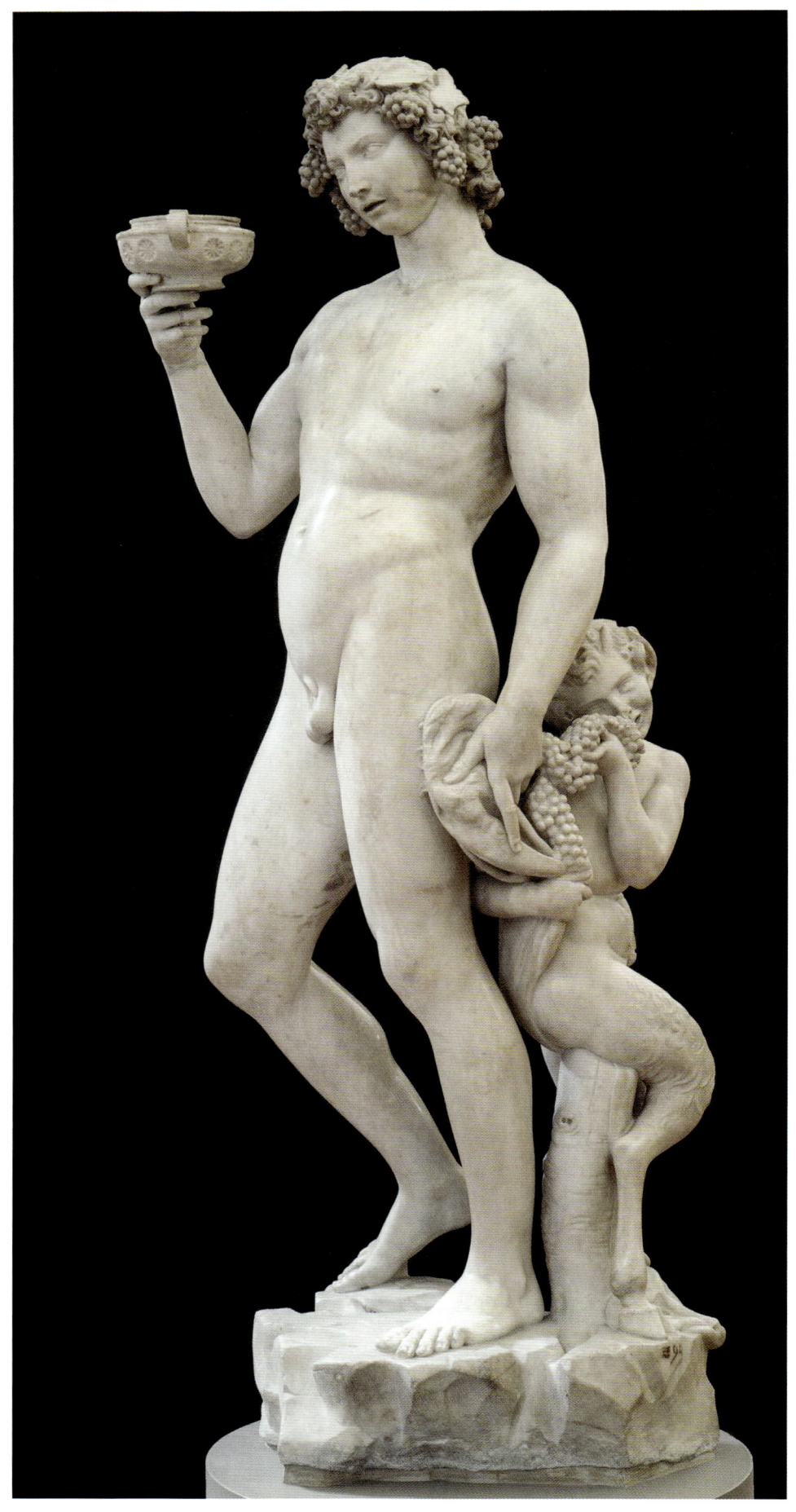

fig. 40   Michelangelo, *Bacchus*, 1496–1497. Marble, height 203 cm. Florence, Museo Nazionale del Bargello, inv. Sculture 10

satyr. Condivi, presumably quoting the septuagenarian Michelangelo, insisted that the 'form and appearance' of Bacchus 'corresponds in every detail to the meaning intended by the ancient writers'.[36]

This raises the question of how Michelangelo, whose Latin was poor, could have known about these references by the Roman author. Many of his patrons, including Cardinal Riario, Riario's banker Jacopo Gallo (of whom more shortly), and Lorenzo di Pierfrancesco probably would have been readers of Pliny. But Michelangelo would almost certainly also have heard a great deal about this Roman author before he left the Medici court. The most likely source of Plinian information was the other person from that household to be warmly mentioned in Condivi's *Life*: the poet and scholar Angelo Ambrogini, usually known as Poliziano. This learned man applied himself to the teenage Michelangelo's education. Condivi states that he 'loved Michelangelo greatly, knowing him for the exalted spirit he was, and, though not needing to, he constantly spurred him on to study, always expounding to him and giving him things to do'.[37] Among other intellectual specialities, Poliziano was a noted authority on Pliny.[38]

Michelangelo's *Bacchus* was a *tour de force* – of a kind. But it did not please the cardinal.[39] Riario paid promptly for the marble block, but he was slow in making the final instalment of 150 ducats, and never took possession of the sculpture.[40] Various reasons have been proposed as to why Riario did not accept the *Bacchus*. But the conclusion that he disliked the work and rejected it seems inescapable. Michelangelo, speaking via Condivi, was clearly still angry about the affair over half a century later. Riario, the text asserts quite wrongly as far as antiquities were concerned, 'little understood or enjoyed statues'. Condivi also claims that the cardinal never commissioned anything from Michelangelo – another striking example of economy with the truth.[41] What was true was that he had never *accepted* a work from the artist. This must have been a blow.

Although Michelangelo remained proud of his *Bacchus*, the sculpture had an unusual fate: for the following three-quarters of a century it was exhibited as antique in the sculpture court of Jacopo Gallo and his heirs. It can be seen there in a drawing by Maarten van Heemskerck from around 1532–36, forming the centrepiece of an array

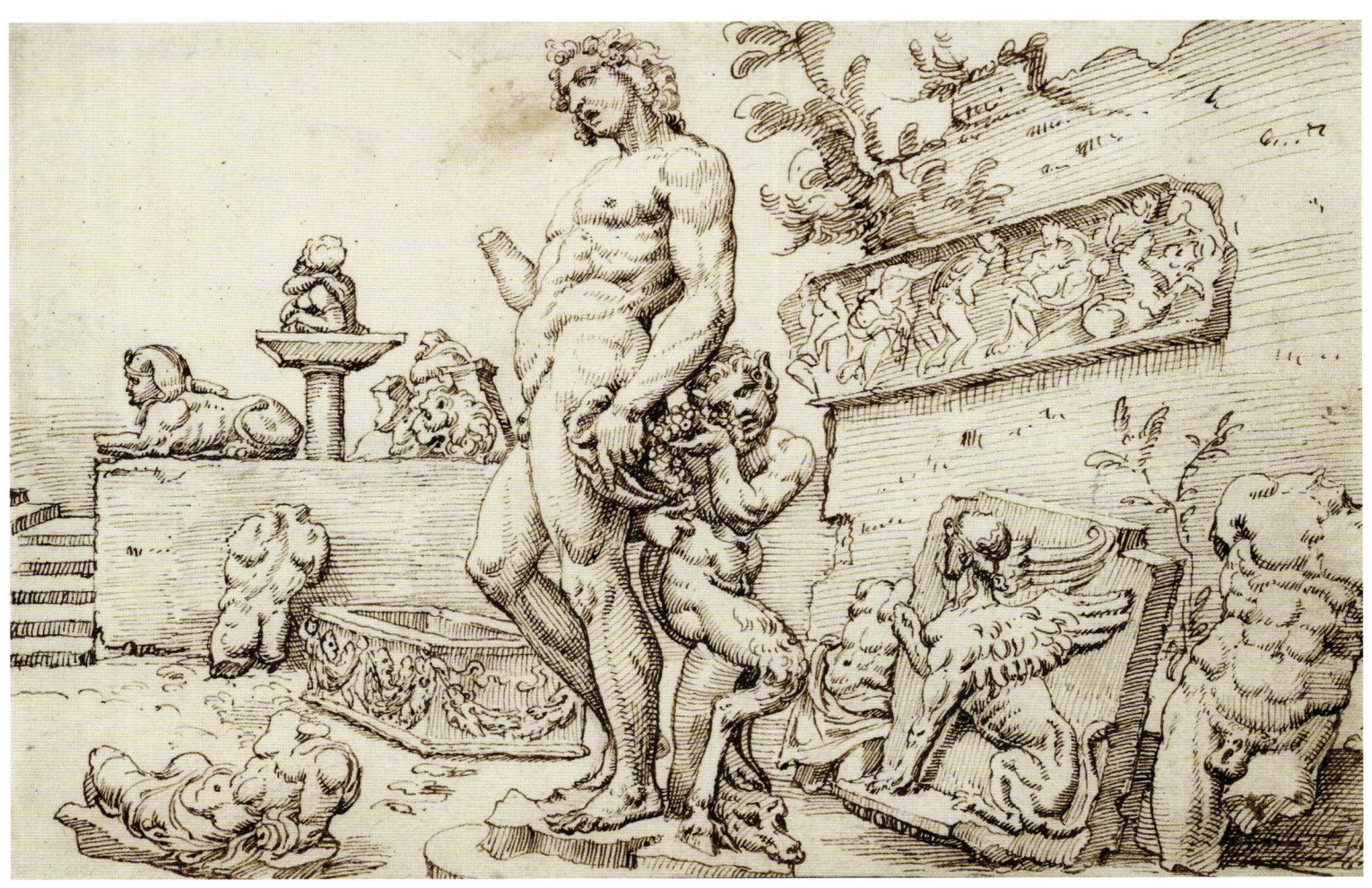

fig. 41   Maarten van Heemskerck, *Statue Court of the Casa Galli,* from his Roman sketchbook, c. 1532–1537. Pen and brown ink, 134 x 208 mm. Berlin, Staatliche Museen, inv. 79 D 2, fol. 72r

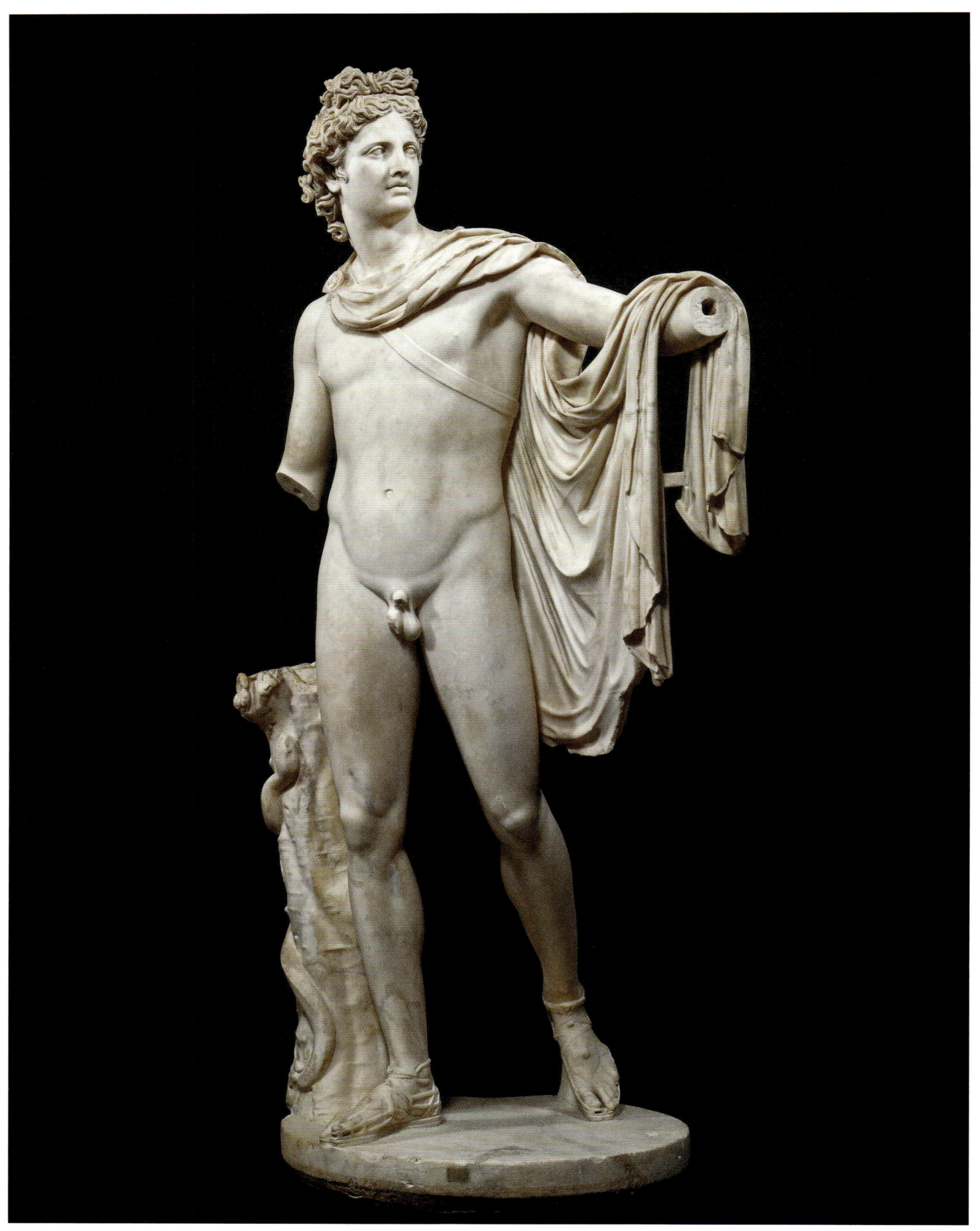

fig. 42   Roman, *Apollo Belvedere*, 2nd century CE copy, possibly of a 4th century BCE Greek original by Leochares. Marble, height 224 cm. Vatican City, Vatican Museums, inv. M.V.1015.0.0

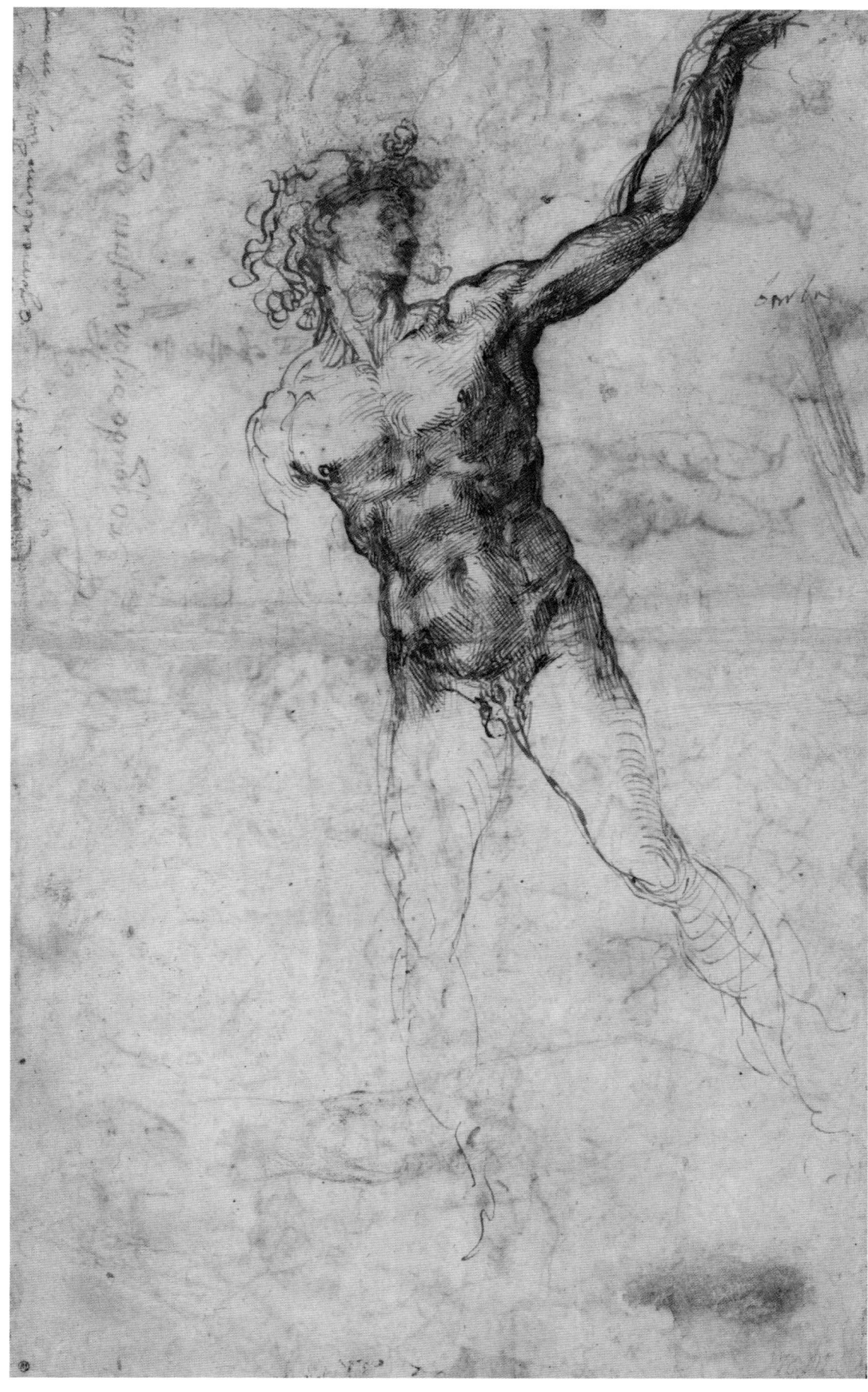

fig. 43   (cat. 10) Michelangelo, *A Male Nude*, c. 1501–1502. Pen and brown ink, black chalk, 374 x 228 mm. London, British Museum, inv. 1887,0502.117

of smaller and more battered antiquities (fig. 41). But the *Bacchus* has sustained damage since it was carved: his right hand and cup are missing, as is his penis.[42] It looks as if the sculpture has been artificially aged to pass as an antiquity.[43]

To Emulate and Surpass

Never again perhaps did Michelangelo try to imitate classical sculpture quite so directly. One reason might have been that the *Bacchus* had been badly received. Another factor, however, was that during this first stay in Rome he widened and deepened his study of ancient art. One work that clearly had an impact on him at this time was the so-called *Apollo Belvedere* (fig. 42). Lorenzo de' Medici had failed to acquire this sculpture when it was first discovered – instead it had been bought by Cardinal Giuliano della Rovere (later Pope Julius II).[44] During the 1490s and early sixteenth century it was on view in the garden attached to the cardinal's palace, next to the church of Santi Apostoli.[45] Michelangelo's interest in this sculpture is suggested by a drawing in the British Museum in which he was clearly thinking about the *Apollo Belvedere,* but musing on the possibilities it offered rather than simply copying it (fig. 43/cat. 10).

The sculpture represents the god poised in midmotion, half turning, one foot raised from the ground. Apollo has just shot an arrow from a bow he once held in his left hand, his other hand drops down having released the string. In his version Michelangelo increased the dynamic effect. His figure balances on one leg, turning more emphatically. The parts of the figure which he has worked up most heavily are the torso and the left arm: both are much more emphatically modelled and muscular than the rather bland body of the classical deity. Clearly, the *Apollo Belvedere* must have affected Michelangelo's thinking about his own *David* (the British Museum drawing might date from the years after his return to Florence in 1501 when he was working on the giant sculpture). David's posture, weight on one leg, and his lordly gaze both echo Apollo, but his chest and abdomen are treated with an anatomical naturalism much closer to the drawing.

The suavity of the *Apollo Belvedere* is not a quality generally associated with Michelangelo. A number of his works, however, lack the rugged dramatic intensity which has been seen as the key quality of his art and personality since the sixteenth century. Instead, they are quieter, calmer, even gentle. These have tended to be less admired by posterity which has largely dismissed them as 'minor' or even denied they were by the master at all.[46] Some of these, including the *Crucifix* in Santo Spirito (fig. 123), and

the *Young Archer* on loan to the Metropolitan Museum, disappeared from the art historical map for centuries and were only re-identified in the late twentieth century.

The majority of this group come from early in Michelangelo's career – but not the two carvings of *The Risen Christ,* which were produced between 1514 and 1521, nor the unfinished so-called *Apollo-David* from around 1530–32 (fig. 44/cat. 38). The latter is another neglected work. It attracts little attention from art lovers and not a great deal from scholars. Nonetheless, it has its own fascination since it is a clear, well-documented example of the mature Michelangelo making a sculpture in a smooth, classicising mode very different from his better-known work. It is, in fact, like the *Bacchus* for Cardinal Riario, an attempt to emulate and at the same time vie with a specific ancient prototype. This aspect has been obscured by a confusion in an early inventory.[47] But two points are now clear. Firstly, this carving is plainly an Apollo.[48] Secondly, the subject is taken from a work by the ancient Greek sculptor Praxiteles. This was described by Pliny: 'a youthful Apollo called in Greek the Lizard-Slayer because he is waiting with an arrow'.[49] The youthful god is seen reaching up to pull out an arrow while looking down at the little reptile; he seems relaxed, even disdainful. This is scarcely a life-and-death tussle.

The *Apollo-David* is a connoisseur's piece, intended for a private collection. It was commissioned by Baccio Valori, a Florentine patrician who was briefly the most powerful person in the city. After the siege of Florence, in August 1530, Valori entered the city in triumph at the head of the pro-Medici army. For a while he served as Governor of Florence for Pope Clement VII, head of the Medici family, and thus had power of life and death over Michelangelo who had taken the opposite, republican, side in the struggle. Vasari wrote that Michelangelo carved the *Apollo-David,* 'to make a friend of Baccio Valori' ('*per farsi amico*').[50] That was doubtless true, although there is reason to suppose Valori's relationship with the artist was more cordial than is usually thought.[51] His understanding of the visual arts is suggested by the fact he commissioned one of Sebastiano del Piombo's greatest portraits.[52] The tone of his surviving letter to Michelangelo, probably from spring 1532, is friendly:

'I do not want to bother you for my figure, because I am sure there is no need, on account of the affection I know you bear me. I assure you that there is nothing I desire more than this for the satisfaction of my mind. And if you need money, or anything else you think I could manage, let me know, so that you lack nothing.'[53]

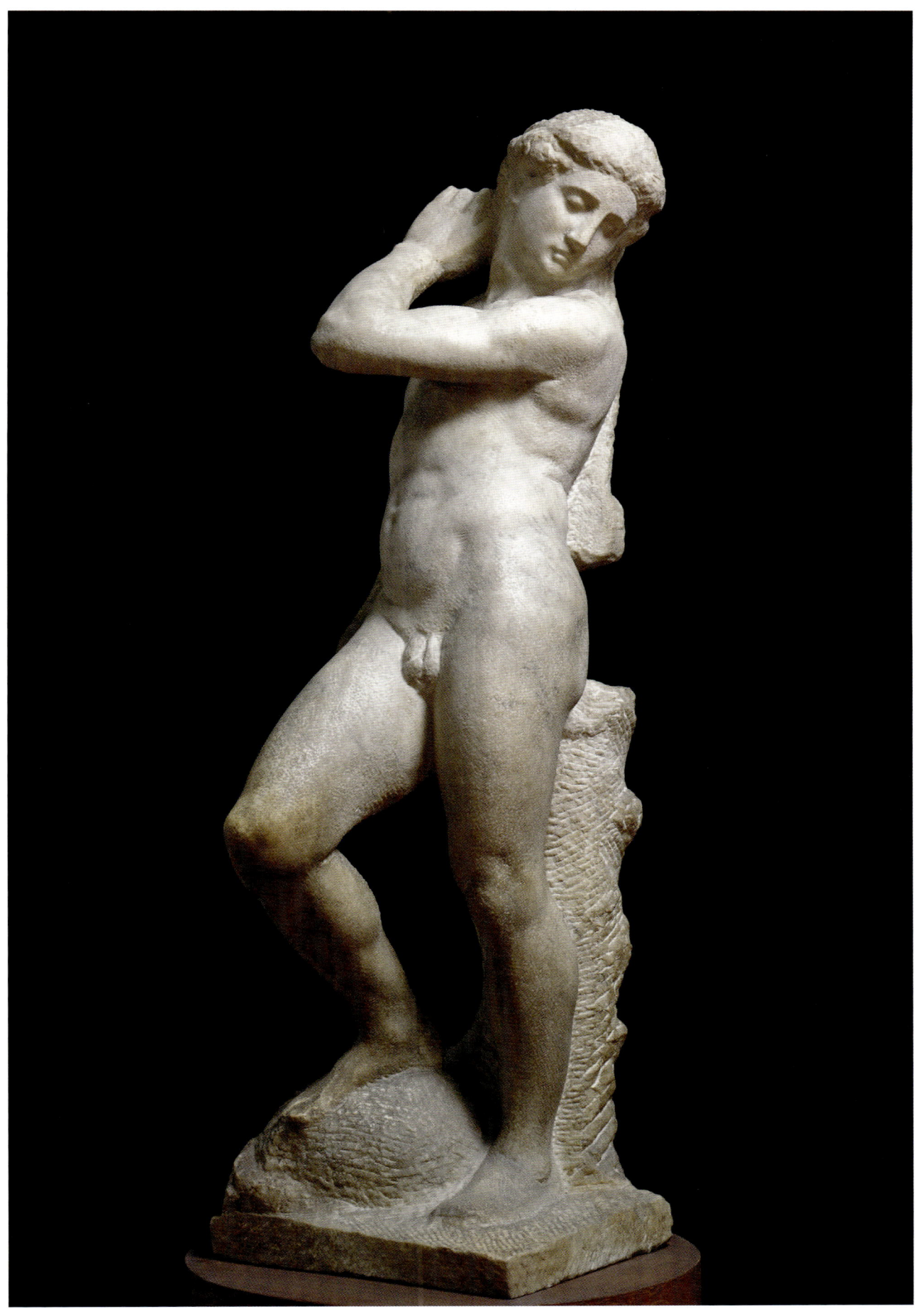

fig. 44   (cat. 38) Michelangelo, *Apollo-David*, c. 1530. Marble, height 146 cm. Florence, Museo Nazionale del Bargello, inv. Sculture 121

This letter is mainly concerned with designs Valori wanted Michelangelo to make for his new Florentine palazzo,[54] which was presumably the intended location for the *Apollo*. Not surprisingly, then, it is a work which would appeal to someone formed, as Valori and Michelangelo both were, by late fifteenth-century Florentine classicism.

Francesco Caglioti has pointed out that the twisting pose with 'a powerful arm bending upwards towards its own shoulder' first makes its appearance in the *Young Archer* from 1496 and the painted *Doni Tondo* from 1504–06, and was repeated in *The Risen Christ*.[55] Thus each figure is given a dynamic twist. In other respects, the body-type and pose of the Apollo are close to those of the so-called 'Seal of Nero' mentioned above, a work which would have been known to Michelangelo (and perhaps Valori too) from his mid-teens and was also one of the best-known antiquities in fifteenth-century Italy.[56]

Subsequently the *Apollo* was displayed in the collection of his enemy Cosimo I de' Medici, the new Duke of Florence, at the Palazzo Vecchio, alongside two sculptures of Bacchus by Baccio Bandinelli and Jacopo Sansovino, and an ancient torso which Benvenuto Cellini had transformed into a figure of Ganymede with the addition of a head, a lower right leg, both feet, a base and an eagle.[57] Michelangelo's work would have fitted into this display of modern imitations – plus one genuine, but heavily restored, antiquity. It is revealing (and intriguing) that Michelangelo was able and willing to produce such a work as an enormously celebrated artist in his mid-50s. Perhaps in making the Apollo, Michelangelo was accommodating his art to the conventional taste of Valori. Others preferred something more adventurous, such as Pope Clement VII who pressed the artist to come up with 'some new fantasy' ('*qualche fantasia nuova*').[58] But it may be that both stylistic possibilities – the conventionally classical and wildly innovatory – existed within Michelangelo's own mind. The central nude of a highly personal work such as *The Dream,* a drawing from around 1533 (fig. 101/cat. 44), has a body type, as far as the arms and upper body are concerned, similar to both the *Apollo-David* and *The Risen Christ*.

The lessons Michelangelo learnt from antiquity were complex, and sometimes contradictory, but so was his own evolution. Ultimately, however, the works which made most impact, both on his contemporaries and on posterity, were more tense, tumultuous and charged with power. They too were inspired by antiquities: the *Belvedere Torso* and the sculptural group *Laocoön and his Sons* (figs 45 and 46). Both of these were intimately connected with his work, his imagination and his life; the latter famously reappeared more or less in front of his eyes.

The rediscovery of *Laocoön and his Sons* on 12 January 1506, was the most sensational event in

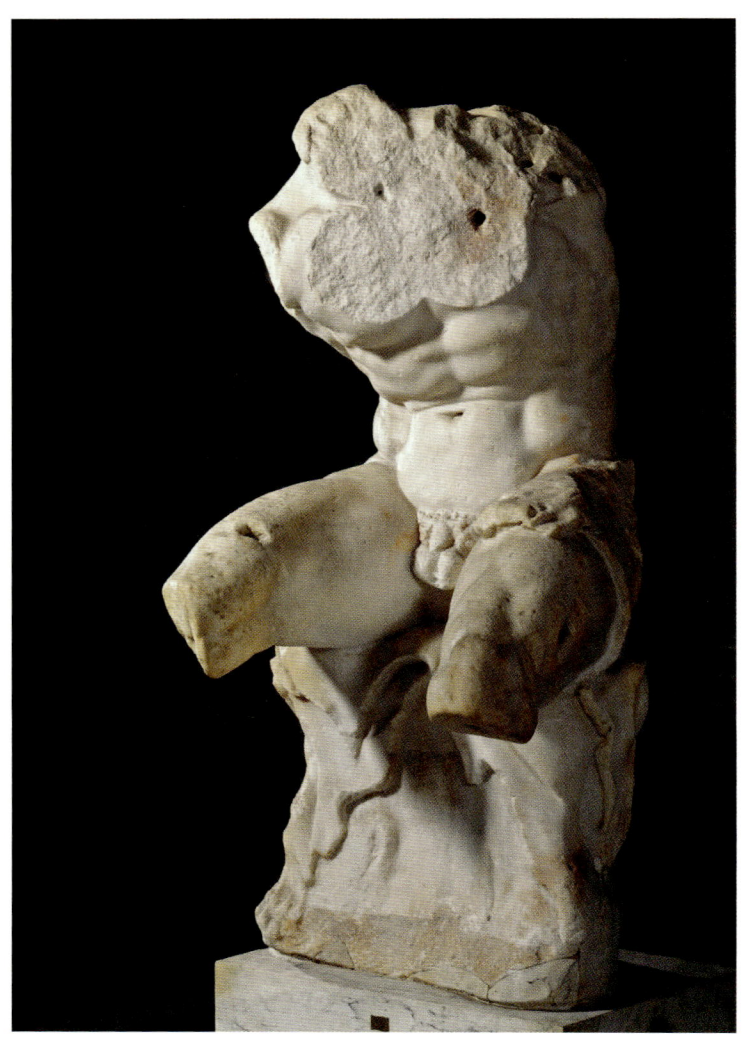

fig. 45   Roman, *Belvedere Torso*, perhaps a copy of a 2nd century BCE Greek sculpture. Marble, height 159 cm. Vatican City, Vatican Museums, inv. M.V. 1192.0.0

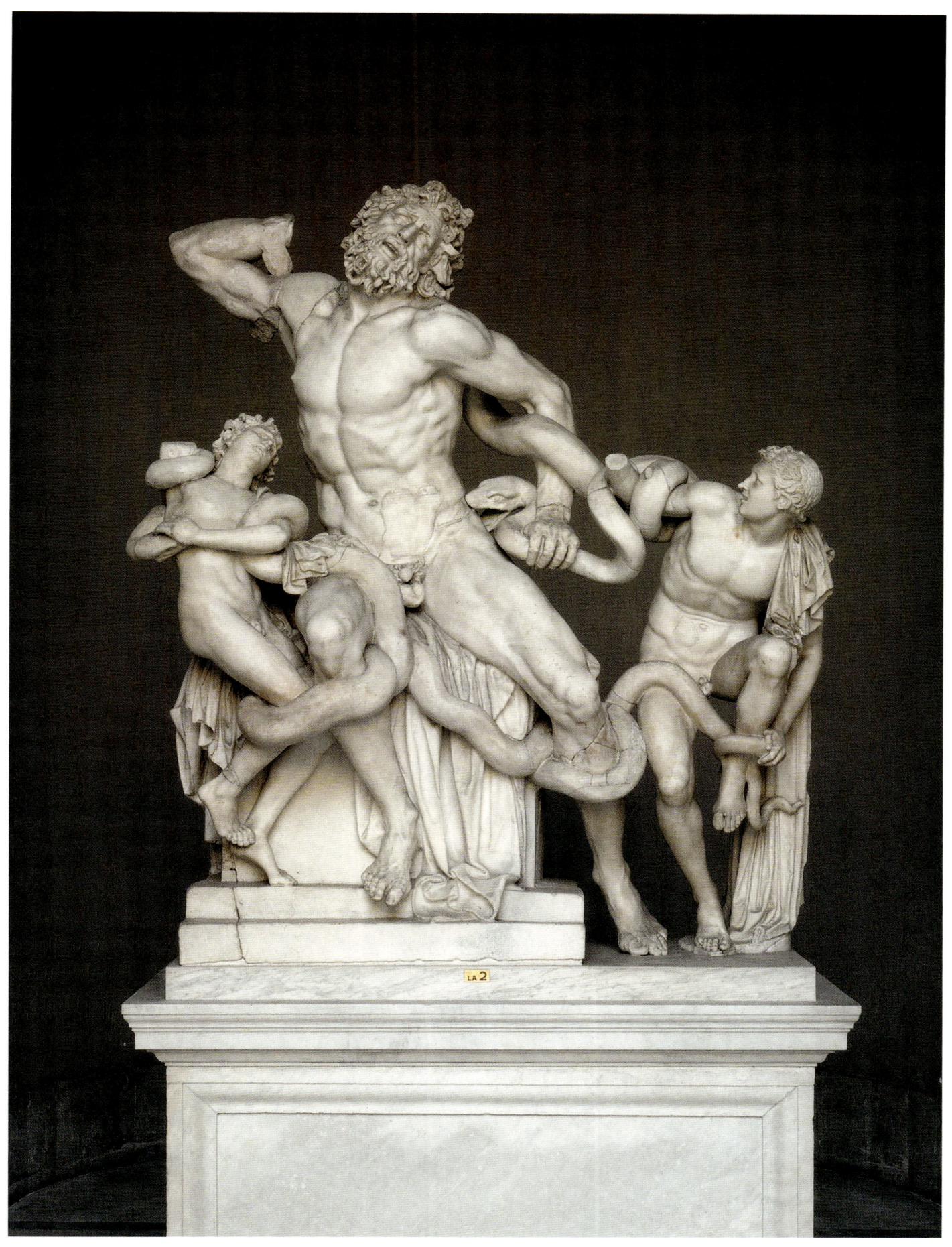

fig. 46　　Hagesander, Polydorus and Athenodorus of Rhodes, *Laocoön and his Sons*, c. 40–20 BCE. Marble, 208 x 163 x 112 cm. Vatican City, Vatican Museums, inv. M.V. 1059.0.0

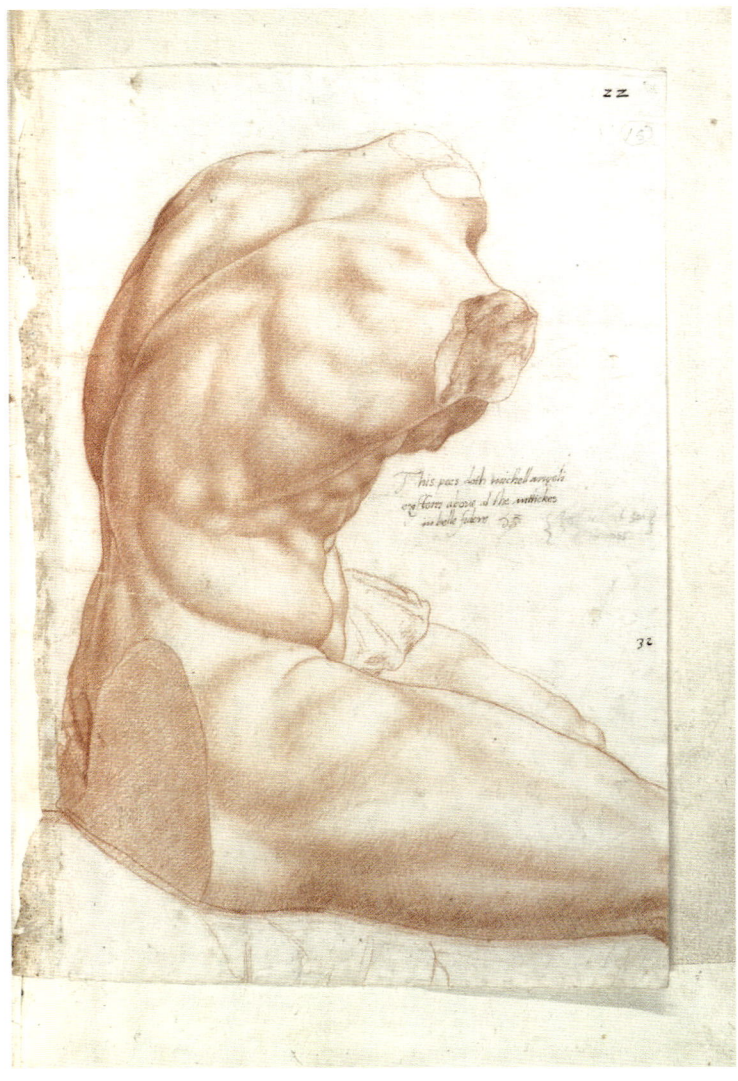

Renaissance archaeology – indeed, one of the most extraordinary of all time. It was found on some land owned by a man named Felice de Fredis not far from the Roman Colosseum and instantly recognised as the celebrated ancient masterpiece described by Pliny. The pope was informed (by this date Giuliano della Rovere had been elected and taken the name Julius II). His first impulse on hearing of the extraordinary find was to send for Giuliano da Sangallo. Sangallo, once a crucial figure in the artistic team of Lorenzo de' Medici, was by then Julius's senior architect and artistic advisor. According to a letter written long afterwards by Sangallo's son, Francesco:

> 'The pope ordered one of his officers to run and tell Giuliano da Sangallo to go and see them. He set off immediately. Since Michelangelo Buonarroti was always to be found at our house, my father having summoned him and having assigned him the commission of the pope's tomb, my father wanted him to come along, too.'[59]

On seeing the work which had emerged from the earth, Sangallo announced, 'That is the *Laocoön*, which Pliny mentions'. At that point, a process of study and discussion began which continued for centuries: 'they dug the hole wider so that they could pull the statue out. As soon as it was visible everyone started to draw, all the while discoursing on ancient things, chatting as well about the ones in Florence.'[60]

Michelangelo plus another sculptor and expert on antiquities, Gian Cristoforo Romano, were charged by the pope with making a technical examination of the *Laocoön*.[61] In his *Natural History*, Pliny made two points about this work. Firstly, that because it was created by three sculptors from Rhodes – Hagesander, Polydorus and Athenodorus – none of them received the level of acclaim they deserved: 'because the credit is shared, nor is it possible to give equal credit to members of a group'. This was a point which would have appealed to Michelangelo, always temperamentally averse to working with collaborators. Secondly, Pliny claimed that the whole group of three figures, plus the 'wonderful coils of the snakes' attacking them had been 'carved from a single block' ('*ex uno lapide*').[62] This was a claim that was testable.

A Milanese gentleman named Cesare Trivulzio described Michelangelo and Gian Cristoforo Romano's technical findings in a letter (although he managed to mangle their names). The two sculptors, Trivulzio reported, deny the *Laocoön*:

fig. 47   Anonymous, *Drawing after the Belvedere Torso*, from a sketchbook with copies after the antique, mid 16th-century. Red chalk, 340 x 225 mm. Cambridge, Master and Fellows of Trinity College, inv. MS R. 17.3, plate 16

'...to be of a single block of marble; and they point to approximately four junction points but fused in such hidden places and so well consolidated and plastered together that only the greatest experts in this art can readily recognise them. They say that Pliny was deceived, or wished to deceive others, in order to render the work more impressive.'[63]

This was a powerful blow to the intellectual foundations of the Renaissance. Pliny was the main source on the subject of ancient art. If he could be wrong, who knew what to think? Trivulzio certainly did not. 'The authority of Pliny is great', he equivocated, 'but our artists can also be right'. For Michelangelo himself, the appearance of the *Laocoön* posed a challenge. This, apparently, was as good as ancient art got. Pliny had described it as 'a work superior to any painting or bronze'.[64]

The question for an artist was whether simply to imitate this model, or to learn from it, even attempt to surpass it. According to Vasari, someone once put exactly this dilemma to Michelangelo. A friend asked him his opinion of someone who had imitated in marble several of the most famous antique statues and boasted that his copies were far better than the originals.[65] Michelangelo's reply was that, 'no one who follows others can ever get in front of them, and those who cannot do good work on their own account can hardly make good use of what others have done'.[66] For his own part, Michelangelo never directly imitated the *Laocoön* but instead made endless variations on it, played with it, improvised on it. Leonard Barkan suggested that we should 'understand Michelangelo as establishing a kind of ownership of the image'.[67] He even suggested that Michelangelo 'copyrighted' the sculpture (and also the *Belvedere Torso,* among other antiquities). The result was such that anyone looking at these ancient works saw Michelangelo in them. Alternatively, you could argue that Michelangelo discovered himself by contemplating those carvings.

More than all other sculptures, whether ancient or modern it seems, Michelangelo revered the *Belvedere Torso*. This, both visual and documentary evidence suggests, was his touchstone – the carving that most fired his imagination and constituted his internal ideal of what his art could be. In his pioneering guidebook to the antiquities of Rome, Ulisse Aldrovandi wrote: 'Michelangelo lavished remarkable praise on this work'.[68] On a beautiful drawing of the *Torso*, from a sketchbook now in Trinity College Library, Cambridge, made around 1550, there is an inscription: 'This pees doth michelangel exstem above all the anttickes in belle fdere' (fig. 47). Though similar to Aldrovandi's claim, this is more specific – and yet more extravagant in its implications. Apparently, Michelangelo

admired the *Belvedere Torso* more than any of the other celebrated works from the papal collection displayed in the Villa Belvedere. That is, he rated it higher than the *Apollo Belvedere*, and higher than the *Laocoön*.

Michelangelo's regard for the *Belvedere Torso* was the subject of legend. Some stories told about him and the marble sound too good to be true.[69] But the notion that Michelangelo hugely admired this object is not just probable, but plainly true. One just has to look at his own works to see that. Numerous variations on the *Belvedere Torso* theme can be seen in his works from the ceiling of the Sistine Chapel to *The Last Judgement*. William Hogarth wrote that in this battered chunk of marble, he 'discover'd a certain principle,' which 'gave his works a grandeur of gusto equal to the best antiques'.[70] About that Hogarth was absolutely correct. Michelangelo probably first saw the *Torso* soon after he arrived in Rome in 1496. Around 1500 the '*prospettivo Milanese*' described it in his poem. In the house of 'Master Andrea' he had seen 'a nude torso without arms or neck the equal of which I have never seen in stone'.[71] 'Master Andrea' was the sculptor and architect Andrea Bregno, to whose collection, as a fellow sculptor, Michelangelo would perhaps have had easy access. The fact that the *Torso* was owned by an artist, even a successful and wealthy one such as Andrea Bregno, rather than a prince of the church or an aristocrat suggests that it was not highly prized. It was not for another thirty years or more that it entered the Vatican collection – apparently between 1530 and 1536. That is, at the end of the pontificate of Clement VII or the beginning of the reign of Paul III: both popes who had great admiration for Michelangelo's judgement. Admiration of the *Torso* was a sophisticated taste.

The writer Anton Francesco Doni noted in his *Disegno*, published in 1549, that the 'torse of Hercules in the Belvedere' (that is, the *Belvedere Torso*) was not much admired by the *hoi polloi* ('*goffi*').[72] So around the same date that Aldrovandi was noting Michelangelo's high opinion of the *Torso*, Doni observed it did not much appeal to the majority of the people who saw it. The reason for this lack of popularity with the wider sixteenth-century public was doubtless its badly damaged state. All the other famous antique statues of Renaissance Rome were more or less 'restored' to look as it was imagined they might have been when new. This did not happen to the *Torso*, and the reason it did not might well have had to do with its high status among a small circle of elite artists: Michelangelo, perhaps Bramante, and by implication, Leonardo.

One of the *Torso*'s qualities that clearly appealed to Michelangelo was the way that – fragmentary as it was – it expressed drama, tension and inner struggle entirely through the structure of the chest, abdomen and thighs.

After all, this is all there is left of it. This gave Michelangelo what he always looked for in his own work: power through concentration. To intensify a work, his instinct was not to expand it, but go inwards, to uncover its essence. In the case of the *Torso,* because of the destruction of so much of the work, all that is left is the poetry of muscles and bones. Even the identity of the figure remains controversial. Apart from the marvellous quality of the carving – its naturalistic beauty and heroic force – the *Torso* is open-ended. In that respect it was like the smoke stains and marks on old walls which Leonardo recommended as aides to the imagination: it was a puzzle which positively demanded to be completed. But there was no single, obvious solution. Instead, there was an infinite range of possible answers. This was not an example of perfection to copy, but a starting point for new explorations.

Terribilità

There are many reincarnations of the *Laocoön* and the *Torso* on the ceiling of the Sistine Chapel. Of these, the one most charged with Michelangelo's trademark quality of awesomeness is the *Separation of Light From Darkness* (fig. 48). In meaning and emotional terms, this is the opposite of the *Laocoön.* Instead of agonised human beings, the hapless victims of divine rage, Michelangelo depicted divine power at its most dynamic. God Almighty makes one of the primary divisions of the universe with one swirl of his body. But the twisting posture and heavy musculature are the same (the latter visible through God's skin-tight robe). So too is what you might call, in musical terms, the tonality: a solemn key, thunderous chords.

It would be easy to multiply iterations of the *Laocoön* and the *Torso* throughout the Sistine Chapel – and the remainder of Michelangelo's *oeuvre*. One of the clearest and greatest recyclings of the latter is the *ignudo* on the right, above the prophet Jeremiah: a version of the *Torso* with missing limbs replaced but also yet more burly than the original (fig. 49). The *ignudo*'s chest is impossibly broad and muscular, yet it creates what you might call anatomical mood-music – slow, heavy, grand – and does so superbly.

In art historical terms, what Michelangelo discovered in both the *Laocoön* and the *Torso* was 'Hellenistic baroque'. This idiom originated in the third century BCE. The scholar Roland R.R. Smith describes it as a style specifically devised 'to characterise the elevated, tumultuous world of epic heroes'.[73] This was the creation of famous sculptors such as Lysippus and Epigonus. It was used for royal monuments created for Alexander the Great and the Attalid monarchs of Pergamon. In literary terms, these sculptural ensembles dealt largely with tragic drama – suffering, defeat, death – and they did so in terms of the struggling and/or dying male body. The *Laocoön,* according to Smith, is 'one of the finest expressions of the full Hellenistic baroque'.[74] As we have seen, Michelangelo encountered it just as he was achieving full artistic maturity. It must have struck him with the force of revelation.

What, then, did Michelangelo find in the *Laocoön* and the *Torso*? In a word, one often applied to Michelangelo himself and his works by his contemporaries: *terribilità.*[75] This capacity to strike awe or – to use another translation, 'terrifying intensity' – came to be regarded as his trademark quality. It was not there right from the beginning. His earliest drawings and carvings have remarkable force and extraordinary quality, but you would not describe the *Bacchus*, the *Apollo-David*, or even the first *Pietà* (fig. 113*),* astonishing masterpieces that they are, as having *terribilità*. This is a quality that appears in his middle period, in the warriors of the *Battle of Cascina* (fig. 133/cat. 51), God the Father, prophets and Sibyls on the ceiling of the Sistine Chapel, and *Moses* (fig. 95) from Julius II's tomb. No doubt Michelangelo found it inside himself but also discovered it in these masterpieces of the Hellenistic sculpture baroque. What he gained from them is as evident in a drawing such as the *Studies for Haman* (fig. 62/cat. 15) as it is in a fresco or a marble. In such works, Michelangelo was transforming anatomy into high drama. The writhing despair of the doomed figure is condensed into the twisting muscles of Haman's throat and the outstretched fingers of his hands. Here the main source is Laocoön, who was also struggling in the throes of an agonising death. In contrast, the Haarlem study of an *ignudo* (fig. 59/cat. 19), or the sheet with studies for the back of *Day* (fig. 65/cat. 28), demonstrate what he learnt from the *Belvedere Torso*.

For him, the muscles, bones and sinews of the upper body, were what John Constable famously said the sky was in his landscapes: the chief organ of sentiment. In these male backs he found rhythm, tension, architecture, dynamism: the expressive world he discovered in these ancient marbles, and the essence of what later artists learnt from him. From a lifetime of going to learn from the school of ancient art, Michelangelo learnt many things. Among them were visual idioms to imitate, and also standards to aim for – and surpass. Finally, perhaps, the most important lesson was how to be himself.

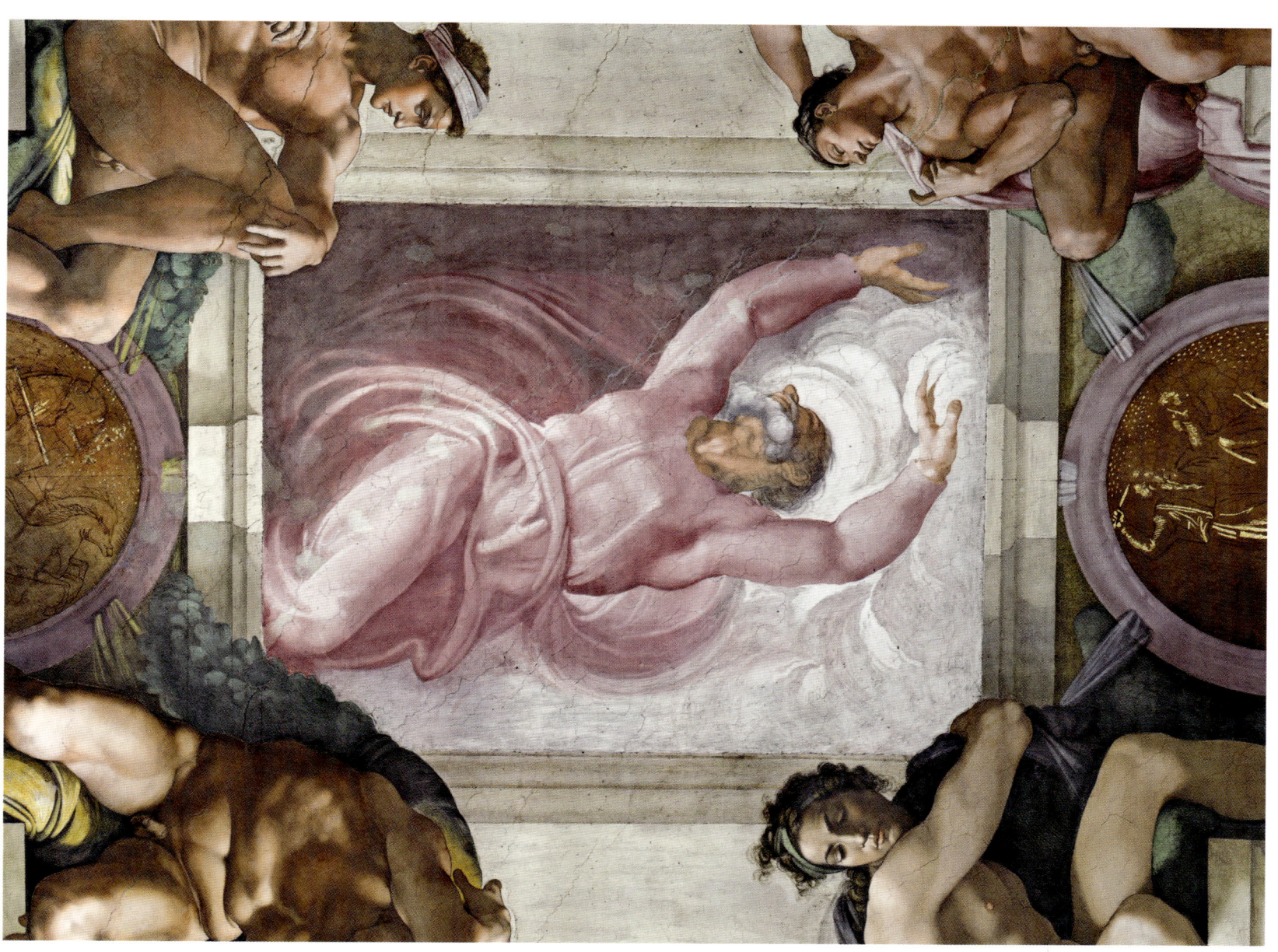

fig. 48   Michelangelo, *The Separation of Light from Darkness*, c. 1511–1512. Fresco. Vatican City, Ceiling of the Sistine Chapel

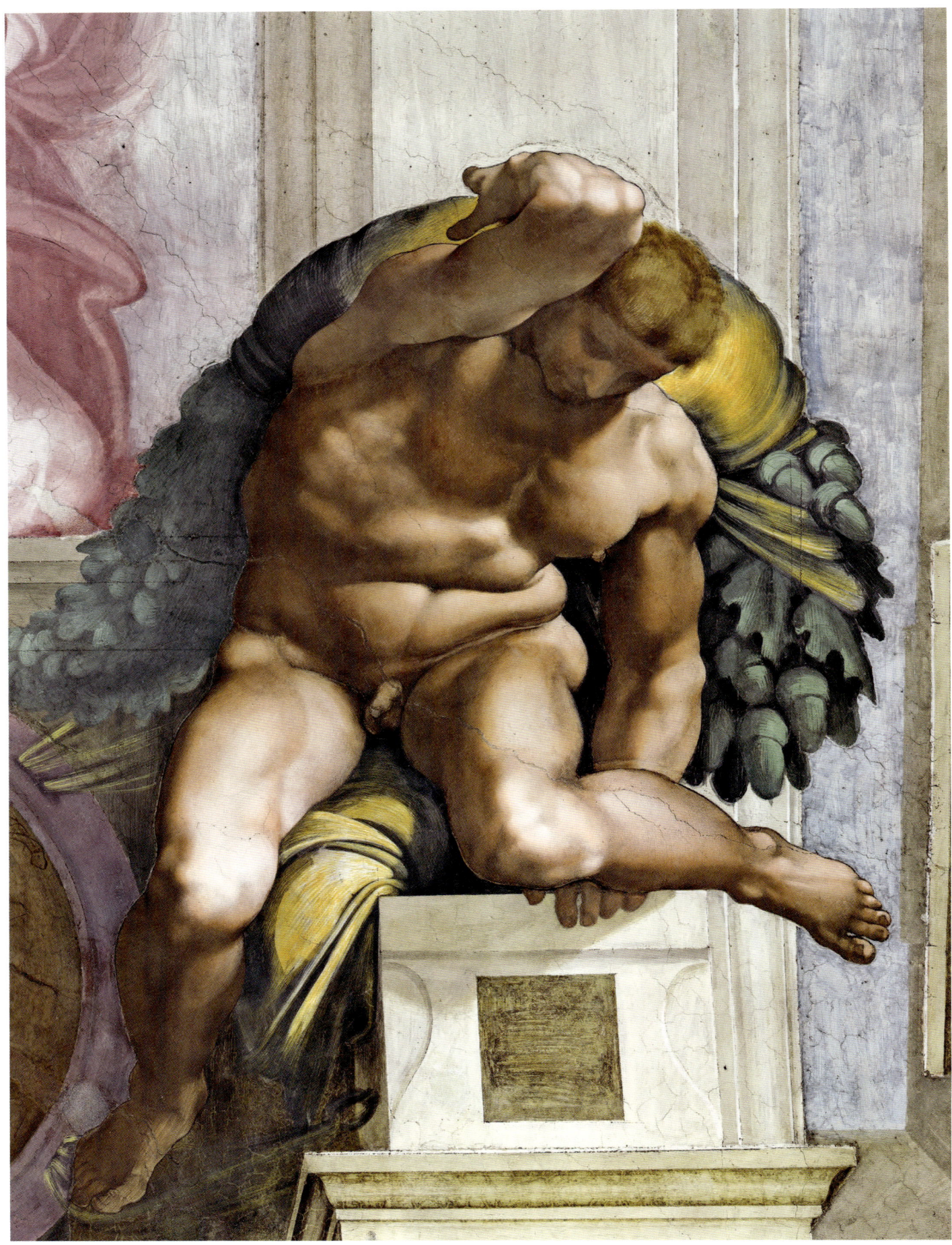

fig. 49   Michelangelo, *Ignudo above Jeremiah*, c. 1511–1512. Fresco. Vatican City, Ceiling of the Sistine Chapel

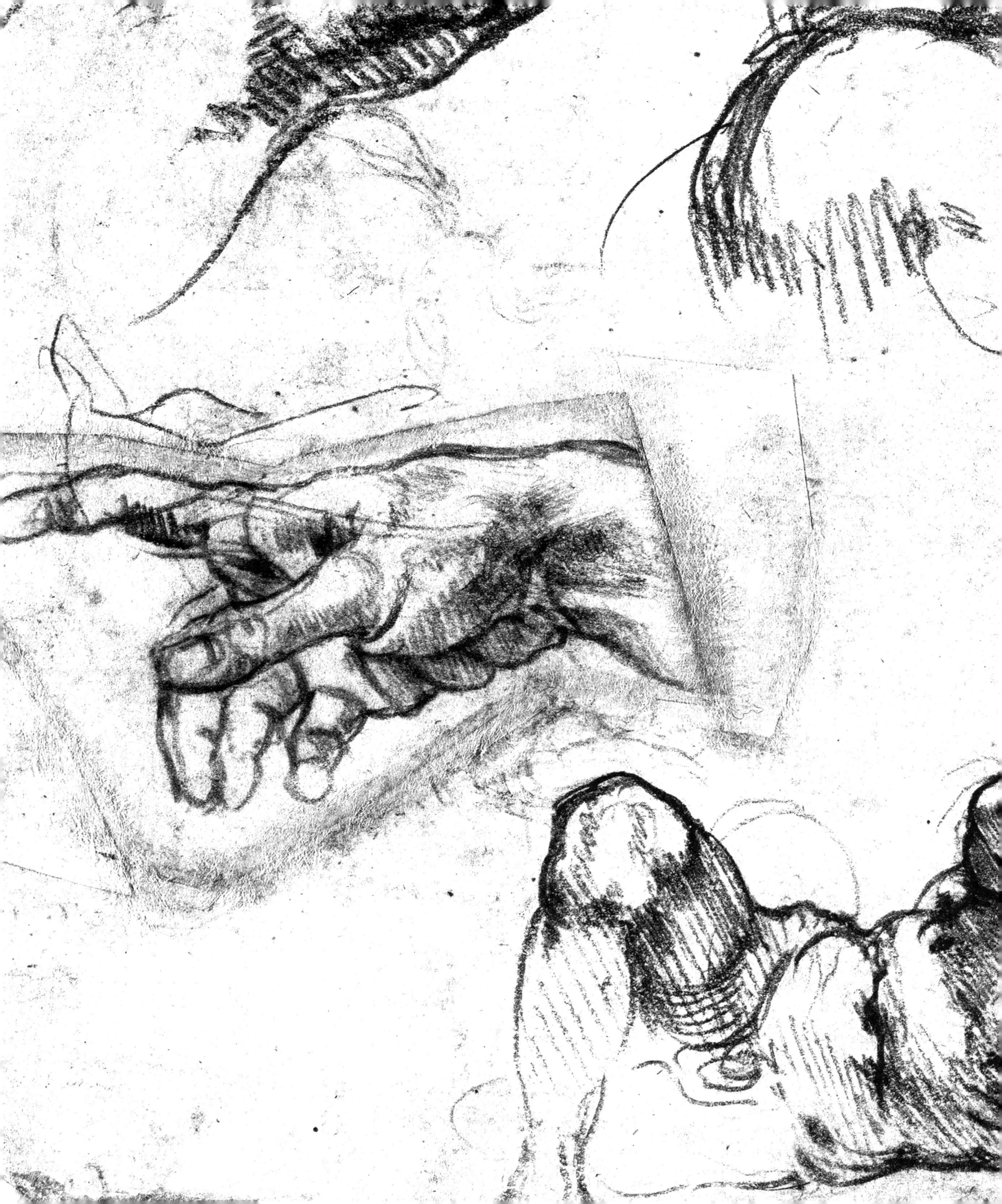

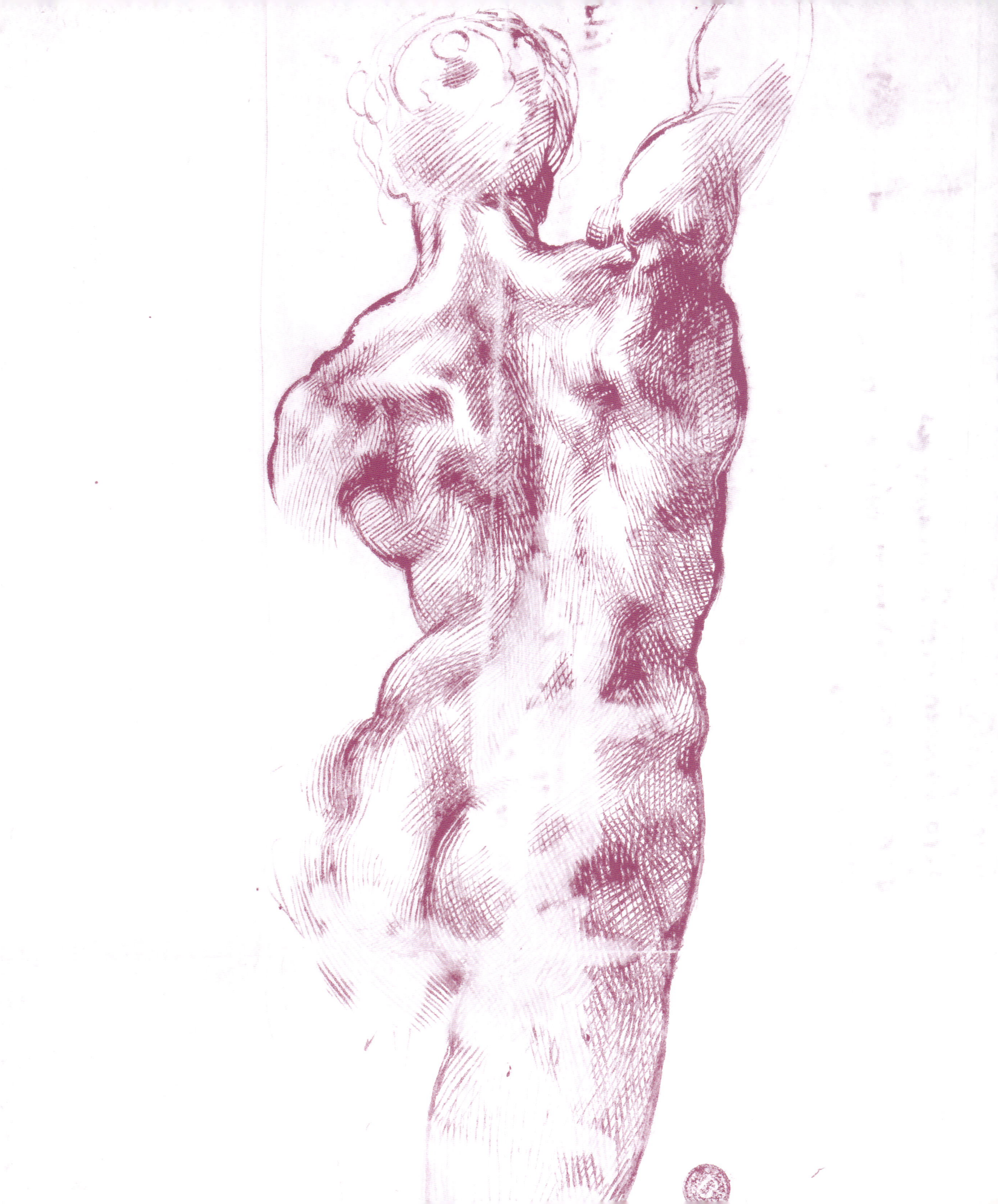

Baccio's Balls.
Michelangelo and the Ideal Model

Terry van Druten

The bulk of Michelangelo's work consists of drawings of human, especially male, figures. Apart from the sheets that formed part of the design process for architectural objects, there is virtually no single drawing by him that does not depict a human being. These drawings represent significant steps towards his sculptures, frescoes and paintings. From the first sketch via the compositional and the detailed study, a central role was played by drawings, many of which give the impression of having been done 'from nature' or a live model.

By the fifteenth century, model drawing had assumed a new and prominent place in creative practice, influenced by the changing artistic ideals of the Renaissance. In the work of earlier artists, figures and objects had chiefly served as symbols within the visual translation of primarily intellectual and, for the most part, religious narratives. The ability to recognise and 'read' them took precedence over naturalism and realism. This had changed significantly by the time Michelangelo took his first steps as a young artist in Domenico Ghirlandaio's workshop. Whereas artists in the early fifteenth century still referred to model books – repositories of more or less standardised images of the natural world – when Michelangelo was born in 1475, drawing from nature, including life drawing, had become an integral part of an artist's training and practice in central Italy.[1] As well as the work of other masters, young artists were expected, above all, to take nature itself as their example. To quote Vasari: 'only objects taken from nature can make pictures and sculptures perfect'.[2] Drawing male models played a central role in this; the human being – the man in particular – was, after all, considered the most perfect part of God's creation, although it was also true that procuring female models was considerably more problematic. Working from nature became even more crucial during Michelangelo's lifetime, when it also spread to the rest of Italy, before gradually developing into an essential part of European art.[3] The male physique in his work – mostly nude and athletic – amounted to a new representation of idealised and heroic bodies that would inspire countless artists in subsequent centuries.[4]

Despite the central place that Renaissance art afforded to nature, the accurate capture of physical reality was not usually an end in itself; the chief aim was to lift nature towards an ideal image, closer to the divine.[5] To use Vasari's words: 'to compose a body so perfect as to make art excel nature'.[6] It is interesting to seek the boundary between observation and idealisation. Most of Michelangelo's frescoes and sculptures likewise seem to have been based on nature and the observation of real, living people. To what extent is this true? And to what extent did he really use live models? At what point in the creative process did this occur? And for which parts of the work? Who exactly were these models? And how did Michelangelo transform their bodies in his art?

Following the Example of Others

While the above questions might be obvious, they are not easy to answer. Drawings only served to a limited degree as direct evidence of workshop practice; the picture they provide is incomplete and moreover distorted.[7] This reflects the fact, firstly, that while a large number of Michelangelo's drawings are known to us, they still represent just a small proportion of his total output. Although the artist's works were already coveted by collectors in his own lifetime, many more of his drawings were lost than have survived. This is due in part to the inherent fragility of the material used and to the almost purely functional role it played in the working process, but equally to Michelangelo's notorious – albeit possibly exaggerated – tendency to 'edit' his legacy by destroying certain groups of drawings.[8]

An even greater obstacle to our understanding of his workshop practice is that in some cases it is simply not clear to which exact source a figure study refers.

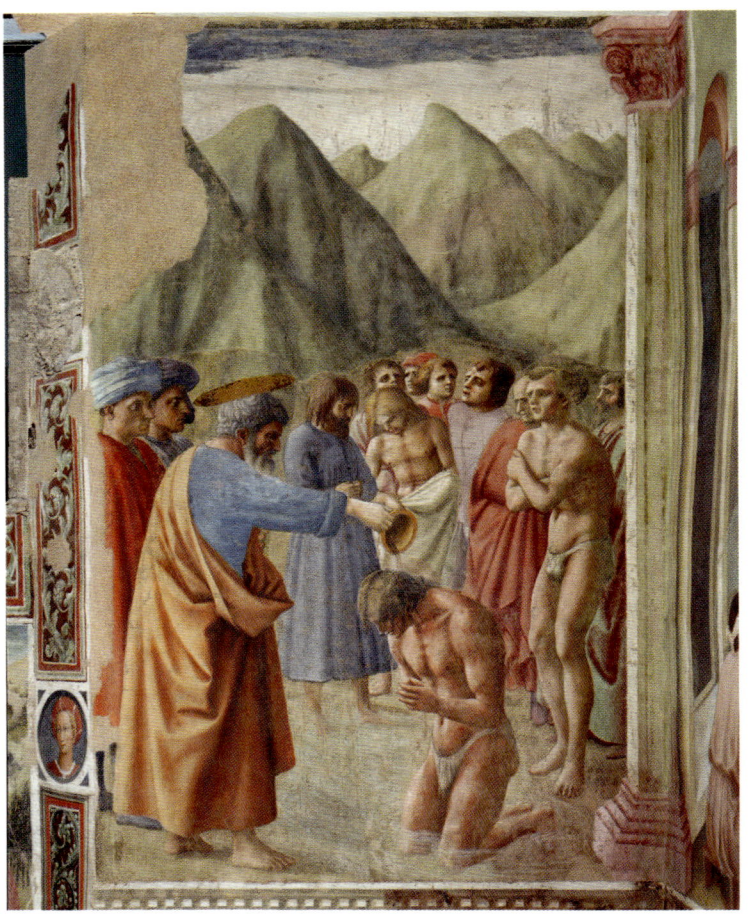

What seems at first to be a study of a live model might not always be so – a significant starting point for several of Michelangelo's figure studies was the work of other artists. His earliest known nude study is a pen drawing – still heavily influenced by his teacher Ghirlandaio, but already extremely powerful – the source of which can be easily identified as one of Masaccio's frescoes in the Brancacci Chapel (figs 50 and 51/cat. 8). Similar drawings might also have been based on the work of other masters, even if we can no longer tell precisely which. An early sheet showing three clothed figures, for instance, has been variously linked to Masaccio, Ghirlandaio and Filippino Lippi (fig. 5/cat. 9).[9] A later drawing in the Louvre contains a study for a sculpture of David with the head of the defeated Goliath, in which the standing figure on the left and the disembodied arm on the right are thought to refer to an example in Donatello (fig. 52/cat. 11).[10]

To Vasari's mind, an artist could only attain the greatest heights through the combined study of nature and the work of others, the latter including both contemporary and antique masters.[11] He described how recent excavations of ancient sculpture had significantly influenced the artists of his time. The naturalism of these classical works significantly stimulated drawing from nature and also provided Michelangelo and his contemporaries with a rewarding example.[12] The similarity has frequently been noted, for instance, between the posture and physique of the nude youth in a drawing from the British Museum and the famous and frequently copied statue of the *Apollo Belvedere* (figs 42 and 43/cat. 10).

The similarities between Michelangelo's drawing and the antique sculpture excavated in his presence around ten years earlier are indeed striking, yet the differences are noticeable too. Where the statue of Apollo is marked by its grounded, vertical majesty with the god's left arm raised to shoulder height, Michelangelo's drawing conveys a forward dynamic, in which the arm is raised much higher, lending the overall figure a more strongly diagonal orientation. It is widely accepted, therefore, that Michelangelo was playing here with the memory of the Roman statue by depicting an even more animated and dynamic pose. So substantial are the differences between the classical sculpture and the drawing that it is entirely plausible that he worked from a live model who assumed a similar pose.[13]

A similar well-known case is a drawing of a male nude seen from behind in the Casa Buonarroti collection (fig. 53), which has traditionally been viewed as a preliminary study for one of the figures in the *Battle of Cascina* fresco (fig. 133/cat. 51). In the early twentieth century, Johannes Wilde linked the drawing with a nude Hercules depicted on Roman sarcophagi, with which Michelangelo's

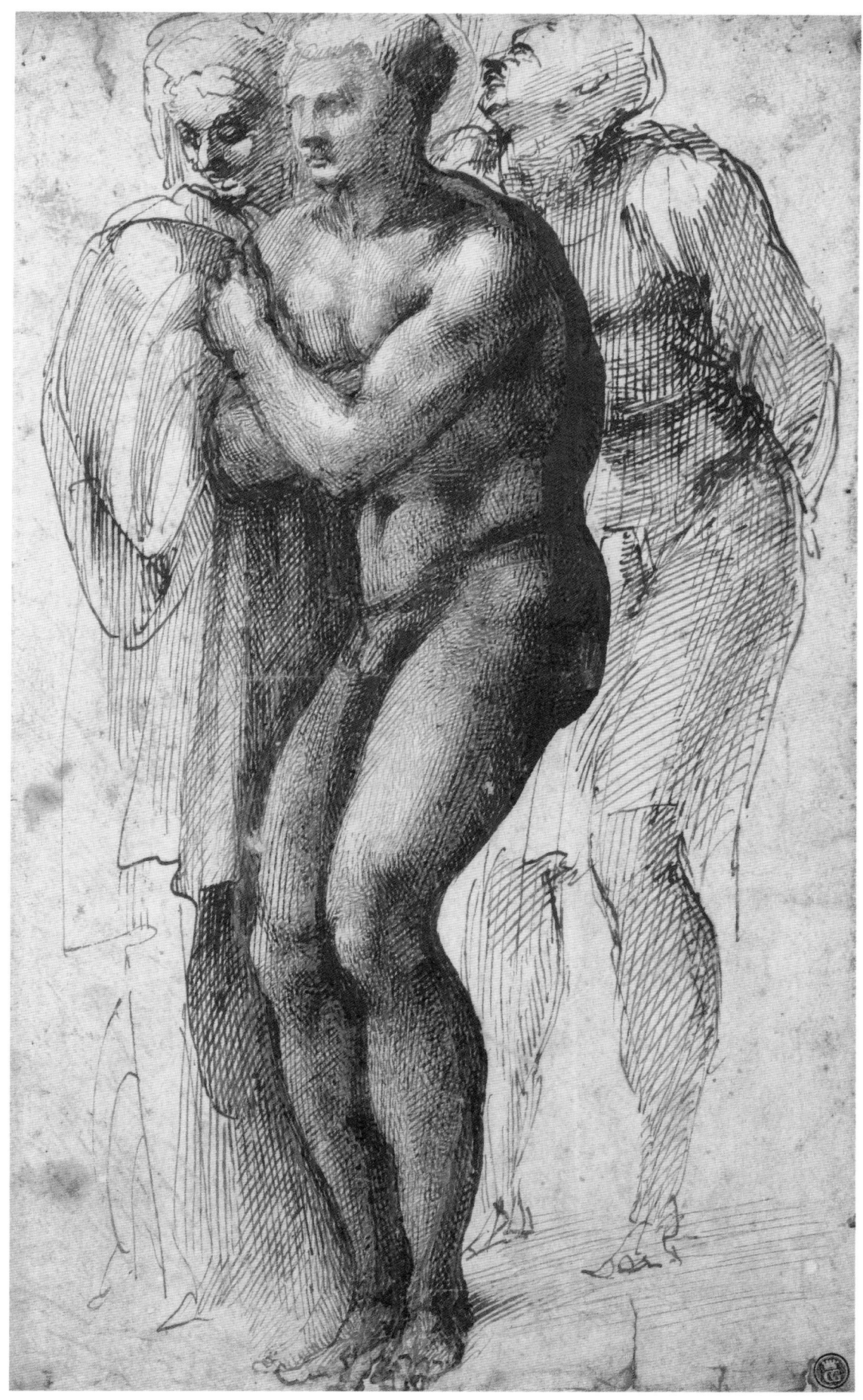

fig. 51   (cat. 8) Michelangelo, *A Male Nude (after Masaccio) and Two Other Figures*, c. 1492–1496. Pen and brown ink, dark brown wash, 330 x 200 mm.
Private collection

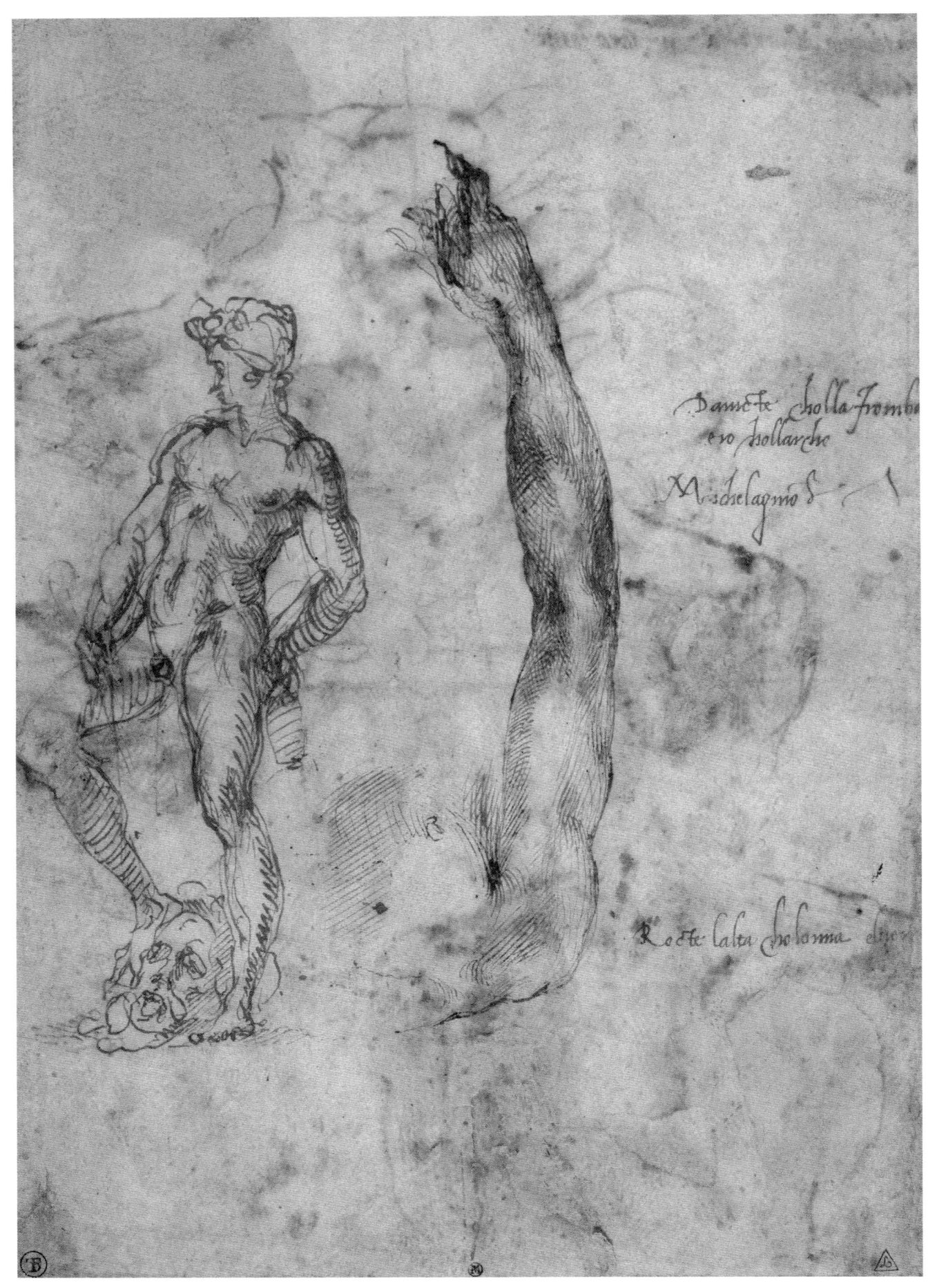

fig. 52   (cat. 11) Michelangelo, *Studies for a Sculpture of David*, c. 1502–1503. Pen and brown ink, 264 x 185 mm. Paris, Musée du Louvre, Département des arts graphiques, inv. 714

figure shares the elongated posture and the focus on the extension of the body from the right foot to the raised right arm. At the same time, the differences between drawing and sculpture are such (combined with doubts as to where the artist might have seen a sarcophagus of this kind) that this sheet too seems more like a mixture of antique inspiration with personal invention, possibly based once more on a model.[14]

To make things yet more complex, the model in question may not have been a live one. The circle drawn in the middle of the head might refer to a protruding element of the armature of a wax model, or else to the peg on which artists' dummies were sometimes hung in the workshop.[15] Clear evidence that Michelangelo – just like earlier artists, including his teacher Ghirlandaio – used dummies of this type is provided by a drapery study for the Eritrean Sibyl on the ceiling of the Sistine Chapel (fig. 54), in which the mannequin sits with infinite patience beneath the folds.[16]

The Model in the Sistine Chapel

The status of the live model in Michelangelo's artistic practice can be clearly inferred from the preparatory drawings for the Sistine Chapel. With the exception of the cartoons that were used to transfer the artist's design to the chapel ceiling (only two small fragments of which are known), several sheets have survived from all the other stages of the working process, although these once again represent a tiny proportion of the hundreds of drawings the artist must have made as he prepared to paint the enormous expanse.[17]

The previously mentioned drapery study based on an artist's dummy dates from around 1508–09, the period in which Michelangelo was working out his ideas for the Sistine Chapel ceiling on paper. The sketchy lines of one of the few surviving compositional studies are proof that this was done directly from his imagination (fig. 55/cat. 12v). It is perhaps significant, however, that other early studies for the ceiling share the paper with later, worked-up chalk studies of arms and hands, which were clearly drawn from a model (fig. 56).

There must have been a phase between the earliest compositional drawings and the later detailed studies in which Michelangelo settled on the poses of his figures, as we see in a series of small drawings from the Ashmolean Museum that he made a few years later in 1510–11, in preparation for the second part of the ceiling.[18] The latter reveal his search for the poses of figures in various parts of the final fresco, most notably the ancestors of Christ in the lunettes. The loose lines with which Michelangelo tested out his ideas and the schematic construction of

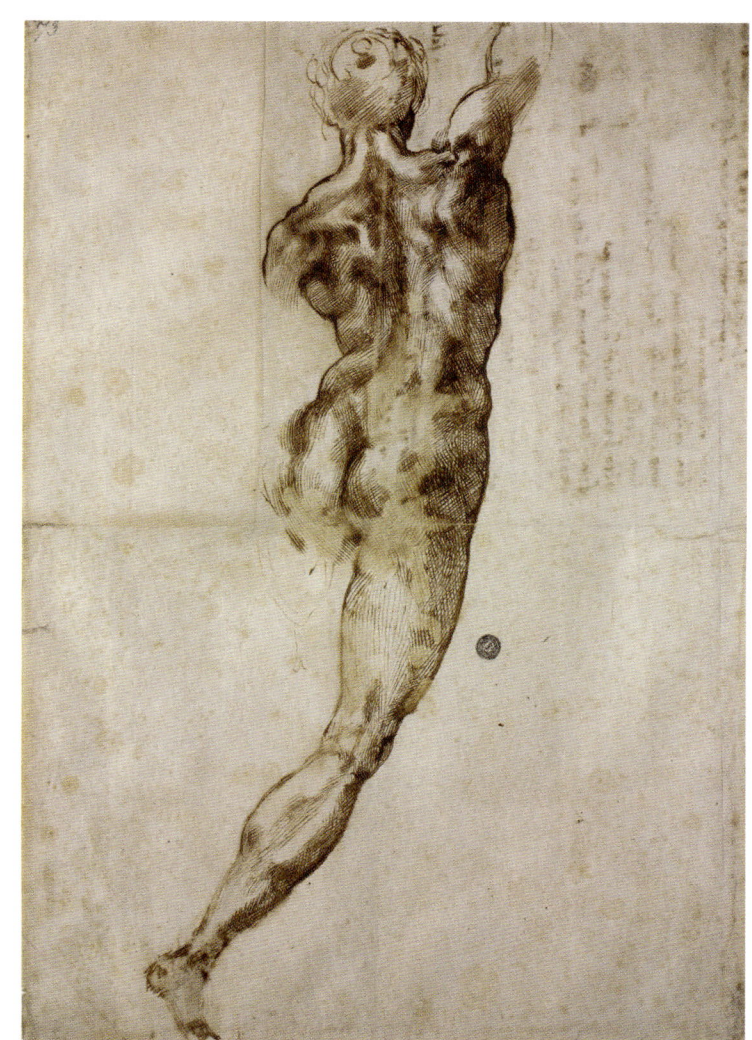

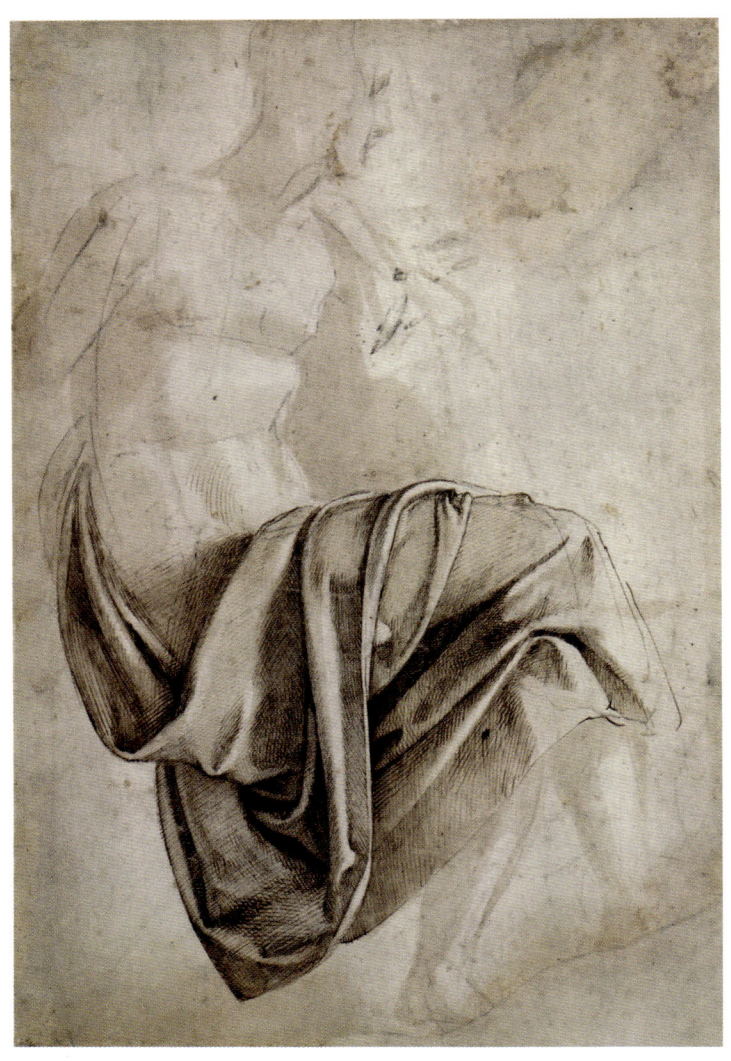

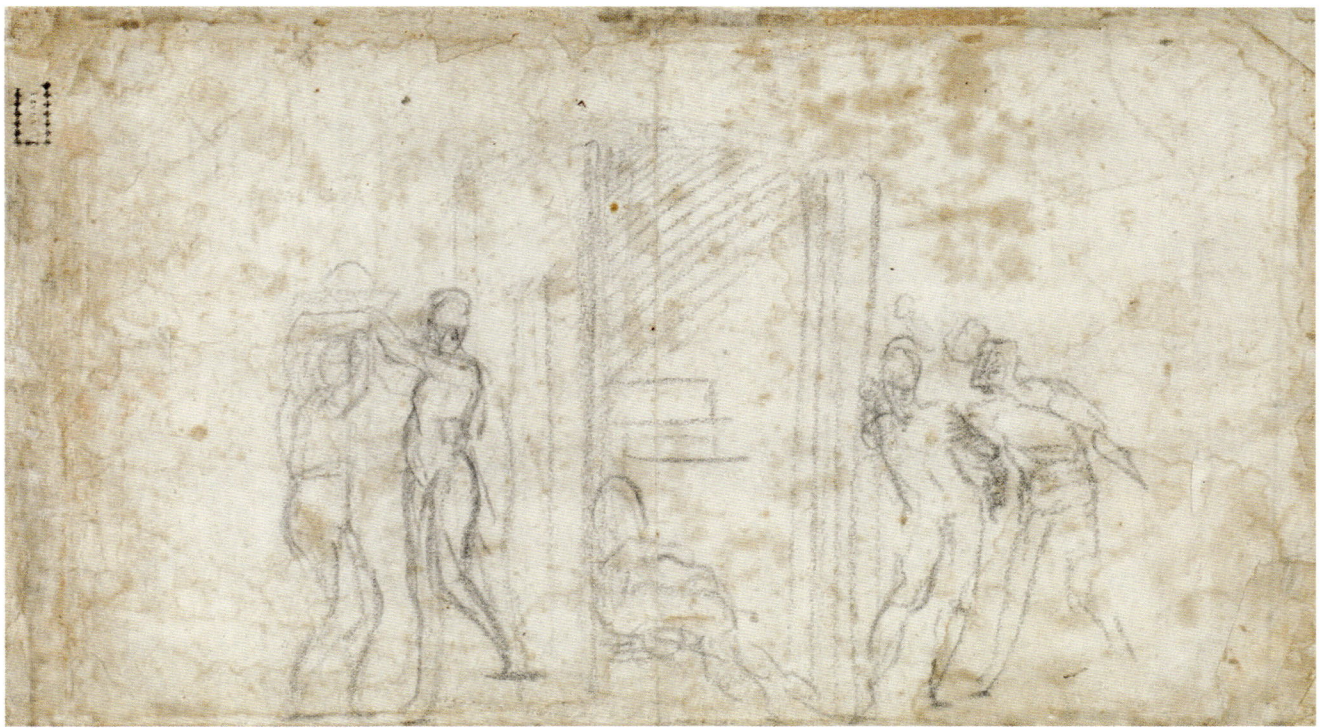

fig. 54   Michelangelo, *Study for the Erythraean Sibyl on the Sistine Chapel Ceiling*, c. 1508–1509. Black chalk, pen and brown ink, brown wash, 387 x 260 mm. London, British Museum, inv. 1887,0502.118

fig. 55   (cat. 12v) Michelangelo, *Study for Judith and Holofernes for the Sistine Chapel Ceiling*, 1508. Black chalk, 225 x 404 mm. Haarlem, Teylers Museum, inv. A 018v

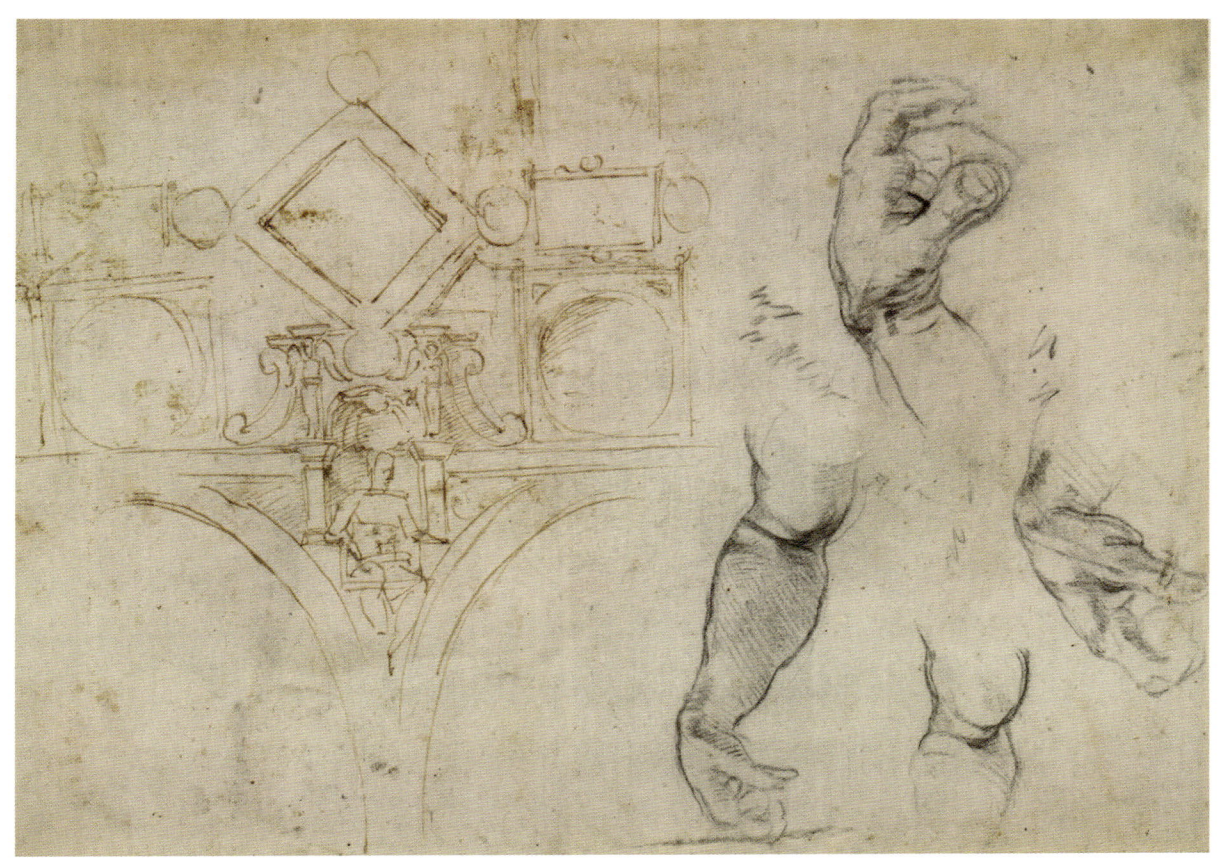

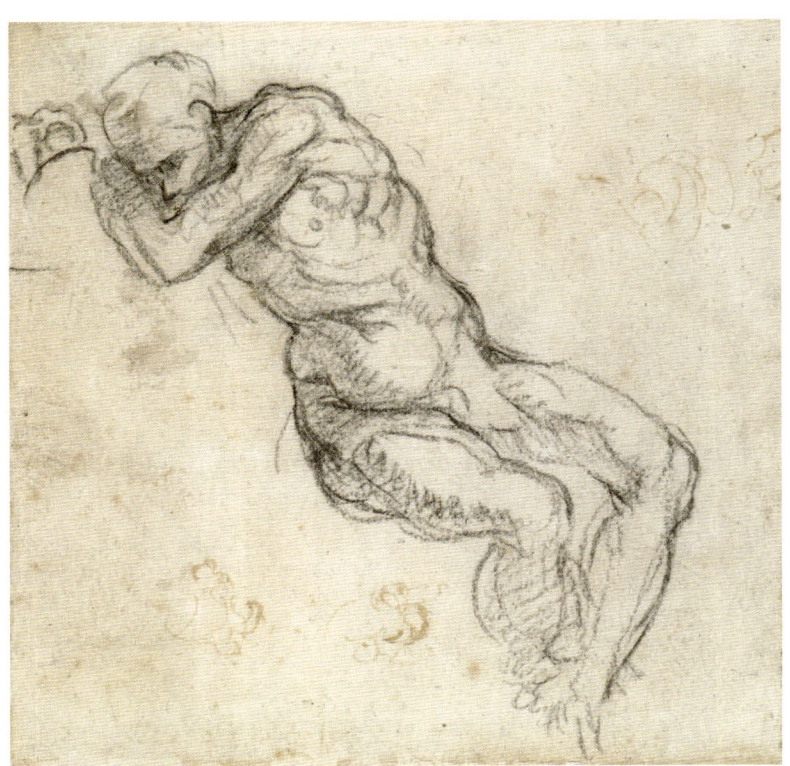

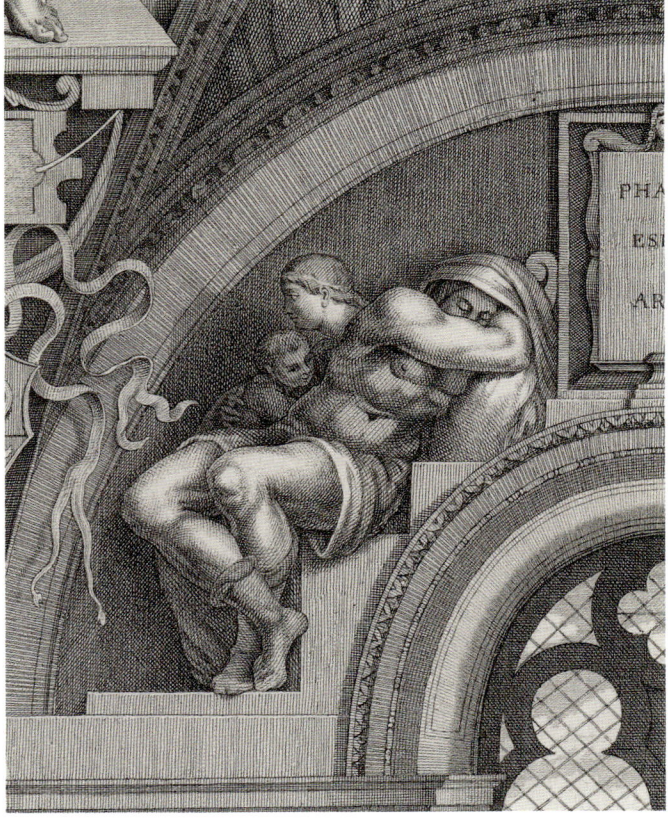

fig. 56   Michelangelo, *Design for the Sistine Chapel Ceiling and Studies of Arms*, 1508. Pen and brown ink, black chalk, 275 x 386 mm. London, British Museum, inv. 1859,0625.567

fig. 57   Michelangelo, *Study of a Male Nude*, c. 1510–1511. Black chalk, pen and brown ink, 135 x 148 mm. Oxford, Ashmolean Museum, inv. WA1846.51

fig. 58   William Young Ottley, after Michelangelo, *Two Destroyed Lunettes from the Sistine Chapel Ceiling* (detail), 1827. Engraving, 488 x 378 mm. London, British Museum, inv. 1851,0208.88

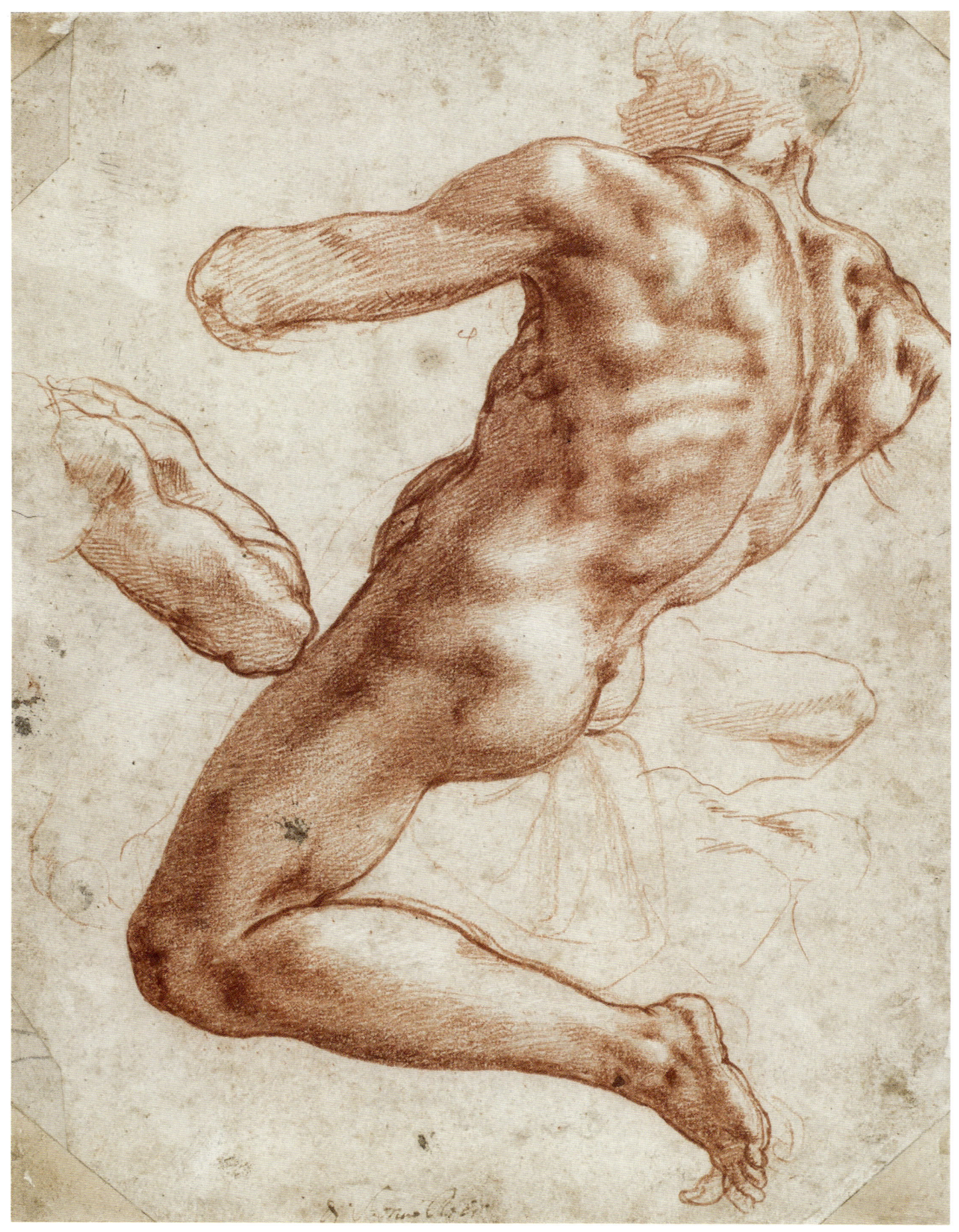

fig. 59   (cat. 19) Michelangelo, *Seated Male Nude* (ignudo) *for the Sistine Chapel Ceiling*, c. 1511. Red chalk with white heightening, 279 x 214 mm.
Haarlem, Teylers Museum, inv. A 027

the figures in some of the sheets suggest that – as with the previously mentioned compositional studies – he set them out directly on paper from his imagination,[19] although it cannot be ruled out that these small sketches were also made with a model at hand. The drawings give us a sense of being present in Michelangelo's workshop, listening to him direct his models to assume one position after another. This would be in keeping with his economical approach to the presence of a model, as described by Michael Hirst.[20] A model was almost certainly used for another sheet in the same series: the anatomical detail of the pose and the shadow effects are striking, especially given the drawing's small size (fig. 57). The realism of the (no doubt young) model's skinny body contrasts sharply with the idealised muscularity of Christ's ancestor in the final fresco. In a print of this part of the chapel, which was later overpainted for *The Last Judgement*, he can readily be identified in an almost identical pose, though now clothed and reversed (fig. 58).

The next step in Michelangelo's process was to work up the selected poses into detailed drawings, by which stage the drawn bodies have been idealised far beyond earthly reality, making it harder to determine whether or not models were used. Even here, however, there are indirect indications. Elements around some of the figures hint at the situation in Michelangelo's workshop and at the presence of a model. Take the telling detail, for instance, of the vaguely sketched cloth on which the *ignudo* from Teylers Museum sits (fig. 59/cat. 19). It is far removed from the pillow on which the figure rests in the final fresco (fig. 60) and most likely alludes to a cloth on which the model sat during the drawing session to keep him warmer and more comfortable than sitting directly on a (possibly dirty) wooden or stone floor.

Vasari describes how, when drawing a foreshortened subject, Michelangelo used wax models 'which more than live models stay put, and from these he obtained the outlines, lights and shadows'.[21] The fact he worked with live models as well, is apparent from traces of the devices used to maintain challenging poses for extended periods. One such proven method for easing the model's discomfort was the use of all manner of supports.[22] For a hard-to-maintain pose, like that of the crucified Haman for instance, the model is likely to have held on to hanging ropes or other aids (fig. 61). Jill Burke noted that this might explain why it is specifically the hands of the central figure in the drawing that are not detailed: they were not correctly positioned and so, partly for that reason, were worked out separately in individual detailed studies (fig. 62/cat. 15).[23]

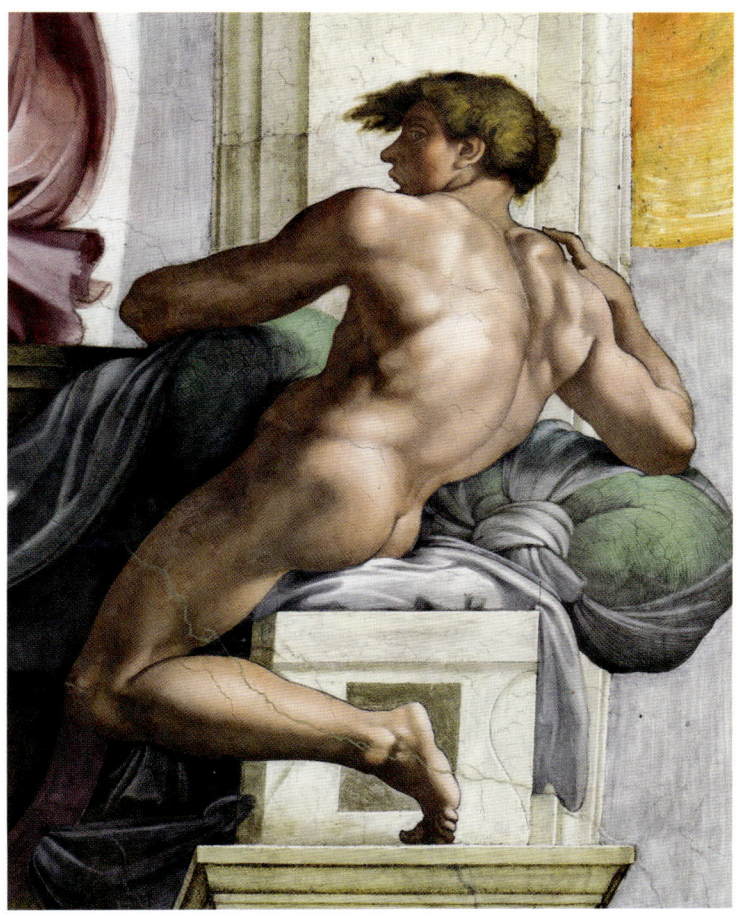

fig. 60   Michelangelo, *Male nude* (ignudo) *near the* Separation of the Waters, c. 1511–1512. Fresco. Vatican City, Ceiling of the Sistine Chapel

Beneath the Underwear

In other drawings, clear evidence of Michelangelo's use of live models can be found directly on the bodies of the depicted figures. Models in the Renaissance most likely wore underwear, which at that time meant a loincloth (fig. 63). While nudity might not have been entirely unknown in everyday life, it was nevertheless surrounded by social and religious taboos. Other than in the bathhouse or during especially heavy or dirty work, it was usual for adult bodies to be largely covered.[24] It was probably not common to undress completely, even during sex.[25] Consequently, even artists' models will not normally have been entirely naked unless strictly necessary.

With this in mind, vestiges of loincloths can also be detected in Michelangelo's drawings. This might explain why in many drawings by him and his contemporaries, the genitals are only sketchily indicated, as in the study for an *ignudo* from the Uffizi (fig. 64/cat. 14), for instance, or the *Studies for a Crucifixion* from Teylers Museum (fig. 90/cat. 41). It is specifically the parts that are likely to have been covered up in the workshop that are depicted in these drawings in much less detail than the surrounding areas of the body. As he worked towards the desired end result, Michelangelo ignored the underwear and depicted the genitals, albeit only sketchily. Swift, circular scribbles like this are found in several drawings, including the aforementioned study for Haman and the study for Adam from the British Museum (fig. 7/cat. 17). In most instances these are preparatory drawings for entirely nude figures in the final frescoes and sculptures.

There is also a drawing of this kind for the nude personification of Day in the Medici Chapel in which a piece of cloth can be made out around the depicted figure's loins (fig. 65/cat. 28).[26] It is not repeated in the final sculpture and so points once more towards the use of a live model, which in turn makes it very likely that a model was used for the other sheets in this series too (fig. 66/cat. 31).[27] The genitals in another drawing for *Day*, by contrast, are clearly worked out, indicating that in this instance the model will actually have been naked (fig. 67).

Incidentally, this series shows how – with the rare exception of a drawing of a young woman (fig. 11) – Michelangelo's models were invariably male, even when they served as the basis for female figures.[28] Social convention prohibited decent women from posing more or less naked as models.[29] Thus, on a study for the female personification of *Night* from the Uffizi, the genitals of the male model can be recognised between the muscular legs on the right side of the sheet (fig. 68/cat. 32).[30] A circular indication of the male member is likewise visible in the drawing that served as the basis for the so-called

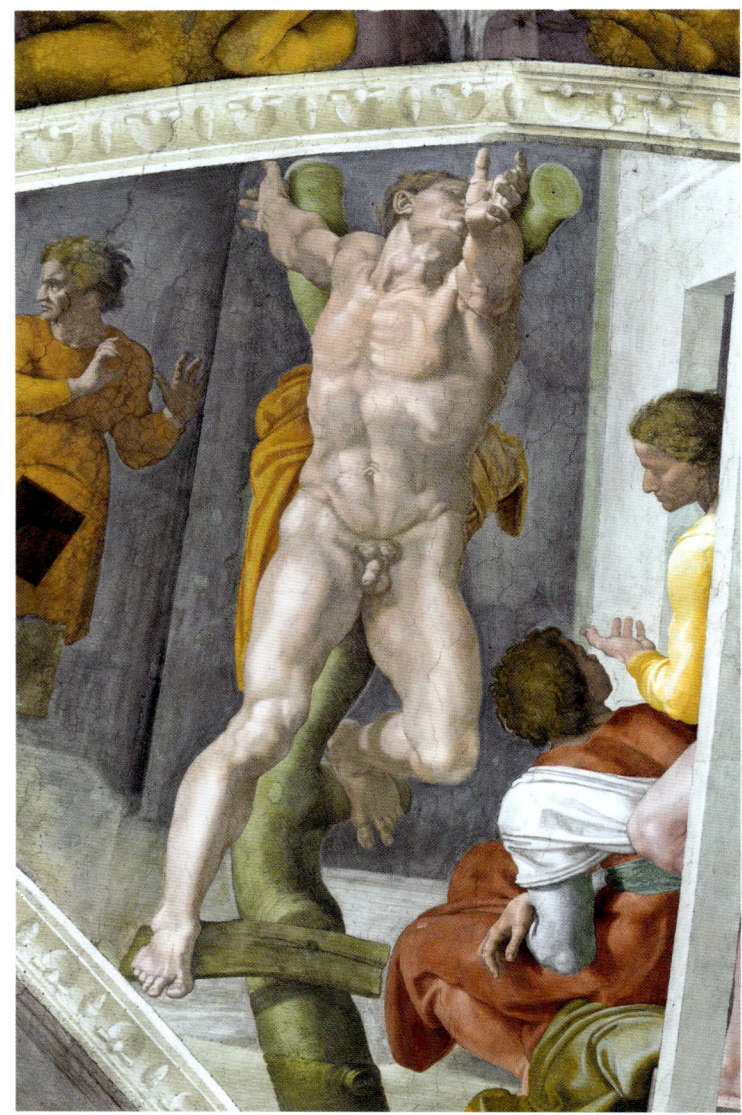

fig. 61   Michelangelo, *The Crucifixion of Haman*, c. 1511–1512. Fresco. Vatican City, Ceiling of the Sistine Chapel

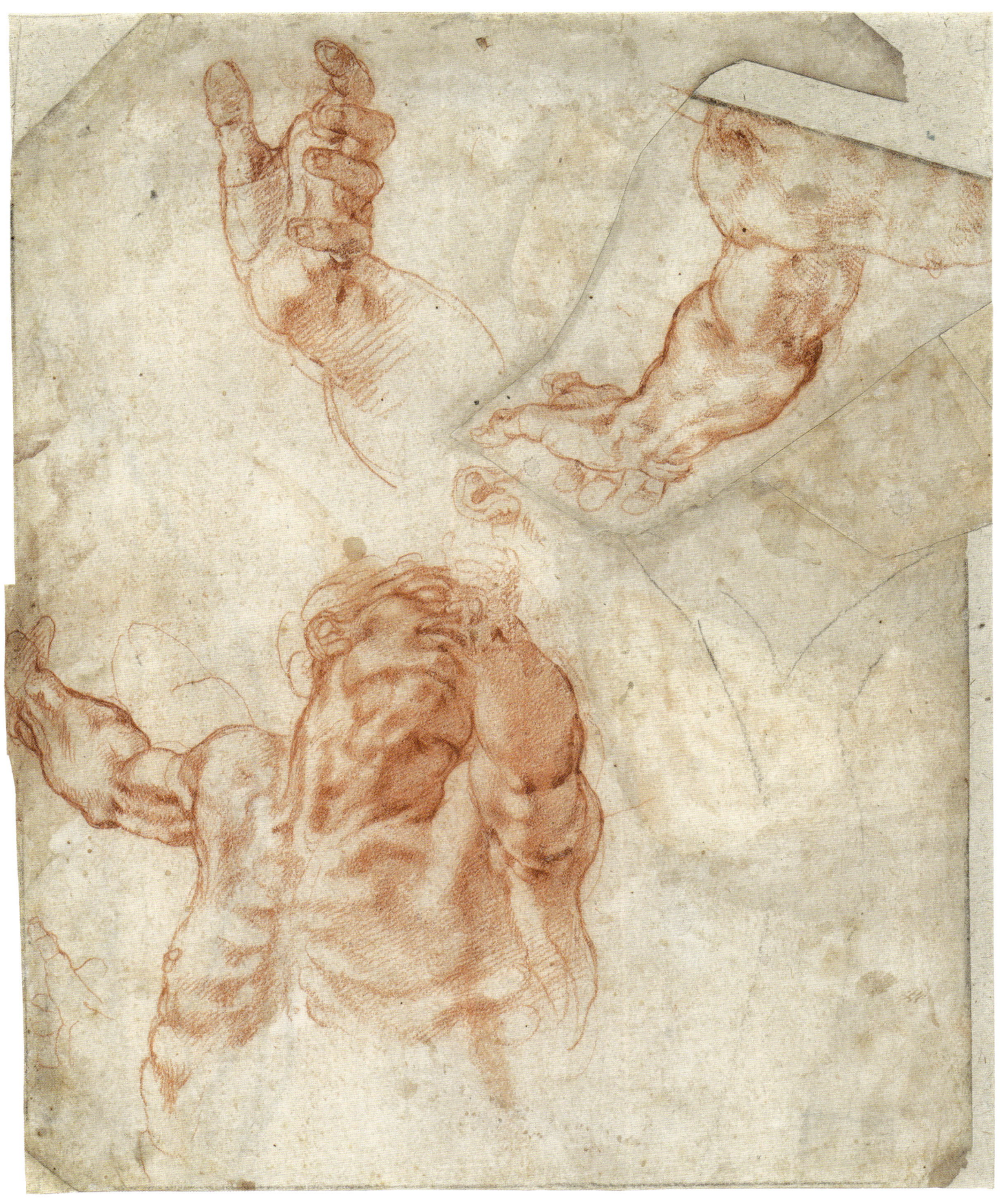

fig. 62   (cat. 15) Michelangelo, *Studies for Haman for the Sistine Chapel Ceiling*, c. 1511. Red and black chalk, 252 x 205 mm. Haarlem, Teylers Museum, inv. A 016

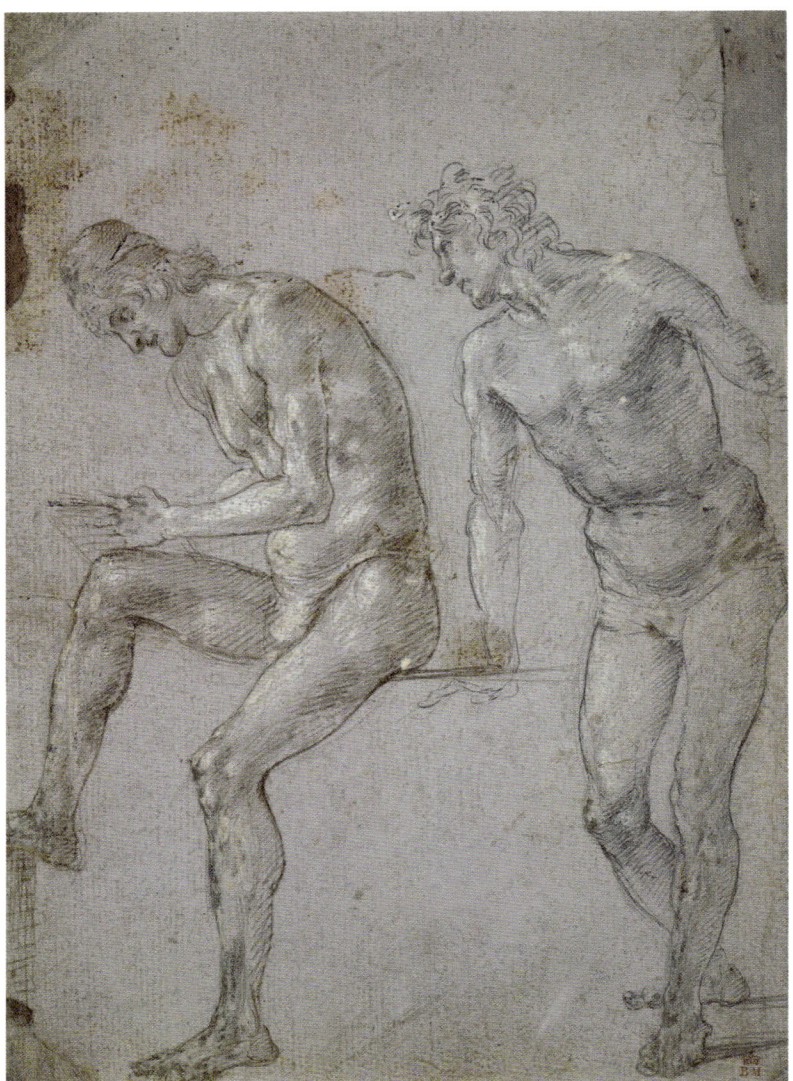

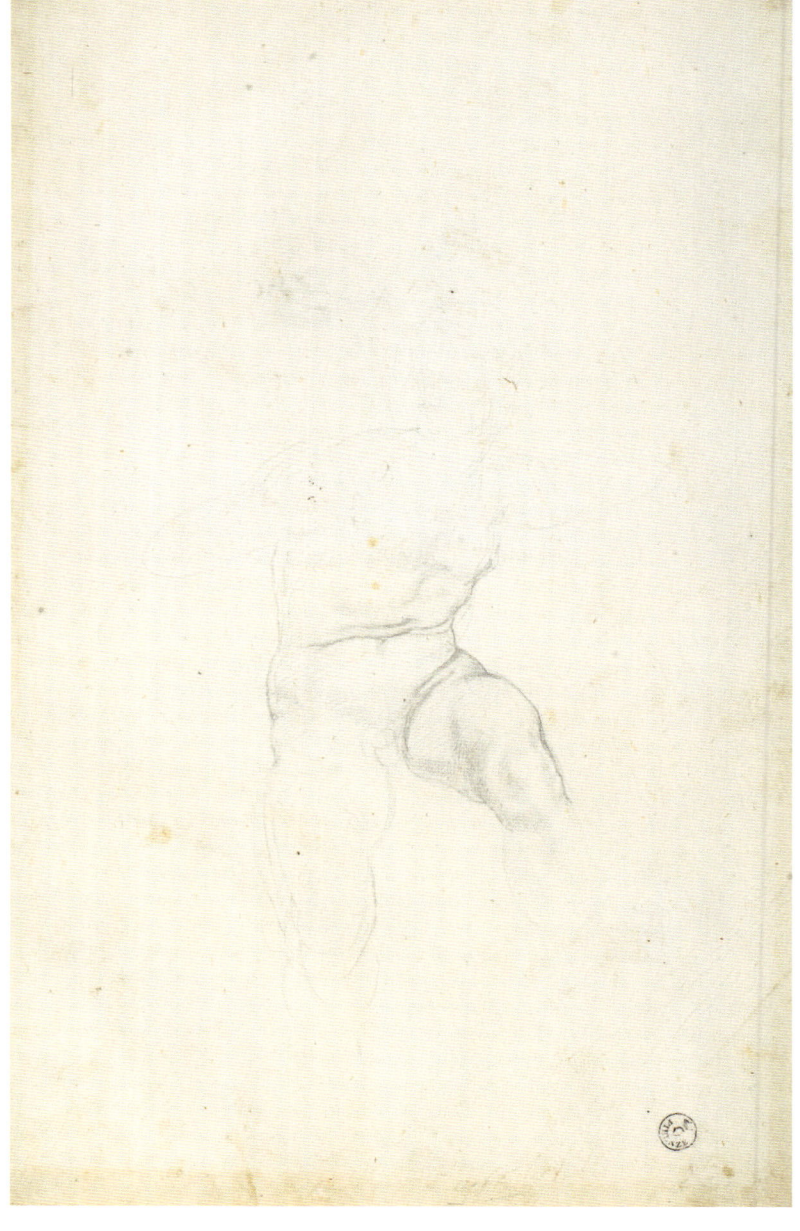

fig. 63   Filippino Lippi, *Two Male Nudes*, c. 1485–1488. Silverpoint and leadpoint with white heightening, 259 x 185 mm. London, British Museum, inv. 1858,0724.4

fig. 64   (cat. 14) Michelangelo, *Study of a Seated Male Nude* (ignudo) *for the Sistine Chapel Ceiling*, c. 1508–1509. Metalpoint, 418 x 265 mm. Florence, Gallerie degli Uffizi, Gabinetto dei Disegni e delle Stampe, inv. 18720 F

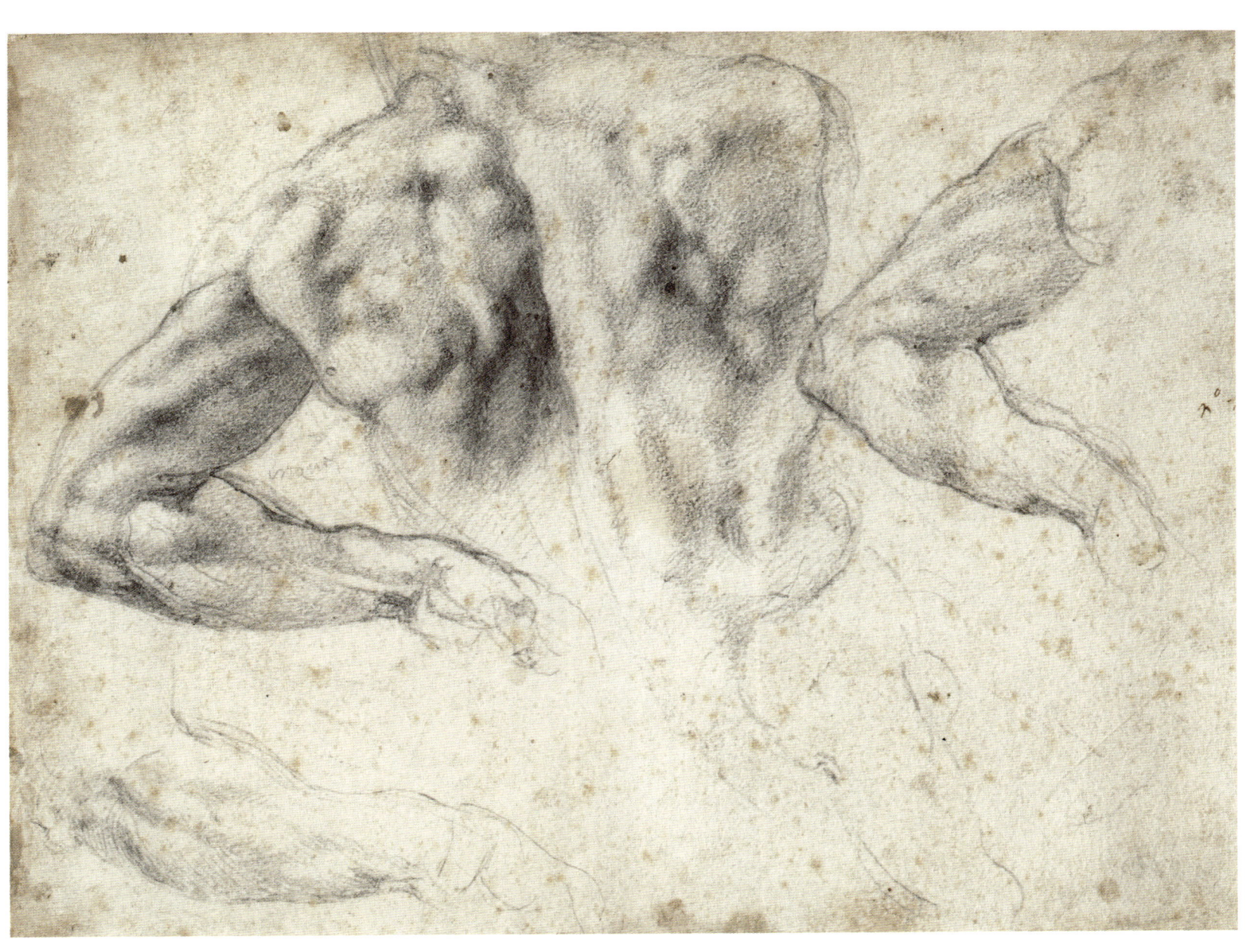

fig. 65   (cat. 28) Michelangelo, *Studies of a Back and Left Arm for the Sculpture of* Day, 1524. Black chalk, 192 x 257 mm. Haarlem, Teylers Museum, inv. A 030

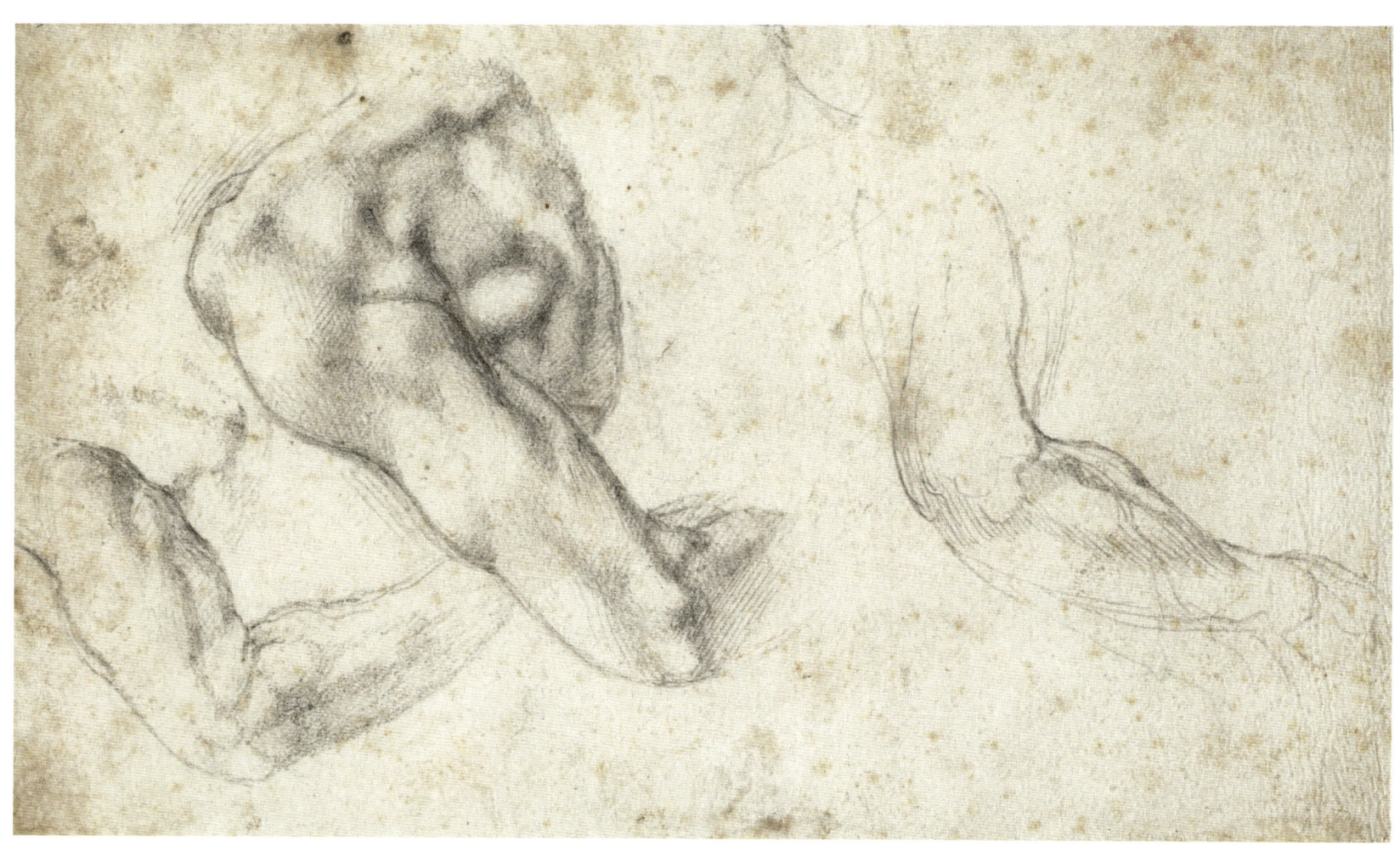

fig. 66   (cat. 31) Michelangelo, *Studies of a Left Arm and Shoulder for the Sculpture of* Day, 1524. Black chalk, 266 x 162 mm. Haarlem, Teylers Museum, inv. A 036

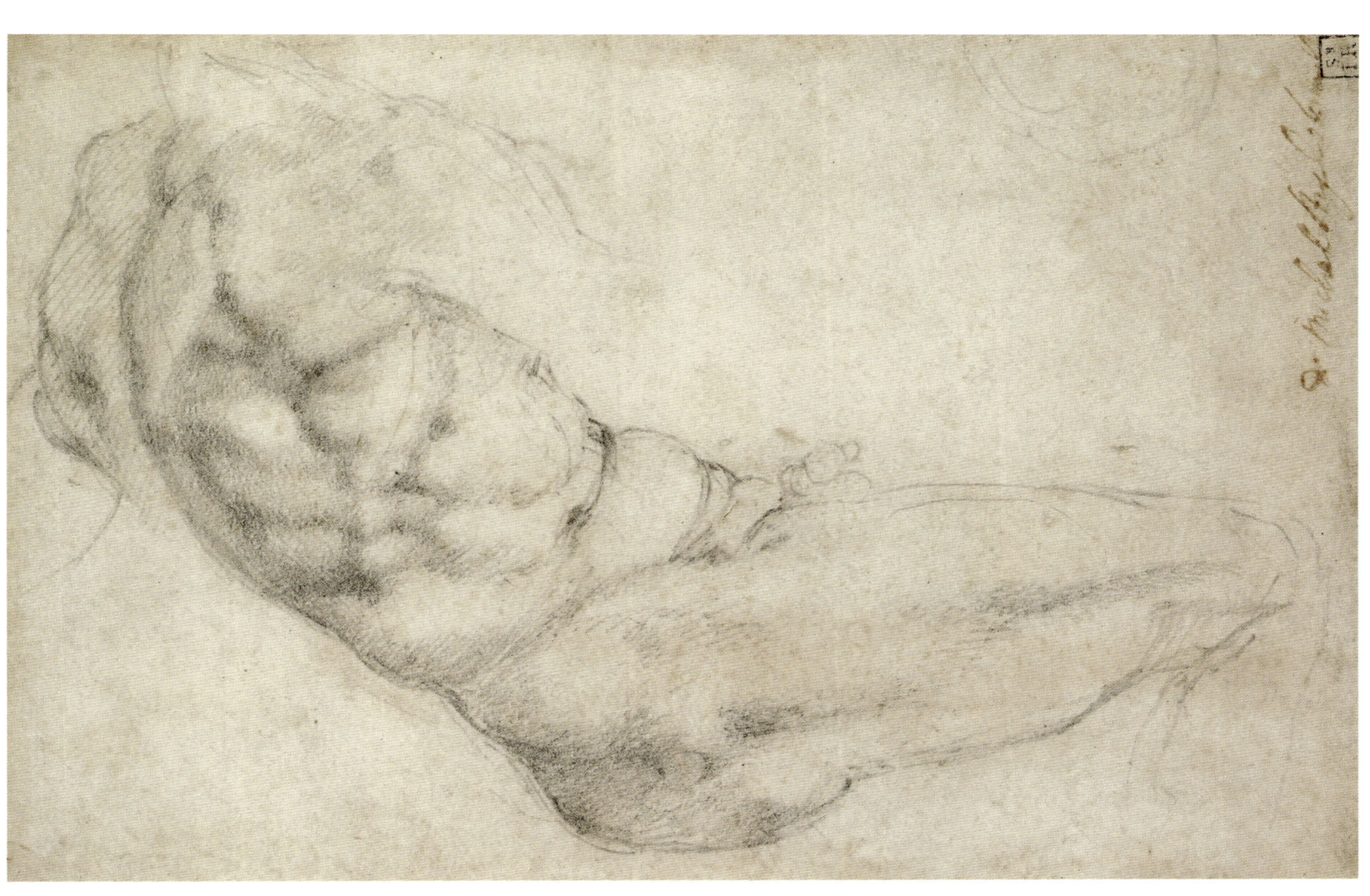

fig. 67   Michelangelo, *Study of a Male Nude for the Sculpture of* Day, 1524. Black chalk, 176 x 270 mm. Oxford, Ashmolean Museum, inv. WA1846.56

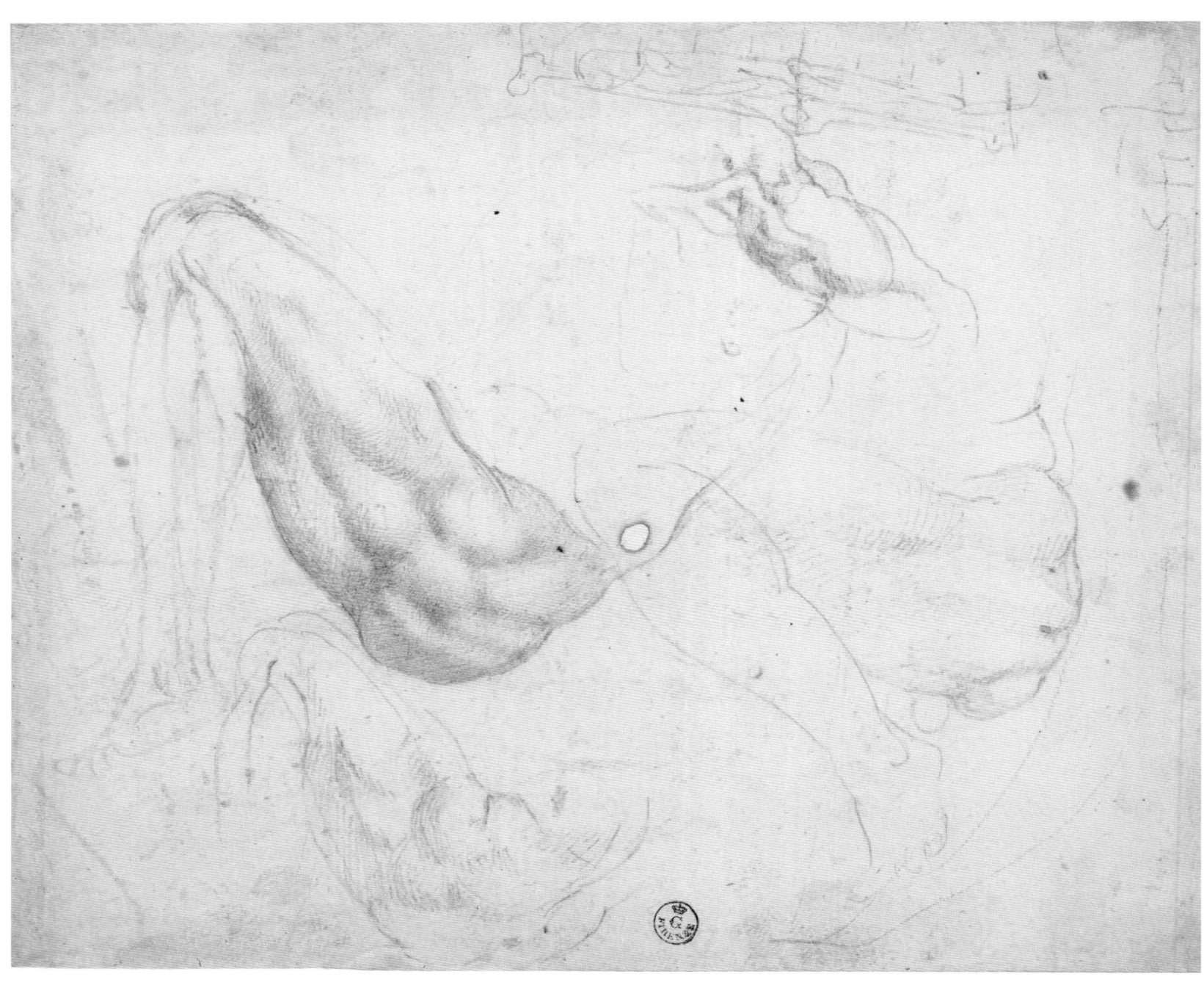

fig. 68   (cat. 32) Michelangelo, *Studies of a Male Nude for the Sculpture of* Night, 1524. Black chalk, 280 x 343 mm. Florence, Gallerie degli Uffizi, Gabinetto dei Disegni e delle Stampe, inv. 18719 F

'Eve' in *The Creation of Adam* fresco (fig. 165/cat. 19v and fig. 36). Another famous example is the drawing from The Metropolitan Museum in which Michelangelo transformed the male features of his youthful model into the mature female Libyan Sibyl in the final fresco (fig. 70/cat. 16 and fig. 71).

Idealisation

It is in drawings such as the Libyan Sibyl that we run up against the limits of the identifiable presence of live models. A drawing from the Casa Buonarroti is a similarly beautiful sheet in which a male model serves as the basis for a female figure. Michelangelo used red chalk to draw the face of what was probably a young man, which ultimately resulted in the head of the female Leda (figs 72/cat. 37 and 22/cat. 4). The androgynous, symmetrical and highly idealised features of the depicted figure might easily lead us to conclude that this is a portrait that sprang directly from the artist's imagination. All the same, vestiges of sketchily depicted textiles – a cap and the hem of a shirt – remind us once more that the scene probably originated in the reality of the workshop and that this is a drawing based once again on a male model. Otherwise, why would this figure be wearing headgear associated, according to the literature, with workshop assistants or *garzoni*?[31]

Should any doubt remain, the magnificent and sensitive detailed study of the eyes and nose are further indications that this drawing must indeed have been done from nature. Michelangelo observed his model's now fully closed eyelids and his eyelashes with even greater attention and from a slightly different angle. Detailed studies of this kind are a recurring element in a great many drawings, including several of the aforementioned sheets for the Sistine Chapel (various *ignudi*, Haman, the Libyan Sibyl and 'Eve') and they can be read as a clear indication that a model was used.

Leda's head shows numerous similarities with a beautiful, worked-up drawing from the Ashmolean Museum (fig. 73/cat. 35). This sheet (formerly called 'Persian Boy', though also long identified as a woman[32]) has likewise been interpreted as a portrait, even one of Michelangelo's favourite, Tommaso de' Cavalieri.[33] The current consensus is that, unlike the Leda, this figure must have sprung entirely from Michelangelo's imagination, as was the case with his *teste divine* drawings. When comparing the two heads, it is nevertheless clear just how tricky it can be to distinguish clearly between drawings in which Michelangelo idealised his model's features, and those purely of his own invention.

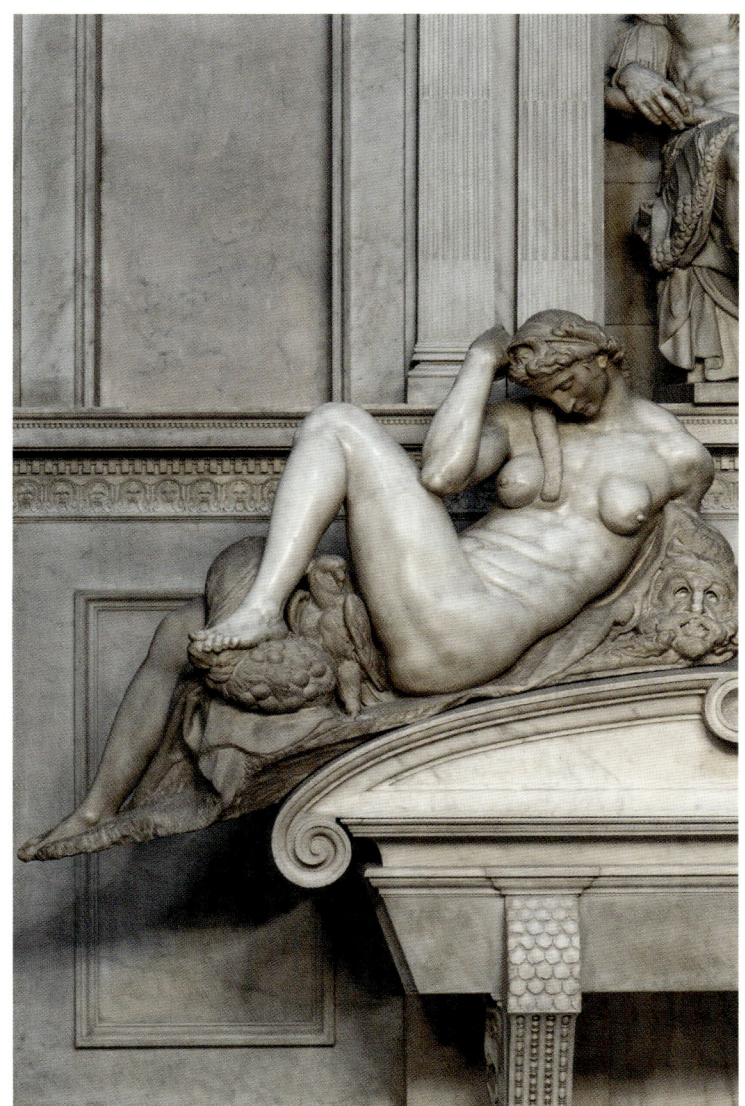

fig. 69   Michelangelo, *Night*, c. 1524–1534. Marble, length 194 cm. Florence, San Lorenzo, Medici Chapel

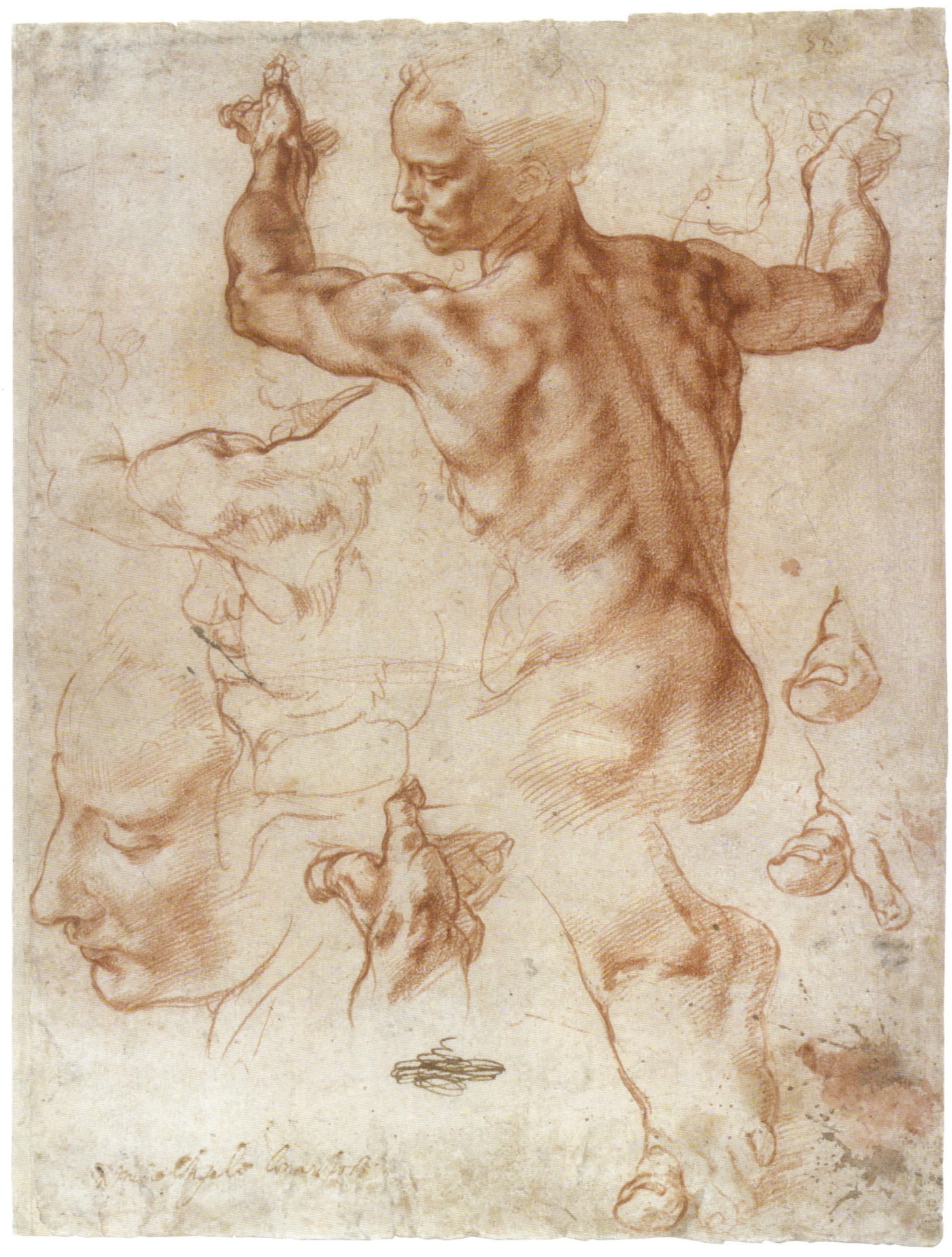

fig. 70   (cat. 16) Michelangelo, *Studies for the Libyan Sibyl for the Sistine Chapel Ceiling*, c. 1511. Red chalk with white heightening, 289 x 214 mm.
New York, The Metropolitan Museum of Art, inv. 24.197.2

Who was the Model?

Johannes Wilde believes that Michelangelo's assistant Antonio Mini might have been the model for Leda, although there seems to be little concrete evidence for this.[34] Compared to a drawing genuinely intended as a portrait, such as that of the young nobleman Andrea Quaratesi, something distinctly different is going on here (fig. 13/cat. 36). The aim in the first instance is to capture a specific personal likeness, whereas in the other, Leda forms one stage of the process to design the mythological female figure for the final painting, in which case the model's identity is irrelevant to the finished result.

Whether or not this Leda was based on Antonio Mini's face, Michelangelo plainly had one of his assistants pose from time to time as part of his creative practice. William Wallace describes how the carpenter Baccio di Puccione posed for a clay model for the personification of Night in the Medici Chapel (fig. 69), but that his posture did not look natural or comfortable.[35] It is intriguing to think that the same Baccio might also have modelled for the previously mentioned drawings for sculptures in the chapel. The idea recalls Vasari's story that, during his apprenticeship with Ghirlandaio, the young Michelangelo used his fellow pupils as models as they worked together on the frescoes in the Santa Maria Novella.[36] Turning to a model who was already present in the workshop still appears to have been a practical solution forty or so years later, when he had Baccio di Puccione pose as Night.

It goes without saying that Michelangelo used a single model for multiple characters during his drawing sessions.[37] The two bathers in Teylers Museum, for instance, are undoubtedly based on the same person's body (figs 140/cat. 12 and 141/cat. 13), and it is likewise easy to imagine that many of the drawings for the Sistine Chapel employed the same model.[38] Will this consistently have been one of Michelangelo's workshop assistants – the *garzoni* who are frequently mentioned in this context, such as Antonio Mini or Baccio di Puccione? Most of them, however, will not have had the physique of a Hercules or an Apollo.[39] It seems unlikely, therefore, that the choice of a model was determined solely by whoever happened to be available at the time. Given the opportunity, Michelangelo will have preferred models with physical features as close as possible to the ideal of the athletically muscular man.[40] This is, after all, the body type we find time and again in his work. While the skinny figure of most of his assistants can be made out in small, individual model sketches, such as those for the ancestors of Christ for the Sistine Chapel, the majority of drawings presumably made from a model show the muscular physique of a man in the prime of his life.

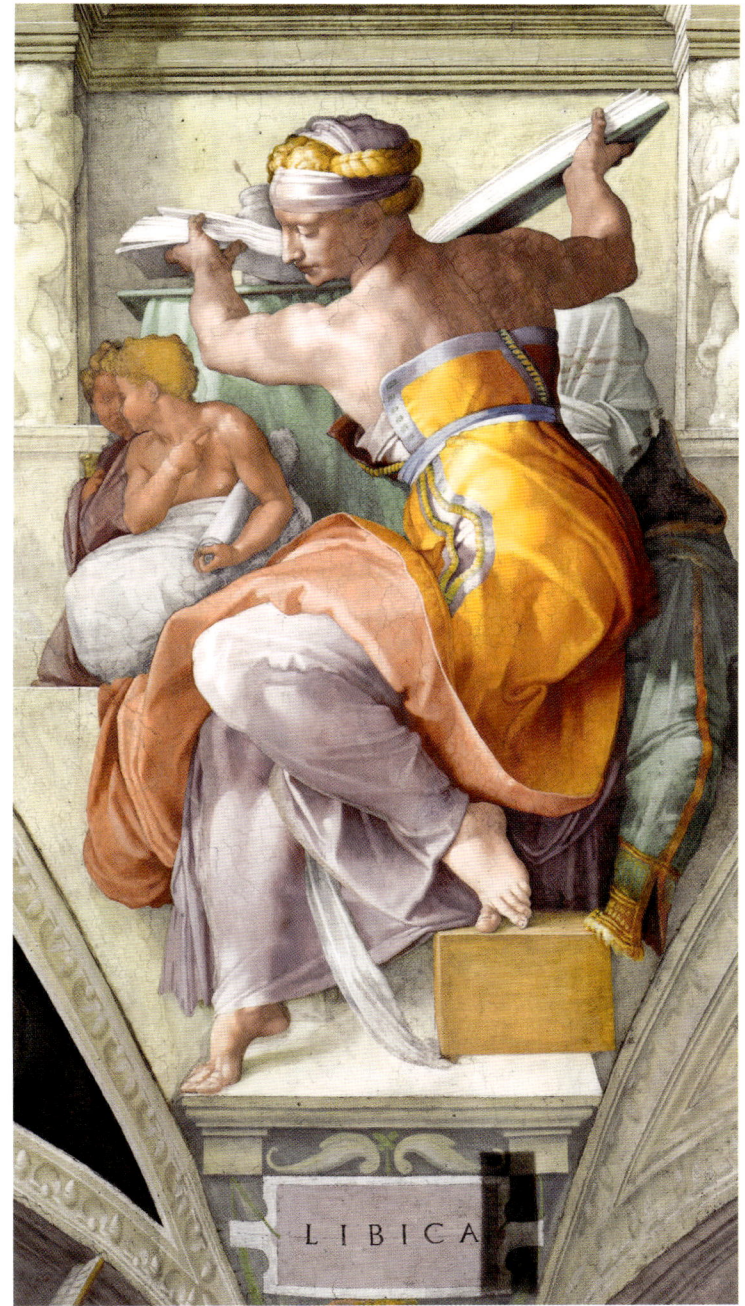

fig. 71   Michelangelo, *The Libyan Sibyl*, c. 1511–1512. Fresco. Vatican City, Ceiling of the Sistine Chapel

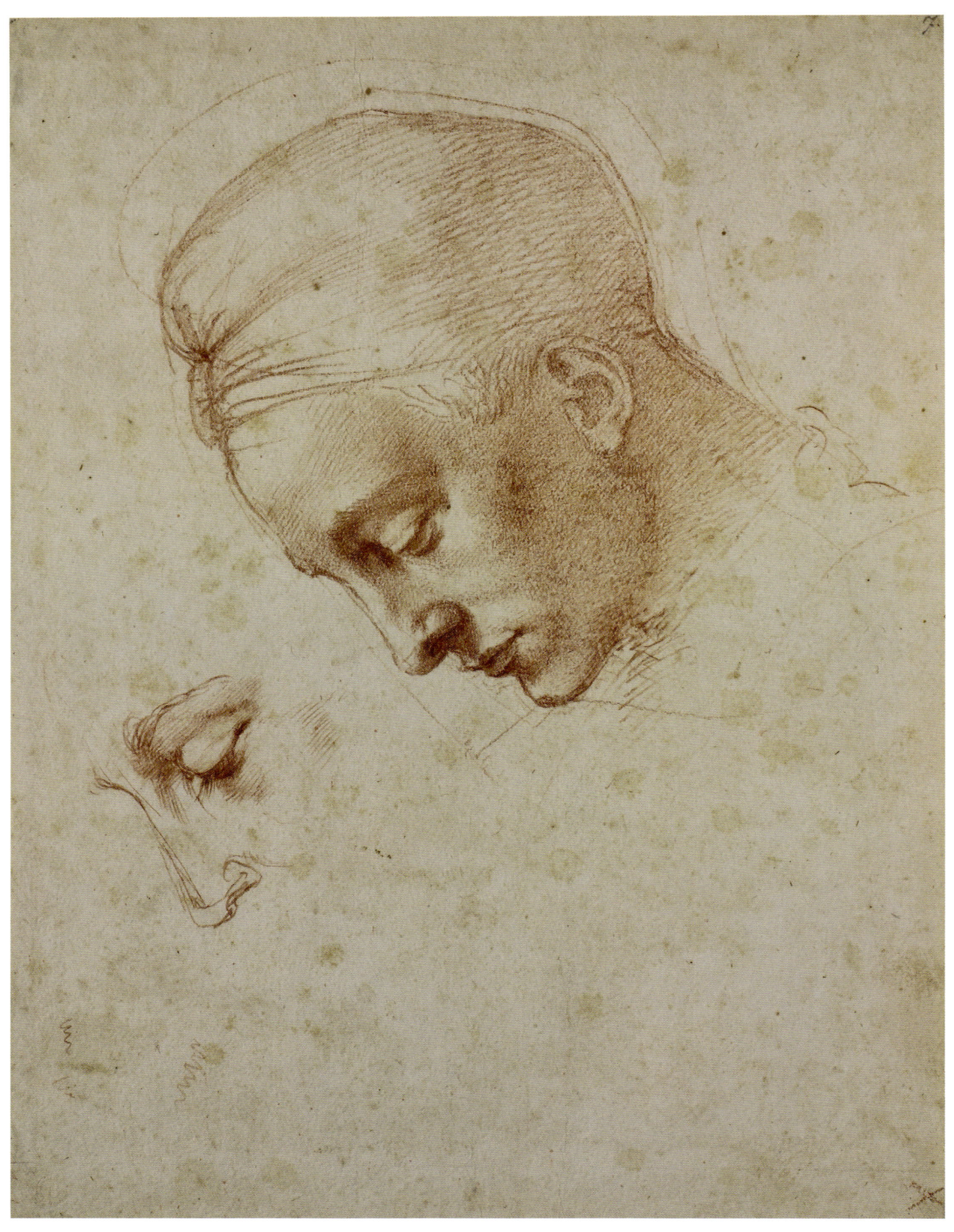

fig. 72   (cat. 37) Michelangelo, *Studies for the Head of Leda,* c. 1530. Red chalk, 355 x 269 mm. Florence, Casa Buonarroti, inv. 7F

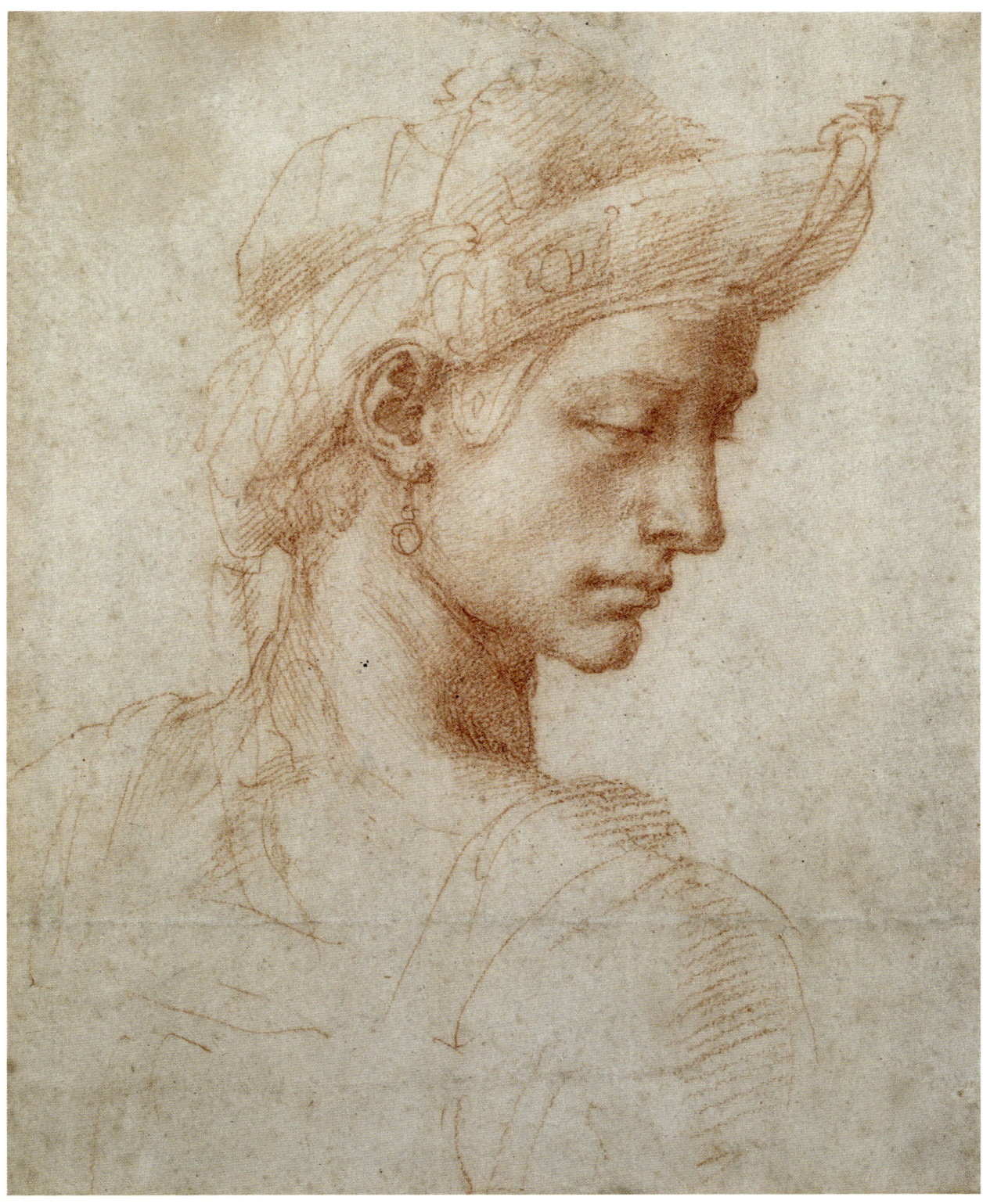

fig. 73   (cat. 35) Michelangelo, *An Idealized Bust*, c. 1525–1530. Red chalk, 205 x 165 mm. Oxford, Ashmolean Museum, inv. WA1846.61

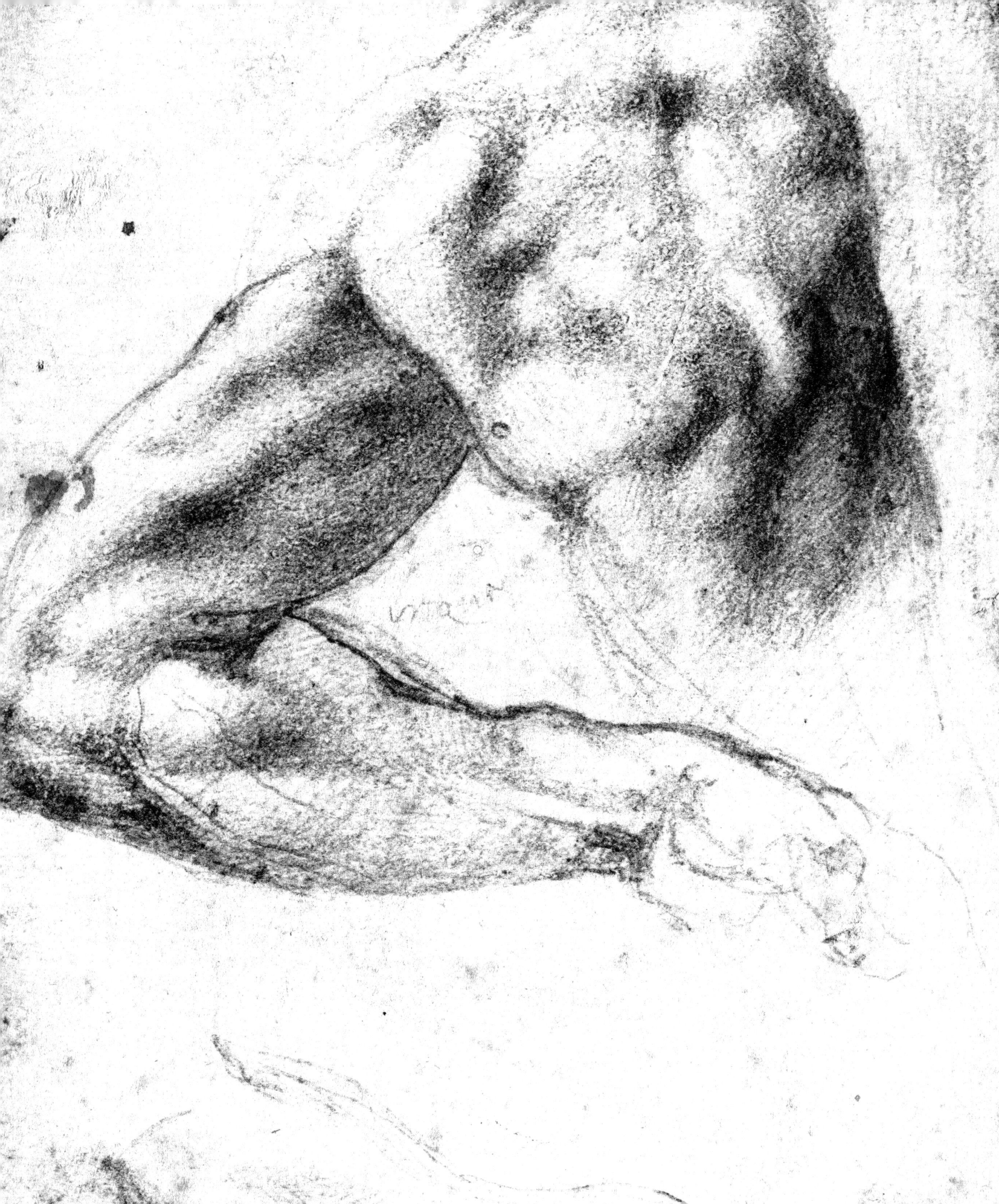

Bodies of this kind that were admired by Michelangelo and his contemporaries were more likely to be found among physical labourers such as porters, farm workers and archers than young *garzoni*.[41] This is also what we read in Condivi's biography of the artist, which describes the memory of a Spanish groom employed by Piero de' Medici and the 'marvelous beauty of his body'.[42] The fact that this was still worthy of mention half a century later speaks volumes about the impression that this 'living David or Adam' (to use Martin Gayford's words) must have made on Michelangelo.[43] It makes sense that men like this would have been happy to earn a little extra money posing for an artist.[44]

No matter how muscular Michelangelo's models might have been in reality, however, they will not have had the physiques we see in his frescoes and sculptures. We cannot know for sure whether Baccio di Puccione really was the origin of the sculptures in the Medici Chapel; all the same, if we picture what his body might actually have looked like – complete with all a human being's natural imperfections – and compare it with the final, larger-than-life figures in Michelangelo's work, we touch on the essence of how the artist interacted with his models, in keeping with the core of his entire oeuvre. What this demonstrates is both an immense knowledge of the body's structure and an extremely precise observation of outward features, combined and elevated by his prodigious imagination. The result is an idealised human image in which hyperrealism and fantastic idealism go hand in hand, based on the body of his model.

Models left their marks in several places in Michelangelo's drawings: in the skinny bodies of the sketches for the Sistine Chapel, the realistic musculature of the bathers beneath a barely drawn loincloth, and in the faces and bodies of the young men he transformed into female characters. Alongside the influence of anatomical study and examples from other artists, both contemporary and antique, they were a key ingredient of his work. At the end of the day, it is thanks to Michelangelo's own, almost superhuman imagination that we are now barely able to distinguish the different influences.

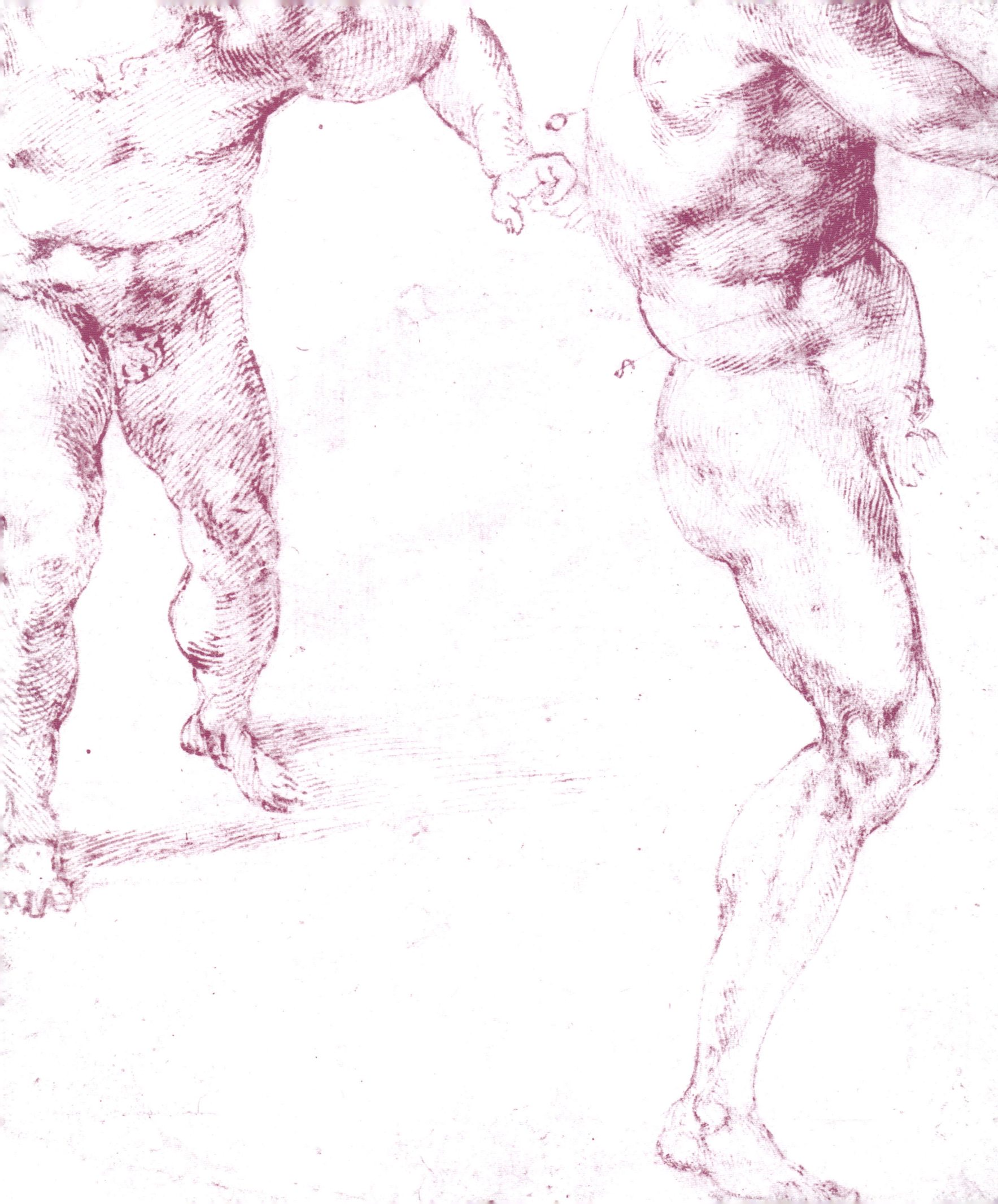

Michelangelo and the Anatomy of the Artist

Eric Boot

When Michelangelo's design for the *Battle of Cascina* was unveiled, the work was immediately heralded as a veritable 'school for artists', to use Giorgio Vasari's words (fig. 133/cat. 51). Curious painters and sculptors flocked from all over Florence to study the cartoon, the young Raphael among them. The monumentality of the nude, male body and the unparalleled complexity of the poses meant that everything he had learnt up until then paled in comparison. If Vasari is to be believed, Raphael immediately set about improving his limited knowledge of the male body, more particularly by immersing himself in the study of anatomy. He quickly realised, however, that 'in this respect he could never attain to the perfection of Michelangelo'.[1]

Whether historically accurate or not, this anecdote shows that Vasari considered anatomical knowledge to be a crucial part of Michelangelo's success: it allowed him to depict the male body – which was, after all, considered to be the most perfect part of God's creation and hence the most challenging subject for the artist – in the best possible way:

> 'In order to be entirely perfect, innumerable times he made anatomical studies, dissecting men's bodies in order to see the principles of their construction and the concatenation of the bones, muscles, veins and nerves, the various movements and all the postures of the human body.... He so executed his works, whether with the brush or with the chisel, that they are almost inimitable, and he gave to his labours, as has been said, such art and grace, and a loveliness of such a kind, that (be it said without offence to any) he surpassed and vanquished the ancients; having been able to wrest things out of the greatest difficulties with such facility, that they do not appear wrought with effort, although whoever draws his works after him finds enough in imitating them.'[2]

During Michelangelo's lifetime, anatomical science in Europe underwent several important developments, including the publication of Vesalius's *De humani corporis fabrica* in 1543, which used empirical study of the human body to question medical theories dating back to antiquity and the Middle Ages. For artists too, anatomy became steadily more important. Members of the Florentine Accademia del Disegno (the art academy founded in 1563), for instance, were required to attend a dissection once a year. The chief motivation for this was the work of Michelangelo, which – as Vasari's quotation makes clear – was thought to have achieved its perfection through his study of anatomy. Widespread acknowledgement of this earned him a near-mythical status as an artist–anatomist.[3] Barely five years after Michelangelo's death, Bartolomeo Passarotti depicted him giving an anatomy lesson to fellow artists (fig. 74).[4] Others were less positive, however, arguing that the master had been led astray by focusing too much on anatomical details. In 1564, for instance, the year in which Michelangelo died, Giovanni Andrea Gilio classified him among the 'insane anatomists' (*notomisti del furioso*).[5]

It was very important to Michelangelo himself that his study of anatomy would be remembered; nowhere, after all, could he delve so deeply into the male body, his principal subject, as during a dissection. Moreover, anatomical knowledge contributed to the artist's status as an intellectual – an important ideal for him.[6] Dissections are thus mentioned several times in the authorised biography published by his pupil Ascanio Condivi in 1553. This book was a response to Michelangelo's biography in the first edition of Vasari's *Lives of the Artists* in 1550, which made no reference to anatomical studies at all. Vasari assiduously corrected his account in the second, revised edition in 1568, which is also the source of the passage quoted above.[7] In other words, Michelangelo's study of anatomy significantly impacted not only his art, it also influenced his own (and later others') view of his artistic practice. According to an early sixteenth-century anatomical manual, removing the skin revealed the secret workings of nature and exposed 'the amazing and divine workmanship of God the Creator'.[8] Since God was frequently described in the Middle Ages and Renaissance as the 'First Artist', opening up the human body offered other artists an insight into the methods of their earliest predecessor, enabling them to mirror their own artistry against that of God himself. Indeed, Michelangelo's depiction of the male body earned him the epithet *divino* as early as his own lifetime.[9] As we will see, this identification with God the Creator was owed in part to the artist's interest in human anatomy.

Pioneering Anatomical Research

The study of anatomy had yet to become common practice for artists when Michelangelo was born in 1475. Although the Florentine sculptor Lorenzo Ghiberti had already written that artists ought to attend dissections, there is little evidence that his advice was followed, let alone that artists themselves dissected human remains – they generally lacked access to places such as the local university where dissections took place, and anatomical study played no part in workshop practice.[10]

Things gradually began to change from around 1490, when Leonardo first started dissecting limbs in Milan, followed by Michelangelo a few years later in Florence.[11] According to Condivi, around 1494 a friendly prior provided Michelangelo, then in his late teenage years, with rooms at the Santo Spirito monastery where he could perform his dissections.[12] The convent's hospital would have been a logical source of bodies. In September 1504, Michelangelo was provided with access to another hospital space – the *sala grande* in the Ospedale dei Tintori near Sant' Onofrio – in which to prepare his cartoon for the *Battle of Cascina*. Dissection might have been possible here too, although this is not mentioned by any of his biographers.[13] A less salubrious tale from the same period can be found in a Florentine artistic chronicle, which reported that Michelangelo secretly dissected a large number of corpses in a crypt, inadvertently includ-

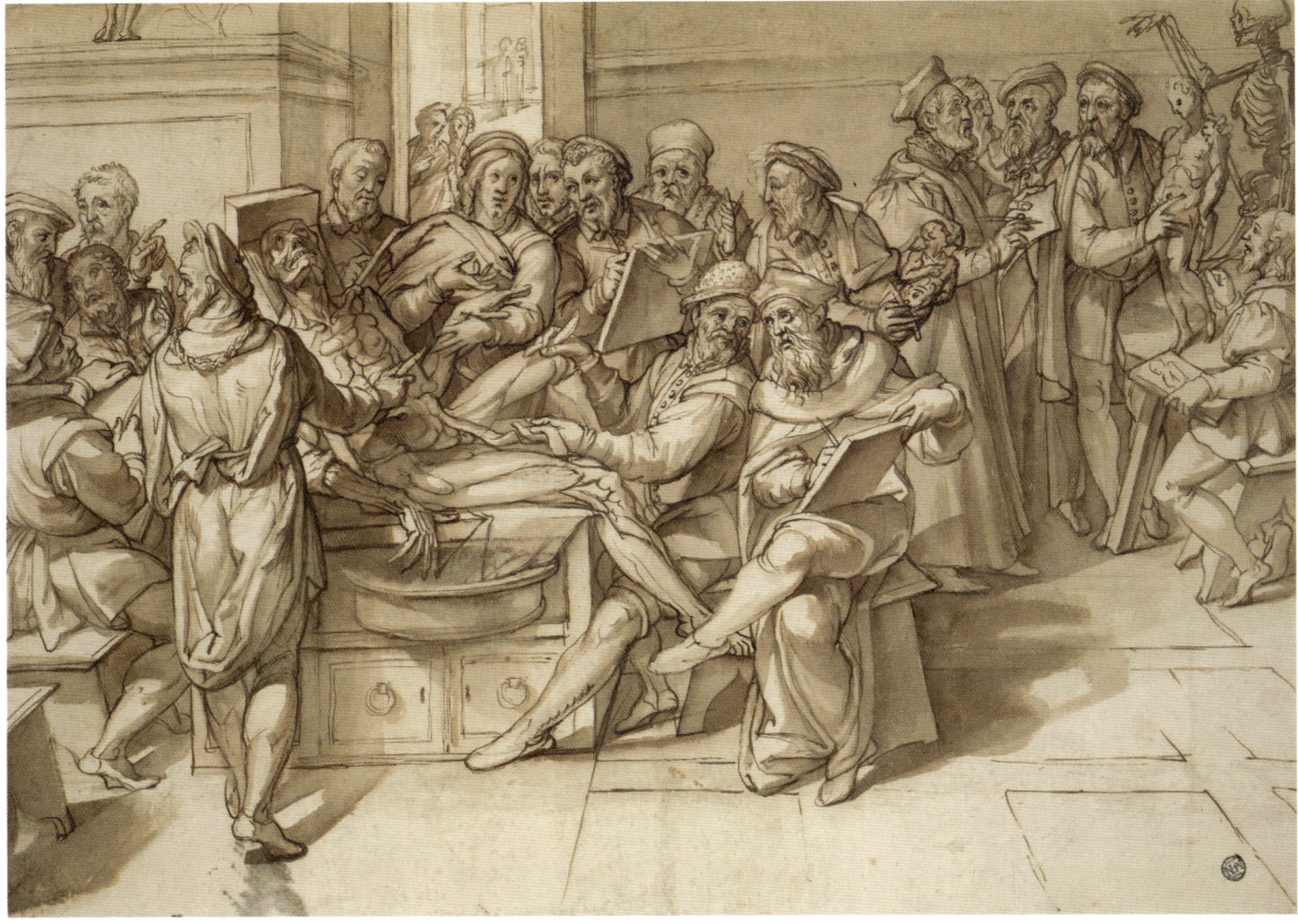

fig. 74   Bartolomeo Passarotti, *Michelangelo Conducting an Anatomy Lesson to his Fellow Artists*, c. 1570. Pen and brown ink, brown wash, black chalk, 385 x 498 mm. Paris, Musée du Louvre, Département des arts graphiques, inv. 8472

ing the body of a member of the city's highly influential Corsini family. When the latter complained about the incident to Piero Soderini, the highest official in Florence, he is said to have guffawed that Michelangelo must have done it 'for his art'.[14]

How credible is this information? The story about the Corsini family may amount to little more than a rumour that circulated in Florence.[15] Condivi's biography is not entirely unproblematic either: it is hard to believe, for instance, that a teenage Michelangelo performed independent dissections with no previous medical knowledge. Like other sixteenth-century artists, he might have kept up contacts with hospital doctors who dissected the bodies of convicted criminals or deceased persons who had not been claimed by relatives.[16] Only one drawing from this period – showing the bones of a hand – testifies to an early interest in anatomy on Michelangelo's part. All the same, parts of skeletons were more readily available than complete cadavers, suggesting that the artist's first introduction to anatomy might well have been limited to the study of bone material.[17] Drawings that can be more securely linked to actual dissections are not found until twenty years later, after the completion of the Sistine ceiling.

It is difficult to determine, therefore, when Michelangelo himself first dissected a human body. What Condivi wrote in 1553 concerning his master's early years might be more a reflection of his own apprenticeship than a historically accurate account. Condivi probably met Michelangelo in the circle of Niccolò Ridolfi, a cardinal with a pronounced interest in medicine.[18] This brought them into contact with the physician Realdo Colombo, with whom Michelangelo would collaborate for many years and who treated him for kidney stones in 1549. Colombo moved to Rome in 1548, because – as he himself claimed – plenty of dead bodies were available there and he was assisted 'by the leading painter in the world' (i.e. Michelangelo).[19] With his medical connections, he could help Michelangelo obtain human remains, including that of 'a most handsome young black man', which the artist dissected together with Condivi. Aside from this passage, we know nothing about the origin, age or gender of the bodies Michelangelo studied.[20] Colombo was working in this period on his magnum opus, *De re anatomica*, which was published posthumously in 1559. There is no evidence for the frequently proposed hypothesis that Michelangelo was to provide illustrations for the text; the book was published without pictures, other than the title page showing Colombo behind a dissection table.[21] The prominent figure in the right foreground is probably Michelangelo (fig. 75).[22] If so, the image might perhaps be read as a tribute to their long-standing friendship and collaboration based on their shared interest in human anatomy.

Theories About the Body

We do not know precisely how long or how often Michelangelo engaged in dissection over the course of his career, but as he grew older he had to abandon the practice, as his frequent handling of dead bodies was making him ill. Anatomical research was not a pleasant activity. The lack of preservatives meant that dissections could only be performed in winter, when the low temperatures would delay the decomposition of the body. Leonardo da Vinci aptly described the 'fear of passing the night hours in the company of these corpses, quartered and flayed and horrible to behold.'[23] Both he and Michelangelo were keen to spare their fellow artists some of this horror by sharing their knowledge with them. Condivi described Michelangelo's intentions as follows:

> 'He gave up dissecting corpses because his long handling of them had so affected his stomach that he could neither eat nor drink salutarily. It is quite true that when he gave it up he was so learned and rich in knowledge of that science that he has often had it in mind to write a treatise, as a service to those who want to work in sculpture and painting, on all manner of human movements and appearances and on the bone structure, with a brilliant theory which he arrived at through long experience.'[24]

Michelangelo had previously made drawings or models of body parts for others, but he now wanted to set down on paper a comprehensive and 'brilliant theory' (*ingegnosa theorica*) about the representation of the human body, of which 'all manner of human movements' formed an important part, as Condivi stated.[25] However, Michelangelo's treatise, like Leonardo's, was never brought to completion.

The Florentine architect and humanist Leon Battista Alberti had been among the first to write about the importance of anatomy to the artist. In his influential treatise on painting he advised those attempting to draw the human figure 'first to sketch in the bones, for, as they bend very little indeed, they always occupy a certain determined position. Then add the sinews and muscles, and finally clothe the bones and muscles with flesh and skin.'[26] Echoing the Roman architect Vitruvius, Alberti also believed that precise measurement of bodies would furnish artists with an understanding of the correct proportions of their various parts.[27]

Just under a century later, the German artist Albrecht Dürer published his views on proportion theory in the *Vier Bücher von menschlicher Proportion* (1528), an illustrated treatise on the proper proportions of the human body. He informs the reader in the introduction

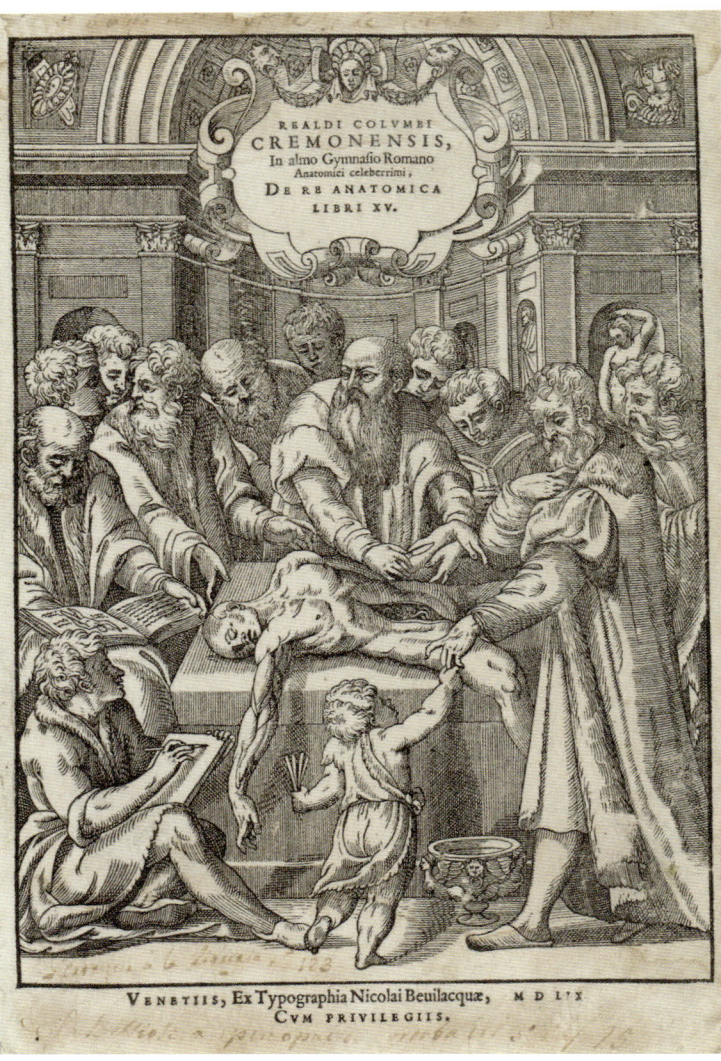

that '[I] write only about the outer lines of forms and figures, and how these are to be drawn from point to point, but not at all about the inner parts.'[28] If these dimensions are adhered to, Dürer stated, the body could be depicted in perspective (fig. 76). This made it less important to resort to anatomical dissection.

It is not certain whether Michelangelo himself read Alberti's treatise, but the method of building up a figure from the skeleton appears several times in his drawings. He was, however, certainly familiar with Dürer's work, because it circulated within his intellectual network.[29] According to Condivi, he was less than impressed by it.

'I know very well that, when he reads Albrecht Dürer, he finds his work very weak, seeing in his mind how much more beautiful and useful in the study of this subject his own conception would have been. And, to tell the truth, Albrecht discusses only the measurements and the varieties of human bodies, for which no fixed rule can be given, and he forms his figures straight upright like poles; as to what was more important, the movements and the gestures of human beings (*atti e gesti humani*), he says not a word.'[30]

Condivi once again refers here to Michelangelo's interest in movement, while his assertion that his master placed little value on studies of proportion is seemingly confirmed by the fact that few such drawings are found in his surviving oeuvre. One exception is a preliminary study for the personification of Night from the Medici Chapel (fig. 68/cat. 32), undoubtedly drawn from a live model, in which Michelangelo made a quick sketch of two bones and a joint, probably from a leg as he wrote *sti[n]cho* (shin-bone) next to it. He also drew measuring lines, indicating that the ratio of the bones is 5:4.

Various prescriptions existed for the correct proportions of the body. Vasari claimed to have several sheets in his collection of drawings in which Michelangelo had constructed figures from 'nine, ten, and even twelve heads (*teste*)'.[31] The drawings he mentions are most likely lost, but they might have been similar to a *Male Nude with Proportions Indicated*, now in the Royal Collection (fig. 77/cat. 24). This magnificent sheet shows the extent to which Michelangelo's views on proportion theory differed from Dürer's.[32] The man stands in *contrapposto* and reaches behind his back with his right hand to his left arm, rotating his impressive torso. In the upper right corner, Michelangelo drew the profile of a head with a hand next to it to indicate that the two are of equal size. The body is then divided into *teste* (heads). The right leg, which bears the weight, is 6 2/3 heads long, for instance, from which one can extrapolate that the height of the entire figure is

fig. 75   Title page of Realdo Colombo, *De re anatomica libri XV* (Nicolò Bevilacqua, 1559). Norman, The University of Oklahoma Libraries

about 10 heads – more or less in keeping with Vitruvius' proportion theory. The artist added precise individual annotations for the joints: the left elbow and the distance between the wrist and fingers, for example, are 1/3 of a head and the ankles 2/3 of a head. He went so far as to sketch the knee again separately.

Michelangelo preferred to base his proportion studies on a dynamic figure rather than a static one, as was customary. In this drawing, he explores whether Vitruvius' theory of proportion was useful to the depiction of movement. His conclusion seems to have been negative, since no measurements have been added to the torso, the rotation of which suggests a sense of motion. Vasari reports that Michelangelo preferred to combine the dimensions of body parts as he saw fit, instead of sticking to a single system of proportion. He describes the master's views as follows:

> 'there should be a certain harmony of grace (*grazia*) in the whole, which nature does not present, with Michelangelo saying that it was necessary to have the compasses in the eyes and not in the hand, because the hands work and the eye judges.'[33]

In a letter written in 1570, Vasari stressed again that Michelangelo 'always went after grace (*grazia*) rather than proportion measurements (*misura*)'.[34] Exact proportions were of little use in depicting a moving body, the limbs of which seem closer at one moment and further away at another. Only Michelangelo's practised eye, informed by his knowledge of anatomy, could achieve this with a grace that surpassed nature.

Under the Skin

According to Condivi, Michelangelo's anatomical research was exclusively concerned with 'the knowledge which is necessary to the art of painting and sculpture and not the other minutiae which anatomists observe'.[35] The surviving drawings confirm that his interest focused on surface anatomy – the muscles and bones visible beneath the skin. In this respect, he differed from Leonardo, who wanted to understand the entirety of the body's functioning and therefore studied more deep-seated organs too, which as an artist he would never be called upon to depict. Anatomical knowledge formed the scientific framework within which Leonardo worked, whereas Michelangelo approached it not as a set of boundaries but rather as a point of departure, a necessary foundation on which to shape the body according to his own artistic ideals. While his anatomical observations are generally very accurate,

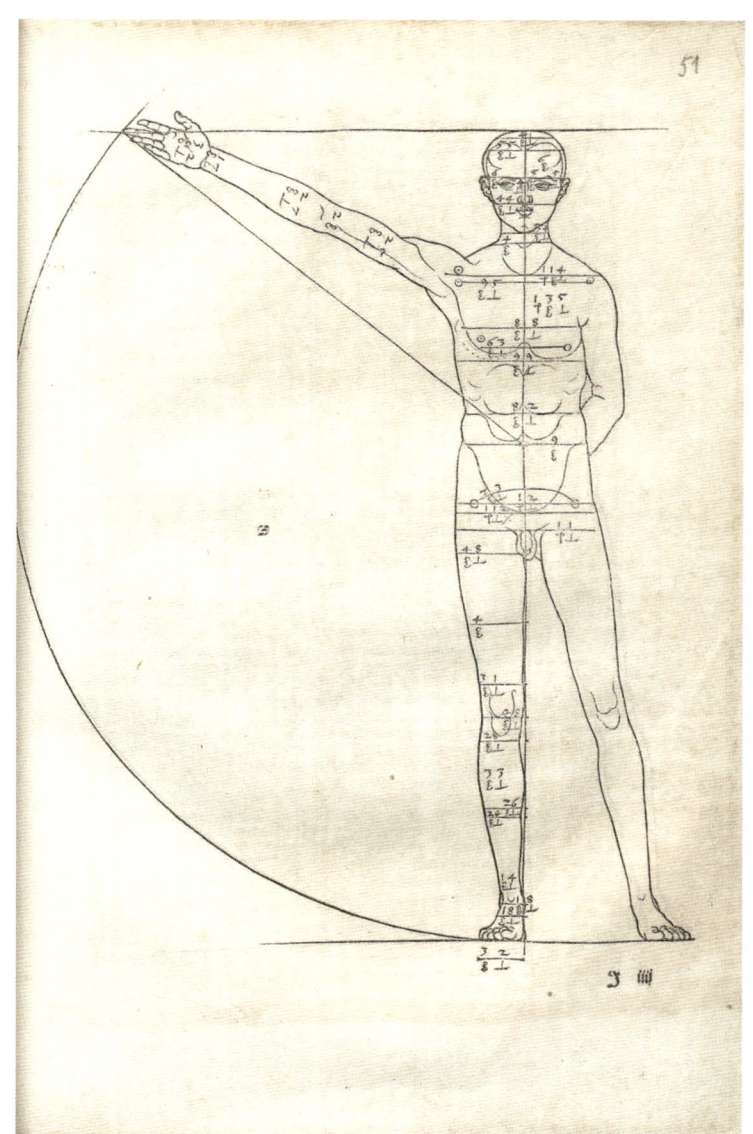

fig. 76   Albrecht Dürer, *Vier Bücher von menschlicher Proportion* (Hieronymus Formschneyder, 1528), fol. I4r. Munich, Bayerische Staatsbibliothek, Rar. 612

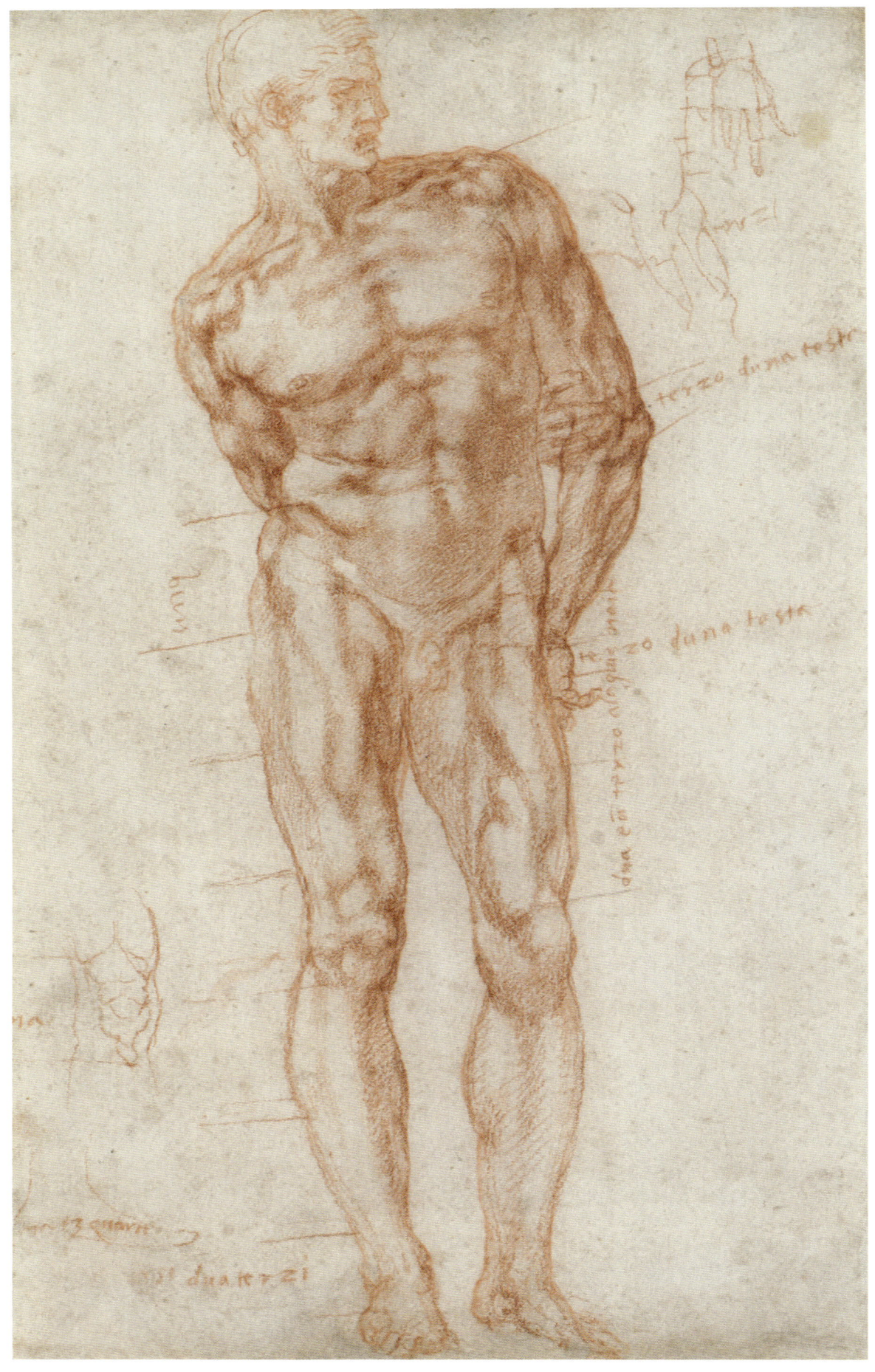

fig. 77   (cat. 24) Michelangelo. *Male Nude with Proportions Indicated*, c. 1515–1520. Red chalk, 291 x 180 mm. Windsor, Royal Collection Trust, inv. RCIN 912765

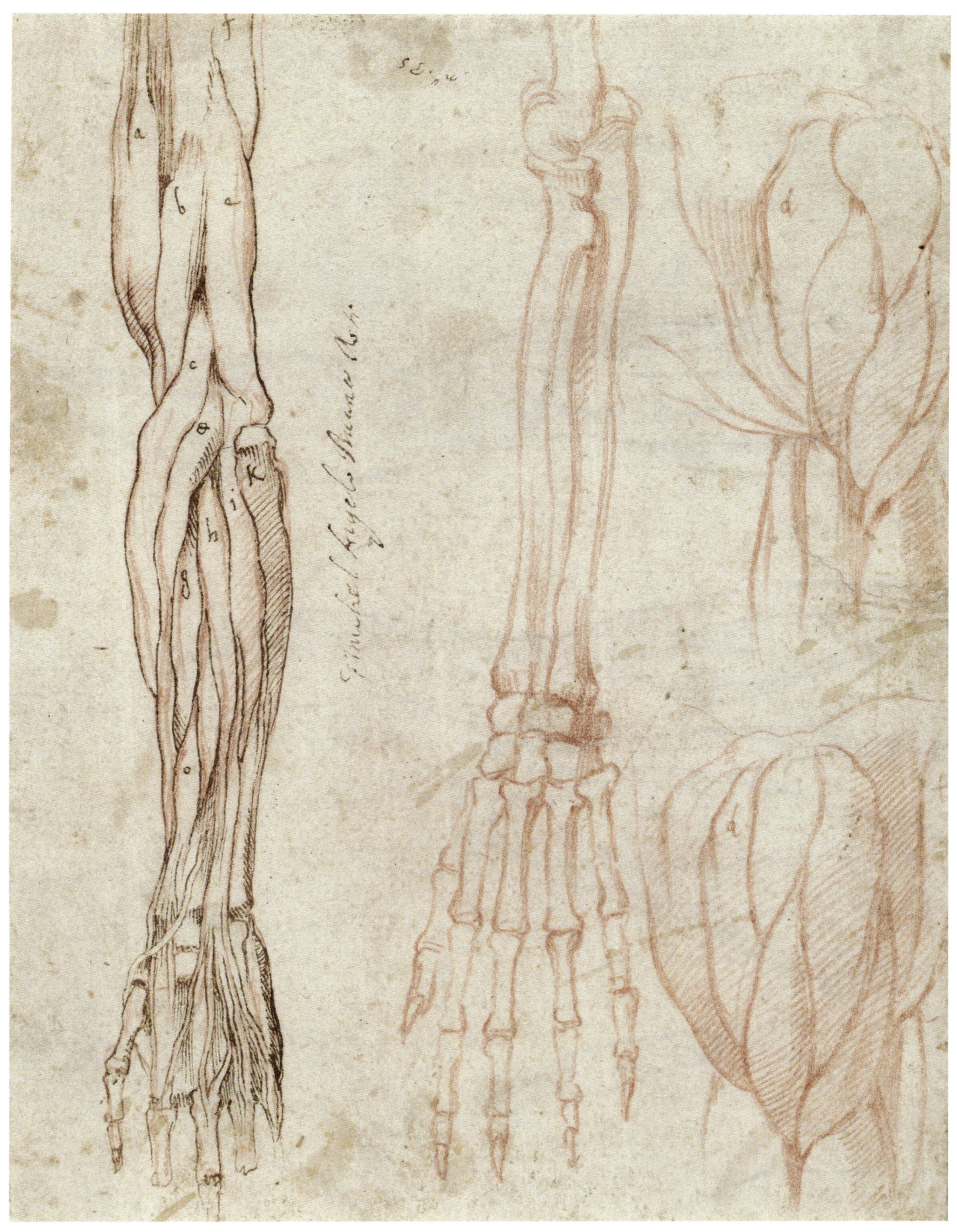

fig. 78   (cat. 22) Michelangelo, *Anatomical Studies of a Left Arm and Shoulder,* c. 1515–1520. Red chalk, partly retraced with pen and brown ink, 263 x 201 mm. Haarlem, Teylers Museum, inv. A 039

he nevertheless drew on his imagination to enhance them when it suited his purpose.[36] Leonardo had already criticised Michelangelo for this in 1513. In one of his notebooks, he reprimanded a certain 'anatomical painter' for 'a too strong indication of bones, sinews and muscles' when seeking to visualise the emotions of his nude figures. He was probably referring to the recently unveiled *ignudi* in the Sistine Chapel.[37]

Michelangelo's anatomical drawings do indeed focus on muscles and bones. His most analytical *écorché* (a drawing of flayed body parts) belongs to the Teylers Museum collection: the recto (fig. 78/cat. 22) shows an arm of which the tendons and muscles have been exposed, as well as the skeleton of the forearm and the left shoulder, which is viewed twice from different angles.[38] Four views of a left leg are featured on the verso (fig. 29/cat. 22v). The recto recalls Alberti's instruction to build a body starting from the skeleton and then covering it with muscles and skin.[39] Michelangelo might have had access to both a flayed body and a prepared skeleton to allow him to compare the two, as can be seen in the drawing by Passarotti (fig. 74). In the Teylers sheet, attention is chiefly focused on the muscular system. Almost all of the muscles of the arm and leg are indicated with letters, as is one muscle in the shoulders.[40] The physician Juan de Valverde, who worked in Rome, viewed Michelangelo's work as proof that an artist 'ought to know not only the muscles at the surface but also those beneath it, where they begin and end and what purpose they serve, so that one knows when one needs to make a particular muscle longer than another, with greater bulging or contraction'.[41] The letters help identify individual muscles and hence to study their location and function.

A more cursorily drawn sheet from the Royal Collection contains similar studies of the muscles of an extended leg, alongside drawings of bent knees, the arm and the neck (fig. 79).[42] Particular attention is paid to the knee joint: Michelangelo seems to have bent the leg into different positions in order to draw its function. He observed the movement of this joint again in another sheet with three muscle studies of a bent left leg in various stages of contraction (fig. 80/cat. 21). On the right, Michelangelo studied how a tensed left arm bends towards the chest. He drew the muscles and tendons that cause the arm to move from shoulder to fingertips. The artist often specifically highlighted the joints in his anatomical research, as was already apparent in his *Male Nude with Proportions Indicated* (fig. 77/cat. 24). These are the places, after all, where muscles and bones meet – nodes at which body parts can be turned, stretched and moved in different ways and where the sense of imminent movement that characterises so many of his figures arises.

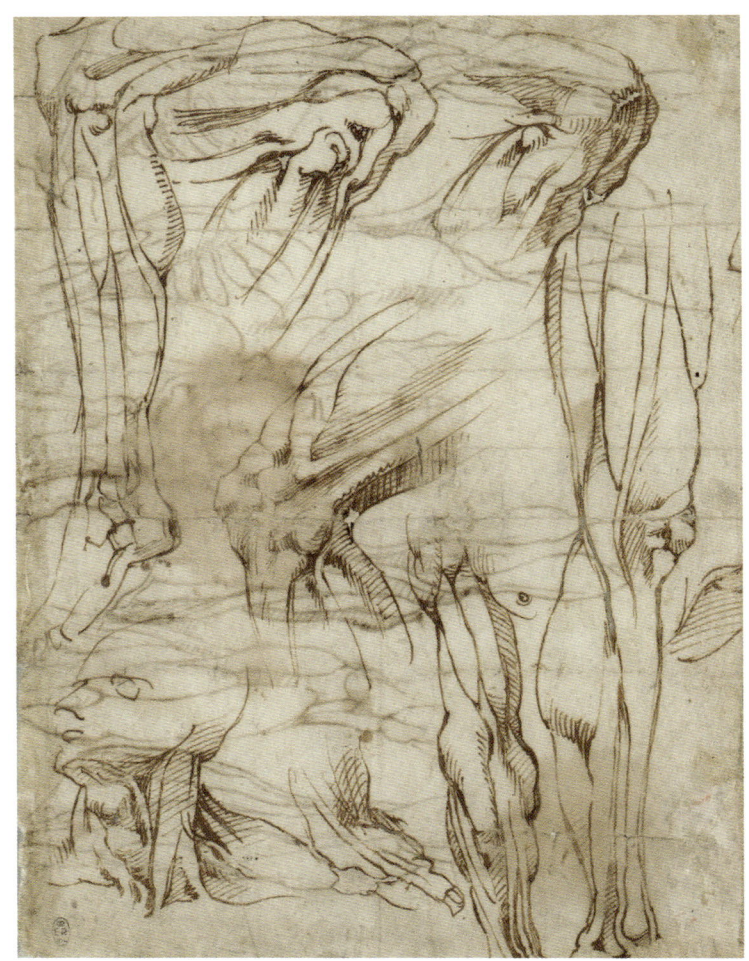

fig. 79   Michelangelo, *Anatomical Studies*, c. 1520–1525. Pen and brown ink, 278 x 203 mm. Windsor, Royal Collection Trust, inv. RCIN 990475

Michelangelo also studied the shoulder joint at length, for the first time around 1504 in two preparatory studies for the *Battle of Cascina*. The drawings in question – done from live models rather than dead bodies – are the earliest ones in Michelangelo's oeuvre that demonstrate how he analytically investigated what lies beneath the skin. One of them contains seven studies of a shoulder with a raised arm, in which various muscles and bones are labelled using symbols (fig. 81). Among other things, this drawing demonstrates Michelangelo's observation that the triceps and biceps are not contracted simultaneously but act as an antagonistic pair to bend the arm.[43] The other drawing shows the complete bodies of two moving models, although the symbols make it clear that the artist was chiefly interested in the shoulders (fig. 82). He labelled various features including the shoulder blade and the acromion, the bony projection on top of the shoulder.[44] These bones are visible when raising and rotating the arm, and the annotations help locate them accurately from different angles. A magnificently worked-up drawing of the figure on the right has been preserved, in which Michelangelo captured the three-dimensional surface of the body in black chalk (fig. 140/cat. 12). Using light and shadow, he clarified how the muscles and bones appear beneath the skin. The rotation of the hips is expressed more strongly in this chalk drawing, bringing the model's torso further forward and making the shoulder more prominent, as we are now looking at it from above. This subtle change in posture allowed Michelangelo to show off his anatomical knowledge to even greater effect. In the *Studies for the Libyan Sibyl for the Sistine Chapel Ceiling,* the acromion is singled out again with a precisely placed marking, indicating how important the bone was to the artist when it came to depicting movement (fig. 70/cat. 16).

A spectacular double-sided sheet from Haarlem features a flayed shoulder, in which Michelangelo depicted the joint with the adjacent muscles from both sides (figs 83 and 84/cat. 23). The arm is raised forwards on the recto, while the opposite movement is depicted on the verso. Whereas in the aforementioned *écorchés* Michelangelo was chiefly concerned with the position and connections of the muscles, here he uses hatching to indicate the volume they assume as they move.

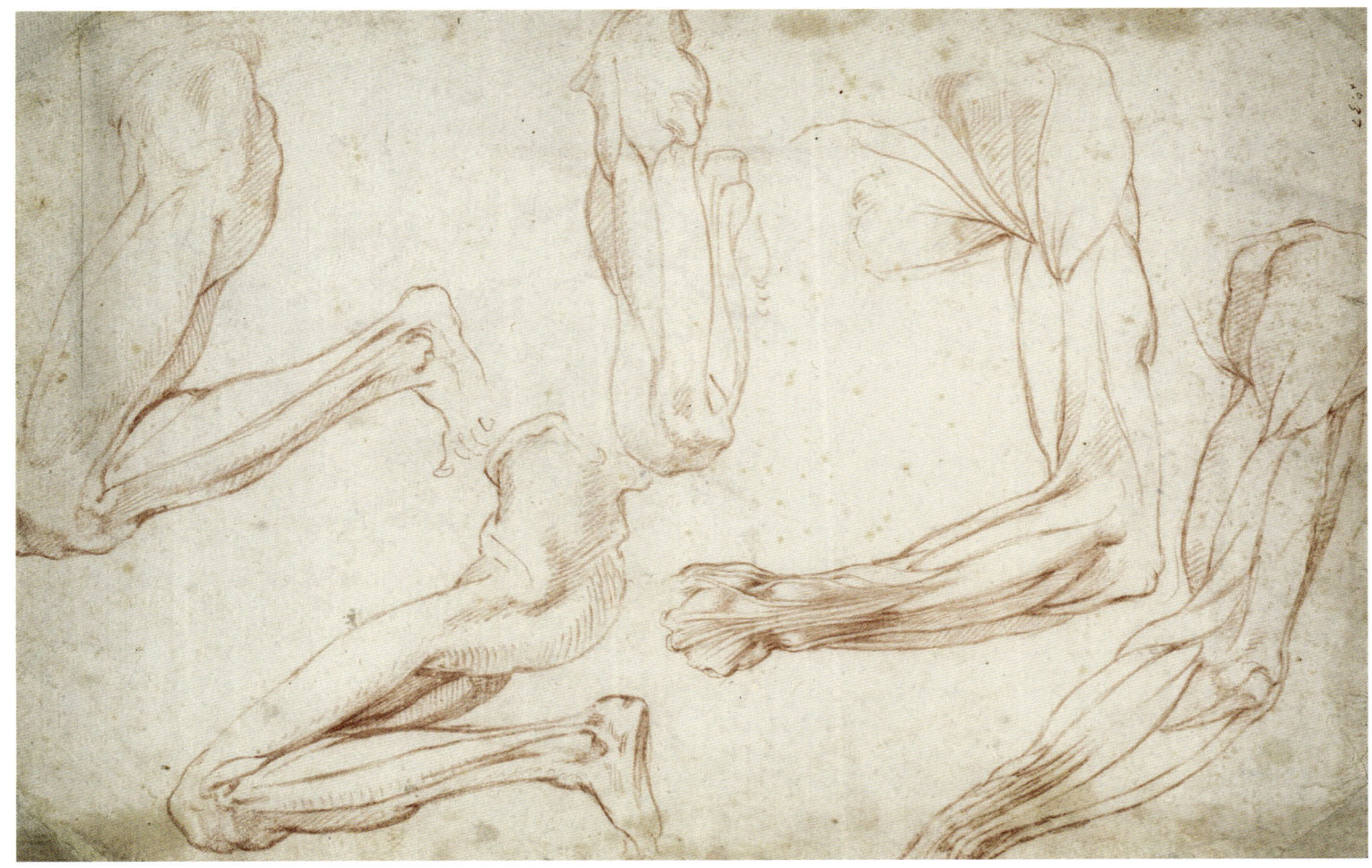

fig. 80   (cat. 21) Michelangelo, *Anatomical Studies of a Left Leg and Arm*, c. 1515–1520. Red chalk, 271 x 419 mm. Haarlem, Teylers Museum, inv. A 037

It is difficult to study the way moving muscles bulge and contract based solely on a rigid and swiftly decomposing dead body. Therefore, from the late sixteenth century onwards, artists frequently resorted to small wax models of dissected bodies in motion when drawing anatomy. Michelangelo might already have done something similar: the most important source for this is Francisco de Holanda, who explains in his *Roman Dialogues* of 1548 how Michelangelo fashioned muscles from dissected bodies in wax and used them to build anatomical models.[45] He might be describing the artist's practice while painting *The Last Judgement*, which was completed shortly before Holanda's book was published. Apart from this passage, there is little direct evidence that Michelangelo used wax anatomical models during his career, nor has a single example survived that can be attributed to him personally. It is very much open to question, therefore, to what extent his anatomical drawings can be traced back to any such sculptural models.[46]

Muscle function could be best studied using live models, as demonstrated by the previously discussed drawings for the *Battle of Cascina* (figs 81 and 82). Hence, alongside dead bodies, live models were another very important subject of study in anatomical research. Sixteenth-century art theorists emphasised the need always to have a living body on hand during dissections for reference purposes. Vasari wrote of Raphael, for instance, that he compared 'the muscles of anatomical subjects and of flayed human bodies with those of the living'.[47] Michelangelo is likely to have done the same. He might have examined an *écorché* (such as fig. 78/cat. 22) in combination with the tensed arm of a muscular model to create the previously discussed study of the left-arm muscles (fig. 80/cat. 21). The study of live models and that of dead bodies were not separate endeavours but steps towards the same goal: the most perfect representation of the human body.

Anatomical Transformation

This brings us to how Michelangelo applied his anatomical knowledge. His *écorchés* served chiefly as study material for himself and his pupils. Most of the sheets have similar dimensions, suggesting that they might have formed part of an anatomical sketchbook that Michelangelo kept in his studio for easy reference.[48] They may well have had a role in his planned treatise. The fact that the drawings remained in the workshop for a long time is shown by the previously discussed sheet with four views of a leg (fig. 29/cat. 22v). At some point around 1542 – more than twenty years after he made the anatomical drawing – Michelangelo reused

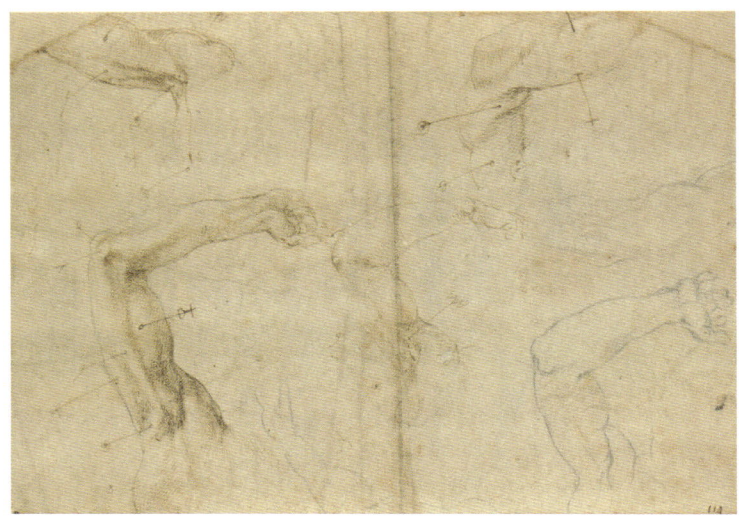

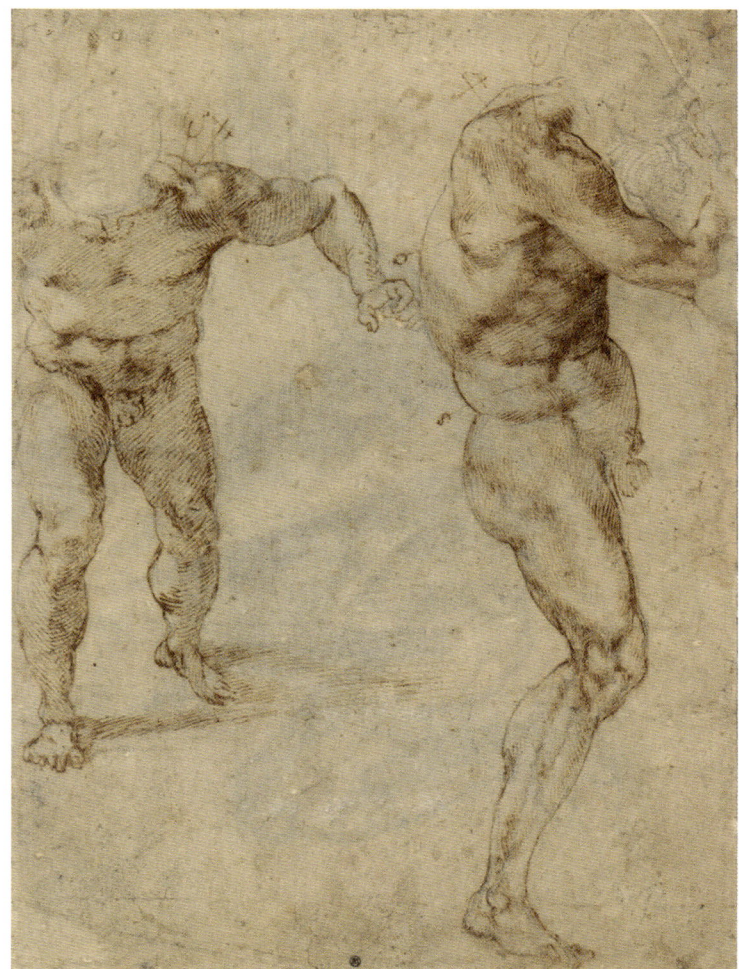

fig. 81   Michelangelo, *Anatomical Studies of a Raised Arm*, 1504. Pen and brown ink, black chalk, 226 x 315 mm. Vienna, The ALBERTINA Museum, inv. 132

fig. 82   Michelangelo, *Anatomical Studies of Two Male Nudes*, 1504. Pen and brown ink, black chalk, 270 x 196 mm. Vienna, The ALBERTINA Museum, inv. 123

the paper to jot down the draft of a sonnet. Perhaps he had dug the drawing out again in recent years when working on *The Last Judgement*.

A sheet with drawings of arms (fig. 85/cat. 20) demonstrates how Michelangelo transformed anatomical material into a preliminary study, in this case for the right arm of the *Dying Captive*. Given the prominence with which this figure (fig. 86) holds his hand in front of his chest, it is no wonder that the artist attached particular importance to the accurate anatomical depiction of this detail. To this end, he reused a sheet (undoubtedly not by chance) on which he had previously made four pen drawings of a flayed arm. The remaining space was then filled with several sketches for the captive's bent right arm.[49] The five topmost studies focus on the muscles of the forearm, after which Michelangelo rotated the sheet to study the anatomy of the bent wrist and hand. The detailed depiction of the muscles and tendons beneath the skin is clearly indebted to the analytical *écorchés* he had previously drawn on this sheet. Michelangelo studied the same hand again on the verso of a large design drawing for the tomb of Julius II, of which the *Dying Captive* was to be a part, this time in even greater detail, from different angles and with yet closer attention to the tendons and bones in the tensed fingers (fig. 87). The rendering of the anatomy is toned down, however, in the final sculpture. Did he feel that the anatomical intensity of the hand was out of keeping with the rest of the figure, who appears more dreamy than forceful in his struggle to escape the bonds that constrain him?

A comparably close adherence to anatomical detail characterises Michelangelo's drawings for the sculptures in the Medici Chapel, as was already apparent from the preparatory study for *Night* (fig. 68/cat. 32). In the *Study of a Left Leg for the Sculpture of Day* (fig. 88/cat. 29), the broad muscle that runs diagonally across the thigh (the sartorius muscle) catches the light, anticipating the lighting of the finished statue.[50] This black chalk drawing was preceded by a study of the same leg with the skin removed.[51] The most astonishing anatomical details of *Day* are found in the figure's ankle and foot, in which the tendons and veins have been captured precisely. The same goes for the veins in the left forearm, which Michelangelo depicted in another black chalk drawing (fig. 65/cat. 28). This time we do find the details in the marble statue (fig. 89), and it comes as no surprise that contemporaries praised these sculptures specifically for their impressive anatomy.[52]

The *Studies for a Crucifixion* (fig. 90/cat. 41) show how consistently Michelangelo applied his knowledge of the body's structure. While the drawing was probably done from a live model, the detailed studies of ribs and shoulder joint speak to a knowledge obtained through anatomical study. Michelangelo had previously studied the powerful protrusion of the ribs in an anatomical drawing of a hanging body (fig. 91).[53] Above the study of the shoulder, he again drew a knee, in such a way that the principal bones are identifiable.[54] Penetrating the skin with his mind's eye, Michelangelo fixed the position of the skeleton in relation to the contours of the leg. While drawing, he envisioned a real body on the paper and not merely its representation, almost as if the muscles and bones were genuinely present beneath the drawing. It is this intention to create a complete body, both internally and externally, that imbues his figures with the grace and vivacity for which Vasari and others praised him.

Anatomy becomes more visible than ever in *The Last Judgement* (fig. 96), the work described by Condivi as a model of 'all that nature can do with the human body'.[55] Since this fresco was meant to depict the moment when the dead rise from their graves and receive a new body, it offered Michelangelo the perfect opportunity to display both his anatomical knowledge and his vision of the perfect nude that surpasses any earthly physique. The resurrected dead are shown bottom left, some still as skeletons, others with a body. Michelangelo's impressive *Studies for Saint Lawrence for the* Last Judgement (fig. 92/cat. 46) present a new ideal: the torso has become even more solid relative to the head, and the shoulders are unnaturally wide, especially in the final fresco (fig. 93).

Michelangelo's creative transformation of the human anatomy reaches a peak here: he presents an idealised image that in many cases is far removed from reality, with the skin apparently barely able to contain what lies beneath it. While it does not appear in the finished fresco, the rapidly sketched figure on the verso of the *Studies for Saint Lawrence* (fig. 94/cat. 46v) typifies the way Michelangelo shaped the body in this period. The legs consist of a series of round and elliptical forms, making the anatomy an agglomeration of bulging and tensed muscle groups.[56] The anatomy of the back is somewhat comparable with the previously mentioned pen study of a hanging body (fig. 91), in which the back likewise consists of elongated, vertical muscles that are hard to identify. Rather than the precise observations in the previously discussed sheets, Michelangelo here set down rapid, cursory suggestions of anatomy. The expressive effect clearly takes precedence over anatomical accuracy. Paul Joannides pointed out that the same anatomy defines the back of the soul in the lower right of *The Last Judgement*, who is dragged from Charon's infernal boat by demons (fig. 96).[57] The muscles in the fresco are rendered almost as distinctly as those in the anatomical drawing, as if a thin membrane of skin is all that conceals

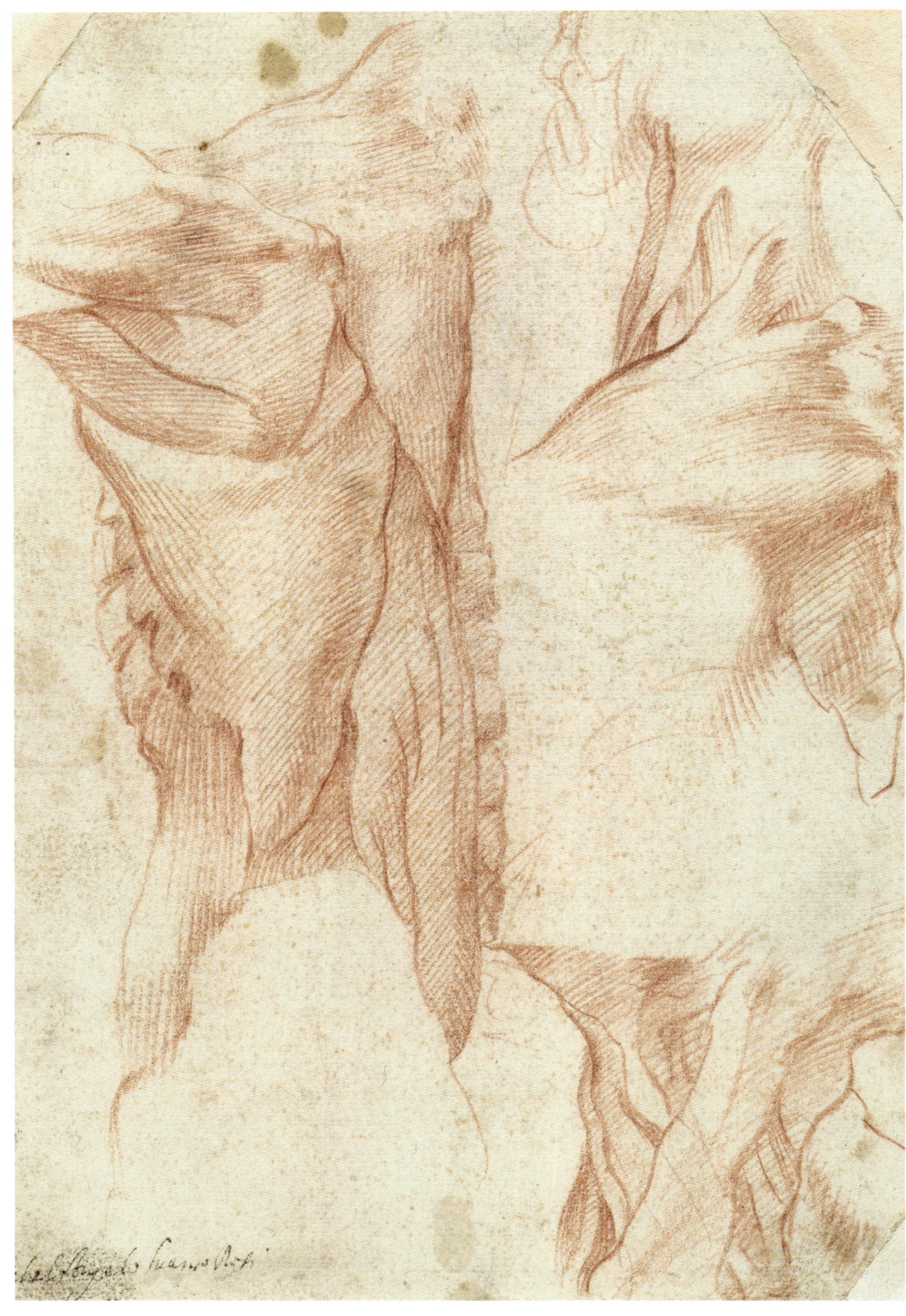

fig. 83   (cat. 23) Michelangelo, *Anatomical Studies of a Neck and Shoulder*, c. 1515–1520. Red chalk, 278 x 189 mm. Haarlem, Teylers Museum, inv. A 042

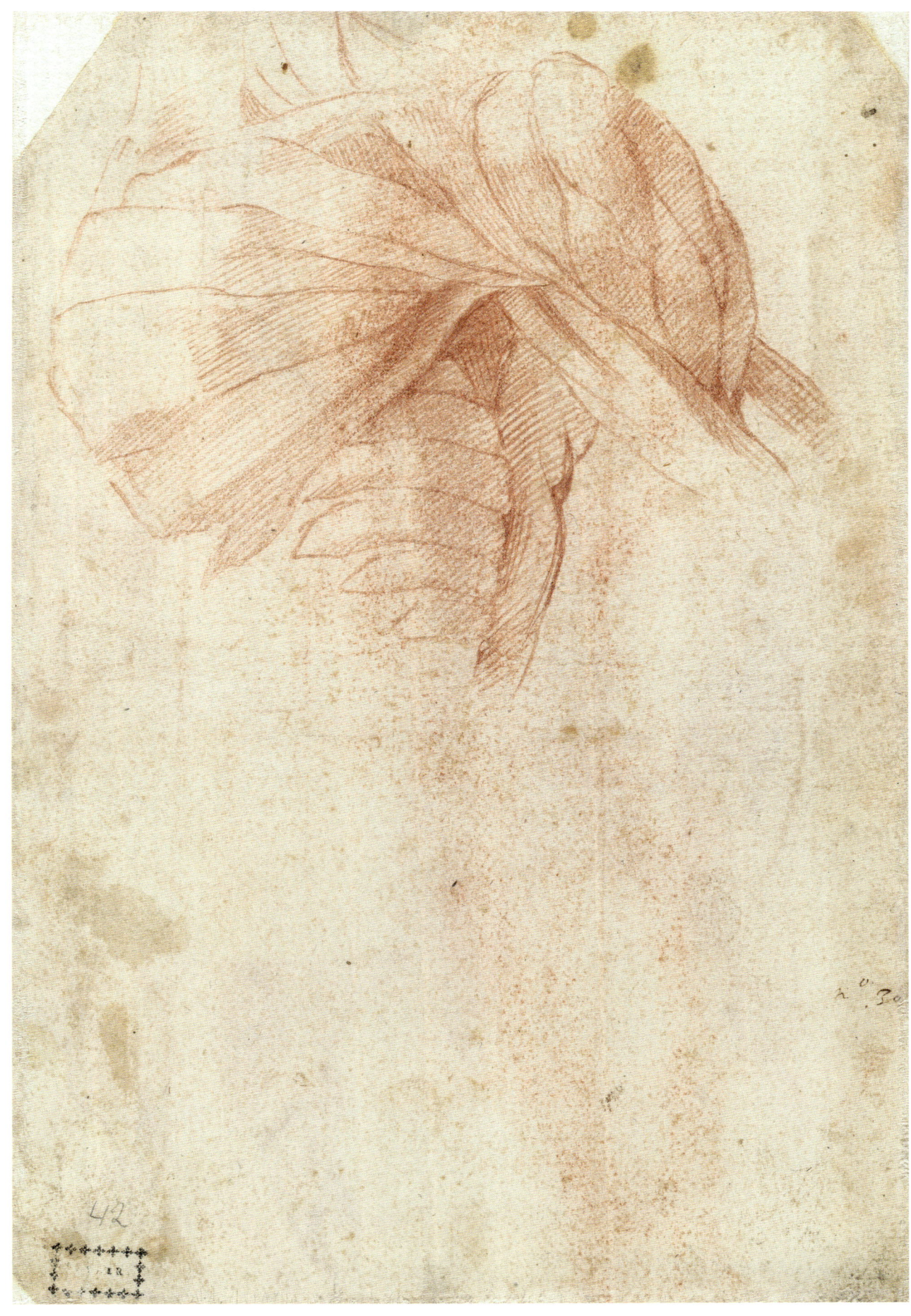

fig. 84   (cat. 23v) Michelangelo, *Anatomical Study of a Shoulder*, c. 1515–1520. Red chalk, 278 x 189 mm. Haarlem, Teylers Museum, inv. A 042v

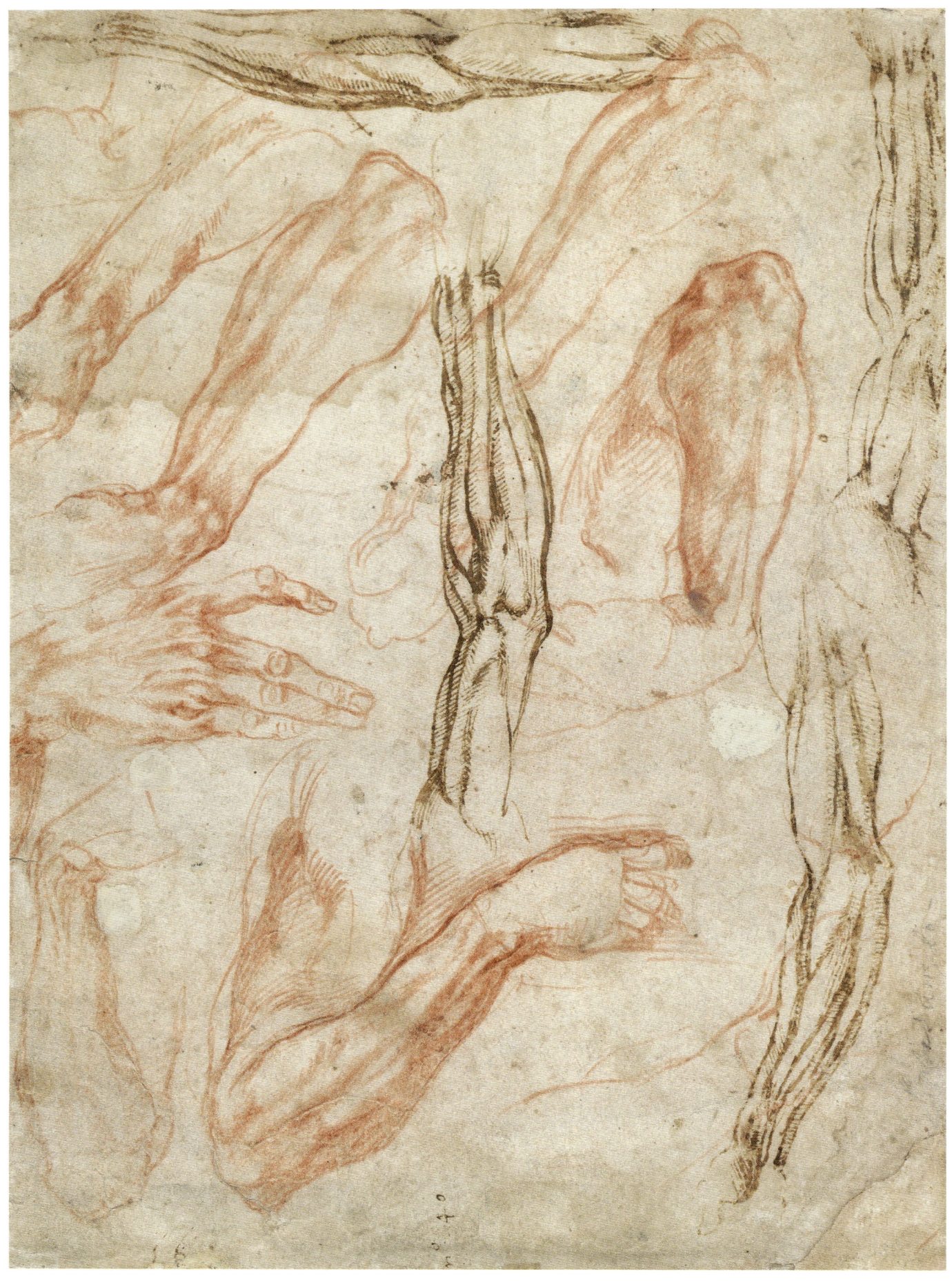

fig. 85   (cat. 20) Michelangelo, *Studies of Arms and Hands*, c. 1513–1514. Pen and brown ink, red chalk, 285 x 207 mm. Haarlem, Teylers Museum, inv. A 028

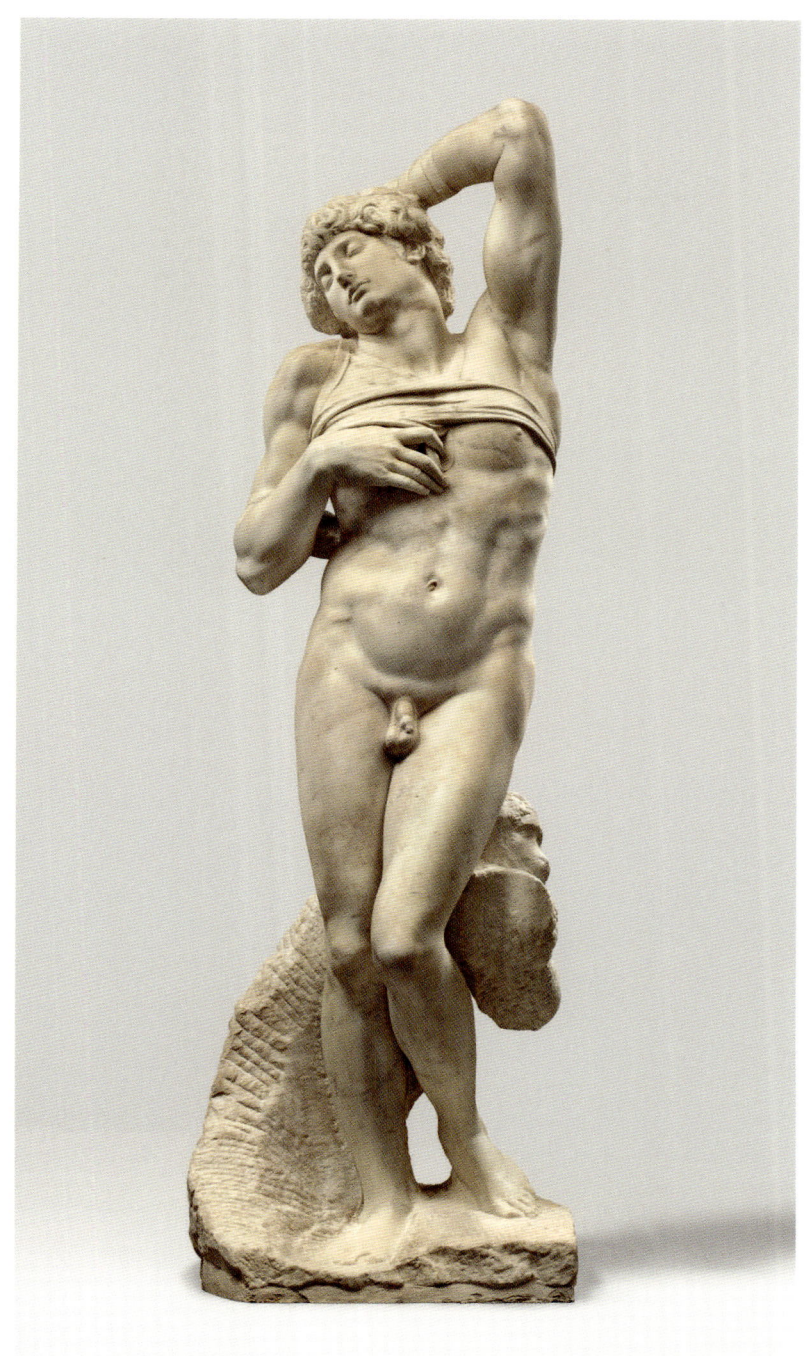

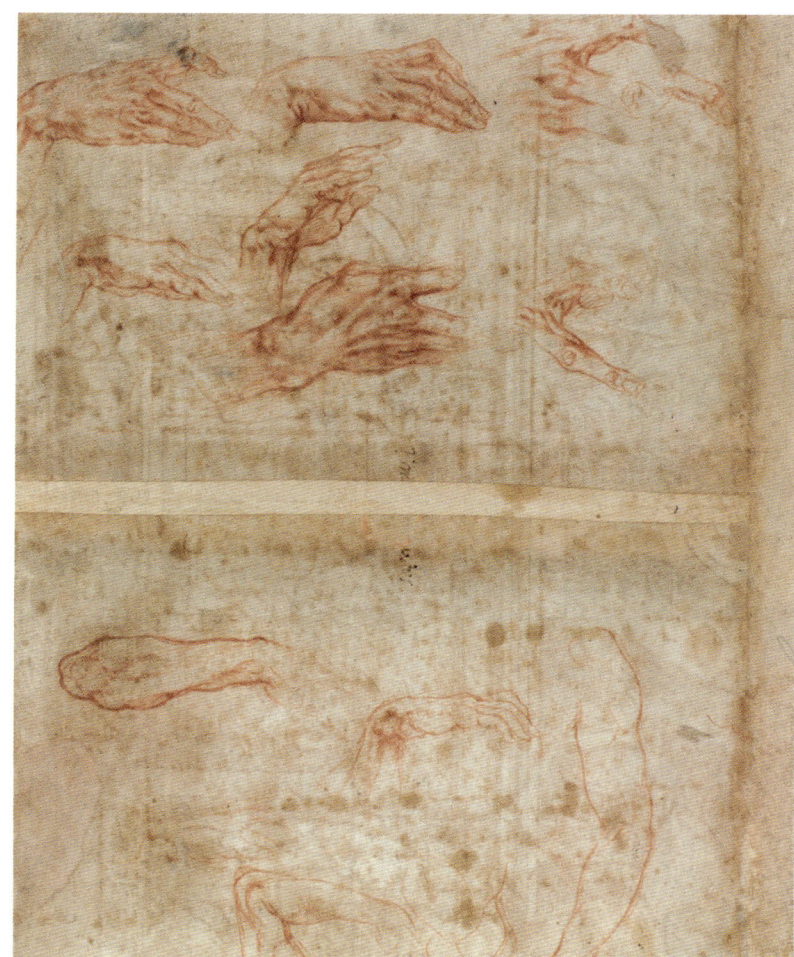

fig. 86   Michelangelo, *Dying Captive*, c. 1513–1516. Marble, height 227 cm. Paris, Musée du Louvre, Département des Sculptures, inv. MR 1590

fig. 87   Michelangelo, *Studies of Arms and Hands*, c. 1513–1514. Red chalk, 292 x 361 mm. Florence, Gallerie degli Uffizi, Gabinetto dei Disegni e delle Stampe, inv. 608 E v

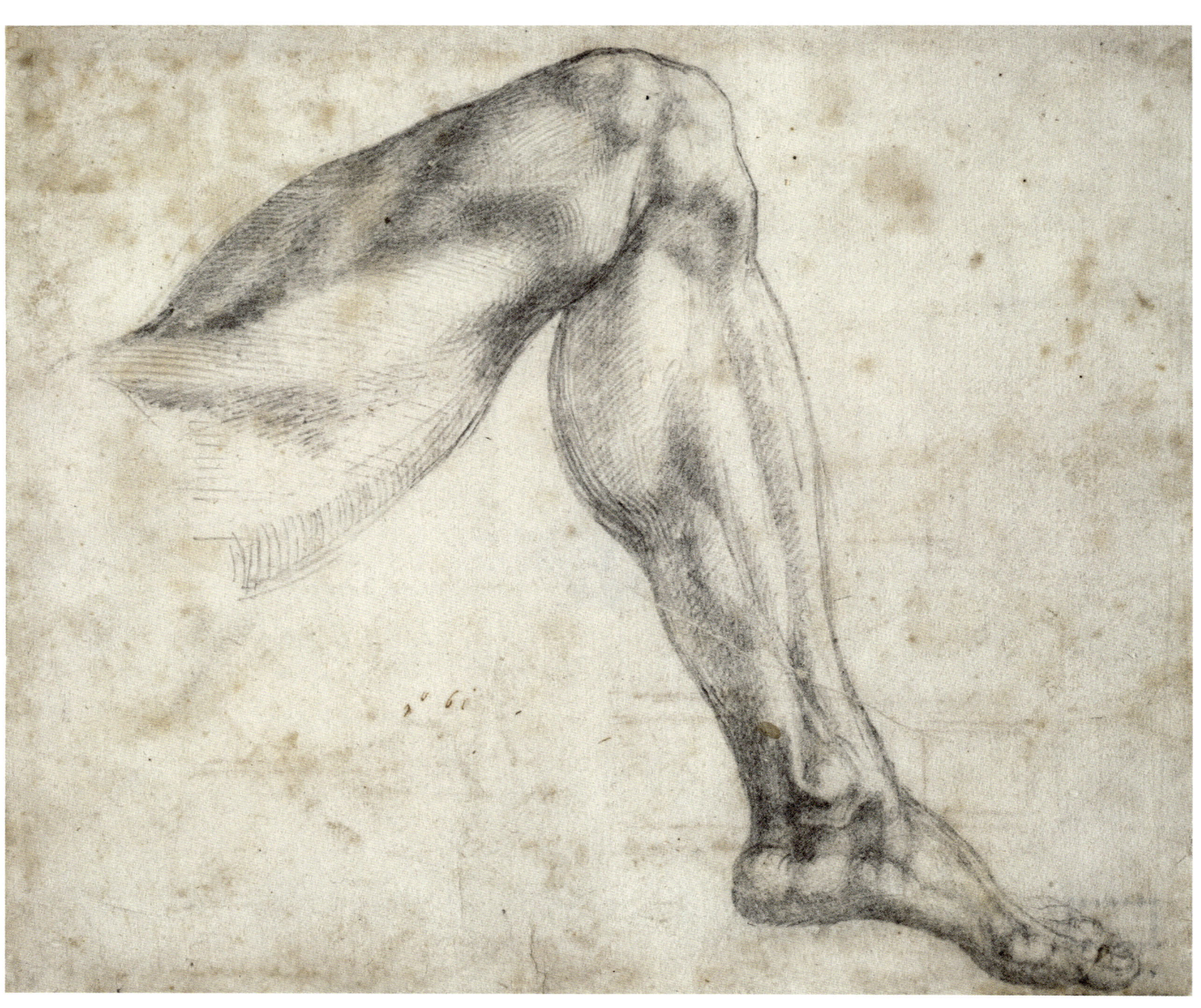

fig. 88   (cat. 29) Michelangelo, *Study of a Left Leg for the Sculpture of* Day, 1524. Black chalk, 207 x 247 mm. Haarlem, Teylers Museum, inv. A 033

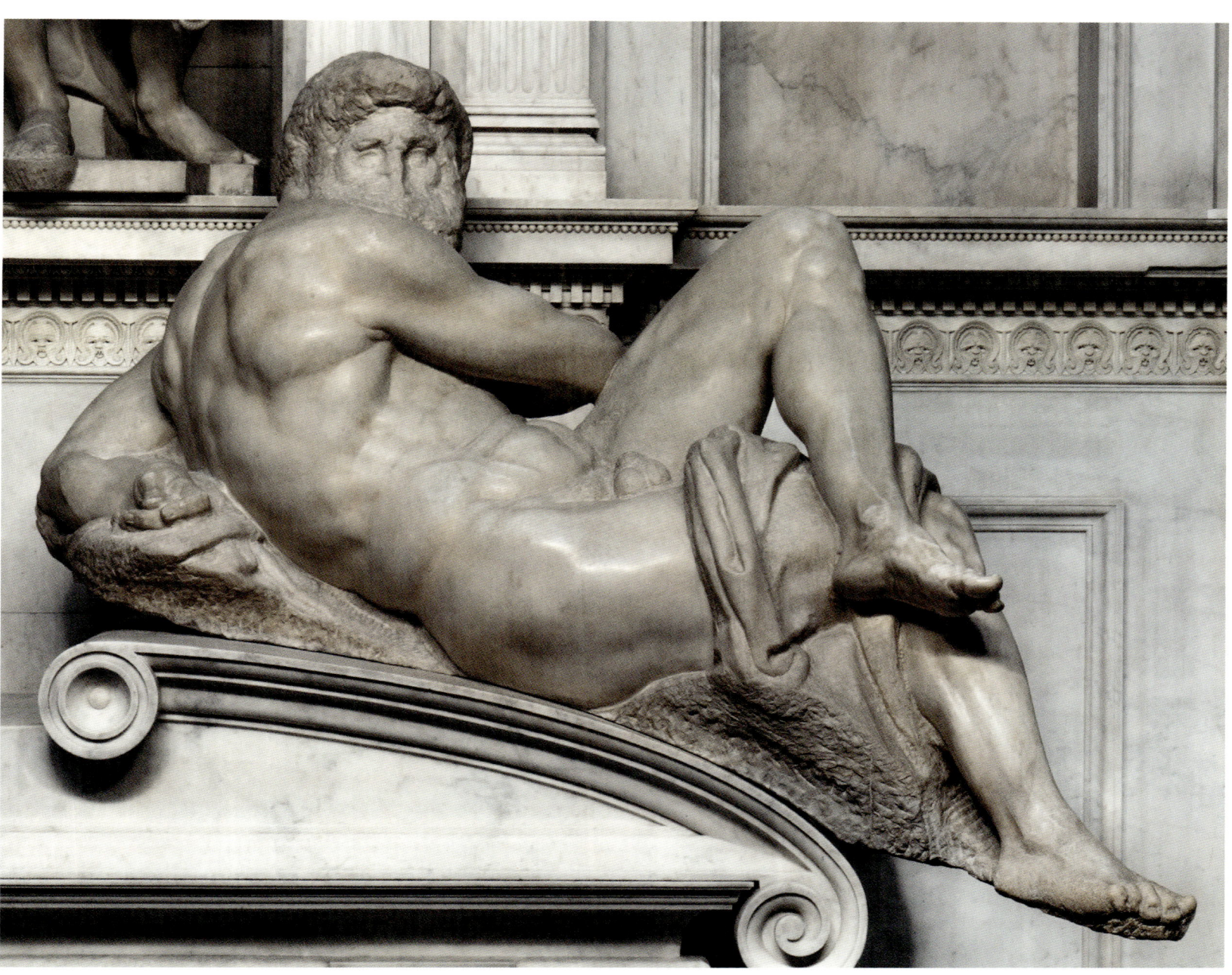

fig. 89   Michelangelo, *Day*, c. 1524–1534. Marble, length 185 cm. Florence, San Lorenzo, Medici Chapel

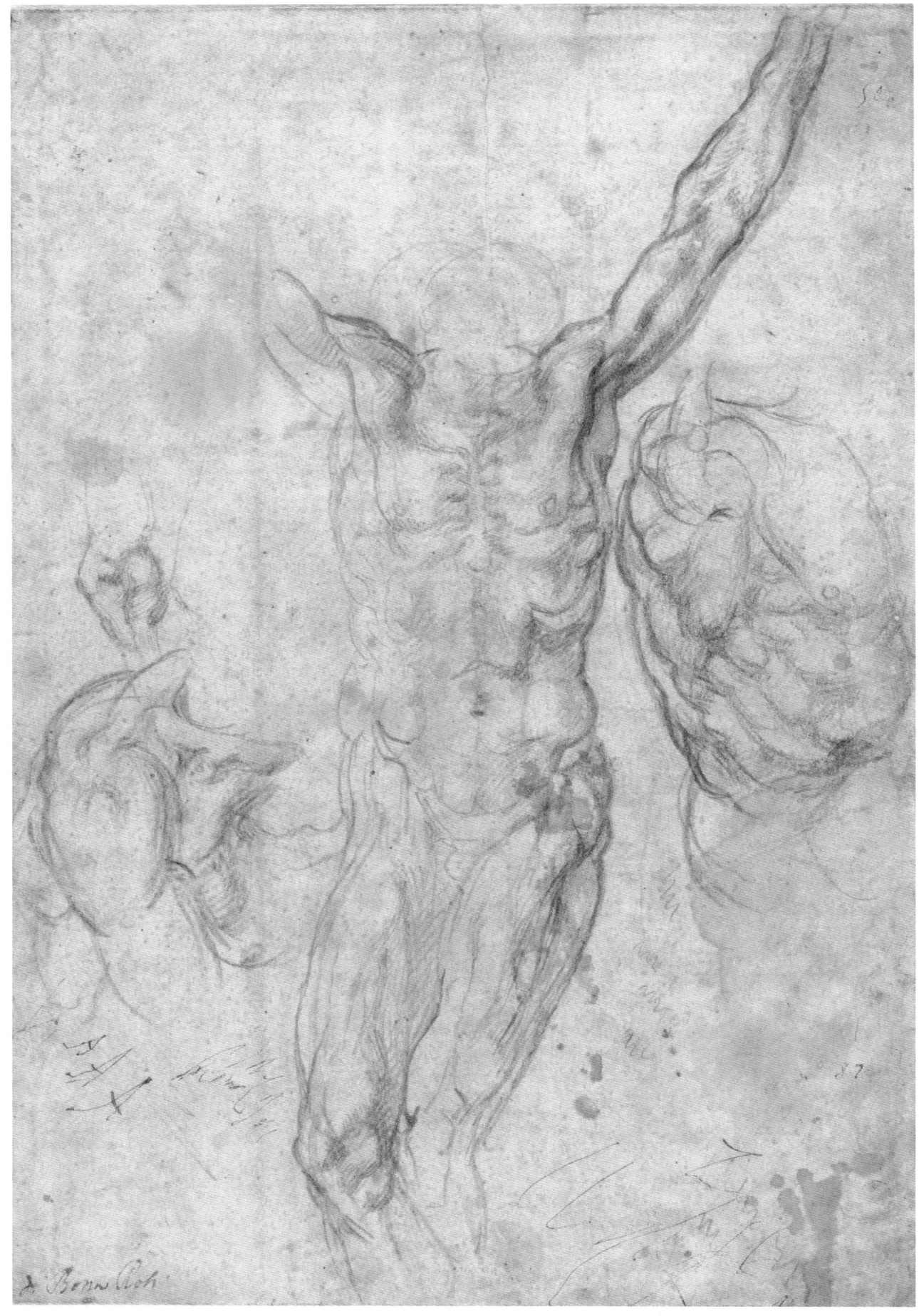

fig. 90   (cat. 41) Michelangelo, *Studies for a Crucifixion,* c. 1530–1536. Black chalk, 331 x 229 mm. Haarlem, Teylers Museum, inv. A 034

their presence. By pushing anatomical detail to its limits in this way, Michelangelo invited not only admiration but also disapproval, as noted earlier.

Body and Mind, Visible and Invisible

According to Vasari, in addition to the human body, Michelangelo intended to depict in *The Last Judgement* 'the play of the passions and contentments of the soul'.[58] Given the circumstances, one can understand why the bodies of the dead are so tensed: the souls being carried off to hell, for instance, struggle vainly to escape their fate. The fresco offers a clear demonstration that the '*atti e gesti humani*' (human movements and gestures) transcend the physical and also express the movements of the soul. A similar connection could already be found in Michelangelo's earlier work, for instance in the depiction of the male body in the *Battle of Cascina* (fig. 133/cat. 51).[59] The soldiers' fear and confusion are evident from the anatomy of their agitated postures, as Vasari aptly put it in his description of the elderly combatant in the right foreground:

> '...and hearing the cries and tumult of the soldiers and the uproar of the drummers, he was struggling to draw on one stocking by force; and, besides that all the muscles and nerves of his figure could be perceived, his mouth was so distorted as to show clearly how he was straining and struggling even to the very tips of his toes.'[60]

Another motif of which Michelangelo understood the emotional effect well was the way in which the neck muscles tense when the head is tilted upwards – a pose we find in his anatomical drawings (fig. 79, for example). He had already used it in his *Studies for Haman for the Sistine Chapel Ceiling* (fig. 62/cat. 15), in which the tension of the chest and neck muscles reveals the figure's inner torment. The *Dying Captive* (fig. 86) displays his neck in a similar manner.

There is more to anatomy, therefore, than simply depicting the human body. Vasari sought to express this added value when he wrote that the artists of Michelangelo's generation set themselves apart from their predecessors by demonstrating a fluidity and naturalness in their *disegno* (the drawing and design of their figures), which lay somewhere 'between the seen and the unseen' (*fra 'l vedi e non vedi*).[61] Although this 'unseen' is open to numerous interpretations, it seems closely connected to the study of anatomy. It denotes the anatomical reality that is obscured from view by the skin, which imbues the artist's representation of the body with a sense of agility

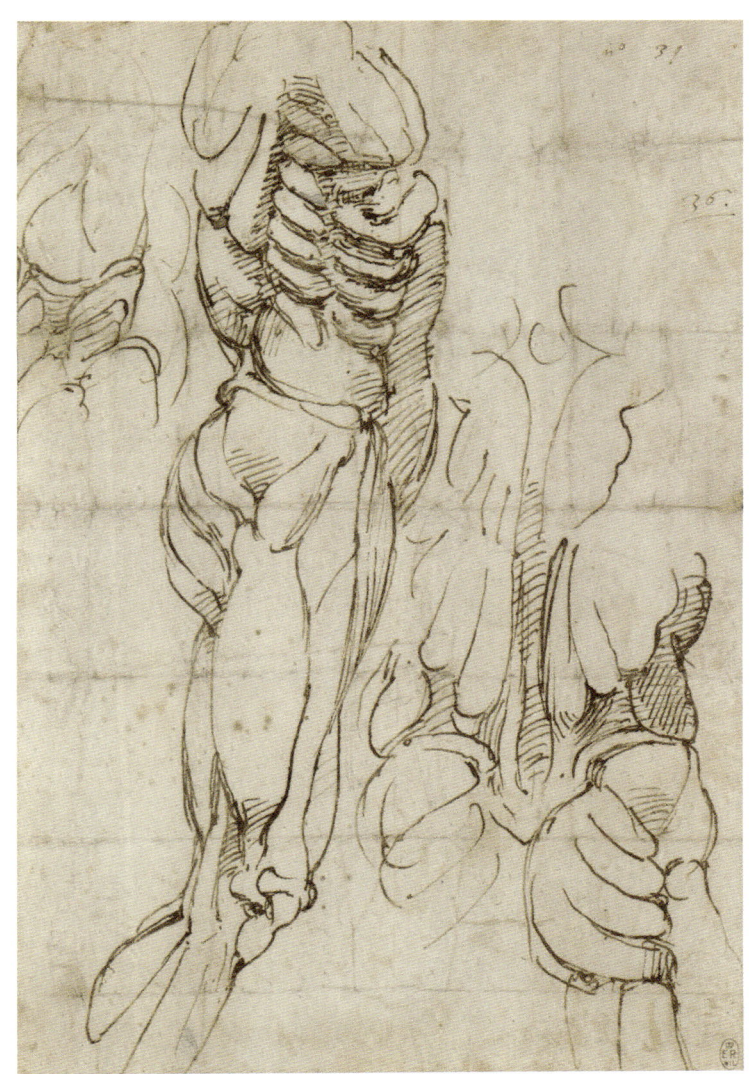

fig. 91   Attributed to Michelangelo, *Anatomical Studies*, c. 1520–1530. Pen and brown ink, 283 x 190 mm. Windsor, Royal Collection Trust, inv. RCIN 990474

141

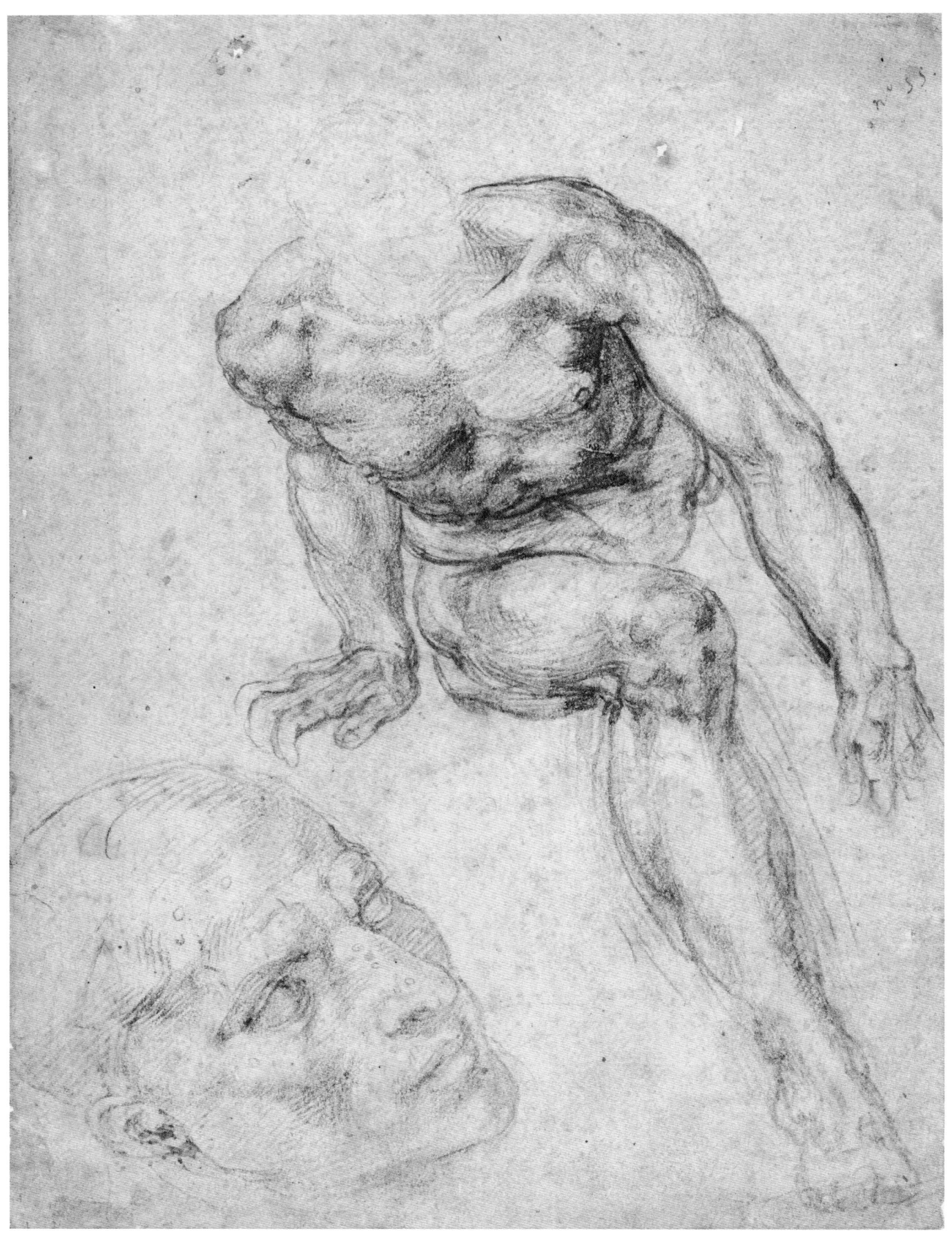

fig. 92   (cat. 46) Michelangelo, *Studies for Saint Lawrence for the* Last Judgement, c. 1534–1538. Black chalk, 242 x 182 mm. Haarlem, Teylers Museum, inv. A 023

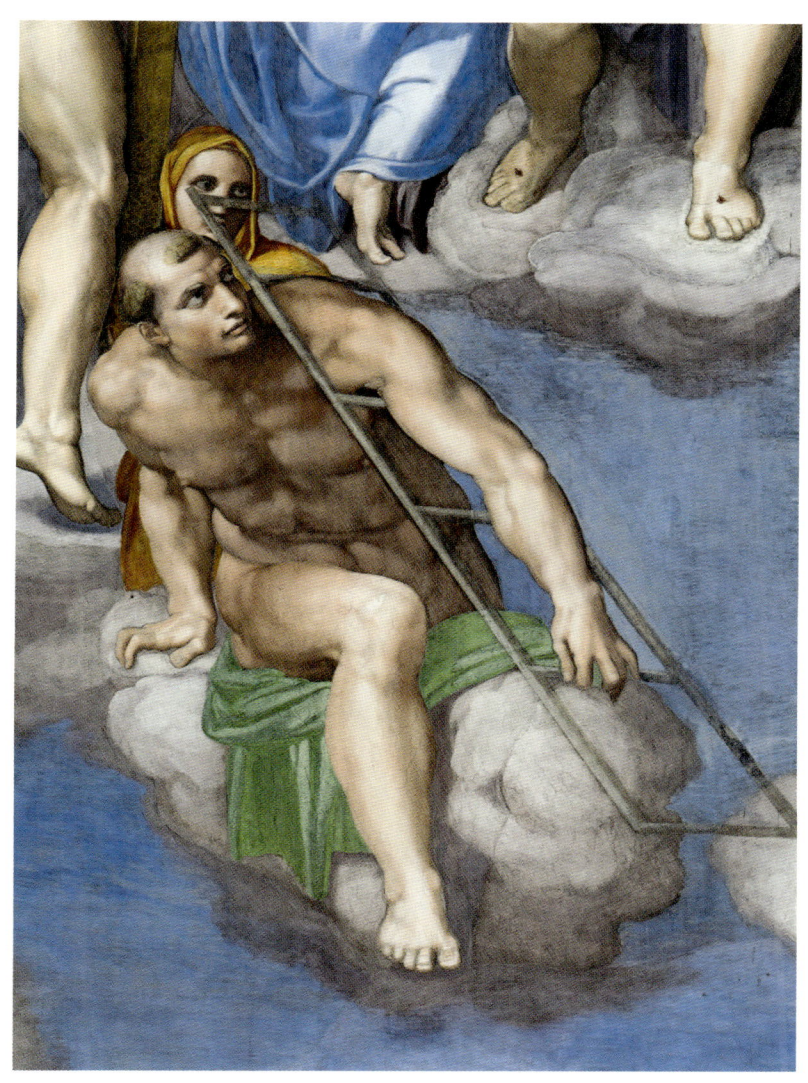

and lifelikeness. Visible anatomical details also express invisible psychological tension, making his figures seem truly animated. In this way, anatomical study adds a certain grace that is not visible yet can be sensed intuitively.

But the quality 'between the seen and the unseen' also alludes to a more abstract form of knowledge, acquired when the artist studies the interior of God's most perfect creature. After all, by opening up the body one uncovers the design of the Creator, the 'First Artist', who wrought living beings from nothing. Vasari therefore argued that the most important result of Michelangelo's initial anatomical study was that he 'began to perfect his *disegno*'.[62] This notion is less concerned with what the artist depicts and more with how he works. His knowledge of the inner structure of the human body affords him direct access to this divine paradigm in which the most perfect method of design is encapsulated. After subdividing the body into separate elements and studying individual limbs in his anatomical drawings, he can subsequently re-unite the parts to create a whole range of new bodies and poses.[63] In this way, anatomical study paves the way for a new vision of what it means to be an artist, in which creation prevails over imitation. The ideal male body now emerges from a metaphysical idea in the artist's mind rather than from the faithful imitation of observed reality through his hand. Michelangelo's previously quoted comment about 'the compasses in the eyes' aptly alludes to this way of thinking. Thus, the artist assumes a godlike role as the creator of new bodies.[64] Nowhere is this parallel expressed so poetically as in Vasari's description of Michelangelo's *Moses.*

From Death to Life

The sculpture of *Moses* (fig. 95) marks the culmination of Michelangelo's study of the '*atti e gesti humani*'. In many respects, it is the most complete embodiment of his work as an artist–anatomist. Michelangelo represents Moses on the verge of motion. The prophet turns his head suddenly to the left and prepares to stand, as if something has caught his attention. The Tablets of Stone are gripped beneath his muscular right arm, while his hands toy with his beard. He stares gravely at what has disturbed him. Condivi describes how Moses' face was filled with so much emotion that the image evoked 'both love and terror'.[65] According to Vasari, he has the expression of one who has just gazed upon the true face of God and has been profoundly affected by His sanctity.[66] This psychological tension finds expression in the muscular arms with their swollen veins and taut tendons. As he sculpted the left arm, Michelangelo was assisted by the aforementioned anatomical drawing of a tensed arm (fig. 80/cat. 21), which is virtually identical to the statue.[67] He will undoubtedly have made equally detailed studies for Moses' right hand, toying with his beard,

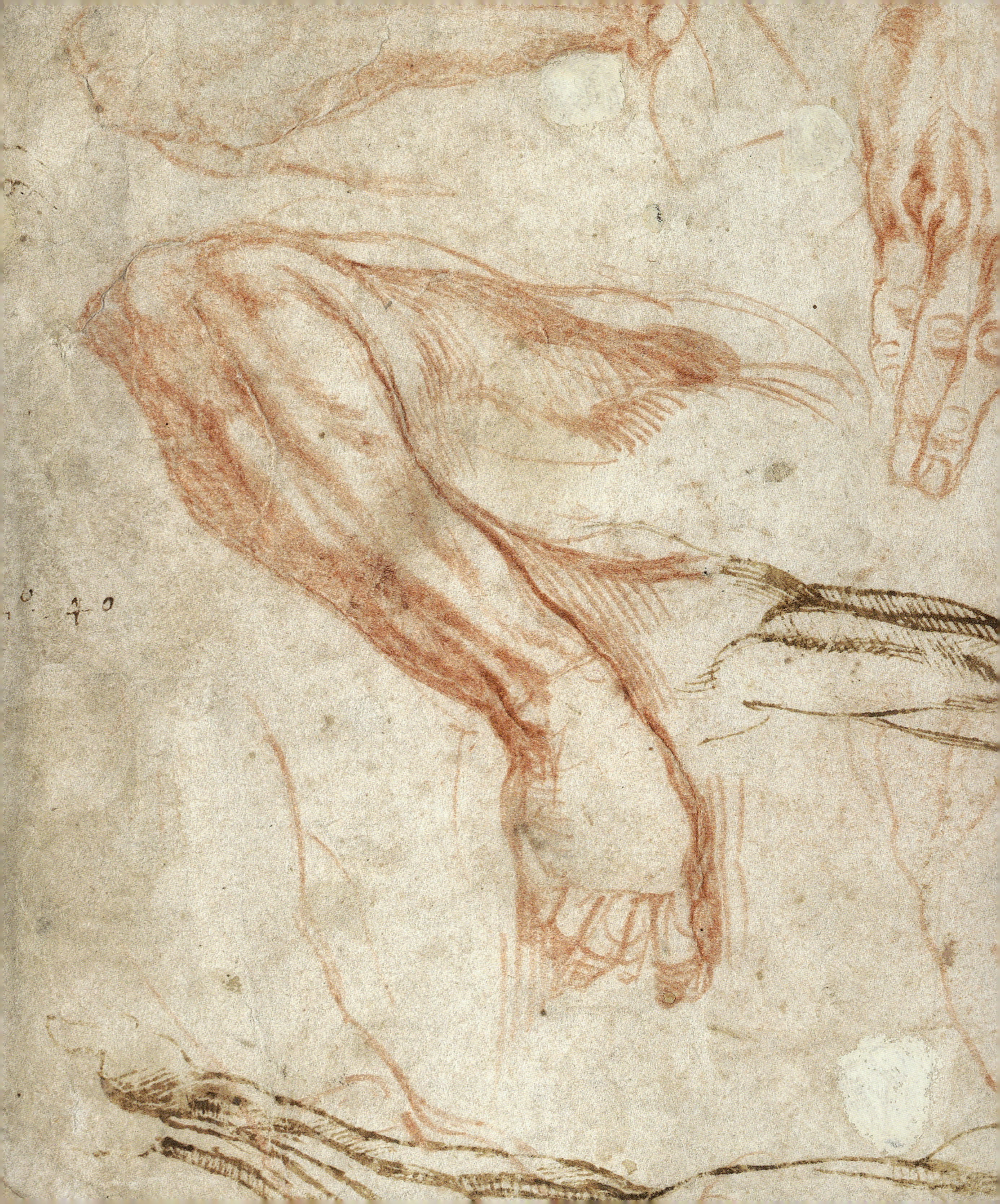

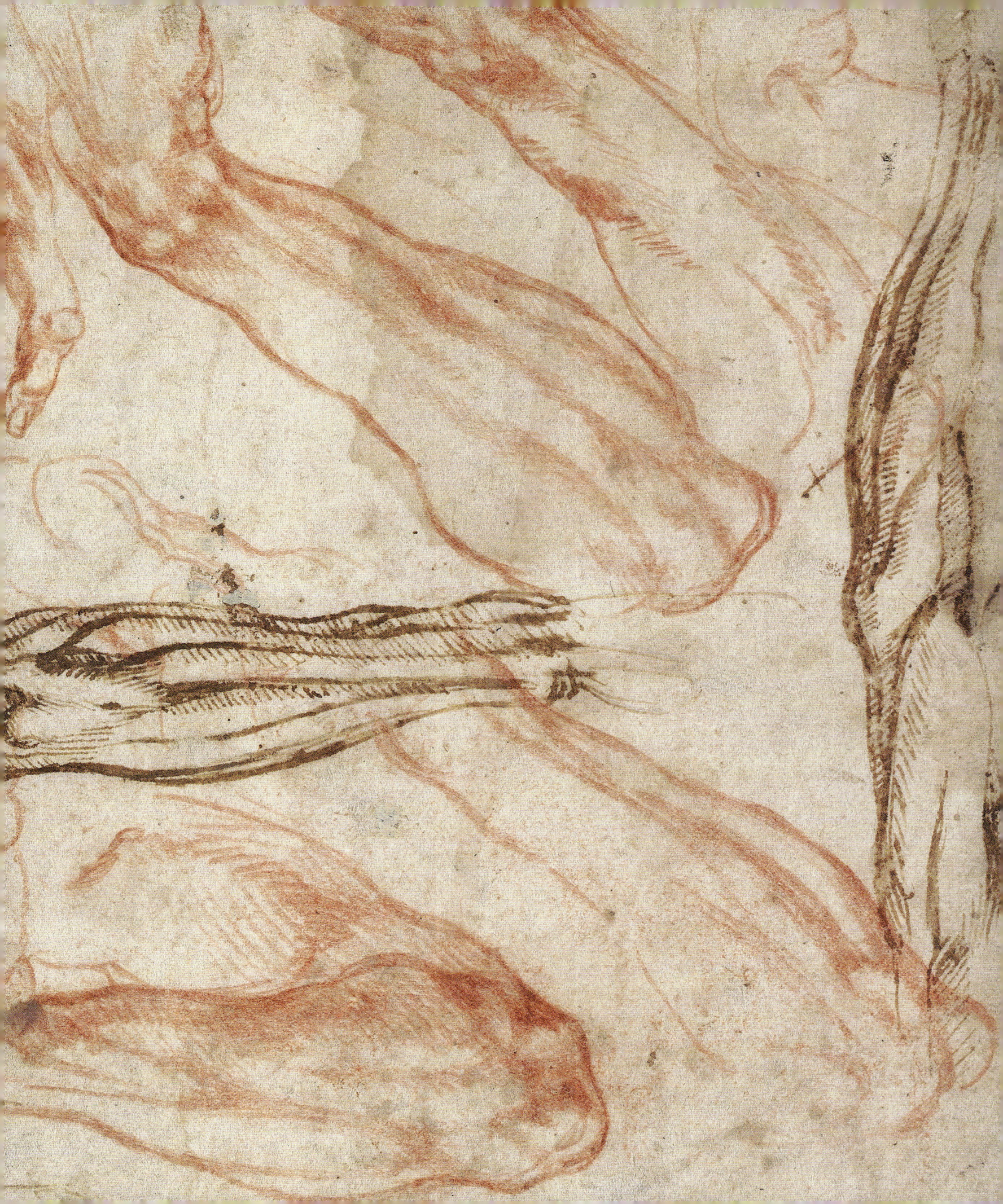

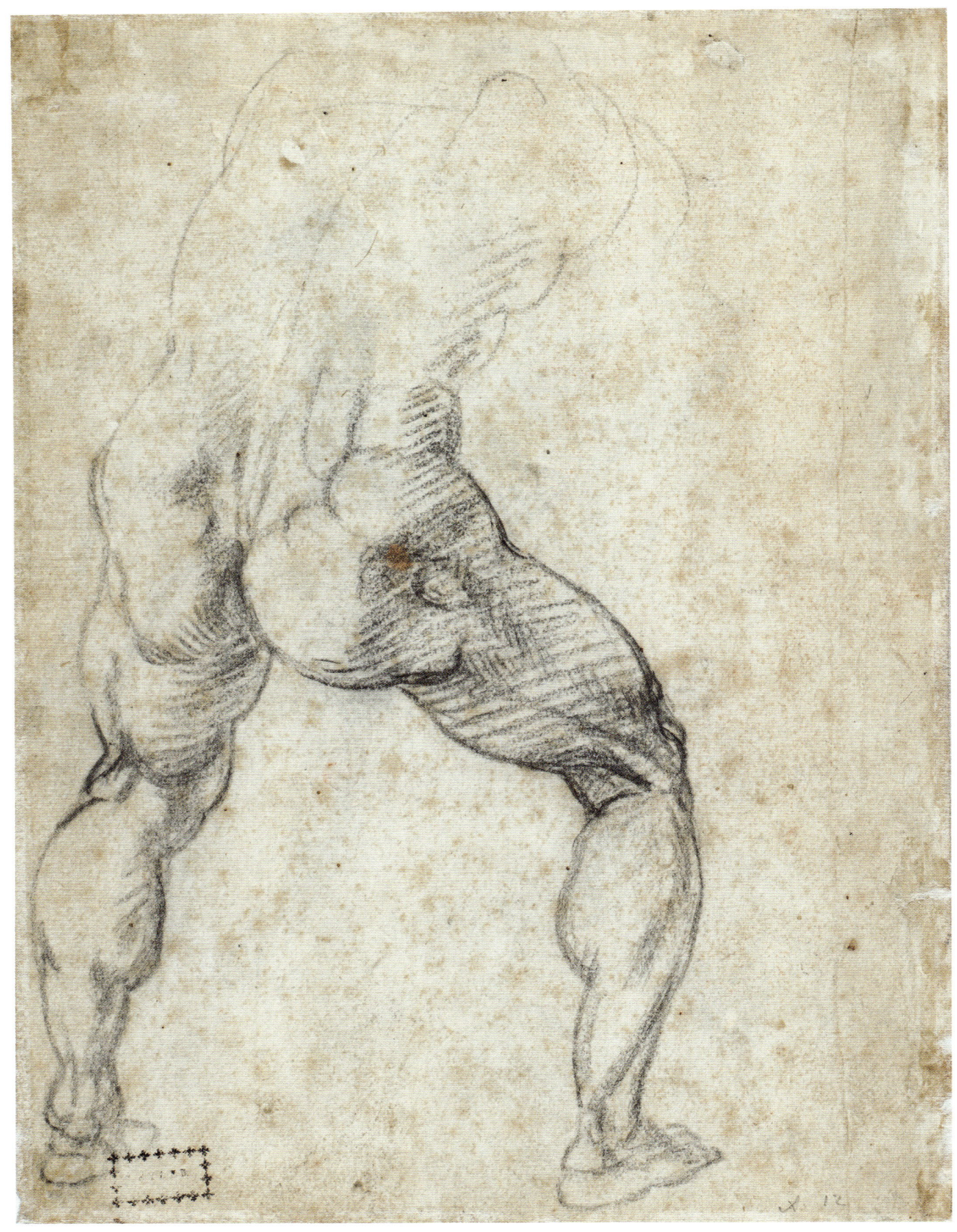

fig. 94   (cat. 46v) Michelangelo, *Study of a Male Nude from the Back*, c. 1534–1538. Black chalk, 242 x 182 mm. Haarlem, Teylers Museum, inv. A 023v

as those for the hand of the *Dying Captive* (fig. 85/cat. 20 and fig. 87).[68] In this case, however, Michelangelo did choose to sculpt these anatomical details. So exact is his observation of anatomy that he does not even overlook the tiny muscle (the *extensor digiti minimis*) with which Moses raises his right little finger.[69] It is thanks to Michelangelo's knowledge of the knee joint, moreover, that the prophet seems on the brink of rising from his seat.

Vasari specifically praised the statue's limbs for their anatomy: 'the arms with their muscles, and the hands with their bones and nerves, are carried to such a pitch of beauty and perfection, and the legs, knees and feet are covered with buskins beautifully fashioned'. No other male body in Michelangelo's oeuvre elicits such high praise from him:

> 'Every part of the work is so finished, that Moses may be called now more than ever the friend of God, seeing that He has deigned to assemble together and prepare his body for the Resurrection before that of any other, by the hands of Michelangelo.'[70]

The perfection with which Michelangelo shaped Moses' body, based on anatomical studies on paper, is compared here to the creative power with which God will one day bestow new, perfect bodies on the resurrected dead. The liveliness of the sculpted body, so highly praised by Vasari, is – paradoxically – made possible only through Michelangelo's study of dead bodies. Working from human remains, he conjures new bodies into life on paper, in paint or in marble. In this way, Michelangelo delved below the skin of the male body to find the essence of his artistry.

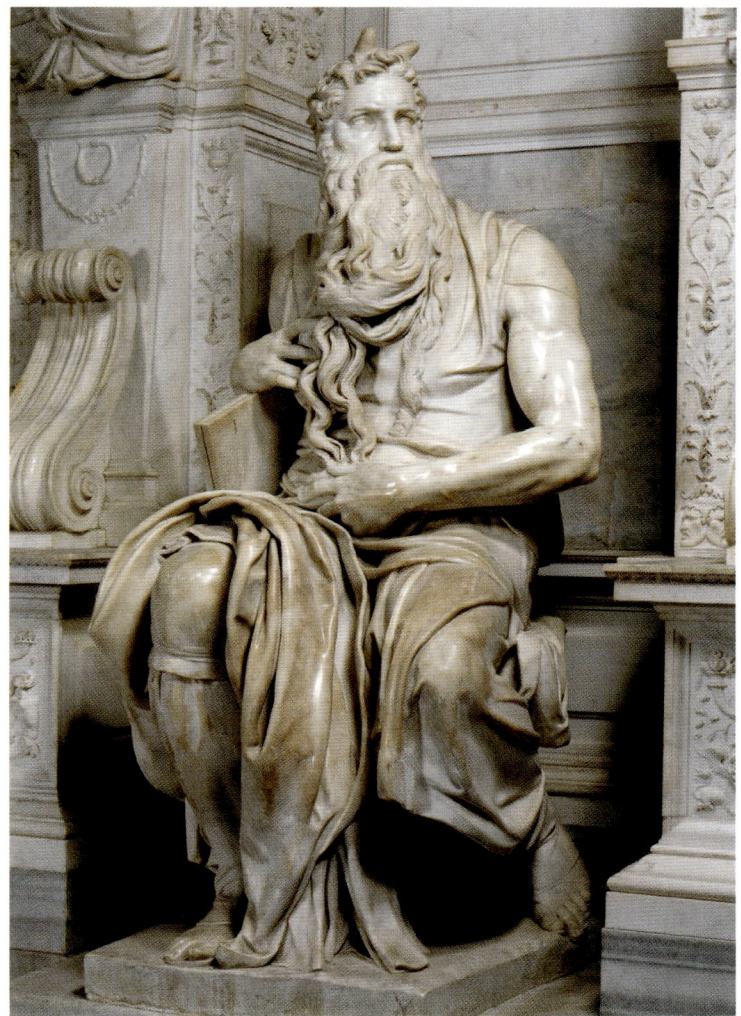

fig. 95   Michelangelo, *Moses*, c. 1513–1516. Marble, height 247 cm. Rome, San Pietro in Vincoli

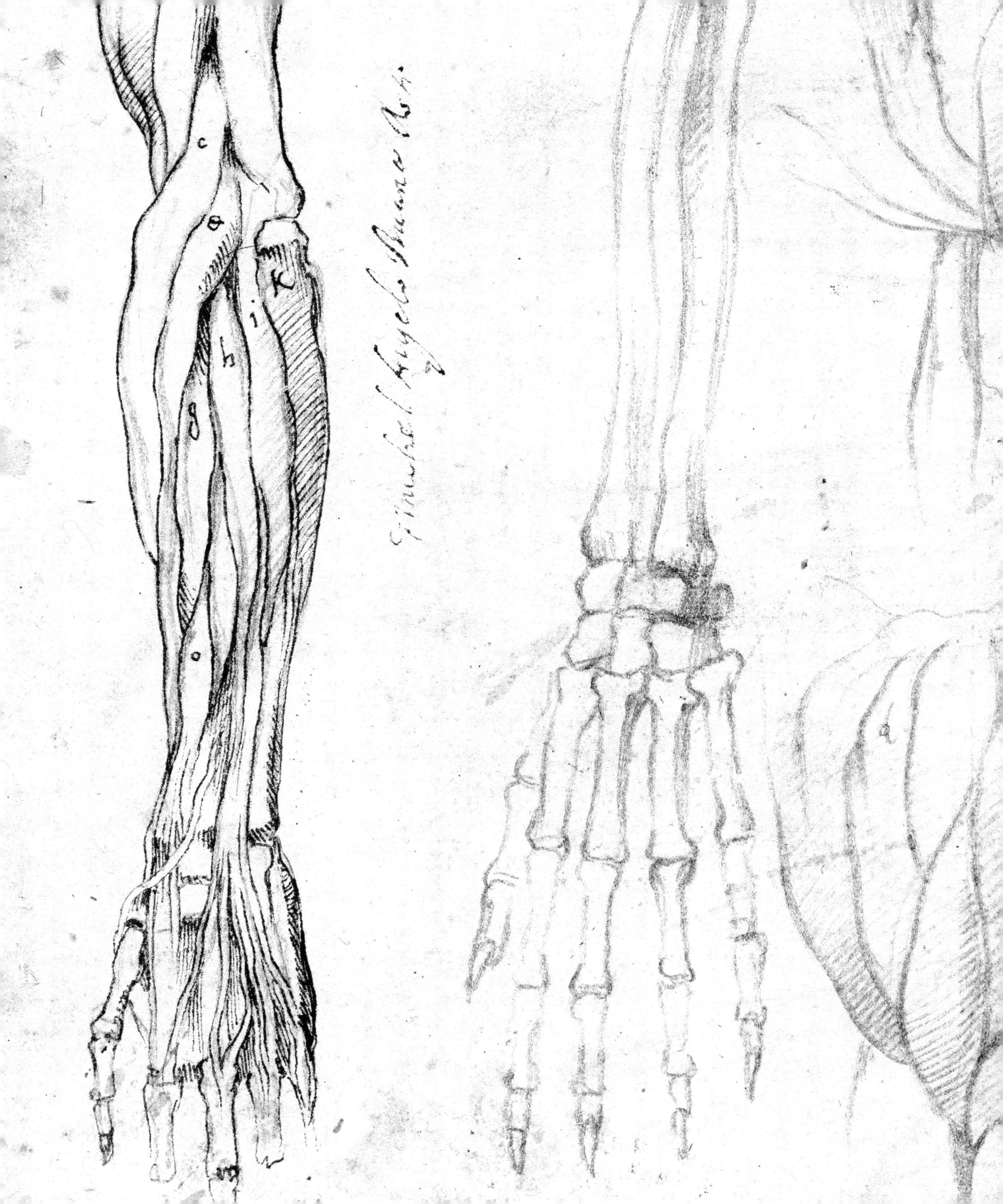

Gezeichnet Angelo Bruné 1809.

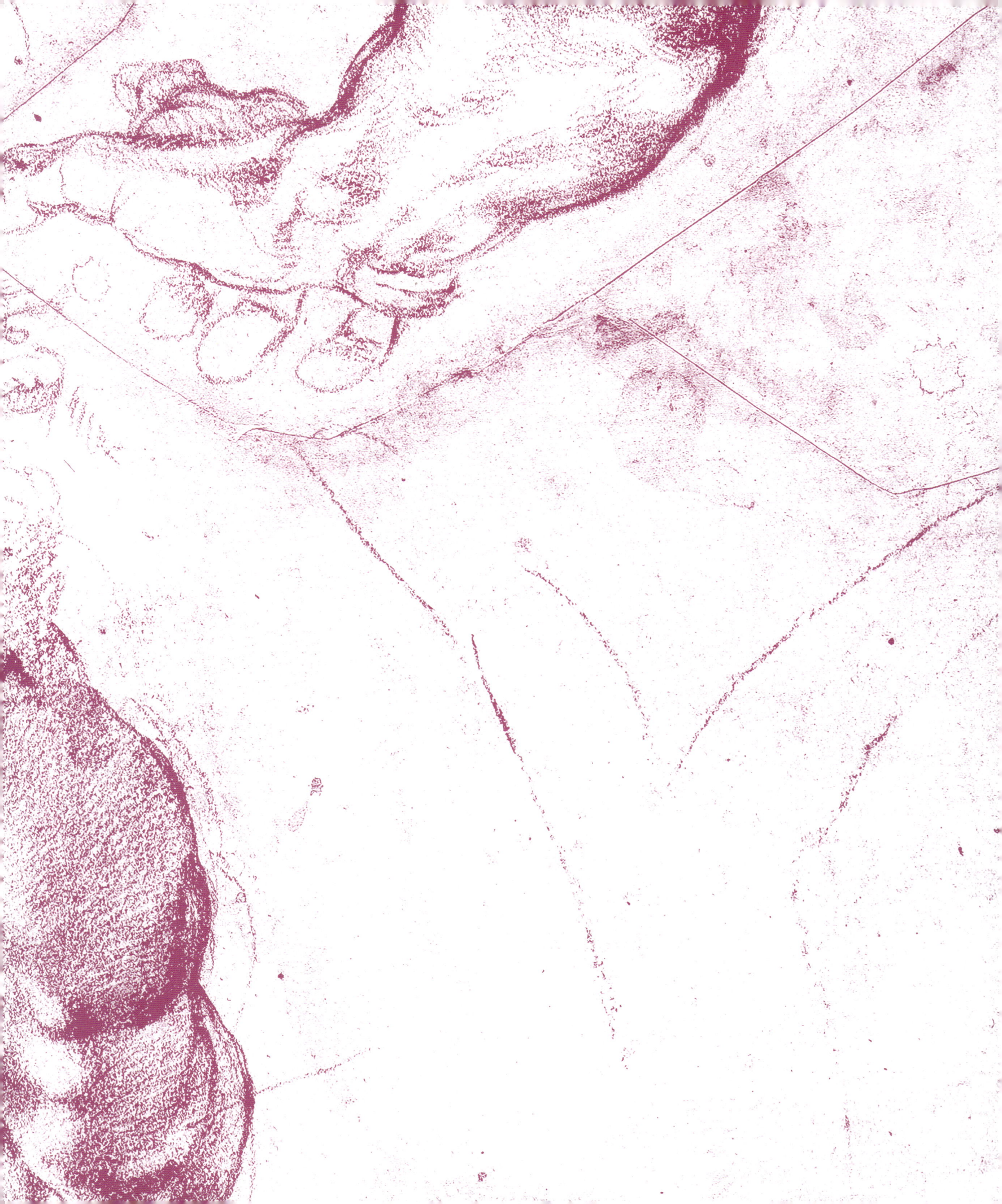

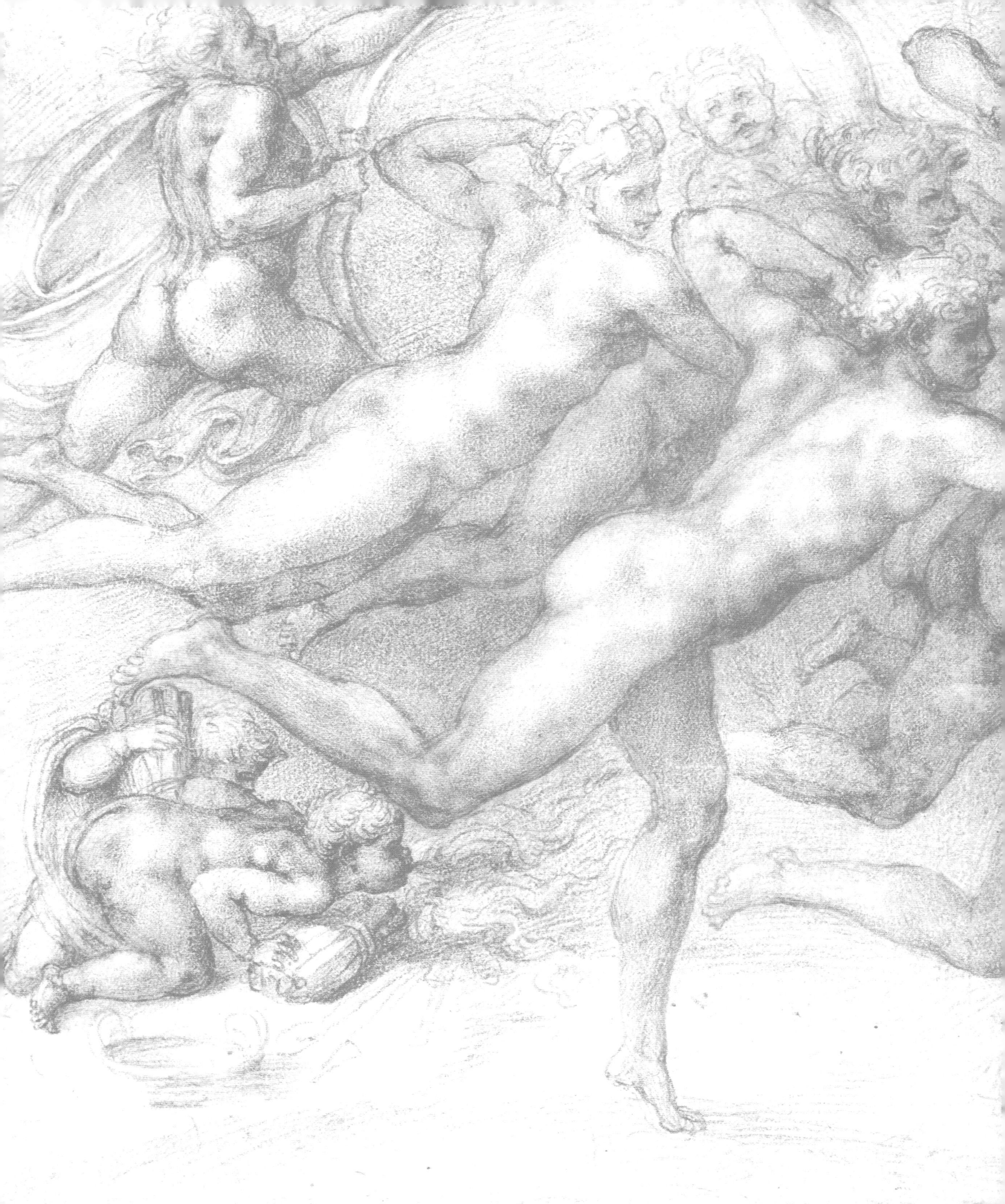

Mind

"L'un tira al cielo, e l'altro in terra tira;
nell'alma l'un, l'altr'abita ne' sensi,
e l'arco tira a cose basse e vile."

'One [love] draws towards heaven, the other draws down to earth;
one dwells in the soul, the other in the senses,
and draws its bow at base and vile things.'

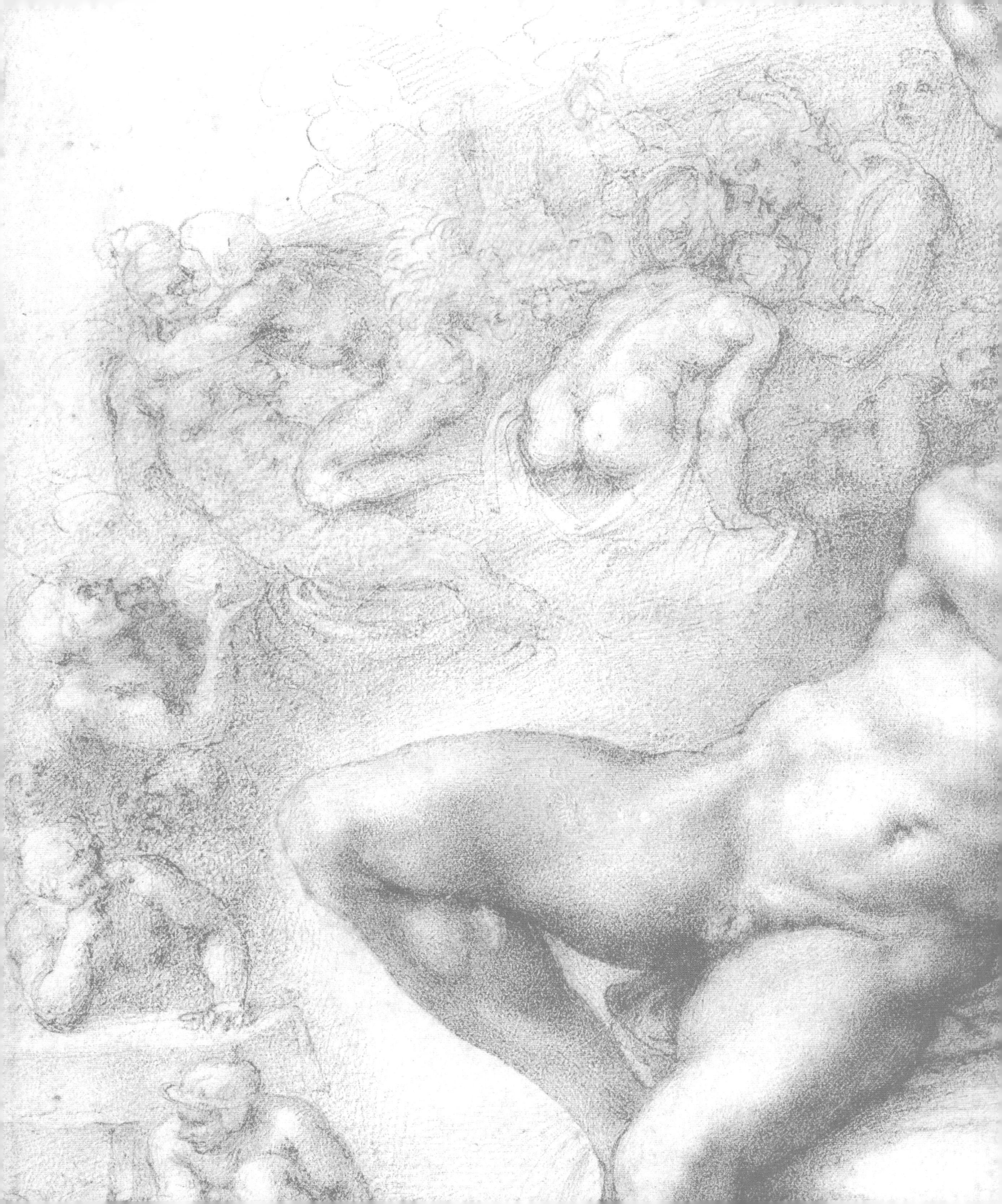

Michelangelo, Neoplatonism and the Idealised Body

Marieke van den Doel

In March 2023, the principal of Tallahassee Classical School in Florida, Hope Carrasquilla, resigned after pupils in a lesson on Renaissance art had been shown Michelangelo's statue of the biblical figure David (fig. 1), prompting parents to complain that children had been exposed to pornography.[1] Although nudity often appeared in Renaissance art, and many free-standing nude sculptures and monumental paintings with naked figures were produced in this period,[2] during Michelangelo's lifetime, a certain discomfort can already be observed towards the lavish nudity in his work. During a visit to *The Last Judgement* in the Sistine Chapel to see the progress of the work, Biagio da Cesena, Papal Master of Ceremonies, told Pope Paul III that: 'it was very disgraceful that in such a sacred place were depicted all those naked figures, exposing themselves so shamefully, and that it was not a work for a papal chapel, but rather for the public baths and taverns'.[3] Giorgio Vasari describes how Michelangelo then depicted the master of ceremonies, naked, among the inhabitants of hell, with donkey ears, referring to King Midas's bad art judgement (fig. 96). After Michelangelo's death in 1564, his former pupil Daniele da Volterra was sent to paint over the genitals in the fresco with draperies, which earned him the nickname '*il braghettone*' (the breeches painter). Criticism by adherents of the Counter-Reformation had clearly now become predominant.

Although not entirely absent in previous centuries, the return of the nude body in art was certainly related to the desire to revive classical art, and antiquity in a broader sense. In the course of the fourteenth, fifteenth and sixteenth centuries, an increasing number of activities was undertaken towards this goal. Humanists rediscovered and translated classical texts and tried to align the contents of these sources with Christian doctrine. Antiquarians studied and collected objects from the past, and artists revived the essence of classical art by combining textual sources with newly acquired knowledge about the visual and material culture of antiquity.[4]

These developments did not occur independently of each other. The interaction between humanists' discoveries and translations and artists' innovations resulted in a growing interest in philosophical matters, and for the first time artists posed the question: what is art?[5] In return, the blossoming of the arts must have had an impact on the visual orientation of the philosophical ideas of the age. As we shall see, the glorification of the ideal and nude body in Michelangelo's work was embedded in such philosophical discussions.

To explain this, we must first elaborate on the ideas of Renaissance philosopher Marsilio Ficino (fig. 97), a humanist in the service of the Medici family in Florence. Ficino, a brilliant scholar, led a relatively quiet life but maintained an extensive network of fellow humanists, students and patrons.[6] As a young man, he was commissioned by Cosimo de' Medici to translate Plato's texts, as well as the text fragments from late antiquity known as the *Corpus Hermeticum* (translation 1463). Later in his life, he translated and wrote commentaries on the works of Plotinus and other classical Neoplatonists, such as Synesius, Iamblichus and Proclus. Some of Ficino's works, including *De Amore* (On Love) (1469), a commentary on Plato's *Symposium*, and *De vita libri tres* (Three Books on Life) (1489), had been widely read for a long time. In these works, and in the eighteen-volume *Platonic Theology* (1482), he expounded his ideas on the power of imagination, human creativity and divine inspiration. Beauty, and the ascension of the human soul it inspires, a notion borrowed from the Platonic tradition, are recurrent themes in his work. In addition, the powers of sight and the imagination are highly valued in Ficino's oeuvre and, although often denied, his philosophy is strongly visually oriented.[7] Art historians have hotly debated the possible relationship between Ficino's thought and Italian Renaissance works of art.[8] This essay is an attempt to contribute to this discussion by demonstrating the influence of Ficino's thought, and that of his pupil Diacceto, on two of Michelangelo's draw-

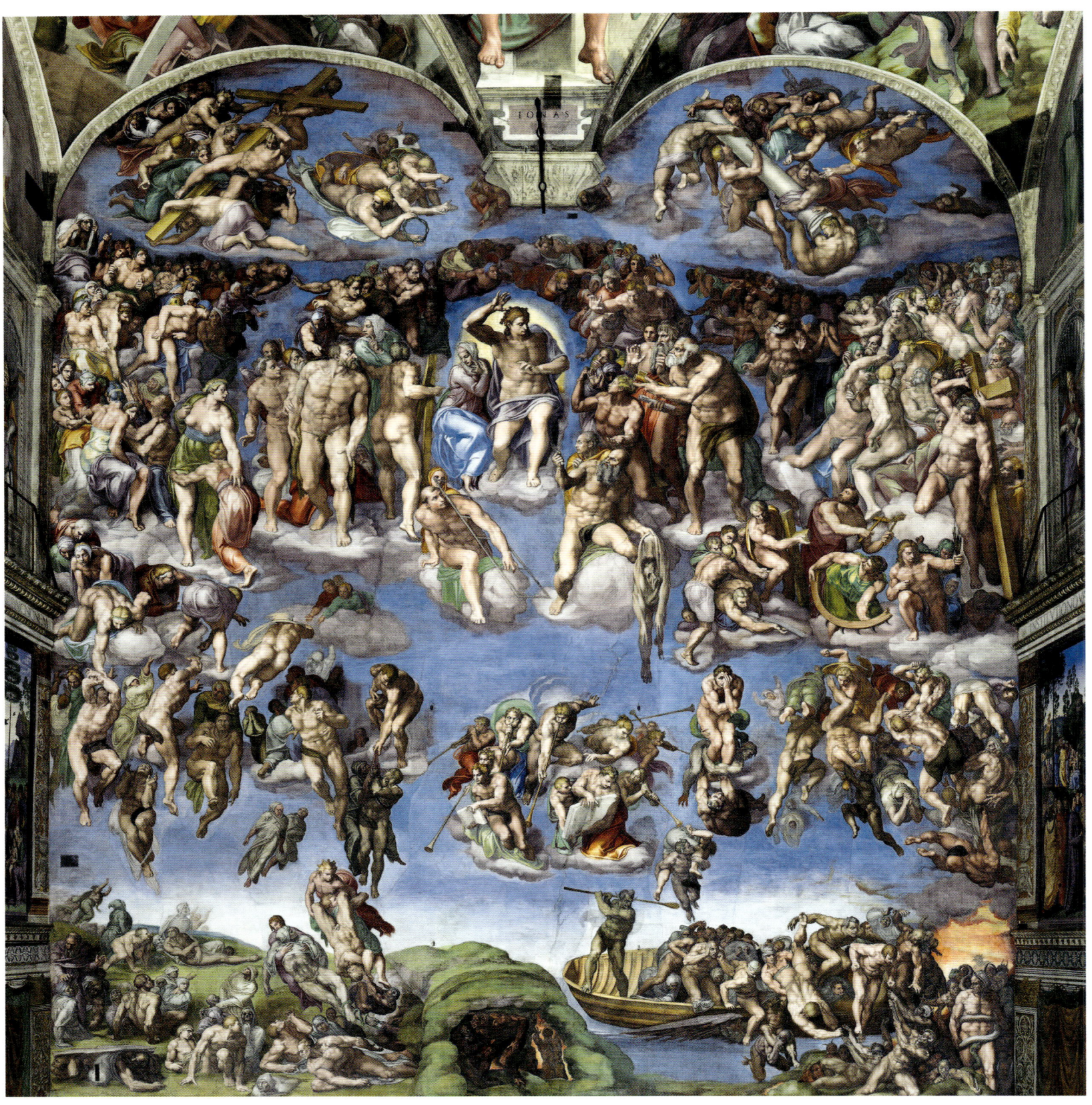

fig. 96   Michelangelo, *The Last Judgement*, 1536–1541. Fresco. Vatican City, Sistine Chapel

ings: *The Dream* and *Archers Shooting at a Herm* (figs 101/cat. 44 and 106).

Michelangelo and Neoplatonism

At an early age, Michelangelo may already have become acquainted with Platonist thought when he became part of Lorenzo the Magnificent's household. There, the ideas of Ficino circulated, and the young Michelangelo could even have met the old man himself. Michelangelo's interest in theories of Platonic love is furthermore shown in his authorised biography by Ascanio Condivi, who would tone down the gossip regarding Michelangelo's 'homosexuality' (or his interest in '*amore masculino*').[9] Condivi says that Michelangelo talked much about love, but not otherwise than described in the works of Plato. After 1516, Michelangelo's Platonism may have intensified, when he became a member of the Accademia Sacra Medicea in Rome.[10] There, he would have met Giovanni Corsi, who became a biographer of Ficino, and Francesco Cattani da Diacceto, Ficino's favourite pupil. The most import-

ant document testifying to the existence of this academy is a petition sent to Pope Leo X in 1519 by its members, including Diacceto, Corsi and Michelangelo (fig. 98); Michelangelo is the only one to sign in Italian rather than Latin, with '*Io, Michelangelo, scultore*' (I, Michelangelo, sculptor).[11]

It was possibly through contact with Diacceto, his *Panegirico all'Amore* (Panegyric to Love) published in Rome in 1526, and his adaptation of Ficino's *De Amore* (in Italian and not in Ficino's Latin), that Platonic thought permeated Michelangelo's artistic work. Diacceto's *I tre libri d'Amore* – on which he worked between 1508 and 1511 – probably circulated long before the publication of the *Panegirico* in 1561. This text can be regarded as a sort of early modern version of a 'Platonic love for dummies'; that is, Diacceto explains clearly, and in Italian, the theory of Platonic love. In short, it is about how non-physical love can lead to divine inspiration. Diacceto provides, in a few short chapters, an overview of Ficinian theories of love, beauty and inspiration. It is precisely this amalgamation of Platonic love, inspiration and the role of imagination that is important for understanding the artistic statements visualised

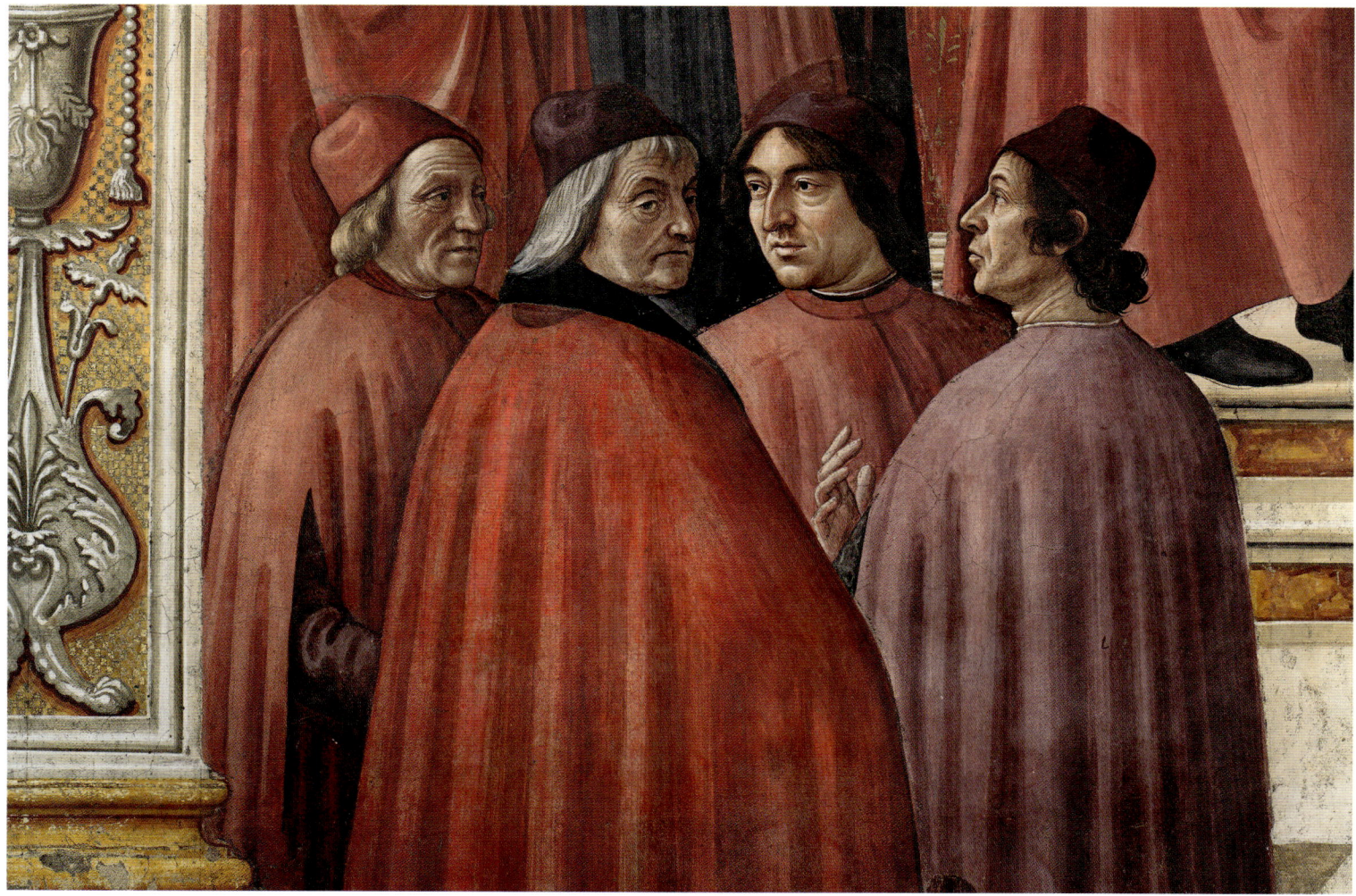

fig. 97   Domenico Ghirlandaio, *Annunciation to Zacharias* (detail with four Florentine philosophers, Ficino is at the far left), c. 1485–1490. Fresco. Florence, Santa Maria Novella, Tornabuoni Chapel

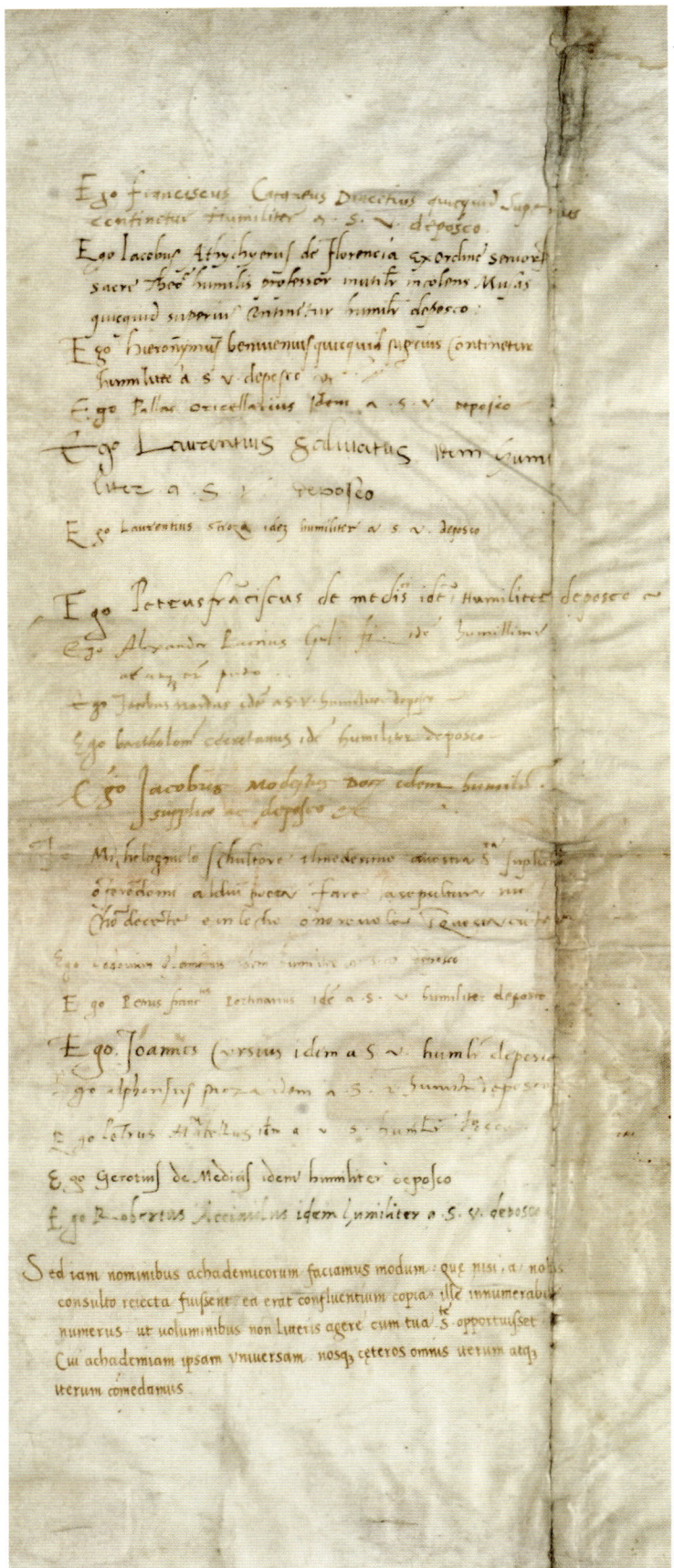

in the two drawings by Michelangelo, as well as their function as refined gifts of love.

Ficino and the Imagination

Ficino worked on the subject of imagination in the thirteenth book of *Platonic Theology*, in which he set out to prove the divinity of the soul by showing what power the imagination, as a faculty of the soul, has over the body. According to Ficino, our imagination alone can make us blush, faint, or induce nausea or sexual desire. And not only our own bodies can be affected. During pregnancy, a mother's imagination, for example, can determine the child's appearance.[12] A strong imagination can make other people sick or fall in love, and it can be the medium through which one can cause natural disasters and receive future-predictive dreams.[13]

According to an Aristotelian tradition, the imagination or fantasy is a faculty of knowledge that stands between the senses and the intellect. Together with the 'common sense' (*sensus communis*) and memory, it belongs to the so-called 'interior senses'.[14] These interior senses were thought to be located in the three 'ventricles of the brain', in which the imagination, along with the *sensus communis*, would have been located at the front of the head (fig. 99). The imagination, then, forms a link between sense perception and intellect. The soul, it was assumed, could not think other than in images or so-called *phantasmata*.[15] Therefore, the fantasy transforms the sensory impressions perceived by the body into these phantasms with which they can be visualised, thought or remembered in the soul.

Sensory impressions were transported from the senses to the soul by means of the *spiritus* or *pneuma,* a semi-material, vaporous substance composed of the same matter as the stars. This *spiritus* is also the instrument by which *phantasmata* are conducted through the soul and by which the soul communicates with the body and causes it to perform all vital activities. Plato states in the *Phaedrus* that the imagination, which is connected to the body as well as to the soul, can drag the soul into the material world through the sensory impressions perceived by the body. On the other hand, by perceiving or imagining earthly beauty, the soul can be reminded of the heavenly beauty of the Ideas and thereby enter a state of *furor* (frenzy), allowing it to fly back to its 'heavenly homeland'.[16]

In summary, it is precisely the beauty of the earthly, visible world – and it can be the beauty of bodies – which reminds humans of the immutable beauty of the world of Ideas. This reminder triggers man's desire to return to this divine realm. In the *furor* that arises, the soul detaches itself from the body and becomes divinely inspired. This line of thinking forms a philosophical basis for the idealised bodies depicted in Michelangelo's work: a beautiful body that triggers divine inspiration. The inspiration resulting from visual experiences, however, cannot always be understood rationally. In his *Timaeus*, Plato states that by means of *furor*, man can be divinely inspired, but nevertheless it will always be God who creates *phantasmata* within the human soul; man may not always understand the images he perceives in this inspirational state of mind. Ficino echoes this notion in the *Platonic Theology* by postulating that:

> 'Men of great prudence and those most learned from their youth have not turned out to be the best poets. Rather, some of the poets were mad, as was said of Homer and Lucretius; ... Poets in a frenzy sing of many things, and marvellous ones at that, which a little later when their frenzy has abated, they do not sufficiently understand: it is as if they themselves had not pronounced the words but God had spoken loudly through them as through trumpets.'[17]

Michelangelo, Melancholy and *The Dream*

These Platonic views are visualised in some of Michelangelo's works and relate to how he saw himself, or maybe even to how he wanted to shape his own personality.[18] Again, Ficino's views are important. He builds further on the theme of inspiration and imagination in his *De vita libri tres,* written during the 1480s, which deals with the melancholic temperament.[19] He considered himself born under the bad constellation of Saturn; these people were believed to be afflicted with melancholy, usually also suffering from such inconveniences as gluttony, avarice, anger, a strong sexual desire and poor health. On the other hand, the melancholic temperament was considered the only 'humour' that offered a predisposition to genius – a concept derived from Aristotle[20] – and therefore it later became, partly thanks to Ficino, the temperament for scholars and artists.[21] This idea became exceedingly popular in the sixteenth century. Ficino explains it as follows: the geniality of the melancholic (artist or scholar) is caused by his subtle and inflammable *spiritus*,[22] combustible like a kind of brandy, which makes him ecstatic and inclined to *furor* in an extreme way. This *furor* makes his soul fly up to heaven, and makes his imagination receptive for inspiration, but it leaves him burnt-out and depressed after his ecstasy.[23] Ficino's opinions on melancholy, *furor* and inspiration also clearly appealed to Michelangelo,

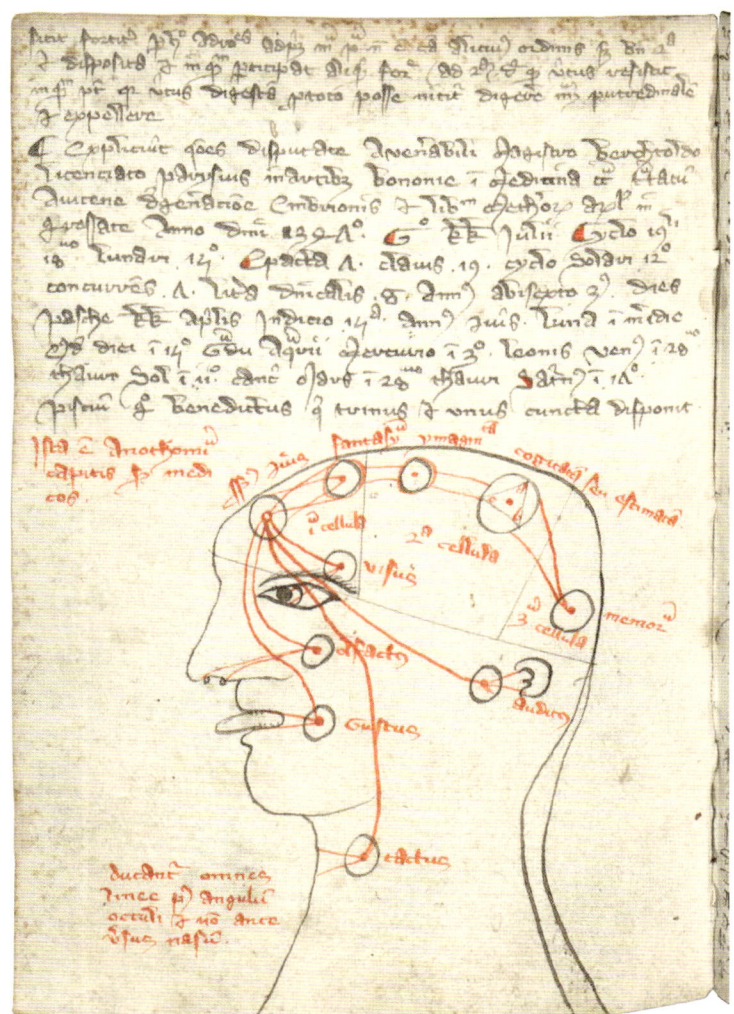

fig. 99   *The ventricles of the brain,* manuscript illustration accompanying Avicenna (Ibn Sina), *De generatione embryonis,* c. 1347. Munich, Bayerische Staatsbibliothek, Clm 527, fol. 64v

and these views seem to have been incorporated into an extraordinary series of detailed and highly finished drawings known as the 'presentation drawings'.

Most of these highly finished drawings were made for Tommaso de' Cavalieri, his alleged lover – or at least the person he was in love with – around 1533, just after his first meeting with the young man. Michelangelo certainly presented himself to the much younger Cavalieri as a melancholic.[24] In his letters and the poetry dedicated to him, Michelangelo complains about his own temperament, his dark sides and depressions. He compares himself with the moon; Cavalieri is the sun.[25] Michelangelo was not alone in making this comparison. Raphael, or some of his assistants, portrayed him in *The School of Athens* in 1509–11 as a melancholic (fig. 100);[26] and in *Idea del tempio della pittura* (Idea of the Temple of Painting) published in 1590, in which painters are linked to planets, Giovanni Paolo Lomazzo explains that Michelangelo 'corresponded' with Saturn.[27] Friend and colleague Francisco de Holanda moreover, tells us that while Michelangelo may have been socially awkward, this was not 'out of pride, but... because... [he does] not want to get corrupted by useless conversation of good-for-nothings and... [his] intellect [is] drawn down from the continuous elevated imaginations that always embellish [his mind]'.[28] We can conclude that Michelangelo was considered a melancholic, with a very sensitive imagination.

Michelangelo's drawing of *The Dream* (fig. 101/cat. 44) can be read as another statement of his melancholic but inspired qualities. Art historian Erwin Panofsky explained the iconography of the drawing as the human soul – represented by the nude young man – surrounded by the seven cardinal virtues and vices.[29] If we look more closely, however, we do not see any virtues, nor all seven cardinal sins. When we follow the figures in the cloud-like formations that surround the young man, we can recognise from left to right: gluttony (people drinking and roasting food), lust (naked and kissing figures, even male genitals, although an attempt was made to erase them), avarice (hands holding a bag of money) and anger (fighting figures), followed by sloth (an apathetic, depressed person); but we seem to be missing the sins of pride and envy. The vices depicted refer to the bad traits belonging to those born under Saturn and reflect the views of the melan-

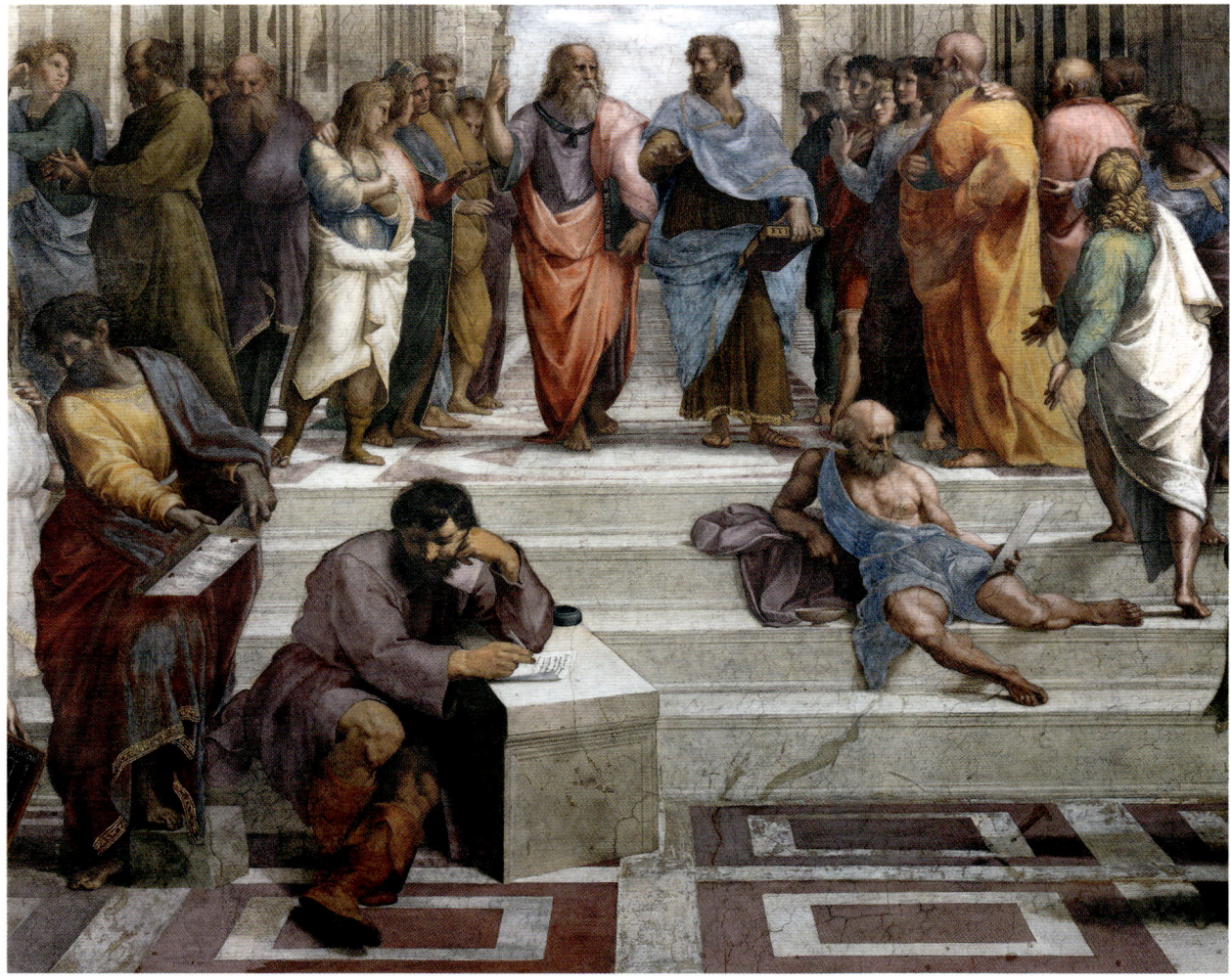

fig. 100   Raphael, *The School of Athens* (bottom left, seated: Michelangelo as the philosopher Heraclitus), 1509–1511. Fresco. Vatican City, Stanza della Segnatura

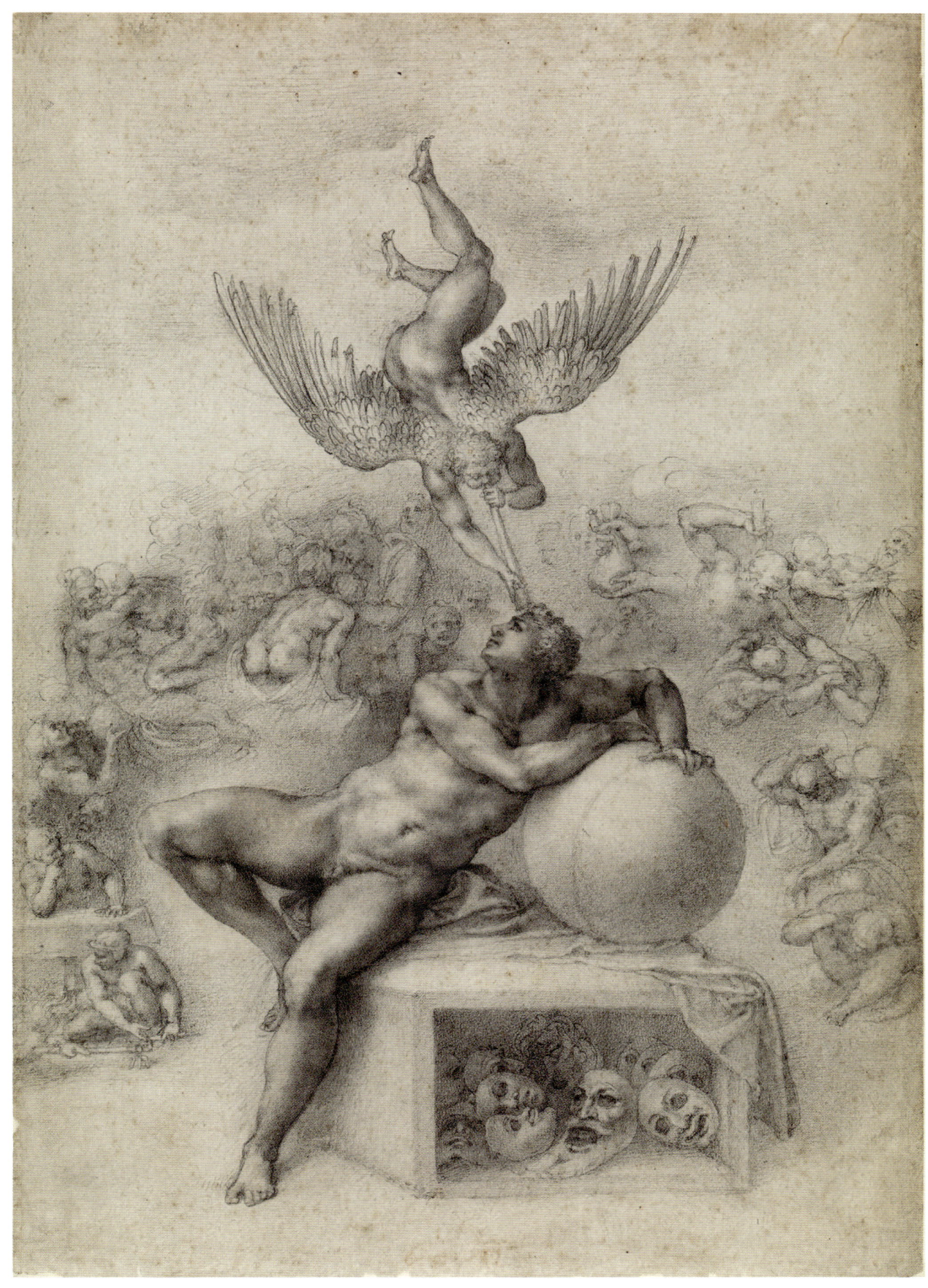

fig. 101   (cat. 44) Michelangelo, *The Dream*, c. 1533. Black chalk, 398 x 280 mm. London, The Courtauld Gallery, inv. D.1978.PG.424

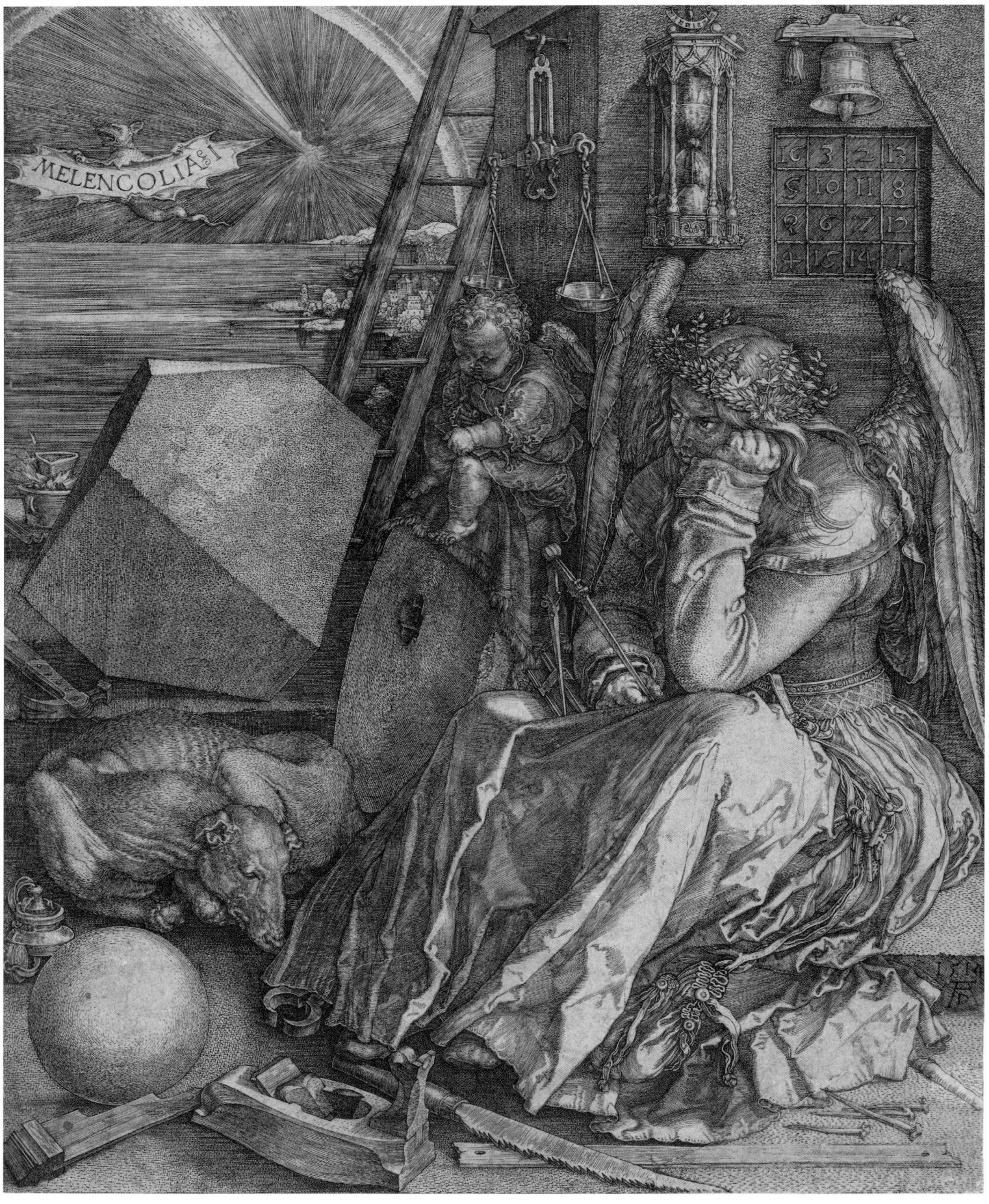

fig. 102   Albrecht Dürer, *Melencolia I,* 1514. Engraving, 239 x 185 mm. Amsterdam, Rijksmuseum, inv. RP-P-OB-11.705

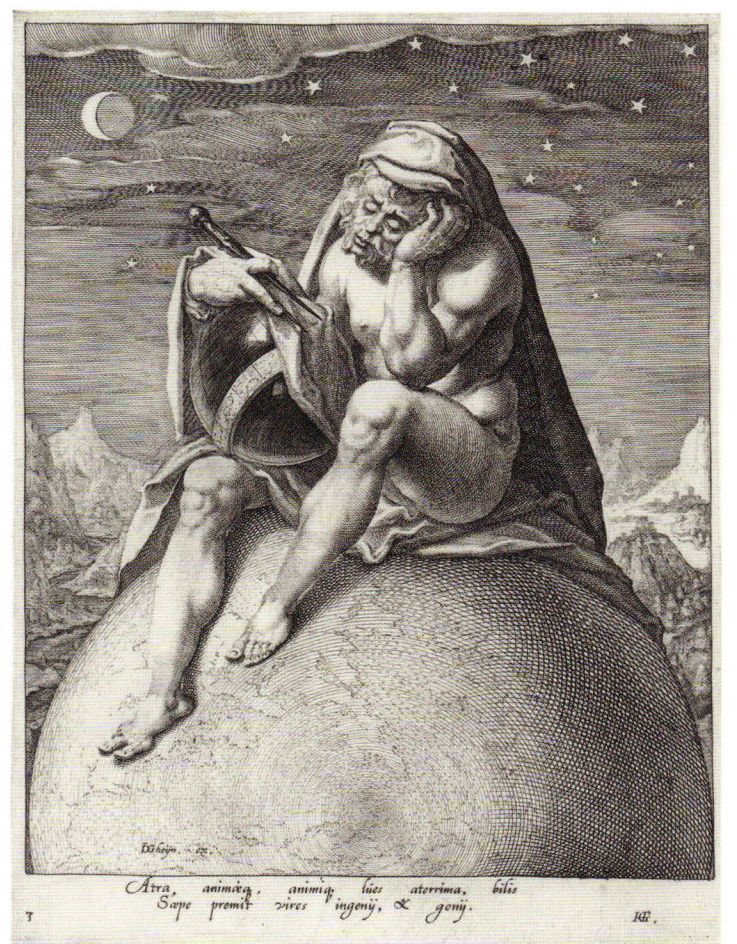

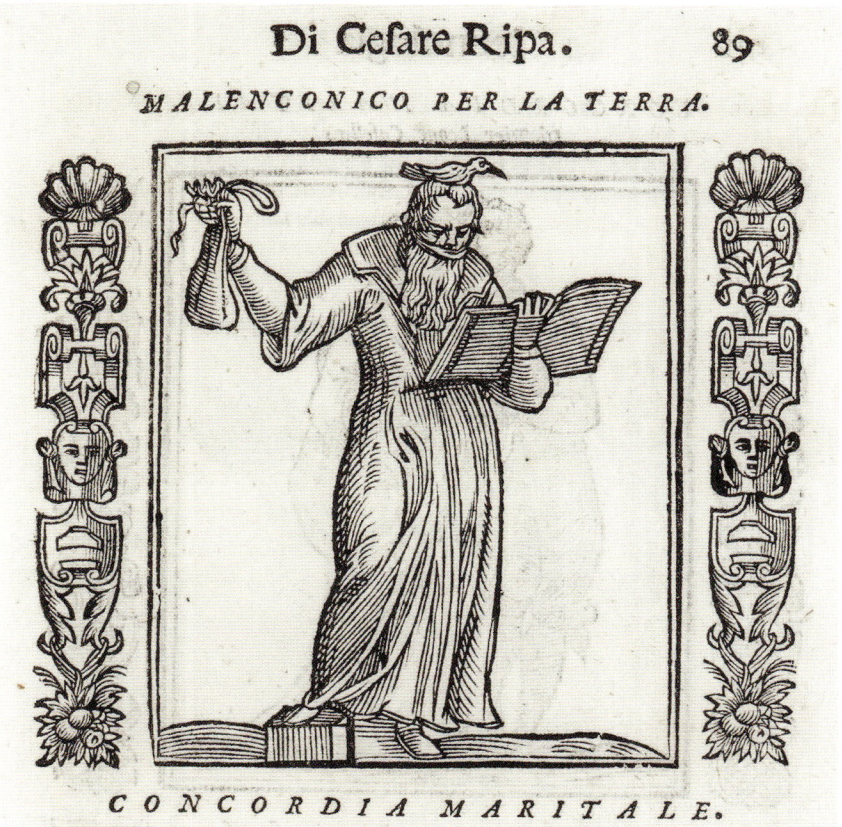

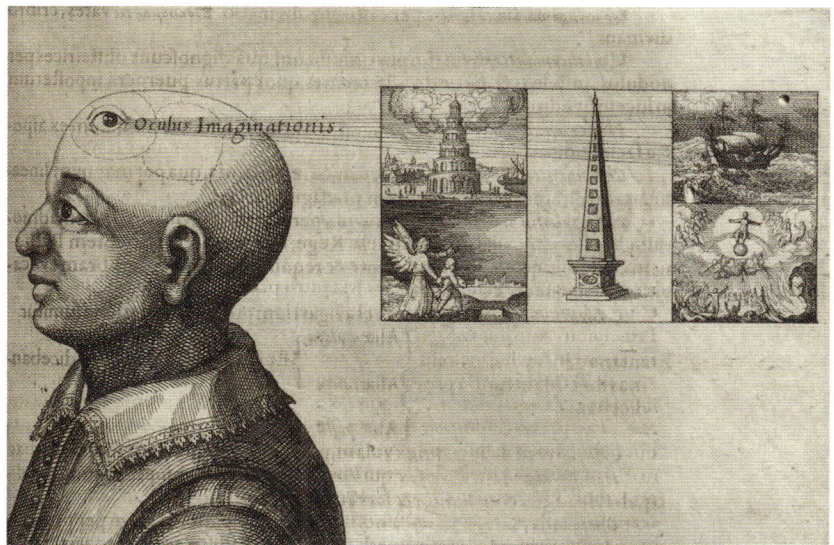

fig. 103   After Jacques de Gheyn II, *Air (Melancholicus),* from *The Four Temperaments*, 1596–1597. Engraving, 230 x 167 mm. Amsterdam, Rijksmuseum, inv. RP-P-1892-A-17247

fig. 104   Engraving from Cesare Ripa, *Iconologia* (Pietro Paolo Tozzi, 1611), p. 89. The Hague, RKD – Netherlands Institute for Art History, inv. 961976

fig. 105   Engraving from Robert Fludd, *Tomus Secundus de supernaturali [...], II, De animae memorativae scientia, quae vulgo ars memoriae vocatur. Ars Memoriae* (J. TH. De Bry/Hieronymus Galler, 1619), p. 47. Frankfurt am Main, Universitätsbibliothek J.C. Senckenberg, inv. 23:233307D

cholic temperament as elaborated by Ficino.[30] The drawing shows us the melancholic (the young man), surrounded by the vices of his temperament: gluttony, lust, anger, avarice and depression. Even the melancholic's inclination for geometry is visualised by means of the globe (geometry literally meaning 'measuring of the Earth').[31] Globes can also be found in other images of melancholics, such as the engravings of Albrecht Dürer and the workshop of Jacques de Gheyn II (figs 102 and 103).[32] The avaricious sides of the melancholic are illustrated by means of a money bag. This traditionally belongs to the iconography of melancholy, as shown by a print in Cesare Ripa's *Iconologia* (fig. 104).

Apparently, the iconography of *The Dream* does not seem to depict the soul surrounded by virtues and vices, as Panofsky suggested, but visualises the qualities belonging to the melancholic temperament, both its negative and positive sides. This can also be concluded from the human figure in the middle, who, although surrounded by his bad character traits, is inspired through his imagination in a very literal way. We see the *spiritus* flying in from above and blowing through a trumpet onto the forehead of the melancholic. This reminds us of Ficino's citation from his *Platonic Theology* on words spoken loudly through inspired people, 'as through trumpets'.[33] Maria Ruvoldt also showed that the place where the melancholic of *The Dream* is inspired, is his forehead, where traditionally the imagination is located.[34] This can also be seen in a later engraving by Robert Fludd (fig. 105). In the course of the sixteenth century, the melancholic temperament, as described by Ficino, had become a model for the artist's temperament: vexed by a problematic character, but with a refined imagination and a strong disposition for inspiration. Ficino created the theoretical background for this, and Michelangelo appropriated these ideas in works of art. After Ficino and Michelangelo, we see a development through time where genius, inspiration and imagination are considered important factors in making art, which are still valid in contemporary art theory today.

Ficino's pupil Diacceto elaborated on the theme of melancholy too. According to Diacceto, melancholy occurs when the soul cannot return to its divine origins. Love, of course, is also a great source for melancholy. In Diacceto's view, love:

> '...is neither Divine nor mortal, but a great demon, whilst the demonic nature is, to a certain extent, placed between man and God as an intermediary, and it leads man's prayers and offerings to the gods, and in reverse order, the will and commandments of the gods to man. And by no other means than by demonic nature, man is, awake or in dreams, inspired by Divine Goodness.'[35]

This remark originates in Ficino's *De Amore* where love is said to be midway between heavenly and earthly things. The winged messenger in the drawing can be seen as the *spiritus*, the subtle substance which permeates everything, which visualises 'love', the 'great demon' or 'demonic nature', which functions as an intermediary between God and human beings and inspires the human soul when it is awake or asleep. There is no better way of showing to what contemplation of love and beauty can lead than by means of Michelangelo's visual masterpiece.

Archers Shooting at a Herm

The Dream contains a complex iconography. This is even more true of the drawing known as *Archers Shooting at a Herm* (fig. 106). Again, the iconography fits very well within the context of a sophisticated love gift. Tommaso de' Cavalieri reported contemplating drawings by Michelangelo sometimes for several hours a day.[36] Although it is not certain whether this drawing was made for Cavalieri, the subject of Platonic love, which seems to be part of a common train of thought, does give reason to suppose so.[37] Michael Hirst has put forward that *Archers Shooting at a Herm* is based on a classical relief from the Domus Aurea.[38] There is also a small visual reference to the Domus Aurea prototype by the hand of Francisco de Holanda (figs 107 and 108). Descriptions of the lost prototype show that Michelangelo made significant changes from the original. He dynamised the group of archers and omitted bows and (most) arrows.

Panofsky suggested that bows and arrows are left out deliberately as we are dealing with a highly finished work, and nothing else reminds us of Michelangelo's famous *non-finito*.[39] The archers are aiming at a shield attached to the herm, a human-like figure whose legs merge into an architectural pedestal. In spite of the absence of bows, some arrows seem to have reached their goal. The left side of the drawing shows two *putti* or *spiritelli* fanning a fire. They do so in the same direction as the archers shoot, adding to the dynamics of the image. On the right side a cupid is depicted, sleeping on top of the only weapons that could have been used to reach the herm's shield. We may thus understand: while love sleeps, everything seems to miss its purpose.

To find an explanation for the iconography of this drawing, we may search for references in Michelangelo's poetry, but none of the presentation drawings appears to have a direct relationship with a specific sonnet. The changes Michelangelo made to the image of the ancient relief, however, on which *Archers* is probably a personal variation, can be clarified from the sixth oration of Ficino's

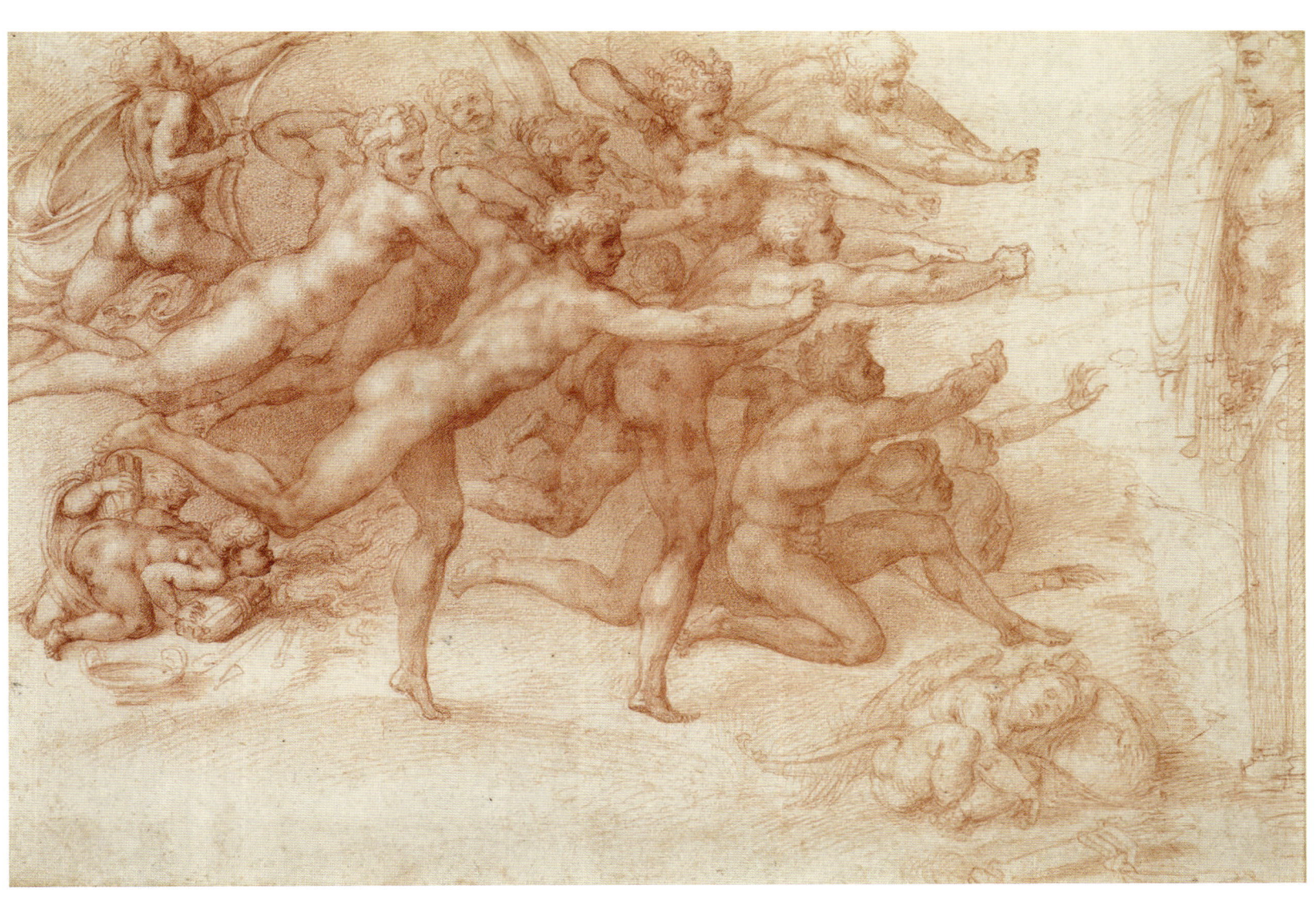

fig. 106   Michelangelo, *Archers Shooting at a Herm*, c. 1530. Red chalk, 219 x 323 mm. Windsor, Royal Collection Trust, inv. RCIN 912778

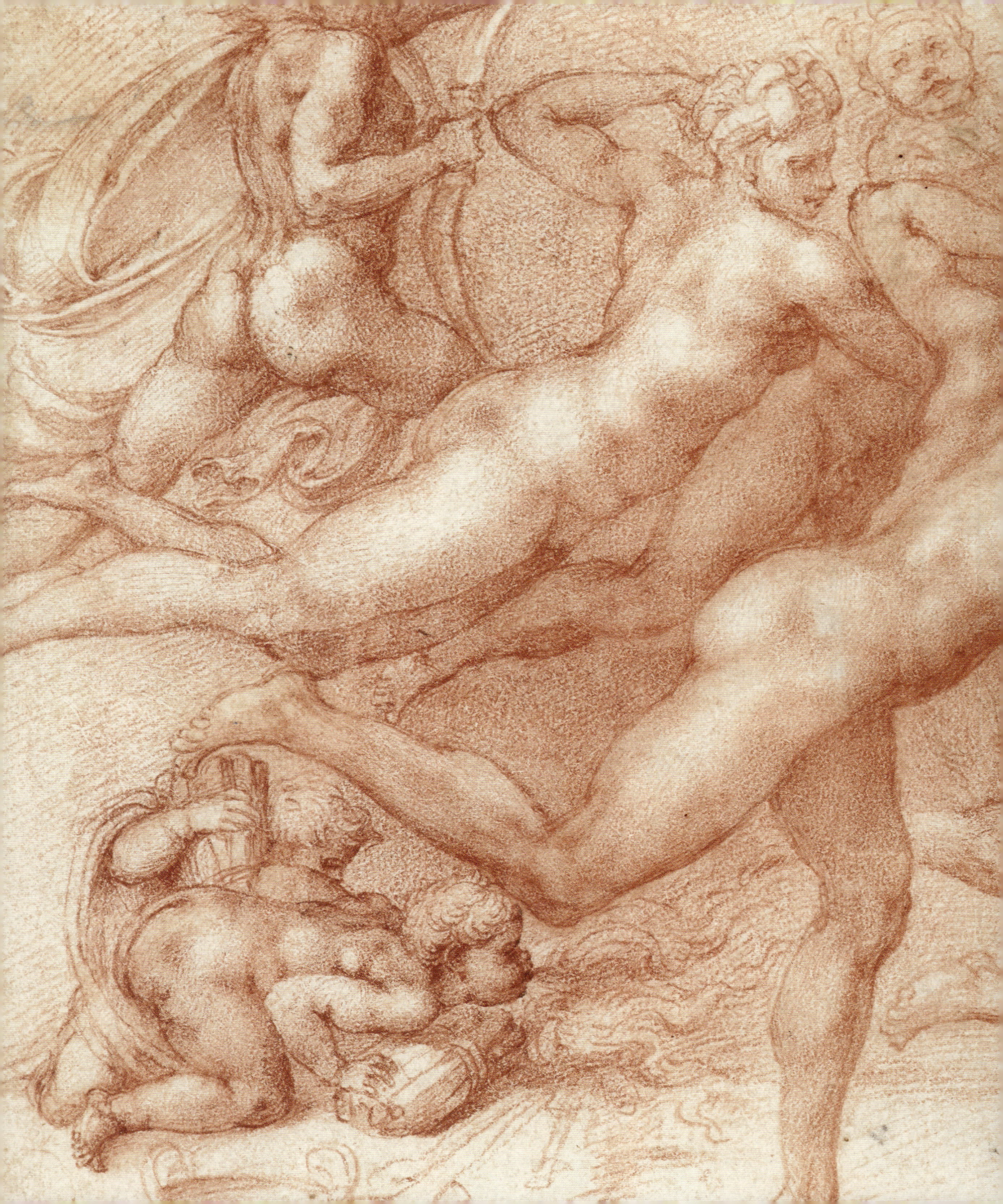

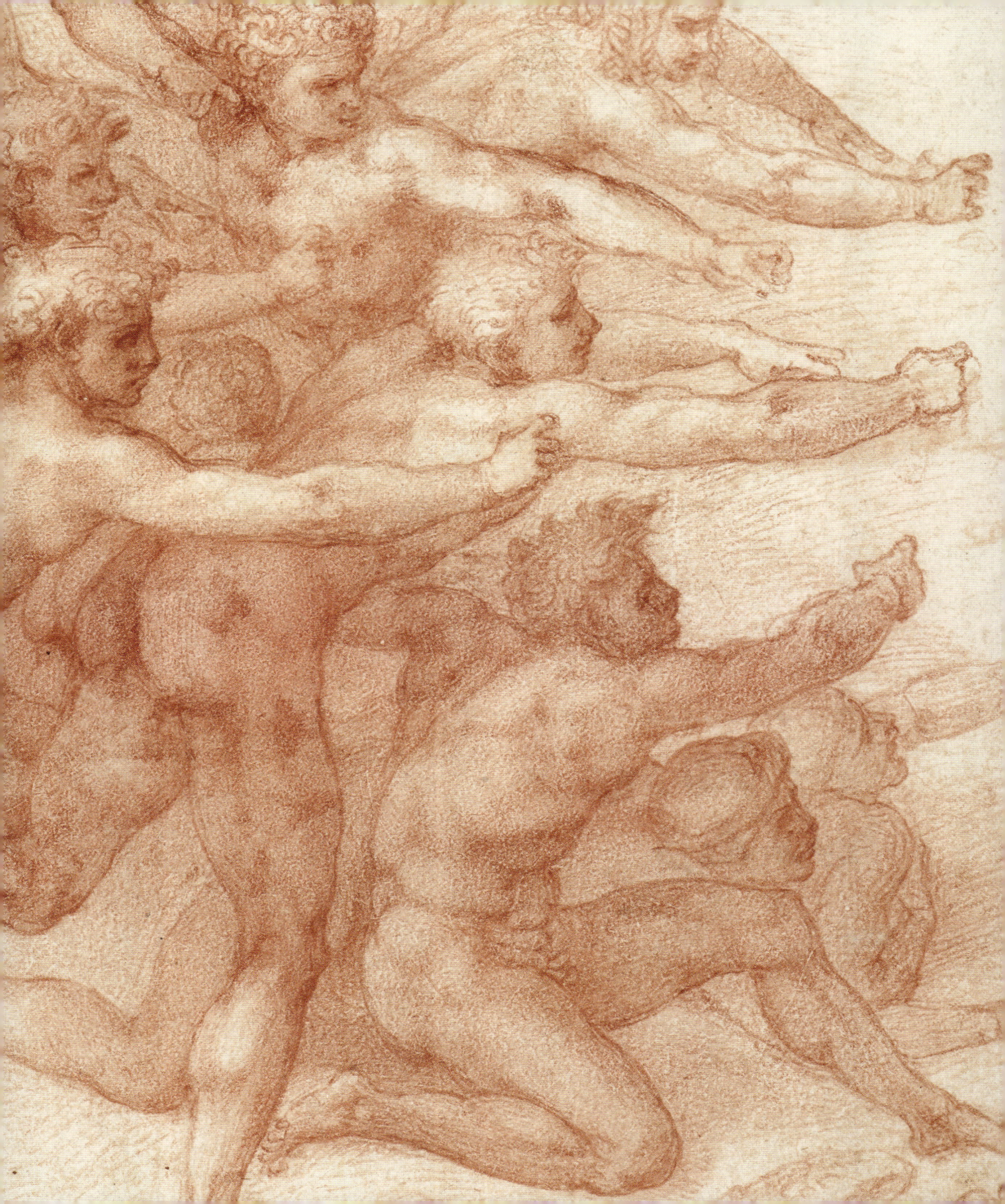

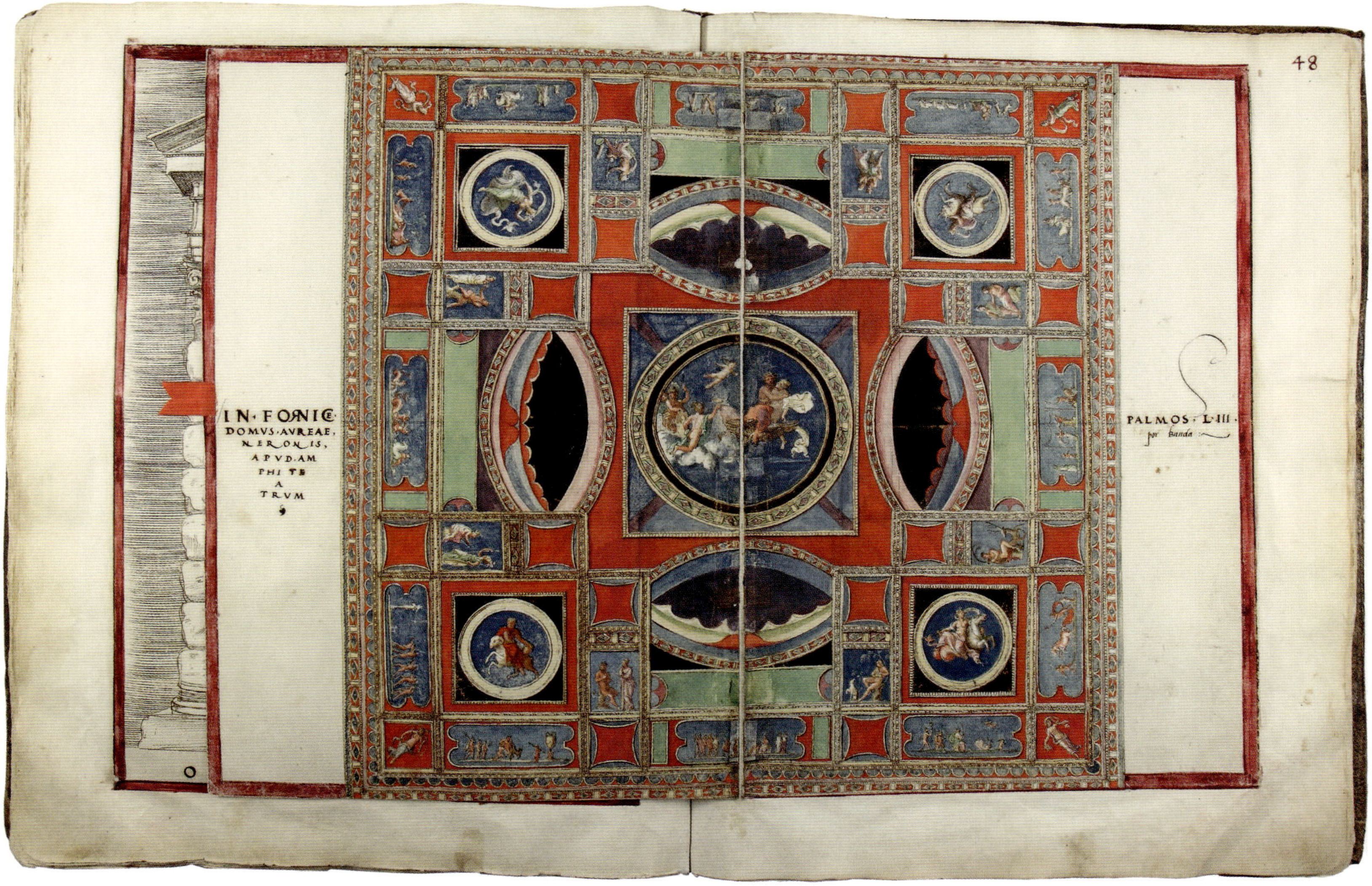

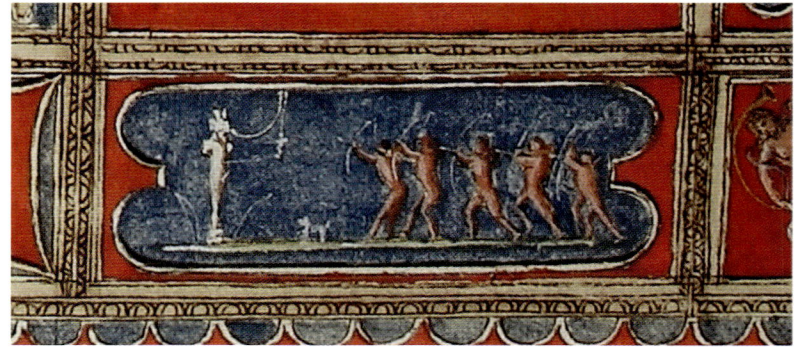

fig. 107   Francisco de Holanda, *The Volta Dorata from the Domus Aurea*,
c. 1538–1541. Watercolour and gouache, 390 x 540 mm.
El Escorial, Biblioteca Real de San Lorenzo, inv. RBME 28-I-20,
fol. 47(bis)v–48r

fig. 108   Detail of fig. 107

De Amore. It is also very plausible that, again, Diacceto's *I tre libri d'Amore* served as a direct source for this drawing. In the aforementioned oration, Ficino explains how a lover's *spiritus* reacts when the latter sees their beloved:

> 'A man's appearance, which is often very beautiful to see, on account of an interior goodness fortunately given him by God, can send a ray of its splendour through the eyes of those who see him and into their soul. Drawn by this spark, *as if by a kind of hook*, the soul hastens toward the drawer.'[40]

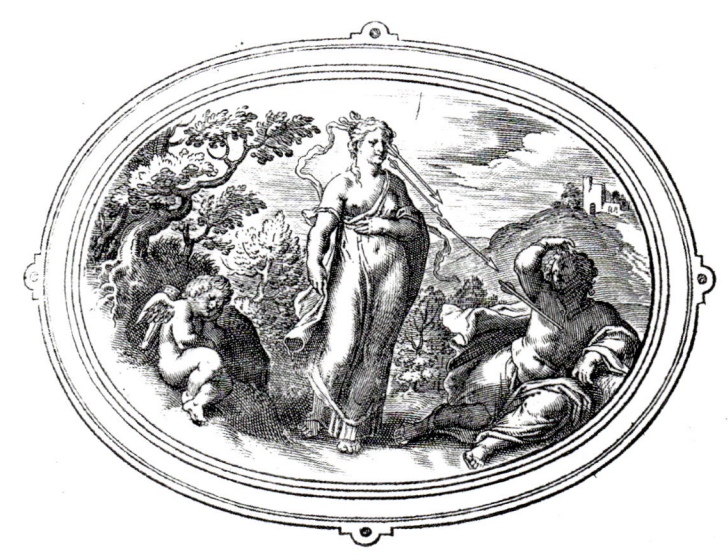

Ficino, moreover, tries to explain the Socratic opinion that the lover only partly possesses his beloved: love is an emotion halfway between the beautiful and the not beautiful. Love is born from Porus (Plenty) and Penia (Poverty) and is a daemon midway between heavenly and earthly things. In Socrates' oration, love, as a son of poverty, is called 'thin, dry and squalid'. Ficino tried to explain this phrase by stating that the tormented lover eats nothing and digests his food badly, because of which he becomes thin and pale and his *spiritus* out of balance:

> 'Wherever the continuous attention of the soul is carried, there also fly the spirits, which are the chariots or instruments of the soul. The spirits are produced in the heart from the thinnest part of the blood. The lover's soul is carried toward the image of the beloved planted in his imagination, and thence toward the beloved himself. To the same place are also drawn the lover's spirits. Flying out there, they are continuously dissipated.'[41]

Ficino subsequently tried to find an allegorical explanation of those negative aspects that Socrates attributed to love because of the fact that love was considered partly beautiful and partly not. In the sixth oration it is formulated that love is called 'humble'.[42] Ficino added to this, that the Greek word Plato used for 'humble', *chamaipetes*, literally means 'low-flying' (*per infima volans,* or in Italian *volante a basso*).[43] He continues that lovers who abuse love seem to be 'low-flying' because they 'live without common sense, and through their trivial preoccupations great causes fail'.[44]

Ficino formulates it thus, that those who are aiming at the divine aspects of love are rewarded by its generous sides, as born from plenty. But love's dark sides spring from poverty: those lovers who focus on bodily, earthly love, are dry, naked and humble or 'low-flying', and they are also dull and unarmed. Lovers focusing only on bodily pleasures are '*unarmed* because they succumb to shameful desire. *Dull* because they are so stupid that they do not

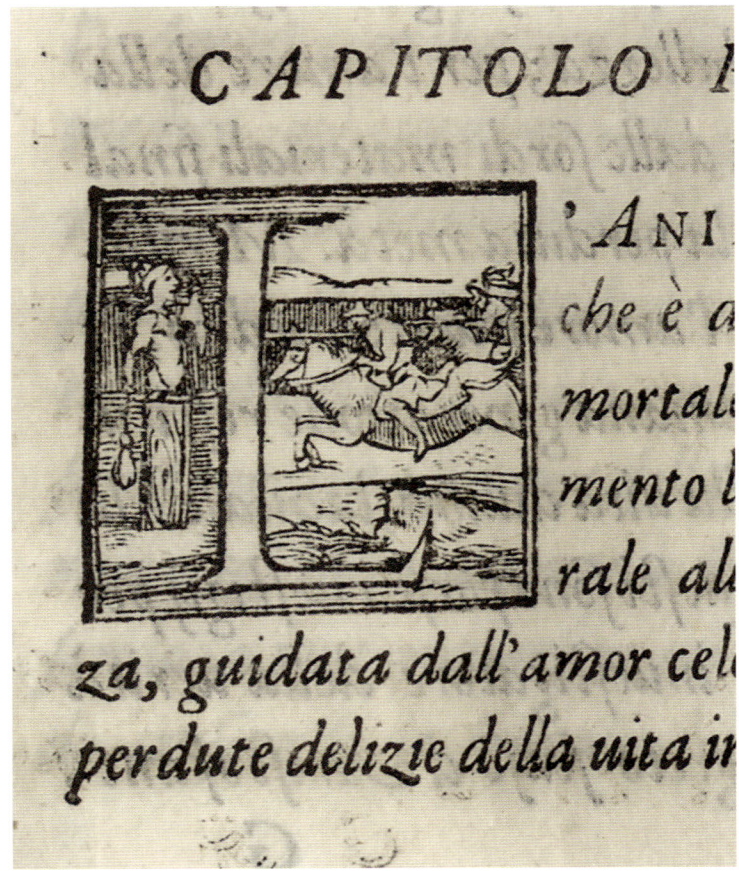

fig. 109   Engraving from Otto Vaenius, *Amorum Emblemata* (Hieronymus Verdussen, 1608), p. 151. Amsterdam, Rijksmuseum Research Library

fig. 110   Illustration in Francesco Cattani da Diacceto, *I tre libri d'amore* (Gabriel Giolito de' Ferrari, 1561), p. 98. Munich, Bayerische Staatsbibliothek, L.eleg.m. 734

know where love is leading them, and they remain *on the road*, and do not arrive at the goal.'[45]

The sixth oration from Ficino's *De Amore* and Diacceto's paraphrase of it are key to understanding the meaning of Michelangelo's *Archers*. The lack of arrows seems to refer to the invisible arrows of love from the *spiritus*, pouring from the lover's eyes. That this was not only an early modern philosophical concept, but also part of a visual tradition, is proven in an emblem by Otto Vaenius (fig. 109). It pictures a woman whose gaze is represented by arrows which penetrate the heart of her beloved.[46] Next to her lies a sleeping cupid, just as we saw in Michelangelo's drawing, which could refer to the absence of higher, divine love. Also, in Michelangelo's masterpiece, the depicted archers only seem to aim at the bodily aspects of love, because of which they become 'naked, humble (low-flying), dull and unarmed', and 'do not arrive at the goal'.

The herm seems to be a defenceless prey to the archers, but we can specify the role of this figure in the drawing, if we know that herms are often depicted without arms and legs, but with a phallus, probably symbolising limitless bodily lust. On the other hand, the figure in this drawing may also represent a tournament target, as shown in one of the initials in a later print of Diacceto's work (fig. 110). Herm or tournament target, the figure is the object of the archers' unavailing aspiration. Finally, there is a striking detail: one of the archers (upper left) seems to possess a bow, but he is not aiming at the target nor even shooting. He holds the bow the wrong way around, albeit not effortlessly; maybe he is tightening his bow. This may be the Platonic lover, who is not deceived by physical temptations, thus overcoming lust and physical pleasures and pursuing a higher goal: divine love. Possibly, this may even be a psychological self-portrait by Michelangelo.

Concluding Remarks

These interpretations of *The Dream* and *Archers Shooting at a Herm* show that the drawings functioned within a philosophical context in which divine significance was given to the sight of earthly and bodily beauty: beholding physical beauty could lead to divine inspiration. Let us now return to *The Last Judgement*. Apparently, Papal Master of Ceremonies Biagio da Cesena had little understanding of the fact that the nude idealised bodies depicted on the wall of the Sistine Chapel had a (well-nigh) religious context.

The fresco of *The Last Judgement* shows the moment when the dead rise to be judged by Christ. Those who are saved are depicted at his right hand (the view-

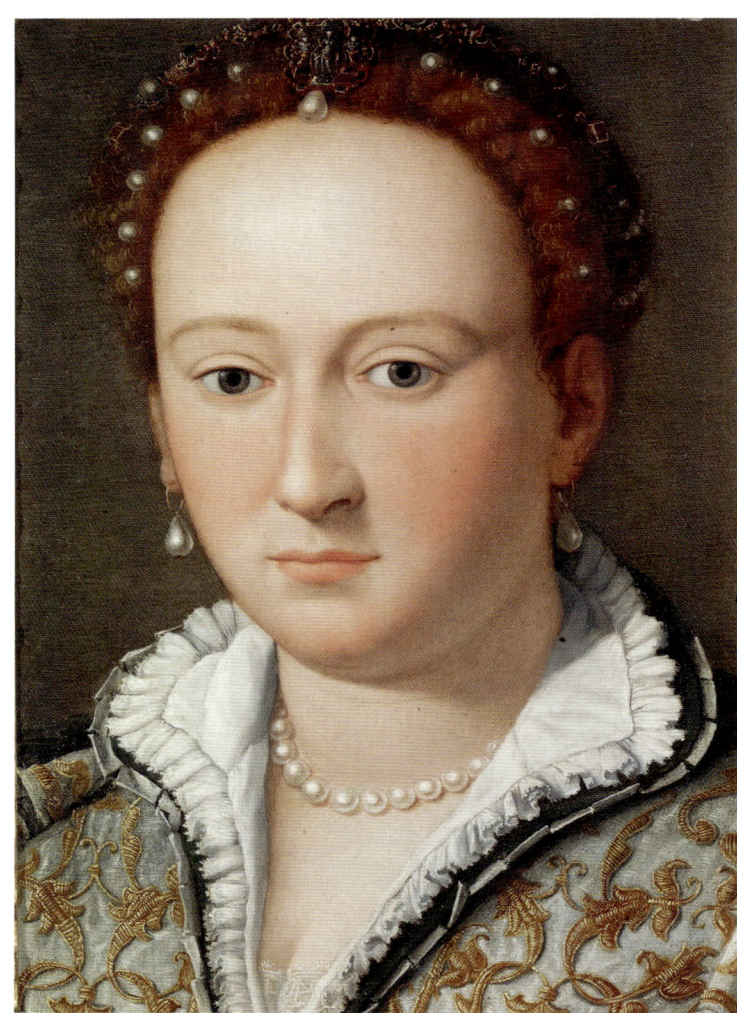

fig. 111   Alessandro Allori, *Portrait of Bianca Cappello*, early 1570s. Oil on copper, 37 x 27 cm. Florence, Gallerie degli Uffizi, inv. 1890 n. 1514

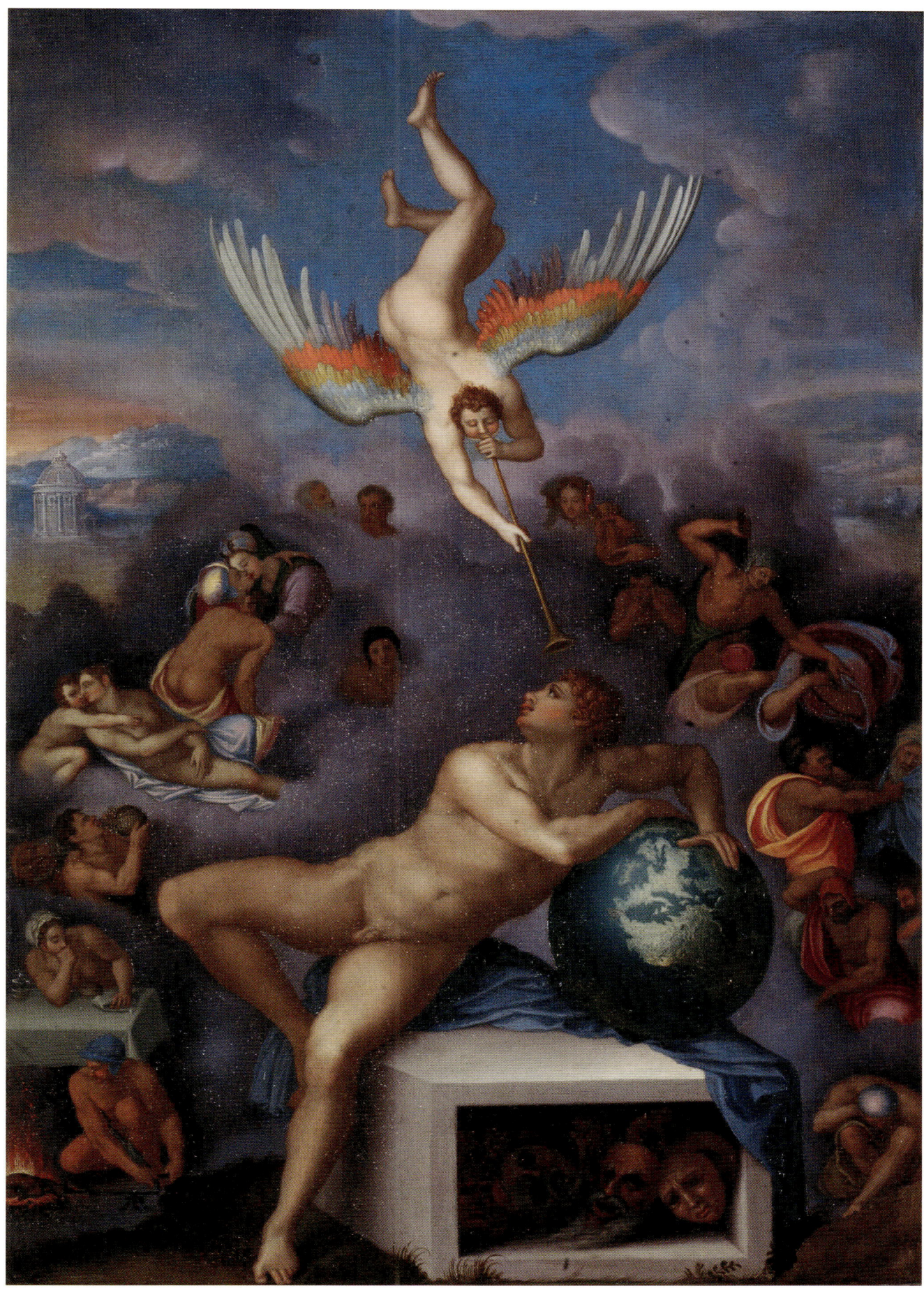

fig. 112   Alessandro Allori, after Michelangelo, *The Dream*, reverse of fig. 111

er's left) and are taken up by saints, while the doomed at his left hand descend to hellfire (or the underworld).[47] The impression is given that Christ's hand gesture initiates a great rotary movement of bodies. According to Christian tradition, during the resurrection, the saved are given back their intact bodies. For this reason, paintings of *The Last Judgement* more often show nude bodies.[48] Michelangelo depicted classical, very muscular and idealised bodies. The figure of Christ may even be based on the *Apollo Belvedere*, the famous classical sculpture in the collection of the Vatican (fig. 42).

As may be clear, nude bodies have a positive and almost religious meaning in Michelangelo's work. The drawings discussed, *The Dream* and *Archers Shooting at a Herm,* thematise the inspirational effect that these beautiful bodies have on the human soul. Ficino's *De Amore* provided the substantive foundation for these views. His work dealt with Platonic relationships between men. According to Sears Jayne, it soon became a 'pet book for court aristocrats' and was very popular at European courts, being used in other relational contexts as well.[49] Similarly, Michelangelo's *The Dream* can be found, for example, on the back of a portrait of Bianca Cappello, painted by Alessandro Allori (figs 111 and 112), a painting that was purportedly a gift from the Grand Duke Francesco I de' Medici to his mistress, and later wife, Bianca. The deeper meaning of this love gift, as we have seen, is the inspiration that love and beauty can give. I hope to have shown what may have really been on Michelangelo's mind when he made these drawings.

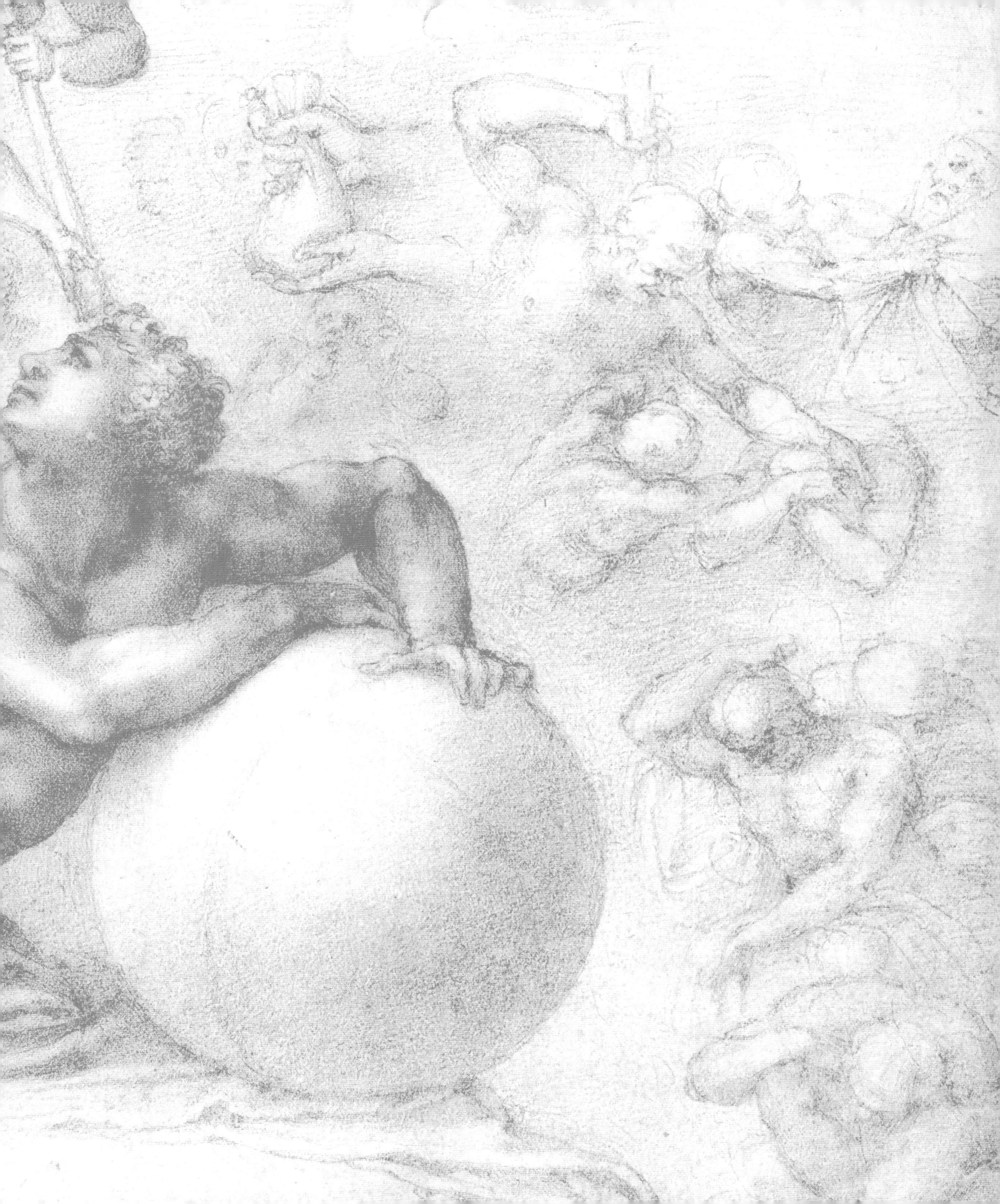

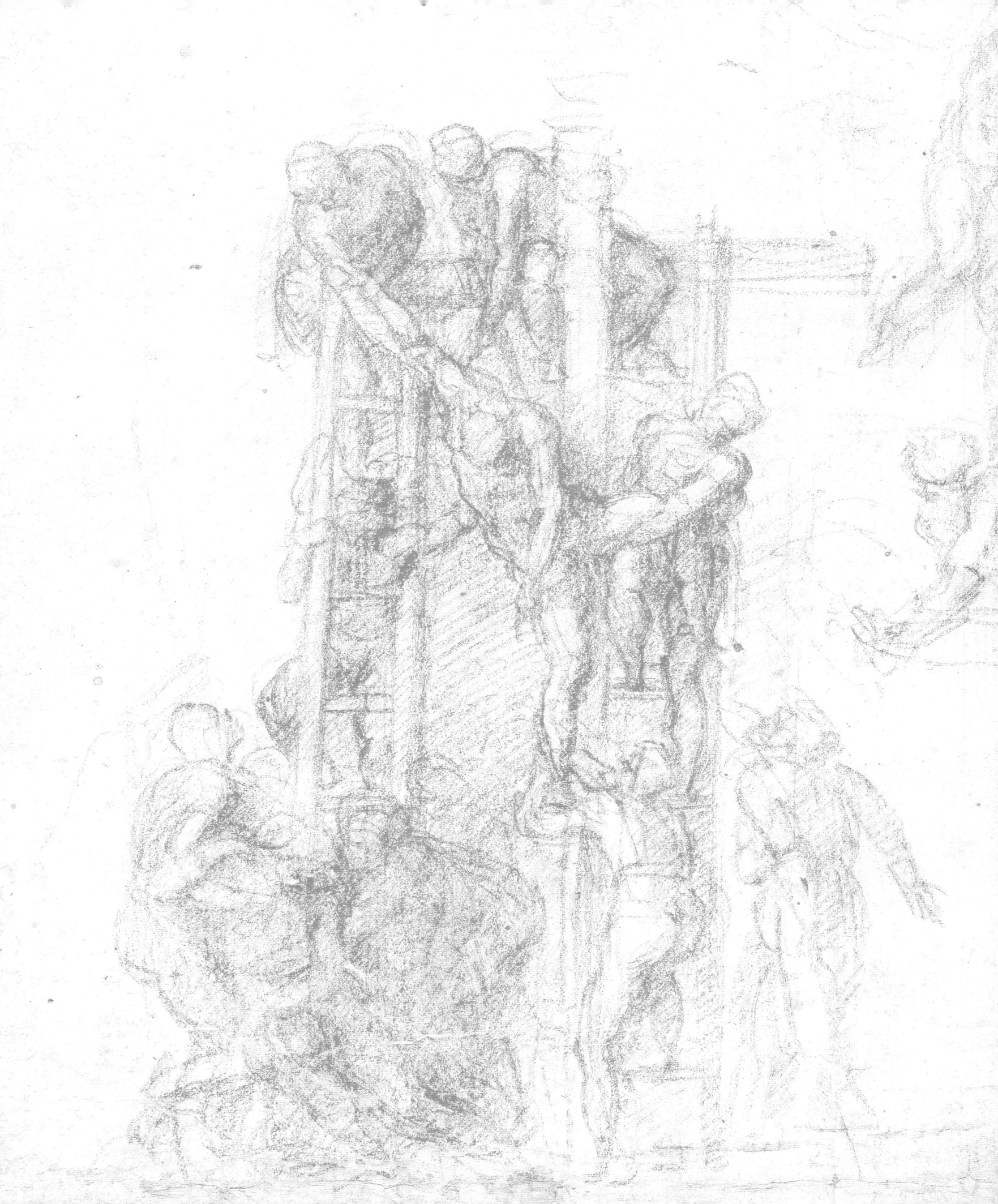

Michelangelo and the Divine Body. Between Crucifixion and Resurrection

Jennifer Sliwka

Michelangelo's deeply held Christian faith informed his profound engagement, preoccupation even, with depicting the body of Christ throughout his long and celebrated career.[1] As his later spiritual sonnets affirm, the artist believed that a new life in heaven awaited him after his earthly death and that this salvation was promised through Jesus Christ's own sacrificial death on the cross.[2] Over the course of his career, Michelangelo repeatedly addressed the subject of the dead Christ in various contexts: on the cross at the Crucifixion, being lowered at the Deposition, cradled in his mother's arms in a Lamentation (or Pietà), carried to the tomb and then reanimated at the Resurrection. These subjects seemed to take on a particularly powerful and personal meaning for the artist in the last three decades of his life, when Christian beliefs around death and resurrection became increasingly important to him as he confronted his own mortality. Michelangelo explored these subjects across various media – in drawing, sculpture and paint – and often used the artistic solutions he devised in one medium to inform his work in another. He is perhaps best known for his treatments of the Pietà, creating at least three sculptures on the subject at key points throughout his career: in 1499, in around 1547–55 and in the year of his death in 1564. What his paintings and especially his drawings reveal, however, is that he continued to rethink and interrogate his ideas about the representation of Christ's dead body in the long periods between these better-known sculpted works.

The Lamented Body

Although he had already completed several sculptures for prestigious patrons by the age of 25, it was the marble *Pietà* that Michelangelo carved for the French cardinal, Jean de Bilhères-Lagraulas, that effectively established his fame as a sculptor (fig. 113). Cardinal of the Basilica of Santa Sabina on the Aventine, Bilhères-Lagraulas commissioned Michelangelo in 1497 to carve the sculpture for his future funerary chapel in Santa Petronilla, a mausoleum with longstanding associations with French royalty. The *Pietà* was installed in the chapel in 1500, a year after the cardinal's death, and remained there until the mausoleum was demolished to make way for the new basilica of St Peter's in around 1517, where it is housed to this day. The surviving contract between the cardinal and the artist specifies that the sculpture was to be a life-size Pietà, an Italian term often translated into English as a Lamentation, but which can also refer to an emotional state such as piety and pity or be applied to other devotional images of the suffering or dead Christ, for example the Man of Sorrows or Christ supported by angels. Curiously, the Pietà as a subject is not described in the gospel accounts but is actually an artistic invention that visualises an unspecified moment following Jesus's Crucifixion and between his Deposition and Entombment. This visual tradition seems to have originated in late thirteenth-century Dominican mysticism in the area around the Rhine valley that had a particular interest in the *Compassio Mariae* or empathy with the sorrow and suffering of the Virgin during Christ's Passion. At the centre of this early meditative practice was the visualisation of Christ and the Virgin in the mind of the worshipper. Over time, however, these ephemeral images of the mind developed into a more concrete visual iconography in the form of a wooden sculpture known as a '*Vesperbild*' or 'image of the vespers (evening prayers)' destined for altars as aids to devotion.[3]

Michelangelo's first interpretation of this *Vesperbild* type, however, is far removed from the aged and grief-stricken Madonnas shown cradling Christ's battered and emaciated body more commonly found in the North. Instead, the Italian artist renders his idealised bodies in highly polished white Carrara marble and represents a serene and unusually youthful Virgin Mary, perhaps to underscore her purity and to evoke images of her cradling the Christ Child in her arms. The Virgin's impossibly wide

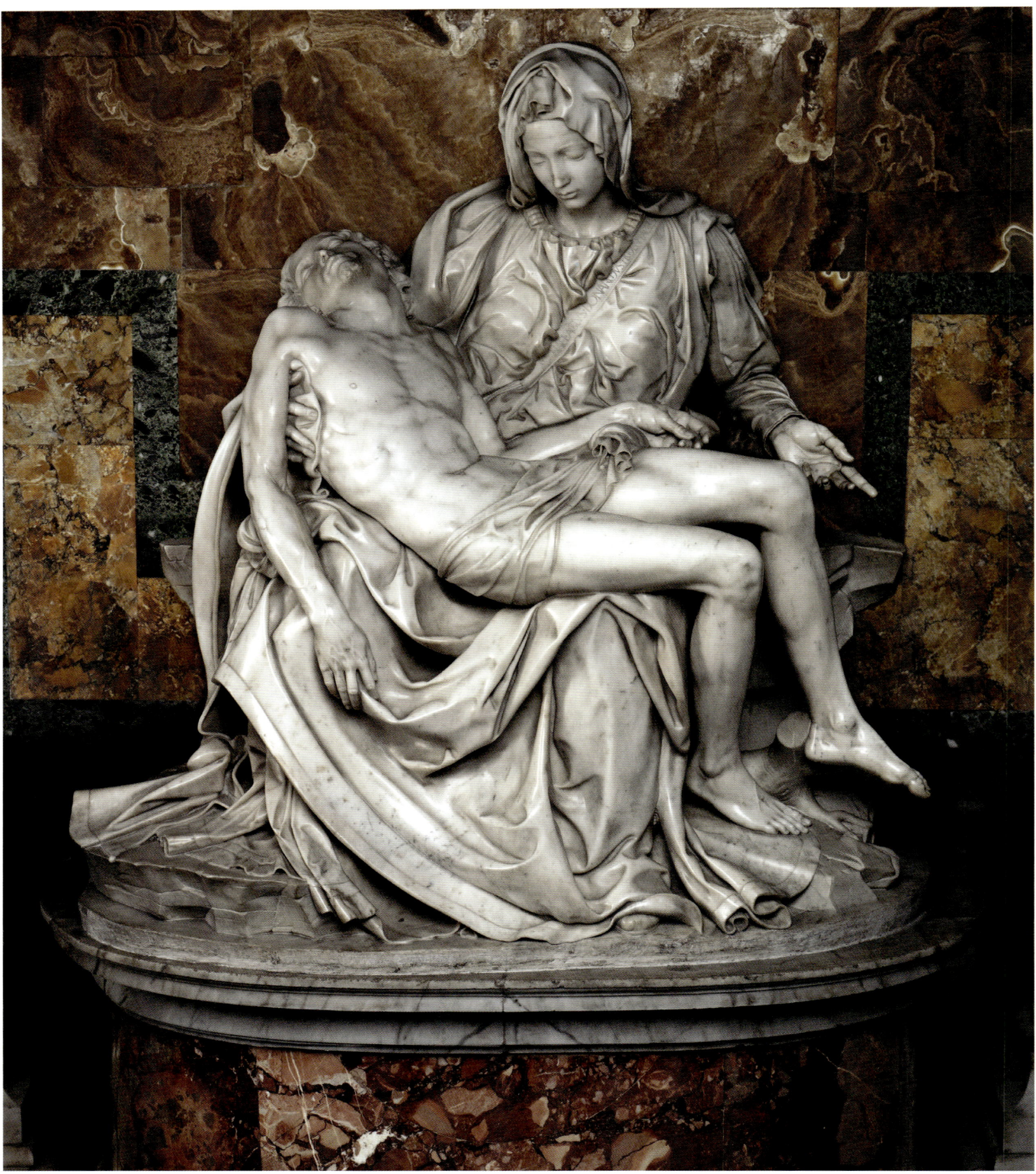

fig. 113   Michelangelo, *Pietà*, c. 1497–1500. Marble, 174 x 195 x 69 cm. Vatican City, St Peter's Basilica

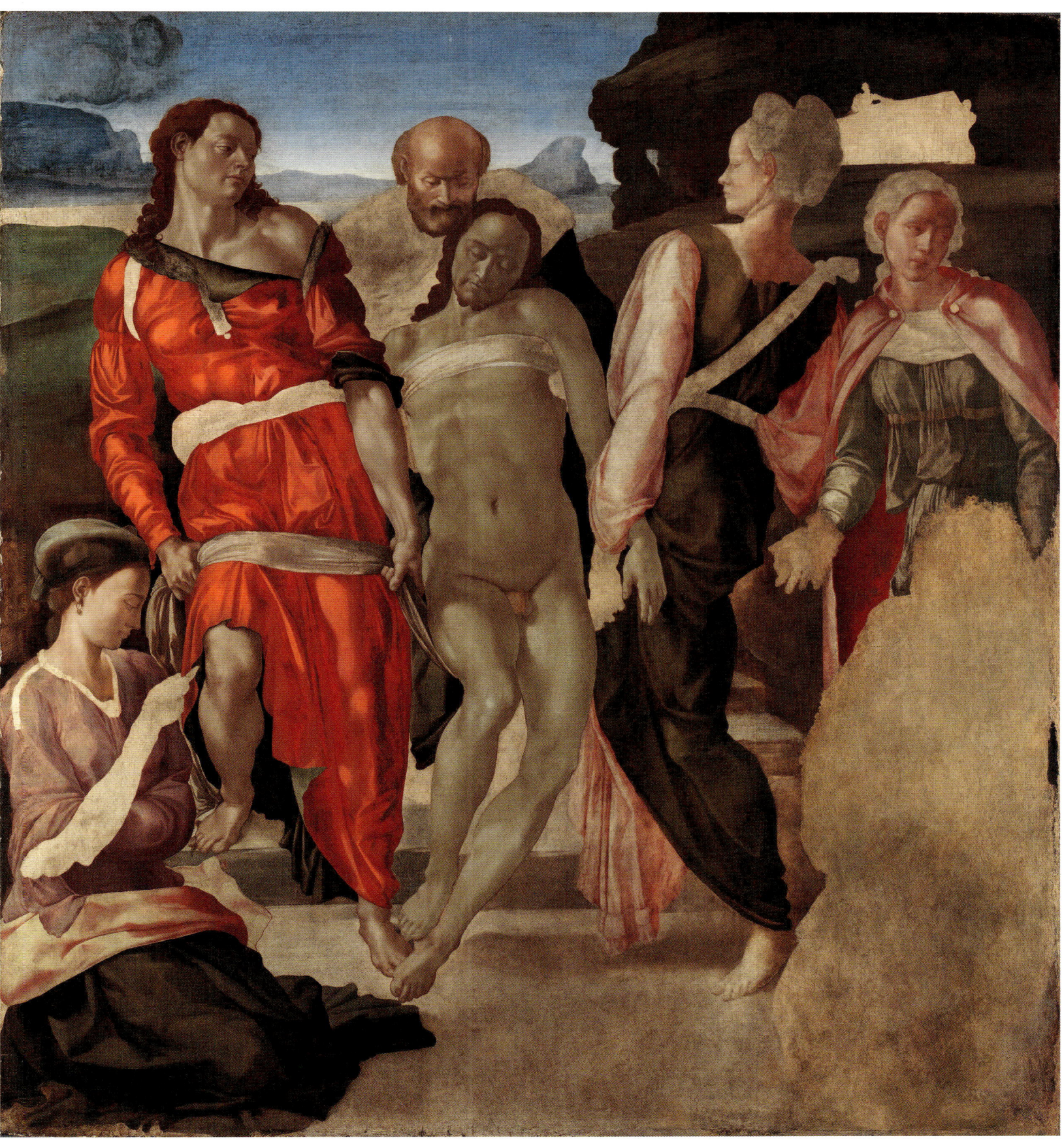

fig. 114   Michelangelo, *The Entombment*, c. 1500–1501. Oil on wood, 162 x 150 cm. London, National Gallery, inv. NG790

lap, her legs spread expansively to both accommodate Christ's body and allude to his birth, is clearly designed to present Christ's athletic body to the viewer. The artist makes this conceit explicit by turning Jesus's lithe nude torso outwards towards the beholder at an angle that, in real life, would likely cause his body to slide to the ground. Furthermore, Mary spreads the fingers of her right hand to draw attention to the wound in Christ's side, the gesture echoing the way Jesus's own dead, but seemingly animate, fingers appear to grasp a fold of her skirt.

In Michelangelo's youthful rendering, the body of Christ evokes the heroic nudes of classical statuary, transforming the Northern *Vesperbild* into a kind of Pietà *all'antica*, that is, in the style of the antique. The artist was clearly drawing upon all the resources available to him – from his early anatomical studies of cadavers in Florence to the recently uncovered ancient sculptures of gods and heroes in the Eternal City – to produce his greatest work to date. Rendering this dead yet astoundingly beautiful, idealised body was certainly a shrewd way of showcasing his precocious talent to potential patrons just a few short years after arriving in Rome. Yet the beauty and perfection Michelangelo strove for was not only aesthetically pleasing, but a highly appropriate way of rendering the divine body of Christ in a period where beauty was highly correlated with virtue.[4] Indeed, beauty and virtue were strongly associated in Renaissance thought and art, drawing on the classical equation of the good and the beautiful, and in particular on the Neoplatonic notion that physical beauty signified an inner beauty of spirit, as expounded, for example, by the Florentine humanist philosopher Marsilio Ficino:

> '…the internal perfection produces the external. The former we can call goodness, the latter beauty. For this reason, we say that beauty is a certain blossom of goodness, by the charms of which blossom, as a kind of bait, the hidden internal goodness attracts beholders. But since the cognition of our intellect takes its origin from the senses, we would never be aware of and never desire the goodness itself hidden in the heart of things if we were not attracted to it by the visible signs of external beauty.'[5]

The lifelikeness and anatomical precision of Jesus's body in the *Pietà*, combined with its idealisation and beauty, underscores Christ's dual nature as both human and divine. At the same time, the rendering of his body in this way commemorates his death on the cross while also alluding to his imminent resurrection – the Christian belief that God raised Jesus from the dead on the third day after his Crucifixion. Critically, in rethinking the *Vesperbild* tradition in this way, Michelangelo shifted attention away from the sorrow and suffering of the Virgin (the *Compassio Mariae* described above) towards a contemplation of Christ's dead body instead.

Shortly after completing his *Pietà* for Bilhères-Lagraulas, Michelangelo produced an even more overtly Christocentric Pietà-type image: his painted *Entombment* (or *Christ being carried to his Tomb*) altarpiece for the funerary chapel of Giovanni da Viterbo, the Bishop of Crotone, for the Roman church of Sant'Agostino (fig. 114). Although left incomplete when Michelangelo left Rome for Florence in 1501, and therefore somewhat difficult to read, the boldness of the composition and the three-dimensionality of the figures suggest an almost high-relief sculpture transposed into paint. At the centre of the composition the figure of the dead Christ is supported and flanked by John the Evangelist and a female figure, probably one of the three Marys described as present at the Crucifixion and/or visiting Christ's tomb. The mature, bearded figure supporting Christ from behind may be either Nicodemus, the Pharisee who secretly visited Christ by night and who helped lower his body from the cross and prepare it for burial or, as he is more often identified, Joseph of Arimathea, the wealthy disciple who offered his own tomb for Christ. The entirely unpainted figure in the lower right must represent the Virgin shown kneeling, with her back to the viewer, probably in an attitude of prayer, gazing directly upon her son. The imagined moment portrayed follows the deposition of Christ's body from the cross and possibly also the mourning over his body by the women. Indeed, the composition seems to suggest that Jesus's body has just been removed from Mary's lap (a Pietà) and is now caught in a moment of suspension as the three figures raise and draw the body away towards the tomb located in the distance at the upper right of the panel. Here, Michelangelo displays Christ's body as startlingly nude, with undefined genitals, placing it before the beholder's eyes even more emphatically than in his earlier Vatican *Pietà*. Indeed, unlike more traditional depictions of the Entombment, in which Christ's body is supported horizontally to be laid in a sepulchre, Michelangelo represents it lifted vertically as if to specifically present it to the viewer.[6]

This unusual upright presentation of the body evokes an early iconographic type known as the Man of Sorrows, a devotional image that traditionally showed Christ standing, naked above the waist, with the wounds of his Passion prominently displayed. While these wounds clearly indicate that Jesus has been crucified on the cross, curiously he is shown upright and with his eyes open. This image type is one that stands outside any specific biblical narrative and is intended instead as a timeless devotional image for meditation. The term 'man of sorrows' derives from the Book of Isaiah in the Hebrew Bible (Old

Testament) which describes a figure who was despised, wounded and punished for the transgressions of others who were miraculously healed and saved through his suffering (Isaiah 53:3–6). The figure was associated by Christians with Jesus and from about the eighth century onwards, was visualised in Christian art in the form of the Man of Sorrows motif which underscored the redemptive efficacy of his suffering and death. Michelangelo's 're-oriented' upright, yet dead, Christ clearly draws on this tradition, presumably as an allusion to Jesus's imminent Resurrection. Indeed, Christ's seemingly weightless and pristine body in *The Entombment* altarpiece, showing no sign of wounds or suffering, might deliberately refer to the immaculate resurrected and heavenly body described in the First Epistle to the Corinthians (15:35–49). This upright presentation of the body may have had even further theological and liturgical meanings. Indeed, the unfinished painting, conceived as an altarpiece, was intended to form a dramatic backdrop to the celebration of the Mass during which the Eucharistic wafer, understood to have been transubstantiated into the body of Christ, would have been raised by the priest in front of the work, aligning it with Michelangelo's painted body. As the decoration for a funerary chapel, the allusions to the Man of Sorrows tradition and to Christ's imminent Resurrection must also have resonated with the deceased's own hopes for the afterlife.

As several of Michelangelo's surviving drawings reveal, he subsequently turned to a different, slightly earlier, moment in the Passion narrative to explore the lowering of Christ's body from the cross. In *Studies for a Deposition from the Cross* in Haarlem, the majority of the sheet is dedicated to a drawing in red chalk of a large number of figures who, with the help of two ladders flanking the cross, are working to lower Christ's flopping, lifeless body to the ground (fig. 115/cat. 26). Here, the muscular body has been released from the cross and is now suspended midway between the crossbar and the earth below. The body is stretched into an extraordinary formation by five figures. One of them pulls Jesus's right arm upwards whilst another has slung Christ's left leg incongruously over his own thigh while perched on a rung of a ladder. Jesus's left arm, right leg and unsupported head hang weightily downwards. A second group of figures at the foot of the left ladder represents the Virgin swooning with grief who, like her son, is caught up by a number of attendants, perhaps Saint John at the left and a bending woman at the right, who lower her to the ground. Surrounding this main study are additional sketches of figures in which Michelangelo reconsiders aspects of the composition elaborated at the centre. These include: studies of a kneeling figure; a man straddling the cross; a man supporting Christ's upright body; and, turning the sheet, two figures support-

ing Christ's body, and above that, the three men who lower the body from the cross. Both this sheet and a related work now in London, *The Three Crosses*, give special attention to the crumpled figure of the Virgin at the foot of the cross (fig. 116). In the London sheet, the collapsed Virgin is given particular prominence as she is substantially larger than the surrounding figures and is movingly shown turning her head to look up at her dying son from the ground below the cross. The Haarlem and London sheets therefore present a strikingly different Mary to the restrained, meditative and composed figure of the unfinished painted *Entombment* and the marble *Pietà* described above. This shift in response may reflect the different functions of each work – the painting and sculpture both intended to adorn a funerary chapel in a sacred but more public context in a church, and in the case of the painting at least, to serve as an altarpiece before which the Body of Christ was ritually raised and lowered in the form of the Eucharist at the celebration of the Mass.

While the original purpose of the *Studies for a Deposition* remains unknown, it was subsequently used for a relief composition known through many examples in various media, including wax and bronze. Indeed, a rough plaster cast in the Casa Buonarroti is thought to have been cast directly from Michelangelo's lost wax model, and many later iterations dating to the late sixteenth and seventeenth centuries have been identified (fig. 117). Accordingly, both the Haarlem and London drawings seem to have been intended for a private devotional work where these more dramatic presentations of the Virgin's suffering would have been especially appropriate and intended to elicit a strong emotive response in the beholder. Beyond its initial preparatory purpose, *Studies for a Deposition* evidently continued to provide Michelangelo with a number of artistic possibilities for presenting the dead body of Christ to the viewer in ways that deliberately solicited different empathetic responses. These responses might range, for example, from a focus on the suffering of the mother to a consideration of the literal and emotional burden of the weight of Christ's body on his followers. Alternatively, the work might shift attention to the viewer themselves in some way, either by implicating their presence in the composition by creating a specific viewing point, or by making them feel that, extracted from a larger narrative, the body is being held up to them for veneration and contemplation.

In *The Descent from the Cross* from the Ashmolean Museum, Oxford, Michelangelo combines ideas initially explored in the Haarlem sheet to new effect (fig. 118/cat. 39). Here, Christ's body has been removed from the cross and is now being lowered to the ground with great effort by at least six figures. Neither the cross nor any wider context is given and the Virgin is seemingly

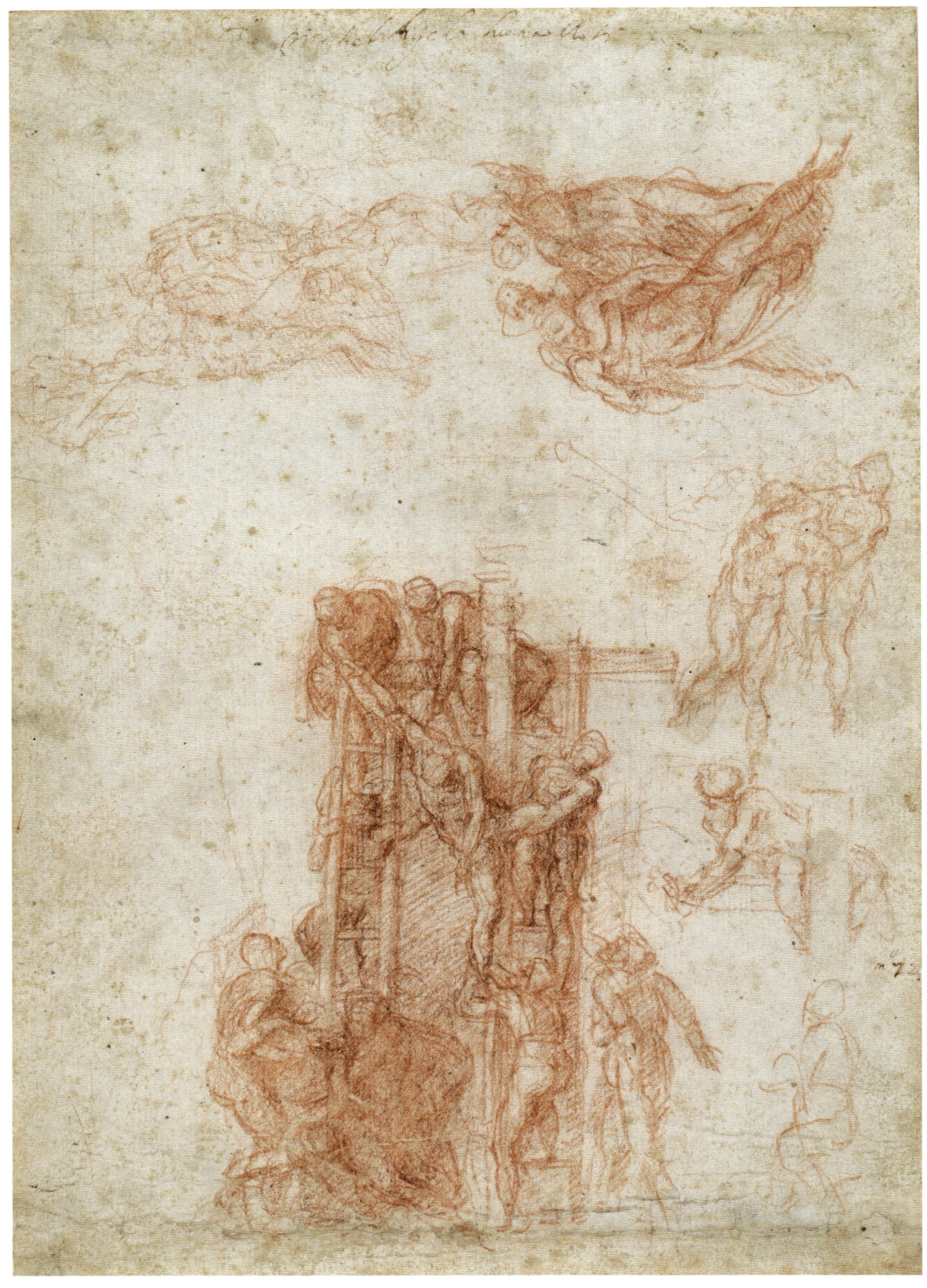

fig. 115   (cat. 26) Michelangelo, *Studies for a Deposition from the Cross*, c. 1522–1524. Red chalk, 273 x 191 mm. Haarlem, Teylers Museum, inv. A 025

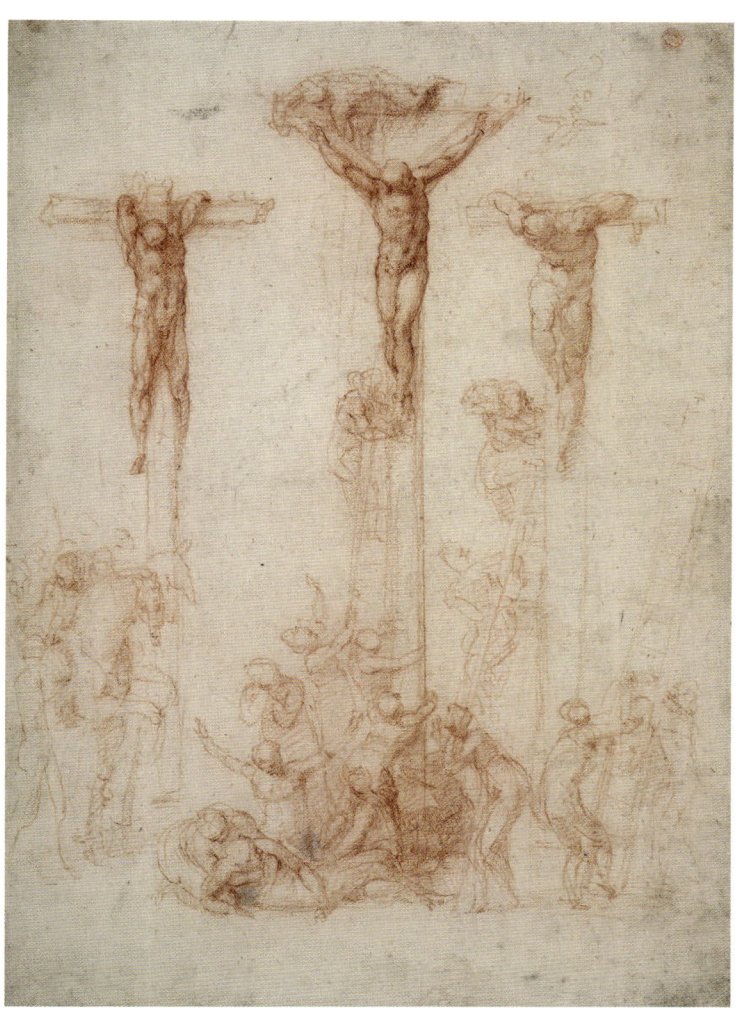

absent. The study seems to combine aspects of two of the marginal sketches on the Haarlem sheet, borrowing and reversing Christ's twisting upper body from one, and the motif of the leg resting on the shoulder of the figure below from the other. Like the Haarlem drawing, this work explores the intimate contact of Christ's body with a large group of mourners while ensuring that he remains at the front and centre of the composition. Michelangelo's effort is clearly concentrated on the figure of Christ, whose torso falls back and to one side, and the two supporting figures closest to the viewer who are seen from behind. Together, these three figures form a compact triangular group that are more intensely worked up than the rest of the figures, some of whom are so summarily sketched, or whose contours overlap with others to such a degree, that they become difficult to distinguish one from the other. Here, the artist's attention is evidently focused on communicating the nature and burden of this dead-weight body, suspended between Crucifixion and Entombment or, theologically speaking, between an earthly death and a divine resurrection, as it is lowered onto these squatting and bending figures and carried to the sepulchre.

Michelangelo continued to experiment with these tightly bound groups of figures and the ways in which they might support or interact with Christ's dead body in a sheet which is unfortunately damaged, yet still highly poignant, and preserved in three fragments: the *Study for a Pietà* (fig. 119).[7] Aspects of the composition recall the artist's earlier unfinished painting of about fifty years earlier as he returns to a frontal and near-upright presentation of Christ's dead body. Here, however, Jesus's head and arm drop to one side, and he is supported at the underarm by a figure standing behind him who raises his right arm with their own and looks down upon his face, almost as if to kiss it. This suggests that the supporting figure is neither Nicodemus nor Joseph of Arimathea, as in the earlier painting, but the Virgin Mary. Mary here plays a far more active role than the passive figure of the swooning Virgin visible at the foot of the cross in Michelangelo's earlier iterations of the theme. At the left of the drawing, an attendant figure, possibly Mary Magdalene, looks outwards as if to present Christ's body to the beholder. A partially preserved figure in the foreground is shown kneeling before the group with his back to the viewer. In this composition, the number of supporting figures has been reduced to five and their postures, even in this fragmentary sheet, are more clearly legible than those in the Oxford drawing. The attention has also shifted to focus specifically on the relationship between mother and son. Indeed, in bringing their faces together in this way, Michelangelo draws on an early tradition most often seen in Orthodox icons of the *Glykophilousa* type known in English as the 'Virgin

fig. 116   Michelangelo, *The Three Crosses*, c. 1522–1524. Red chalk, 394 x 281 mm. London, British Museum, inv. 1860,0616.3

of the Sweet Kiss.' In these images, the Virgin and Christ Child are shown cheek to cheek or even kissing, demonstrating their particularly close and tender relationship. While some early Italian Renaissance artists adopted this Eastern visual tradition, few represented the Virgin pressing her face to that of her dead adult son instead of to her living child. In transposing this motif to the mourning Virgin Mother, Michelangelo may have been drawing on a second association between mother and son, one derived from the *Song of Songs*, a book of the Hebrew Bible containing an anthology of love poems. Since about the twelfth century, Christians interpreted the bride and bridegroom described in the poems as the Virgin and Christ, likening their love to a kind of spiritual marriage in which they are simultaneously mother and son and betrothed lovers. If read through this theological lens, the intimate embrace between mother and son in Michelangelo's drawing suggests Mary's longing for her 'bridegroom'/son and her fervent desire for their ecstatic reunion in heaven.

This exploration between the intimacy of the two figures was a subject Michelangelo would return to in his second marble *Pietà* (known as the *Florentine Pietà*) of around 1547–55 (fig. 120), which he intended for his own tomb in Santa Maria Maggiore in Rome.[8] Now in his seventies, Michelangelo worked on the block of marble for eight years, and would ultimately leave the work both unfinished and partially destroyed after taking a hammer to it and severing Christ's left arm (now repaired) and leg (now absent). The precise reasons for his frustration with the work remain obscure. Some believe the marble was flawed and the sculpture could not be completed, while others have hypothesised over Michelangelo's dissatisfaction with a composition which had already preoccupied him for decades.[9] Here, the artist distils the number of figures down to four, and presents Christ's twisting dead body upright and supported on the lap of the Virgin, who threads her hand under his left arm and presses her hand to his chest. She also presses her face to his own following the *Glykophilousa* type. Above them, the hooded figure of Nicodemus (or possibly Joseph of Arimathea) stands at the top of this pyramidal composition, his left arm wrapped around the Virgin and his right under Christ's right arm supporting his weight as the figure slumps into a zigzag of folded limbs. As Giorgio Vasari noted, the hooded figure, even in its roughly hewn and unfinished state, reveals the features of the artist who therefore takes on the role of bearer and burier of Christ himself.[10] Touchingly, Christ's right arm seems to enfold the kneeling figure of Mary Magdalene at his side, his hand gently resting on her shoulder while she, in turn, supports his bent right leg. The central figure of Christ is the only one that seems to have been relatively

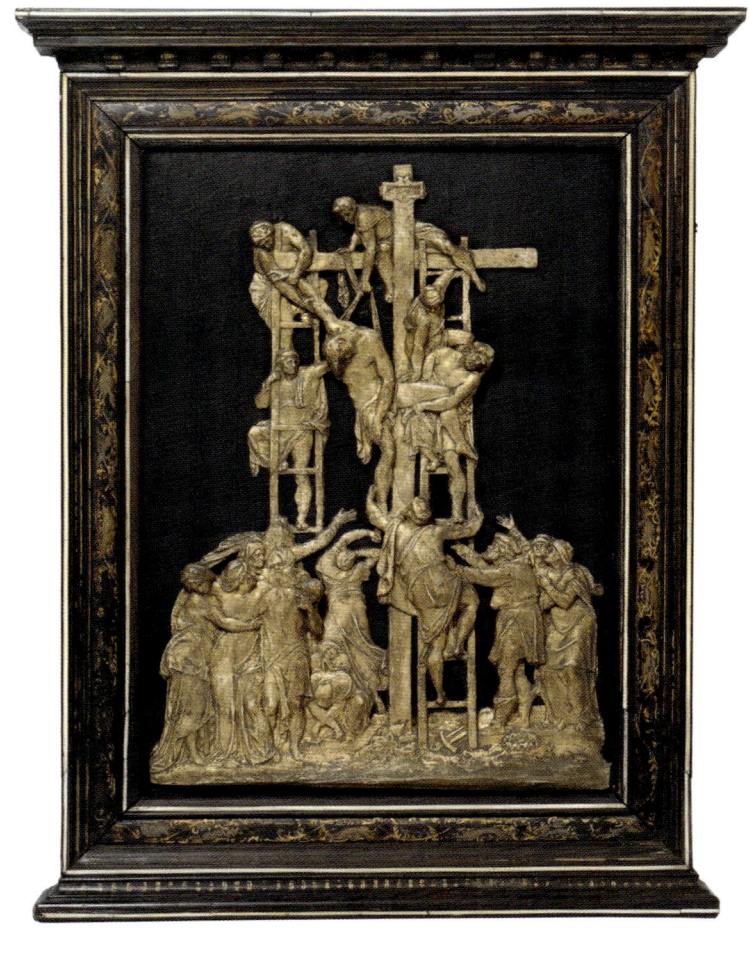

fig. 117   Anonymous, after Michelangelo, *The Deposition,* second half of the sixteenth century. Relief in gilded gesso on a slate ground, 38.1 x 27.9 cm. London, Victoria and Albert Museum, inv. A.1:1-1941

180

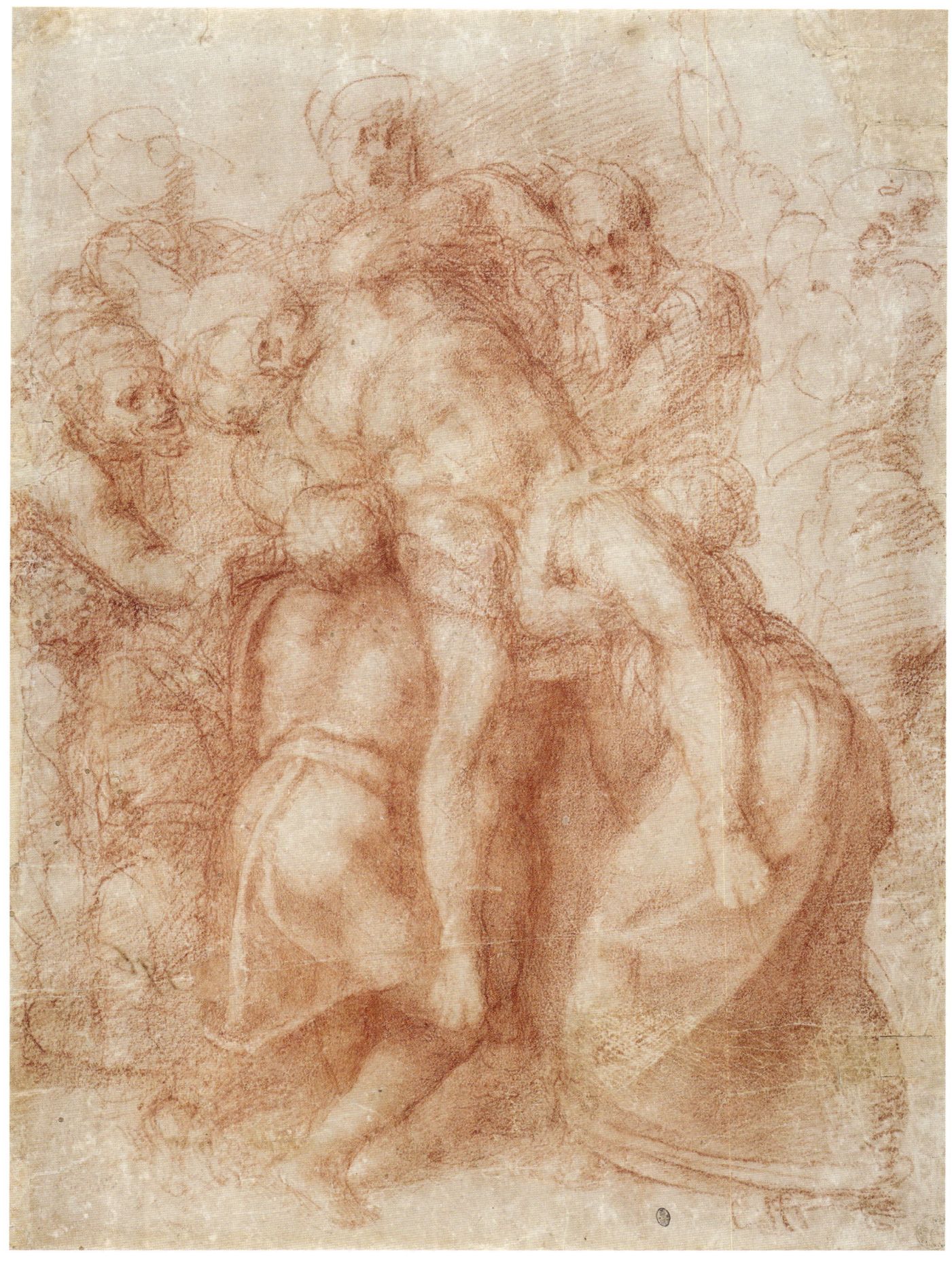

fig. 118   (cat. 39) Michelangelo, *The Descent from the Cross*, c. 1530–1532. Red chalk, 375 x 280 mm. Oxford, Ashmolean Museum, inv. WA1846.88

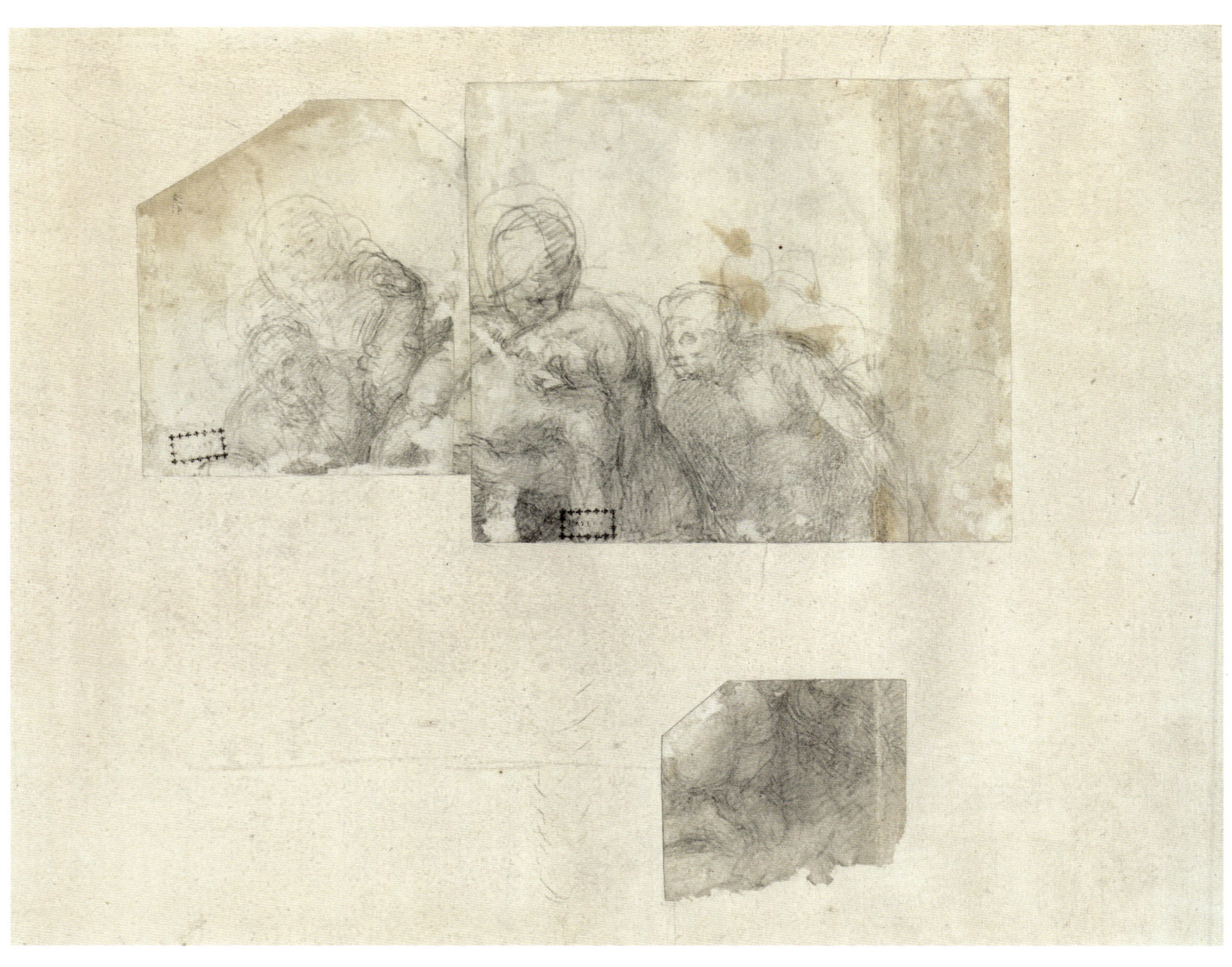

fig. 119   Michelangelo, *Study for a Pietà*, c. 1550–1555. Black chalk, 3 paper fragments (165 x 189 mm, 133 x 116 mm, 75 x 81 mm). Haarlem, Teylers Museum, inv. A 035v

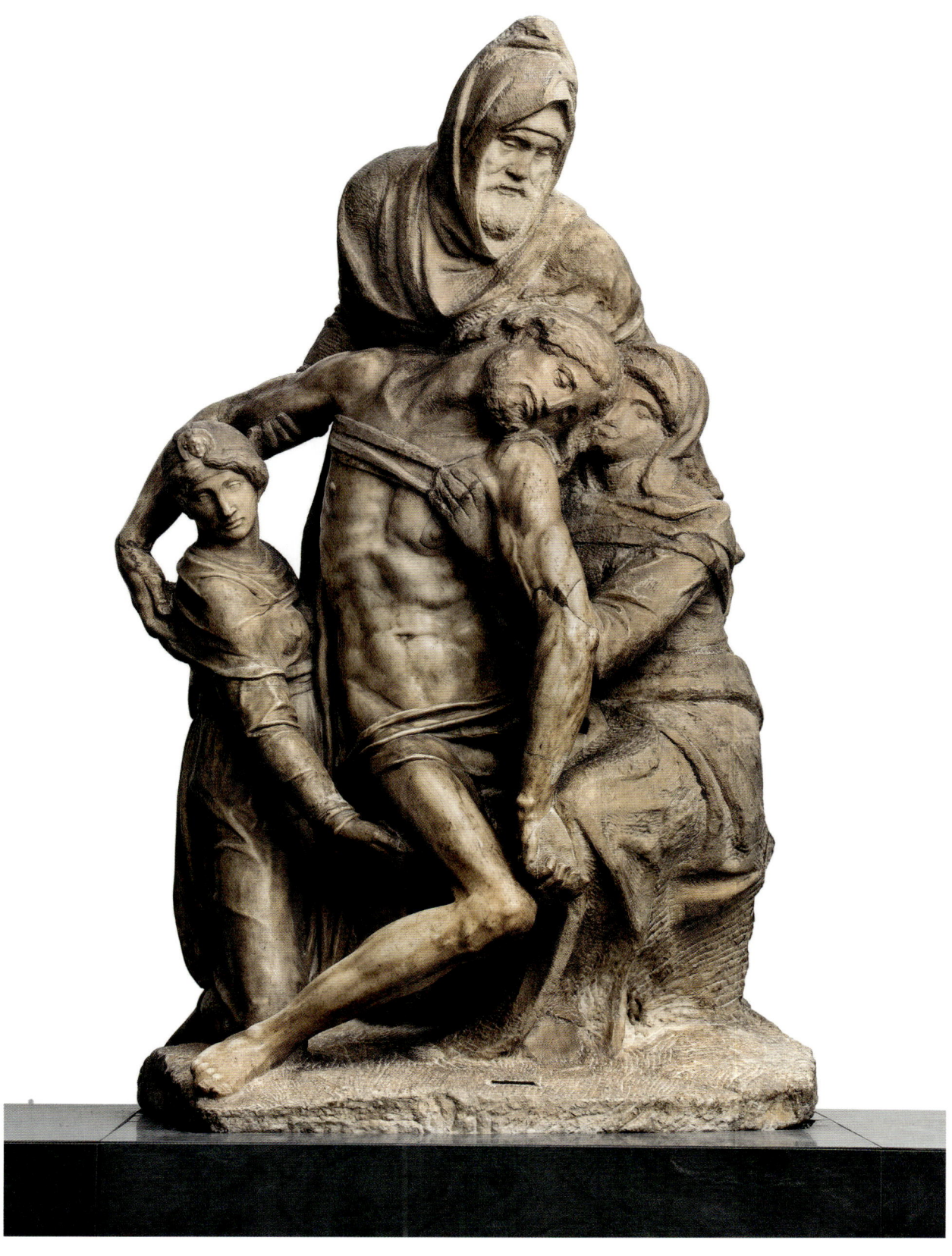

fig. 120   Michelangelo, *Pietà*, c. 1547–1555. Marble, height 226 cm. Florence, Museo dell'Opera del Duomo, inv. 289

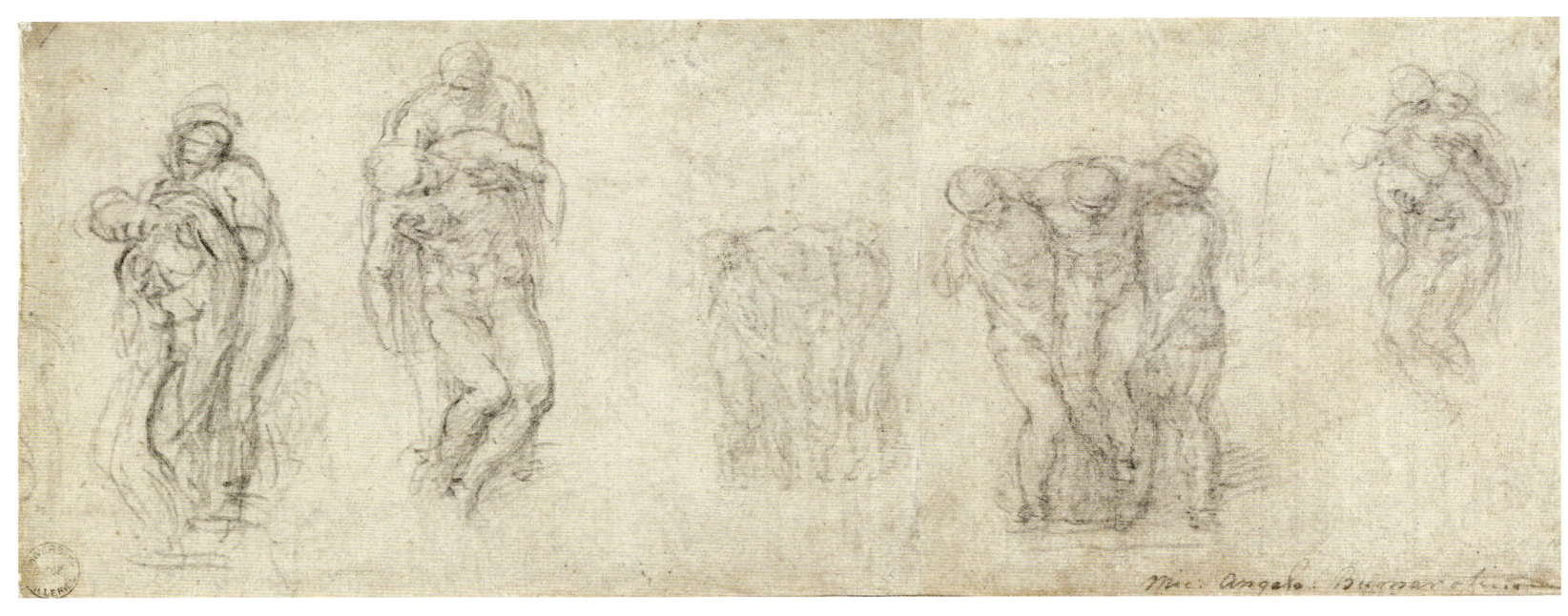

fig. 121   Michelangelo, *Studies for a Two-Figure Pietà and a Three-Figure Entombment*, 1550s. Black chalk, 108 x 281 mm. Oxford, Ashmolean Museum,
         inv. WA1846.85

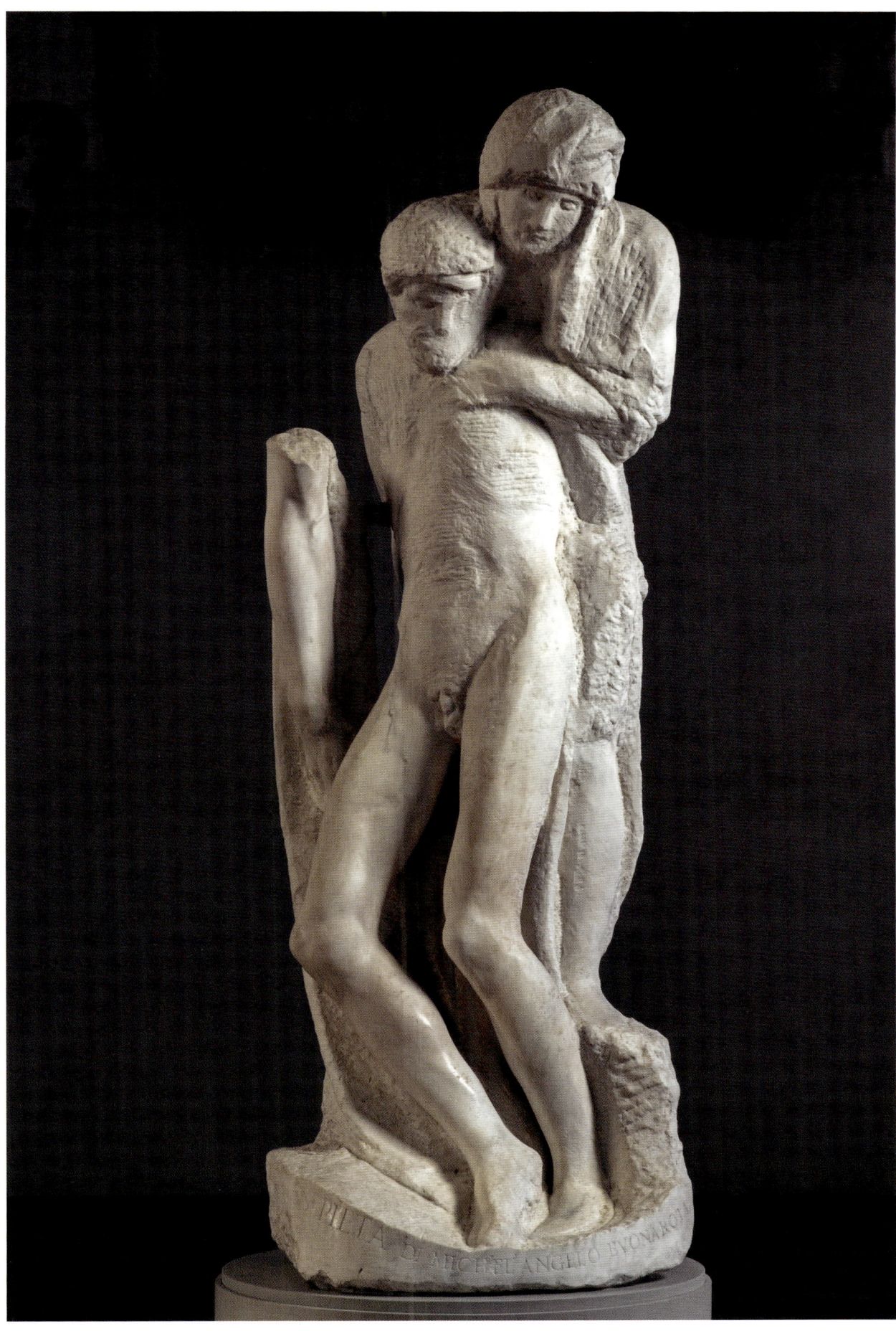

fig. 122   Michelangelo, *Rondanini Pietà*, c. 1552–1564. Marble, height 195 cm. Milan, Castello Sforzesco

finished by the master (the Magdalene is a later work by Michelangelo's assistant Tiberio Calcagni), and originally his left leg slung over the Virgin's thigh with his foot touching the ground. This posture, as Leo Steinberg has demonstrated, was a 'common and unmistakable symbol of sexual union'.[11] Indeed, it was adopted by Renaissance artists after the antique as a symbolic form implying a context of heroic or sacred love, or as in this case, of a kind of divine marriage. Accordingly, the motif underscores the Virgin's role as both mother and 'spouse of Christ' in the tradition of the *Song of Songs*. The use of the sexual metaphor here, however, would have been on a scale unprecedented in Christian devotional art where it was only previously used in a few prints, drawings and small paintings, and not for broad public consumption.[12] Furthermore, the religious climate in Western Europe had changed since the earlier Renaissance period, becoming more cautious and increasingly didactic following the Protestant Reformation and the Council of Trent (1545–63). It has been argued that Michelangelo may have been concerned that once placed in a public sacred space, before the eyes of an audience less familiar with the visual histories and theological meanings of this posture, his marble sculpture would have been misunderstood.[13] Given that the work was intended to mark Michelangelo's tomb, making it a testament both to his divinely given artistic skills and the profound spiritual faith described in his spiritual sonnets, he may have given up on the composition part way through carving, concerned about the response it might elicit in this more conservative and reform-minded religious context.

Indeed, the artist appears to redress this potential issue in several of his subsequent drawings and sculptures on the subject. An important work in this respect is the sheet of *Studies for a Two-Figure Pietà and a Three-Figure Entombment* (fig. 121) in the Ashmolean Museum.[14] In these five sketches, Michelangelo abandoned the problematic motif of the adult Christ shown in the lap or between the legs of the Virgin and instead presents his body fully upright and supported by standing figures. Three of the sketches show Christ supported by a single figure and can be associated with the first version of the artist's final marble Pietà, known as the *Rondanini Pietà* after the Palazzo Rondanini in Rome where it was housed for centuries (fig. 122). The large right arm and the legs on this sculpture are remnants of this first version and will be discussed in greater detail below. The other two sketches on the Oxford sheet show Christ carried by two figures, an idea elaborated in several other surviving studies.[15] What this set of sketches reveals, however, is that as late as the 1550s, Michelangelo was still grappling with the artistic challenges he had encountered over fifty years earlier in the London painting, such

as how to express Christ's humanity whilst simultaneously suggesting his divinity and alluding to his miraculous return to life after death. In the studies from the 1550s, even while Christ is being carried upright, his feet touch the ground in a way that suggests he is animate, even in death, much as he appears in the London *Entombment* (fig. 114). Unlike, however, the London painting and the *Descent from the Cross* drawing in Oxford (fig. 118/cat. 39), in which Christ's body is shown falling backwards and in the process of being drawn away from the viewer towards the tomb, in these sketches, the artist presents the figures proceeding forward, as if into the space of the beholder.

The three sketches showing Christ held up by a single figure directly informed the artist's final *Pietà* (Rondanini) which marks a dramatic shift from his earlier sculptures (fig. 122). Even here, however, Michelangelo seems to be composing and then re-thinking his composition in marble. That he was unsatisfied with the result is revealed by the block itself, which was clearly sculpted, re-sculpted and then left unfinished at his death. While little remains of the first version of this two-figure group, the most conspicuous element is the vestigial muscular right arm which hangs untethered from Christ's re-carved body, its long, thin and near-emaciated torso dissociated from the heroic arm of its predecessor. Fascinatingly, Michelangelo did not remove the arm and elected to keep it, linked to the rest of the block by a thin bridge of marble, as if to hold it up as a negative exemplum of what he was trying to achieve. In re-carving the two figures, the artist was left with a much thinner block of stone which left little room for dramatic gestures or dynamic movement. Indeed, in order to re-work the block, Michelangelo had to sculpt the second figure of Christ out of the figure of the Virgin. In this new configuration, Jesus's head is carved out of his mother's shoulder, and his arms out of her body so that they are fixed against her legs. Although she presses her dead son's shoulder against her chest, the Virgin cannot really be described as supporting him. Here, the energetic pulling, hoisting and supporting of the body, as seen in Michelangelo's earlier compositions, has disappeared and has been replaced with a kind of resigned acceptance and profound stillness. The two bodies seem to press against each other as if propping each other up in a way that defies earthly laws of gravity, as if to suggest that they are no longer of this world but entirely of another.

The Crucified Body

According to Michelangelo's biographer Ascanio Condivi, the artist's earliest representation of the Crucifixion was the wooden crucifix he carved around 1492 for the prior of the church of Santo Spirito in Florence, as a thank you for allowing him to study the anatomy of corpses before their burial (fig. 123).[16] Most scholars have associated this precocious work, made when the artist was just seventeen, with the delicately modelled and serene-faced sculpture that hangs to this day in the church for which it was made. This near life-sized figure of the naked crucified Christ was originally placed above the high altar, and was presumably provided with a real loincloth, as was the custom in this period. The body is painted a pale flesh tone with red articulating his side, hand and foot wounds, as well as droplets on his forehead to indicate where the crown of thorns was fixed. This slender, gently twisting and seemingly fragile body is quite at odds with the later heroic muscular bodies of Michelangelo's maturity, but not far from the body presented to the viewer in the London *Entombment* (fig. 114). It has been suggested that the appearance of this early work may have been informed by the charismatic Dominican preacher Girolamo Savonarola, whose sermons in Florence in this period had a lasting effect on Michelangelo. Indeed, in one sermon, Savonarola described Christ's body as 'delicate, and very sensitive' presumably in part to encourage his audience to imagine the intensity of Jesus's suffering at the Crucifixion.[17]

Michelangelo would return to the subject again much later in life with a markedly different approach; for example, in a black-chalk drawing produced almost forty years later, *Studies for a Crucifixion*, Michelangelo presents a frontal view of a crucified male body with the head lightly sketched in two positions and the legs slightly bent at the knees at the centre of the sheet (fig. 90/cat. 41). The artist concentrates his attention on the figure's right flank and its contours, leaving the left side more summarily sketched in. On the right, he made a second study, this time observing a suspended figure as seen from the right. At the left of the sheet, he added a study for a right knee and a shoulder as seen from above. All these sketches appear to be studies from life and suggest Michelangelo was posing and moving around his model in the studio, exploring different viewpoints and spatial arrangements. While the drawing cannot be definitively associated with a known project, scholars have suggested it is a study for a Golgotha group that was designed by Michelangelo in the early 1530s but never produced. A number of later bronze statuettes, however, seem to reflect the artist's original intention for these drawings, as seen, for example, in a bronze Christ of around 1560–70, now in New York,

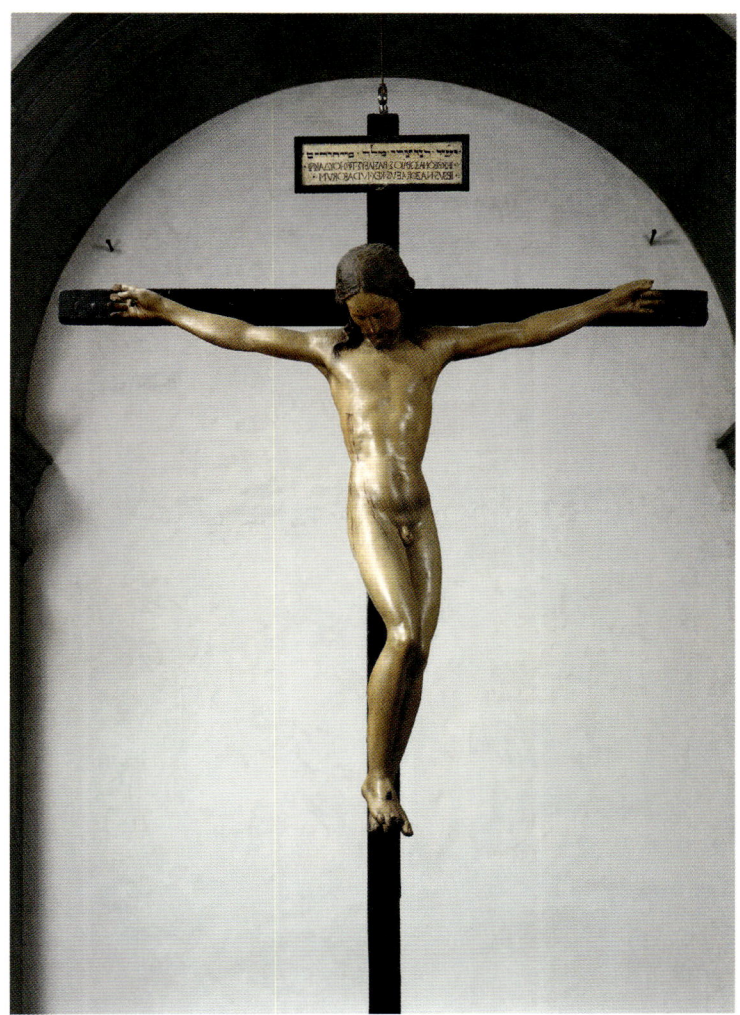

fig. 123   Michelangelo, *Crucifix*, c. 1492. Polychrome wood, height 142 cm. Florence, Basilica di Santo Spirito

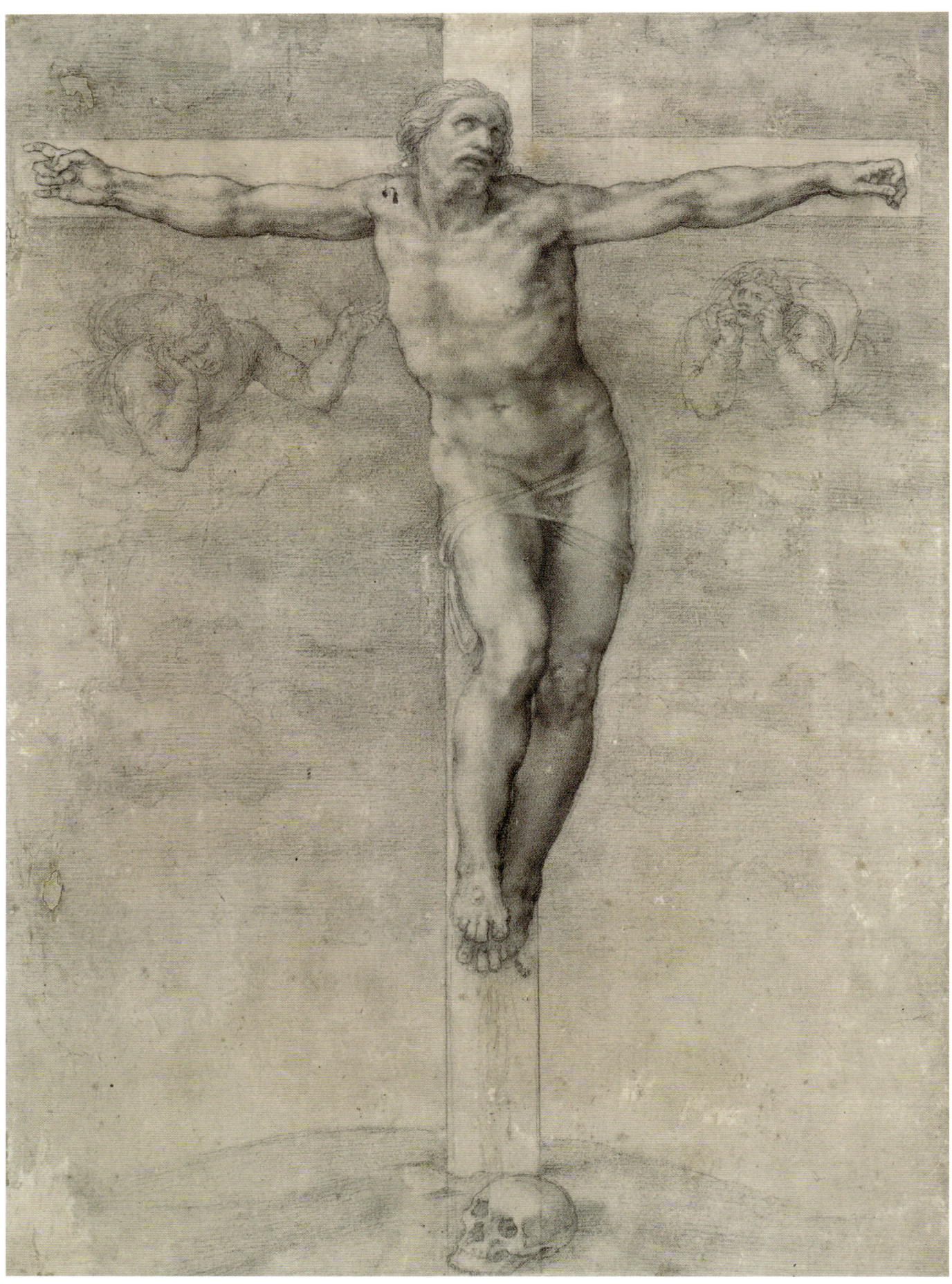

fig. 124   Michelangelo, *Crucifixion,* c. 1538–1541. Black chalk, 370 x 270 cm. London, British Museum, inv. 1895,0915.504

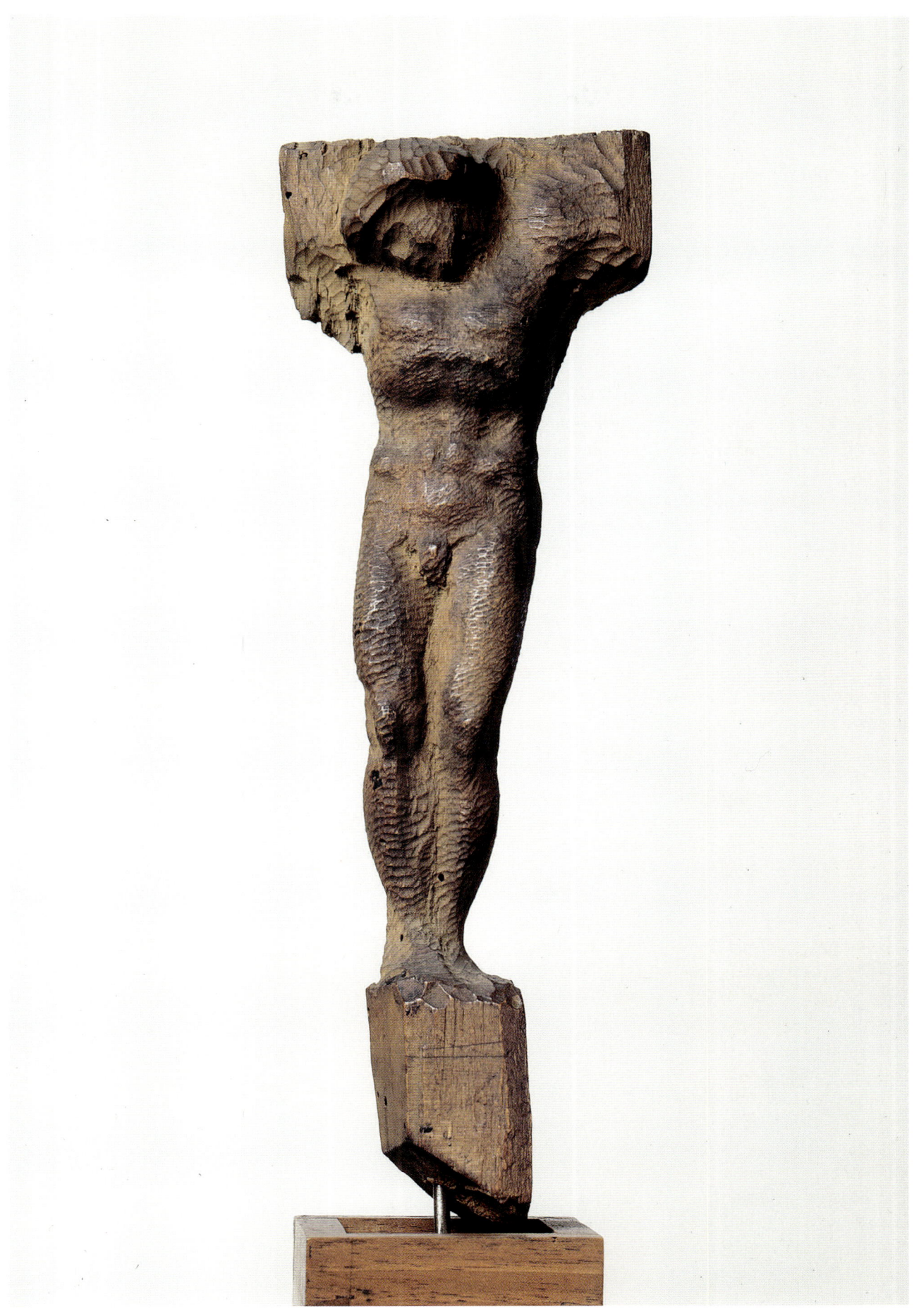

fig. 125   (cat. 47) Attributed to Michelangelo, *Bozzetto for a Crucifixion*, c. 1562–1563. Wood, height 25 cm. Florence, Casa Buonarroti, inv. 195

in which the slim and highly articulated naked muscular body hangs in a similar posture.[18]

One of Michelangelo's most important representations of the Crucifixion is the highly finished 'presentation' drawing he made as a gift for his friend and spiritual confidante, the poet and religious reformer Vittoria Colonna, in around 1538–41 (fig. 124).[19] Colonna was an important member of the growing number of reform-minded Catholics who were seeking an intense personal spirituality, that is, one less mediated by the clergy and the church, and more centred on Christ, the Scriptures and on the theological writings of the early Church Fathers as advocated by Luther and other Protestant thinkers. Rome, especially, became a centre for spiritual renewal in this period and for this group of *spirituali* who sought the personal revelation of God's grace through the working of the Holy Spirit.[20] Intriguingly, Michelangelo's Crucifixion drawing for Colonna represents Christ on the cross flanked only by two lamenting angels and no additional figures. Colonna describes the drawing in a letter to Michelangelo saying 'I have received your letter and seen the Crucifix which has certainly crucified itself in my memory more than any other picture that I have ever seen'.[21] Here, Michelangelo's spiritual confidante poetically identifies the affective nature of the work which, with its rich modelling and powerful three-dimensionality, largely achieved through the use of a stippling technique rather than hatching, provides an intense and meditative spiritual focus. The emotional lamenting postures of the angels may be seen as modelling different responses to the subject for the viewer. Most striking, however, is Michelangelo's highly original representation of Christ as triumphant in the moment of his sacrifice. He is shown alive, his side unpierced by Longinus' lance, and with his eyes cast upwards towards heaven. His heroic body, undiminished by suffering, seems deliberately to evoke the ancient sculptures of gods and heroes being discovered in Rome in this period, such as the *Laocoön Group*, which was put on public display in the Vatican's Cortile delle Statue, where it remains to this day (fig. 46).

After completing his Crucifixion for Vittoria Colonna (fig. 124), most of Michelangelo's time was dedicated to the monumental *The Last Judgement*, with which he frescoed the entire altar wall of the Sistine Chapel in the Vatican (fig. 96). He would return to the subject of the crucified body again, however, in a flurry of activity in the 1550s. Indeed, around 1557–62 Michelangelo drew a series of arresting three-figure compositions on the theme of the Crucifixion, including six complete drawings and four fragments.[22] In almost all these studies, Christ's head hangs limply on his chest, a posture that

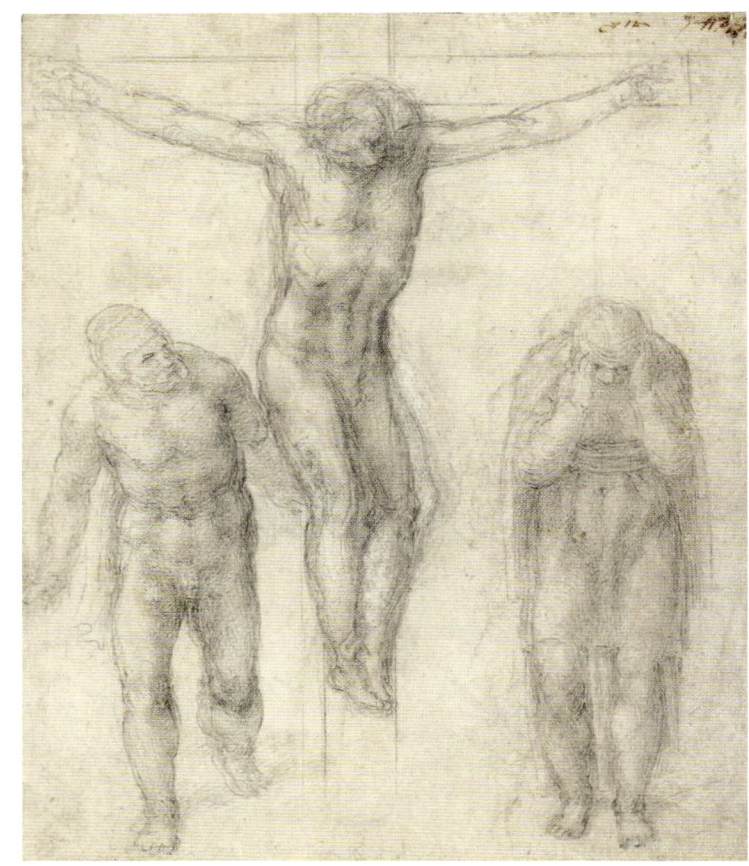

fig. 126   Michelangelo, *Crucifixion with Two Figures*, c. 1557–1562. Black chalk with white heightening, 278 x 234 mm. Oxford, Ashmolean Museum, inv. WA1846.89

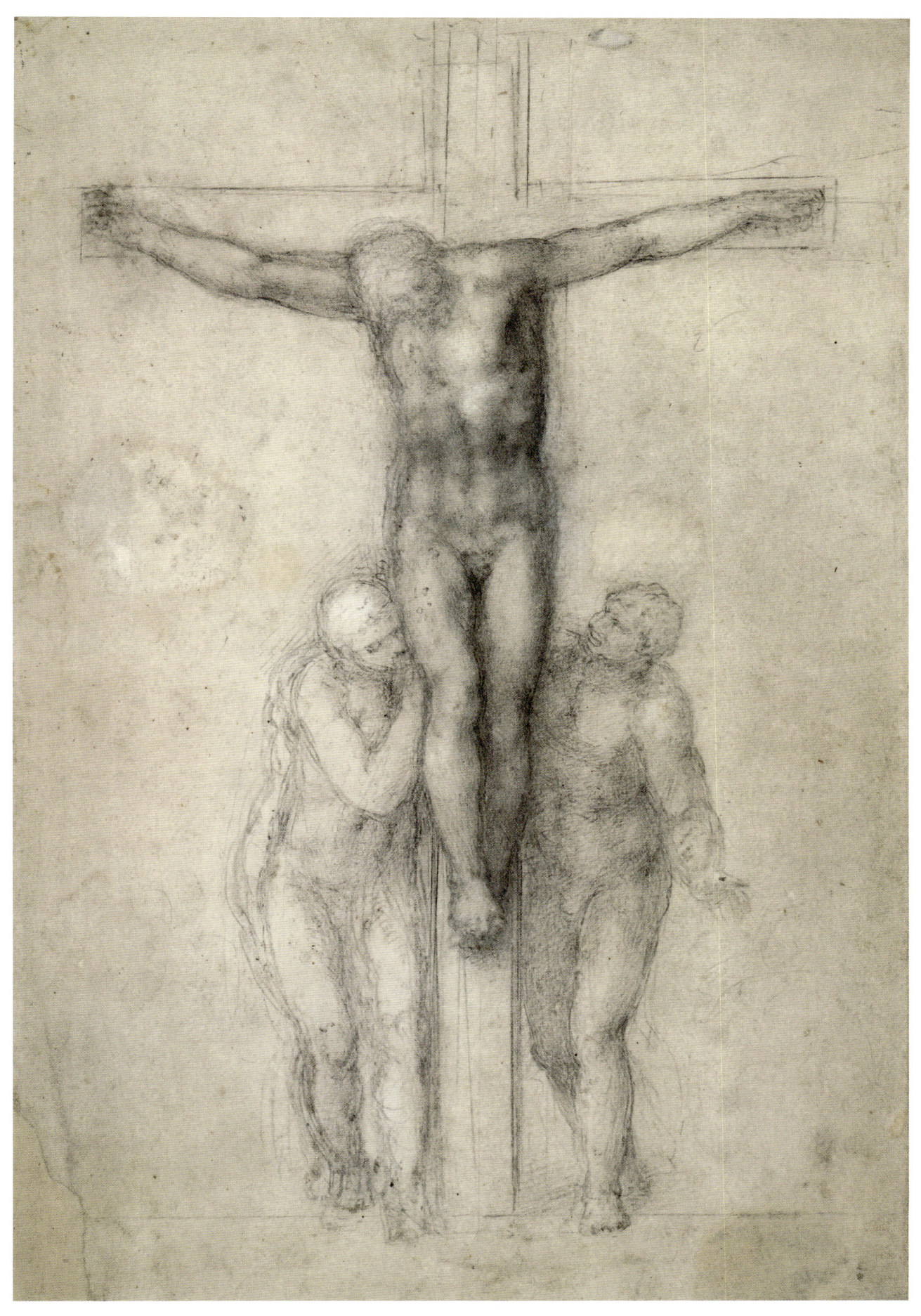

fig. 127   Michelangelo, *Crucifixion with the Virgin and Saint John*, c. 1557–1562. Black chalk with white heightening, 410 x 278 mm. London, British Museum, inv. 1895,0915.510

encourages an even more intense emotional response in the viewer. Again, the precise purpose of these drawings remains unknown, and while they may have been preparatory for a sculpture or painting, it is also possible that they were being used as a kind of spiritual exercise by the artist. Indeed, in his old age, Michelangelo became increasingly preoccupied with the challenge of conveying Christ's divine love as expressed in his acceptance of the cross for the salvation of humankind. In what may be interpreted as a poetic counterpart to these drawings, Michelangelo wrote in a sonnet of 1554: 'There's no painting or sculpture now that quiets / The soul that's pointed toward that holy Love / That on the cross opened Its arms to take us.'[23]

In addition to these drawings and poems, around 1562 Michelangelo carved a small, fragmentary wooden *bozzetto* (sketch) of the head, torso and legs of the Crucified Christ (fig. 125/cat. 47).[24] As in the drawn studies, Christ's head is dropped to one side. Curiously however, rather than following tradition and portraying one leg or ankle crossed over the other to suggest where Christ's feet were nailed to the cross, this figure's feet appear quite firmly planted one beside the other. This work, left unfinished and considered one of Michelangelo's last known sculpted works, may be related to two letters of the same date that he wrote to his nephew, Lionardo, indicating his intention to carve a wooden crucifix for him.[25] Interestingly, Vasari reveals that Michelangelo also made a small crucifix as a gift for his friend Menighella.[26] It is clear therefore that, for Michelangelo, the Crucifixion was a particularly appropriate subject for gifts for his nearest and dearest, and one wonders, given his deep faith, whether this practice was intended to underscore Christ's ultimate gift in sacrificing himself on the cross for the salvation of humankind.

While the sequential order of Michelangelo's late Crucifixion drawings (*c.* 1557–62) is still debated, Carmen Bambach has convincingly suggested that they may move from a marked three-quarter view of Christ on the cross, with flanking figures who gesture dramatically but do not interact, as in *The Crucifixion with Two Figures* in Oxford (fig. 126), to a crucified Christ in an iconic frontal view that harmonises with the Virgin and Saint John at the foot of the cross, such as the *Crucifixion with the Virgin and Saint John* in London (fig. 127).[27] Indeed, in the Oxford drawing, Michelangelo made several changes to Christ's head, first representing it turned to the right, before bringing it back to the centre to hang limply over the chest, and repeatedly reworked the torso and legs to adjust an earlier *contrapposto* twisting pose to a more frontal position. The muscular figure to the left is positioned so close to the cross that his left arm coincides uncomfortably with it and appears to disappear behind it, while his feet seem, incongruously, to stride out in front. The mourning figure to the right appears caught up in grief and ignores the others. The discordant combination of the figures here is such that each requires its own distinct consideration – taking attention away from the drama of the central event. By contrast, in the London Crucifixion drawing, Christ is represented in a clear, frontal view, while the two flanking saints embrace the cross, uniting all three figures into a harmonious grouping with a clear focus. Moving from one iteration of the subject to the next, one senses the artist using the drawings as a kind of meditation on the mystery of Christ's dual nature, on his suffering and sacrifice for the redemption of humankind from sin and its consequences, and on the promise of eternal life through Jesus's death and resurrection.

The Resurrected Body

Given this life-long focus on the dead body of Christ, it is perhaps unsurprising that Michelangelo should also explore the great mystery of Christ's resurrected body. In Christian theology, the Resurrection of Jesus is considered one of the mysteries – if not the central mystery – of the faith which holds that God raised Jesus from the dead on the third day after his Crucifixion, marking his exalted life as Christ (that is, as the Messiah or the Anointed One) and Lord. Jesus's bodily Resurrection is described in biblical texts as being transformed into a spiritual or celestial body, and it is this restoration to life that guarantees that all the Christian dead will be resurrected at Christ's Second Coming, his return to earth at the moment of the Last Judgement.[28] Michelangelo first treated the subject in two sculpted versions of *The Risen Christ* dating from around 1514–21 intended for the Porcari chapel in Santa Maria sopra Minerva in Rome. The first version of these appears to have been abandoned due to a fault in the marble, but both represent a heroic standing nude Christ holding a cross, and reveal Michelangelo's close study of the magnificent ancient Greek and Roman sculptures such as the *Belvedere Torso*, the *Laocoön Group*, and the *Apollo Belvedere*, all recently rediscovered in Rome.[29] Michelangelo would return to the subject of the Resurrection in earnest in the years after 1530, and arguably one of his greatest treatments of the subject is *The Last Judgement* fresco of around 1536–41 for the altar wall of the Sistine Chapel (fig. 96). Here, the artist again draws on the antique to represent the figure of the resurrected Christ at the top centre of the composition, who is shown raising the dead at this moment of reckoning.

At around the same time as he was working on *The Last Judgement*, that is from about 1530 onwards, Michelangelo executed some sixteen linked drawings on

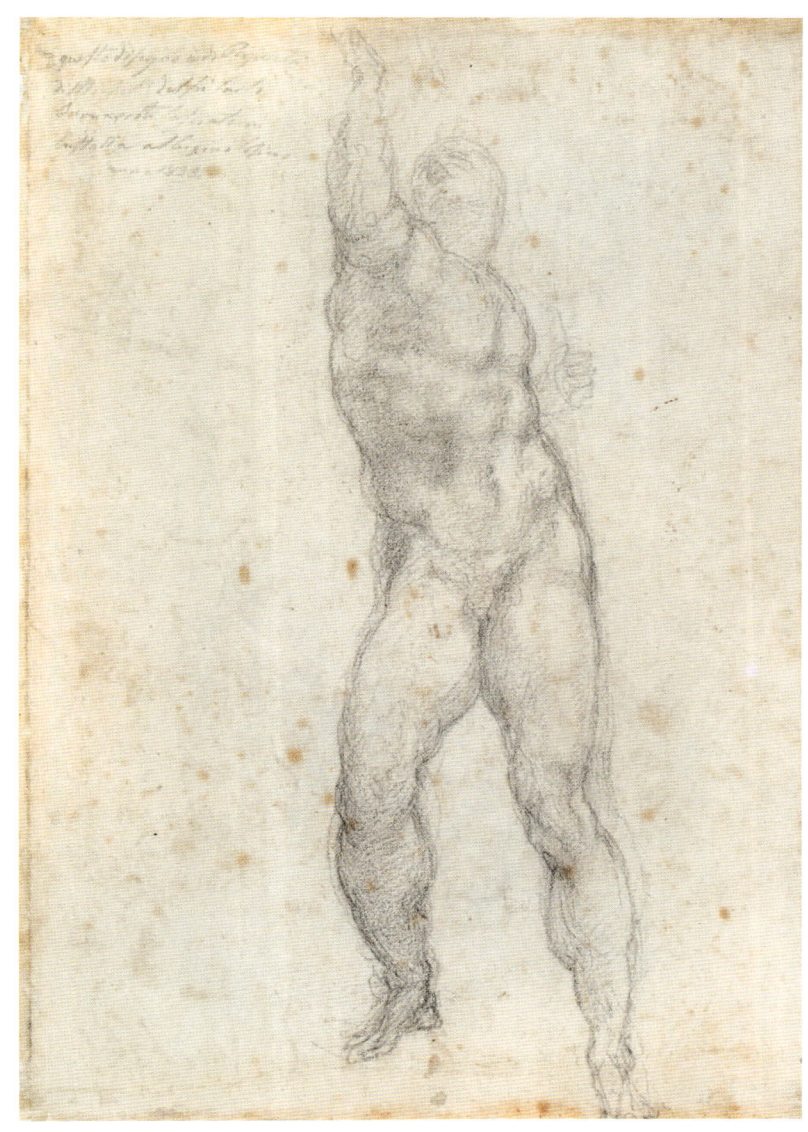

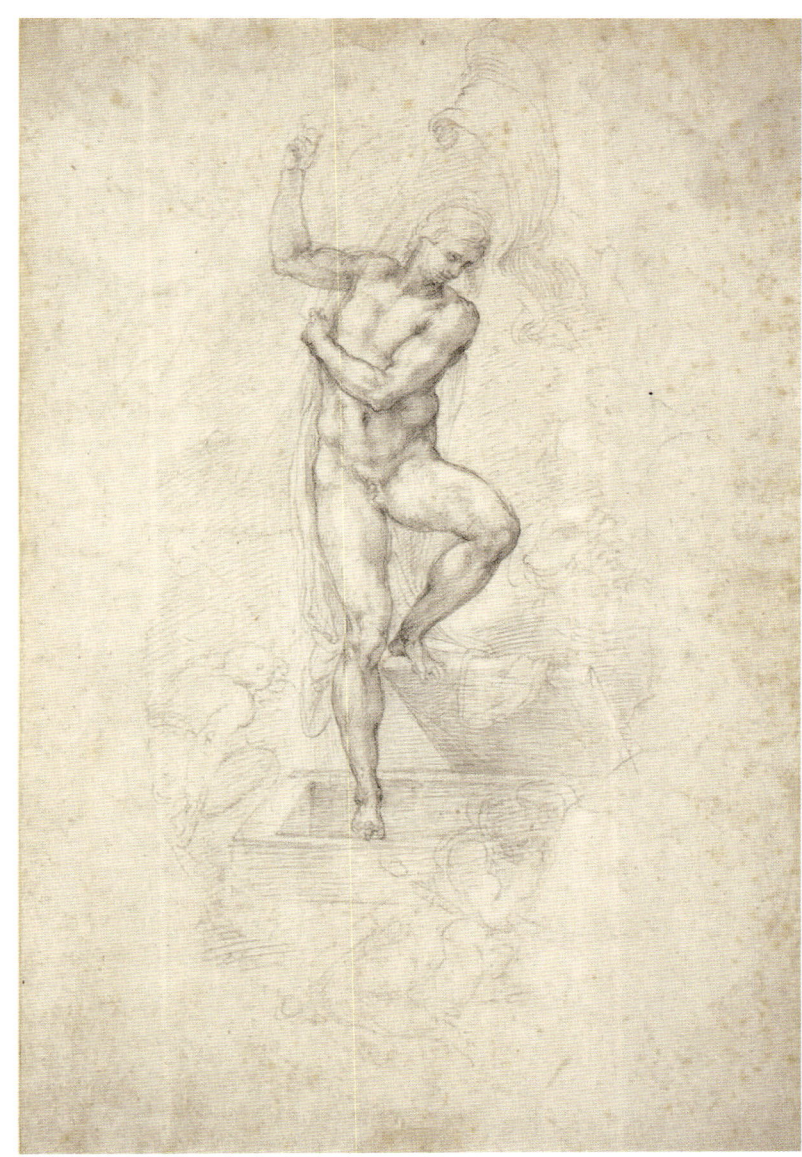

fig. 128   Michelangelo, *The Risen Christ*, c. 1532–1533. Black chalk,
            418 x 288 mm. Florence, Casa Buonarroti, inv. 65F

fig. 129   Michelangelo, *The Risen Christ*, c. 1532–1533. Black chalk,
            406 x 271 mm. London, British Museum, inv. 1887,0502.119

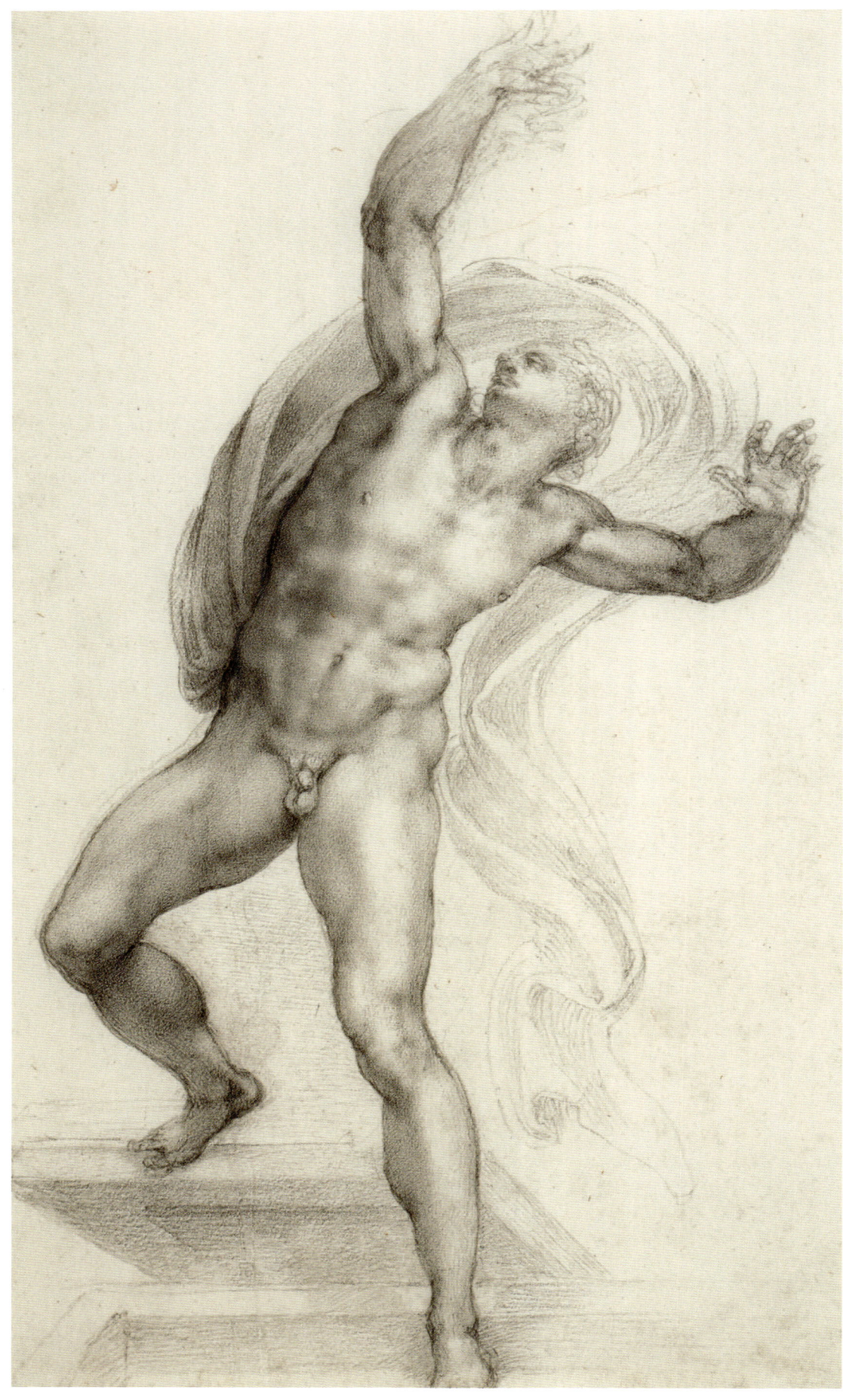

fig. 130   Michelangelo, *The Risen Christ*, c. 1532–1533. Black chalk, 372 x 221 mm. Windsor, Royal Collection Trust, inv. RCIN 912768

the theme of the Resurrection and further independent studies of the Risen Christ. While Michelangelo's compositional studies of the Resurrection may have been intended as preparation for a specific project, no firm documentary evidence on these exists, and neither of Michelangelo's biographers mentions a Resurrection project. Scholars have suggested, however, that these drawings relate to a design for an altarpiece, perhaps to assist Michelangelo's collaborator Sebastiano del Piombo in his commission for an altarpiece in the Chigi Chapel in Santa Maria della Pace, or for the decoration of the entrance wall of the Sistine Chapel.[30] By contrast, the highly finished single-figure drawings of the Risen Christ may have been intended, not as preparatory sketches, but as 'presentation drawings' of the type Michelangelo gifted to Vittoria Colonna, as discussed above.[31] Regardless of their original purpose – or purposes – what becomes apparent is that, like his drawings of the Crucifixion and Lamentation, these works go beyond mere practical studies and appear to serve the artist's own spiritual needs.

Within this large group of Resurrection drawings, the sheets fall fairly neatly into two distinct types. The first consists of largely horizontal multi-figure configurations in which guards scatter in astonishment as Christ rises from the tomb, while the second, which will be considered in greater depth here, comprises vertically oriented compositions focusing primarily on the single figure of Christ at his moment of triumph over death. These single-figure compositions are worked up into various states of finish, ranging from loose sketches (fig. 128), to more worked-up compositions (fig. 129) and highly finished works (fig. 130). Taken together, these drawings reveal Michelangelo's seemingly inexhaustible ability to investigate a range of physical, emotional and spiritual states through very nuanced adjustments to the figure's posture, such as bending a leg or widening the gestures of his arms.[32] The drawings also explore different ways the Saviour might emerge from the tomb, from propelling himself upwards from the sarcophagus with great energy, to a calm, almost floating, ascent (fig. 131). In *The Risen Christ* (fig. 128), all extraneous detail (the soldiers, the cave, the shroud) is removed, and it is only with comparison with other works in the series (such as fig. 129) that one can 'fill in the blanks' and imagine Jesus leaping out of the open tomb, his front, left leg stepping over the threshold with his back, right foot pushing away the cover of the sarcophagus. This posture suggests a twisting forward and upward propulsion. The figure's receding left hand, just faintly sketched in, was presumably meant to be holding the shaft of the flag traditionally held by Jesus in representations of this scene. This banner, usually described as a 'Resurrection' or 'Triumphal' cross is often borne by Christ as a stand-

ard of power, evoking his ability to conquer death and hell. With his dramatically raised right arm and thrown-back head just lightly sketched in, Michelangelo implies a rising movement heavenward. Indeed, lacking the more defined shadows and contours of the rest of the torso, the arm and head of the figure appear as if they are disappearing, almost dissolving into a bright light emanating from above. This posture already seems to allude to Christ's immanent Ascension into heaven which, according to the gospels, only occurred forty days after his Resurrection.

Of all these related studies, Michelangelo's most famous treatment of the subject is probably the highly finished black-chalk drawing *The Risen Christ* (fig. 130), which represents Jesus dramatically springing from his tomb. In this extraordinary drawing, Christ's limbs span the entire sheet and his head, thrown back, is reduced in size as if to draw greater attention to the magnificently modelled torso at the centre. Here, Michelangelo used a particularly innovative technique: tiny, stippled strokes of chalk to build up the three-dimensionality of the body which appears to stand out from the plane of the paper, leaving the shroud behind him to appear flattened and almost decorative. In the Windsor sheet, Christ is represented as young, muscular and powerful, like an Olympian god, with only the lightly drawn sarcophagus below him signalling the wider context. The extraordinary energy, both in Christ's pose and in the rendering of his body, express this triumph of the soul over death. Indeed, the way the bright light appears to reflect off Jesus's torso makes it appear to transcend the earthly, material world and ascend towards an otherworldly sphere composed of light and spirit.

The dramatic contrast between this triumphant Olympian body of the Risen Christ and the thin, almost emaciated appearance of Christ's torso in the *Rondanini Pietà*, dated around thirty years later (fig. 122), may be attributed in part to the different materials used and to the different moments of the Christian story each presents. Indeed, we might compare the solemnity of the treatment of the end of Jesus's earthly life with the celebratory energy of the beginning of his new life after death. There seems to be more, however, to Michelangelo's change in approach to the representation of Christ's body in his later career, one that appears to transcend the physical, to focus instead on the emotional and the spiritual. In these late works we observe a move away from extraneous figures and narrative detail in favour of a near-obsessive reworking of the body of Christ. This approach is particularly evident in the Crucifixion drawings and the *Rondanini Pietà*, which forms seem to both preoccupy and elude the artist as he works towards a deeper understanding of Christ's sacrifice on the cross and what this means for his own salvation. Indeed, the young artist who, if Vasari's anecdote is to be

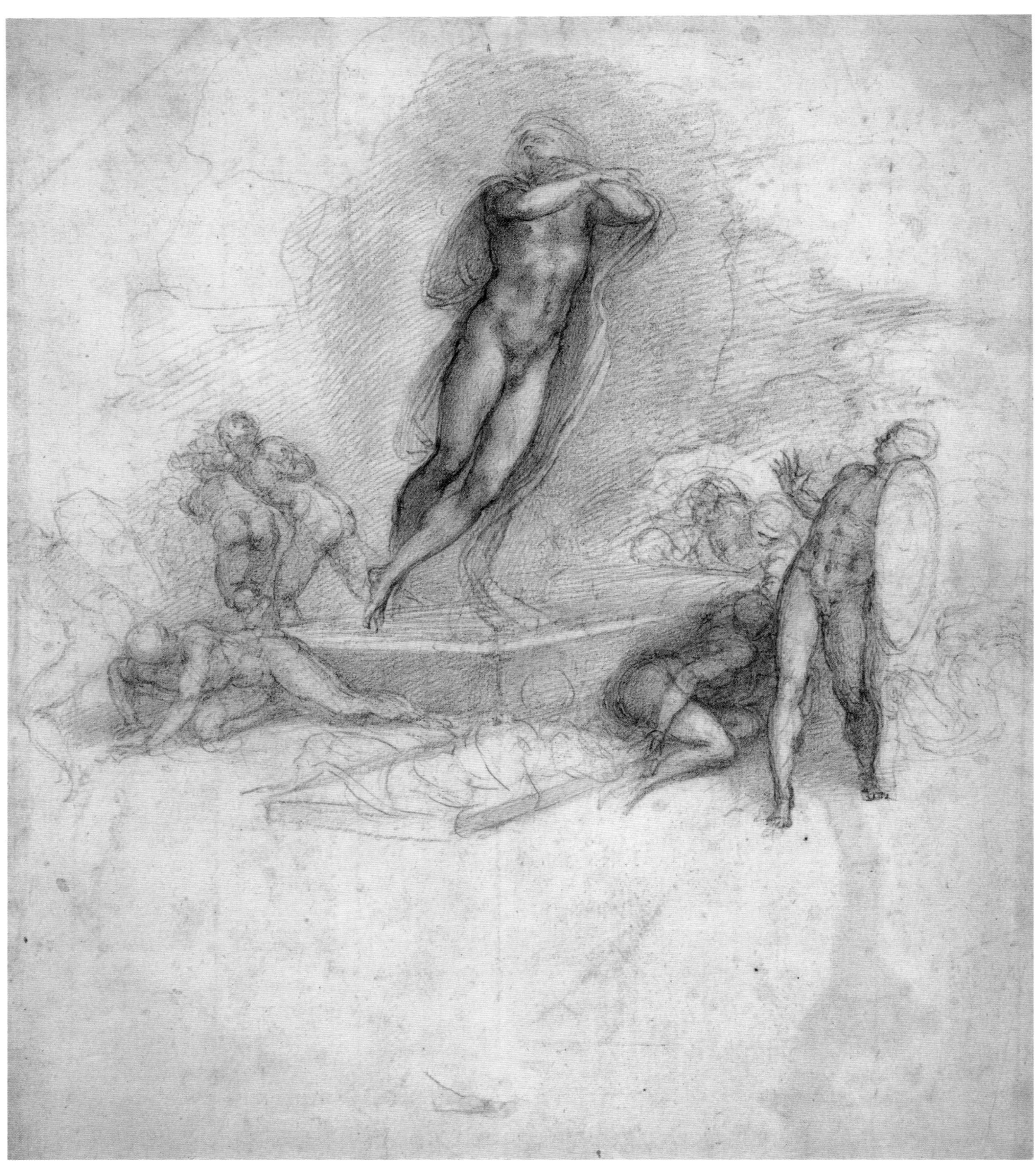

fig. 131   Michelangelo, *The Resurrection of Christ*, c. 1532–1533. Black chalk, 326 x 286 mm. London, British Museum, inv. 1860,0616.133

believed, later regretted signing the Vatican *Pietà* (fig. 113) as a prideful act, seems to become increasingly humble in his later years when attempting to represent the divine body of Christ.

These later works reveal Michelangelo's emotional intensity and investment in the subject and it is perhaps unsurprising that, according to his assistant, in 1561 the aged artist was drawing barefoot for three hours with such a concentrated exertion that it eventually caused him to faint.[33] Michelangelo's deep life-long commitment to understanding and portraying Jesus's life, death and sacrifice is at once highly theological and deeply personal, and his treatment of the subject reflects his changing ideas about the nature of Christ's sacrifice and his own relationship with God. Indeed, Michelangelo's anxieties about this relationship are especially evident towards the end of his life, as testified by the poetry of his last years. In sonnet 285 for example, he describes himself as a Christian pilgrim facing death, and repents his past artistic vanity in failing to subordinate art and love to God as his soul turns towards the open and loving arms of Christ on the cross.[34] In sonnet 290, Michelangelo craves reunion with God in heaven and implores Christ to shorten his time on earth in order to be liberated from his 'troublesome and heavy corpse' and to bring him closer to the 'sweet calm' of the afterlife in Paradise.[35]

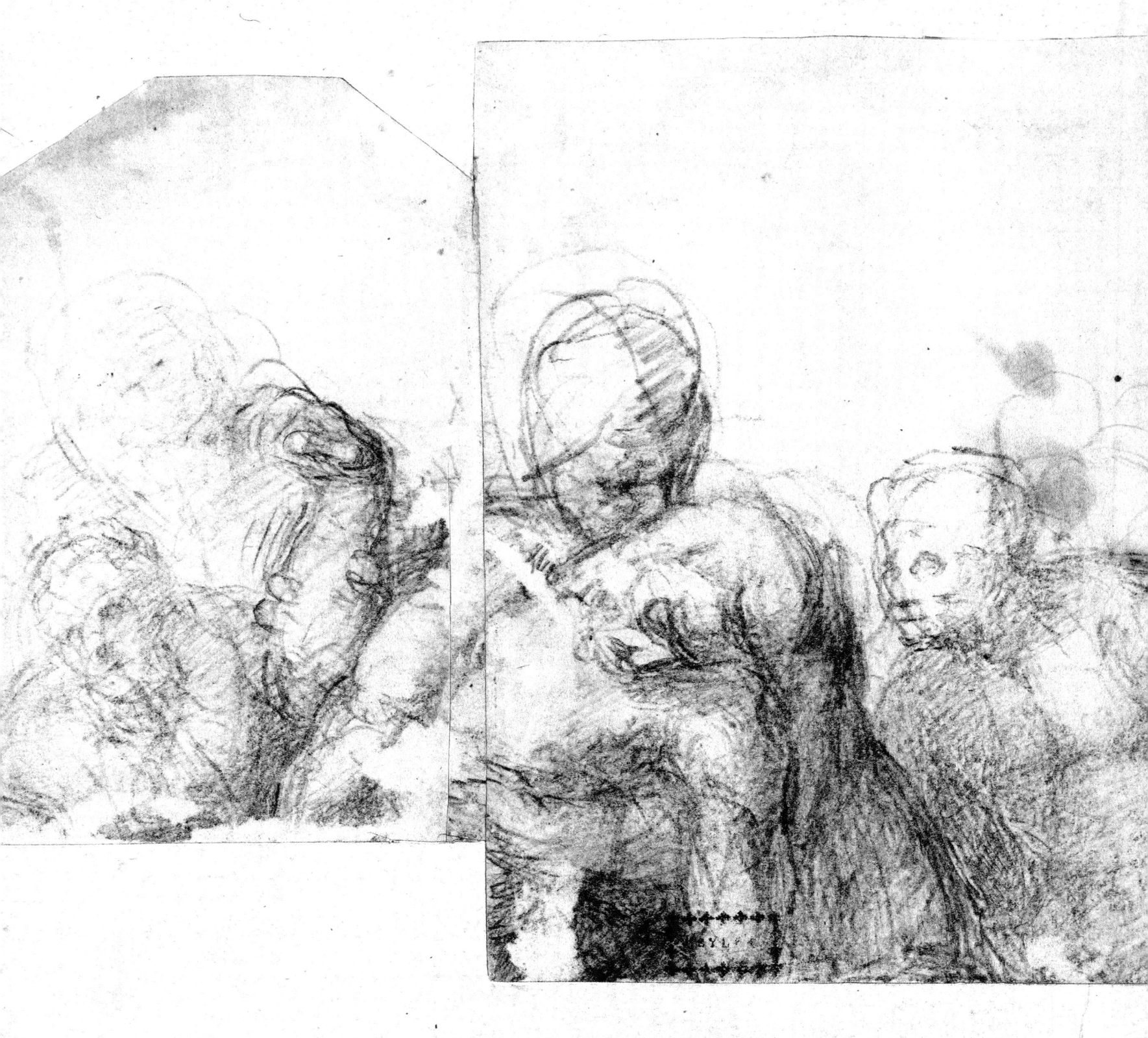

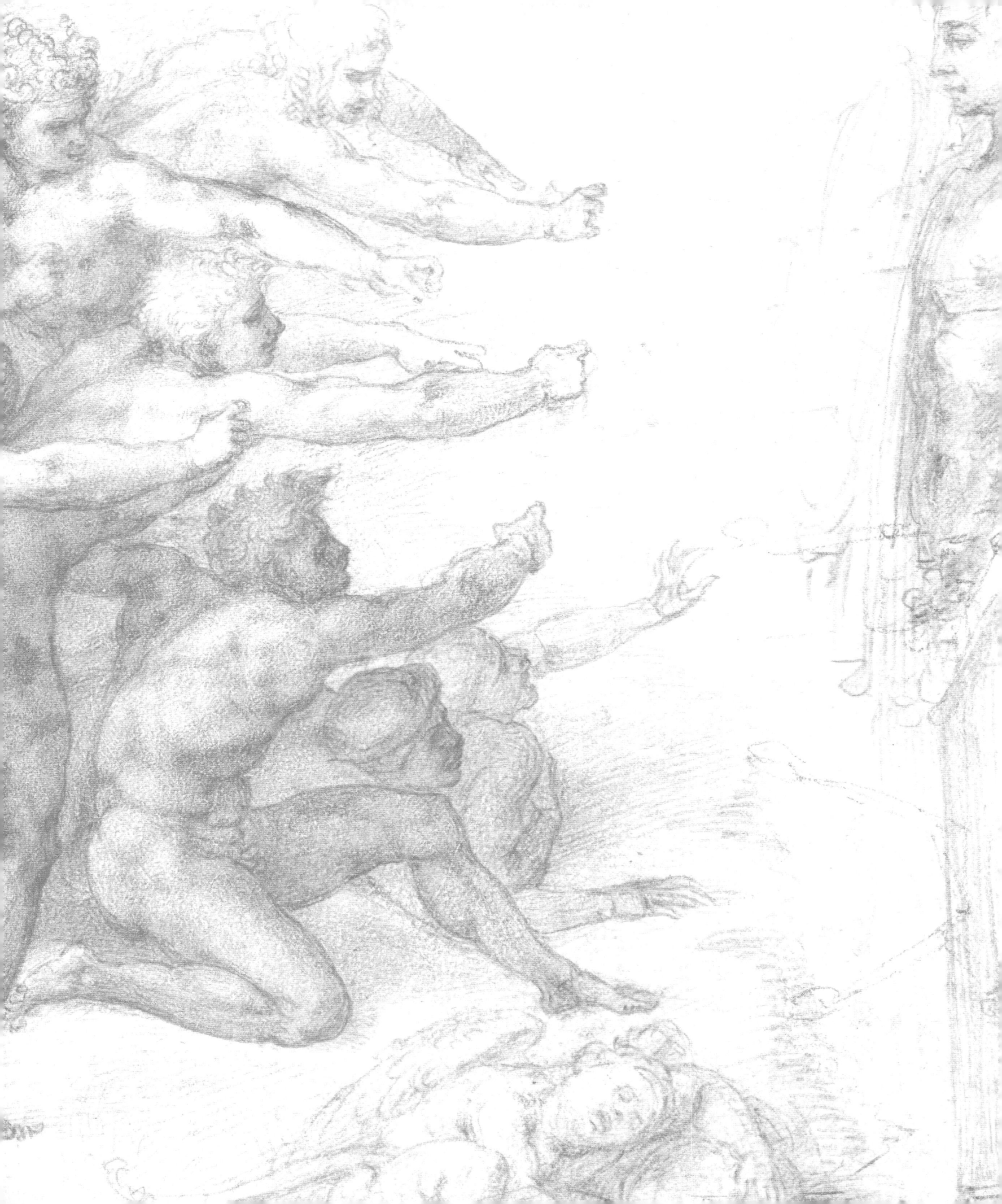

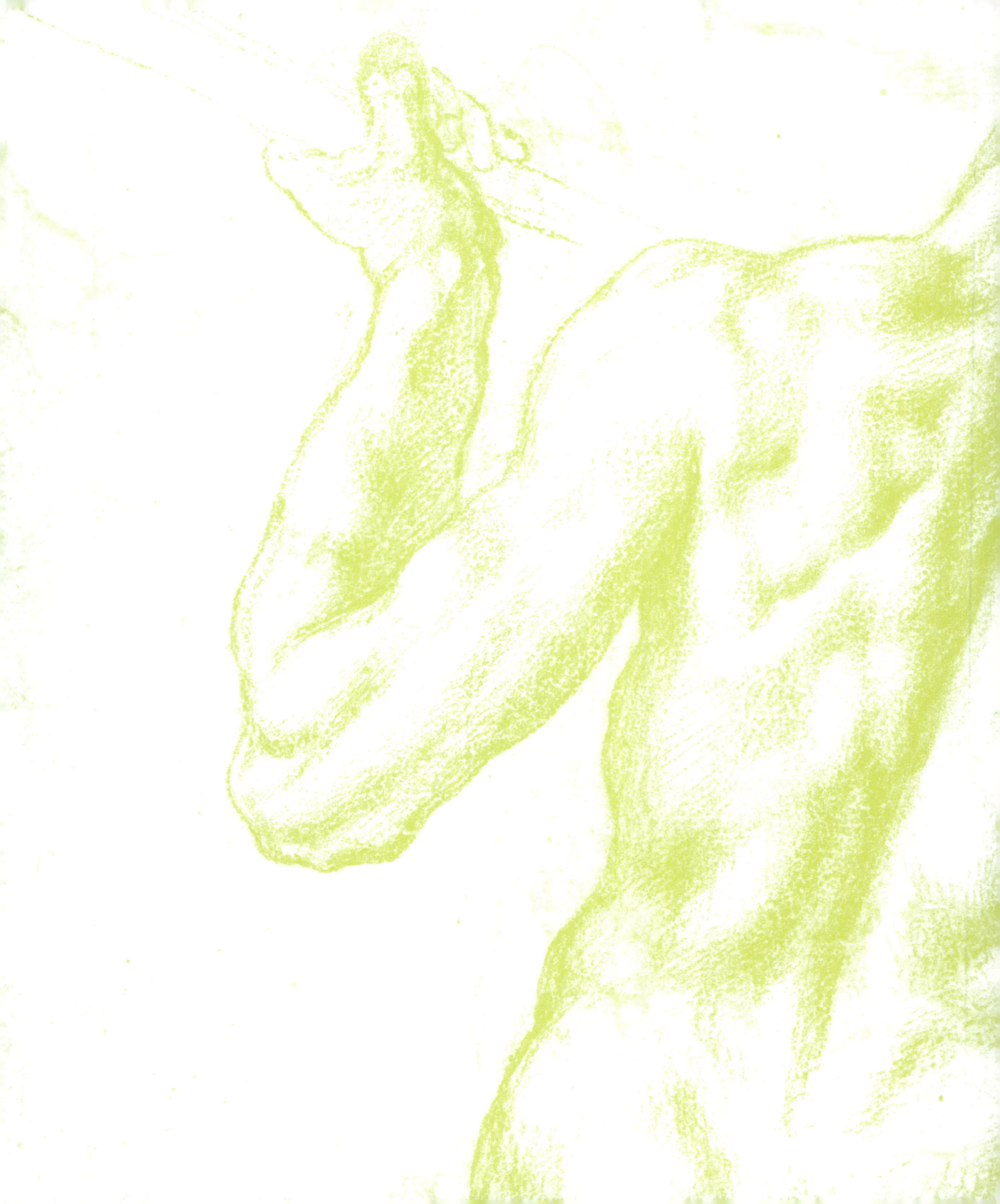

Connection

"Com'io ebbi la vostra, signor mio,
cercand'andai fra tutti e' cardinali
e diss'a tre da vostra part' addio.

Al Medico maggior de' nostri mali
mostrai la detta, onde ne rise tanto
che 'l naso fe' dua parti dell'occhiali."

'After I had received [your letter], my lord,
I went searching among all the cardinals
and greeted three of them on your behalf.

I showed the letter to the greatest Medic
of our ills, who laughed at it so much
that his nose split his eyeglasses in two halves.'

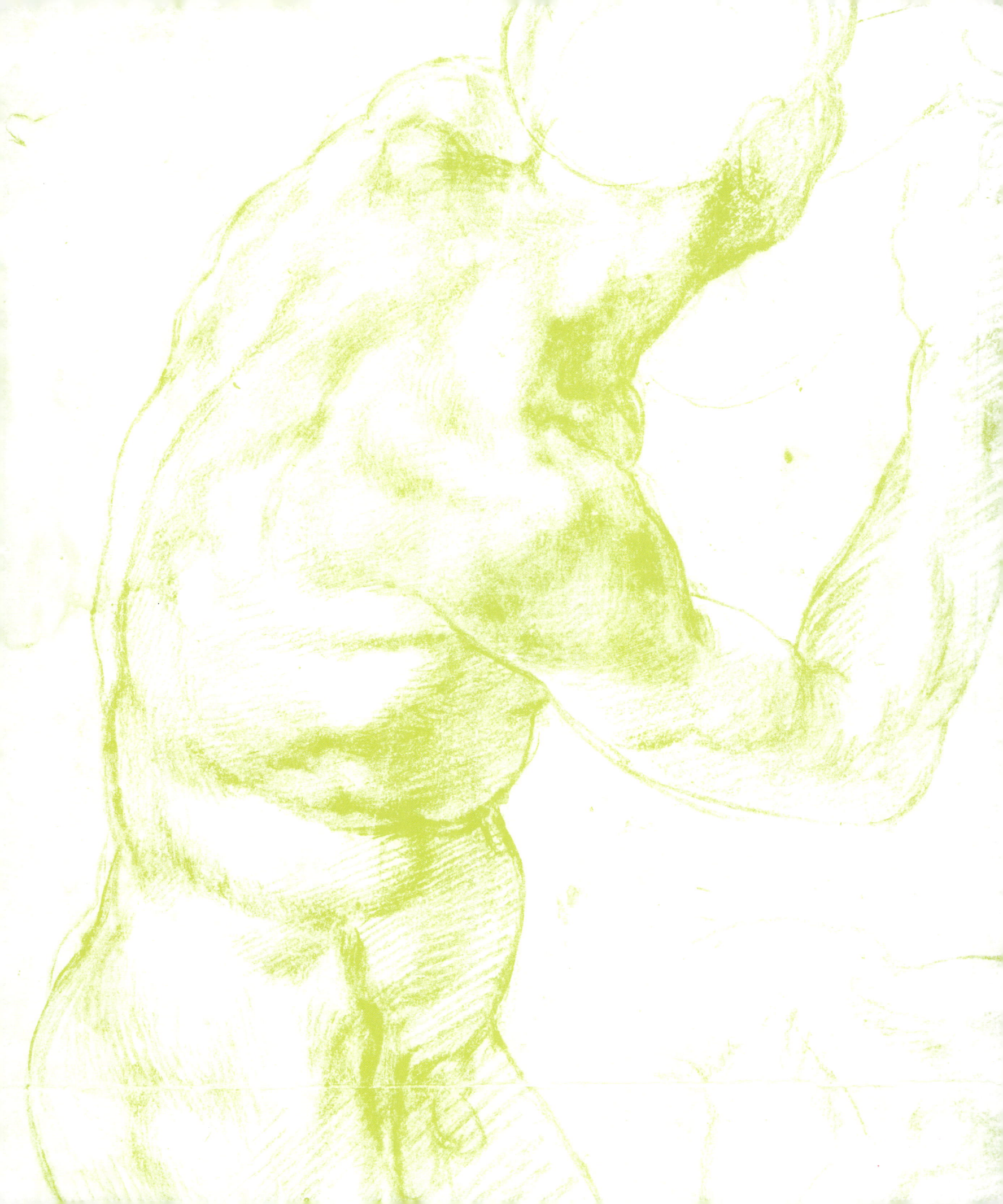

Michelangelo's *Battle of Cascina*.
Its Context and Development

Paul Joannides, assisted by Luka Pajovic

In renewed memory of Cecil Gould

Leonardo da Vinci's *Battle of Anghiari* and Michelangelo's *Battle of Cascina* were the most ambitious, innovative and influential mural projects to be undertaken in Italy at the dawn of the High Renaissance (figs 132 and 133/ cat. 51). No later treatment of a cavalry battle could ignore Leonardo's aims and ambitions – and his design – and no treatment of expressive male nudity was unaffected by Michelangelo's. The paintings and drawings of Raphael, Titian, Pietro da Cortona and Rubens, among many others, testify to the enduring influence of both battles, echoes of which can be found as late as the end of the nineteenth century: Frederic Leighton, for example, borrowed extensively from *Cascina*.[1]

The twinned projects excited contemporaries from their inception: according to Vasari, the young Raphael was enticed to Florence by rumours of the Battles (and the battle of the Battles). If, as seems likely, he arrived in October 1504, he was no doubt hoping to be at the front of the queue for a ringside seat: for Leonardo had not yet begun to apply paint to the wall and Michelangelo had not started his cartoon (the full-size drawing of the composition, used to transfer it to the surface to be painted). Unfortunately, no part of that cartoon is known today, although a few fragments survived into the seventeenth century. We have no written record of Raphael's reactions to Michelangelo's work, but we do have those of Benvenuto Cellini who, writing many years later, remembered vividly his excitement as a teenager on seeing the two compositions when they were still more-or-less intact: Michelangelo produced his cartoon in:

'…competition with another painter, Lionardo da Vinci [sic], who also made a cartoon; and both were intended for the council hall in the palace of the Signory. They represented the taking of Pisa by the Florentines [sic]; and our admirable Lionardo had chosen to depict a battle of horses, with the capture of some standards, in as divine a style as could possibly be imagined. Michel Agnolo in his cartoon portrayed a number of foot soldiers, who, the season being summer, had gone to bathe in the Arno. He drew them at the very moment the alarm is sounded, and the men all naked run to arms; so splendid in their actions that nothing survives of ancient or of modern art which touches the same lofty point of excellence; and, as I have already said, the design of the great Lionardo was itself most admirably beautiful. These two cartoons stood, one in the palace of the Medici, the other in the hall of the Pope. So long as they remained intact, they were the school of the world. Though the divine Michel Agnolo in later life finished that great chapel of Pope Julius, he never rose half-way to the same pitch of power; his genius never afterwards attained to the force of those first studies.'[2]

Leonardo did begin the task of painting his mural, but the project was effectively abandoned in September 1506 when he returned to Milan. What he left on the wall was executed in an unstable encaustic medium (in which pigments are mixed with beeswax, among other things) that soon deteriorated. Its remains were eventually covered or destroyed by Vasari when he reorganised the decoration of the council hall in the 1560s. Michelangelo set aside his cartoon for *Cascina* when he was called to Rome in the spring of 1505, and whether or not he reprised it when he returned to Florence for several months in mid-1506 is conjectural. In any case, he never began his fresco, and by about 1520, perhaps earlier, his cartoon had been dismembered.

That neither Leonardo nor Michelangelo completed their designs, and that the *Battles* had such short lives, makes their continuing impact all the more astonishing. Vasari provides a list of artists who studied the two compositions, including the Florentines Andrea del Sarto, Pontormo and Franciabigio, among others; but it was Raphael, far outstripping all his contemporaries in versatility, intelligence and ambition, who made the earliest and most accomplished use of both. His *Expulsion of Heliodoros from the Temple* of 1511 in the Vatican's Stanze, is inconceivable without Leonardo's example; and *The Battle of the Milvian Bridge*, similar in size to *Anghiari* and also planned for execution in a novel medium in the Vatican's *Sala di Costantino*, brilliantly exploits Leonardo's ideas, setting individual encounters within a panoramic account of a clash of armies. In 1511–12, projecting a *Resurrection* that never proceeded beyond the planning stage, Raphael exploited *Cascina*'s lexicon of emotional effects in a group of black-chalk drawings for astounded guards. Raphael's nude studies come near equalling Michelangelo in invention and intensity – indeed, more than one of them has been attributed to him. But the most inventive and powerful fusion of Leonardo's and Michelangelo's designs came not, as one might have expected, from a Central Italian painter, but from a Venetian: Titian's great, and also short-lived, canvas of the *Battle of Cadore* (or *Spoleto*) completed in 1538 for the Palazzo Ducale in Venice, and consumed in the devastating fire of 1577, combined the equestrian energy of Leonardo's composition with the expressive figure construction of Michelangelo's, and it had, through prints and copies, equal influence on later art (fig. 134).

The two ill-starred murals were components of an ill-starred scheme, masterminded by Florence's gonfalonier Piero Soderini, to decorate the new council hall, the Salone dei Cinquecento, of the Palazzo della Signoria. Constructed following the fall of the populist, quasi-dictatorship of the Medici dynasty in November 1494, the Salone dei Cinquecento expressed Florence's desire to extend its government, under God, to a broadly-based republic influenced by at least some of the ideas of the Dominican friar Girolamo Savonarola. The Palazzo's *salone* was loosely inspired by the hall of the Doge's Palace in Venice, whose constitution was the model for that of Florence.

By 1498 building-work was completed, and attention turned to its furnishing and decoration.[3] This was analysed in a fundamental article by Johannes Wilde who provided a visual reconstruction (fig. 135).[4] The council was to be seated on a *tribuna* in the centre of the East wall; facing the council, on the West wall, was a chapel with a large altarpiece representing the Virgin and Child with Saint Anne accompanied by Florence's patron saints. This was commissioned in May 1498 from the city's leading painter,

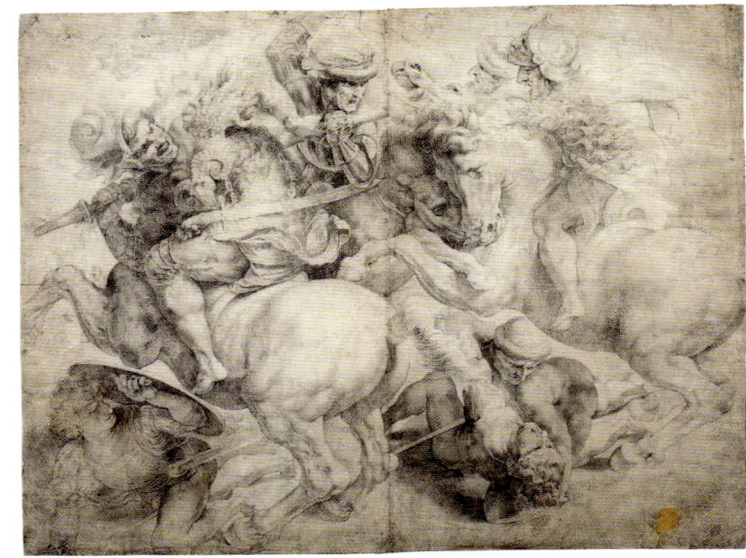

fig. 132   Studio of Rubens, after a Rubens drawing of c. 1607, after Leonardo da Vinci, *The Fight for the Standard*, c. 1620. Black chalk, 435 x 565 mm. Private collection

Filippino Lippi, but he died before he could begin it.[5] In June 1502, Andrea Sansovino was commissioned to carve a statue of Christ to stand on the *tribuna* above the throne of the gonfalonier, but of this nothing further is heard. As with his *Baptism of Christ* group on the Baptistery, it was no doubt put aside when Andrea (like Michelangelo) was called to Rome in 1505, and was not resumed.

Flanking the *tribuna* were two large same-size picture fields: the right-hand one (Leonardo's) illuminated from the right, the left-hand one (Michelangelo's) from the left. Wilde calculated the fields' dimensions at about 7 metres high by 17.5 metres wide. He later revised these figures upwards a little to 7.3 x 18.3, but an aspect ratio of about 1:2.5 remains relatively constant.[6] Any reconstruction of Leonardo's and Michelangelo's final designs for their murals that fails to respect these dimensions and lighting directions is irretrievably compromised.

A government constituted under the aegis of the Saviour, represented on the canopy above its representatives, meeting in a hall dedicated to the Virgin and Saint Anne, might have been expected to select emollient subjects for these frescoes: scenes of council, civic cer-emonies, diplomatic triumphs and the like; or evocations of good government, following the precedent of Siena's Palazzo Pubblico. Had an historical event, with topical resonance, been desired, the expulsion of the tyrant Walter of Brienne, the so-called Duke of Athens, on Saint Anne's day 1343 could have been selected. Instead, the choice fell on two battles. Florence was in a dangerous position, threatened on several sides and, from 1494, at war with Pisa, a conflict in which Leonardo was involved as an engineer. It was decided to represent old victories against both Pisa and Milan in a spirit of new defiance.

The *Battle of Anghiari*

The commission of the *Battle of Anghiari* is undocumented, but it was probably awarded late in 1503. Details of the subject would have been determined in discussions between Leonardo and Soderini. Leonardo had demonstrated his command of horsemen in action two decades earlier in the *Adoration of the Magi*, and his knowledge of equine anatomy in his model for the great horse of the

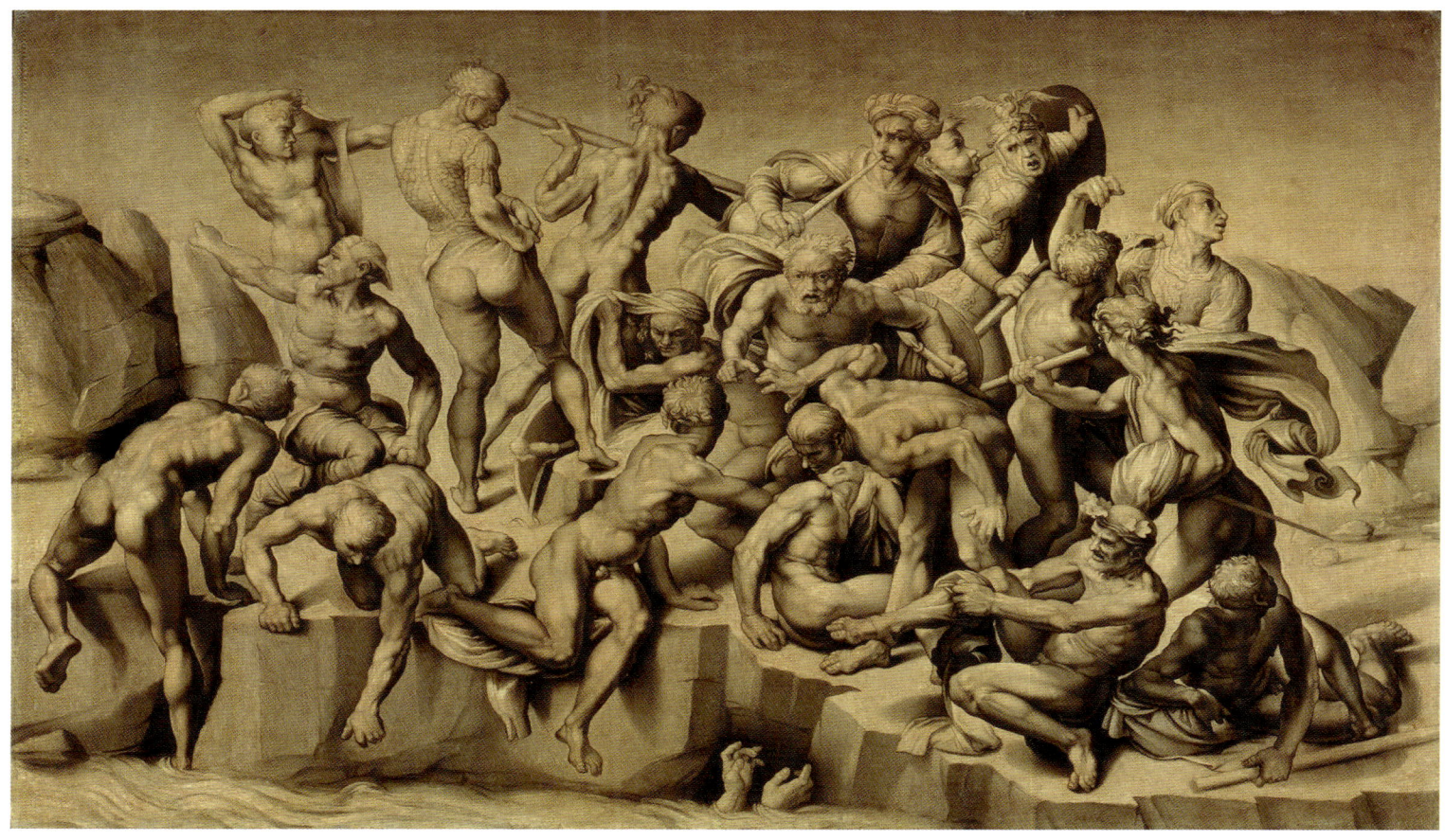

fig. 133   (cat. 51) Bastiano da Sangallo, after Michelangelo, *The Bathers* (part of the *Battle of Cascina*), c. 1542. Oil on wood, 76.5 x 129 cm. Norfolk, Holkham Hall, Collection of the Earl of Leicester

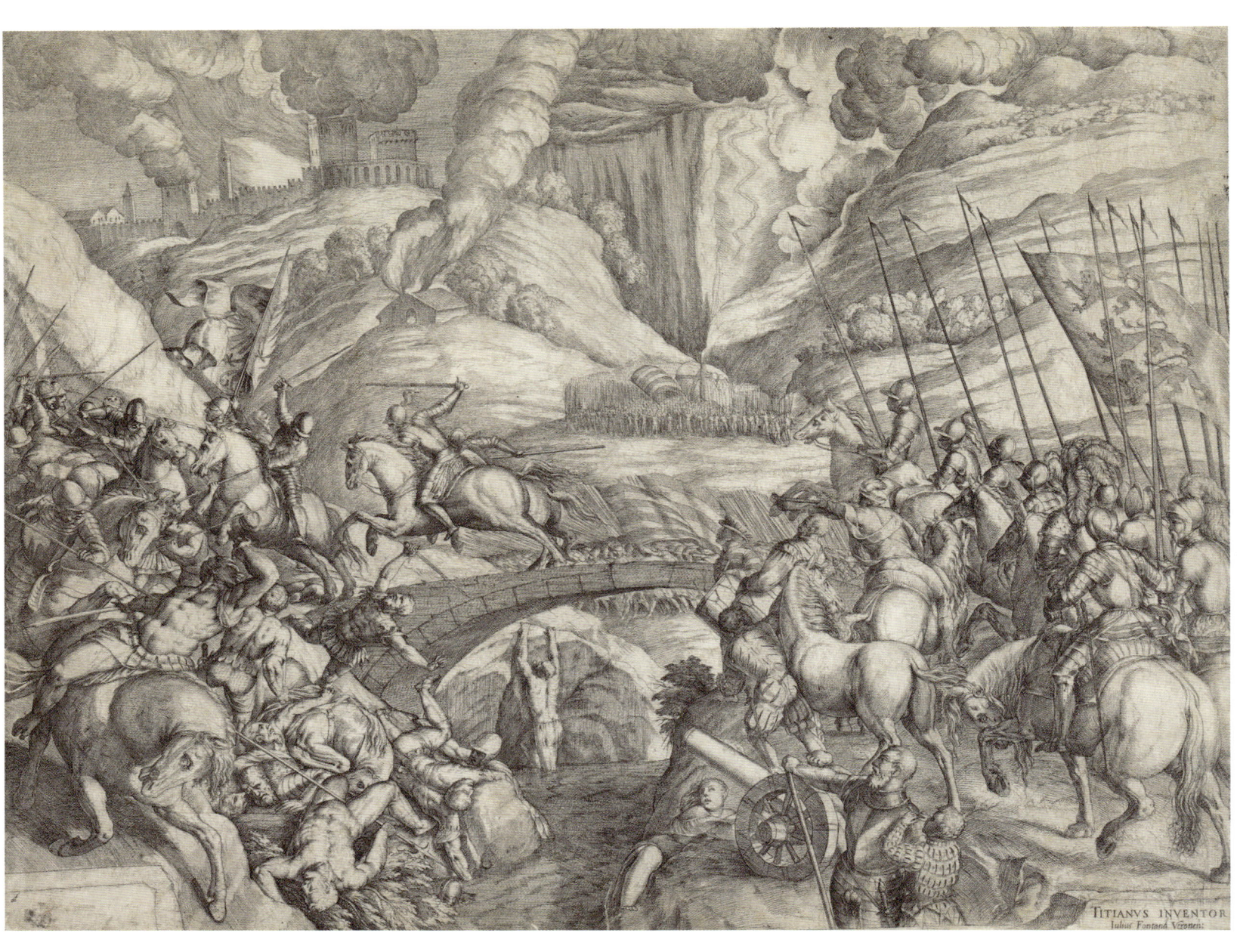

fig. 134   Giulio Fontana, after Titian, *The Battle of Cadore (or Spoleto)*, c. 1570. Engraving, 436 x 558 mm. Amsterdam, Rijksmuseum, inv. RP-P-OB-36.120

Sforza monument. His skills, plus his enormous reputation, made him an obvious candidate.

In January and April 1504, Leonardo was allocated paper for his cartoon: the quantity was about double that received by Michelangelo in October. This discrepancy has been variously interpreted but the most plausible explanation is Carmen Bambach's: that Leonardo intended to prepare two cartoons, a finished one for reference and preservation, and a rough copy of it by an assistant to be used on the wall.[7] In Leonardo's own account, the working cartoon was damaged when he began painting on 6 June 1505: 'At the very moment I applied the brush, the weather deteriorated and the bell resounded, calling the men to their deliberations. The cartoon tore, the jar of water being carried broke and water spilled.'[8] A fragment of it is in Oxford (fig. 136).[9]

Few preparatory drawings for *Anghiari* survive. There are four or five pages (totals are uncertain because some have been cut from larger sheets) of tiny pen *concetti* (first sketches).[10] Ferociously inventive, they present a cauldron of motifs, some of which were developed in *The Fight for the Standard*, the only section of *Anghiari* to be brought to an advanced stage and the only one of which we have fairly precise knowledge. Of course, other motifs generated on these pages may have been taken further in unrecorded areas of Leonardo's composition.

Naturally, critical attention has been attracted by these astonishing *concetti*; but also distracted, for they were made at an early stage in Leonardo's thoughts about his mural and are uninformative – and potentially misleading – about his final intentions. Innumerable stages would have intervened between them and the cartoon, but for these we have minimal evidence. Apart from various studies of horses, which are not particularly informative about the composition's progress, intermediary drawings are confined to three sketches, one in black chalk and two in red, of the same charging horseman, probably to be placed at the left, plus an unfinished red-chalk sketch, for the right-hand cavalryman attempting to seize the standard.[11] There is also a black-chalk study for a spearman, preparing a subsidiary episode that appears elsewhere *only* in the mid-seventeenth-century drawing discussed below (fig. 137).[12] We have two loose, charcoal sketches of a group,[13] no compositional drafts, no detailed figure-drawings, and no *modelli* (elaborated studies). In contrast, there survive over twenty pages of drawings by Raphael, including examples of all these types, for his *Entombment* of 1507 in the Galleria Borghese.[14]

The dramatic and emotional centre of *Anghiari* was *The Fight for the Standard*, in which opposing cavalrymen struggle for possession of a flag. What Leonardo put on the wall survived long enough to generate cop-

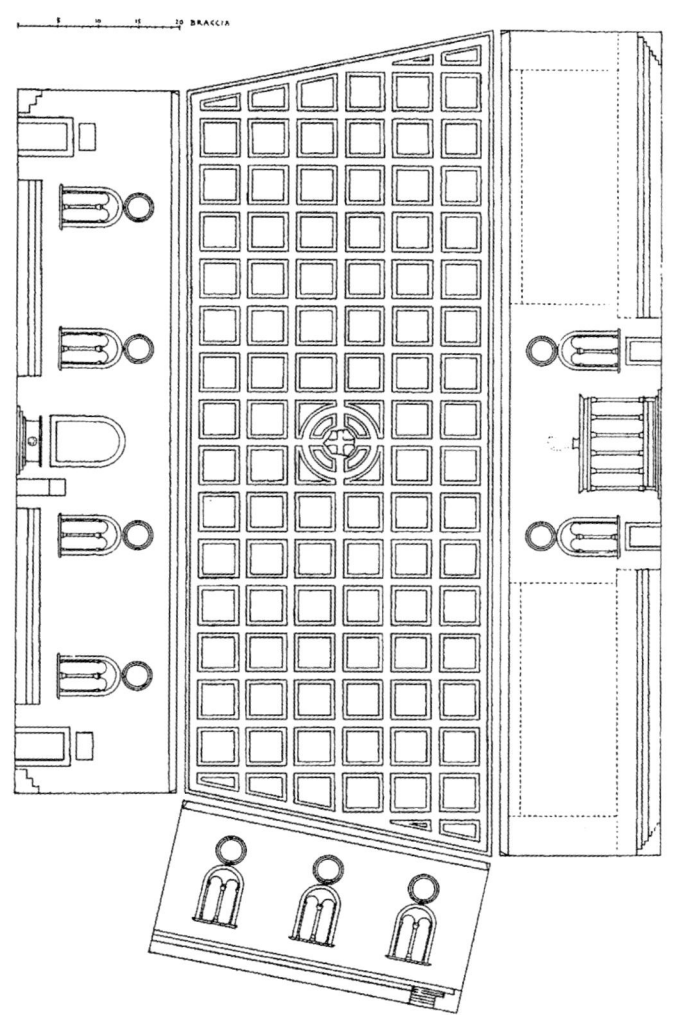

fig. 135   Johannes Wilde's reconstruction of the Salone del Cinquecento before 1512

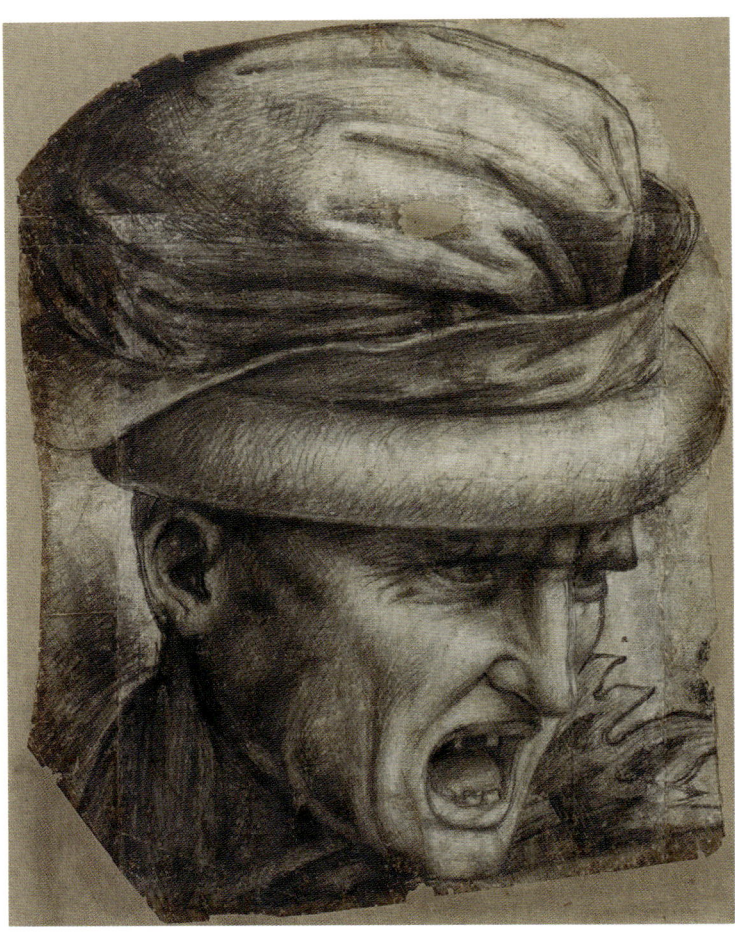

ies, direct or indirect. Painted, drawn or engraved, of widely varying competence, these cannot be trusted for every detail, but they are broadly in agreement and can be used with some confidence. The most dynamic and exciting, though not the most complete, is a large drawing – whose textural variety and energy suggest that it was made from a painted, not a drawn, reduction of Leonardo's group – executed by Rubens around the middle of his Italian sojourn. He subsequently overworked it, modulating and enriching it with layers of wash and body colour to produce what is, effectively, a painting in grisaille; later engraved by Gérard Edelinck, it became canonical. But a studio replica of Rubens's drawing (fig. 132), made before he submerged it, preserves much of his vitality of hand and richly varied employment of chalk and, by extension, his intense response to the powers and energies of Leonardo's design. This drawing, long inaccessible and known only from old photographs, did not reappear until 2019.[15]

The dimensions of *The Fight for the Standard* can be calculated approximately. The Oxford fragment (fig. 136) measures 505 x 375 mm, and when these figures are extrapolated and applied, for example, to Rubens's copy (which is trimmed all round), it can be estimated that the group was to measure approximately 4.4 m high by 5 m wide.[16] It would have occupied over half the height of the picture field and a little over a quarter of its width. A mid-seventeenth century Florentine drawing (fig. 137), presumably by a draughtsman with access, direct or indirect, to a now-lost *modello* or *ricordo* by Leonardo or an assistant, allows us to extend the group by about two metres at the right-hand side, so it would have occupied over a third of the field's width. This drawing, of which an early chalk copy exists (fig. 138), adds several memorable figures to *The Fight for the Standard*, and enables us to approach Leonardo's final intentions a little more closely.[17]

The *Battle of Cascina*

The commission of the *Battle of Cascina* was probably received by Michelangelo about a year later, in the autumn of 1504.[18] Whether Soderini had intended to involve Michelangelo from the outset is uncertain – Filippino Lippi would have been a more obvious choice, but his death in April 1504, the month that Michelangelo finished *David*, may have prompted Soderini to turn to the new artistic hero. Michelangelo had not, so far as we know, previously executed work in fresco, but his technical competence was assured for he had trained with the most accomplished frescoist of the late Quattrocento,

fig. 136   Assistant of Leonardo da Vinci, *Fragment of the working cartoon for the* Battle of Anghiari, 1504–1505. Black chalk, 505 x 375 mm. Oxford, Ashmolean Museum, WA1863.618

Domenico Ghirlandaio. And even as a teenager he had shown his ability to create scenes of conflict in his *Battle of the Centaurs* (fig. 38).

Michelangelo always claimed to be a sculptor rather than a painter, but he had not yet begun to carve the *Apostles* for the Duomo, although he was planning them – and the opportunity for so rapid a worker to serve his city and a government whose ideals he seems to have shared would have been powerful incentives. So would the challenge of competing publicly with Leonardo.

Nevertheless, despite his dislike of Leonardo, Michelangelo could hardly avoid some accommodation to his plans. The most obvious and dramatic feature of Leonardo's design was its panoply of dynamic horses, whose emotions evoke those of their riders. *Cascina*, historically, did not require horses as the Pisans lacked cavalry, but to exclude them would have impoverished his fresco comparatively, so Michelangelo made the (invented) Pisan charge the engine of his drama.

Johannes Wilde insisted that Michelangelo never copied works by contemporaries, but it is hard to believe that his sketches of riders in action were entirely independent of those of his rival.[19] Whether Michelangelo would have included any of these groups verbatim in his final design is an open question – they may have constituted research rather than development – but they can hardly be detached from Leonardo's example. To prepare further, Michelangelo made several life studies of horses, the only such drawings in his oeuvre.[20]

The emotional, if not physical, centre of Michelangelo's projected mural was the *Bathers* (fig. 133/cat. 51). He must have been responsible for choosing the event, although he would have required Soderini's acquiescence. On the face of it, his selection was unlikely: on a stiflingly hot day in 1364, young Florentine troops sought relief by bathing in the Arno. A veteran (whose name we know to have been Manno Donati), observing their vulnerability, sounded the alarm, prompting them to rush for their weapons and don their armour.[21] In actuality, battle was joined only the next day and Michelangelo elided the false alarm and the real engagement in a feat of dramatic compression. But why this episode? To show Florence's soldiers 'caught with their pants down' was hardly positive propaganda. But the literal was trumped by the metaphorical and allusive: Michelangelo saw in the subject poetic and spiritual imperatives that would fuse apparent disparities and potential absurdities into an epic unity.

There were strong reasons for Michelangelo's nudes. One was to situate his composition within classical precedent: Roman reliefs of battles and combats, except when strictly reportorial, generally showed their actors, or many of them, nude. This was followed in the

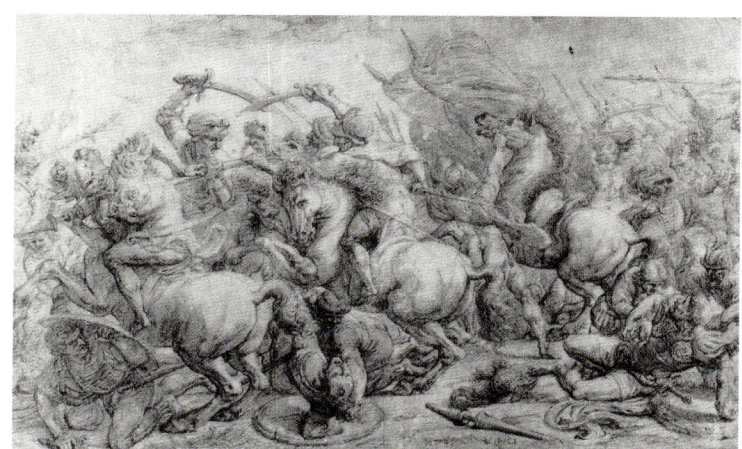

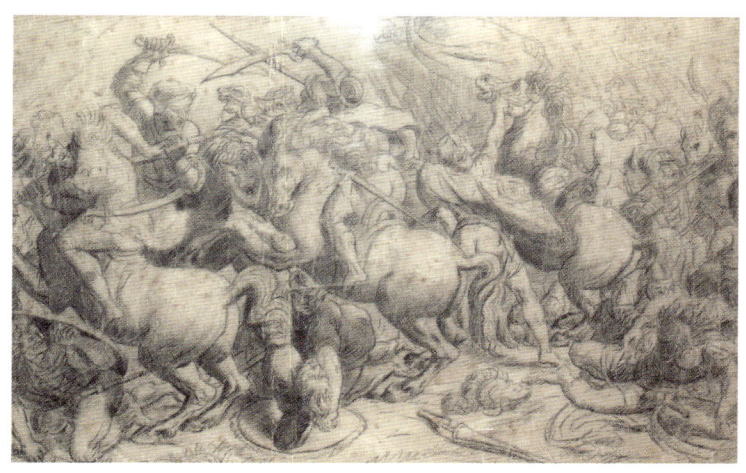

fig. 137 Unidentified Florentine draughtsman, after Leonardo da Vinci, *The Fight for the Standard*, mid-seventeenth century. Pen and wash, 265 x 440 mm. Private collection

fig. 138 Unidentified Flemish draughtsman, after fig. 137, seventeenth century. Black chalk, dimensions unrecorded. Private collection

209

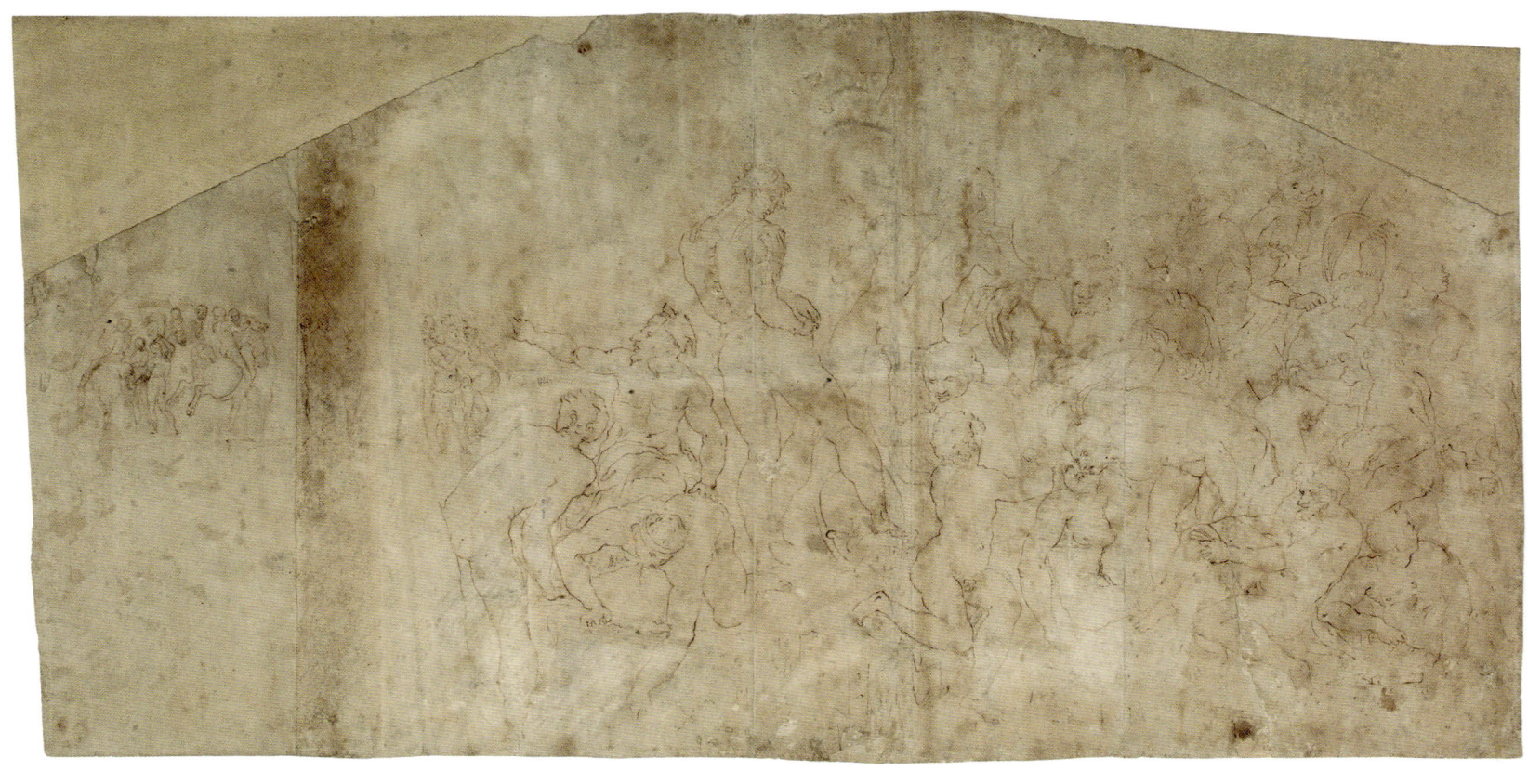

fig. 139   Unidentified Florentine draughtsman, after Michelangelo, *The Battle of Cascina*, sixteenth century. Pen and brown ink, black chalk, 458 x 890 mm.
London, British Museum, inv. 1946,0713.593

renowned bronze *Battle* relief, a modern interpretation of an antique marble, by Michelangelo's sculptural master, Bertoldo (fig. 37), and by the greatest Florentine exponent of male anatomy, Antonio Pollaiuolo, who had produced a combat of nude men in a famous engraving (fig. 3).

Obviously, the subject indulged Michelangelo's principal vehicle of expression and his central artistic – and spiritual – preoccupation, the male nude. But nudity was a vehicle, not a destination. It evoked the grandest of themes: these naked men, answering the trumpet, are the dead called from their graves by the trumpets of the *Dies irae* (Judgement Day) – a preferred topic in Savonarola's sermons – which had recently been depicted in a large fresco by Fra Bartolommeo and Mariotto Albertinelli, and which was to be painted by Michelangelo himself thirty years later (fig. 96; in it he re-employed the soldier reaching down to rescue a comrade at the lower left of the *Bathers*). A potentially embarrassing – and historically unimportant – incident is transformed into a spiritual allegory in which each man must confront himself and his destiny under the eye of eternity. In this optic, the waters of the Arno serve a double purpose: of course, they provide a pretext for nudity, but thematically and spiritually they embody the efficacy of baptism. Cleansed, imbued, as it were, by the Holy Spirit, these men address their fate in the purity of their souls. In the thematically vital duo of a soldier helping his comrade don his cuirass, Michelangelo offers a foresight of spirits re-united after Judgement. Comparison with Leonardo crystallises a fundamental divergence between them: Leonardo was fascinated by the movements of the mind; Michelangelo was committed to the aspirations of the soul.

The ineluctable record of the cartoon's appearance is, of course, Bastiano da Sangallo's grisaille at Holkham Hall, commissioned from him by Giorgio Vasari (fig. 133/cat. 51). There is also a loose sketch by an unknown hand, perhaps made from memory, which repeats the group – with various inaccuracies – and sets it in a broader landscape (fig. 139). It may be that the soldiers in the left background of the drawing reflect Michelangelo's ideas for the far distance of his design, but they can have been little more than extras.[22]

The cartoon had long been dismembered by the time Bastiano came to paint his panel, and he had to reconstruct Michelangelo's composition. We do not know by what processes he did so, or precisely what visual evidence he had at his disposal, but no serious objections have been raised to his reliability; and no evidence has come to light to contradict it. Engravings made after three of Michelangelo's figures were reproduced by Marcantonio Raimondi in around 1510, and a couple of other engraved copies of single figures are known (fig. 4/cat. 49, as well as

cat. 48, 52 and 53).[23] There is also a dynamic pen sketch of two figures, drawn *da sotto in su* (seen from below) from the suspended cartoon, by Raphael of about 1507 – the only surviving copy of whose immediate contemporaneity we can be sure.[24] Early drawings after individual figures and small groups, including at least two fine ones by Francesco Salviati, support Bastiano's accuracy. But more important is a series of magnificent figure studies by Michelangelo himself, in pen and ink and black chalk, some with body colour, in Haarlem (figs 140/cat. 12 and 141/cat. 13), London (fig. 142) and Vienna (fig. 143). These unmatched drawings, and others, confirm that Bastiano's rendering, to the best of his abilities, was loyal.

Cascina is unlike *Anghiari* in that we can form some idea of the stages by which Michelangelo took the subject from its beginnings to its refined conclusion. The starting point is a compositional sketch in soft black chalk, with recognisable links to Bastiano's image, but with several fast-moving figures at the left, presumably initiating a flanking manoeuvre (fig. 144).[25] One follow-up survives of this moment, the sole drawing for *Cascina* in red chalk, of two running men (fig. 145).[26] How many others Michelangelo might have made at this stage is anyone's guess.

Shortly thereafter, Michelangelo decided to shift rapid movement to subsidiary areas of his composition and to reserve the largest part for the eighteen statuesque figures. With one soldier, we can chart a development over three drawings: a small full-length sketch showing him from the rear, apparently engaged in defensive action (fig. 146);[27] a large follow-up of the same man, more clearly realised in pose and now, probably, proactive, but still uncertainly balanced (fig. 147).[28] And finally, no doubt following other lost studies, in the sublime drawing in the Albertina which excises the lower part of the figure, Michelangelo concentrated on the expressive topography of the back, combining ease of moment and contained energy with incomparable grace (fig. 143).[29] This is the longest run of drawings for the same figure in the *Bathers*, but we do have a calm pen drawing in Vienna (fig. 82) and a black-chalk drawing in Haarlem for the soldier helping his comrade don armour (fig. 140/cat. 12), an abbreviated sequence which implies Michelangelo employed pen to establish structure and chalk to evoke surface.[30] A famous study in London for the turning man in the immediate foreground, however, the pivotal figure of the pivotal group, is executed in a hard, aggressive penline, appropriate for one who seems to burst from the picture field (fig. 142).[31]

Michelangelo developed his composition from a near *melée* into a 'forest of statues'; we cannot follow his refining processes in much detail, but he evidently turned

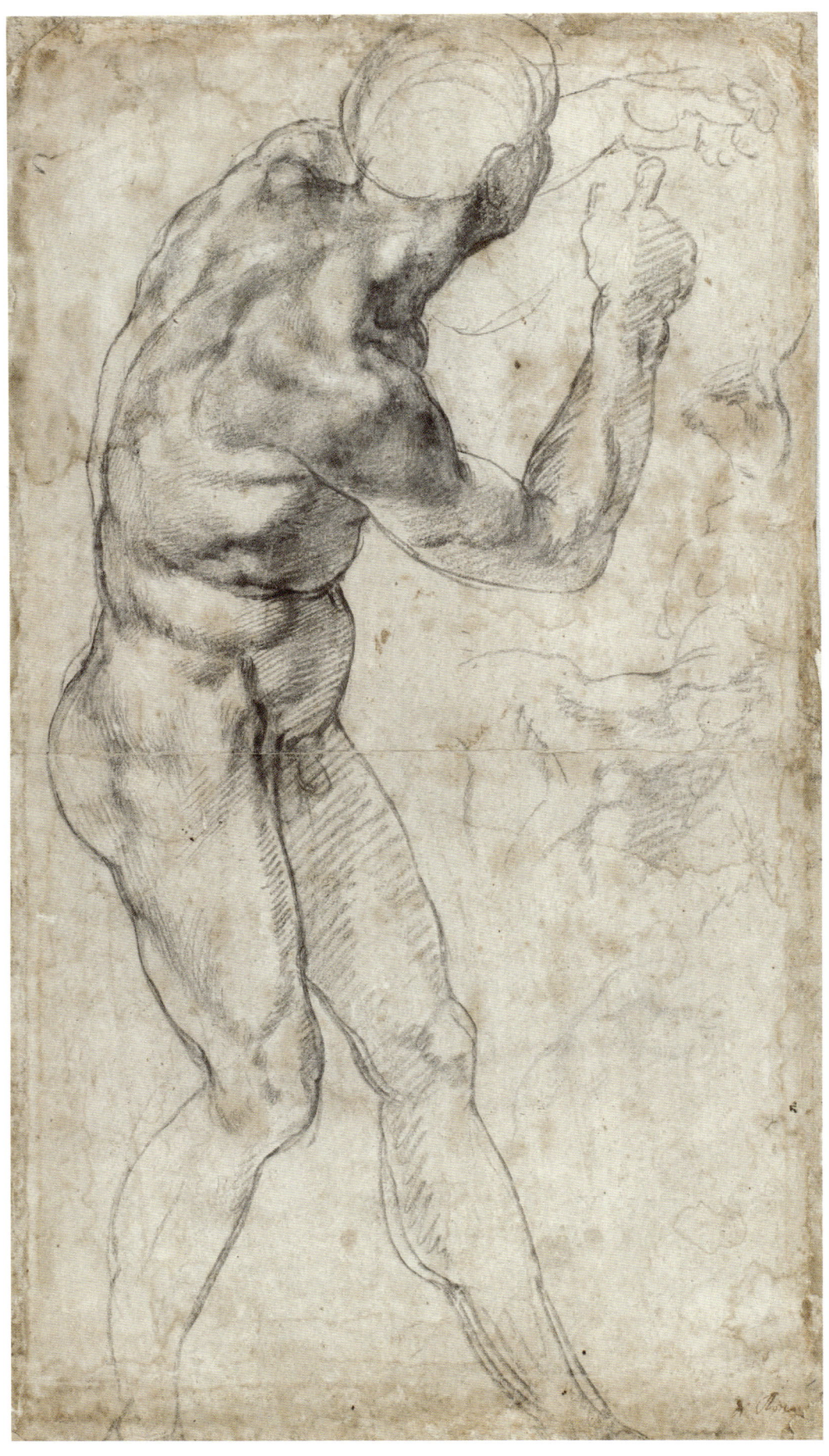

fig. 140   (cat. 12) Michelangelo, *Study of a Male Nude*, 1504. Black chalk with white heightening, 404 x 225 mm. Haarlem, Teylers Museum, inv. A 018

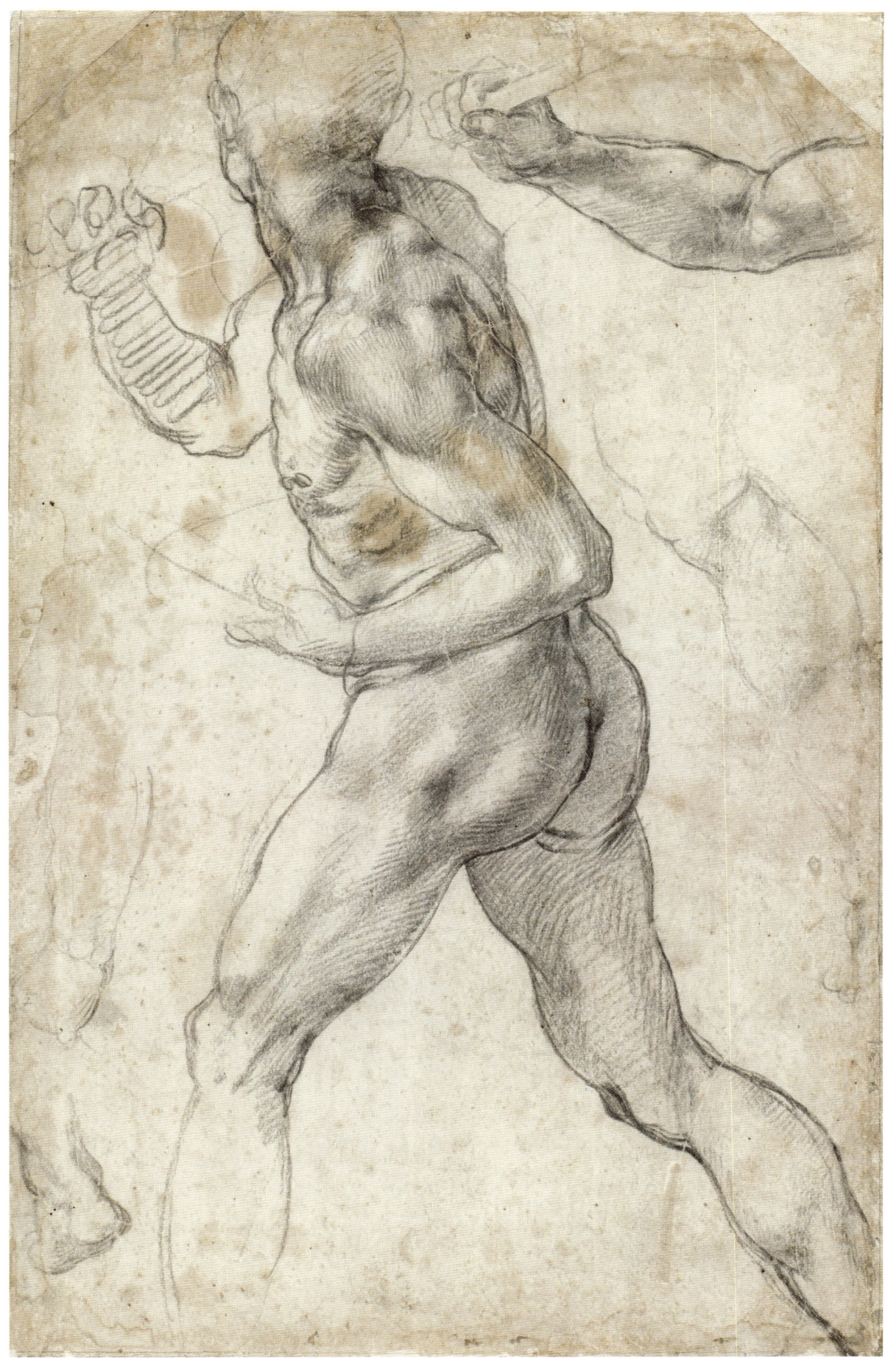

fig. 141   (cat. 13) Michelangelo, *Study of a Male Nude*, 1504. Black chalk with white heightening, 404 x 258 mm. Haarlem, Teylers Museum, inv. A 019

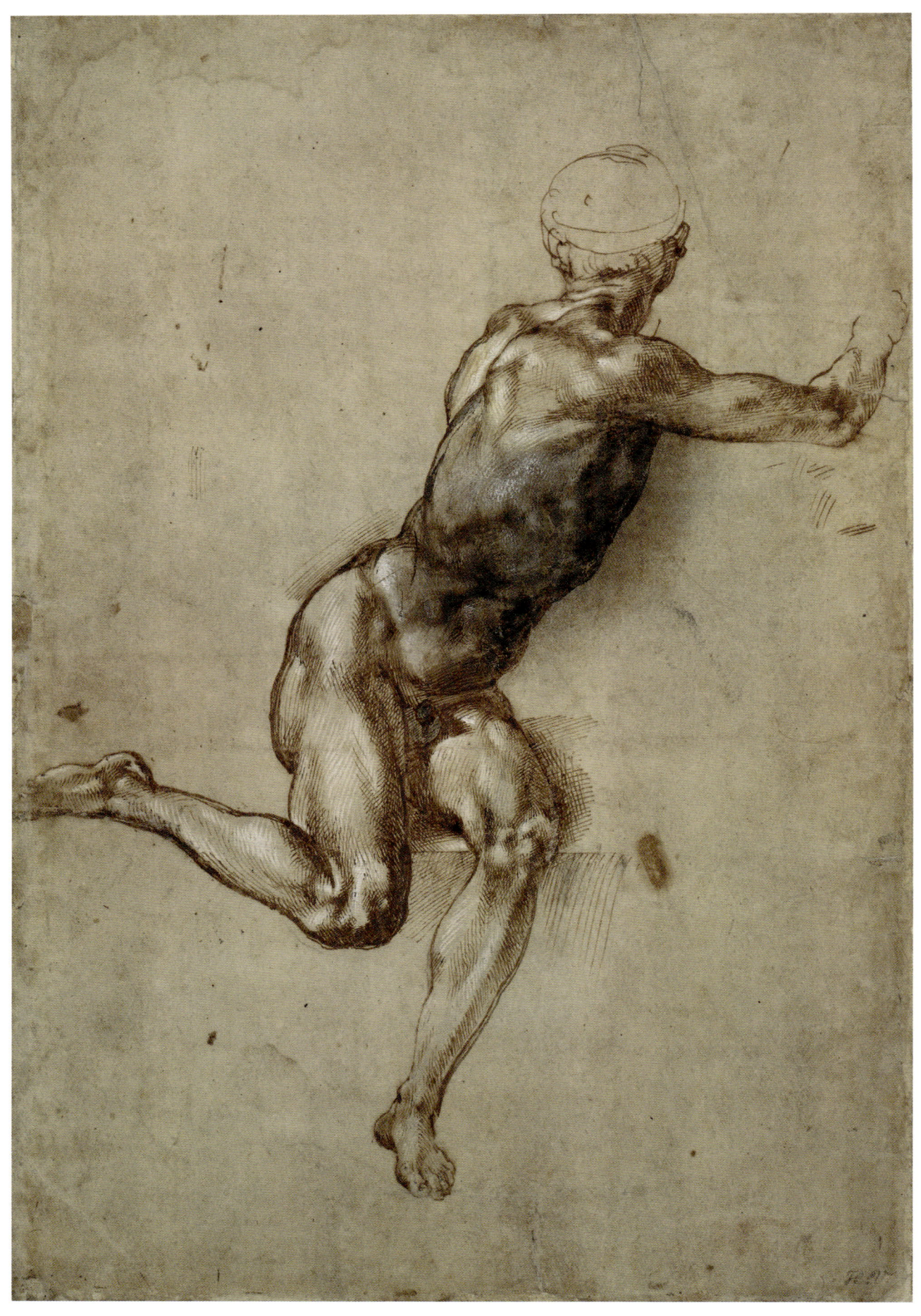

fig. 142   Michelangelo, *Study of a Twisting Male Nude*, 1504. Pen and brown ink, brown and grey wash, with white heightening, 421 x 287 mm. London, British Museum, inv. 1887,0502.116

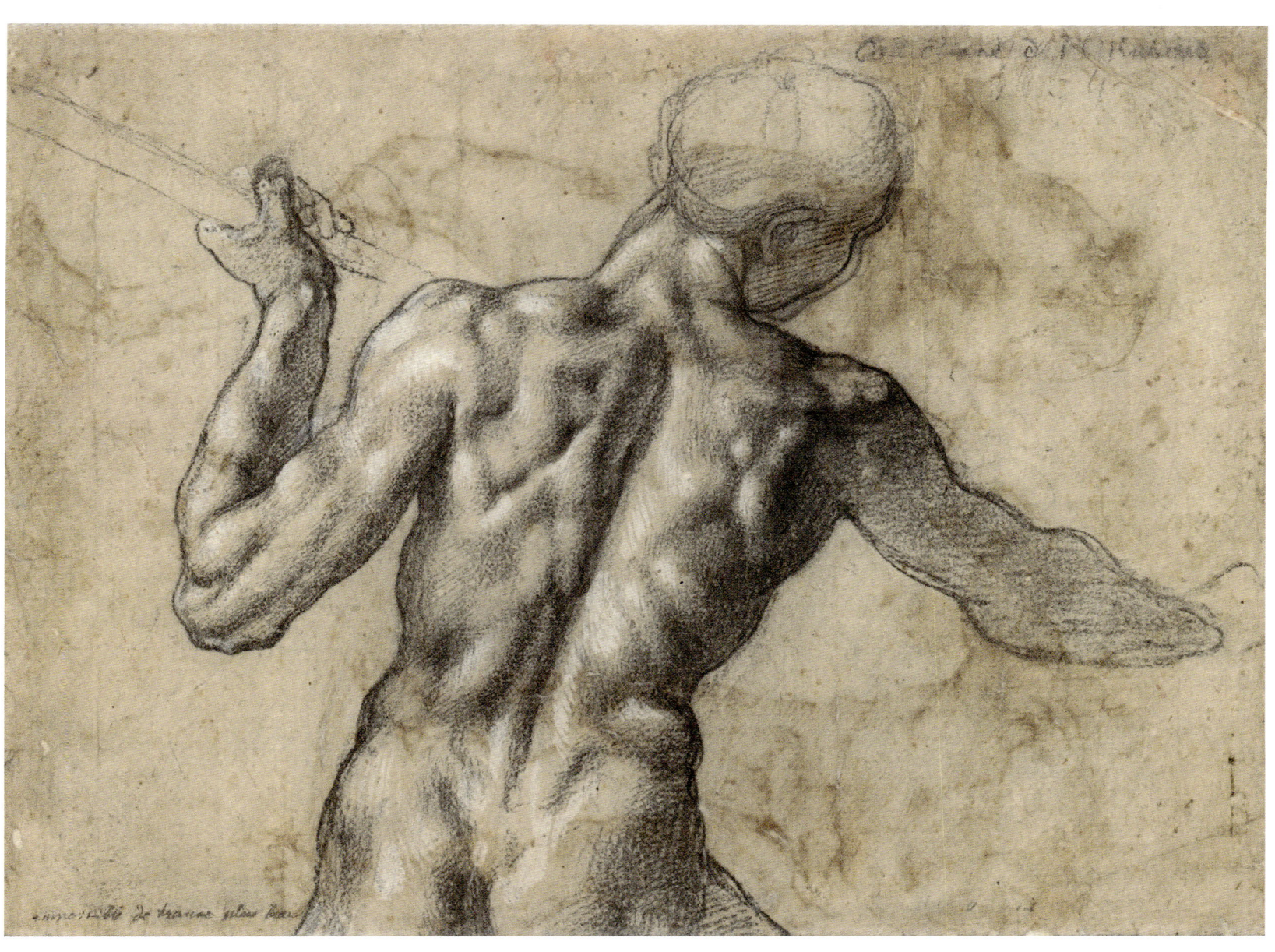

fig. 143   Michelangelo, *Study of a Male Nude from the Back*, 1504. Black chalk with white heightening, 196 x 270 mm. Vienna, The ALBERTINA Museum, inv. 123v

fig. 144   Michelangelo, *Composition Study for the Bathers*, 1504. Black chalk, 235 x 356 mm. Florence, Gallerie degli Uffizi, Gabinetto dei Disegni e delle Stampe, inv. 613 E

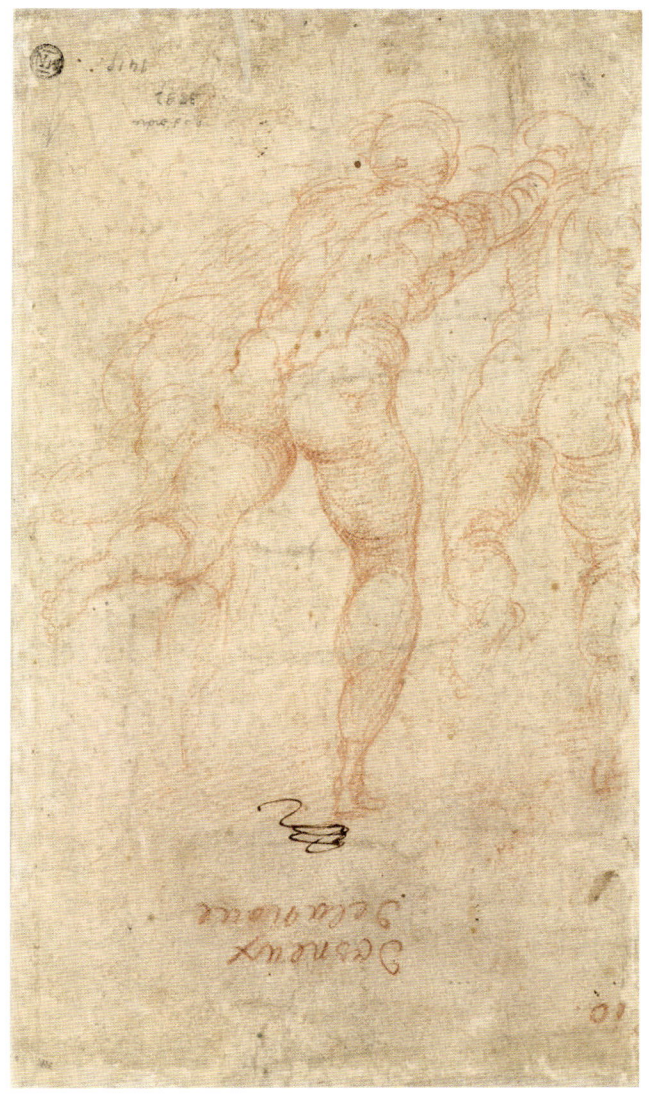

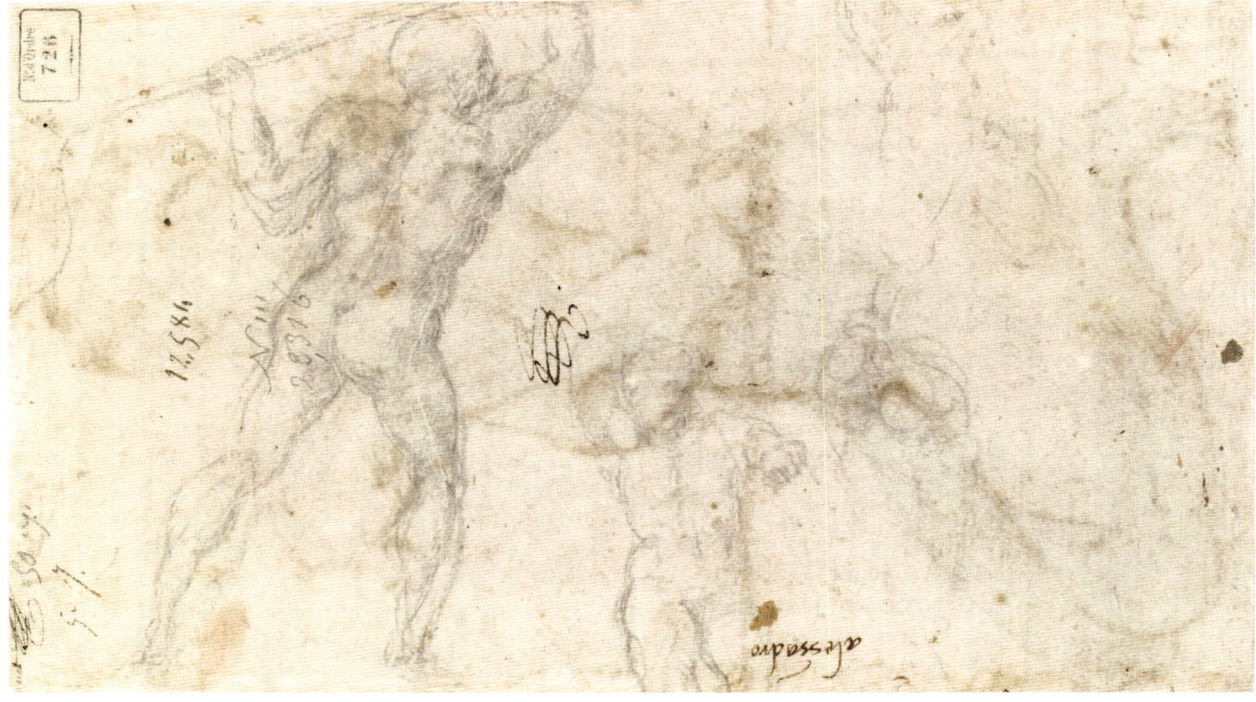

fig. 145   Michelangelo, *Study of Running Men*, 1504. Red chalk, 326 x 187 mm. Paris, Musée du Louvre, Département des arts graphiques, inv. 3897v

fig. 146   Michelangelo, *Study of a Male Nude from the Back*, 1504. Black chalk, 163 x 258 mm. Paris, Musée du Louvre, Département des arts graphiques, inv. 726v

to certain prototypes. The soldier at the far left, climbing the river bank, seen from the rear, recalls closely a figure in Bertoldo's *Battle Scene* relief (fig. 37); and the soldier running from right to left, now in Haarlem (fig. 141/cat. 13), was inspired by a soldier in Donatello's late relief of the Crucifixion. A decade after Bertoldo's death, Michelangelo continued to reflect upon the work of his sculptural mentor and of that mentor's mentor, the sculptor he admired most.

We have nothing of Michelangelo's dismembered cartoon for the *Bathers*, but fragments surviving in the early seventeenth century are described as larger than life.[32] We cannot know from which parts of the cartoon these came, nor can we know how much larger than life they were, nor can we be sure that Michelangelo's figures respected approximately the same scale as Leonardo's. But if we assume that the heads of the foreground figures were about 50 cm high, we arrive at dimensions for the *Bathers* group of about 5 x 9 m. Obviously such a calculation is very rough, but it suggests that the top of Michelangelo's *Bathers* group rose about as high in the picture field as Leonardo's, and that it probably occupied just over half its width.

The *Bathers* group is composed like sculpture in high relief and firmly controlled by a grid of verticals and horizontals. The grid was one of Michelangelo's most fundamental compositional formulae, adaptable to fields of very different dimensions: it organises, for example the *Battle of the Centaurs* (fig. 38), *The Entombment* in the National Gallery (fig. 114), and, on a massive scale, *The Last Judgement* (fig. 96). But the grid controlled only a section of *Cascina*'s picture field. How might we go about reconstructing the events occurring at either side of the *Bathers*, and in the background? In his famous diagram (fig. 148), Cecil Gould took the example of the Sistine *Flood* to suggest the kinds of relationship between the *Bathers* and other areas of the foreground and background that we might expect to find, and his insight is surely incontestable.

The main difficulty in reconstructing areas of Michelangelo's composition outside that covered by the *Bathers* cartoon is evident. Although we have a number of autograph drawings – plus a couple of copies – that are likely to prepare figures and groups set in various places and depths, these figures and groups are hard to situate with confidence and I now think that my earlier attempt to suggest where various figures might have been located was over-ambitious; it has been modified in fig. 157.[33]

Furthermore, we can never be fully sure of the positions of the known drawings in Michelangelo's preparatory sequence.[34] With the *Bathers* group we can usually match drawings to stages for which we have fairly secure

starting points and end points, even if moving from one to another risks too rigid a teleology. But with the scenes at the left and right, we are deprived of anchorage: we have no clear picture of Michelangelo's final intentions; indeed, he may not fully have formulated them before he abandoned his project.

In broad terms we can probably accept, from Vasari's account and Gould's elucidation, that the Pisan attack came from the right, while the Florentine response formed at the left. Such a narrative would fit the outward-facing gestures of the bathers at either side, and it would correspond roughly with the known drawings. But how can we assess which drawings were experiments without sequel, and which had a place in a progressive sequence?

One way of addressing the question is to consider the drawings' level of finish: in principle, a higher finish is likely to bring us closer to Michelangelo's final intentions. A related approach is to assume that if the content and forms of one drawing are developed in another, it probably constitutes a sequence. This is particularly significant in attempting to reconstruct the left-hand side for which we have no drawings containing more than two figures.

For the right-hand side, we have a rapidly drawn but informative pen study of a charging Pisan cavalryman about to be unhorsed by Florentine infantry (fig. 149).[35] The forms are simplified, of course, but the drawing is compositionally coherent and remarkably dynamic. Outlines at the left imply that other foot soldiers were involved, one of whom may be sketched out in a black-chalk drawing of a leaping, helmeted male nude in the Louvre.[36] The group would presumably have been situated somewhat deeper in space than the *Bathers*, and the helmeted and the shield-bearing soldier at the top right in the back row would be about to join his comrades in a brutal struggle.

No such drawings exist for the left side, but two suggestions might be made. On the verso of a double-sided sheet is a chalk sketch for a soldier helping a comrade mount a horse, while on the recto is a more advanced chalk study overworked in pen (by the assistant), inspired by a version of the *Discobolus* (figs 150, 151 and 152).[37]

Probably related to this moment of preparation are two small drawings, on the same page. The most sharply defined is of a nude soldier, clinging to the back of a comrade while kneeling on the rump of his horse as it advances into depth (fig. 153). The page also carries a quick sketch for the kneeling soldier at the left side of the *Bathers*, who points with his right arm into depth and thus makes the connection with the upper group evident. The extraordinary invention of the kneeling pillion rider

218

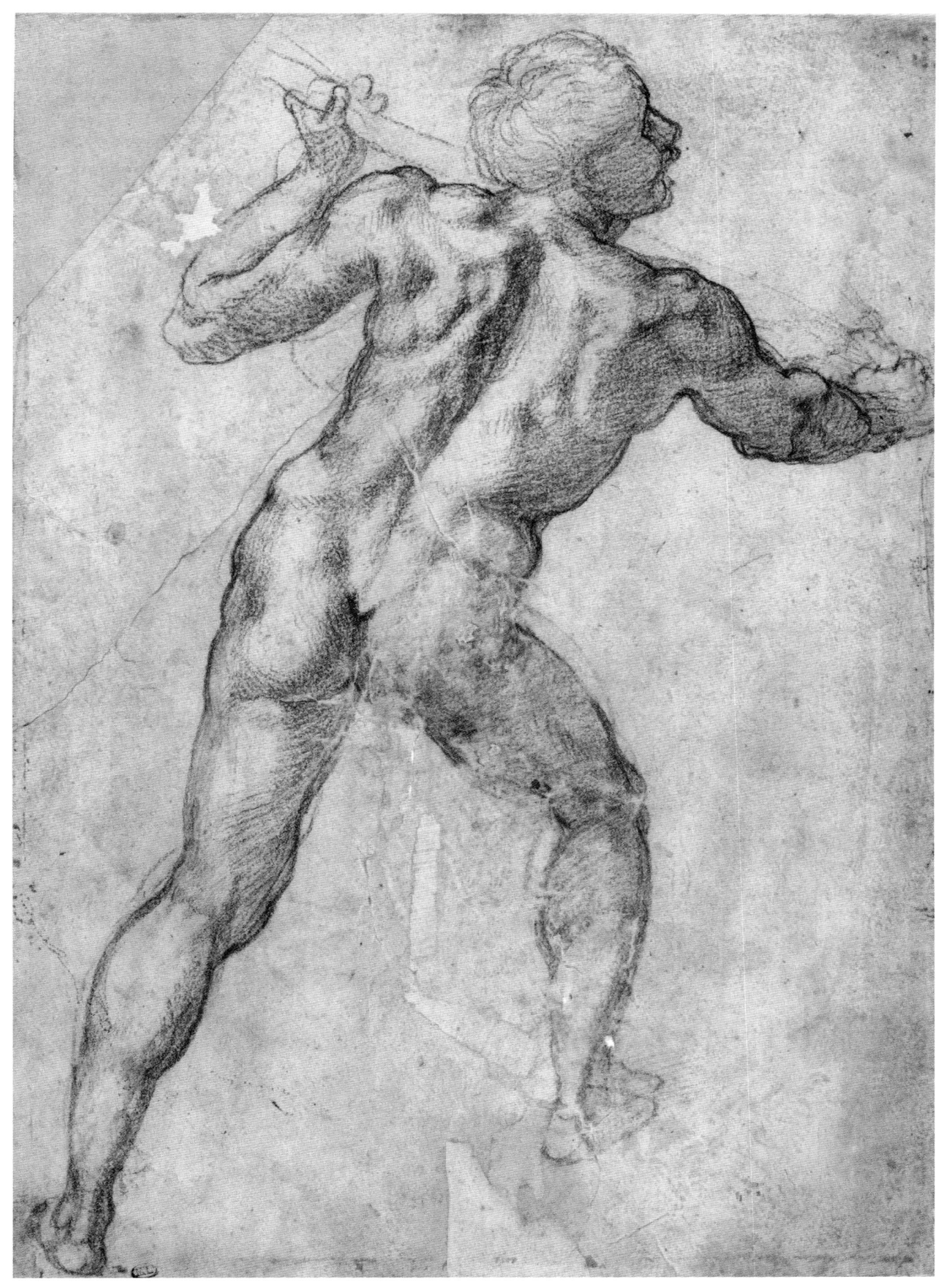

fig. 147   Michelangelo, *Study of a Male Nude from the Back*, 1504. Black chalk, 282 x 203 mm. Paris, Musée du Louvre, Département des arts graphiques, inv. 713

was developed further in a dynamic drawing in the Casa Buonarroti (figs 154 and 155).[38]

No other sequences of drawings can be linked with *Cascina* with confidence, although a group of two men lifting a third, essayed over three sketches and finalised(?) in a more developed drawing, is generally considered to have been made for it. Two are on either side of a sheet in the British Museum, a group sketch on the recto and a single-figure study on the verso; a third, very similar to the verso of the London sheet, is in the Uffizi, while the most detailed group study, on a larger scale than the sketches, is in the Louvre.[39] I suspect that critics are correct in thinking that this group was planned for the mural, but I can find no plausible place for it, and an attempt to force the issue would be counterproductive.[40]

In addition to these drawings, there are three *concetti* of fighting horsemen, probably intended for placement in the background: one of a cavalryman in profile hurling a javelin, a second of a soldier pulling another from a horse, and a third of a cavalryman wielding a mace. The first is autograph, the other two are copies.[41] I attempted to incorporate all three in the reconstruction illustrated in my article of 2013, but I think it is sensible to omit the second one here. A linear drawing in the British Museum (fig. 156), however, which shows a frontal clash of two cavalrymen – obviously a riposte to Leonardo's central group but also recalling Paolo Uccello's famous *Battles* series – could well have found a place near the centre of the background, a kind of capstone.[42] It has therefore been included here in the graphic reconstruction prepared by Luka Pajovic (fig. 157).[43]

The *Bathers* was the only part of *Cascina* to be taken to cartoon stage, and it was certainly the most significant section of the mural, both for Michelangelo himself and his contemporaries and followers; but it was only a part, and it would be unwise to assume that the peripheral areas held no interest for Michelangelo. When Gould argued that an approximation of the overall layout of *Cascina* could be inferred from the *Flood* – the first of the large histories to be painted on the ceiling of the Sistine Chapel – he was surely correct. But his argument also implies the opposite: *Cascina* preceded and inspired the *Flood*, not the other way around. Michelangelo treated the *Flood* as though it were a wall painting to be studied

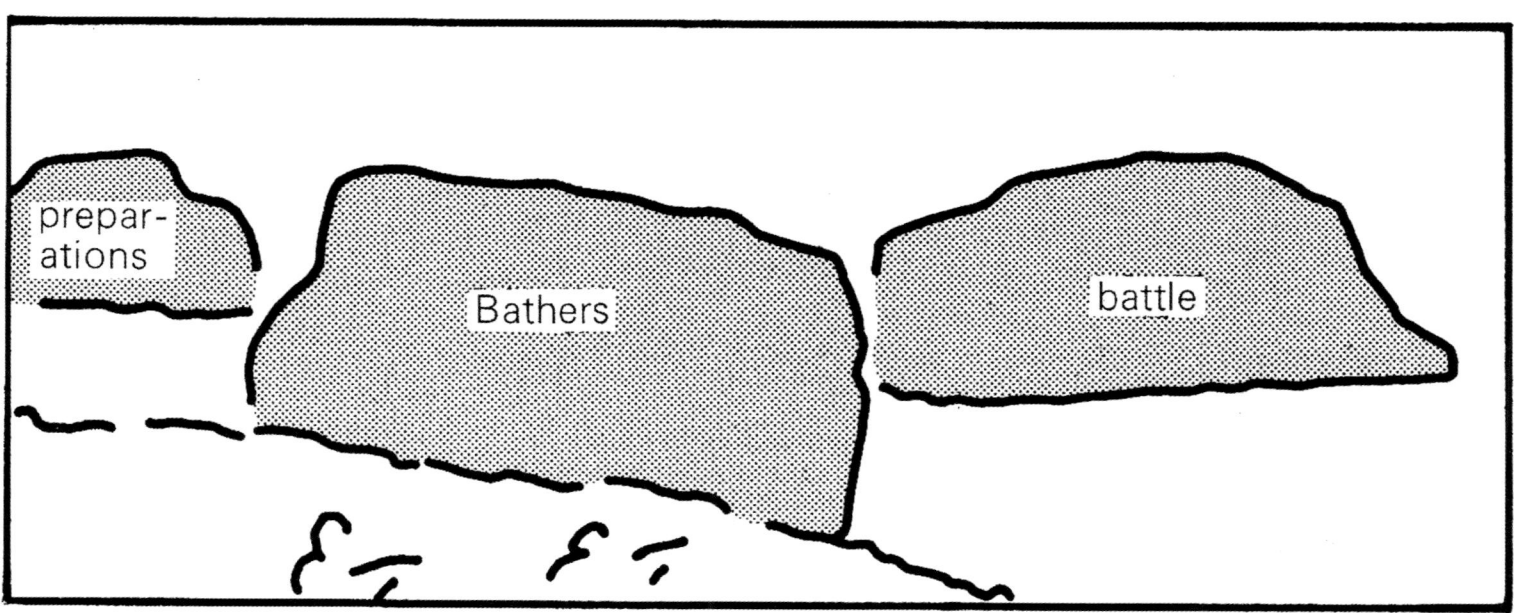

fig. 148   Cecil Gould's conjectural reconstruction of the layout of *Cascina*

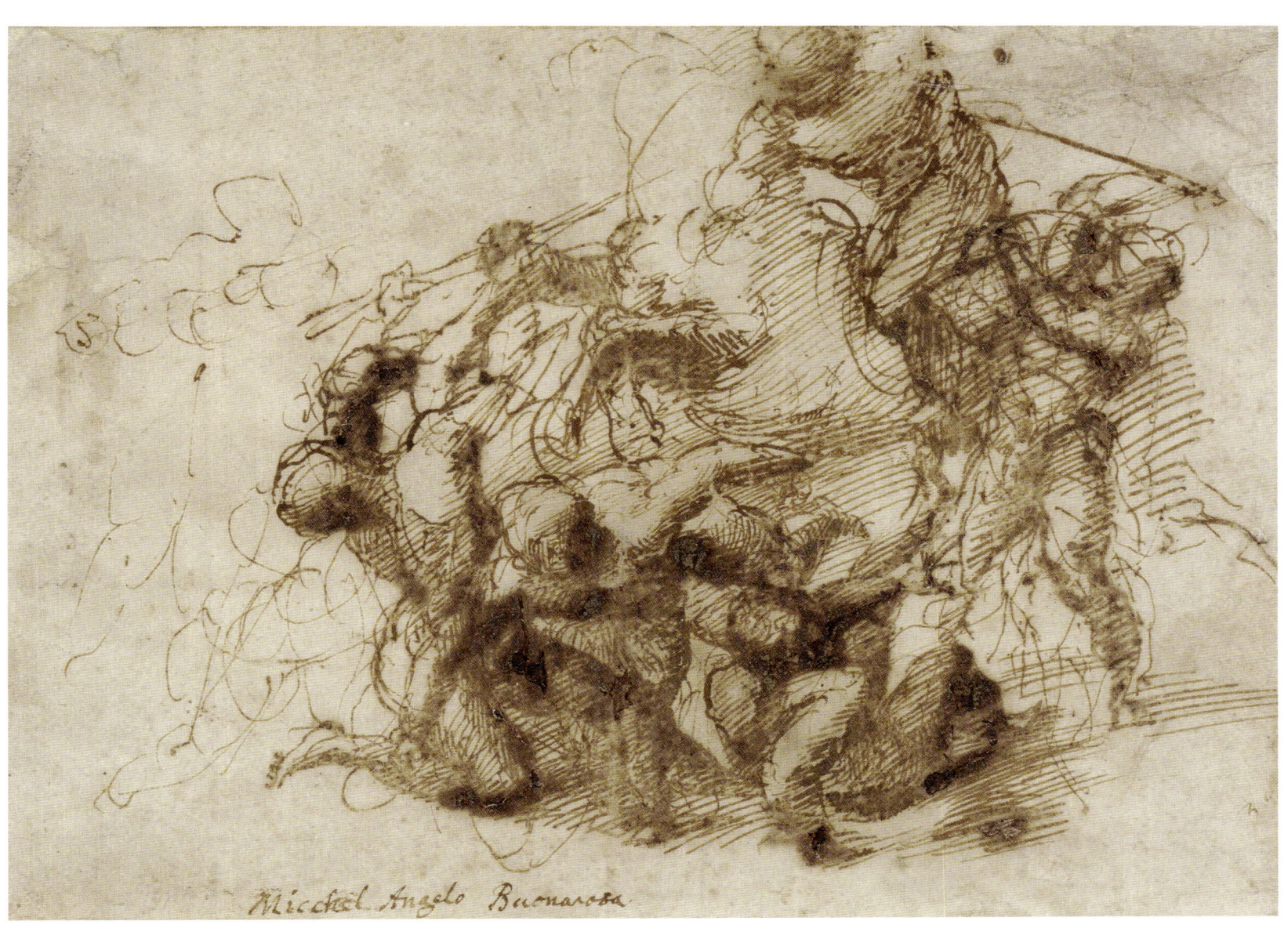

fig. 149   Michelangelo, *A Cavalryman Attacked by Infantrymen*, 1504. Pen and brown ink, 179 x 251 mm. Oxford, Ashmolean Museum, inv. WA1846.40

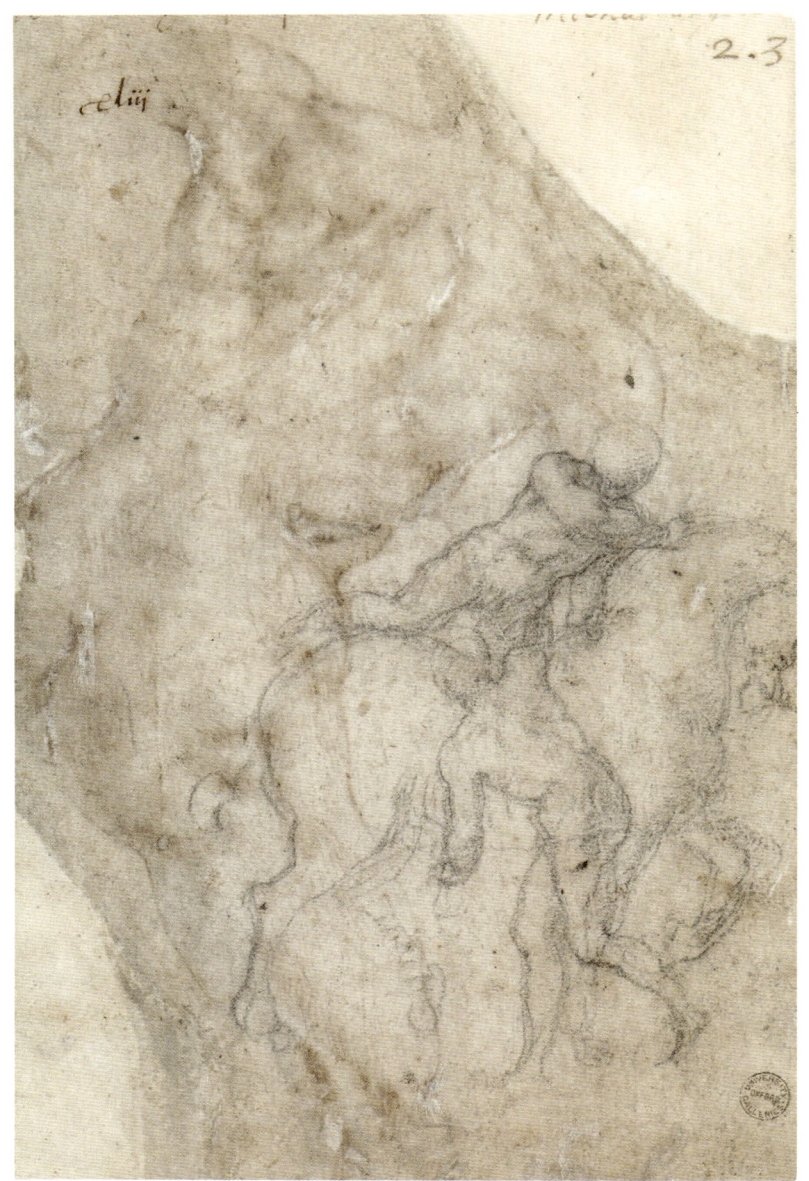

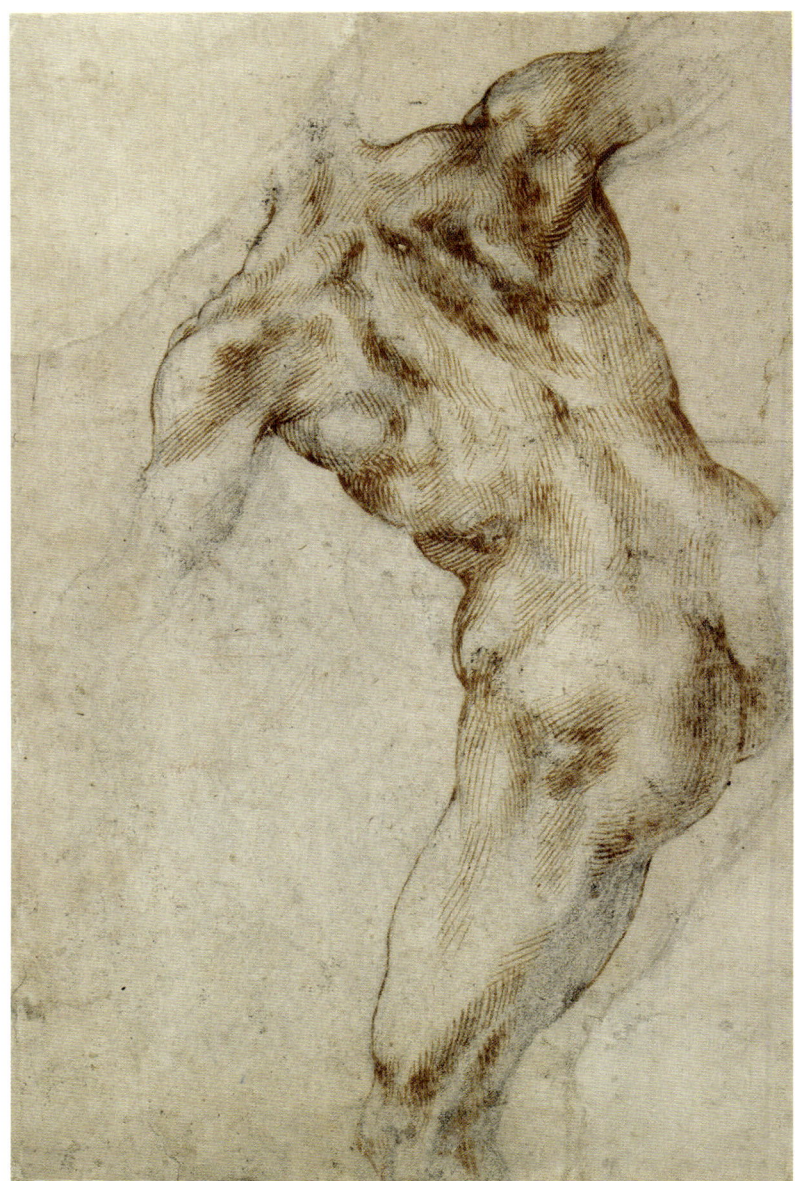

fig. 150   Michelangelo, *A Soldier Assisting Another to Mount a Horse*, 1504.
            Black chalk, 262 x 173 mm. Oxford, Ashmolean Museum,
            inv. WA1846.42v

fig. 151   Michelangelo, *Study of the Back of a Nude Male*, 1504.
            Pen and brown ink, black chalk, 262 x 173 mm. Oxford,
            Ashmolean Museum, inv. WA1846.42

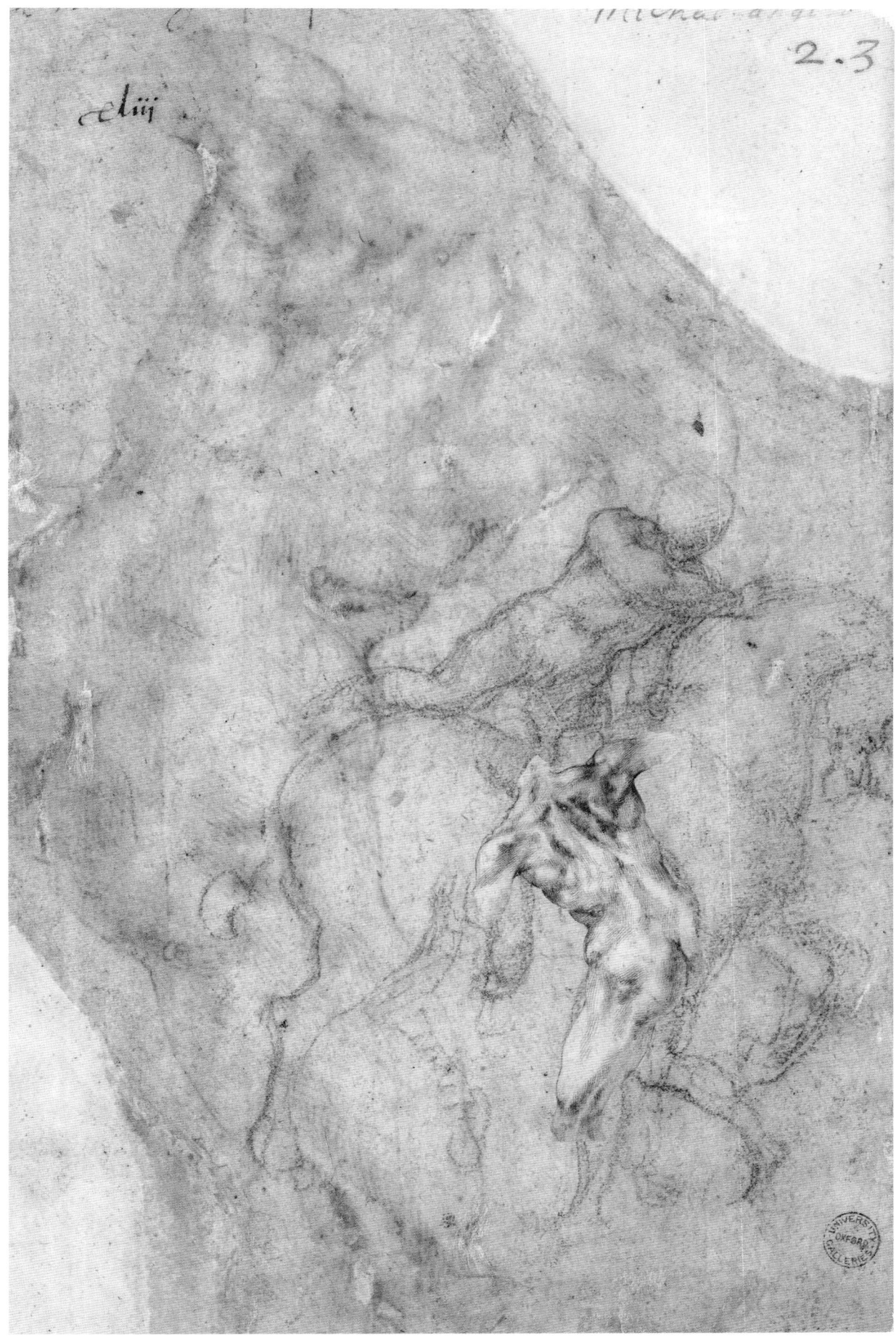

fig. 152   Figs 150 and 151 combined, with the courtesy of Vannessa Timmermans

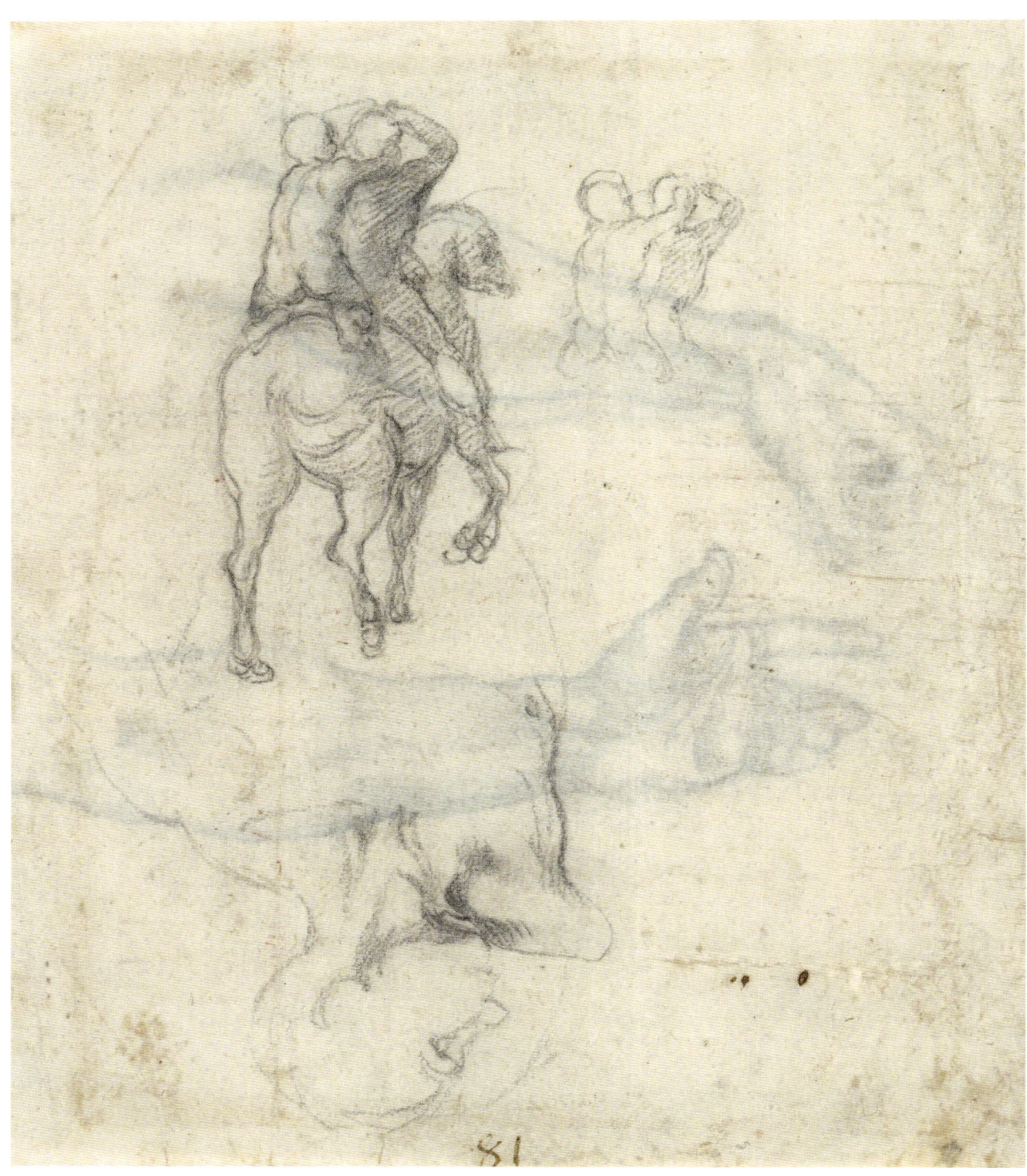

fig. 153   Michelangelo, *Studies of Two Male Nudes on Horseback and a Pointing Soldier*, 1504. Black chalk, 198 x 222 mm. Rotterdam, Museum Boijmans van Beuningen, inv. I 513

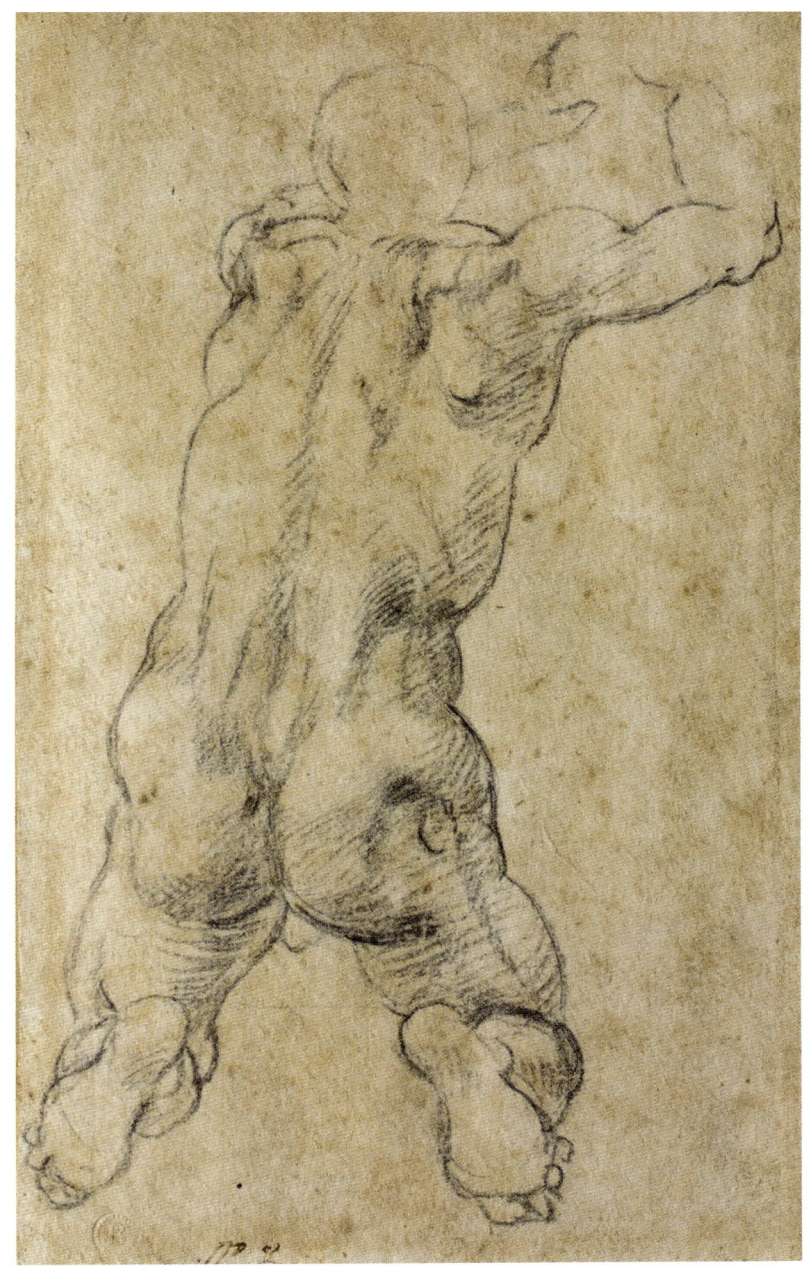

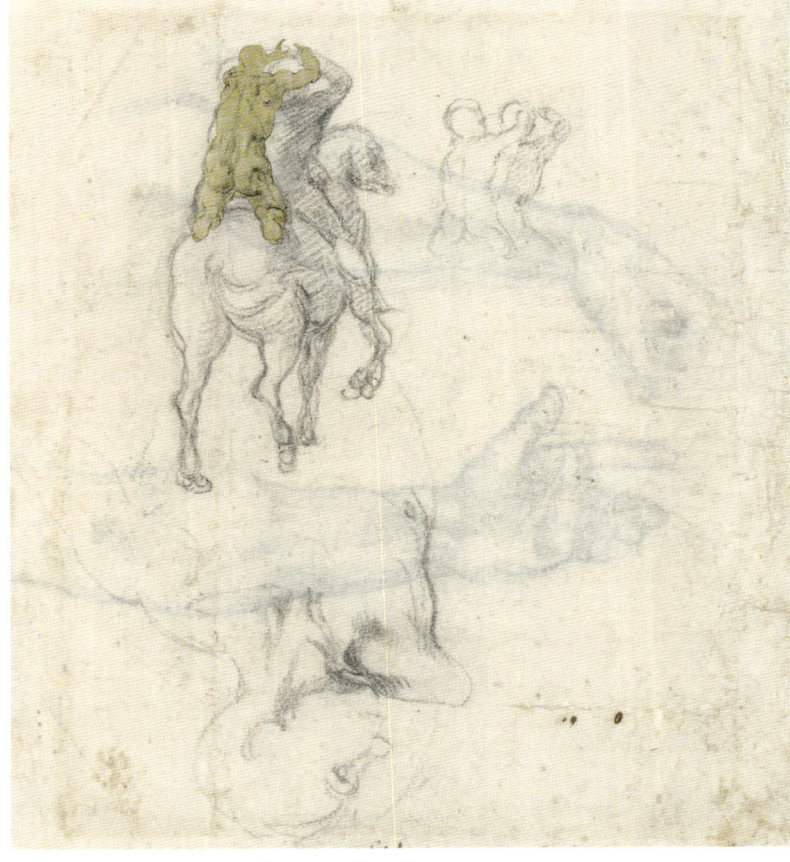

fig. 154   Michelangelo, *Study of A Male Nude from the Back,* 1504.
Black chalk, 258 x 157 mm. Florence, Casa Buonarroti, inv. 54F

fig. 155   Figs 153 and 154 combined, with the courtesy of Vannessa
Timmermans

from a few metres away and on the same level, not as a ceiling painting visible only from a considerable distance. It was a major miscalculation, as Michelangelo realised when he saw from the chapel's floor that many of the *Flood*'s background incidents are virtually impossible to decipher. It was an error Michelangelo did not repeat elsewhere on the ceiling.

Yet that he even thought of reproducing in the *Flood* the 'scattered' organisation of the outskirts of *Cascina*, is surely significant. There was, in Michelangelo, an element of the disruptor, a desire to discard the limiting effects of one-point perspective and rational spatial diminution in favour of a free-form visual poetry, where verses (or figural groups), or words (or figures) are placed without much more than a conceptual relationship to one another. It is this approach that one sees in the lower left-hand section of *The Last Judgement* where there is something of a reprise of the background figures of the *Flood*. But it is also the overall mode of *The Conversion of Saul* (fig. 158), where the vertical axis is tilted and everything is thrown off-balance; figure-scales and figural actions are uncoordinated. In his vision of Saul's soldiers, disorientated by a deafening blast of sound, Michelangelo was playing against the positive responses of the soldiers in the *Bathers* to the trumpet call – and in the soldiers moving away at the left-hand side of *The Conversion*, and in Saul's frightened horse at the centre, Michelangelo was surely recalling the men and horses planned for the left-hand side of *Cascina*. In *The Conversion*, ideas tried in the periphery of *Cascina* are elevated to founding concepts, with the result that the fresco violates most of the accepted visual syntaxes of Renaissance painting.[44] These ideas had little effect in Italy, even among the wildest inventors, such as Francesco Salviati or Pellegrino Tibaldi; their only true recipient was Pieter Bruegel, perhaps Michelangelo's least anticipated student.[45]

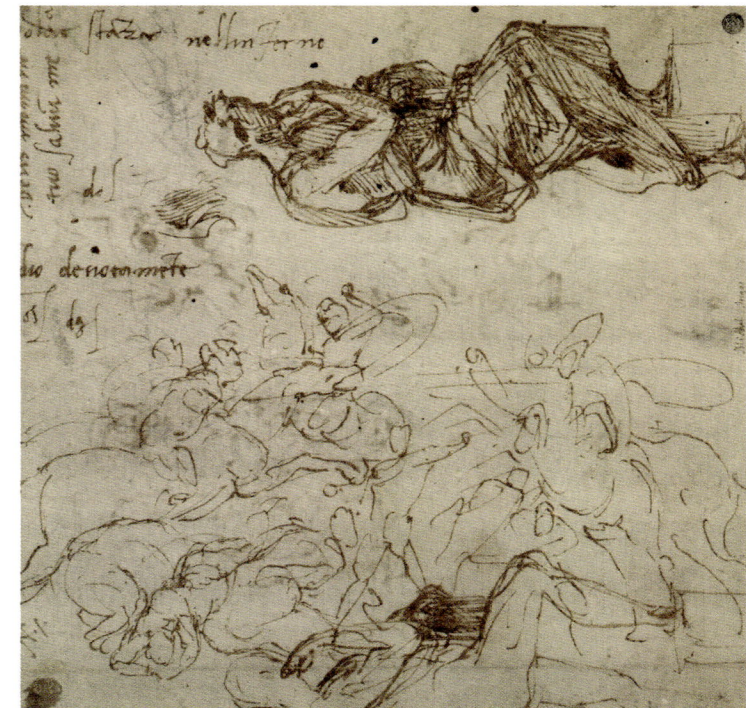

fig. 156   Michelangelo, *Studies of a Battle Scene and a Standing Man*, 1504. Pen and brown ink, 185 x 181 mm. London, British Museum, inv. 1895,0915.496

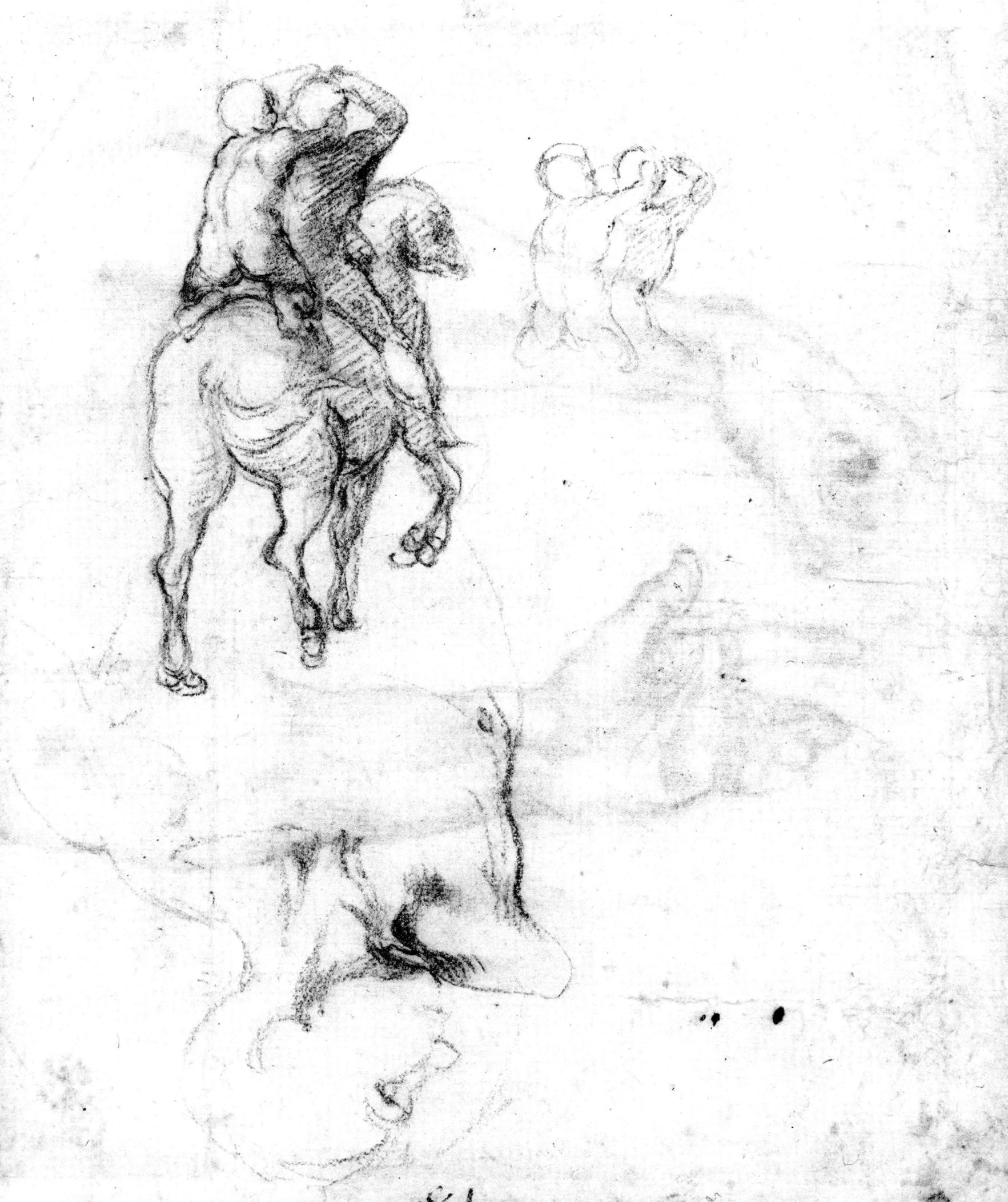

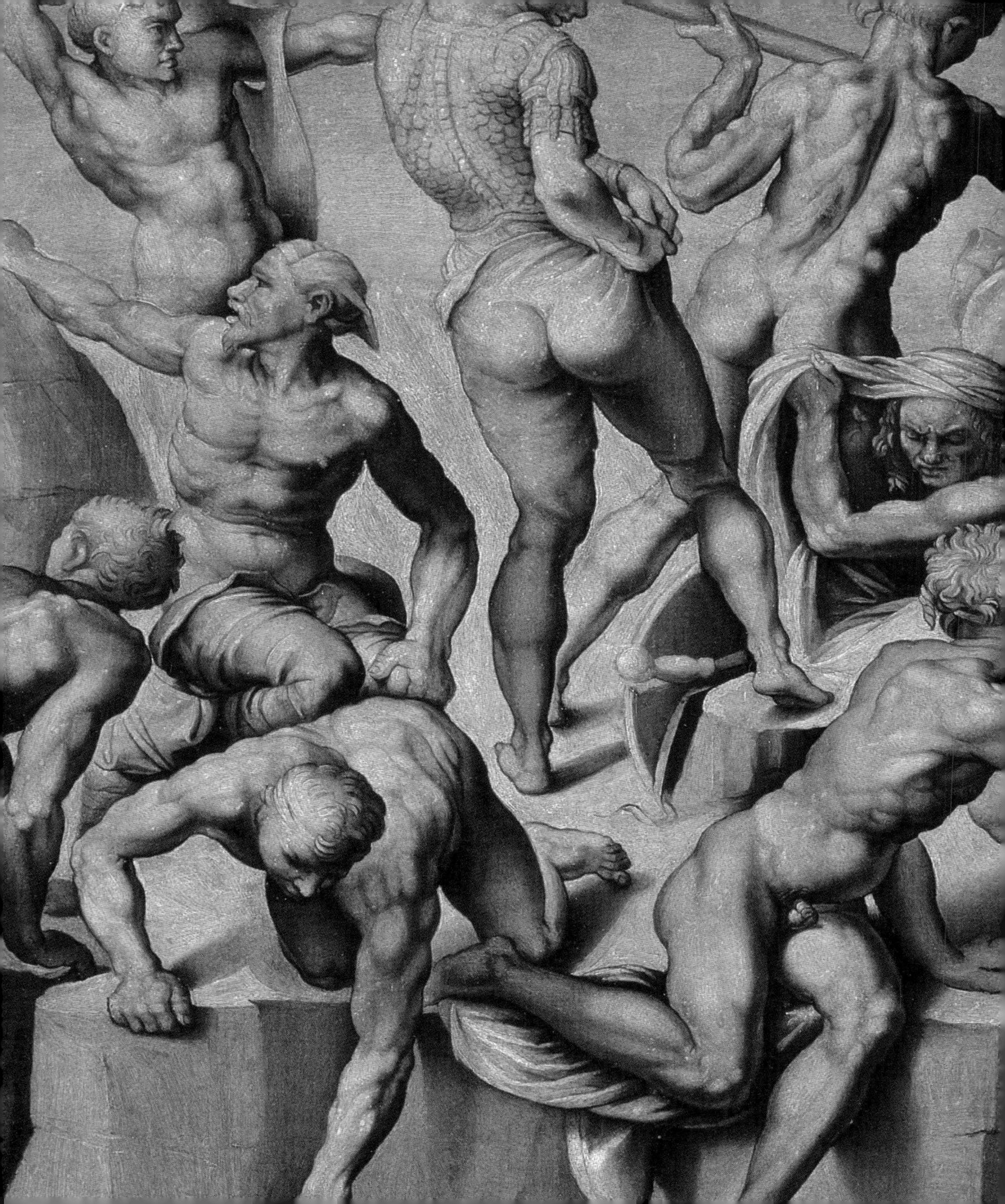

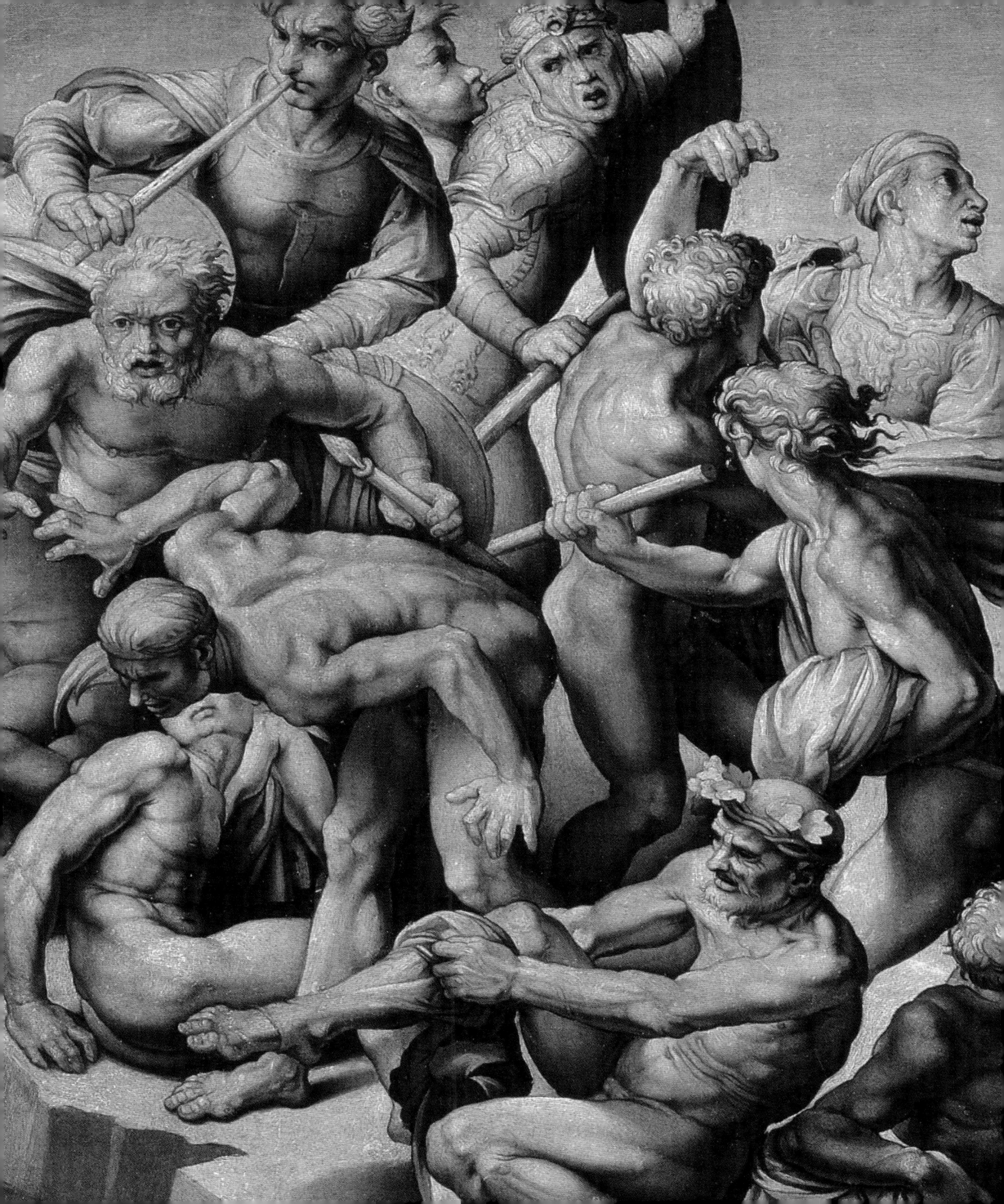

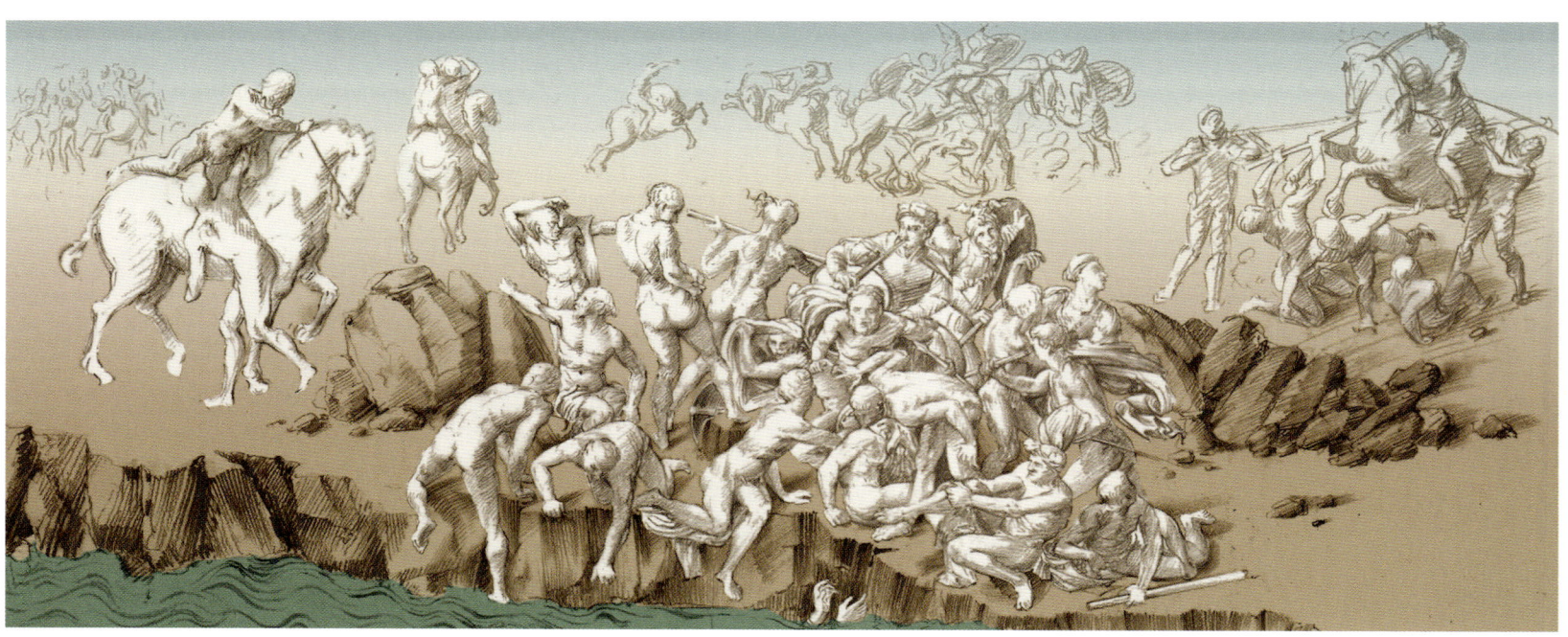

fig. 157   Conjectural reconstruction of Michelangelo's *Battle of Cascina*, by courtesy of Luka Pajovic

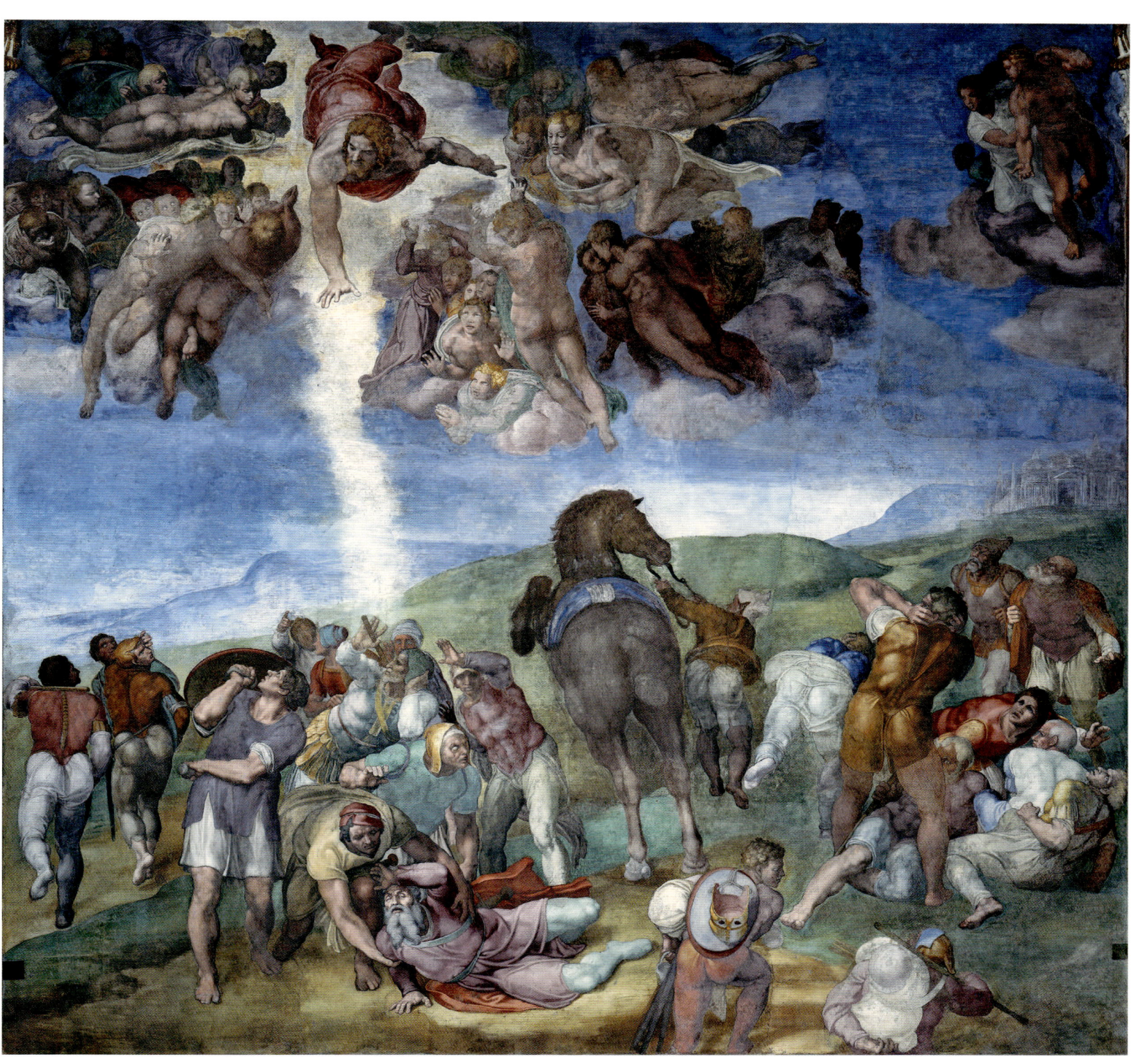

fig. 158   Michelangelo, *The Conversion of Saul*, c. 1542–1545. Fresco. Vatican City, Cappella Paolina

Friend and Enemy.
The Men in Michelangelo's Life

Klazina Botke

Friendship

Direct visual representations of friendship are scarce in the Renaissance; as well as Raphael's famous self-portrait with a male friend, the most revealing is probably Jacopo Pontormo's double portrait of 1523–24.[1] Two men, dressed in black, their bodies turned towards one another, gaze at us out of the panel. The one in front points towards a sheet of paper he is holding, the white of which contrasts strongly with their dark clothing. It appears to be a letter containing a passage from Cicero's *Laelius de amicitia*: 'friendship embraces innumerable ends; turn where you will it is ever at your side; no barrier shuts it out; it is never untimely and never in the way.'[2] While we no longer know who the depicted men are, the text leaves us in no doubt that the two were true friends. To the celebrated Roman orator, the notion of *amicitia* (friendship) was 'nothing else than an accord in all things, human and divine, conjoined with mutual goodwill and affection', and more important to a person than wealth, power, pleasure or even good health.[3] According to Cicero, true friendship was a deep form of connection in which two people, who were not seeking their own advantage, could identify with each other. This Ciceronian idea clearly drew fresh attention in the Renaissance, as it aligned with the humanist emphasis on the autonomous individual.

Aristotle's views on the subject of *philia* (friendship) likewise played a role in early modern society. In his *Nicomachean Ethics*, the Greek philosopher – like Cicero – described friendship as a bond, but now as part of the pursuit of a common social life.[4] Personal friendships, he stressed, require a community of citizens and vice versa. Aristotle further distinguished between three types of *philia*: friendship that arises from pleasure, from utility, and from moral goodness or virtue.[5] His ideas were developed in the thirteenth century by the influential Dominican theologian Thomas Aquinas, who sought in his commentaries on the *Ethics* to connect them with Christian theol-

ogy. In Aquinas's view, there are indeed three types of love: a person can 'be loved for the sake of the good, for the sake of pleasure or because it is useful. As the act of friendship is a loving one, it follows that there are also three types of friendship.'[6] All the same, humankind's true goal, to his mind, remained the all-transcending 'friendship' with God.

By Michelangelo's time, this classical notion of friendship had become embedded in a Christian context and was deeply intertwined with Florentine society. In her book *Friendship, Love and Trust*, Dale Kent shows that in practice there was mainly a difference between the ideal friendship (based on mutual affection and trust), and patronage relationships. The latter were useful and functional friendships on which most artists relied for protection and support.[7] The two were not, however, mutually exclusive: a beneficial friendship could also be a pleasant or even loving relationship. At any rate, as far as artists in Florence were concerned, the ties with patrons and with friends who depended on them were an indispensable form of friendship.[8]

Like all artists during the Renaissance, Michelangelo belonged to a network of family, friends and work relationships. But who were his friends, what kind of relationships did he keep up, and what did they mean to him? Did he have enemies too? The biographies written during the artist's lifetime by Paolo Giovio, Giorgio Vasari and Ascanio Condivi give us some idea, allowing for their somewhat biased character. Our knowledge of the artist's personal relationships has been greatly enriched, moreover, by his 538 or so surviving letters in which he corresponded with relatives, friends, fellow artists, lovers, employees and patrons.[9] His work too – including the drawings and sonnets he gave to his friends – is likewise full of deep, personal feelings for another. This is taken to an extreme in the works he made for Tommaso de' Cavalieri (fig. 14/cat. 6) and Vittoria Colonna, but also in the few rare portraits he drew, such as that of Andrea Quaratesi (fig. 13/cat. 36). The drawing in Teylers Museum

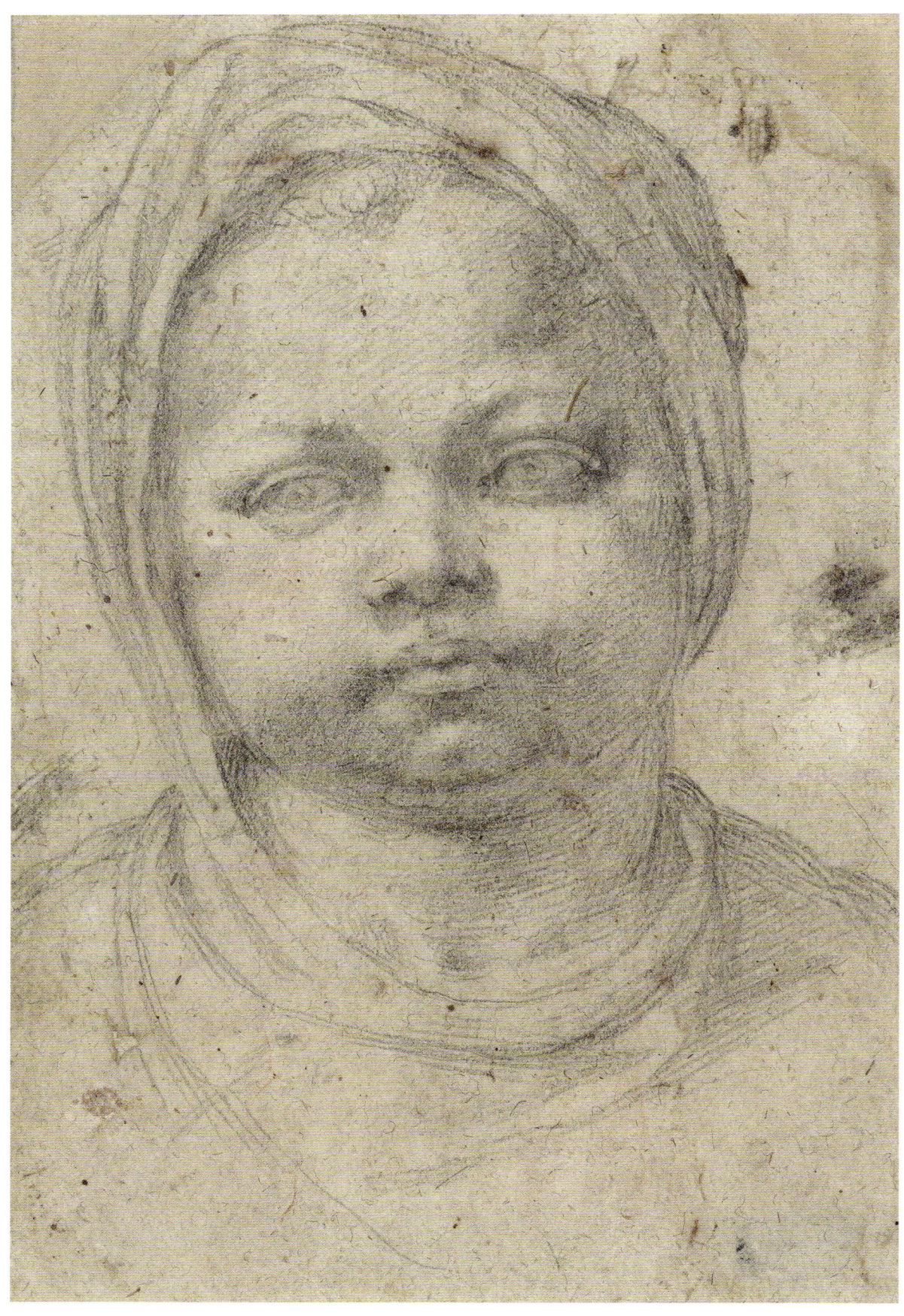

fig. 159   (cat. 34) Michelangelo, *Head of a Child*, c. 1525. Black chalk, 237 x 160 mm. Haarlem, Teylers Museum, inv. K I 53

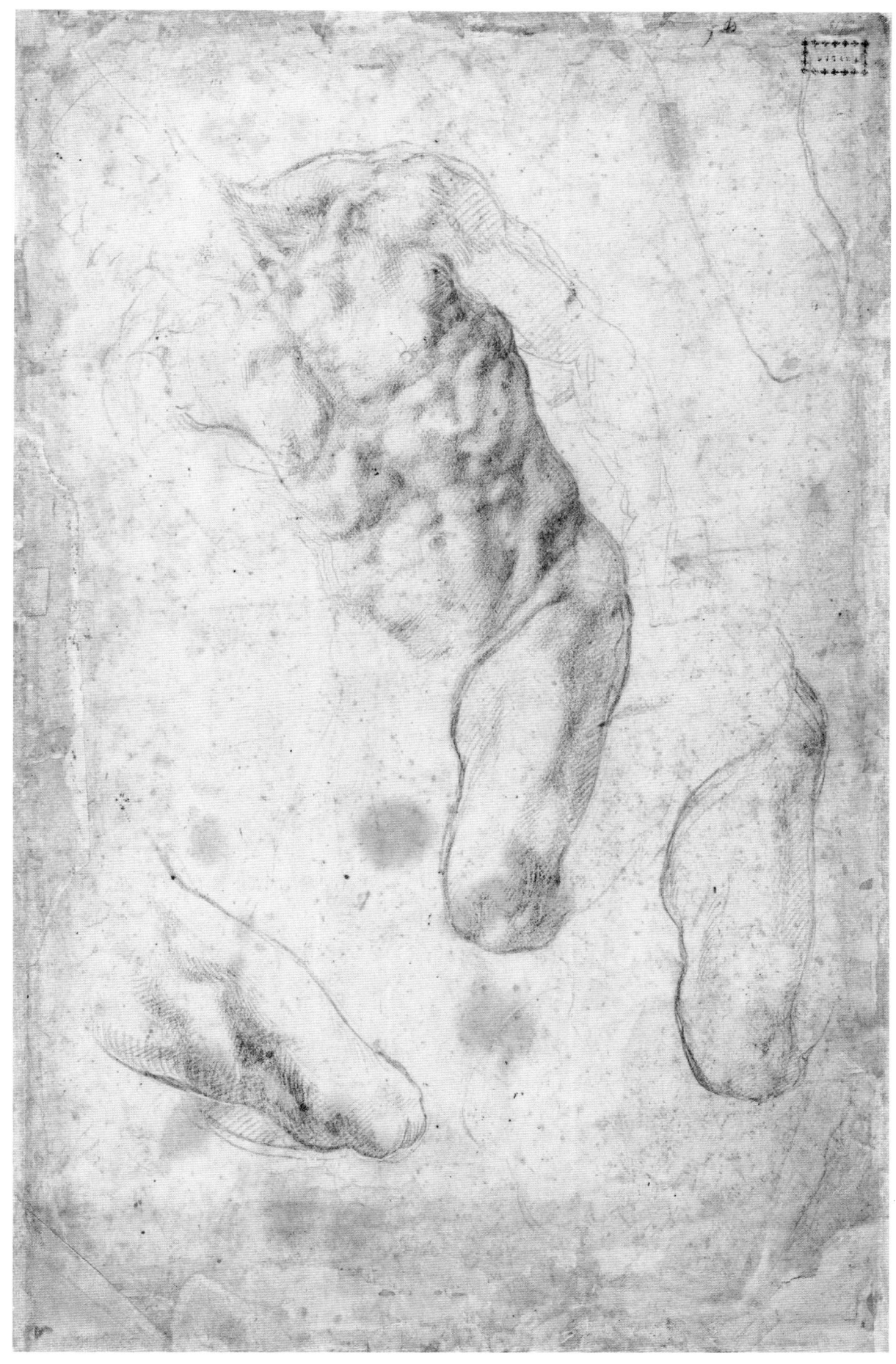

fig. 160   (cat. 13v) Michelangelo, *Study of a Male nude for the* Genius of Victory, c. 1527–1530. Black chalk, 404 x 258 mm. Haarlem, Teylers Museum,
inv. A 019v

with the likeness of a young boy (fig. 159/cat. 34) – soft yet direct – expresses a similarly intimate proximity. While it is not entirely certain that this is a portrait, it is possible that Michelangelo's nephew – one of the three children of Buonarroto, his favourite brother – posed for it.

Michelangelo's friendships – in the classical sense – did indeed bring him pleasure (and heartache) and a sense of inner worth, but undoubtedly also new commissions. In this way, in their role as relatives, lovers, students, models, colleagues, political leaders, clients or even rivals, the people in his life all influenced not only his art but also his fame and reputation.

Strategic Relationships

The most effective and strategic relationships in Michelangelo's life were undoubtedly those with his patrons. Even at a young age, he forged valuable connections at the Palazzo Medici where he had been taken into the household of Lorenzo 'Il Magnifico' and grew up alongside Giovanni de' Medici, the future Pope Leo X.[10] Friends he made in his youth would help advance Michelangelo's career via their connections and recommendations. Building on the Medici family as his starting point, he developed a network of important patrons: from Cardinals Raffaele Riario and Jean Bilhères in Rome and wealthy patrician families such as the Pitti, Strozzi, Doni and Salviati in Florence, to multiple generations of popes. These key relationships clearly did not rely solely on a one-sided dependency. Michelangelo needed commissions, but before long he was highly sought-after. He was able to turn work down and to set demands, and he failed to complete a commission more than once. The efforts of influential men such as Alfonso d'Este and King Francis I of France, who tried to acquire a work by Michelangelo, are also well documented, as are those of the writer Pietro Aretino, who – after failed attempts to obtain a drawing by Michelangelo – became increasingly critical of the artist.

The relationship between Michelangelo and Pope Julius II (Giuliano della Rovere), one of his most prominent patrons, has assumed an almost legendary status over the past century, due in part to Irving Stone's popular novel in which their difficult relationship is strongly emphasised.[11] In 1505, the pope asked Michelangelo to come to Rome where he received the commission to design Julius's tomb, originally for the new St Peter's Basilica. The artist had been recommended to the pontiff by his Florentine friends Alamanno Salviati and Giuliano da Sangallo, whom he had first met at the home of Lorenzo de' Medici. Michelangelo wrote to Giuliano, stating that he expected to receive respect and fair treatment from the pope – plainly a different attitude from the customary relationship between artist and patron, with the former now dictating terms.[12] Julius summoned Michelangelo to Rome again in 1508, this time to paint the ceiling of the Sistine Chapel. Both Condivi and Vasari stressed the discussions and exchanges that subsequently took place between pope and artist, with the aim, as Carmen Bambach notes, of suggesting 'a social equality of sorts between the superlative artist and the supreme authority of the Church'.[13] After Julius's death in 1513, Michelangelo received a new contract specifying a simplified version of the tomb. Work on the monument was repeatedly interrupted in the years that followed: the artist did not complete the assignment until forty years later and in an entirely different form. A drawing in Teylers Museum might be linked to the commission (fig. 160/cat. 13v). The pose of the muscular male figure with the raised knee is comparable to that of the *Genius of Victory*, a sculpture that was probably intended for one of the lower niches in one of the final designs for the tomb.[14] The sculpture, which later found a place in the Salone dei Cinquecento under Cosimo I de' Medici, was never finished, any more than the four *Captives* which, according to Vasari, partly represent the provinces subject to the pope's rule and partly the free arts.[15] In response to comments by Condivi, the latter figures have also been interpreted as embodying Michelangelo's own sense of being held prisoner by his papal patron:

> 'So that it seems as if Julius cared more than for anything else to keep this man for himself; nor was he contented with his services during his life only, but required them after his death; wherefore coming to die he commanded that the Tomb which Michael Angelo had formerly begun should be finished for him.'[16]

The relationship with the Medici family was another significant but complicated one, coloured by politics. Michelangelo grew up under the protection of Lorenzo 'Il Magnifico', and after the Medici returned in 1512 he undertook several important projects for the family: the facade for San Lorenzo – ultimately never executed – the New Sacristy (the Medici funerary chapel), on which he worked from 1519 onwards, and a few years after that, the design for the Laurentian Library.[17] After 1527, however, when Florence rejected Medici rule for a second time, he adopted a different political stance. When pro-Medici imperial troops laid siege to the city in 1529, Michelangelo was appointed governor-general for its fortifications – a position created especially for him. He also served several times on the Gran Consiglio and accepted a position on the Council of Nine – a republican administrative body for military affairs.[18]

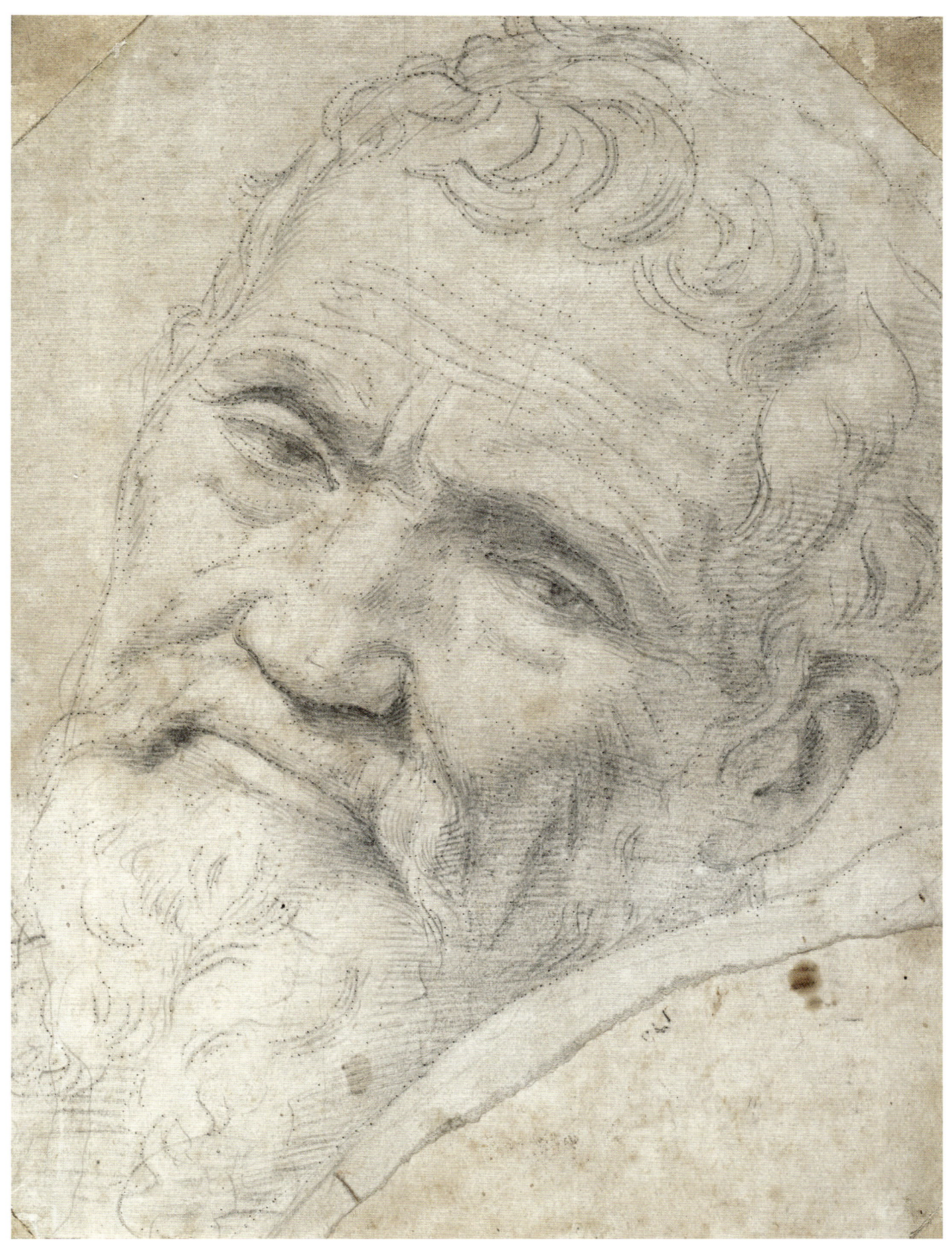

fig. 161   (cat. 7) Daniele da Volterra, *Male Head (Portrait of Michelangelo)*, 1547–c. 1553. Metalpoint and black chalk with white heightening, pricked, 295 x 218 mm.
Haarlem, Teylers Museum, inv. A 021

When the Florentine republic finally came to an end in 1530 and Alessandro de' Medici was appointed head of state, Michelangelo went into hiding, afraid that his republican sympathies would invite punishment. His fears proved groundless: the Medici were eager to have him resume work on the San Lorenzo commissions, which had been on hold since 1527. The exceptional power of Michelangelo's work and the prestige it commanded seem to outweigh their political differences. But whether Michelangelo was able to put his personal views aside remains to be seen. The artist quit Florence for good in 1534, leaving behind an unfinished chapel. For the Medici, even the imperfect work appears to have had the desired effect, for when Holy Roman Emperor Charles V visited the New Sacristy in May 1536 he praised the sculptures in the chapel, including the imposing *Night* (fig. 69).[19]

In Rome, Michelangelo maintained good relations with a number of *fuoriusciti* – republican Florentines who had fled the city-state out of fear of the Medici or who had been exiled, including Cardinal Niccolò Ridolfi and Roberto Strozzi. Strozzi had cared for Michelangelo when he suffered a serious illness in 1544, and received the sculptures of the *Rebellious* and the *Dying Captive* as a gift in return (figs 33 and 86). Not long after, Strozzi presented the sculptures to King Francis I in the hope that he would continue to promote the political agenda of the *fuoriusciti*. Michelangelo thus supported the resistance against the Medici with politically motivated gifts, allowing him to convey, in a subtle manner, his criticism of the Medici regime.[20]

That political differences were not an insurmountable obstacle to effective relationships is in keeping with the ideas of Thomas Aquinas, whose view on concord within friendships differed somewhat from Aristotle's. According to Aquinas, a shared opinion is not essential to a good understanding as it is not formed by the equality of views but by a harmony of wills. Furthermore, love creates a bond that allows for a 'blameless diversity of opinions' as a result of differences in personal circumstances and/or degrees of knowledge.[21] Mere political disagreement is therefore not enough to undermine a relationship, Aquinas said, although it is questionable whether this can be applied to Michelangelo's already difficult relationship with the Medici.[22]

Artistic Collaboration

Michelangelo maintained professional friendships with younger artists throughout his life. This includes his apprentices, who can be divided into two categories: the *garzoni* (assistants) who helped in his workshop, and the *gentiluomini amici* (aristocratic male friends) with whom he corresponded.[23] He enjoyed an emotional bond with some of them and a powerful love with others, as Michael Rocke and Raymond Carlson describe in their essays in this publication. The way Michelangelo's friendships intertwined with his artistic practice is apparent in the exchange of artistic ideas, often in the form of drawings.

There was a small group of artists with whom he developed a collaborative relationship.[24] Marcello Venusti – the protégé who created the most works based on Michelangelo's designs – reproduced his religious compositions, often on a small scale and extremely faithfully.[25] Among other things, this working relationship provided the master with control over the dissemination of his art.[26] Daniele da Volterra, a loyal friend who supported the artist until his death, likewise turned his designs into large-scale paintings when Michelangelo no longer wished to undertake the task himself. He also gained access to his friend's other inventions, including the two drawings of bathers now in Teylers Museum (figs 140/cat. 12 and 141/cat. 13). These figures, viewed from the back, appear in paintings produced in Daniele's workshop between 1560 and 1570. The famous portrait of Michelangelo (fig. 161/cat. 7) – a cartoon for the fresco *The Assumption of the Virgin* (1548–62) in the Santissima Trinità dei Monti, in which his likeness features as one of the apostles – is also by da Volterra's hand. The master's timeworn face looks at us with a resigned gaze. It might be a stretch to detect in this the profound friendship that existed between the two artists, but Michelangelo's expression does seem to have been caught by someone who knew him well.

Michelangelo had already struck up a relationship with the Venetian painter Sebastiano del Piombo by the time he was working on the ceiling of the Sistine Chapel.[27] When Sebastiano came to Rome, Michelangelo took him under his wing and gave him drawings and figure studies to use while creating his works. Michelangelo's drawing of *Christ in Limbo* (fig. 162/cat. 40) was very probably an example of this, although it is not certain to which of Sebastiano's projects the study can be linked.[28] Their collaboration was, in Carmen Bambach's view, 'a professional friendship, though one with a complex personal side not equally felt by both parties'.[29] Artistically speaking, Sebastiano benefited more from their relationship than Michelangelo, although we know from their correspondence that Sebastiano also gave Michelangelo advice. Above all, he admired the much older artist. The friendship between the two seems to have ended around 1533–34 after a remarkable conflict over *The Last Judgement*. Sebastiano had had the wall of the Sistine Chapel prepared for the use of oil paint – the medium with which Raphael had also experimented in the Sala di Costantino in the papal apartments.[30] According to Vasari, Michelangelo took this as a grave insult, on the grounds that working in oil was for lazy painters and women. Such was the scale of the *faux pas* that he promptly severed the relationship for good.[31] The fact that their friendship had in part been based on mutual utility and benefit puts the quarrel into some perspective. Aristotle also argued that accusations and reproaches only arise within friendships formed out of utility: those who become friends on the grounds of virtue will, on the contrary, only seek to benefit one another.[32]

Rivalry and Criticism

Some artists went to great lengths to gain access to Michelangelo's work. In 1529, his workshop on the Via Mozza in Florence was reportedly broken into by a group of rivals who stole more than fifty drawings and four models.[33] The sculptor Baccio Bandinelli was named as one of the burglars. Vasari later specifically accused the same man of tearing up the Cascina cartoon, supposedly out of jealousy.[34] The rivalry was further inflamed when Benvenuto Cellini poured scorn on Bandinelli's *Hercules and Cacus*, the sculpture installed at the Palazzo della Signoria in 1534 next to *David*, and which had been intended to outdo Michelangelo.[35]

Leonardo da Vinci was, however, a more important artistic rival to Michelangelo. The competition between the two men was expressed in the designs for *Battle of Cascina* and *Battle of Anghiari* for the Palazzo della Signoria, as Paul Joannides describes elsewhere in this publication. Vasari also noted the contempt in which they held one another and recounted several anecdotes about the way their rivalry played out. These are set out in *The Codex of the Anonimo Magliabechiano* – an unfinished collection of artists' biographies penned between 1540 and 1547 – and include an account of how a group of men gathered at the Santa Trinità to discuss the work of Dante. They asked Leonardo da Vinci to explain a particular passage, but since Michelangelo happened to walk by at that moment, Leonardo suggested that he answer the question instead. Michelangelo responded brusquely, 'Explain it yourself, you, who designed a giant horse to cast in bronze and failed!' (referring to a botched equestrian monument for Francesco Sforza).[36] Carl Frey even believed the source for these anecdotes might actually have been Bandinelli.

Michelangelo came in for even more venomous criticism from the Venetian writer Lodovico Dolce in his *Dialogo della Pittura*, a text he published in 1557 while the master was still alive. It takes the form of a three-part dialogue between the writer Pietro Aretino, representing the Venetian viewpoint, and the Florentine humanist Giovanni Francesco Fabrini, who defends the art produced in his own city. There are several passages in which the rivalry between Michelangelo and Raphael is settled in Raphael's favour. It is well known, Arentino declares, that Michelangelo is responsible for the design (*disegno*) of Sebastiano's work and that he put pressure on his younger colleague to join in the rivalry with Raphael. Raphael supposedly responded by expressing his pleasure that Michelangelo had helped Sebastiano out, because now he knew it was Michelangelo himself whom he had surpassed.[37] Fabrini continues to defend Michelangelo in the *Dialogo*, stating that he 'stands alone', whereas Aretino responds that comparable painters certainly exist, as well as those who surpass him, such as Titian.[38] When it comes to the rendering of fabrics and clothing, Fabrini has to concede that Raphael's draperies are the more praiseworthy, but adds that this is also because Michelangelo focuses more on the nude figure.[39] Aretino counters with the criticism that Michelangelo is unable to distinguish clearly between men, women and children in terms of robustness, delicacy and softness,[40] before haranguing the many nudes in the Sistine Chapel that 'display their fronts and backs in an immodest way', unworthy of the location.[41] Several letters dating from the 1540s and 1550s confirm that this really was Aretino's opinion. He wrote to Michelangelo that 'in reviewing the entire sketch of your Day of Judgement, I have come to recognise the illustrious grace of Raphael in the pleasing beauty of his invention'.[42] Aretino continued: 'I, as a baptised person, am ashamed of the licence, so offensive to the spirit, that you have taken in expressing the ideas in which is resolved the end towards which every sense of our truest faith strives'.[43] He also referred to *David*, whose genitals had been covered with gold leaves, even though the statue was not located in a sacred place but on a public square.[44]

The design of *The Last Judgement* in the Sistine Chapel (fig. 96) elicited further criticism.[45] While the work was still in progress, Biagio da Cesena, Pope Paul III's master of ceremonies, complained to the pope that Michelangelo's fresco would be more at home in a bathhouse or brothel than in a papal chapel; there was simply too much nudity. Michelangelo responded by placing Biagio's face on the figure of King Minos in hell.[46] Not everyone shared this opinion, however; shortly after the fresco was unveiled on 19 November 1541, Nino Sernini reported as follows to his patron, Cardinal Ercole Gonzaga of Mantua, putting the criticism in perspective:

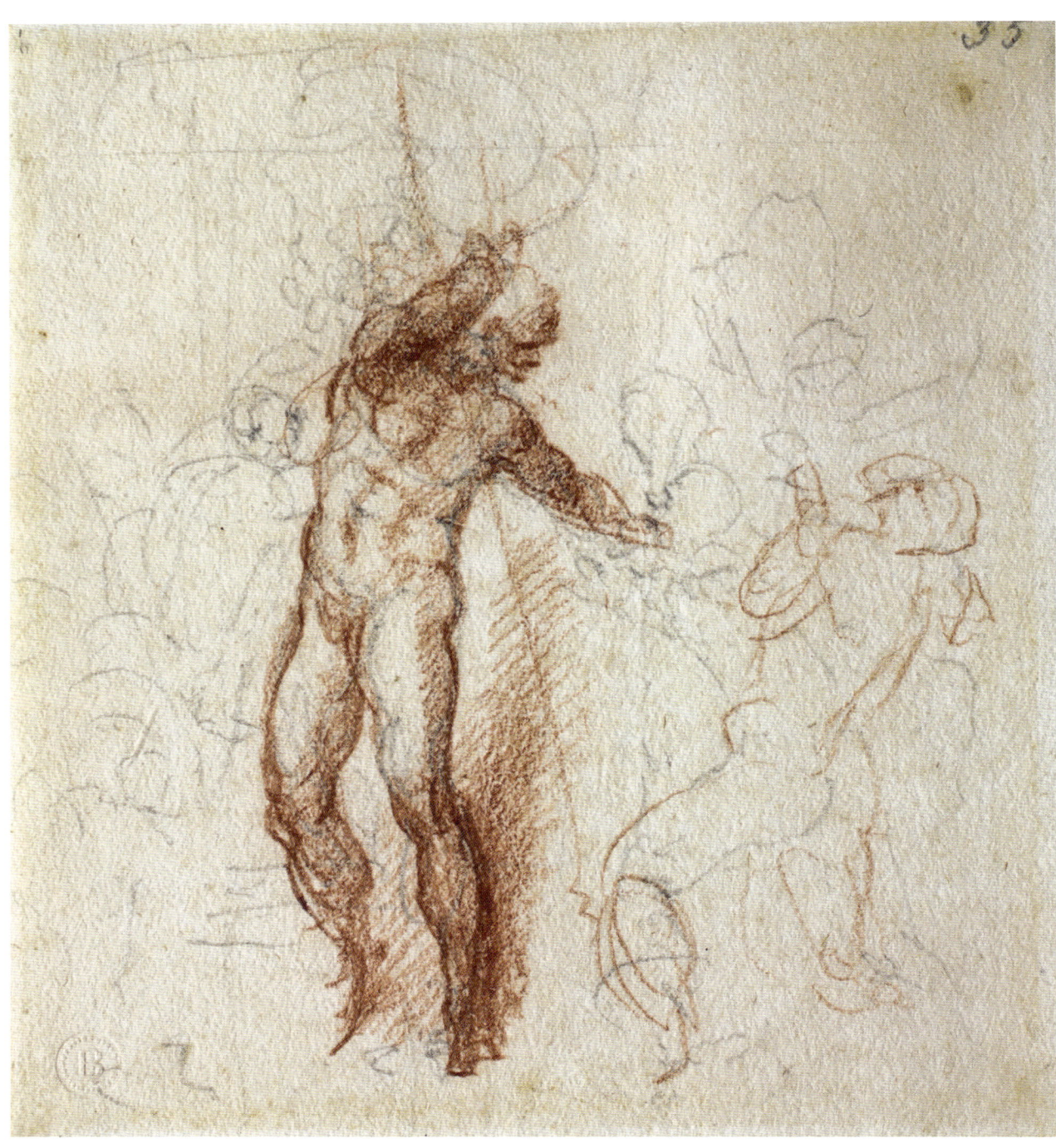

fig. 162   (cat. 40) Michelangelo, *Christ in Limbo*, c. 1530–1533. Red and black chalk, 163 x 148 mm. Florence, Casa Buonarroti, inv. 35F

'...the work is of such beauty as Your Illustrious Lordship may imagine, there are not lacking those who damn it. The Theatine fathers are the first to say that it is not good to have nudes displaying themselves in such a place, even though [Michelangelo] has paid great attention to this, and only in about ten out of so great a number can one see anything indecent. Others say that he has made Christ beardless and too young, and He does not have that majesty which is suitable for Him, and so there is no lack of talk.'[47]

In 1564, after the Council of Trent ruled that saints ought to be represented with propriety and decorum, Daniele da Volterra was employed by Pope Pius IV to paint clothing or drapery over some of the nude figures.

Spiritual Intimacy

The idea that Michelangelo's depiction of nudes was meant to encourage licentiousness in the manner claimed by (the not unbiased) Aretino is inconsistent with his actual religious practice, as attested by his friendship with the Roman noblewoman Vittoria Colonna, from 1536–38 until her death in 1547. Vittoria was Michelangelo's spiritual confidante, of whom Queen Marguerite de Navarre went so far as to claim that she showed the most serious and celebrated of men 'the light that is a guide to the haven of salvation'.[48] Both were members of the *Spirituali*, a reformist movement within the Catholic Church that focused on an intense personal experience of faith, as previously discussed in this publication by Jennifer Sliwka.[49] It was in this same period that Michelangelo composed a substantial proportion of his 302 surviving poems. The numerous spiritual compositions he devoted to Colonna clearly express a deep, emotional bond between the two – a relationship that also resulted in some of the artist's most refined meditative drawings: the *Pietà* and the *Crucifixion* (fig. 124).[50] It was 'for love of her' that he created these works.[51]

In one of his most famous madrigals he represents her as a divine instrument, she who has changed the poet forever:

'A man in a woman, or rather a god
speaks through her mouth,
so that in listening to her,
I am made such that I shall never again be mine.'[52]

The 'man' or 'god' who speaks through her can be read as a reference to Christ or the Holy Spirit.[53] In the letter Michelangelo wrote to Giovan Francesco Fattucci after Vittoria's death, he referred to her, moreover, using a male form, calling her *un grande amico*, a great (male) friend, rather than *una grande amica*, a great (female) friend.[54] This testifies to his high regard for her, given that women in the Renaissance period were considered imperfect, incapable of absolute virtue and hence also of true friendship. As gender, however, was not determined directly by physical sex but rather by culture, women could become male and vice versa,[55] opening the way for an intimate friendship. Furthermore, shared spiritual contemplation of redemption through Christ, in both text and image, was in keeping with the ideas of Thomas Aquinas that true bliss lay in communing with the goodness of the deity, that the true purpose of humankind is intimate communication with God.[56] Even for Michelangelo, as he confirmed in one of his last sonnets, Christ remained the only perfectly reliable and true friend.[57]

'Day after day, ever since my early years,
Lord, you have been my helper and my guide;
therefore my soul is even now confident
of doubled support in my doubled sufferings.'[58]

Virtù e Fama

An artist's network consists of all manner of relationships and friendships, with scope for advocacy and artistic exchange, emotional support and love, but also for criticism and rivalry. Some friendships have a lasting impact on fame and reputation. A bound collection of letters preserved at the Casa Vasari shows how the relationship between Giorgio Vasari and Michelangelo evolved in the final years from formality to true friendship. The artist wrote them during his time in Rome between 1550 and 1557, while Vasari was mostly residing in Florence. Carmen Bambach has shown how their friendship shaped the rewritten 1568 *Vita* of Michelangelo.[59]

When Michelangelo died in Rome on 18 February 1564, he was initially interred in the Santi Apostoli. He had made clear to his friends and his cousin Lionardo, however, that he wished to find his eternal rest in Florence. His body was thus smuggled from Rome to Florence, allowing the ceremony finally to take place five months later, on 14 July 1564, at San Lorenzo. The humanist Benedetto Varchi delivered the eulogy, which was published shortly afterwards.[60] Like Vasari in his *Vita*, Varchi presented Michelangelo as an artist whose talent for *disegno* enabled him to surpass all his predecessors in painting, sculpture, architecture and poetry – praise that would not soon be forgotten.

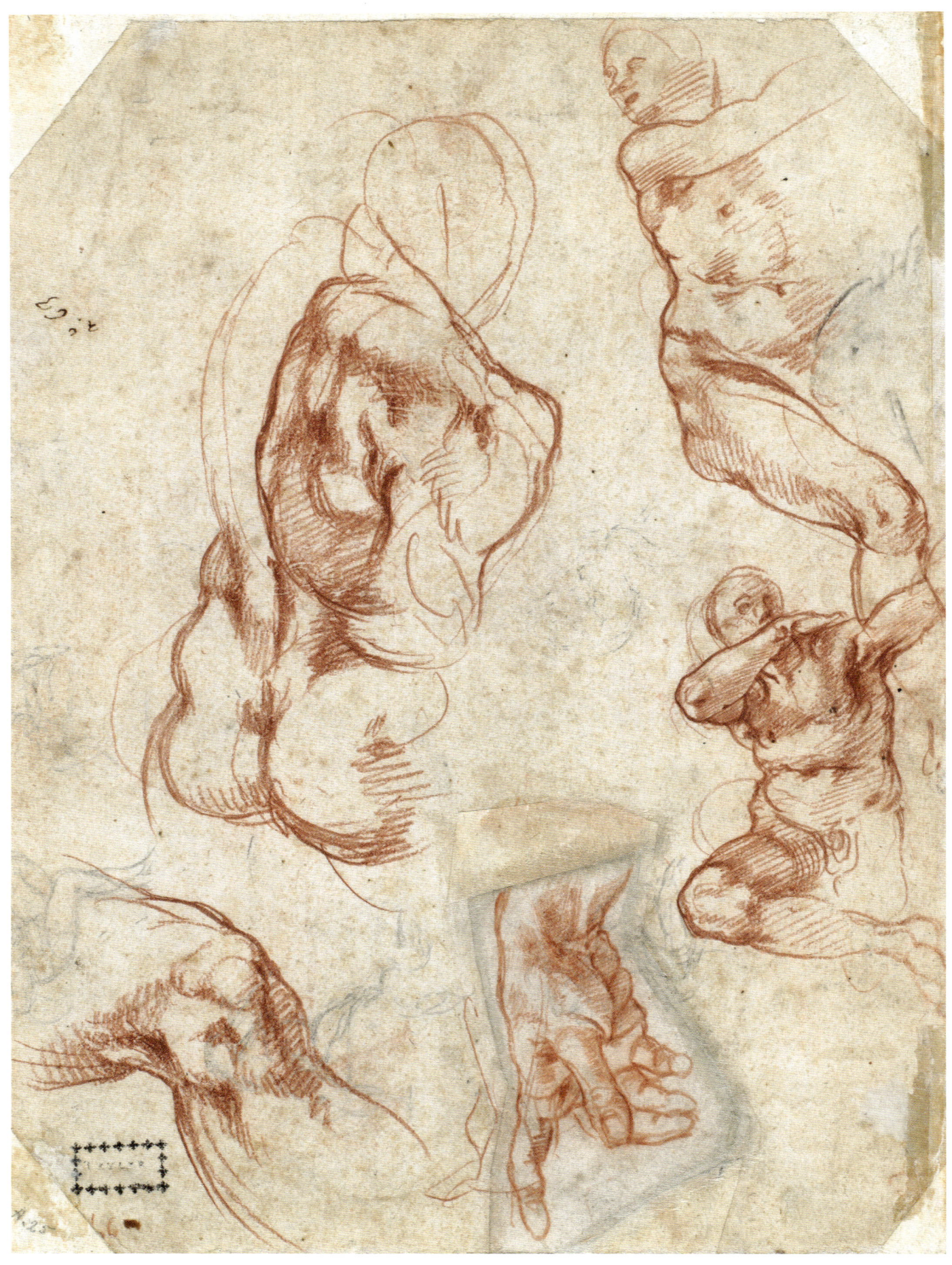

fig. 163   (cat. 18v) Michelangelo, *Figure Studies for the Sistine Chapel Ceiling*, c. 1511. Red chalk, 296 x 195 mm. Haarlem, Teylers Museum, inv. A 020v

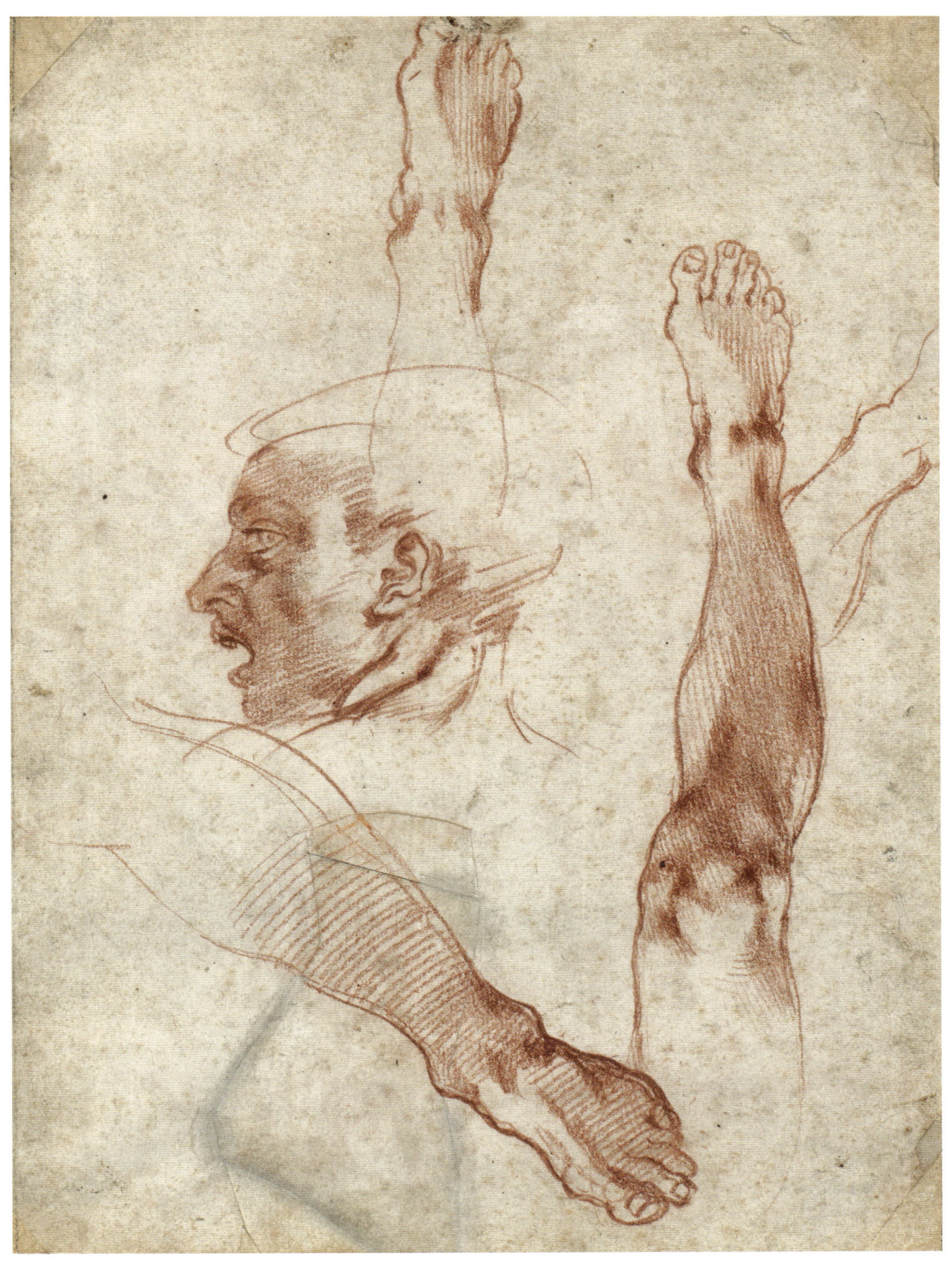

fig. 164   (cat. 18) Michelangelo, *Studies of a Head and Limbs for the Sistine Chapel Ceiling*, c. 1511. Red chalk, 296 x 195 mm. Haarlem, Teylers Museum, inv. A 020

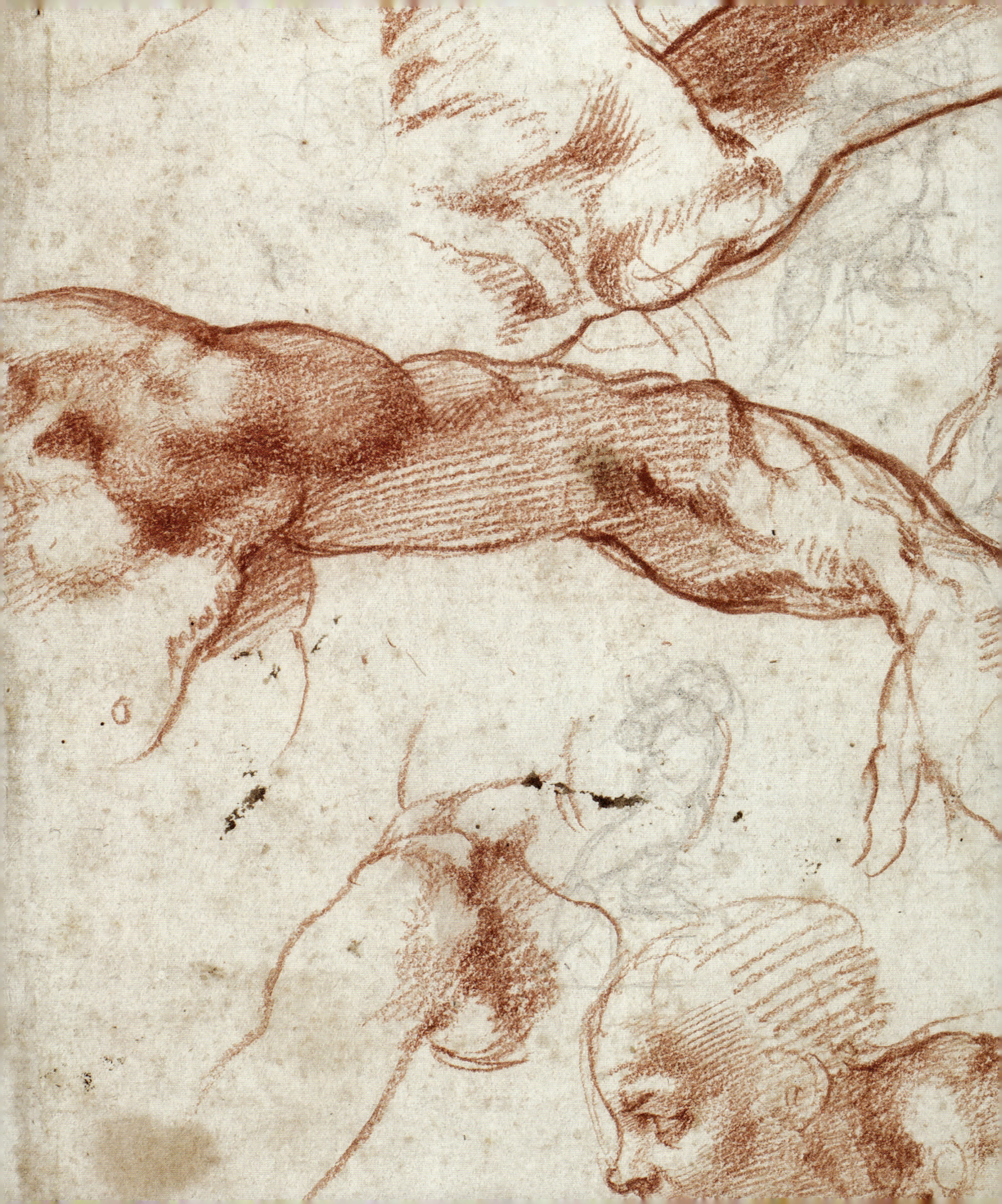

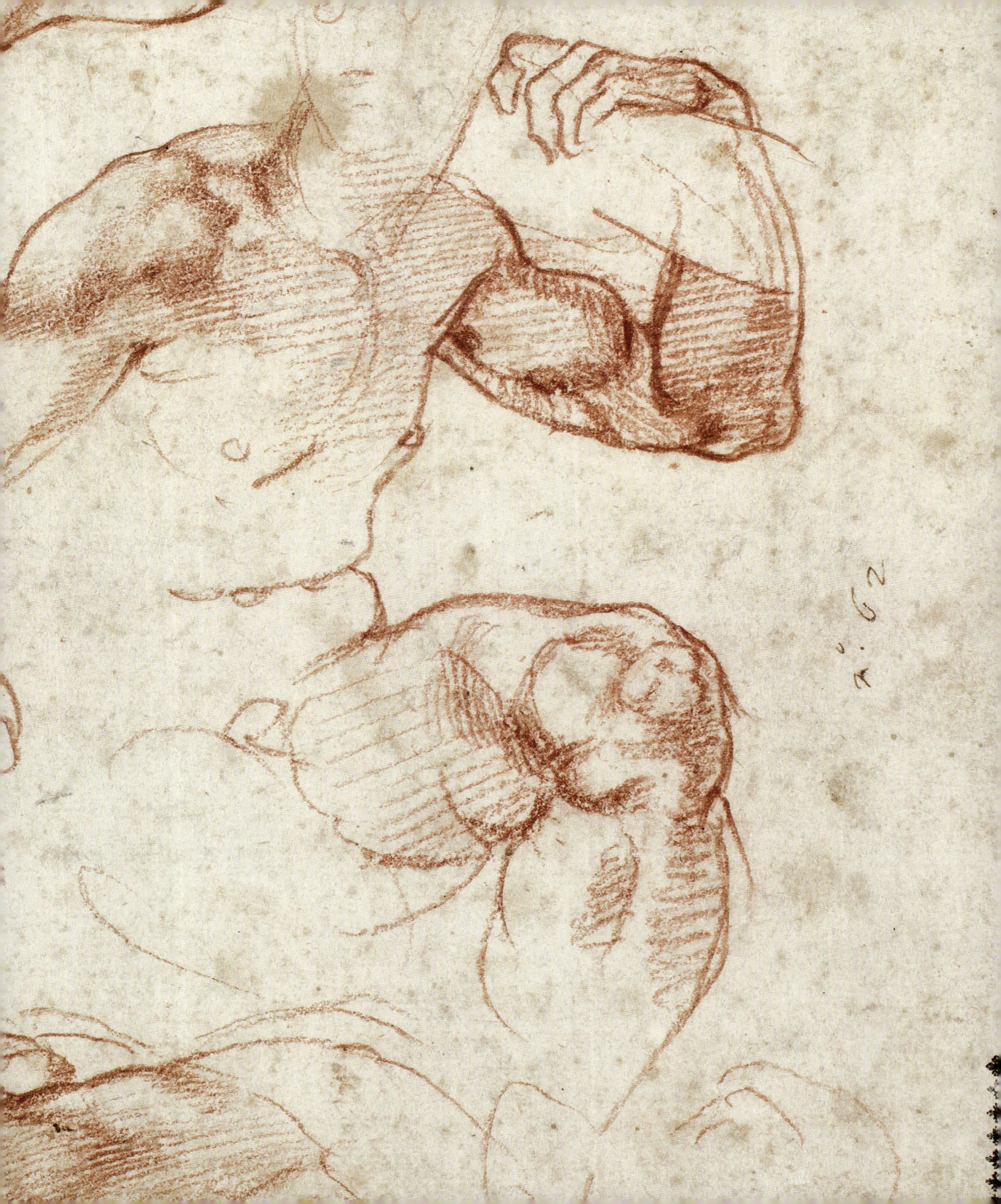

Michelangelo Buonarroti the Younger, the master's great-nephew, was largely responsible for the expansion of Michelangelo's reputation in the century that followed. The extensive decoration of the additions to the Casa Buonarroti in Florence between 1615 and 1637 was intended to contribute to this.[61] The biographies of Filippo Baldinucci (published in 1682) and Domenico Bernini (published in 1713) and the diary of Paul Fréart de Chantelou (published in 1665) offer further important documentary evidence regarding the fate of Michelangelo's art and reputation in the subsequent period.[62]

His drawings, too, continued to inspire artists over the course of those centuries, as the following modest but illustrative example demonstrates. Teylers Museum holds some of Michelangelo's studies in red chalk for the figures in the later part of the Sistine Chapel ceiling. The preliminary study for the hand of God (figs 163 and 164/cat. 18) – perhaps Michelangelo's most famous work after *David* – was cut out at some stage and pasted to a sheet with preliminary studies for his Haman, possibly because it was mistaken for that figure's hand. The fragment was returned to its original place during restoration in 1952.[63] The expressive face of one of the *ignudi* on the other side of the sheet was fortunately spared when the hand of God was cut out. A second study for the ceiling of the Sistine Chapel shows the famous *ignudo* viewed from the back, with preliminary studies for Eve and for God's arms on the other side (fig. 165/cat. 19v). The separate studies on the two sheets were copied by an unknown artist in around 1600–50 and combined in a single sheet now in Windsor (fig. 166). It appears that either Michelangelo gave these drawings away at a very early stage or that they were taken from his studio, and that they have been inseparable for more than 500 years.

The fact that Michelangelo's fame has extended as far as our own twenty-first century reflects the power of his work, to which his friendships and relationships also contributed. Thanks to the wealth of information we now possess regarding the artist's personal life, not only have we gained a deeper insight into his art and methods, we also seem to be getting steadily closer to the artist himself. Almost as if Michelangelo had become a friend of ours.

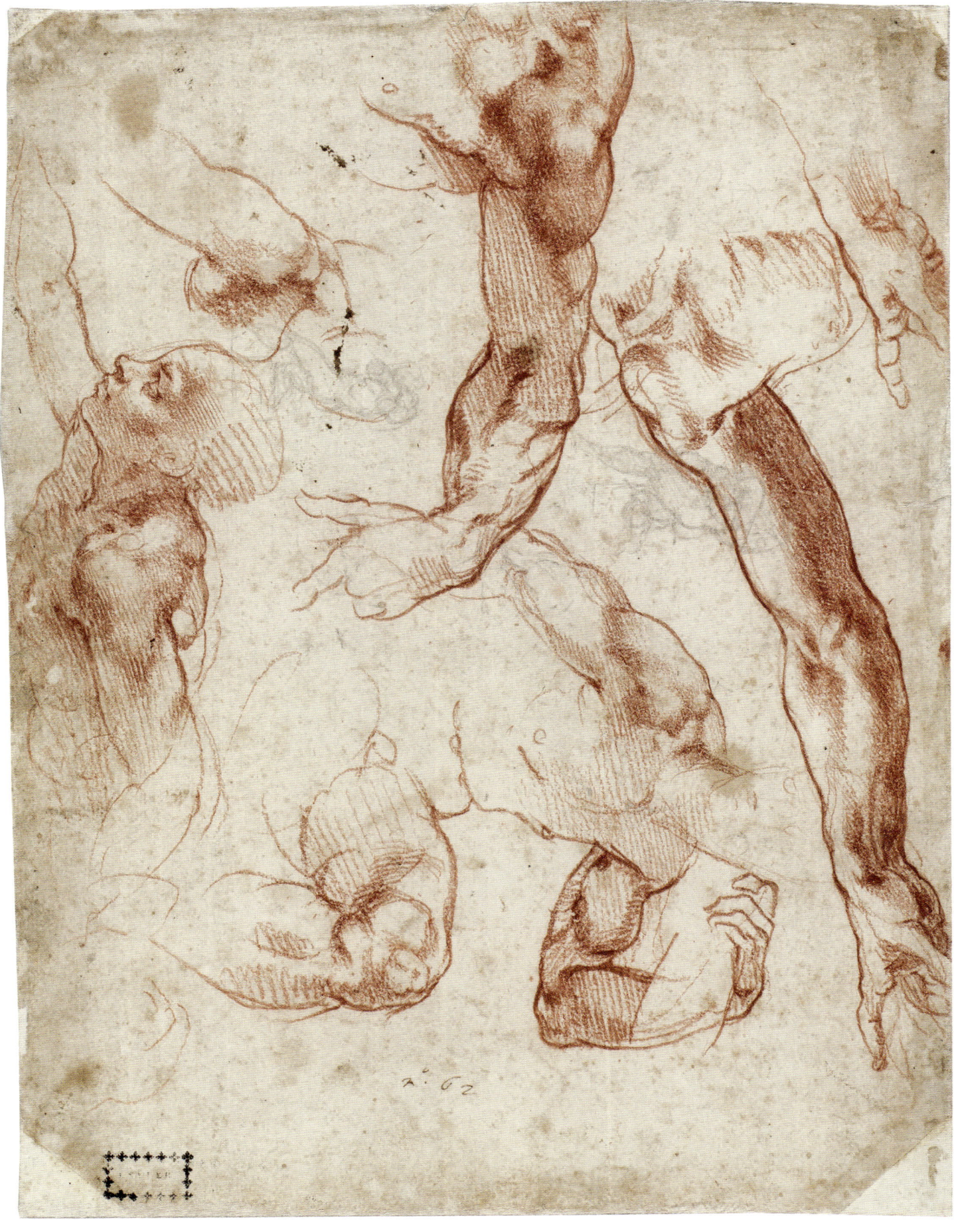

fig. 165   (cat. 19v) Michelangelo, *Figure Studies for the Sistine Chapel Ceiling*, c. 1511. Red chalk, 279 x 214 mm. Haarlem, Teylers Museum, A 027v

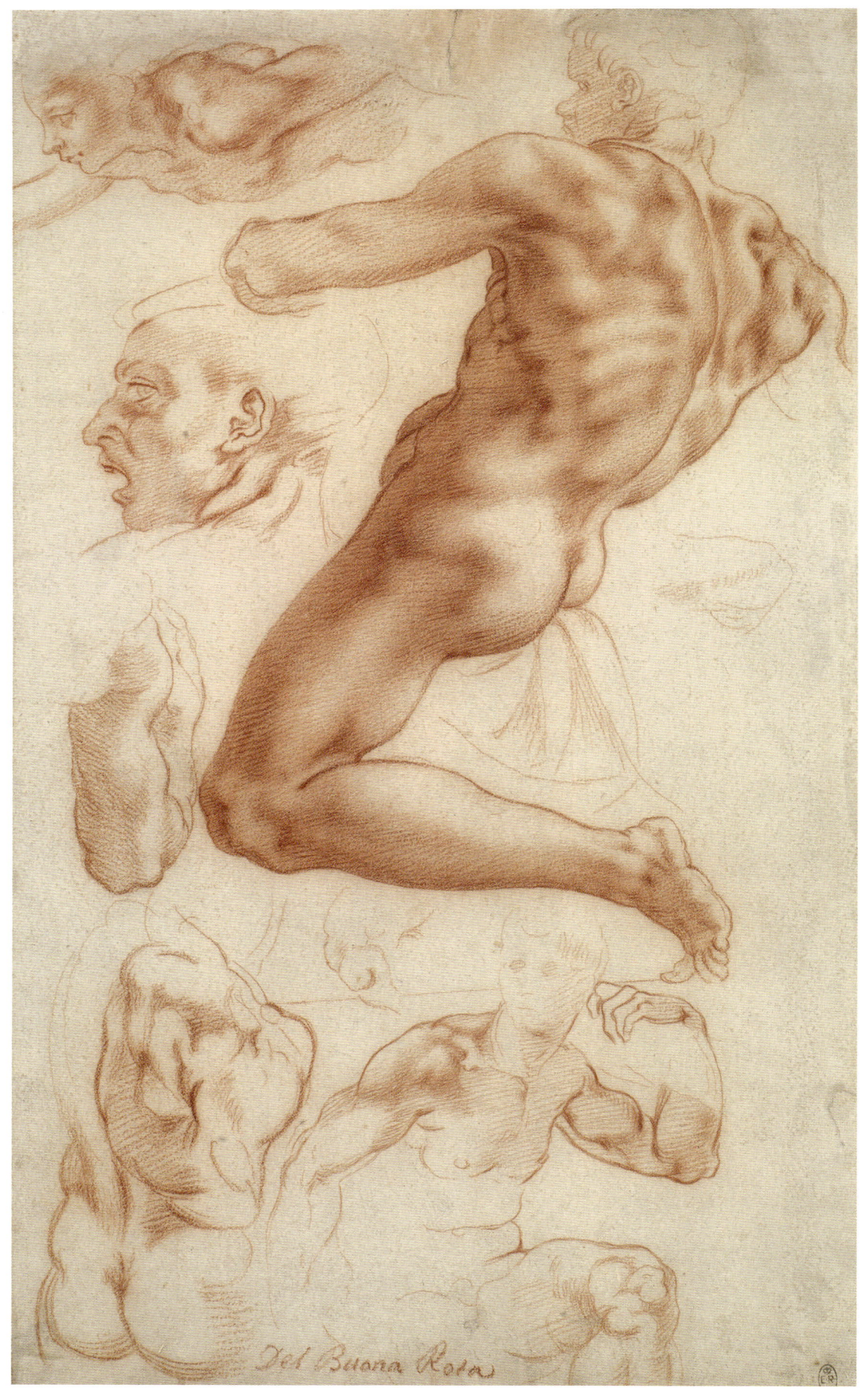

fig. 166   Unidentified draughtsman, *Copies after Michelangelo's Studies for the Sistine Chapel Ceiling*, c. 1600–1650. Red chalk, 390 x 235 mm.
Windsor, Royal Collection Trust, inv. RCIN 990441

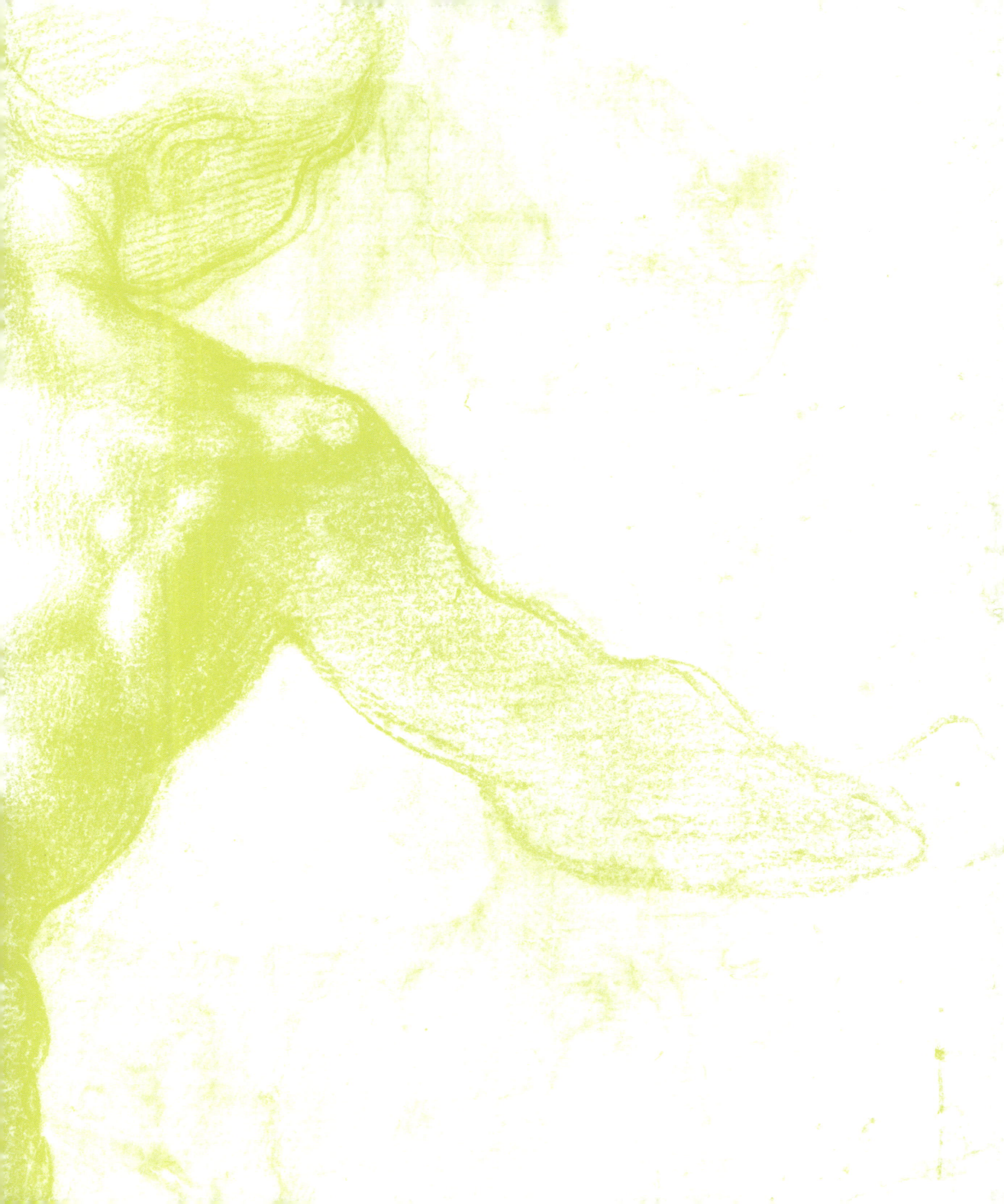

Notes

Introduction. Michelangelo's Men (pp . 17-30)

1. See, among others, Chapman, *Michelangelo*, p. 65.
2. For the history of the Florentine republic, see Jurdjevic, *Guardians of Republicanism*.
3. See Hirst, *Michelangelo in Florence*; Chapman, *Michelangelo*, p. 66.
4. This would have been less of an issue at the originally planned location; see Olszewski, 'Michelangelo's David', p. 118.
5. Chapman, *Michelangelo*, p. 66; see also Caglioti, *Donatello e i Medici*, I, pp. 334–38.
6. Garrard, 'The Cloister and the Square', p. 22; Johnson, 'Idol or Ideal', pp. 233–36.
7. Olszewski, 'Michelangelo's David', p. 121.
8. Garrard, 'The Cloister and the Square', p. 17.
9. Garrard, 'The Cloister and the Square', p. 29; for prints after *Cascina* see, among others, Barnes, *Michelangelo in Print*.
10. Vasari, *Le vite*, ed. by Bettarini and Barocchi, VI, p. 12. See also Rinaldi, *Looking at Masaccio*.
11. Keizer, 'Michelangelo, Drawing, and the Subject of Art', p. 312.
12. Joost Keizer suggests that this might have been to allow the process of making art, the *disegno*, to remain visible; see Keizer, 'Michelangelo, Drawing, and the Subject of Art', p. 312. See also Burke, *The Italian Renaissance Nude*, p. 132.
13. *Bozzetti* were not intended to last: models were utilitarian objects that were discarded once the final marble sculptures were completed.
14. Examples include: inv. 685 (study for Saint Anne with the Virgin and Child), Musée du Louvre, Paris; inv. DE 35 (female figures, possibly after antique sculpture), Musée Condé, Chantilly; inv. 1F (study for Doni Tondo), Casa Buonarroti, Florence.
15. The other drawings are: inv. 16F, Casa Buonarroti, Florence; inv 1859,0625.570 and 1859,0625.571, British Museum, London.
16. Hirst, *Michelangelo and his Drawings*, p. 61.
17. See Van Tuyll van Serooskerken, *The Italian Drawings*, no. 52, for the different interpretations of this sheet.
18. The attribution of this sheet to Michelangelo was long contested, see Joannides, *Michel-Ange*, no. 2.
19. Hirst, *Michelangelo and his Drawings*, pp. 63–64; Joannides, *Michel-Ange*, no. 2.
20. Bambach, *Michelangelo*, p. 91.
21. Bambach, *Michelangelo*, p. 91. The nude, seated Sibyl is depicted again on the verso of the sheet, but here the body seems softer and more feminine in its shapes.

22. Hibbard, *Michelangelo*, p. 151; Clark, *The Nude*, p. 330. See also Evan, 'The Heroine as Hero', p. 29.
23. Evan, 'The Heroine as Hero', p. 29; Garrard, *Artemisia Gentileschi*, p. 7.
24. For more about Leda, see Hirst, *Michelangelo and his Drawings*, pp. 73–74. Antonio Mini, Michelangelo's pupil, might have posed for this drawing: see Wilde, 'Notes on the Genesis of Michelangelo's *Leda*'; Ragionieri, *Michelangelo*, no. 8.
25. The androgynous appearance and the discussion surrounding the figure's gender can also be seen in the case of RCIN 912764, Royal Collection, Windsor.
26. See also Coonin, 'Beyond the Binary', pp. 258–59.
27. For more in this regard, see Vowles and Lewis, *Michelangelo*.
28. For a brief discussion on the scale of the corpus, see Bambach, *Michelangelo*, pp. 28–29.
29. '*La fama tiene gli epitaffi a giacere; non va né inanzi né indietro, perché sons morti, e el loro operare è fermo*' (Buonarroti, *The Poetry of Michelangelo*, trans. and ed. by Saslow, no. 13). The fame in question is that of the Medici. The text is found on a preliminary study for the tombs of Giuliano and Lorenzo de' Medici: inv. 1859,0625.543r, British Museum, London.

'Masculine Love'. Michelangelo and Boys (pp. 35-46)

1. This essay began as a paper presented at the British Museum in 2006 in connection with a memorable exhibition of Michelangelo's drawings held there that year, after having opened at Teylers Museum the previous year. I would like to thank Curator Hugo Chapman for that kind invitation, which led to numerous other speaking engagements and multiple revisions of the paper over the years. My thanks also go to Paul Barolsky, Bill Wallace, Jonathan Nelson and Patricia Rubin, in particular, for their attentive reading of various versions of the paper and for their many helpful suggestions.
2. Buonarroti, *Rime*, ed. by Michelangelo Buonarroti il Giovane (Florence: Giunti, 1623).
3. Buonarroti, *Le Rime*, ed. by Cesare Guasti (Florence: Le Monnier, 1863[1864]). Guasti revealed the great-nephew's falsification of Michelangelo's original verses on pp. xliii–xlvi.
4. Østermark-Johansen traces the development in the late nineteenth and

early twentieth centuries of what she calls 'Michelangelo as Platonic Lover' in *Sweetness and Strength*, pp. 191–257. See also Saslow, 'Inventing Michelangelo'.
5. Pioneers in this area include Havelock Ellis, Edward Carpenter and John Addington Symonds in England, and Karl Heinrich Ulrichs and Magnus Hirschfeld in Germany; among others, see Anderson, *Fraternity of the Estranged*; Mancini, *Magnus Hirschfeld*.
6. Symonds, *Life*, pp. 125–66, 381–85 (citation on p. 384). Symonds also published the first translation into English of Michelangelo's poetry, based on Guasti's unexpurgated edition of 1863: *Sonnets*. In private, Symonds was blunter about Michelangelo's sexuality: 'One thing is certain, that if he had any sexual energy at all (which is doubtful), he was a U.' – for Urning, or Uranian, an early precursor of the term homosexual; letter from Symonds to Edmund Gosse (18 September 1891), in Symonds, *Letters*, III, pp. 606–07. For a fascinating recent study of Symonds, see Butler, *Passions*, whom I thank for the reference to Symonds's letter.
7. Many works in the vast bibliography on Michelangelo mention or allude briefly to his sexuality. General studies that have addressed the issue in greater detail include Clements, *Poetry*; Liebert, *Michelangelo*; and especially several important studies by James Saslow, including 'A Veil of Ice'; *Ganymede*; *Poetry*.
8. Chapman, *Michelangelo Drawings*, p. 224.
9. James Saslow provides an excellent survey of how notions about Michelangelo's homosexuality have been linked to his creative genius as an artist through to his apotheosis as an iconic symbol in modern gay culture in 'Inventing Michelangelo'.
10. To cite here only the most relevant studies on male same-sex relations in Italy, see Rocke, *Forbidden Friendships*; Ruggiero, *The Boundaries of Eros*, pp. 109–45; Grassi, *L'Offizio sopra l'Onestà*; Baldassarri, *Bande giovanili*; Ferguson, *Same-sex Marriage*. For a recent magisterial overview and comparison of same-sex relations among males across Europe and the Mediterranean region, with extensive bibliography, see Malcolm, *Forbidden Desire*.
11. On the Office of the Night and its work, see Rocke, *Forbidden Friendships*, pp. 45–84.
12. Rocke, *Forbidden Friendships*, pp. 60, 66. These figures combine data regarding the Officers of the Night with those from other courts that also policed sodomy.
13. Rocke, *Forbidden Friendships*, pp. 67–73.
14. On the widespread nature of age-differentiated sexual relations around the Mediterranean, see Malcolm, *Forbidden Desire*, esp. pp. 28–68.
15. Rocke, *Forbidden Friendships*, pp. 87–111.

16. Rocke, *Forbidden Friendships*, pp. 113–42.

17. Condivi, *Vita di Michelagnolo Buonarroti*, ed. by Nencioni, p. 13.

18. On Poliziano's homoeroticism generally, see Saslow, *Ganymede*, pp. 30–32; Rocke, *Forbidden Friendships*, p. 317 n. 11; and especially Butler, 'Things Left Unsaid'. William Wallace raises the possibility that the teenage Michelangelo may have been the object of the sexual attentions of Poliziano and others in the Medici household; *Michelangelo*, p. 43.

19. Rocke, *Forbidden Friendships*, pp. 202–03. The events recounted here come from unpublished parts of a letter written by 25-year-old Niccolò di Braccio Guicciardini, a young man from a minor branch of the family and outside the regime's inner circles, suggesting knowledge of the accusation was widespread.

20. Rocke, *Forbidden Friendships*, p. 317 n. 11.

21. Dionisotti, 'Considerazioni'; Stewart, 'Singing Boy'.

22. To my knowledge there is no evidence to suggest such a connection and it has not been put forth elsewhere, but neither is there much reason to believe Condivi's strange account of the 'bizarre episode' (Hirst) surrounding Michelangelo's hasty departure; Condivi, *Vita di Michelagnolo Buonarroti*, ed. by Nencioni, pp. 15–16; and Hirst, *Michelangelo*, pp. 21–22.

23. 14 December 1521: 'nonne a[n]dare di notte e lasc[i]are le pratiche nocive all'animo e al chorpo, – perché a vo' non nuochono a l'anima', (*Il Carteggio di Michelangelo*, II, p. 336); 'Sopra a tutte le nuove mi date, una passa tutte, e questo è l'essere guarito d'una malatia che pochi ne guarischo... Perseverete', (*Il Carteggio di Michelangelo*, II, p. 339; 4 January 1522); 'siate libero d'una malatia che danava l'anima e 'l chorpo' (*Il Carteggio di Michelangelo*, II, p. 341; 22 January 1522).

24. Liebert, *Michelangelo*, pp. 306-07; Bull, *Michelangelo*, p. 432 n. 156. Gayford, *Michelangelo*, pp. 348-50, suggests, as I do here, that illicit sexual activity was most likely the subject of Sellaio's concern.

25. Rocke, *Forbidden Friendships*, pp. 151–61.

26. See Arrizabalaga, Henderson and French, *The Great Pox*, pp. 34–37.

27. Saslow in his introduction of Buonarroti, *The Poetry of Michelangelo*, trans. and ed. by Saslow, p. 13.

28. 'quegli che voi sapete che più vi amano', (*Il Carteggio di Michelangelo*, II, p. 342; early February, 1522). The three extant letters from Perini to Michelangelo are on pp. 342, 352–53.

29. Michael Hirst was the first, in 2011, to correctly identify Perini's birthdate, in *Michelangelo*, pp. 202, 344 n. 156, citing the birth registers of the Florentine

electoral rolls (ASF, Tratte, Libri di Età, Leon d'Oro, c. 428). In his 1949 biography, Giovanni Papini argued that Perini was born in 1480, making him only five years younger than Michelangelo, but he had mistakenly found the birthdate of someone else with the same name. He exulted – imprudently, in hindsight – that Perini's presumed older age meant he was no ephebe or catamite, and therefore Michelangelo could not have engaged in sexual sins with him; Papini, *Vita di Michelangelo*, p. 243.

30. Vasari, *La vita di Michelangelo*, ed. by Barocchi, I, p. 122. On the drawings for Perini, Hirst, *Michelangelo and his Drawings*, pp. 107–09.

31. 'Io vi prego che non mi facciate disegnare stasera perchè e' non c'è Perino'; Gallerie degli Uffizi, Florence, inv. 621Er; De Tolnay, *Corpus*, I, no. 70r; Barkan, *Michelangelo*, pp. 199–204; Liebert, *Michelangelo*, pp. 295–96. On Perini see also Bull, *Michelangelo*, p. 163; Clements, *Poetry*, pp. 211–12.

32. Michelangelo's letter is in *Il Carteggio di Michelangelo*, III, p. 413; Barkan, *Michelangelo*, pp. 197–99. Andrea's letters to Michelangelo are in *Il Carteggio di Michelangelo*, III, p. 292 (24 November 1530); p. 314 (22 June 1531); p. 400 (14 May 1532); and p. 431 (July-August 1532).

33. Ashmolean Museum, Oxford, inv. WA1846.69; Parker, *Italian Schools*, no. 323v; De Tolnay, *Corpus*, I, no. 96v; Barkan, *Michelangelo*, pp. 197–99; Liebert, *Michelangelo*, p. 297. My reading and translation of the phrase differs somewhat from both Barkan's and Liebert's. Specialists disagree about whose hand wrote this particular phrase.

34. Rocke, *Forbidden Friendships*, p. 118.

35. *Il Carteggio di Michelangelo*, I, p. 150 (August-September?, 1514).

36. The British Museum, which holds the Quaratesi portrait (inv. 1895,0915.519), dates it to 1530; https://www.britishmuseum.org/collection/object/P_1895-0915-519 [accessed 22 February 2024]. See also Wilde, *Italian Drawings*, pp. 96–98, who suggests the date 1532. Carmen Bambach dates the drawing to between 1531 and 1534; *Michelangelo*, p. 142.

37. Ruvoldt provides an excellent account of their relationship in 'Michelangelo's Open Secrets'. See also Frommel, *Michelangelo und Tommaso dei Cavalieri*. The bibliography on Michelangelo and Cavalieri is extensive.

38. The evidence on Cavalieri's birthdate is summarised by Ruvoldt in 'Gossip', p. 379 n. 13. Marongiu proposes a birthdate of 1513–14 in 'Tommaso de' Cavalieri', p. 258

n. 4, but as Ruvoldt observes, the evidence is inconclusive.

39. Vasari, *La vita di Michelangelo*, ed. by Barocchi, IV, pp. 1905–06; Hirst, *Michelangelo*, p. 263 and p. 375 n. 89.

40. Joannides, *Michel-Ange*, p. 253 n. 107; Hirst, *Michelangelo*, pp. 263, 375–76 n. 90. Critics have not reached a consensus as to the attribution to Michelangelo; see Bambach, *Michelangelo*, p. 142, who suggests it may be a copy, but does not dispute the sitter's resemblance to early descriptions of Cavalieri's portrait.

41. Simone's letter is mentioned briefly by Wallace, *Michelangelo*, p. 166; and by Ruvoldt, 'Michelangelo's Open Secrets', p. 112.

42. 'non so dove mi rivoltare, sì che io trovi la mia quiete, se non in te. Tu adunche se' quello che puoi rendermi ogni contento et piacere'; 'perchè io desidero che tu sia mio e io il tuo cordialissimo amico'; 'Et però, M mio soavissimo, ricevi gratamente la mia amichevol lettera, insieme con l'anima et cor mio, e' quali tutti ti dono in senpiterno; et di me puoi a tuo modo disporre, perché sono parato a soportar per te ogni passione, purché la tua amicitia mi sia renduta', (*Il Carteggio di Michelangelo*, IV, p. 65; before 23 September 1534).

43. For the poems, see Buonarroti, *The Poetry of Michelangelo*, trans. and ed. by Saslow, nos. 99–101, 117, 246. On Febo see also Clements, *Poetry*, pp. 212–15; Liebert, *Michelangelo*, pp. 299–302.

44. 'benché voi mi portiate odio grandissimo – non so perché, no credo già per l'amore che io porto a voi ma per le parole d'altri, le quale non doverresti credere, avendomi provato...', (*Il Carteggio di Michelangelo*, IV, p. 66; before 23 September 1534).

45. *Il Carteggio di Michelangelo*, IV, p. 67 (14 January 1535).

46. On teenage male prostitutes and 'gifts' from older lovers to boys, see Rocke, *Forbidden Friendships*, pp. 164–69; Rocke, '"Whoorish boyes"'.

47. Rocke, *Forbidden Friendships*, p. 102.

48. Clements, *Poetry*, pp. 134–53; Liebert, *Michelangelo*, pp. 302–05.

49. Ruvoldt, 'Michelangelo's Open Secrets'.

50. *Il Carteggio di Michelangelo*, IV, pp. 215–17 (November 1545).

51. 'uomini carnali, e che non sanno intendere amor di bellezza se non lascivo e disonesto' (Condivi, *Vita di Michelagnolo Buonarroti*, ed. by Nencioni, p. 62).

52. Condivi, *Vita di Michelagnolo Buonarroti*, ed. by Nencioni, p. 62.

53. Condivi, *Vita di Michelagnolo Buonarroti*, ed. by Nencioni, p. 65.

54. 'Del coito. Questo ho io fatto sempre, e se ti vòi prollungar la vita, non lo usare o pure quanto puoi 'l meno' (Condivi, *Vita di*

Michelagnolo Buonarroti, ed. by Nencioni, p. XXII); Elam, '"*Che utima [sic] mano?*"', pp. xliv–xlv.

55. Saslow concurs that Michelangelo's typical remorse later in his life about his past 'sin' and his 'wicked, depraved desires' is an indicator 'that there must have been some component of physical desire in his earlier loves'; Buonarroti, *The Poetry of Michelangelo*, trans. and ed. by Saslow, p. 17.

56. Michelangelo Buonarroti, *Rime*, ed. by Guasti, p. xlv; Symonds, *Life*, p. 128.

57. On Renaissance efforts to downplay Plato's sensuous, same-sex understanding of love and distort it into a sexless and heterosexual form, see Reeser, *Setting Plato Straight*.

58. Cady, '"Masculine Love"'; Cady, '"Princes of Sodom"'. See also Kenneth Borris's introduction to *Same-Sex Desire*, pp. 6–9 and *The Sciences of Homosexuality*, esp. pp. 5–9.

59. '*il gioco, che tanto ameno i fiorentini, di dretto*'; '*massimo nei quindici anni*'; '*Sappi che l'amore masculino è opera sollamente di virtù che, congiungendo insieme gli uomini, con diverse affezioni di amicizia, acciò che da una età tenera vengano nella virile più fortificati amici*' (Lomazzo, *Il Libro dei Sogni*, in *Scritti sulle arti*, I, p. 104). Though he presumably knew this passage, since he cites my book *Forbidden Friendships* where it appears prominently, Borris disregards it in his discussions of 'masculine love' cited in the previous note.

60. The author of *Erōtes* is disputed, and it is sometimes attributed alternatively to an unknown writer dubbed pseudo-Lucian. For a standard English translation, Lucian, *Lucian, Volume VIII*, pp. 148–236.

61. For the translation and publishing history of this dialogue in Italy, see De Faveri, *Le traduzioni di Luciano*, pp. 319–20.

62. Rocco, *L'Alcibiade*, p. 75. Although Borris, one of the proponents of the 'egalitarian' interpretation of 'masculine love', provides an English translation of long parts of this work in *Same-Sex Desire*, pp. 365–71, he chose to omit this inconvenient passage.

Poems and Letters. How Michelangelo Wrote the Unseeable and Drew the Unsayable (pp. 49-67)

1. Such poetic expositions were a regular part of the academy's endeavours. The lecture was published in print several years later: Varchi, *Due lezzioni di M. Benedetto Varchi* (Lorenzo Torrentino, 1549). On the academy, see especially Plaisance, *L'accademia e il suo principe*. On the *Due lezzioni*, see Mendelsohn, *Paragoni*; Cascio, *Michelangelo in Parnaso*, pp. 41–51; Gamberini, *New Apelleses and New Apollos*, pp. 71–78; as well as the introductions in Varchi, *Paragone – Rangstreit der Künste*, ed. by Bätschmann and Weddigen; and Varchi, *Deux leçons sur l'art*, ed. by Dubard de Gaillarbois.

2. On Tommaso de' Cavalieri, see Frommel, *Michelangelo und Tommaso dei Cavalieri*; Marongiu, 'Tommaso de' Cavalieri nella Roma di Clemente VII e Paolo III'.

3. '*Nel quale io conobbi già in Roma (oltra l'incomparabile bellezza del corpo) tanta leggiadria di costumi et cosi eccellente ingegno, et graziosa maniera, che ben meritò, et merita ancora, che più l'amasse chi maggiormente il conosceva*' (Varchi, *Due lezzioni*, p. 47).

4. Castiglione, *Il Cortigiano*, ed. by Quondam, I, p. 295.

5. Gramatzki, *Zur lyrischen Subjektivität in den Rime*; Ott, *Cambiare pelle*.

6. For detailed studies on the punishment of sodomy in Renaissance Italy, see Ruggiero, *The Boundaries of Eros*, pp. 109–45; Rocke, *Forbidden Friendships*; Grassi, *L'offizio sopra l'onestà*.

7. '*Il sonetto vien bene da me, ma il comento viene dal cielo; et veramente è cosa mirabile, non dico al giudizio mio, ma degli huomini valenti*' (*Il Carteggio di Michelangelo*, IV, p. 257).

8. '*prego voi facciate per me parole verso di lui come si conviene a tanto amore, affezzione et cortesie*' (*Il Carteggio di Michelangelo*, IV, p. 257).

9. '*Messer Tomao de' Cavalieri m'ha pregato ch'io ringrazi da sua parte il Varchi per un certo Libretto mirabile che c'è di suo in istampa, dove dice che parla molto honorevolmente di lui, et non manco di me*' (*Il Carteggio di Michelangelo*, IV, p. 340).

10. On different historical treatments of Michelangelo and same-sex love, see Østermark-Johansen, *Sweetness and Strength*, pp. 191–257; Saslow, 'Inventing Michelangelo'.

11. Exceptions to this trend signal the rewards of considering such media together, as in the case of Barkan, *Michelangelo*; and Parker, *Michelangelo and the Art of Letter Writing*, pp. 87–115. On connections between Michelangelo's letters and drawings for Cavalieri, see Ruvoldt, 'Michelangelo's Open Secrets'.

12. A seventeenth-century book of some of Michelangelo's poems, edited by his great-nephew, was revised in a way that eliminated potential references to same-sex desire: Buonarroti, *Rime*, ed. by Michelangelo Buonarroti il Giovane (Giunti, 1623). The first comprehensive edition to restore the poems fully was: Buonarroti, *Die Dichtungen des Michelagniolo Buonarroti*, ed. by Carl Frey (Berlin: G. Grote, 1897).

13. For over a century, different editions of Michelangelo's poems have sought to name different intended recipients for his verses, but a lack of details surrounding the original poems makes many such endeavours speculative.

14. Cf. Barkan, *Michelangelo*.

15. *Il Carteggio di Michelangelo*. Michelangelo's drawings for Cavalieri notably lack visible folds, although their exact mode of transit to shield their delicate chalk surfaces remains an important question.

16. Charles De Tolnay's enumeration of 633 autograph drawings is an informative if contested benchmark: De Tolnay, *Corpus*. On the range of connoisseurial approaches to Michelangelo's drawings and resultant totals, see Bambach, *Michelangelo*, pp. 28–29.

17. These drawings have generated an extensive bibliography. For an excellent study that considers the range of sources and scholarly assessments, see Marongiu, '"… perché egli imparassi a disegnare gli fece molte carte stupendissime…"'.

18. '*Infinitamente amò più di tutti Messer Tommaso de' Cavalieri, gentiluomo romano*'. See Vasari, *La vita di Michelangelo*, ed. by Barocchi, I, p. 118.

19. On this portrait, see Chapman, *Michelangelo Drawings*, pp. 209–11; Bambach, *Michelangelo*, p. 142.

20. For Michelangelo's poems that name Febo, see Buonarroti, *Rime e lettere*, pp. 190–92, 432.

21. On Cavalieri's family and his ancestry, see Kirkendale, *Emilio de' Cavalieri*, pp. 13–27; and Ruvoldt, 'Tommaso de' Cavalieri'.

22. Sickel, 'Die Sammlung des Tommaso de' Cavalieri'; Bedon, 'La professione di Tommaso de' Cavalieri'.

23. On Cavalieri's marriage to Della Valle, see Ruvoldt, 'Gossip and Reputation in Sixteenth-Century Rome'.

24. On the likely objectives for Varchi's sharing of Michelangelo's verse at the Florentine Academy, see Carlson, '"Eccellentissimo poeta et amatore divinissimo"'.

25. Corsaro, '*La prima circolazione manoscritta delle rime di Michelangelo*'; and Lo Re, 'Varchi e Michelangelo'.

26. '*Fui mosso a scrivere a Vostra Signoria*' (*Il Carteggio di Michelangelo*, III, pp. 443–44). There is scholarly disagreement as to whether this is Michelangelo's first letter to Cavalieri or instead a draft of an original missive that postdated Cavalieri's

response, a debate which does not make a significant difference to the arguments presented here.

27. *Il Carteggio di Michelangelo*, III, pp. 443–44.

28. '*Mi pigliarò almanco doi hore del giorno piacere in contemplare doi vostri desegni che Pier Antonio me à portai, quali quanto più li miro, tanto più li piacciono*' (*Il Carteggio di Michelangelo,* III, p. 445); on Cecchini, see Schlitt, '"…viri studiosi et scientifici…"'.

29. *Il Carteggio di Michelangelo*, III, p. 444.

30. *Il Carteggio di Michelangelo*, IV, p. 1. As if for emphasis, Michelangelo incorporated the words 'and no less pleasure' ('*e non manco piacere*') at the base of the letter and then re-wrote the whole draft separately, see *Il Carteggio di Michelangelo*, IV, p. 3.

31. On the eroticism of Michelangelo's rendering of the subjects of both drawings, see Saslow, *Ganymede*, pp. 17–47; and Barkan, *Transuming Passion*, pp. 78–98.

32. '*E perché l'ingegno suo lo tirava al dilettarsi del disegno*' (Vasari, *La vita di Michelangelo*, ed. by Barocchi, I, p. 5). On this, see Nancy, *The Pleasure in Drawing*, pp. 15–19.

33. The epistolary resonances of this phrase and the sheet's function through such means of exchange are reflected in this statement's inclusion in the collected edition of Michelangelo's letters, see *Il Carteggio di Michelangelo*, IV, p. 12.

34. '*Vostra S[ignori]a*' (*Il Carteggio di Michelangelo*, III, p. 443; IV, p. 1).

35. '*E se creata a Dio non fusse eguale / altro, che 'l bel di fuor, / ch'agli occhi piace, / più non vorria, ma perch'è sì fallace / trascende nella forma universale*'. Varchi's citation offers the only known version of the sonnet, which a number of scholars have taken to be for Cavalieri, an assessment that aligns with the context of Varchi's own lecture. Even if this sonnet were not necessarily written for Cavalieri, it could have informed others for him that likewise may not survive. See Buonarroti, *Rime e lettere*, p. 195.

36. '*Tutti i componimenti pieni d'Amore Socratico, et di concetti Platonici*' (Varchi, *Due lezzioni*, p. 52).

37. The foundational study on the Neoplatonic features of Michelangelo's art is: Panofsky, *Studies in Iconology*, pp. 181–230.

38. '*Voglia sfrenata el senso è, non amore, / che l'alma uccide, e 'l nostro fa Perfetti / gl'amici qui, ma più per morte in cielo*', (Buonarroti, *Rime e lettere*, p. 195).

39. '*Né mai desiderai amicitia più che la vostra*' (*Il Carteggio di Michelangelo*, III, p. 445); '*nessuna cosa possa impedire l'amicitia nostra*' (*Il Carteggio di Michelangelo*, IV, p. 29).

40. On Italian Renaissance representations of friendship (*amicizia*) as informed by Cicero's *De Amicitia*, see Kent, *Friendship, Love, and Trust*, pp. 17–85. In her correspondence with Michelangelo, Vittoria Colonna likewise expounded upon their '*amicitia*' (*Il Carteggio di Michelangelo*, IV, p. 169).

41. On changes in Michelangelo's script and spellings over time, see Bardeschi Ciulich, *Costanza ed evoluzione nella scrittura di Michelangelo*; and Parker, *Michelangelo and the Art of Letter Writing*, pp. 5–7.

42. Petrucci, *Scrivere lettere*, p. 96. Lucilla Bardeschi Ciulich singled out the 'beautiful writing' that characterised Michelangelo's letter drafts for Cavalieri; Bardeschi Ciulich, 'Michelangelo: un percorso attraverso gli autografi', pp. 21–29, esp. 25–26.

43. For an exemplary attestation of this association, see McCahill, 'Finding a Job as a Humanist'.

44. Printed editions of Petrarch's letters appeared in the late fifteenth century, see, for example, Petrarch, *Epistolae familiares* (1492). In the same decade that Michelangelo was writing to Cavalieri, there began in Italy an important trend of assembling and publishing one's collected letters, on which see Quondam, *Le 'carte messaggiere'*.

45. On the rhetorical achievements of Michelangelo's letters, see Parker, *Michelangelo and the Art of Letter Writing*, pp. 47–86.

46. On copies after Michelangelo's drawings for Cavalieri, see Alberti, Rovetta and Salsi, *D'après Michelangelo*, pp. 90–204.

47. *Il Carteggio di Michelangelo*, IV, p. 49. On this episode, see Rebecchini, *Un altro Lorenzo*, pp. 235–39.

48. On the stylus marks, see Buck and Bissolati, *Michelangelo's Dream*, p. 116.

49. *Il Carteggio di Michelangelo*, IV, p. 49.

50. Vasari, *La vita di Michelangelo*, ed. by Barocchi, I, p. 118.

51. *Il Carteggio di Michelangelo*, III, p. 444.

52. '*Le vive voci m'erano interditte, / ond'io gridai con carta et con incostro*' (Petrarch, *Rerum vulgarium fragmenta*, XXIII, vv. 98–99).

53. '*Per non vi tediare non scriverrò altro. Molte cose conveniente alla risposta restano nella penna*' (*Il Carteggio di Michelangelo*, IV, p. 3).

54. '*Sarebbe lecito dare il nome delle cose che l'uomo dona, a chi le riceve: ma per buon rispecto non si fa in questa*' (*Il Carteggio di Michelangelo*, IV, p. 2).

55. Hirst, *Michelangelo and His Drawings*, p. 113.

56. '*Ma perché più dolermi, po' chi'i' veggio / negli occhi di quest'angelo lieto e solo / mie pace, mie riposo e mie salute? / Forse che prima sarie stato il peggio / vederlo, udirlo, s'or di pari a volo / seco m'impenna a seguir suo virtute*' (Buonarroti, *Rime e lettere*, p. 164, vv. 9–14).

57. Dante, a vital poetic model for Michelangelo, used this same verb to comparable effect to signal flight toward the divine: 'whoever does not gain wings to fly up there, / waits therefore for news from the mute [*chi non s'impenna sì che là sù voli, / dal muto aspetti quindi le novelle*]' (Dante, *Paradiso*, X, 74–75). On these intertexts, cf. Buonarroti, *Rime e lettere*, p. 968.

58. '*Son certo che de la affetione che mi portate la causa sia questa, che, essendo voi virtuosissimo, o per dir meglio essa virtù, sete forzato amar coloro che di essa son seguaci e che l'amano, tra li quali son io*' (*Il Carteggio di Michelangelo*, III, p. 445). Marcella Marongiu has admirably explored how beauty and virtue appear as guiding inspirations across Michelangelo and Tommaso de' Cavalieri's creative exchange: Marongiu, '"…perché egli imparassi a disegnare gli fece molte carte stupendissime…"'.

59. On this history, see Finlay, *Western Writing Implements*.

60. On the profundity of Michelangelo's visual and textual engagement with Ovid through his exchange with Cavalieri, see Parker, 'Ovidian Influences and Figural Obsessions'.

61. On these commissions, see Wallace, 'Michelangelo's *Leda*'; Aste, 'Bartolomeo Bettini'.

62. On this project, see Marongiu, 'Michelangelo e la "maniera di figure piccole"', pp. 13–73, esp. 43–49.

63. Michelangelo had known Angelini since 1521, when he first sent a batch of letters on behalf of Sebastiano, and a decade later Sebastiano encouraged Michelangelo to trust Angelini as the main courier for their correspondence after a breach of trust by a previous intermediary (*Il Carteggio di Michelangelo*, III, p. 304).

64. On Sebastiano's guile as a letter writer, see Carlson, 'Epistolary Criticism'.

65. *Il Carteggio di Michelangelo*, IV, p. 13.

66. '*Sabato passato vi mandai una sua conn una di messer Thomao vostro, e per la vostr'à inteso quanto sia l'afezione li portate, che invero che, per quanto in lui ò visto, non vi ama mancho che vi amiate voi lui*' (*Il Carteggio di Michelangelo*, IV, p. 25).

67. *Il Carteggio di Michelangelo*, IV, p. 14.

68. '*Amor così mi tiene, / né vuol che altro brami, / se a te non s'assomiglia, / ché sol dalle tuo ciglia / dipende mie salute: / di sì calda virtute / ch'all'alma grave ognior chiaro revela / quante natura e 'l ciel nasconde e cela*' (Buonarroti, *Rime e lettere*, p. 425).

69. '*dipende ogni virtute, / onor, vita e salute*' (*Il Carteggio di Michelangelo*, IV, p. 15 n. 1).

253

70. Cf. Barkan, *Michelangelo*, p. 217.
71. *Il Carteggio di Michelangelo*, IV, pp. 14–15.
72. Wallace, *Michelangelo at San Lorenzo*.
73. On these sheets, see Peters and Brooks, *Michelangelo*, pp. 90–97. On the broader means whereby Michelangelo's figural drawings informed his architectural designs, see Brothers, *Michelangelo, Drawing, and the Invention of Architecture*.
74. 'A me parebbe [che] li staese bene de Ganimede, e farli la diadema che paresse San Ioanni de l'Apochalipse quando el fu rato in cielo' (*Il Carteggio di Michelangelo*, IV, p. 18).
75. For the other related poems, see Buonarroti, *Rime e lettere*, pp. 22–23, 174–77.
76. *Il Carteggio di Michelangelo*, IV, p. 22.
77. On the social practices of madrigal performance for young men in Italy during the 1530s, see Coelho, 'Bronzino's Lute Player'.
78. Feldman, *City Culture and the Madrigal at Venice*, pp. 3–46; and Gerbino, 'Florentine Petrarchismo and the Early Madrigal'.
79. On this practice in the period, see Quaintance, *Textual Masculinity and the Exchange of Women*, pp. 61–76.
80. On this endeavour, see Costa, 'Michelangelo e la stampa'; Corsaro, 'Intorno alle rime di Michelangelo Buonarroti'; and Buonarroti, *Canzoniere*, ed. by Tarsi.
81. '*Socto duo belle ciglia / chom pace e maraviglia / a posto l fre[n] de mie pe[n] sieri amore*'. On the sheet, see Peters and Brooks, *Michelangelo*, pp. 76–79.
82. For the related poem, see Buonarroti, *Rime e lettere*, p. 52.
83. Consider the terms '*maravigliarrssi*' and '*[maravi]glierei*' in Michelangelo's letter, see *Il Carteggio di Michelangelo*, IV, p. 14.

Michelangelo and Antiquity. Ongoing Training (pp. 73-94)

1. Schütze, "*Anchora inparo*". The story was related by the late sixteenth-century art theorist and painter, Giovanni Paolo Lomazzo, but he did not say exactly when this encounter happened. Since Alessandro Farnese was not made a councillor until 1534, when he was 14 (and Michelangelo was 59), it cannot have occurred before then but probably years afterwards. So it was an elderly artist that was walking through the frozen Roman landscape that day – perhaps he was in his 70s or 80s, at an age when his attention turned mainly to architectural projects. In any case, he decided he needed to take another look at how the walls of the great amphitheatre had been designed by their Roman builders.
2. Condivi, 'Life of Michelangelo Buonarroti', trans. by Bull, p. 11.
3. For Michelangelo's apprenticeship, see Bambach, 'The Young Artist and the Traditions of Fifteenth Century Art' in *Michelangelo*, esp. p. 33.
4. Vasari also described this event, though in less detail.
5. See Hickson, 'Gian Cristoforo Romano in Rome', p. 5.
6. Condivi, 'Life of Michelangelo Buonarroti', trans. by Bull, p. 14.
7. See Elam, 'Lorenzo de' Medici's Sculpture Garden'.
8. A surviving letter from Bertoldo to his master from 1479 is surprisingly informal and full of private, coded jokes about cooking, spicy stews and grilled songbirds, see Draper, *Bertoldo di Giovanni*, pp. 7–12.
9. See Fusco and Corti, *Lorenzo de' Medici*.
10. In a letter from 9 May 1490, perhaps a few weeks after Michelangelo joined the household, Lorenzo instructed his son Piero to show an honoured guest all his antiquities, including the large ones outside and the smaller ones 'which are in the study', see Fusco and Corti, *Lorenzo de' Medici*, p. 314, doc. 136.
11. Vasari, 'Life of Michelangelo Buonarroti', trans. by Bull, p. 332.
12. Quoted by Dunkelman, 'From Microcosm to Macrocosm', p. 369.
13. Michelangelo could scarcely have avoided seeing *Diomedes and the Palladium* since it was copied in a roundel in the courtyard of the Palazzo Medici. But he would also have been intimately acquainted with the original, small enough to hold in the palm of one's hand, one of the most prized objects in the Medici collection.
14. Dunkelman, 'From Microcosm to Macrocosm', p. 369.
15. This suggests that whatever the iconographical meaning of the nudes on the ceiling of the Sistine Chapel in the background of the *Doni Tondo* and the 'prisoners' of the tomb, the images for these figures were lodged in his imagination well before any iconographical scheme for these works could have been devised.
16. *Diomedes and the Palladium* and the *Sigillo di Nerone* were two of the most valuable items in Lorenzo's possession. The former was listed at 1,500 florins in his inventory and the latter at 1,000, both sums far more than a work of then-contemporary art such that a Botticelli painting would fetch. But the most precious thing he owned by far was the *Tazza Farnese* (so called from a later owner), priced at 10,000 florins.
17. Dunkelman, 'From Microcosm to Macrocosm', p. 371.
18. See Draper, *Bertoldo di Giovanni*. The glazed terracotta frieze on the entrance loggia to the Medici villa at Poggio a Caiano, a major work in a classical idiom, is discussed on pp. 197–220, and the stucco reliefs in the courtyard of the Palazzo Scala-della Gherardesca, possibly executed around the time Michelangelo entered the Medici household, on p. 253.
19. See Draper, *Bertoldo di Giovanni*, p. 133.
20. Fusco and Corti, *Lorenzo de' Medici*, p. 52.
21. Fusco and Corti, *Lorenzo de' Medici*, pp. 52, 55.
22. Many years later Michelangelo mentioned the piece to an agent of the Duke of Mantua, explaining that it had been made for 'a great lord', i.e. Lorenzo; see Hirst, *Michelangelo*, pp. 223–24, 353. The agent's letter states that Michelangelo had made '*un certo Quadro di figure nude che combatteno, di marmore, quale havea principiato ad instantia d'un gran signore ma non e finito*'. This unfinished marble relief of battling nudes can only be the *Battle of the Centaurs*, and the '*gran signore*' Lorenzo.
23. The *Battle of the Centaurs* is on a similar scale to Bertoldo's *Battle*, each being around 90 cm across, though Michelangelo's relief is higher. If Lorenzo had wished, the relief could easily have been installed in the same room as the antique sculpture with three fauns (today called *Three Satyrs Fighting a Serpent*) itself, which at 641 x 800 mm is slightly smaller.
24. Condivi, 'Life of Michelangelo Buonarroti', trans. by Bull, p. 11.
25. According to Condivi, il Magnifico even suggested Michelangelo knock out a few of the faun's teeth to add comic verisimilitude, after which 'within a few days he brought it to perfection, supplying from his imagination all that was lacking in the antique, namely the mouth open in the manner of a man laughing, so that one could see the inside with all the teeth' (Condivi, 'Life of Michelangelo Buonarroti', trans. by Bull, p. 12).
26. Probably the one given to Lorenzo by Ferrante d'Aragona (Ferdinand I) of Naples in 1488; see Fusco and Corti, *Lorenzo de' Medici*, p. 44.
27. This still exists in the Chapel of the Saviour, Úbeda, Spain, having been smashed to fragments during the Civil War and recently subject to a radical restoration.
28. Condivi, 'Life of Michelangelo Buonarroti', trans. by Bull, p. 19.
29. For a discussion of the story of Michelangelo's Cupid and Cardinal

Raffaele Riario, see Hirst and Dunkerton, *Making and Meaning*, pp. 21–22.

30. Hirst and Dunkerton, *Making and Meaning*, p. 23.

31. Hirst and Dunkerton, *Making and Meaning*, p. 23.

32. Buonarroti, *The Letters of Michelangelo*, I, p. 3.

33. Buonarroti, *The Letters of Michelangelo*, I, p. 3.

34. Buonarroti, *The Letters of Michelangelo*, I, p. 3.

35. Pliny, *Natural History*, IX, pp. 178–79 (book 34.69-70). Praxiteles would have been of particular interest to Michelangelo because Pliny describes him as 'excelling above all as a sculptor in marble', which of course Michelangelo regarded as his own *arte* (profession) above all.

36. Condivi, 'Life of Michelangelo Buonarroti', trans. by Bull, p. 21.

37. Condivi, 'Life of Michelangelo Buonarroti', trans. by Bull, p. 14.

38. There were many topics on which Poliziano could have, and probably did, 'expound' to the young Michelangelo. One was the question of signatures. At once modestly and immodestly, Pliny compared himself to the great painters and sculptors of Greece who were in the habit of inscribing their masterpieces with formulae such as 'Faciebat Apelles or Polyclitus' ('Apelles or Polyclitus was making this'). This was, Pliny went on, 'as though art was always a thing in process and not completed' (Pliny, *Natural History*, I, p. 16–17 (prefatio, 26)). In 1488 Poliziano had himself discovered a Greek inscription in a house on Piazza Navona which he translated as '*Seleucus rex, Lysippus faciebat*' ('King Seleucus, Lysippus was making this'). This was exactly the formula with which Michelangelo signed his Pietà: MICHAEL • A[N]GELUS • BONAROTUS • FLORENT[INUS] •FACIEBA[T].

39. On 1 July 1497, Michelangelo complained to his father that he had still not been paid. 'I've not yet been able to settle up my affairs with the Cardinal and I do not want to leave without first receiving satisfaction and being remunerated for my pains', (Buonarroti, *The Letters of Michelangelo*, trans. by Ramsden, I, p. 4, letter 2). Riario paid up shortly afterwards.

40. It has been suggested that the death of the Duke of Gandia, son of Pope Alexander VI, on 14 June 1497, led to a crackdown on pagan, classical pastimes by the College of Cardinals; see Sutherland Minter, 'Discarded Deity'. But this does not explain why Riario did not reclaim the *Bacchus* when the fuss had died down, especially when his kinsman Giuliano della Rovere

had become pope – nor why Michelangelo remained enraged over the affair.

41. Condivi, 'Life of Michelangelo Buonarroti', trans. by Bull, p. 20.

42. See the mid-sixteenth-century drawings by Maarten van Heemskerck and in the Cambridge Sketchbook (Trinity College, Cambridge); Barkan, *Unearthing the Past*, pp. 203, 205.

43. Whether this damage was deliberate or not is not clear, but it is intriguing that the annotation in the Cambridge Sketchbook (Trinity College Library, inv. R. 17 3 fol. 16) confuses *Bacchus* with the lost *Sleeping Cupid*, noting it is a 'Scoltur de michelangeli / the which was buried / in the grownd & fond for / antick'. Aldrovandi listed it among the ancient works of Rome, but noted at the end of the description that it was a 'modern work' by Michelangelo. The hand and cup were stored and reattached, presumably after the sculpture was bought by the Medici in 1572, but the missing penis was not. A plausible hypothesis would be that the damage to the hand and cup was accidental, but that the penis was deliberately omitted to make the work look more like an antiquity, and more suitable for a cardinal's courtyard.

44. See Fusco and Corti, *Lorenzo de' Medici*, pp. 52–5.

45. It was seen there around 1500 by a poet signing himself '*prospettivo milanese*' – who might be identifiable as Bramante or Bramantino and was a discerning Northern Italian connoisseur. Barkan, *Unearthing the Past,* pp. 196–97. The poem was dedicated to Leonardo da Vinci.

46. For an outline of this group, especially among the early works, see Caglioti, 'Michelangelo the Sculptor', pp. 279–86.

47. It was described as a David in an inventory of the Medici collection from 1553, but twice described as 'an Apollo drawing an arrow from his quiver' by Vasari in both editions of the *Lives* (1550 and 1568). Vasari was in a good position to know, as he was in contact with the artist in Florence shortly after it was made, he probably knew the patron and almost certainly the work as well.

48. Caglioti makes a clear and convincing case, in Caglioti, 'Michelangelo the Sculptor', pp. 284–85.

49. Pliny, *Natural History*, IX, p. 178–79 (book 34.70).

50. Vasari, *Le vite de'più eccellenti pittori, scultori ed architettori* (Giunti, 1568), p. 743.

51. Valori was an almost exact contemporary of the artist. He came from a patrician Florentine family that aimed to combine the Neoplatonism of Marsilio Ficino with the Republican religious reformism of

Girolamo Savonarola (which was roughly Michelangelo's own position). Like the artist, Valori was attached to the court of Pope Clement VII. His name was blackened by later Florentine writers, such as Benedetto Varchi, for good reason, as Valori turned against the Medici, fought with the Republican rebels at the battle of Montemurlo, and was tortured and executed as a result.

52. Florence, Palazzo Pitti, inv. Palatina 409.

53. Pope-Hennessy, *Italian High Renaissance and Baroque Sculpture*, p. 325.

54. It has been suggested that Michelangelo was responsible for the window tabernacles of Valori's palace on the Via de' Pandolfini; see Hirst, *Michelangelo*, p. 351.

55. Caglioti, 'Michelangelo the Sculptor', p. 284. It is worth noting that these were all commissions from patrons of much the same generation.

56. Before it was in Lorenzo's collection it had been owned first by Cardinal Ludovico Trevisan, who commissioned Ghiberti to make a mount for it, then by Pope Paul II; see Fusco and Corti, *Lorenzo de' Medici*, p. 124.

57. Mangone, *Generation and Ruination*, pp. 77–79.

58. Giovanni Battista Fattucci's letter to Michelangelo, *Il Carteggio di Michelangelo*, III, pp. 41–42 (10 March 1524).

59. Barkan, *Unearthing the Past*, p. 3.

60. Barkan, *Unearthing the Past*, p. 3.

61. Jointly they had a claim to be the greatest experts on ancient sculpture in Rome, Michelangelo having been the trusted artist/advisor to Lorenzo and Piero de' Medici, and Gian Cristoforo Romano having had the same role in the court of Isabella d' Este.

62. Pliny, *Natural History*, X, pp. 28–31 (book 36.37–38).

63. Barkan, *Unearthing the Past*, p. 112. It seems Michelangelo and Gian Cristoforo slightly underestimated the number of joints: modern researchers have determined that the sculpture is made up of a minimum seven pieces of stone.

64. Pliny, *Natural History*, X, pp. 28–31 (book 36.37–38). Furthermore, though some have argued it is based on an earlier bronze, the carving itself was in marble, Michelangelo's preferred medium.

65. This boastful sculptor would have been Baccio Bandinelli, who made a copy of the *Laocoön* in 1520, proclaiming in advance that 'he was confident that he could make [a version] not merely equal to it, but even surpassing it in perfection'. Michelangelo had a low opinion of Bandinelli and his abilities, see Vasari, 'Life of Michelangelo Buonarroti', trans. by Bull, pp. 426–27.

255

66. Vasari, 'Life of Michelangelo Buonarroti', trans. by Bull, pp. 426–27.
67. Barkan, *Unearthing the Past*, p. 14.
68. '*E stato questo busto singularmente lodato da Michel' Angelo*' (Aldrovandi, *Tutte Le Statue Antiche*, p. 121). It is likely that Aldrovandi had the *entre* to Michelangelo's inner circle, since he was related to Gian Francesco Aldrovandi, the artist's friend and patron during his stay in Bologna in 1494–95; see Bentz, *Ulisse Aldrovandi*, p. 969 n. 31.
69. For example, that he was discovered kneeling before it. Though it turned out this was only to examine it in greater detail, or that he declared of it that, 'This is the work of a man who knew more than nature'; see Barkan, *Unearthing the Past*, p. 200.
70. Hogarth, *The Analysis of Beauty*, p. v.
71. Barkan, *Unearthing the Past*, p. 196.
72. Haskell and Penny, *Taste and the Antique*, p. 312.
73. Smith, *Hellenistic Sculpture*, p. 99.
74. Smith, *Hellenistic Sculpture*, p. 108.
75. People who knew Michelangelo well described him in exactly those terms. Pope Leo X was Giovanni, the second son of Lorenzo de' Medici, Il Magnifico, and had known the artist well since his mid-teens. He gave the painter Sebastiano del Piombo a succinct account of Michelangelo's primacy as a creative fore, but also why he preferred not to give him commissions. 'Look at the works of Raphael, who as he saw the works of Michelangelo, immediately abandoned Perugino's style, and as much as he was able, moved closer to that of Michelangelo. But he is terrible, as you see; one cannot deal with him'; see Golzio, *Raffaello*, p. 135.

Baccio's Balls. Michelangelo and the Ideal Model (pp. 99-121)

I am grateful to Eric Boot for his input and feedback on this article.

1. Ames-Lewis, *Drawing in Early Renaissance Italy*, Chap. 5; Forlani Tempesti, 'Studiare dal nature nella Firenze'; Wood, 'Indoor-Outdoor', pp. 36–37; Burke, *The Italian Renaissance Nude*, pp. 98–99; Chapman and Faietti, *Fra Angelico to Leonardo*, pp. 60–64; Lazzarini, 'The Nude in Central Italian Painting and Sculpture', pp. 83–86.
2. Vasari, *Lives*, trans. De Vere, p. 590.
3. Burke, *The Italian Renaissance Nude*, p. 19.
4. Rubin, *Seen from Behind*, pp. 187–217; Hirst, *Michelangelo and His Drawings*, p. 61.
5. Burke, *The Italian Renaissance Nude*, Chap. 3.
6. Vasari, *Lives*, trans. De Vere, p. 590.
7. Burke, *The Italian Renaissance Nude*, p. 95.
8. Bambach, *Michelangelo*, pp. 26–29; Hirst, *Michelangelo and His Drawings*, pp. 16–21; Wallace, 'Drawing Limits'.
9. Lack of evidence makes the precise work on which Michelangelo drew uncertain; see also Van Tuyll van Serooskerken, *The Italian Drawings*, no. 45.
10. Joannides, *Michel-Ange*, pp. 72–73; Kárpáti, *Triumph of the Body*, pp. 67–87. The drawing is often regarded as a preliminary study for the now-lost bronze *David* of 1502–1508. Saul Levine has argued, however, that it can be linked to the marble *David* (1504), see Levine, 'Michelangelo's David'.
11. Vasari, *Lives*, trans. De Vere, p. 590.
12. Vasari, *Lives*, trans. De Vere, p. 773; see also Aymonino and Varick Lauder, *Drawn from the Antique*, pp. 24–29; Hirst, *Michelangelo and His Drawings*, p. 61; Bambach, *Michelangelo: Divine Draftsman and Designer*, pp. 56–68; and Martin Gayford's essay in this publication.
13. Rubin, *Seen from Behind*, pp. 214–16; Hartt, *Michelangelo Drawings*, p. 28; Chapman and Faietti, *Fra Angelico to Leonardo*, pp. 290–91.
14. Wilde, 'Eine Studie Michelangelos nach der Antike'; Hirst, *Michelangelo and His Drawings*, p. 65; Rubin, *Seen from Behind*, pp. 212–16.
15. De Tolnay, *Corpus*, I, p. 59; Rubin, *Seen from Behind*, p. 216.
16. Hirst, *Michelangelo and His Drawings*, p. 71; Bambach, *Michelangelo*, p. 39; Chapman, *Michelangelo Drawings*, pp. 117–20.
17. Hartt, *Michelangelo Drawings*, p. 78; Bambach, *Michelangelo*, pp. 27, 86–91.
18. Joannides, *The Drawings of Michelangelo*, pp. 92–117.
19. See the drawing inv. WA1846.49 in the Ashmolean Museum, Oxford, for instance.
20. Hirst, *Michelangelo and His Drawings*, p. 71. According to Hartt, all the 300–400 detailed studies Michelangelo must have made for the figures on the Sistine Chapel ceiling were drawn from models: Hartt, *Michelangelo Drawings*, p. 78.
21. Vasari, *Le vite*, ed. by Milanesi, I, pp. 177–78; Bambach, *Michelangelo*, p. 209.
22. Lazzarini, 'The Nude in Central Italian Painting and Sculpture', p. 105.
23. Burke, *The Italian Renaissance Nude*, pp. 122–23; see also Chapman, *Michelangelo Drawings*, p. 108.
24. Burke, *The Italian Renaissance Nude*, Chap. 1 and p. 99; Lazzarini, 'The Nude in Central Italian Painting and Sculpture', Chap. 2.
25. Burke, *The Italian Renaissance Nude*, pp. 50–51.
26. Van Tuyll van Serooskerken, *The Italian Drawings*, no. 56.
27. Bambach, *Michelangelo*, p. 118.
28. See also Hirst, *Michelangelo and His Drawings*, pp. 73–74.
29. Burke, *The Italian Renaissance Nude*, pp. 48–58; Lazzarini, 'The Nude in Central Italian Painting and Sculpture', pp. 107–09.
30. Hartt, *Michelangelo Drawings*, p. 179; Bambach, *Michelangelo*, p. 118.
31. Hartt, *Michelangelo Drawings*, p. 216; Hirst, *Michelangelo and His Drawings*, pp. 73–74.
32. Joannides, *The Drawings of Michelangelo*, pp. 175–76.
33. Perrig, *Michelangelo's Drawings*, p. 78.
34. Wilde, 'Notes on the Genesis of Michelangelo's *Leda*', p. 277.
35. Wallace, 'A Week in the Life of Michelangelo', p. 216. For the relationship between Michelangelo and Baccio di Puccione, see also Wallace, 'Michelangelo at Work', p. 245 n. 25.
36. Vasari, *Lives*, trans. De Vere, p. 1835; see also Varchi, *Orazione*, p. 13.
37. Hirst, *Michelangelo and His Drawings*, p. 71.
38. Hartt, *Michelangelo Drawings*, p. 83.
39. Burke, *The Italian Renaissance Nude*, p. 101; Lazzarini, 'The Nude in Central Italian Painting and Sculpture', pp. 99–107.
40. Burke, *The Italian Renaissance Nude*, pp. 96, 101–04; Lazzarini, 'The Nude in Central Italian Painting and Sculpture', pp. 60–72.
41. Lazzarini, 'The Nude in Central Italian Painting and Sculpture', pp. 103–06.
42. Condivi, *The Life of Michelangelo*, trans. by Sedgwick Wohl, ed. by Wohl, pp. 15–17.
43. Gayford, *Michelangelo: His Epic Life*, p. 103.
44. Forlani Tempesti, 'Studiare dal nature nella Firenze', p. 11.

Michelangelo and the Anatomy of the Artist (pp. 123-147)

I am very grateful to Machtelt Brüggen Israëls, Martin Clayton, Michael Kwakkelstein and Frits Scholten for sharing their insights, suggestions and critique. Special thanks are due to Dr Gert-Jan Kleinrensink, Emeritus Professor of Anatomy at Erasmus MC, Rotterdam, whose medical knowledge made an important and inspiring contribution to this essay.

1. Vasari, *Le vite*, ed. by Bettarini and Barocchi, IV, pp. 205–06; Vasari, *Lives*, trans. De Vere, p. 910. For Raphael's drawings after the cartoon, see Chapman, Henry and Plazzotta, *Raphael*, nos. 55–57; the small body of anatomical drawings attributed to him is discussed in Cazort,

Kornell and Roberts, *The Ingenious Machine of Nature*, nos. 6–7; and Laurenza, 'Art and Anatomy in Renaissance Italy', pp. 17–20.

2. Vasari, *La vita di Michelangelo*, ed. by Barocchi, I, pp. 116–17; Vasari, *Lives*, trans. De Vere, p. 1923.

3. Jacobs, '(Dis)assembling'.

4. Serra, *Dessins bolonais du XVIème siècle*, no. 312.

5. Quoted in Campbell, '"Fare una Cosa Morta Parer Viva"', pp. 611–12. Amerson, 'The Problem of the Écorché', pp. 19–22 discusses the sixteenth-century reception of Michelangelo's anatomical studies.

6. One of the speakers in Donato Giannotti's *Dialoghi* (1546), in which Michelangelo also appears, comments that besides a knowledge of poetry and geometry, artists should have a *grandissima notitia* (great knowledge) of anatomy, see Giannotti, *Dialoghi*, pp. 5–6. Benedetto Varchi's funeral oration likewise numbered anatomy among the liberal arts Michelangelo had mastered; see Varchi, *Orazione funerale*, p. 54.

7. Vasari, *La vita di Michelangelo*, ed. by Barocchi, II, pp. 120–21 and Kornell, 'Artists and the Study of Anatomy', I, p. 149.

8. Alessandro Benedetti, *Anatomice: Sive, de historia corporis humani libri quinque* (1493), quoted and translated in Jacobs, '(Dis)assembling', p. 436 n. 65. Leonardo da Vinci owned this book, see Reti, 'The Two Unpublished Manuscripts'. We do not know whether Michelangelo possessed any anatomical manuals.

9. Burke, 'The Body in Artistic Theory', pp. 185–87. See note 64 for further literature on this subject.

10. Ghiberti, *Lorenzo Ghibertis Denkwürdigkeiten*, ed. by Schlosser, pp. 6, 222 *et seq.* Vasari stated that Antonio del Pollaiuolo was the first artist to perform dissections himself, but this claim has rightly been questioned by, among others, Fusco, 'The Nude as Protagonist', pp. 136–67 and Schultz, *Art and Anatomy*, pp. 51–59. Dissections at the university of Florence are discussed by Park, *Doctors*, pp. 198–236. There is little evidence that these were accessible to laypeople, and the Florentine medical faculty had, moreover, relocated to Pisa in 1483; see Fusco, 'The Nude as Protagonist', pp. 139 and 238.

11. See Clayton and Philo, *Leonardo*, pp. 7–29, regarding dissections performed by Leonardo da Vinci.

12. Condivi, *Vita di Michelagnolo Buonarroti*, fols. 7v–8r. According to Kornell, 'Artists and the Study of Anatomy', I, pp. 150–51, this must have occurred in the winter of

1494, when Michelangelo was nineteen.

13. Vasari, *La vita di Michelangelo*, ed. by Barocchi, I, pp. 24–25 and Morozzi, 'La "Battaglia di Cascina" di Michelangelo'.

14. The story can be found in *Anonimo Magliabechiano*, see *The Codex of the Anonimo Magliabechiano*, ed. by Wierda, Van ter Toolen and Van Veen, pp. 300–01.

15. The same passage links Michelangelo to a murder, but in the commentary in the recent edition it is rightly stated that this is not confirmed by any other source, see *The Codex of the Anonimo Magliabechiano*, ed. by Wierda, Van ter Toolen and Van Veen, p. 301 n. 737.

16. Hughes, *Michelangelo*, pp. 30–32. Regarding private autopsies and dissections by physicians in hospitals, see Fusco, 'The Nude as Protagonist', pp. 232–35; Park, 'The Criminal and the Saintly Body', pp. 16–17. Michelangelo's patron Piero de' Medici, who was *operaio* of Santo Spirito, might have put him in touch with a doctor; see Hirst, *Michelangelo*, p. 20. Diana, 'Anatomy between Public and Private', pp. 340–45, describes examples of collaboration between doctors and artists.

17. The drawing in question is a poorly preserved sheet in Munich; see Harprath, *Italienische Zeichnungen*, no. 57 and Gnann, *Michelangelo*, no. 2. According to Fusco, 'The Nude as Protagonist', p. 147, bone material was more widely available from sources including ossuaries. In addition, Katherine Park points out that dissection does not produce a clean skeleton as flesh requires time to decompose, and boiling bones to remove it was prohibited; see Park, 'Masaccio's Skeleton', pp. 128–29 n. 38.

18. Byatt, *Niccolò Ridolfi*, p. 224–36.

19. Coppola, 'The Discovery of the Pulmonary Circulation'; Carlino, *Books of the Body*, pp. 57–68. Condivi and Vasari both described Colombo as 'a close friend' (*amicissimo*) of Michelangelo. See Steinberg, 'Michelangelo and the Doctors', regarding Michelangelo's kidney stones.

20. Condivi, *Vita di Michelagnolo Buonarroti*, verso of the second folio between fols. 42 and 43.

21. Hillard, 'Michelangelo and Realdo Colombo'.

22. This identification was proposed by Ciardi, 'Michelangelo come Galeno'.

23. Leonardo da Vinci, *The Literary Works of Leonardo da Vinci*, ed. by Richter, II, no. 796.

24. Condivi, *Vita di Michelagnolo Buonarroti*, recto of the second folio between fols. 42 and 43; Condivi, *The Life of Michelangelo*, trans. by Sedgwick Wohl, ed. by Wohl, pp. 97-99.

25. He did so for Sebastiano del Piombo, for instance, who asked him in 1532 to 'bring some figures, legs, bodies or arms' (*Il Carteggio di Michelangelo*, III, pp. 419–20).

26. Alberti, *On Painting and on Sculpture*, ed. by Grayson, p. 74; Burke, 'The Body in Artistic Theory', pp. 187–90.

27. By way of assistance he listed the dimensions of body parts at the end of *De statua* (§12–13, Alberti, *On Painting and on Sculpture*, ed. by Grayson, pp. 134–39).

28. Dürer, *Vier Bücher von menschlicher Proportion*, ed. by Hinz, p. 22.

29. One of the interlocutors in Donato Giannotti's *Dialoghi*, states that 'he received a book a few days ago by Albrecht Dürer, a German painter', to which Michelangelo replies that he too would like to write a treatise like that 'if God allows him the time for it'; Giannotti, *Dialoghi*, pp. 5–6.

30. Condivi, *Vita di Michelagnolo Buonarroti*, recto and verso of the second folio between fols. 42 and 43; Condivi, *The Life of Michelangelo*, trans. by Sedgwick Wohl, ed. by Wohl, p. 99.

31. Vasari, *La vita di Michelangelo*, ed. by Barocchi, I, p. 117; Vasari, *Lives*, trans. De Vere, p. 1924.

32. Summers, *Michelangelo and the Language of Art*, pp. 385–87.

33. Vasari, *La vita di Michelangelo*, ed. by Barocchi, I, p. 117; Vasari, *Lives*, trans. De Vere, p. 1924, slightly adapted.

34. Barocchi, *Scritti*, II, p. 1824, quoted and discussed in Summers, *Michelangelo and the Language of Art*, pp. 368–79. The complex notion of *grazia* is discussed by Jacobs, 'Aretino and Michelangelo'.

35. Condivi, *Vita di Michelagnolo Buonarroti*, fol. 40v; Condivi, *The Life of Michelangelo*, trans. by Sedgwick Wohl, ed. by Wohl, p. 93.

36. I am grateful to Gert-Jan Kleinrensink for his observations on the accuracy of the anatomical drawings from Teylers Museum. The degree of anatomical precision in Michelangelo's drawings is also discussed by Elkins, 'Michelangelo and the Human Form' and Ruston and Abrahams, 'An Anatomical "Whodunnit"', and – in relation to artistic transformation of the body – by Kleinbub, *Michelangelo's Inner Anatomies*, pp. 6–8.

37. Quoted in Clark, *Leonardo*, p. 132; Schultz, *Art and Anatomy*, pp. 91–92. According to Chastel, 'Treatise', p. 226, the idea that Leonardo was critical of Michelangelo's anatomy was already current in the sixteenth century.

38. The attribution history of Michelangelo's *écorchés* can be found in Van Tuyll van Serooskerken, *The Italian Drawings*, no. 53. Regarding similar drawings, not all of

which however are securely attributed, see Kornell, 'Artists and the Study of Anatomy', I, pp. 156–58.

39. See in particular inv. 598Ev, Gallerie degli Uffizi, Florence (known as *Zenobia*), in which the structure of the head is visualised in keeping with these rules.

40. Regarding these and similar annotations, see Kornell, 'Artists and the Study of Anatomy', I, pp. 161–65.

41. Quoted in Vasari, *La vita di Michelangelo*, ed. by Barocchi, II, p. 123.

42. Joannides, *Michelangelo and His Influence*, no. 27 with, among other things, the profile of a hanging body on the verso.

43. Schultz, *Art and Anatomy*, pp. 82–88.

44. Elkins rightly interpreted the symbols as referring to muscles and bones alike, noting that no consistent system exists between the different drawings (Elkins, 'Michelangelo and the Human Form', pp. 179–80, 184–85); Schultz believed incorrectly that they refer to muscles alone (Schultz, *Art and Anatomy*, pp. 89–90) and Kornell, also wrongly, only to bones (Kornell, 'Artists and the Study of Anatomy', I, p. 163). A drawing from Oxford (inv. 0068v, Christ Church Picture Gallery) contains similar annotations.

45. 'It is said that Michelangelo removed all the muscles and sinews from a dead body with a knife and then moulded them in wax, so that he could place them in another body as he saw fit, exactly as they were in the flesh, and that he used this in his sculptures.' Kornell, 'Artists and the Study of Anatomy', I, p. 187, provides the original; see also Summers, *Michelangelo and the Language of Art*, pp. 398–99.

46. Numerous art historians have cited wax models as the source for Michelangelo's anatomical drawings, including Joannides, *Michelangelo and His Influence*, p. 134, Peters and Brooks, *Michelangelo*, p. 77 and Kwakkelstein, *Rubens*, pp. 42–62. While models of this kind do occasionally display some affinity with his work (see Amerson, 'The Problem of the Ecorché', nos. 15–27, 32–33, for examples), there are insufficient grounds to attribute them to him personally. For the best-known examples, see Pope-Hennessy, 'The Gherardini Collection'. Michelangelo's drawings do not provide any clear indications for the use of an anatomical wax model either.

47. Vasari, *Le vite*, ed. by Bettarini and Barocchi, IV, pp. 205–06; Vasari, *Lives*, trans. De Vere, p. 910. Giovanni Paolo Lomazzo wrote that when studying anatomy, the painter should work from 'the example of both dead and living bodies'; see Kornell, 'Artists and the Study of Anatomy', I, p. 31 n. 14. See also Terry

van Druten's essay in this publication in this regard.

48. All the sheets have similar dimensions apart from the drawing in Teylers Museum (inv. A 037; fig. 80/cat. 21). A possible sketchbook is mentioned by Popham and Wilde, *The Italian Drawings*, p. 262; Wilde, *Michelangelo: The Group of Victory*, p. 16; Hirst, *Michelangelo and His Drawings*, p. 14.

49. Van Tuyll van Serooskerken, *The Italian Drawings*, no. 51, notes that the pen drawings pre-date the ones in chalk.

50. Chapman, *Michelangelo Drawings*, p. 185; Mussolin, 'I disegni di Michelangelo per le "Allegorie del Tempo"', p. 81.

51. Ms. Add. 21907, fol. 1, British Library, London. This is discussed by Chapman, *Michelangelo Drawings*, p. 185, no. 51; Mussolin, 'I disegni di Michelangelo per le "Allegorie del Tempo"', p. 91.

52. Francesco Bocchi (quoted in Campbell, '"Fare una Cosa Morta Parer Viva"', p. 619, n. 88), for instance, commented on these sculptures in his *Le bellezze della città di Firenze* (1591) that they could never have been done 'without the aid of anatomy'.

53. The attribution is contested; while Popham and Wilde, *The Italian Drawings*, no. 442, identify it as 'school of Michelangelo', many later authors attribute the drawing to Michelangelo himself, among them Hirst, *Michelangelo and His Drawings*, p. 14 and Joannides, *Michelangelo and His Influence*, no. 26.

54. Cf. also Oxford's Christ Church Picture Gallery (inv. 0068v) and Ashmolean Museum (inv. WA1846.63).

55. Condivi, *Vita di Michelagnolo Buonarroti*, fol. 39r; Condivi, *The Life of Michelangelo*, trans. by Sedgwick Wohl, ed. by Wohl, p. 87.

56. Similar figure studies are discussed at length in Chapman, *Michelangelo Drawings*, pp. 233–46; Vowles and Lewis, *Michelangelo: The Last Decades*, pp. 64–71.

57. Joannides, *Michelangelo and His Influence*, p. 100.

58. Vasari, *La vita di Michelangelo*, ed. by Barocchi, I, p. 74; Vasari, *Lives*, trans. De Vere, p. 1882.

59. This connection was important to Leonardo too: Kemp, '"Il Concetto dell'Anima"'.

60. Vasari, *La vita di Michelangelo*, ed. by Barocchi, I, p. 25; Vasari, *Lives*, trans. De Vere, p. 1848.

61. This comes from the preface to the third volume of *Lives*, of which Michelangelo marks the culmination: Vasari, *Le vite*, ed. by Bettarini and Barocchi, IV, p. 5; Vasari, *Lives*, trans. De Vere, p. 772.

62. 'Michelangelo made a Crucifix of wood … doing this to please the prior, who placed rooms at his disposal, in which he was

constantly flaying dead bodies, in order to study the secrets of anatomy, thus beginning to give perfection to the *great knowledge of design* [*disegno*] that he afterwards acquired.' Vasari, *La vita di Michelangelo*, ed. by Barocchi, I, p. 13.

63. Assembling a figure from separate body parts became commonplace in the sixteenth century and is discussed in the context of sculpture by De Haseth Möller, 'Anatomical Study Models', pp. 157–62, and that of drawing by Van den Akker, *Sporen*.

64. Regarding the 'divinity' of Michelangelo's art and the role played in it by anatomy, see Campbell, '"Fare una Cosa Morta Parer Viva"'. The relationship between anatomy and *disegno* is beautifully expressed by Bohde, 'Skin and the Search for the Interior', pp. 20–22. See Burke, *The Italian Renaissance Nude*, pp. 117–23, regarding the parallel between the way the Creation is depicted in the ceiling of the Sistine Chapel and the divine creative power of Michelangelo as an artist.

65. Condivi, *Vita di Michelagnolo Buonarroti*, fol. 36r; Condivi, *The Life of Michelangelo*, trans. by Sedgwick Wohl, ed. by Wohl, p. 79.

66. Vasari, *La vita di Michelangelo*, ed. by Barocchi, I, p. 30.

67. First noted by Hartt, *Michelangelo Drawings*, no. 132A.

68. According to Christoph Frommel, it is even plausible that Michelangelo also used the studies on the sheet in the Gallerie Degli Uffizi, Florence (inv. 608Ev)(fig. 87) for *Moses*; see Frommel and Forcellino, *Michelangelo's Tomb for Julius II*, p. 41.

69. The author is grateful to Gert-Jan Kleinrensink.

70. Vasari, *La vita di Michelangelo*, ed. by Barocchi, I, pp. 30–31; Vasari, *Lives*, trans. De Vere, pp. 1851-52.

Michelangelo, Neoplatonism, and the Idealised Body (pp. 153-170)

1. https://www.theguardian.com/us-news/2023/mar/25/florida-principal-resigns-michelangelo-david [accessed 23 December 2024].

2. See, for example, Masaccio's *Expulsion of Adam and Eve from Eden* (1424–25) and Masolino's *The Temptation of Adam and Eve* (1424) in the Brancacci Chapel in the Santa Maria del Carmine, Florence. Donatello's *David* (fig. 2) is the first freestanding male nude statue and dates to the 1440s; Botticelli's *Birth of*

Venus (Florence, Gallerie degli Uffizi, inv. 1890 n. 878) from *c.* 1484–86 is the first monumental female nude after antiquity; and Michelangelo's *David* (fig. 1) was created between 1501 and 1504.

3. Vasari, *Le vite,* ed. by Marini, p. 1231. Translation is taken from Vasari, *Artists of the Renaissance,* trans. and ed. by Bull, p. 274.

4. This research has been published earlier in different but overlapping publications: Van den Doel, 'Marsilio Ficino on Melancholy and Artistic Genius', pp. 107–32; Van den Doel, *Ficino and Fantasy,* pp. 1–7, 202–67.

5. Van den Doel, *Ficino and Fantasy,* pp. 2–14; Cf. Ames-Lewis, *The Intellectual Life.*

6. Allen, 'Ficino, Marsilio', pp. 360–61.

7. Van den Doel, *Ficino and Fantasy,* pp. 3–14, 132–201.

8. Van den Doel, *Ficino and Fantasy,* pp. 5–14.

9. I am aware of the fact that 'homosexuality' is a modern term. Noel Malcolm research-es in *Forbidden Desire* the predominantly early modern Mediterranean phenomenon called 'sodomy', where adult men were seeking sex with teenage boys. Earlier research by James Saslow shows that this was not the only practice. As Saslow puts forward 'the surviving evidence of [homosexual] relations is incomplete and biased because of the gravity of the crime and the nature of the sources' (Saslow, 'Homosexuality in the Renaissance', p. 91). On this topic see also Michael Rocke's es-say in this publication, as well as Saslow, 'Homosexuality in the Renaissance', Malcolm, *Forbidden Desire*, and Palmer, *Inventing the Renaissance.* The gossip came, for example, from Pietro Aretino. Condivi's *Vita di Michelagnolo Buonarroti* was a rebuttal of hostile rumours about the artist, and also corrected inaccura-cies Michelangelo found in the biography of him in Vasari's *Le Vite.* Condivi wrote: 'He also loved the beauty of the human body, as one who best understands it; and in such wise that certain carnal-minded men, who are not able to comprehend the love of beauty unless it be lewd or shame-ful, have taken the occasion to think and speak evil of him, as if Alcibiades, a youth of perfect beauty, had not been pure-ly loved by Socrates, from whose side he arose as from the side of his father' (Condivi, *The Life of Michelangelo,* trans. by Holroyd, intro. by Robertson, p. 166). Cf. Ruvoldt, 'Michelangelo's Open Secrets', pp. 105–25.

10. Frommel, *Michelangelo und Tommaso dei Cavalieri,* p. 33; Kristeller, 'Francesco da Diacceto and Florentine Platonism'. The Accademia Sacra Medicea was supported by Pope Leo X and active from 1515 until

the end of 1519/20. It took the form of a revival of the Platonic Academy of Lorenzo il Magnifico.

11. Van den Doel, *Ficino and Fantasy,* pp. 217–20; this signature shows that Michelangelo did not pretend that he could read Latin.

12. This idea is derived from the Roman rhetorician Quintillian, see Van den Doel, *Ficino and Fantasy,* pp. 34–35; Freedberg, *The Power of Images*, pp. 2 ff.

13. Van den Doel, *Ficino and Fantasy,* p. 34; Van den Doel and Hanegraaff, 'Imagination', pp. 606–16.

14. Aristotle says that *phantasia* derives from 'φῶς' (*phoos*), 'light' or 'glow', and that it is primarily visually oriented, see Aristotle, *De Anima*, III, 3, 427 a17–b26, 427 b27–429–a9; Van den Doel, *Ficino and Fantasy,* p. 33.

15. Van den Doel, *Ficino and Fantasy,* p. 33. Nowadays we would say 'the brain', but Renaissance psychology is focused on the soul.

16. Van den Doel, *Ficino and Fantasy,* p. 47.

17. Ficino, *Theologia Platonica*, XIII, p. 2; Ficino, *Platonic Theology,* ed. by Hankins and Bowen, trans. by Allen and Warden, IV, p. 127.

18. We see this phenomenon, described by Stephen Greenblatt as 'self-fashioning', emerging during the Renaissance, see Greenblatt, *Renaissance Self-Fashioning.*

19. It was believed that there were four temperaments or 'humours', which arose from an excess or deficiency of certain substances in the body. The melancholic temperament was said to arise from a large amount of black bile in the body, the choleric temperament from yellow bile. The phlegmatic temperament was caused by phlegm and the sanguine by blood. The latter temperament was believed to be the most balanced. The theory goes back to the Roman physician Galen and predominated throughout the Middle Ages and early modern period.

20. (Pseudo)Aristotle, *Problemata*, 30.1 (935a); Ficino, *De vita libri tres,* I, V.

21. Ficino, *De vita libri tres,* I, II; Ficino, *Three Books on Life,* trans. by Kaske and Clark, p. 113.

22. This is caused by the black bile in the blood of the melancholic – 'melancholy' literally means 'black bile'. According to Ficino, the soul of the melancholic is 'filled from above with divine influences and oracles', and it always invents new and unaccustomed things and predicts the future. Not only do Democritus and Plato affirm this but also Aristotle confesses it in his book of *Problemata*, and Avicenna in his *Liber divinorum* and in his *De anima*; Ficino, *De vita libri tres* I, VII; Ficino, *Three Books on Life,* p. 123.

23. Ficino, *De vita,* I, II; Ficino, *Three Books on Life,* p. 113.

24. Van den Doel, *Ficino and Fantasy,* pp. 208–09.

25. For example, Buonarroti, *The Poetry of Michelangelo*, trans. and ed. by Saslow, no. 89.

26. Van den Doel, *Ficino and Fantasy,* p. 209: The figure of Heraclitus was added later to the fresco, and it is considered a portrait of Michelangelo. Heraclitus was 'the weeping philosopher' and Michelangelo is portrayed in a pose that has become standard for the melancholic.

27. Lomazzo, *Idea*, pp. 44 ff.

28. Holanda, *Romeinse dialogen,* trans. by Boon, pp. 19–20 (my translation).

29. This interpretation began with Hieronymus Tetius, a seventeenth-century visitor to the Palazzo Barberini, who saw a copy of *The Dream* there. In the young man he saw the human mind surrounded by an angel and the representation of sins. Panofsky, *Studies in Iconology*, pp. 171 ff; see also Vollmer, 'The Vices in Michelangelo's Dream'.

30. Van den Doel, *Ficino and Fantasy,* pp. 203–04.

31. Ficino, *De vita tres libri,* I, IV; Ficino, *Three Books on Life,* p. 113. Ficino writes about the supposed connection between planetary influences of the Earth and a melancholic disposition with the following: 'The natural cause seems to be that for the pursuit of the sciences, especially the difficult ones, the soul must draw in upon itself from external things to internal as from circumference to the centre, and while it speculates, it must stay immovable at the very centre... of man. Now to collect oneself from the circumference to the centre, and to be fixed in the centre, is above all the property of Earth itself, to which black bile is analogous.'

32. Albrecht Dürer, *Melencolia I*, 1514 (Schoch, Mende and Scherbaum, no. 71ii); Jacques de Gheyn II (after), *Air, Melancholicus*, 1596–97 (New Hollstein, I. no. 204. 137; Hollstein, VII. no. 134. 127; Passavant, III, no. 121. 79).

33. See Ficino, *Theologia Platonica*, XIII, p. 2; Ficino, *Platonic Theology,* ed. by Hankins and Bowen, trans. by Allen and Warden, IV, p. 127.

34. Ruvoldt, 'Michelangelo's Dream'; Ruvoldt, *The Italian Renaissance Imagery of Inspiration*, p. 146.

35. '*Onde eßi chimarono lo amore non Iddio, non mortale, ma grande demone, perche la natura demonica, posta in mezzo fra gli huomini e li Dij quasi interprete, conduce a li Dij li prieghi e sacrificij de gli huomini, alli huomini la volontà e commandamenti*

delli Dij. Ne per altro mezzo gli huomini, o uigilanti o dormienti sono inspirati dalla diuina bontà, che per la natura demonica' (Cattani da Diacceto, *I tre libri d'Amore*, p. 144); English translation is mine. The citation refers to Plato, *Symposium*, 202e–203b.

36. The letter is published in Frommel, *Michelangelo und Tommaso dei Cavalieri*, p. 17.

37. If the drawing was made for Tommaso, it should be dated after autumn 1532.

38. Hirst, *Michelangelo and his Drawings*, p. 111.

39. Michelangelo often left parts of his work, especially sculptures and drawings, unfinished ('*non-finito*'). There is debate as to whether this was an artistic choice or had to do with practical circumstances (or both).

40. Ficino, *De Amore,* VI, 2 (my italics); trans. by Jayne, in Ficino, *Commentary on Plato's Symposium on Love*, p. 108.

41. Ficino, *De Amore,* VI, 9; trans. by Jayne, in Ficino, *Commentary on Plato's Symposium on Love*, p. 121.

42. Plato, *Symposium*, 201d ff.

43. Ficino translates χαμαιπετής as '*humi et per infima volans*' or '*volante a basso*'. Ficino, *De Amore,* VI, 9.

44. Ficino is citing Propertius; Ficino, *Commentary on Plato's Symposium on Love,* trans. by Jayne, p. 149.

45. Ficino, *De Amore,* VI, 10 (my italics); trans. by Jayne, in Ficino, *Commentary on Plato's Symposium on Love*, p. 125.

46. Vaenius, *Amorum emblemata*, p. 151, no. 76: '*Amor, ut lacryma, ex oculis oritur, in pectis cadit*'.

47. Cf. Matthew 25:33.

48. Cf. Rogier van der Weyden, *Beaune Altarpiece*, c. 1443–51, Hospices de Beaune; Hans Memling, *The Last Judgement,* 1467–71, National Museum of Gdansk, inv. MNG/SD/413/M.

49. Jayne, 'Introduction', in Ficino, *Commentary on Plato's Symposium on Love,* trans. by Jayne, pp. 19–20.

Michelangelo and the Divine Body. Between Crucifixion and Resurrection (pp. 173-197)

1. On the artist's early religious education see Verdon, 'The Infancy, Passion and Resurrection'; on his faith and religious poetry see Eisenbichler, 'The Religious Poetry of Michelangelo'.

2. On Michelangelo's poetry see Buonarroti, *The Poetry of Michelangelo*, trans. and ed. by Saslow; on the themes of longed-for death and resurrection see, in particular, sonnets 284–85, 288, 290, 293, 296 and 298.

3. On the history of this visual tradition see Mazzotta and Salsi, *Vesperbild*.

4. This association applied to both men and women although it was more often discussed in the case of the latter. For more on this topic see Brown, *Virtue and Beauty*.

5. Ficino, *Commentarium in Convivium Platonis: De amore*, ed. by Marcel, pp. 178–79. See also Ficino's letter to the Venetian ambassador and humanist Bernardo Bembo, which can be dated to 1477/78, in which he explores the relationship between virtue and its 'lovely form' in *The Letters of Marsilio Ficino*, IV, no. 51, pp. 66–67.

6. On this work see Sliwka in Wivel, *Michelangelo and Sebastiano*, pp. 94–95; Nagel, *Michelangelo and the Reform of Art*, esp. pp. 25–48.

7. On this work see Van Tuyll van Serooskerken, *The Italian Drawings*, no. 65.

8. Vasari, *Le vite*, ed. by Milanesi, VII, p. 218: '*ancora che egli avessi avuto animo che la dovessi servire per la sepoltura di lui, a piè di quello altare dove e'pensava di porla*'.

9. These speculations begin with Vasari himself who, because he could not imagine why Michelangelo would damage the work, offers three slightly contradictory reasons: 1) he suggests the marble was marred by many flaws; 2) the marble was hard, making the sparks fly from the chisel; 3) the artist's standards were so high that he could never be content with what he had done. Vasari subsequently reports that Michelangelo's assistant Tiberio Calcagni told him that Michelangelo grew frustrated with the nagging of his servant about finishing the work and that because there were many mishaps due to a vein in the stone, he grew frustrated and attacked it; see Vasari, *Le vite,* ed. by Milanesi, VII, pp. 242 ff, and 281 ff.

10. Vasari, *Le vite,* ed. by Milanesi, VIII, p. 377. In Vasari's letter to Michelangelo's nephew he refers to the work as intended for the artist's own sepulchre and to the figure of Joseph of Arimathea as an intended self-portrait.

11. Steinberg, 'Michelangelo's Florentine Pietà'.

12. Steinberg provides a survey of these images from antiquity through the Renaissance, including both sacred and profane subjects in a variety of media, see Steinberg 'Michelangelo's Florentine Pietà'.

13. This is argued in Steinberg, 'Michelangelo's Florentine Pietà' and in Hibbard, *Michel-angelo*, p. 284. Wasserman provides an alternative proposal, arguing that the 'destruction' was a premeditated disassembly of the leg so as to re-carve it in another position and create a composition more akin to a Deposition than a Pietà. The author, however, does not suggest why this would have a more desirable composition, see Wasserman, *Michelangelo's Florence Pietà*, pp. 68–73.

14. On this work see Joannides, *The Drawings of Michelangelo*, no. 48.

15. On these studies see Nagel, 'Observations on Michelangelo's Late Pietà Drawings and Sculptures'.

16. Condivi, 'Life of Michelangelo Buonarroti', trans. by Bull, p. 16.

17. This association with Savonarola's sermons, as recorded in his *Trattato dell'amore di Gesù Christo*, written in 1492, is made in Barnes, *Michelangelo and the Viewer in His Time*, p. 26.

18. New York, The Metropolitan Museum of Art, inv. 37. 28a.

19. See Chapman, *Michelangelo Drawings,* pp. 250 ff.

20. For a useful short guide to the defining characteristics of the *spirituali*, see Collett, *A Long and Troubled Pilgrimage*.

21. '*ho havta la vostra et visto il crucifixo, il qual certamente ha crucifixe nella memoria mia quante altre picture viddi mai*' (London, British Library, Ms. 23139, fol. 10; translation taken from Chapman, *Michelangelo Drawings*, Appendix II, no. 7).

22. On these compositions see Bambach, *Michelangelo,* pp. 225 ff.

23. Buonarroti, *Complete Poems*, trans. by Gilbert, no. 283, p. 159.

24. This work is discussed in Ragionieri, *I bozzetti michelangioleschi*, no. 8, pp. 64–67. The work was recently more cautiously attributed to Michelangelo in Vowles and Lewis, *Michelangelo: The Last Decades*, p. 226.

25. This is noted in one of two letters written by Michelangelo to Lionardo in August 1562, see *Il Carteggio Indiretto di Michelangelo,* II, no. 324, p. 126; and Joannides, '"Primitivism" in the Late Drawings of Michelangelo'.

26. Vasari, *Le vite*, ed. by Milanesi, VII, p. 282.

27. Bambach, *Michelangelo,* pp. 222 ff. On the Oxford drawing see also Bambach, *Michelangelo*, no. 204, p. 229; Joannides, *The Drawings of Michelangelo*, no. 57. More recently, Michelangelo's late crucifixion drawings have all been discussed together in Vowles and Lewis, *Michelangelo: The Last Decades*, pp. 209–18.

28. It should be noted that the moment of the Resurrection is not described in any of the gospels, but all four contain passages in which Jesus is portrayed as predicting his death and resurrection, and accounts of

an empty tomb and the appearances of Jesus. One of the letters sent by Paul the Apostle to one of the early Greek churches, the First Epistle to the Corinthians, contains one of the earliest Christian creeds referring to post-mortem appearances of Jesus and expressing the belief that he was raised from the dead (1 Corinthians 15:3–8).

29. For an in-depth discussion of this project see Wivel, *Michelangelo and Sebastiano*, pp. 171–81.

30. On these drawings see Chapman, *Michelangelo Drawings*, pp. 217–21; Bambach, *Michelangelo*, pp. 161–64; and Joannides in Wivel, *Michelangelo and Sebastiano*, pp. 198–205.

31. These include London, British Museum, inv. 1895,0915.501 (De Tolnay, *Corpus*, II, no. 263); Florence, Casa Buonarroti, inv. 61F and 66F (De Tolnay, *Corpus*, II, nos. 261-262); and another now lost, but known through copies.

32. On this series of *Resurrection* and *Risen Christ* drawings, see Bambach, *Michelangelo,* pp. 161–64.

33. This was reported in a letter from Tiberio Calcagni to Lionardo Buonarroti; see Daelli, *Carte Michelangiolesche inedite*, no. 23, pp. 34–35.

34. 'Giunto è già 'l corso della vita mia, con tempestoso mar, per fragil barca, al comun porto, ov'a render si varca conto e ragion d'ogni opra trista e pia. Onde l'affettüosa fantasia che l'arte mi fece idol e monarca conosco or ben com'era d'error carca e quel c'a mal suo grado ogn'uom desia.Gli amorosi pensier, già vani e lieti,che fien or, s'a duo morte m'avvicino? D'una so 'l certo, e l'altra mi minaccia. Né pinger né scolpir fie più che quieti l'anima, volta a quell'amor divino c'aperse, a prender noi, 'n croce le braccia' (Buonarroti, *Rime*, ed. by Girardi; for an English translation, see Buonarroti, *The Poetry of Michelangelo*, trans. and ed. by Saslow).

35. 'Scarco d'un'importuna e greve salma, Signor mie caro, e dal mondo disciolto, qual fragil legno a te stanco rivolto da l'orribil procella in dolce calma. Le spine e' chiodi e l'una e l'altra palma col tuo benigno umil pietoso volto prometton grazia di pentirsi molto, e speme di salute a la trist'alma. Non mirin co' iustizia i tuo sant'occhi il mie passato, e 'l gastigato orecchio; non tenda a quello il tuo braccio severo. Tuo sangue sol mie colpe lavi e tocchi, e più abondi, quant'i' son più vecchio, di pronta aita e di perdono intero' (Buonarroti, *Rime*, ed. by Girardi; for an English translation, see Buonarroti, *The Poetry of Michelangelo*, trans. and ed. by Saslow).

Michelangelo's *Battle of Cascina*. Its Context and Development (pp. 203-226)

This essay was more or less complete in Autumn 2024, but I was prompted to make a few minor changes by Per Rumberg and Scott Nethersole's *Michelangelo, Leonardo, Raphael: Florence c. 1504*, the catalogue of an exhibition at the Royal Academy, London, 9 November 2024–16 February 2025, which inevitably covers some of the same ground; and especially by Nethersole's catalogue essay 'The Battles of Leonardo and Michelangelo', pp. 57–69.

1. I hope to return to this topic elsewhere.
2. Cellini, *The Life of Benvenuto Cellini*, pp. 18–19.
3. Elsewhere in the Palazzo della Signoria, the Pollaiuolo brothers' canvases of three of Hercules' Labours, sequestered from the Palazzo Medici, were installed in the Old Council Hall as examples of virile virtue. Outside, Michelangelo's *David*, intended to be placed on one of the buttresses of the Duomo, was re-purposed in 1504 to stand before the Palazzo as an emblem of resolute defiance. In 1507–08, Soderini intended it to be accompanied by a Hercules and Antaeus, also to be carved by Michelangelo, but it was set aside when he was recalled to Rome.
4. Wilde, 'The Hall of the Great Council'; Rubinstein, *The Palazzo Vecchio 1298–1532*, pp. 73 ff. Other reconstructions have been put forward, but only Wilde's is satisfactory.
5. In 1510, the commission was transferred to Fra Bartolommeo, whose large (4.44 x 3.06 m) panel was inserted, only to be abandoned when the Medici regained power in 1512.
6. Wilde, 'Michelangelo and Leonardo', p. 75.
7. Bambach, 'The Purchases of Cartoon Paper'.
8. Conveniently cited in Jones's evocative *The Lost Battles*, p. 251.
9. Parker, *Italian Schools*, no. 20; discussed in detail by Martin Kemp and Juliana Barone in *I disegni di Leonardo da Vinci*, pp. 142–46.
10. Most of the relevant sheets are reproduced by Bambach in *Leonardo da Vinci*, II, pp. 386–416; the grouping by Popham in *The Drawings of Leonardo da Vinci* (and later editions), nos. 190–204, also remains useful.
11. Windsor, Royal Collection Trust, inv. RCIN 912540; Popham, *The Drawings of Leonardo da Vinci*, no. 190; Bambach, *Leonardo da Vinci*, no. 8.41. Venice, Gallerie dell' Accademia, inv. 236; Popham, *The*

Drawings of Leonardo da Vinci, no. 191; Bambach, *Leonardo da Vinci,* no. 8.64. Windsor, Royal Collection Trust, inv. RCIN 912340; Popham, *The Drawings of Leonardo da Vinci*, no. 200; Bambach, *Leonardo da Vinci,* no. 8.68. Budapest, *Szépművészeti Múzeum*, inv. 1774; Bambach, *Leonardo da Vinci,* no. 8.59 (verso of the head study for the same cavalryman).

12. See also London, British Museum, inv. 1854,0513.17; Popham and Pouncey, *Italian Drawings*, no. 109 verso; Bambach, *Leonardo da Vinci,* no. 8.46.

13. Windsor, Royal Collection Trust, inv. RCIN 912338; for this double-sided sheet, absent from Popham and Bambach, see Clark and Pedretti, *The Drawings of Leonardo da Vinci*, I, p. 33–34; Rumberg and Nethersole, *Michelangelo, Leonardo, Raphael*, no. 20.

14. Rome, Galleria Borghese, inv. 170.

15. Published, as by Rubens, by I.Q. Van Regteren Altena in 'Rubens as a Draughtsman'. The later twentieth century, counter-traditional opinion that what Rubens overworked in his Louvre drawing was an earlier Italian copy of *Anghiari*, of which the drawing *The Fight for the Standard* (fig. 132), would be a replica, has been widely followed. The matter is most thoroughly treated by Jeremy Wood but, of course, no-one holding this view before 2019 knew the drawing 'in the flesh' (Wood, *Copies and Adaptations*, pp. 75–98). Carmen Bambach assigns it, without visual comparisons, to Giovanni Stradano (Jan van der Straet), and although that attribution is unacceptable to the present author, it least recognises in the drawing a Flemish element (Bambach, 'Rubens, *Pictor Doctus*', p. 55). I examined the drawing in London in early 2019, prior to its sale at Sotheby's New York, 30 January 2019, lot 10 (that it fetched some twenty-five times its upper estimate suggests at least two collectors thought well of it), and had no doubt that it loyally replicated a superb original by Rubens.

16. For a calculation of a range of dimensions, but geared to what Leonardo actually succeeded in painting rather than what he intended to paint, see Kemp and Barone, *I disegni di Leonardo da Vinci*, fig. 81 and pp. 206–07.

17. Joannides, 'Leonardo da Vinci, Peter-Paul Rubens, Pierre-Nolasque Bergeret', pp. 76–86. This article, and the drawing published in it have, I think, been avoided – if not evaded – by all later writers on the subject except Frank Zöllner, '"La Battaglia di Anghiari"', p. 39; but he addressed neither the evidence nor the arguments – otiose to repeat here. When I studied the (framed and glazed) drawing, at the

time in a Parisian private collection, in the mid-1980s, I thought it was by Andrea Commodi. I later consulted Philip Pouncey, who was sceptical of that attribution, but neither he nor Michael Jaffé, who thought it close to Stefano della Bella, doubted that the drawing was seventeenth-century Florentine work. Much to my surprise, I was informed by David Weingarten (email of 25 May 2024) that the drawing had been offered by Artcurial, Paris, on 20 March 2024, lot 6, as 'Ecole Flamande, vers 1600'. From enquiries kindly made on my behalf by Diederick Poncelin de Raucourt, it transpired that the drawing had been withdrawn from sale and returned to its owners, but Artcurial kindly provided me with an image of it, reproduced here with their permission. Some years ago I was sent, by an American collector, a photograph of a rather coarse, probably same-size, copy, made in black chalk, seemingly seventeenth-century Flemish and perhaps from the circle of Jacob Jordaens (fig. 138). Unfortunately, I am ignorant of its whereabouts.

18. Some of what follows adapts and reworks Joannides, assisted by Clifford, 'On a War-Horse at Cascina', pp. 237–52.

19. Frommel, 'Michelangelos Handschrift', pp. 137–44; see note 42 below.

20. Oxford, Ashmolean Museum, inv. WA 1846.39; Joannides, *Drawings of Michelangelo*, no. 4; De Tolnay, *Corpus*, I, no. 102.

21. Gould, *Michelangelo: Battle of Cascina*.

22. Wilde, *Italian Drawings*, no. 85.

23. For engravings after *Cascina*, see Barnes, *Michelangelo in Print*, pp. 9–27.

24. Vatican City, Biblioteca Apostolica Vaticana, inv. Vat. Lat. 13991, fol. 1v; Joannides, *The Drawings of Raphael*, no. 27 verso; Knab, Mitsch and Oberhuber, *Raffaello, I disegni*, no. 160.

25. Barocchi, *Michelangelo e la sua scuola*, I, no. 4; De Tolnay, *Corpus*, I, no. 45. Nethersole provides a perceptive analysis of this drawing in Rumberg and Nethersole, *Michelangelo, Leonardo, Raphael*, pp. 64–65, which Elizabeth Pilliod kindly discussed with me.

26. Joannides, *Michel-Ange*, no. 3 verso; De Tolnay, *Corpus*, I, no. 68. The recto is a copy of Masaccio's *Expulsion of Adam and Eve from Eden*.

27. Joannides, *Michel-Ange*, no. 2v; De Tolnay, *Corpus*, I, no. 31.

28. Joannides, *Michel-Ange*, no. 5r; De Tolnay, *Corpus*, I, no. 54. A little-studied drawing first attributed to Michelangelo by Konrad Oberhuber and associated, by him, with the *Bathers* (sold at Christie's, London, 5 July, 2010, lot 63), may be an offshoot of this phase.

29. Birke and Kertész, *Die Italienischen Zeichnungen*, I, pp. 68–70; De Tolnay, *Corpus*, I, no. 53

30. Vienna, Albertina, inv. 123r; Birke and Kertész, *Die Italienischen Zeichnungen*, I, pp. 68–70; De Tolnay, *Corpus*, I, no. 53 (387 x 195 mm).

31. Wilde, *Italian Drawings*, no. 6; De Tolnay, *Corpus*, I, no. 52.

32. Cited by Gould, *Michelangelo: Battle of Cascina*, p. 10.

33. This reconstruction was based on scans of various photographs which could not be harmonised to achieve convincing renderings of the figures' positions in space. See also Joannides, 'On a War-Horse at Cascina'.

34. I have omitted several other figure studies often linked with *Cascina*, not because I feel certain that they are unconnected, but because at present, I can find no plausible place for them.

35. Joannides, *The Drawings of Michelangelo*, no. 5; De Tolnay, *Corpus*, I, no. 103. The small sketch in Oxford prepares this drawing: Oxford, Ashmolean Museum, inv. WA1846.39; Joannides, *The Drawings of Michelangelo*, no. 4r; De Tolnay, *Corpus*, I, no. 102. Although the relationship is far from certain, a barely visible black-chalk drawing in the Uffizi, which seems to show an infantryman attempting to unseat a rider, may also have formed part of the preparation: Florence, Gallerie degli Uffizi, inv. 18737F; Barocchi, *Michelangelo e la sua scuola*, I, no. 3; De Tolnay, *Corpus*, I, no. 44.

36. Paris, Musée du Louvre, inv. 707; Joannides, *Michel-Ange*, no. 8; De Tolnay, *Corpus*, I, no. 71.

37. Joannides, *The Drawings of Michelangelo*, nos. 7r and 7v; De Tolnay, *Corpus*, I, no. 41. The assistant was also studied in a quick line drawing which treats the back with more suppleness: Florence, Casa Buonarroti, inv. 9F; Barocchi, *Michelangelo e la sua scuola*, I, no. 5; De Tolnay, *Corpus*, I, no. 40.

38. The inverted figure on the Rotterdam drawing was first linked to *Cascina* by the present author, who also attached it to the group in Florence, Casa Buonarroti, inv. 54F (Barocchi, *Michelangelo e la sua scuola*, I, no. 146; De Tolnay, *Corpus*, II, no. 284) which had previously been associated with *The Last Judgement*; see Joannides, 'On a War-Horse at Cascina', pp. 240–41.

39. London, British Museum, inv. 1859,0625.564; Wilde, *Italian Drawings*, nos. 5r, 5v; De Tolnay, *Corpus*, I, no. 46. Florence, Gallerie degli Uffizi, inv. 233Fr; Barocchi, *Michelangelo e la sua scuola*, I, no. 1r; De Tolnay, *Corpus*, I, no. 37. Paris, Musée du Louvre, inv. 718; Joannides,

Michel-Ange, no. 9; De Tolnay, *Corpus*, I, no. 47. I previously suggested that the group might be connected with the *Martyrdom of the Ten Thousand* which Michelangelo seems to have been planning at this time, but I am now less attracted by this idea. The upper of the two episodes in Michelangelo's *Brazen Serpent* (Oxford, Ashmolean Museum, inv. WA.1846.64; Joannides, *The Drawings of Michelangelo*, no. 34; De Tolnay, *Corpus*, II, no. 266) from c. 1530 reprises the fleeing soldier from fig. 143, while the lower cites the three-figure group.

40. Wilde takes the well-known pen drawing of a gesturing man (fig. 43/cat. 10) to be a further development of the supported man, but the pose differs sufficiently to make this debatable; see Wilde, *Italian Drawings*, no. 4r.

41. Oxford, Ashmolean Museum, WA1846.41; Joannides, *The Drawings of Michelangelo*, no. 6; De Tolnay, *Corpus*, I, no. 39. The two copies are found in London, British Museum, inv. 1946,0713.635; Joannides, 'On a War-Horse at Cascina', fig. 7, p. 243. The second, perhaps adumbrated, in the small black chalk sketch of an, apparently, fallen horse, in Oxford, Ashmolean Museum, WA1846.41.

42. Wilde, *Italian Drawings*, no. 3r; De Tolnay, *Corpus*, I, 36. Compare the left-hand cavalryman in this drawing with Leonardo's sketch, RCIN 912340, mentioned in note 13.

43. Luka Pajovic has made better visual sense of my speculations than I could have hoped for. Michelangelo made several drawings of heads of soldiers wearing elaborate helmets in this period. See, for example, the sheet in the Hamburger Kunsthalle, inv. 21094, De Tolnay, *Corpus*, I, no.35, and Rumberg and Nethersole, *Michelangelo, Leonardo, Raphael*, no. 40 but, as Nethersole remarks (p. 65): 'the association with the Cascina cartoon is not certain and even if it were, the faces themselves are fairly expressionless.' To which one might add that all such heads are portrayed statically and it is hard to see where any of them might have fitted into Michelangelo's composition.

44. Martin Gayford reminds me that in one of his *postille* to Condivi's life, as recorded by Tiberio Calcagni, Michelangelo loftily remarked that he had never paid attention to perspectival construction: '*Alla prospettiva no, ché mi pareva perdervi troppo tempo*' (see Condivi, *Vita di Michelagnolo Buonarroti*, ed. by Nencioni, pp. XXII and 58).

45. Charles de Tolnay wrote extensively on Bruegel the Elder before concentrating on Michelangelo, and although he once told

me that this was not by design, he clearly had a fundamental sympathy.

Friend and Enemy. The Men in Michelangelo's Life (pp. 233-246)

1. Inv. 614, Musée du Louvre, Paris; inv. 40025, Galleria di Palazzo Cini, Fondazione Giorgio Cini, Venice.
2. 'amicitia res plurimas continet; quoquo te verteris, praesto est, nullo loco excluditur, numquam intempestiva, numquam molesta est' (Cicero, *Laelius de amicitia*, VI.22).
3. '*Est enim amicitia nihil aliud nisi omnium divinarum humanarumque rerum cum benevolentia et caritate consensio*' (Cicero, *Laelius de amicitia*, VI.20).
4. See Leontsini, 'The Motive of Society', p. 23.
5. Aristotle, *Ethica Niomachea*, VIII and IX; Langer, 'Friendship, Renaissance Understanding'.
6. 'quod amationes secundum haec tria differant specie: ut scilicet alia sit species amationis qua amatur aliquid propter bonum, et alia qua amatur aliquid propter delectabile, et alia qua propter utile. Et quia amicitiae actus est amatio, consequens est, quod etiam sint tres species amicitiae, aequales numero amabilibus. Quarum una est amicitia propter honestum, quod est bonum simpliciter; alia propter delectabile; et tertia, propter utile' (Thomas Acquinas, *Sententia Libri Ethicorum*, VIII, 3.2)
7. Kent, *Friendship, Love and Trust*, pp. 1–3.
8. Kent, *Friendship, Love and Trust*, p. 7.
9. Bambach, *Michelangelo*, p. 17. See *Il carteggio di Michelangelo* for the letters.
10. Leo X spoke about Michelangelo in tears, as if he were his brother and said that they had grown up together. Kent, *Friendship, Love and Trust*, p. 214.
11. Stone, *The Agony and the Ecstasy*, Chap. 7 'The Pope'.
12. Wallace, *Michelangelo: The Artist, the Man and his Times*, pp. 73 and 78; Frommel and Forcellino, *Michelangelo's Tomb for Julius II*, pp. 19 and 30; Bredekamp, *Michelangelo*, pp. 177–191.
13. Bambach, *Michelangelo*, p. 82.
14. For an extensive study of the tomb, see Frommel and Forcellino, *Michelangelo's Tomb for Julius II*.
15. Vasari, *Le vite* (1568), p. 727.
16. Condivi, *Michael Angelo Buonarroti*, trans. by Holroyd, p. 51
17. Pope Leo X (Giovanni de' Medici) gave Michelangelo the commission for the facade in 1516. There is some discussion in the literature as to whether Cardinal Giulio de' Medici (the later Pope Clement VII) took the initiative for Michelangelo's building of the New Sacristy in 1519, or whether Lorenzo 'Il Magnifico' had already given Giuliano da Sangallo the commission around 1491. There is documentary evidence for the first view: see Elam, 'The Site and Early Building History of Michelangelo's New Sacristy'. Giulio de' Medici commissioned the Laurentian Library in 1524, as Pope Clement VII.
18. Keizer, 'History, Origins, Recovery', p. 263; Hatfield, *The Wealth of Michelangelo*, p. 215.
19. Jacobs, 'Aretino and Michelangelo', p. 51.
20. See Elam, 'Art in the Service of Liberty'; Vasari, *Lives* (1568), p. 727; Ruvoldt, 'Michelangelo's "Slaves" and the Gift of Liberty', p. 1047. Michelangelo also donated several works to anti-Medici Florentines and their allies in the 1530s and 1540s.
21. Schwartz, *Aquinas on Friendship*, pp. 41, 44–45
22. One of the last works Michelangelo oversaw was for a Medici: the project for the Porta Pia in the 1560s, commissioned by Pope Pius IV (Giovanni Angelo de' Medici). This client, however, was at most a distant (possibly even non-existent) relative of Michelangelo's earlier patrons and the ruling Grand Ducal Medici in Florence.
23. Bambach, *Michelangelo*, p. 130.
24. See Vowles and Lewis, *Michelangelo: The Last Decades*, p. 126; Bambach, *Michelangelo*, p. 169.
25. Bambach, *Michelangelo*, p. 218.
26. Vowles and Lewis, *Michelangelo: The Last Decades*, p. 131–32.
27. For more on the relationship between the two artists, see Wivel, *Michelangelo and Sebastiano*.
28. In this regard, Michael Hirst suggested Sebastiano's painting *Christ's Descent into Limbo*, which shows Christ at the gates of the underworld, holding the banner of the cross. His pose is a mirror image of that in the drawing, see inv. P000346, Museo del Prado, Madrid; Hirst, *Sebastiano del Piombo*, p. 130. The drawing and its relationship with Sebastiano's work is discussed by Perrig, 'Über eine verkannte Michelangelo-Zeichnung', pp. 34–36; Acidini, *The Medici, Michelangelo and the Art of Late Renaissance Florence*, p. 326.
29. Bambach, *Michelangelo*, p. 169.
30. Bambach, *Michelangelo*, p. 171.
31. Vasari, *Le vite* (1568), p. 347.
32. Aristotle, *Ethica Niomachea*, VIII, 13.5–10.
33. Smithers, 'Michelangelo's Suicidal Stone', p. 218; Barocchi, *Michelangelo e la sua scuola*, p. 124–25.
34. Vasari, *Lives*, p. 1440 and 1849.
35. *Vita di Benvenuto Cellini*, ed. by Bacci, p. 353.
36. Frey, *Il codice Magliabechiano*, p. 115; *The Codex of the Anonimo Magliabechiano*, ed. by Wierda, Van ter Toolen and Van Veen, p. 300 (fol. 121v). The text is currently attributed to Bernardino Vecchietti.
37. 'o quanto egli mi piace, M. Pietro, che Michel'Angnolo aiuti questo mio novello concurrente, facendogli di sua mano i disegni: percioche dalla fama, che le sue Pitture non istiano al paragone delle mie, portà avendersi molto bene Michel'Angnolo, ch'io non vinco Bastiano […] ma lui medesimo, che si reputa (e meritamente) la Idea del disegno' (Roskill, *Dolce's Aretino*, pp. 94–95).
38. Roskill, *Dolce's Aretino*, pp. 84–89.
39. 'Che se ben vedete nelle Pitture di Michel'Angnolo la distintione in geneatl dell'età e de'sessi (cosa, che sanno far tutti) non la troverete gia partitamente ne muscoli' (Roskill, *Dolce's Aretino*, pp. 176–77).
40. Roskill, *Dolce's Aretino*, pp. 160–63.
41. Roskill, *Dolce's Aretino*, pp. 162–63.
42. 'Signor mio. Nel rivedere lo schizzo intiero di tutto il vostro dì del Giudicio, ho fornito di conoscere la illustre gratia di Rafaello ne la grata bellezza de la inventione' (Il Carteggio di Michelangelo, IV, p. 215–17 (31 October 1545)).
43. 'Intanto io, come battezzato, mi vergogno de la licentia, sì illecita a lo spirito, che havete preso ne lo isprimere i concetti u' si risolve il fine al quale aspira ogni senso de la veracissima credenza nostra' (Il Carteggio di Michelangelo, IV, p. 215–17 (31 October 1545)).
44. 'Sì che risuscitatele il nome col fare di fiamme di fuoco le vergogne dei dannati, et quelle dei beati di raggi di sole, o imitate la modestia fiorentina, la quale sotto alcune foglie auree sotterra quelle del suo bel colosso' (Il Carteggio di Michelangelo, IV, pp. 215–17 (31 October 1545)).
45. Stollhans, 'Michelangelo's Nude', p. 26. Scipione Saurolo wrote to Cardinal Borromeo in 1561 concerning the 'indecency of the nudity in certain figures in The Last Judgement'. Andrea Gilio also criticised Michelangelo's style, but actually did so based on a print after the work rather than the original; see also Bambach, *Michelangelo*, p. 22.
46. Barolsky, 'The Meaning of Michelangelo's Minos', pp. 30–31; Smithers, 'Michelangelo's Suicidal Stone', p. 216; Melinda Schlitt, 'Painting, Criticism, and Michelangelo's Last Judgement', p. 119.
47. Quoted in Chastel, *A Chronicle of Italian Renaissance Painting*, pp. 188–89; Stollhans, 'Michelangelo's Nude', p. 26.
48. Regarding the relationship between Marguerite de Navarre and Vittoria Colonna, see Low, 'Receiving Vittoria'; Adler, 'Strong Mothers, Strong Daughters'.

49. The anonymous *Beneficio di Cristo*, published in Venice in 1543, provided the *Spirituali* with a guide. The Holy Office, however, banned it in 1549 on the grounds that it was inspired by the ideas of Calvin.

50. Rolfe Prodan, *Michelangelo's Christian Mysticism*, p. 121; Maratos, 'Michelangelo, Vittoria Colonna, and the Afterlife of Intimacy', p. 69. The *Pietà* is in the British Museum, London (inv. 1895,0915.504) and Isabella Stewart Gardner Museum, Boston (inv. 1.2.0.16).

51. Kent, *Friendship, Love and Trust*, p. 217.

52. Madrigal G235: '*Un uomo in una donna, anzi uno dio / per la sua bocca parla, / ond'io per ascoltarla / son fatto tal, che ma' più sarò mio*'. For further interpretation of the madrigal, see Rolfe Prodan, *Michelangelo's Christian Mysticism*, pp. 121–22.

53. Rolfe Prodan, *Michelangelo's Christian Mysticism*, p. 122.

54. Quoted in Liebert, *Michelangelo: A Psychoanalytic Study*, pp. 312, 315, 322, 325.

55. Baker, 'Power and Passion in Sixteenth-Century Florence', pp. 434–35; Rocke, 'Gender and Sexual Culture in Renaissance Italy', pp. 150–70. For more on the subject of gender shifts, see Bassanese, 'Vittoria Colonna's Man/God'; Agoston, 'Male/Female, Italy/Flanders, Michelangelo/Vittoria Colonna'; Evan, 'The Heroine as Hero', p. 33; and Bassanese, 'Vittoria Colonna, Christ and Gender'.

56. Wadell, 'Charity: How Friendship with God Unfolds in Love for Others', p. 369.

57. Kent, *Friendship, Love and Trust,* p. 218.

58. "*Di giorno in giorno insin da' mie prim'anni, / Signor, soccorso tu mi fusti e guida, / onde l'anima mia ancor si fida / di doppia aita ne' mie doppi affani.*" Fragment of a sonnet, see *The poetry of Michelangelo*, trans. Saslow, no. 287.

59. Bambach, 'Letters from Michelangelo', pp. 58–60.

60. Varchi, *Orazione funerale*. Varchi had previously delivered a public lecture on Michelangelo's poems at the Accademia Fiorentina in 1547. This lecture went on to play a significant role in the dissemination of the artist's poetry to a wide audience; see Carlson, '"Eccellentissimo poeta et amatore divinissimo"'.

61. Soussloff, 'Imitatio Buonarroti', p. 593.

62. Soussloff, 'Imitatio Buonarroti', p. 582.

63. Van Tuyll van Serooskerken, *The Italian Drawings*, no. 49.

Catalogue of Exhibited Works

Compiled by Eric Boot

The selected bibliographies include the most significant recent publications that provide information on the provenance of the artworks, along with more detailed bibliographies. These publications also contain transcriptions of letters and poems.

Alciato, Andrea
1.
Emblemata, 1551
Guliel Rouilium, Lyon (pages 10–11 displayed)
RKD – Netherlands Institute for Art History, The Hague, inv. 201402142
Selected literature: Landwehr, *French, Italian, Spanish and Portuguese Books of Devices and Emblems,* no. 53; Daly, *Andreas Alciatus,* I, p. 236, II, pp. 361–62; Kruszynski, *Der Ganymed-Mythos,* pp. 26–33; Adams, Rawles and Saunders, *A Bibliography of French Emblem Books,* I, no. F.031.
(fig. 12)
p. 30

Anonymous
2.
Ganymede, after Michelangelo, 1542
Engraving, 430 x 278 mm
Inscribed: GANIMEDIS × IVVENIS × TROIANVS × RAPTVS × A × IOVE
Teylers Museum, Haarlem, inv. KG 00214
Selected literature: Marongiu, *Il mito di Ganimede,* no. 26; Gramaccini-Meier, *Die Kunst der Interpretation,* no. 124 (as Nicolas Beatrizet); Barnes, *Michelangelo in Print,* no. 81; Alberti, Rovetta and Salsi, *D'après Michelangelo,* II, no. 231.
(fig. 20)
pp. 55, 56

3.
Plaster Cast of Michelangelo's Dying Captive, 19th century
Plaster, height 227 cm
Collection Maastricht Institute of Arts, Zuyd Hogeschool, Maastricht
(not illustrated)

Bos, Cornelis
4.
Leda and the Swan, after Michelangelo, 1544–1545
Engraving, 302 x 410 mm
Rijksmuseum, Amsterdam, inv. RP-P-BI-2785
Selected literature: Hollstein, *Dutch and Flemish Engravings,* III, 124. 54; Van der Coelen, 'Cornelis Bos', pp. 126–27; Barnes, *Michelangelo in Print,* no. 74; Alberti, Rovetta and Salsi, *D'après Michelangelo,* II, no. 206.
(fig. 22)
pp. 58, 60, 115

Cavalieri, Tommaso de'
5.
Letter to Michelangelo, 1 January 1533
Pen and brown ink, 300 x 220 mm
Casa Buonarroti, Archivio Buonarroti, Florence, VII, 143
Selected literature: *Il carteggio di Michelangelo,* III, pp. 445–46; Frommel, *Michelangelo und Tommaso dei Cavalieri,* pp. 15–18; Marongiu, *Il mito di Ganimede,* no. 16; Acidini, Cecchi and Capretti, *Michelangelo, divino artista,* no. 90a.
(fig. 17)
pp. 50, 52

Clovio, Giulio
6.
Ganymede, after Michelangelo, c. 1540.
Black chalk, 192 x 260 mm
Royal Collection Trust, Windsor, inv. RCIN 913036
Selected literature: Popham and Wilde, *The Italian Drawings,* no. 457; Joannides, *Michelangelo and His Influence,* no. 15; Marongiu, *Il mito di Ganimede,* no. 24; Alberti, Rovetta and Salsi, *D'après Michelangelo,* I, pp. 127–30; Bambach, *Michelangelo,* no. 125.
(fig. 14)
pp. 28, 40, 41, 53, 55, 233

Daniele da Volterra (Daniele Ricciarelli)
7.
Male Head (Portrait of Michelangelo), 1547–c. 1553
Metalpoint and black chalk with white heightening, pricked, 295 x 219 mm
Teylers Museum, Haarlem, inv. A 021
Selected literature: Van Tuyll van Serooskerken, *The Italian Drawings,* no. 142; Romani, *Daniele da Volterra,* no. 27; Chapman, *Michelangelo Drawings,* no. 108; Gnann, *Michelangelo,* no. 121; Vowles and Lewis, *Michelangelo: The Last Decades,* pp. 111–12.
(fig. 161)
pp.237, 238

Michelangelo Buonarroti
8.
A Male Nude (after Masaccio) and Two Other Figures, c. 1492–1496
Pen and brown ink, dark brown wash, 330 x 200 mm
Private collection
Selected literature: Rinaldi, 'Looking at Masaccio'; Michel and Schröder, *Michelangelo and Beyond,* pp. 28–33.
(fig. 51)
pp. 19, 100, 101

9.
Three Figures in Adoration, c. 1496–1503
Verso: *Two Figures, Leaning Forward,* c. 1496–1503
Pen and brown ink, black chalk; verso: pen and brown ink, 269 x 194 mm
Teylers Museum, Haarlem, inv. A 022
Selected literature: De Tolnay, *Corpus,* I, no. 10; Van Tuyll van Serooskerken, *The Italian Drawings,* no. 45; Chapman, *Michelangelo Drawings,* no. 6; Gnann, *Michelangelo,* no. 6.
(figs 5 (recto) and 6 (verso))
pp. 19, 22, 23, 100

10.
A Male Nude, c. 1501–1502
Verso: *Studies of Children*, c. 1503–1505 (not exhibited)
 Pen and brown ink, black chalk, 374 x 228 mm
 Inscribed by Michelangelo, on the recto: *barba; Ero ig[n]udo or son vestito ogni mal me*; in a different hand: *charissimo sa … chome abiano visto meno*; on the verso, by Michelangelo: *[a]lessandro manecti*; in a different hand: *chosse de bruges*
 British Museum, London, inv. 1887,0502.117
 Selected literature: Wilde, *Italian Drawings*, no. 4; De Tolnay, *Corpus*, I, no. 48; Turner, *Florentine Drawings*, no. 11; Chapman, *Michelangelo Drawings*, no. 13; Chapman and Faietti, *Fra Angelico to Leonardo*, no. 92; Bambach, *Michelangelo*, pp. 52–53; Wivel, *Michelangelo and Sebastiano*, no. 5.
 (fig. 43)
 pp. 87, 88, 100

11.
Studies for a Sculpture of David, c. 1502–1503
Verso: *Figure studies*, c. 1502–1503 (not exhibited)
 Pen and brown ink, 264 x 185 mm
 Inscribed by Michelangelo, on the recto: *Davicte cholla frombe / e io chollarcho / Michelagniolo*; and lower right: *Rocte lalta cholonna el verd[e lauro]*
 Musée du Louvre, Département des arts graphiques, Paris, inv. 714
 Selected literature: De Tolnay, *Corpus*, I, no. 19; Natali, *L'officina della maniera*, no. 23; Echinger-Maurach 'Zu Michelangelos Skizze für den verlorenen Bronzedavid'; Joannides, *Michel-Ange*, no. 4; Ekserdjian, 'Michelangelo's Bronze "David"'.
 (fig. 52)
 pp. 100, 102

12.
Study of a Male Nude for the Battle of Cascina, 1504
Verso: *Study for Judith and Holofernes for the Sistine Chapel Ceiling*, c. 1508 (not exhibited)
 Black chalk with white heightening; verso: black chalk, 404 x 225 mm
 Teylers Museum, Haarlem, inv. A 018
 Selected literature: De Tolnay, *Corpus*, I, no. 51; Hirst, *Michelangelo Draftsman*, no. 7; Van Tuyll van Serooskerken, *The Italian Drawings*, no. 46; Chapman, *Michelangelo Drawings*, no. 9; Gnann, *Michelangelo*, no. 25.
 (figs 55 (verso) and 140 (recto))
 pp. 103, 104, 117, 131, 211, 212, 238

13.
Study of a Male Nude for the Battle of Cascina, 1504
Verso: *Study of a Male Nude for the* Genius of Victory, c. 1527–1530 (not exhibited)
 Black chalk with white heightening; verso: black chalk, 404 x 258 mm
 Teylers Museum, Haarlem, inv. A 019
 Selected literature: De Tolnay, *Corpus*, I, no. 50; Van Tuyll van Serooskerken, *The Italian Drawings*, no. 47; Chapman, *Michelangelo Drawings*, no. 10; Echinger-Maurach, *Michelangelos Grabmal für Papst Julius* II, pp. 53, 58; Gnann, *Michelangelo*, no. 26.
 (figs 141 (recto) and 160 (verso))
 pp. 17, 117, 211, 213, 218, 235, 236, 238

14.
Study of a Seated Male Nude (ignudo) *for the Sistine Chapel Ceiling*, c. 1508–1509
Verso: *Studies of Legs*, c. 1508–1509 (not exhibited)
 Metalpoint, 418 x 265 mm
 Gallerie degli Uffizi, Gabinetto dei Disegni e delle Stampe, Florence, inv. 18720 F
 Selected literature: Barocchi, *Michelangelo e la sua scuola*, I, no. 19; De Tolnay, *Corpus*, I, no. 141; Gnann, *Michelangelo*, no. 33; Kárpáti, *Triumph of the Body*, no. 26.
 (fig. 64)
 pp. 108, 110

15.
Studies for Haman for the Sistine Chapel Ceiling, c. 1511
Verso: *Fragmentary Cartoon for Haman and Other Figures*, c. 1511 (not exhibited)
 Red and black chalk, 252 x 205 mm
 Teylers Museum, Haarlem, inv. A 016
 Selected literature: De Tolnay, *Corpus*, I, no. 164; Hirst, *Michelangelo Draftsman*, no. 18; Van Tuyll van Serooskerken, *The Italian Drawings*, no. 50; Chapman, *Michelangelo Drawings*, no. 30; Gnann, *Michelangelo*, no. 43.
 (fig. 62)
 pp. 94, 107, 109, 141

16.
Studies for the Libyan Sibyl for the Sistine Chapel Ceiling, c. 1511
Verso: *Studies for the Libyan Sibyl for the Sistine Chapel Ceiling and Sketch for a Seated Figure*, c. 1511 (not exhibited)
 Red chalk with white heightening; verso: black chalk, 289 x 214 mm
 The Metropolitan Museum of Art, New York, inv. 24.197.2
 Selected literature: De Tolnay, *Corpus*, I, no. 156; Hirst, *Michelangelo Draftsman*, no. 16; Franklin, *From Raphael to Carracci*, no. 10; Gnann, *Michelangelo*, no. 41; Bambach, *Michelangelo*, no. 64.
 (fig. 70)
 pp. 28, 115, 116, 131

17.
Studies for Adam for the Sistine Chapel Ceiling, c. 1511
Verso: *Study of a Youthful Head for the Sistine Chapel Ceiling*, c. 1511 (not exhibited)
 Red chalk, 193 x 259 mm
 British Museum, London, inv. 1926,1009.1
 Selected literature: Wilde, *Italian Drawings*, no. 11; De Tolnay, *Corpus*, I, no. 134; Chapman, *Michelangelo Drawings*, no. 25; Bambach, *Michelangelo*, pp. 28–29.
 (fig. 7)
 pp. 20, 24, 108

18.
Studies of a Head and Limbs for the Sistine Chapel Ceiling, c. 1511
Verso: *Figure Studies for the Sistine Chapel Ceiling*, c. 1511
 Red chalk; verso: red chalk, metalpoint, black chalk, 296 x 195 mm
 Teylers Museum, Haarlem, inv. A 020
 Selected literature: De Tolnay, *Corpus*, I, no. 135; Van Tuyll van Serooskerken, *The Italian Drawings*, no. 49; Chapman, *Michelangelo Drawings*, no. 27; Gnann, *Michelangelo*, no. 39.
 (figs 163 (verso) and 164 (recto))
 pp. 242, 243, 246

19.
Seated Male Nude (ignudo) *for the Sistine Chapel Ceiling,*
c. 1511
Verso: *Figure Studies for the Sistine Chapel Ceiling,* c. 1511
   Red chalk with white heightening; verso: red chalk, metalpoint,
   279 x 214 mm
   Teylers Museum, Haarlem, inv. A 027
   Selected literature: De Tolnay, *Corpus,* I, no. 136; Van Tuyll van
   Serooskerken, *The Italian Drawings,* no. 48; Chapman, *Michelangelo
   Drawings,* no. 26; Gnann, *Michelangelo,* no. 38.
   (figs 59 (recto) and 165 (verso))
   pp. 94, 106, 107, 115, 246, 247

20.
Studies of Arms and Hands, c. 1513–1514
Verso: *Study of a Male Torso and Various Figure Studies,*
c. 1514–1518
   Pen and brown ink, red chalk, 285 x 207 mm
   Teylers Museum, Haarlem, inv. A 028
   Selected literature: De Tolnay, *Corpus,* I, no. 108; Van Tuyll van
   Serooskerken, *The Italian Drawings,* no. 51; Chapman, *Michelangelo
   Drawings,* no. 31; Echinger-Maurach, *Michelangelos Grabmal für
   Papst Julius* II, pp. 39, 43; Gnann, *Michelangelo,* no. 47.
   (fig. 85)
   pp. 132, 136, 143

21.
Anatomical Studies of a Left Leg and Arm, c. 1515–1520
Verso: *Anatomical Study of a Kneeling Man,*
c. 1515–1520
   Red chalk, 271 x 419 mm
   Teylers Museum, Haarlem, inv. A 037
   Selected literature: De Tolnay, *Corpus,* I, no. 109; Van Tuyll van
   Serooskerken, *The Italian Drawings,* no. 54; Peters and Brooks,
   Michelangelo, no. 12.
   (fig. 80)
   pp. 130, 131, 132, 143

22.
Anatomical Studies of a Left Arm and Shoulder,
c. 1515–1520
Verso: *Anatomical Studies of a Left Leg,* c. 1515–1520
   Red chalk, partly retraced with pen and brown ink, 263 x 201 mm
   Inscribed by Michelangelo, on the verso: *Socto due belle ciglia /
   chom pace e maraviglia / a postol fren de mie pensieri amore*
   Teylers Museum, Haarlem, inv. A 039
   Selected literature: De Tolnay, *Corpus,* I, no. 111; Van Tuyll van
   Serooskerken, *The Italian Drawings,* no. 53; Peters and Brooks,
   Michelangelo, no. 10.
   (figs 29 (verso) and 78 (recto))
   pp. 64, 68, 129, 130, 132

23.
Anatomical Studies of a Neck and Shoulder, c. 1515–1520
Verso: *Anatomical Study of a Shoulder,* c. 1515–1520
   Red chalk, 278 x 189 mm
   Teylers Museum, Haarlem, inv. A 042
   Selected literature: De Tolnay, *Corpus,* I, no. 115; Van Tuyll van
   Serooskerken, *The Italian Drawings,* no. 55; Peters and Brooks,
   Michelangelo, no. 9.
   (figs 83 (recto) and 84 (verso))
   pp. 131, 134, 135

24.
Male Nude with Proportions Indicated, c. 1515–1520
Verso: *Male Nude,* c. 1515–1520 (not exhibited)
   Red chalk, 291 x 180 mm
   Inscribed by Michelangelo, on the recto: *2 terzi* (upper arm sketched
   separately at the upper right), *terzo duna testa* (twice, right elbow
   and wrist), *dua e u[n] terzo a l a[n]guinaia* (right leg), *una* (left waist),
   due terzi (left ankle), *[u]na* (knee in the lower left), *una e 3 quarti* (foot
   in the lower left)
   Royal Collection Trust, Windsor, inv. RCIN 912765
   Selected literature: Popham and Wilde, *The Italian Drawings,* no.
   421; De Tolnay, *Corpus,* I, no. 61; Joannides, *Michelangelo and His
   Influence,* no. 33a; Kren, *The Renaissance Nude,* no. 57; Bormand,
   Paolozzi Strozzi and Tasso, *Il corpo e l'anima,* no. 131.
   (fig. 77)
   pp. 126, 128, 130

25.
Male Nude and Woman with a Hoe, c. 1517–1523
Verso: not by Michelangelo, *Studies of a Left Foot* (not
exhibited)
   Pen and brown ink, black chalk, 210 x 233 mm
   Inscribed by Michelangelo (?), on the recto: *rafiotare hora*
   Teylers Museum, Haarlem, inv. A 017
   Selected literature: De Tolnay, *Corpus,* I, no. 130; Van Tuyll van
   Serooskerken, *The Italian Drawings,* no. 52; Gnann, *Michelangelo,* no. 7.
   (fig. 10)
   pp. 20, 27

26.
Studies for a Deposition from the Cross, c. 1522–1524
Verso: Michelangelo and pupils, *Copies after Giotto,*
c. 1522–1524 (not exhibited)
   Red chalk, 273 x 191 mm
   Teylers Museum, Haarlem, inv. A 025
   Selected literature: De Tolnay, *Corpus,* I, no. 89; Hirst, *Michelangelo
   Draftsman,* no. 24; Nagel, 'Observations on Michelangelo's
   Late Pietà Drawings and Sculptures', pp. 548–50; Van Tuyll van
   Serooskerken, *The Italian Drawings,* no. 60; Chapman, *Michelangelo
   Drawings,* no. 72; Gnann, *Michelangelo,* no. 64.
   (fig. 115)
   pp. 177, 178

27.
Studies of a Classical Female Sculpture, c. 1523–1526
   Black chalk, 200 x 147 mm
   Casa Buonarroti, Florence, inv. 41F
   Selected literature: Barocchi, *Michelangelo e la sua scuola,* I, no. 70;
   De Tolnay, *Corpus,* II, no. 231; Falletti and Nelson, *Venere e amore,*
   no. 2; Cole, *Donatello, Michelangelo, Cellini,* no. 12; Acidini, Cecchi
   and Capretti, *Michelangelo, divino artista,* no. 44a.
   (fig. 9)
   pp. 20, 26

28.
Studies of a Back and Left Arm for the Sculpture of Day, 1524
Verso: *Study of a Shoulder for the Sculpture of* Day, 1524
(not exhibited)
> Black chalk; verso: red chalk, 192 x 257 mm
> Inscribed by Michelangelo on the recto: *in qua*
> Teylers Museum, Haarlem, inv. A 030
> Selected literature: De Tolnay, *Corpus*, II, no. 216; Hirst, *Michelangelo Draftsman*, no. 28; Van Tuyll van Serooskerken, *The Italian Drawings*, no. 56; Chapman, *Michelangelo Drawings*, no. 49; Gnann, *Michelangelo,* no. 58; Mussolin, 'I disegni di Michelangelo per le "Allegorie del Tempo"', pp. 81–84.
> (fig. 65)
> pp. 94, 108, 111, 133

29.
Study of a Left Leg for the Sculpture of Day, 1524
Verso: *Studies for the Vestibule of the Laurentian Library,*
1524 (not exhibited)
> Black chalk; verso: pen and brown ink, black chalk, 207 x 247 mm
> Teylers Museum, Haarlem, inv. A 033
> Selected literature: De Tolnay, *Corpus*, II, no. 218; Van Tuyll van Serooskerken, *The Italian Drawings*, no. 58; Chapman, *Michelangelo Drawings*, no. 52; Gnann, *Michelangelo*, no. 60; Mussolin, 'I disegni di Michelangelo per le "Allegorie del Tempo"', pp. 73–81.
> (fig. 88)
> pp. 64, 133, 138

30.
Studies of a Left Leg and Knee for the Sculpture of Day,
1524
Verso: *Studies for the Vestibule of the Laurentian Library,*
1524 (not exhibited)
> Black chalk; verso: pen and brown ink, 206 x 248 mm
> Teylers Museum, Haarlem, inv. A 033bis
> Selected literature: De Tolnay, *Corpus*, II, no. 219; Van Tuyll van Serooskerken, *The Italian Drawings*, no. 59; Chapman, *Michelangelo Drawings*, no. 53; Gnann, *Michelangelo*, no. 61; Mussolin, 'I disegni di Michelangelo per le "Allegorie del Tempo"', pp. 73–81.
> (figs 27 (recto) and 28 (verso))
> pp. 64, 65, 66

31.
Studies of a Left Arm and Shoulder for the Sculpture of
Day, 1524
> Black chalk, 266 x 162 mm
> Teylers Museum, Haarlem, inv. A 036
> Selected literature: De Tolnay, *Corpus*, II, no. 215; Van Tuyll van Serooskerken, *The Italian Drawings*, no. 57; Chapman, *Michelangelo Drawings*, no. 50; Gnann, *Michelangelo*, no. 59; Mussolin, 'I disegni di Michelangelo per le "Allegorie del Tempo"', pp. 81–84.
> (fig. 66)
> pp. 108, 112

32.
Studies of a Male Nude for the Sculpture of Night, 1524
Verso: *Studies of Legs,* 1524 (not exhibited)
> Black chalk, 280 x 343 mm
> Inscribed by Michelangelo, on the recto: *sti[n]cho*
> Gallerie degli Uffizi, Gabinetto dei Disegni e delle Stampe, Florence, inv. 18719 F
> Selected literature: Barocchi, *Michelangelo e la sua scuola,* I, no. 76; De Tolnay, *Corpus*, II, no. 210; Bambach, *Michelangelo*, no. 91; Mussolin, 'I disegni di Michelangelo per le "Allegorie del Tempo"', pp. 64–73.
> (fig. 68)
> pp. 108, 114, 126, 133

33.
Bozzetto of a River God, c. 1524
> Wax, length 22 cm
> Casa Buonarroti, Florence, inv. 542
> Selected literature: O'Grody, 'Un semplice modello', no. 4; Ragionieri, *I bozzetti michelangioleschi,* no. 3; Acidini, Cecchi and Capretti, *Michelangelo, divino artista*, no. 74.
> (fig. 8)
> pp. 20, 25

34.
Head of a Child, c. 1525
Verso: after Michelangelo, *Anatomical Studies of Legs*
(not exhibited)
> Black chalk; verso: red chalk, 237 x 160 mm
> Teylers Museum, Haarlem, inv. K I 53
> Selected literature: De Tolnay, *Corpus*, II, no. 330; Van Tuyll van Serooskerken, *The Italian Drawings*, no. 69; Chapman, *Michelangelo Drawings*, no. 69; Wallace, 'Michelangelo's Baby'; Gnann, *Michelangelo,* no. 70.
> (fig. 159)
> pp. 233, 234

35.
An Idealized Bust, c. 1525–1530
> Red chalk, 205 x 165 mm
> Ashmolean Museum, Oxford, inv. WA1846.61
> Selected literature: Parker, *Italian Schools*, no. 315; De Tolnay, *Corpus*, II, no. 323; Hirst, *Michelangelo Draftsman,* no. 23; Chapman, *Michelangelo Drawings*, no. 67; Joannides, *The Drawings of Michelangelo*, no. 31; Bambach, *Michelangelo*, no. 115.
> (fig. 73)
> pp. 28, 115, 119

36.
Portrait of Andrea Quaratesi, c. 1528–1532
> Black chalk, 410 x 290 mm
> British Museum, London, inv. 1895,0915.519
> Selected literature: Wilde, *Italian Drawings*, no. 59; De Tolnay, *Corpus*, II, no. 329; Turner, *Florentine Drawings*, no. 85; Chapman, *Michelangelo Drawings*, no. 70; Bambach, *Michelangelo*, no. 119.
> (fig. 13)
> pp. 37, 41, 50, 117, 233

37.
Studies for the Head of Leda, c. 1530
Red chalk, 354 x 269 mm
Casa Buonarroti, Florence, inv. 7F
Selected literature: Barocchi, *Michelangelo e la sua scuola*, I, no.
122; De Tolnay, *Corpus,* II, no. 301; Hirst, *Michelangelo Draftsman*,
no. 38; Gnann, *Michelangelo*, no. 75; Acidini, Cecchi and Capretti,
Michelangelo, divino artista, no. 84.
(fig. 72)
pp. 28, 115, 118

38.
Apollo-David, c. 1530
Marble, height 146 cm
Museo Nazionale del Bargello, Florence, inv. Sculture 121
Selected literature: Echinger Maurach, 'Michelangelos Statuen
des 'Apollo Pubes'', pp. 448-58; Acidini Luchinat, *The Medici,
Michelangelo*, no. 80; Acidini, *Michelangelo scultore*, pp. 210-14, 305;
Bambach, *Michelangelo*, no. 164.
(fig. 44)
pp. 88, 89, 90, 94

39.
The Descent from the Cross, c. 1530–1532
Red chalk, 375 x 280 mm
Ashmolean Museum, Oxford, inv. WA1846.88
Selected literature: Parker, *Italian Schools*, no. 342; De Tolnay,
Corpus, III, no. 431; Nagel, 'Observations on Michelangelo's Late
Pietà Drawings and Sculptures', pp. 561, 563–66; Chapman,
Michelangelo Drawings, no. 101; Joannides, *The Drawings of
Michelangelo*, no. 40; Bambach, *Michelangelo*, no. 141.
(fig. 118)
pp. 177, 181, 186

40.
Christ in Limbo, c. 1530–1533
Red and black chalk, 162 x 148 mm
Casa Buonarroti, Florence, inv. 35F
Selected literature: Barocchi, *Michelangelo e la sua scuola*, I, no.
135; De Tolnay, *Corpus*, I, no. 90; Acidini Luchinat, *The Medici,
Michelangelo,* no. 185; Gnann, *Michelangelo*, no. 51.
(fig. 162)
pp. 238, 240

41.
Studies for a Crucifixion, c. 1530–1536
Verso: *A Crucifixion and Architectural Profiles*,
c. 1530–1536 (not exhibited)
Black chalk; verso: black and red chalk, 331 x 229 mm
Teylers Museum, Haarlem, inv. A 034
Selected literature: De Tolnay, *Corpus*, II, no. 250; Ferino-Pagden,
Vittoria Colonna, no. 4.48; Van Tuyll van Serooskerken, *The Italian
Drawings*, no. 62; Chapman, *Michelangelo Drawings*, no. 89; Gnann,
Michelangelo, no. 108.
(fig. 90)
pp. 108, 133, 140, 187

42.
Draft of a letter to Tommaso de' Cavalieri, end of
December 1532
Verso: *Draft of a letter to Tommaso de' Cavalieri*,
1 January 1533
Pen and brown ink, 292 x 222 mm
Casa Buonarroti, Archivio Buonarroti, Florence, V, 61
Selected literature: *Il carteggio di Michelangelo,* III, pp. 443–44, IV,
pp. 1–2; Frommel, *Michelangelo und Tommaso dei Cavalieri*,
pp. 18–21; Bardeschi Ciulich and Ragionieri, *Michelangelo: grafia e
biografia*, no. 23; Buck, *Michelangelo's Dream*, pp. 82–83.
(fig. 16)
pp. 50, 51

43.
The Fall of Phaeton, 1533
Black chalk, 312 x 215 mm
Inscribed by Michelangelo: *[Mess]e toma[s]o se questo scizzo no[n]
ui piace ditelo a urbino [acci]o / ch[e] io abbi tempo d auerne facto un
altro doma[ni]dassera / [co]me ui promessi e se ui piace e uogliate
ch[e] io lo finisca / [rim]andante me lo*
British Museum, London, inv. 1895,0915.517
Selected literature: Wilde, *Italian Drawings,* no. 55; De Tolnay,
Corpus, II, no. 340; Hirst, *Michelangelo Draftsman*, no. 44; Chapman,
Michelangelo Drawings, no. 81; Buck, *Michelangelo's Dream*, no.
4; Marongiu, 'Le tre versioni della *Caduta di Fetonte*'; Alberti,
Rovetta and Salsi, *D'après Michelangelo*, I, pp. 162–63; Bambach,
Michelangelo, no. 127; Vowles and Lewis, *Michelangelo: The Last
Decades*, pp. 50–54.
(fig. 19)
pp. 53, 54

44.
The Dream, c. 1533
Black chalk, 398 x 280 mm
The Courtauld Gallery, London, inv. D.1978.PG.424
Selected literature: De Tolnay, *Corpus*, II, no. 333; Winner,
'Michelangelo's *Il Sogno*'; Ruvoldt, 'Michelangelo's Dream'; Buck,
Michelangelo's Dream, no. 1; Alberti, Rovetta and Salsi, *D'après
Michelangelo*, I, pp. 189–93; Bambach, *Michelangelo,* no. 131.
(figs 21 and 101)
pp. 57, 60, 90, 155, 158, 159, 162, 168, 170

45.
Draft of a letter to Bartolomeo Angelini, July-September
1533
Verso: *Fragments of love poetry and architectural studies*,
July-September 1533
Pen and brown ink, 290 x 218 mm
Casa Buonarroti, Archivio Buonarroti, Florence, V, 67
Selected literature: Barocchi, *Michelangelo e la sua scuola*, III, no.
354; De Tolnay, *Corpus*, IV, no. 562; *Il carteggio di Michelangelo,* IV,
pp. 14–15; Frommel, *Michelangelo und Tommaso dei Cavalieri,* pp.
49–50.
(figs 25 (recto) and 26 (verso))
pp. 61, 62, 63, 64

46.
Studies for Saint Lawrence for the Last Judgement,
c. 1534–1538
Verso: *Study of a Male Nude from the Back*, c. 1534–1538
(not exhibited)
> Black chalk, 242 x 182 mm
> Teylers Museum, Haarlem, inv. A 023
> Selected literature: De Tolnay, *Corpus*, III, no. 357; Ferino-Pagden,
> *Vittoria Colonna,* no. 4.51; Van Tuyll van Serooskerken, *The Italian
> Drawings*, no. 64; Chapman, *Michelangelo Drawings*, no. 84; Gnann,
> *Michelangelo*, no. 104; Vowles and Lewis, *Michelangelo: The Last
> Decades*, p. 68.
> (figs 92 (recto) and 94 (verso))
> pp. 133, 142, 146

47.
Attributed to Michelangelo, *Bozzetto for a Crucifixion*,
c. 1562–1563
> Wood, height 25 cm
> Casa Buonarroti, Florence, inv. 195
> Selected literature: O'Grody, 'Un semplice modello', no. 9;
> Ragionieri, *I bozzetti michelangioleschi*, no. 8; Acidini Luchinat, *The
> Medici, Michelangelo*, no. 82; Ragionieri, *Michelangelo, il piccolo
> crocifisso*; Rovetta, *L'ultimo Michelangelo*, no. 2.7; Acidini, Cecchi
> and Capretti, *Michelangelo, divino artista*, no. 121; Vowles and Lewis,
> *Michelangelo: The Last Decades*, pp. 225–27.
> (fig. 125)
> pp. 189, 192

Raimondi, Marcantonio
48.
Bather, after Michelangelo's Battle of Cascina,
c. 1508–1509
> Engraving, 203 x 136 mm
> Inscribed: IV × MI × AG × FLO × MAF
> Teylers Museum, Haarlem, inv. KG 00005
> Selected literature: Bartsch, *Le peintre graveur*, XIV, no. 488;
> Gramaccini and Meier, *Die Kunst der Interpretation,* no. 54; Barnes,
> *Michelangelo in Print*, no. 2; Alberti, Rovetta and Salsi, *D'après
> Michelangelo*, II, no. 1.
> (not illustrated)
> p. 211

49.
Bathers, after Michelangelo's Battle of Cascina, 1510
> Engraving, 288 x 228 mm
> Inscribed: *1510*
> Teylers Museum, Haarlem, inv. KG 00004
> Selected literature: Bartsch, *Le peintre graveur*, XIV, no. 487;
> Gramaccini and Meier, *Die Kunst der Interpretation,* no. 55; Barnes,
> *Michelangelo in Print*, no. 3; Alberti, Rovetta and Salsi, *D'après
> Michelangelo*, II, no. 3.
> (fig. 4)
> pp. 17, 21, 211

Raphael (Raffaello Sanzio)
50.
Study of Hebe and Proserpina for the Villa Farnesina, 1518
> Red chalk, 257 x 164 mm
> Teylers Museum, Haarlem, inv. A 062
> Selected literature: Knab *et al.*, *Raffaello*, no. 552; Van Tuyll van
> Serooskerken, *The Italian Drawings*, no. 236; Gnann and Plomp,
> *Raphael and His Age*, no. 40.
> (not illustrated)

Sangallo, Bastiano (Aristotile) da
51.
Bathers, Copy after the Central Segment of Michelangelo's
Battle of Cascina, c. 1542
> Oil on wood, 76.5 x 129 cm
> Holkham Hall, Norfolk, Collection of the Earl of Leicester
> Selected literature: Natali, *L'officina della maniera*, no. 20; Chapman,
> Henry and Plazotta, *Raphael*, no. 55; Franklin, *Leonardo da Vinci,
> Michelangelo and the Renaissance in Florence*, no. 13; Bambach,
> *Michelangelo*, no. 39; Delieuvin and Frank, *Léonard de Vinci*, no. 121.
> (fig. 133)
> pp. 17, 94, 100, 123, 141, 203, 205, 209, 211

Veneziano, Agostino
52.
Soldier Fastening his Breeches, after Michelangelo's
Battle of Cascina, 1517
> Engraving, 162 x 121 mm
> Inscribed: *A.V. 1517*
> Teylers Museum, Haarlem, inv. KG 00008
> Selected literature: Bartsch, *Le peintre graveur*, XIV, no. 463A;
> Barnes, *Michelangelo in Print*, no. 4; Alberti, Rovetta and Salsi,
> *D'après Michelangelo*, II, no. 8.
> (not illustrated)
> p. 211

53.
Bathers, after Michelangelo's Battle of Cascina, 1524
> Engraving, 335 x 440 mm
> Inscribed: *Michael Angelus bonarota florentinus inventor /
> MCXXIII A.V.*
> Teylers Museum, Haarlem, inv. KG 00007
> Selected literature: Bartsch, *Le peintre graveur*, XIV, no. 423;
> Gramaccini and Meier, *Die Kunst der Interpretation,* no. 85; Barnes,
> *Michelangelo in Print,* no. 5; Alberti, Rovetta and Salsi, *D'après
> Michelangelo*, II, no.11.
> (not illustrated)
> p. 211

Bibliography

PRIMARY SOURCES

Alberti, Leon Battista, *On Painting and on Sculpture. The Latin Texts of 'De Pictura' and 'De Statua'*, trans. and ed. by Cecil Grayson (Phaidon, 1972)

Aldrovandi, Ulisse, *Tutte le statue antiche, che in Roma in diversi luoghi, e case particolari si veggono, raccolte e descritte per Ulisse Aldrovandi*, in Lucio Mauro, *Le Antichità de la Città di Roma* (Ziletti, 1556)

Aristotle, *Nicomachean Ethics,* trans. and ed. by Robert C. Bartlett and Susan D. Collins (The University of Chicago Press, 2012)

Buonarroti, Michelangelo, *Canzoniere,* ed. by Maria Chiara Tarsi (Fondazione Pietro Bembo, 2015)

Buonarroti, Michelangelo, *Il Carteggio di Michelangelo*, posthumous edition by Giovanni Poggi, ed. by Paola Barocchi and Renzo Ristori, 5 vols (S.P.E.S., 1965–1983)

Buonarroti, Michelangelo, *Il Carteggio indiretto di Michelangelo*, ed. by Paula Barocchi, Kathleen Loach Bramanti and Renzo Ristori, 5 vols (S.P.E.S., 1988–1995)

Buonarroti, Michelangelo, *Complete Poems and Selected Letters of Michelangelo*, trans. by Creighton Gilbert (Modern Library, 1963)

Buonarroti, Michelangelo, *Die Dichtungen des Michelagniolo Buonarroti*, ed. by Carl Frey (Grote, 1897)

Buonarroti, Michelangelo, *The Letters of Michelangelo*, trans. by E.H. Ramsden, 2 vols (Owen, 1963)

Buonarroti, Michelangelo, *The Poetry of Michelangelo. An Annotated Translation*, trans. and ed. by James M. Saslow (Yale University Press, 1991)

Buonarroti, Michelangelo, *Rime*, ed. by Enzo Noè Girardi (Laterza, 1960)

Buonarroti, Michelangelo, *Le Rime di Michelangelo Buonarroti, pittore, scultore e architetto*, ed. by Cesare Guasti (Le Monnier, 1863[1864])

Buonarroti, Michelangelo, *Rime di Michelagnolo Buonarroti: Raccolte da Michelagnolo suo nipote*, ed. by Michelangelo Buonarroti il Giovane (Giunti, 1623)

Buonarroti, Michelangelo, *Rime e lettere*, ed. by Antonio Corsaro and Giorgio Masi (Bompiani, 2016)

Castiglione, Baldassarre, *Il Cortegiano,* ed. by Amedeo Quondam (Mondadori, 2002)

Cattani da Diacceto, Francesco, *I tre libri d'amore: con un panegirico all'amore et con la vita del detto autore fatta da m. Benedetto Varchi* (Gabriel Giolito de' Ferrari, 1561)

Cellini, Benvenuto, *The Life of Benvenuto Cellini written by Himself*, trans. by John Addington Symonds, ed. by John Pope-Hennessy (Phaidon, 1949)

Cellini, Benvenuto, *Vita di Benvenuto Cellini. Testo critico con introduzione e note storiche*, ed. by Orazio Bacci (Sansoni, 1901)

The Codex of the Anonimo Magliabechiano. Newly edited with a transcription faithful to the original manuscript and provided with an Introduction, ed. by Bouk Wierda, Lotte van ter Toolen and Henk Th. van Veen (Brill, 2024)

Il codice Magliabechiano, cl. XVII, 17, contente notizie sopra l'arte degli antichi e quella de' fiorentini da Cimabue a Michelangelo Buonarroti, scritte da Anonimo Fiorentino, ed. by Carl Frey (G. Grote'sche Verlagsbuchhandlung, 1892)

Condivi, Ascanio, *The Life of Michelangelo*, trans. by Alice Sedgwick Wohl, ed. by Hellmut Wohl (Penn State University Press, 1976)

Condivi, Ascanio, *The Life of Michelangelo,* trans. by Charles B. Holroyd, intro. by Charles Robertson (Pallas Athene, 2006)

Condivi, Ascanio, 'Life of Michelangelo Buonarroti', in Michelangelo Buonarroti, *Life, Letters, and Poetry*, trans. by George Bull (Oxford University Press, 1999)

Condivi, Ascanio, *Michel Angelo Buonarroti*, trans. by Charles Holroyd (Duckworth, 1903)

Condivi, Ascanio, *Vita di Michelagnolo Buonarroti* (Antonio Blado, 1553)

Condivi, Ascanio, *Vita di Michelagnolo Buonarroti*, ed. by Giovanni Nencioni (S.P.E.S., 1998)

Daelli, Giovanni, *Carte Michelangiolesche inedite* (Achille Migliavacca, 1865)

Dürer, Albrecht, *Vier Bücher von menschlicher Proportion (1528): Mit einem Katalog der Holzschnitte*, trans. and ed. by Berthold Hinz (Akademie Verlag, 2011)

Ficino, Marsilio, *Commentarium in Convivium Platonis: De amore*, ed. by Raymond Marcel (Les Belles Lettres, 1956)

Ficino, Marsilio, *Commentary on Plato's Symposium on Love,* trans. by Sears R. Jayne (Spring, 1985).

Ficino, Marsilio, *De vita libri tres* (Antonio Miscomini, 1480–1489)

Ficino, Marsilio, *The Letters of Marsilio Ficino*, trans. and ed. by Members of the Language Department of the School of Economic Science London, 11 vols (Shepheard-Walwyn, 1975–2015)

Ficino, Marsilio, *Platonic Theology*, ed. by James Hankins and William Bowen, trans. by Michael J.B. Allen and John Warden, 6 vols (Harvard University Press, 2001–2006)

Ficino, Marsilio, *Sopra lo amore o ver' Convito di Platone* [*De Amore*], ed. by Cosimo Bartoli (Neri Dortelata, 1544)

Ficino, Marsilio, *Theologia Platonica*: *De immortalitate animorum* (Antonio Miscomini, 1482)

Ficino, Marsilio, *Three Books on Life,* trans. by Carol V. Kaske and John R. Clark (Medieval & Renaissance Texts & Studies, 1989)

Fludd, Robert, *Tomus secundus... de supernaturali, naturali, praeternaturali et contranaturali microcosmi historia, in tractatus tres distributa. Tomi secundi, tractatus primi, sectio secunda, de technica microcosmi historia* (J. Th. de Brij/Hieronymus Galler, 1619)

Ghiberti, Lorenzo, *Lorenzo Ghibertis Denkwürdigkeiten (I commentarii)*, ed. by Julius von Schlosser (Julius Bard, 1912)

Giannotti, Donato, *Dialoghi de' giorni che Dante consumo nel cercare l'Inferno e'l Purgatorio (1546)* (Tipografia Galileiana, 1859)

Hogarth, William, *The Analysis of Beauty* (Reeves, 1753)

Holanda, Francisco de, *Romeinse dialogen: Gesprekken met Michelangelo en Vittoria Colonna,* trans. by Adri Boon (Meulenhoff, 1993)

Leonardo da Vinci, *The Literary Works of Leonardo da Vinci*, ed. by Jean Paul Richter, 2 vols (Phaidon, 1970)

Lomazzo, Giovanni Paolo, *Idea del tempio della pittura di Gio. Paolo Lomazzo pittore. Nella quale egli discorre dell'origine, & fondamento delle cose contenute nel suo trattato dell'arte della pittura* (Paolo Gottardo Ponto, 1590)

Lomazzo, Giovanni Paolo, *Scritti sulle arti*, ed. by Roberto Ciardi, 2 vols (Marchi & Bertolli, 1973–1974)

Lucian of Samosata, *Lucian, Volume VIII*, trans. by A.M. Harmon (Harvard University Press, 1967)

Petrarch, *Epistolae familiares* (Johannes & Gregorius de Gregoriis, 1492)

Petrarch, *Rerum vulgarium fragmenta*, ed. and annot. by Giuseppe Savoca (Olschki, 2008)

Pliny the Elder (Gaius Plinius Secundus), *Natural History,* trans. by H. Rackham, W.H.S. Jones and D.E. Eichholz, 9 vols (Harvard University Press, 1938–1963)

Ripa, Cesare, *Iconologia overo descrittione de diverse imagini* (Pietro Paolo Tozzi, 1611)

Rocco, Antonio, *Alcibiade a Scola*, ed. by Laura Coci (Salerno editrice, 1988)

Vaenius, Otto, *Amorum emblemata* (Venalia apud auctorem, 1608)

Varchi, Benedetto, *Deux leçons sur l'art*, ed. by Frédérique Dubard de Gaillarbois (Classiques Garnier, 2020)

Varchi, Benedetto, *Due lezzioni di M. Benedetto Varchi, nella prima delle quali si dichiara un Sonetto di M. Michelagnolo Buonarroti. Nella seconda si disputa quale sia piu nobile arte la Scultura, o la Pittura, con una lettera d'esso Michelagnolo, et piu altri Eccellentiss. Pittori, et Scultori, sopra la Quistione sopradetta* (Lorenzo Torrentino, 1549)

Varchi, Benedetto, *Orazione funerale di Messer Benedetto Varchi fatta, e recitata da lui pubblicamente nell'essequie di Michelagnolo Buonarroti in Firenze nella chiesa di San Lorenzo* (I Giunti, 1564)

Varchi, Benedetto, *Paragone – Rangstreit der Künste*, ed. by Oskar Bätschmann and Tristan Weddigen (Wissenschaftliche Buchgesellschaft, 2013)

Vasari, Giorgio, *Artists of the Renaissance; A Selection from Lives of the Artists,* trans. and ed. by George Bull (Book Club Associates, 1979)

Vasari, Giorgio, *La vita di Michelangelo nelle redazioni del 1550 e del 1568*, ed. and comm. by Paola Barocchi, 5 vols (Ricciardi, 1962–1964)

Vasari, Giorgio, *Le vite de' più eccellenti architetti, pittori, e scultori Italiani* (Torrentino, 1550)

Vasari, Giorgio, *Le vite de'più eccellenti pittori, scultori ed architettori* (Giunti, 1568)

Vasari, Giorgio, *Le vite de' più eccellenti pittori, scultori ed architettori. Con nuove annotazioni e commenti di Gaetano Milanesi,* ed. by Gaetano Milanesi, 9 vols (Sansoni, 1878–1885)

Vasari, Giorgio, *Le vite de' più eccellenti pittori, scultori ed architettori: nelle redazioni del 1550 e 1568*, ed. by Rosanna Bettarini and Paola Barocchi, 6 vols (Sansoni, 1966–1987)

Vasari, Giorgio, *Le vite dei più eccellenti pittori, scultori e architetti,* ed. by Maurizio Marini (New Compton, 1991)

Vasari, Giorgio, 'Life of Michelangelo Buonarroti', in *The Lives of the Artists*, trans. by George Bull (Penguin, 1987)

Vasari, Giorgio, *Lives of the Most Eminent Painters Sculptors and Architects*, trans. by Gaston Du C. de Vere (Abrams, 1979)

SECONDARY LITERATURE

Acidini Luchinat, Cristina, *Michelangelo scultore* (Federico Motta Editore, 2006)

Acidini Luchinat, Cristina *et al.*, *The Medici, Michelangelo and the Art of Late Renaissance Florence* (Yale University Press, 2002)

Acidini, Cristina, Alessandro Cecchi and Elena Capretti (eds), *Michelangelo, divino artista* (Sagep Editori, 2020)

Adams, Alison, Stephen Rawles and Alison Saunders, *A Bibliography of French Emblem Books of the Sixteenth and Seventeenth Centuries*, 2 vols (Librairie Droz, 1999)

Adler, Sara M., 'Strong Mothers, Strong Daughters: The Representation of Female Identity in Vittoria Colonna's Rime and Carteggio', *Italica* 77, no. 3 (2000), pp. 311–30

Agoston, Laura Camille, 'Male/Female, Italy/Flanders, Michelangelo/Vittoria Colonna', *Renaissance Quarterly* 58, no. 4 (2005), pp. 175–219

Akker, Paul van den, *Sporen van vaardigheid. De ontwerpmethode voor de figuurhouding in de Italiaanse tekenkunst van de renaissance* (Uniepers, 1991)

Alberti, Alessia, Alessandro Rovetta and Claudio Salsi (eds), *D'après Michelangelo*, 2 vols (Marsilio, 2015)

Allen, M.J.B., 'Ficino, Marsilio', in *Dictionary of Gnosis and Western Esotericism,* ed. by Wouter J. Hanegraaff *et al.* (Brill, 2005), pp. 360–61

Amerson, L. Price, 'The Problem of the Ecorché: A Catalogue Raisonné of Models and Statuettes from the Sixteenth Century and Later Periods' (unpublished dissertation, Pennsylvania State University, 1975)

Ames-Lewis, Francis, *Drawing in Early Renaissance Italy* (Yale University Press, 1981)

Anderson, Brian, *The Fraternity of the Estranged: The Fight for Homosexual Rights in England, 1891–1908* (Matador, 2018)

Annas, Julia, 'Plato and Aristotle on Friendship and Altruism', *Mind* 86, no. 344 (1977), pp. 532–54

Arrizabalaga, John, John Henderson and Roger French (eds), *The Great Pox: The French Disease in Renaissance Europe* (Yale University Press, 1997)

Aste, Richard, 'Bartolomeo Bettini e la decorazione della sua "camera" fiorentina', in *Venere e Amore: Michelangelo e la nuova bellezza ideale*, ed. by Franca Falletti and Jonathan Katz Nelson (Giunti, 2002), pp. 2–25

Aymonino, Adriano and Anne Varick Lauder, *Drawn from the Antique: Artists & the Classical Ideal* (Sir John Soane's Museum, 2015)

Baker, Nicholas Scott, 'Power and Passion in Sixteenth-Century Florence: The Sexual and Political Reputations of Alessandro and Cosimo I de' Medici', *Journal of the History of Sexuality* 19, no. 3 (2010), pp. 432–57

Baldassarri, Marina, *Bande giovanili e 'vizio nefando': violenza e sessualità nella Roma barocca* (Viella, 2005)

Bambach, Carmen C., *Leonardo da Vinci Rediscovered*, 4 vols (Yale University Press, 2019)

Bambach, Carmen C., 'Letters from Michelangelo', *Apollo* 177, no. 608 (2013), pp. 58–67

Bambach, Carmen C., *Michelangelo: Divine Draftsman and Designer* (The Metropolitan Museum of Art, 2017)

Bambach, Carmen C., 'The Purchases of Cartoon Paper for Leonardo's "Battle of Anghiari" and Michelangelo's "Battle of Cascina"', *I Tatti Studies* 8 (1999), pp. 105–33

Bambach, Carmen C., 'Rubens, "Pictor Doctus", and His Response to Leonardo', in *The Touch of Pygmalion: Rubens and Sculpture in Rome*, ed. by Francesca Cappelletti and Lucia Simonato (Electa, 2023), pp. 33–58

Bardeschi Ciulich, Lucilla, *Costanza ed evoluzione nella scrittura di Michelangelo* (Cantini, 1989)

Bardeschi Ciulich, Lucilla 'Michelangelo: un percorso attraverso gli autografi', in *Michelangelo: Grafia e biografia*, ed. by Lucilla Bardeschi Ciulich and Pina Ragionieri (Mandragora, 2004), pp. 21–29

Bardeschi Ciulich, Lucilla and Pina Ragionieri (eds), *Michelangelo: grafia e biografia. Disegni e autografi del Maestro* (Mandragora, 2004)

Barkan, Leonard, *Michelangelo: A Life on Paper* (Princeton University Press, 2011)

Barkan, Leonard, *Transuming Passion: Ganymede and the Erotics of Humanism* (Stanford University Press, 1991)

Barkan, Leonard, *Unearthing the Past: Archaeology and Aesthetics in the Making of Renaissance Culture* (Yale University Press, 1999)

Barnes, Bernardine, *Michelangelo and the Viewer in His Time* (Reaktion, 2017)

Barnes, Bernadine, *Michelangelo in Print. Reproductions as Response in the Sixteenth Century* (Routledge, 2010)

Barocchi, Paola, *Michelangelo e la sua scuola: I disegni dell'Archivio Buonarroti* (Olschki, 1964)

Barocchi, Paola, *Michelangelo e la sua scuola: I disegni di Casa Buonarroti e degli Uffizi*, 2 vols (Olschki, 1962)

Barocchi, Paola (ed.), *Scritti d'arte del Cinquecento*, 3 vols (Ricciardi, 1971–77)

Barolsky, Paul, 'The Meaning of Michelangelo's Minos', *Notes in the History of Art* 25, no. 4 (2006), pp. 30–31

Bartsch, Adam von, *Le peintre graveur*, 22 vols (Olms, 1970)

Bassanese, Fiora A., 'Vittoria Colonna, Christ and Gender', *Il Veltro* 40, nos. 1–2 (1996), pp. 53–57

Bassanese, Fiora A., 'Vittoria Colonna's Man/God', *Annali d'Italianistica* 25 (2007), pp. 263–74

Bedon, Anna, 'La professione di Tommaso de' Cavalieri', in *Michelangelo: Arte, materia, lavoro*, ed. by Alessandro Nova and Vitale Zanchettin (Marsilio, 2019), pp. 137–51

Bentz, Katherine M., 'Ulisse Aldrovandi, Antiquities, and the Roman Inquisition', *Sixteenth Century Journal* 43, no. 4 (2012), pp. 963–88

Birke, Veronika, and Janine Kertész, *Die Italienischen Zeichnungen der Albertina*, 4 vols (Hirmer, 1992)

Bohde, Daniela, 'Skin and the Search for the Interior: The Representation of Flaying in the Art and Anatomy of the Cinquecento', in *Bodily Extremities: Preoccupations with the Human Body in Early Modern European Culture*, ed. by Florike Egmond and Robert Zwijnenberg (Ashgate, 2003), pp. 10–47

Bolzoni, Marco Simone, 'In the Footsteps of Michelangelo', in *Triumph of the Body: Michelangelo and Sixteenth-Century Italian Draughtsmanship*, ed. by Zoltán Kárpáti (Museum of Fine Arts Budapest, 2019), pp. 111–36

Bormand, Marc, Beatrice Paolozzi Strozzi and Francesca Tasso (eds), *Il corpo e l'anima, da Donatello a Michelangelo. Scultura italiana del Rinascimento* (Officina Libraria, 2021)

Borris, Kenneth (ed.), *Same-Sex Desire in the English Renaissance: A Sourcebook of Texts, 1470–1650* (Routledge, 2004)

Borris, Kenneth and George Rousseau (eds), *The Sciences of Homosexuality in Early Modern Europe* (Routledge, 2008)

Bredekamp, Horst, *Michelangelo* (Verlag Klaus Wagenbach, 2021)

Brothers, Cammy, *Michelangelo, Drawing, and the Invention of Architecture* (Yale University Press, 2008)

Brown, David Alan, *Virtue and Beauty. Leonardo's 'Ginevra de' Benci' and Renaissance Portraits of Women* (Princeton University Press, 2001)

Buck, Stephanie and Tatiana Bissolati (eds), *Michelangelo's Dream* (Paul Holberton, 2010)

Bull, George, *Michelangelo: A Biography* (Viking, 1995)

Burke, Jill, 'The Body in Artistic Theory and Practice', in *The Renaissance Nude*, ed. by Thomas Kren (Getty Publications, 2018), pp. 183–99

Burke, Jill, *The Italian Renaissance Nude* (Yale University Press, 2018)

Butler, Shane, *The Passions of John Addington Symonds* (Oxford University Press, 2022)

Butler, Shane, 'Things Left Unsaid', *I Tatti Studies* 21, no. 2 (2018), pp. 245–74

Byatt, Lucinda, *Niccolò Ridolfi and the Cardinal's Court. Politics, Patronage and Service in Sixteenth-Century Italy* (Routledge, 2022)

Cady, Joseph, '"Masculine Love" of the "Princes of Sodom" "Practising the Art of Ganymede" at Henri III's Court: The Homosexuality of Henri III and his *Mignons* in Pierre de L'Estoile's *Mémoires-Journaux*', in *Desire and Discipline: Sex and Sexuality in the Premodern West*, ed. by Konrad Eisenbichler and Jacqueline Murray (University of Toronto Press, 1996), pp. 123–54

Cady, Joseph, '"Masculine Love," Renaissance Writing, and the "New Invention" of Homosexuality', *Journal of Homosexuality* 23 (1992), pp. 9–40

Caglioti, Fancesco, *Donatello e i Medici, storia del 'David' e della 'Giuditta'*, 2 vols (Olschki, 2000)

Caglioti, Francesco, 'Michelangelo the Sculptor: A Lifetime of Formal Obsessions', in *Michelangelo: Divine Draftsman and Designer*, ed. by Carmen C. Bambach (The Metropolitan Museum of Art, 2017), pp. 279–86

Campbell, Stephen J., '"Fare una Cosa Morta Parer Viva": Michelangelo, Rosso, and the (Un)Divinity of Art', *The Art Bulletin* 84, no. 4 (2002), pp. 596–620

Carlino, Andrea, *Books of the Body. Anatomical Ritual and Renaissance Learning*, trans. by John Tedeschi and Anne C. Tedeschi (University of Chicago Press, 1999)

Carlson, Raymond, '"Eccellentissimo poeta et amatore divinissimo": Benedetto Varchi and Michelangelo's Poetry at the Accademia Fiorentina', *Italian Studies* 69, no. 2 (2014), pp. 169–88

Carlson, Raymond, 'Epistolary Criticism, the Minerva *Christ*, and Michelangelo's "Garzone" Problem', *Mitteilungen des Kunsthistorischen Institutes in Florenz* 63, no. 1 (2021), pp. 126–45

Cascio, Gandolfo, *Michelangelo in Parnaso: La ricezione delle Rime tra gli scrittori* (Marsilio, 2019)

Cazort, Mimi, Monique Kornell and K.B. Roberts, *The Ingenious Machine of Nature. Four Centuries of Art and Anatomy* (National Gallery of Canada, 1996)

Chapman, Hugo, *Michelangelo Drawings: Closer to the Master* (British Museum Press, 2005)

Chapman, Hugo and Marzia Faietti, *Fra Angelico to Leonardo. Italian Renaissance Drawings* (British Museum Press, 2010)

Chapman, Hugo, Tom Henry and Carol Plazzotta, *Raphael: From Urbino to Rome* (National Gallery Company, 2004)

Chastel, André, *A Chronicle of Italian Renaissance Painting,* trans. by Linda Murray and Peter Murray, (Cornell University, 1984)

Chastel, André, 'Treatise on Painting', in *The Unknown Leonardo*, ed. by Ladislao Reti (Hutchinson, 1974), pp. 216–39

Ciardi, Roberto Paolo, 'Michelangelo come Galeno. Un'ipotesi iconological', in *Studi in onore di Giulio Carlo Argan*, vol. 1, ed. by Silvana Macchioni and Bianca Tavassi la Greca (Multigrafica Editore, 1984), pp. 173–81

Clark, Kenneth, *Leonardo da Vinci. An Account of His Development as an Artist* (Cambridge University Press, 1939)

Clark, Kenneth, *The Nude: A Study in Ideal Form* (Pantheon Books, 1956)

Clark, Kenneth and Carlo Pedretti, *The Drawings of Leonardo da Vinci in the Collection of Her Majesty the Queen at Windsor Castle*, 2nd ed., 2 vols (Phaidon, 1968)

Clayton, Martin and Ron Philo, *Leonardo da Vinci: Anatomist* (Royal Collection Publications, 2012)

Clements, Robert J., *The Poetry of Michelangelo* (New York University Press, 1965)

Coelen, Peter van der, 'Cornelis Bos: Where Did He Go? Some New Discoveries and Hypotheses about a Sixteenth-Century Engraver and Publisher', *Simiolus* 23, nos. 2–3 (1995), pp. 119–46

Coelho, Victor, 'Bronzino's Lute Player: Music and Youth Culture in Renaissance Florence', in *Renaissance Studies in Honor of Joseph Connors*, ed. by Machtelt Israëls and Louis Alexander Waldman, 2 vols (Villa I Tatti, 2013), II, pp. 650–59

Cole, Michael W. (ed.), *Donatello, Michelangelo, Cellini: Sculptor's Drawings from Renaissance Italy* (Paul Holberton, 2014)

Collett, Barry, *A Long and Troubled Pilgrimage: The Correspondence of Marguerite D'Angoulême and Vittoria Colonna 1540–1545* (Princeton Theological Seminar, 2000)

Coonin, A. Victor, 'Beyond the Binary: Michelangelo, Tommaso de' Cavalieri, and a Drawing at Windsor Castle', *Artibus et Historiae* 78 (2018), pp. 255–66

Coppola, Edward D., 'The Discovery of the Pulmonary Circulation: A New Approach', *Bulletin of the History of Medicine* 31, no. 3 (1957), pp. 44–77

Corsaro, Antonio, 'Intorno alle rime di Michelangelo Buonarroti: La silloge del 1546', *Giornale storico della letteratura italiana* 185 (2009), pp. 536–69

Corsaro, Antonio, 'La prima circolazione manoscritta delle rime di Michelangelo', *Medioevo e Rinascimento* 25, no. 22 (2011), pp. 279–97

Costa, Giorgio, 'Michelangelo e la stampa: la mancata pubblicazione delle "Rime"', *ACME: Annali della Facoltà di lettere e di filosofia dell'Università degli Studi di Milano* 60 (2007), pp. 211–44

Daly, Peter M. (ed.), *Andreas Alciatus*, 2 vols (University of Toronto Press, 1985)

De Faveri, Lorena, *Le traduzioni di Luciano in Italia nel XV e XVI secolo* (Hakkert, 2002)

Delieuvin, Vincent and Louis Frank, *Léonard de Vinci* (Louvre Éditions/Éditions Hazan, 2019)

De Tolnay, Charles, *Corpus dei Disegni di Michelangelo*, 4 vols (Istituto geografico De Agostini, 1975–80)

Diana, Esther, 'Anatomy between Public and Private in 14th–16th Century Europe: Social Contexts, Scenarios and Personages', in *Anatomy and Surgery: From Antiquity to the Renaissance*, ed. by Hélène Perdicoyianni Paléologou (Hakkert, 2016), pp. 329–74

Dionisotti, Carlo, 'Considerazioni sulla morte di Poliziano,' in *Culture et société en Italie du Moyen-Age à la Renaissance: Hommage à André Rochon* (Université de la Sorbonne nouvelle, 1985), pp. 145–56

Doel, Marieke J.E. van den, *Ficino and Fantasy: Imagination in Renaissance Art and Theory from Botticelli to Michelangelo* (Brill, 2022)

Doel, Marieke J.E. van den, 'Marsilio Ficino on Melancholy and Artistic Genius', in *The Making of the Humanities: The Emergence of the Humanities in Early Modern Europe,* ed. by Rens Bod, Jaap Maat and Thijs Weststeijn (Amsterdam University Press, 2009), pp. 107–32

Doel, Marieke J.E. van den and Wouter J. Hanegraaff, 'Imagination', in *Dictionary of Gnosis and Western Esotericism,* ed. by Wouter J. Hanegraaff *et al.* (Brill, 2005), pp. 606–16

Draper, James, *Bertoldo di Giovanni, Sculptor of the Medici Household: Critical Reappraisal and Catalogue Raisonné* (University of Missouri Press, 1992)

Dunkelman, Martha, 'From Microcosm to Macrocosm: Michelangelo and Ancient Gems', *Zeitschrift für Kunstgeschichte* 73, no. 3 (2010), pp. 363–76

Echinger-Maurach, Claudia, *Michelangelos Grabmal für Papst Julius II* (Hirmer Verlag, 2009)

Echinger Maurach, Claudia, 'Michelangelos Statuen des "Apollo Pubes" und Raffaels "Apollo Citharoedus" in der "Schule von Athen"', *Mitteilungen des Kunsthistorischen Institutes in Florenz* 43, nos. 2–3 (1999), pp. 420–70

Echinger-Maurach, Claudia, 'Zu Michelangelos Skizze für den verlorenen Bronzedavid und zum Beginn der gran maniera degli ignudi in seinem Entwurf für den Marmordavid', *Zeitschrift für Kunstgeschichte* 61, no. 3 (1998), pp. 301–38

Eisenbichler, Konrad, 'The Religious Poetry of Michelangelo: The Mystical Sublimation,' *Renaissance and Reformation/Renaissance et Réforme* 11, no. 1 (1987), pp. 121–34

Ekserdjian, David, 'Michelangelo's Bronze "David", Its Ancestry and Progeny', in *Scritti per Eugenio: 27 testi per Eugenio Riccòmini*, ed. by Marco Riccòmini (Modigliana, 2007), pp. 30–41

Elam, Caroline, 'Art in the Service of Liberty: Battista della Palla. Art Agent for Francis I', *I Tatti Studies* 5 (1993), pp. 33–109

Elam, Caroline, '"Ché ultima mano!"': Tiberio Calcagni's Marginal Annotations to Condivi's Life of Michelangelo', *Renaissance Quarterly* 51, no. 2 (1998), pp. 475–97

Elam, Caroline, '"Che ultima mano?"': Tiberio Calcagni's "Postille" to Condivi's Life of Michelangelo', in Ascanio Condivi, *Vita di Michelagnolo Buonarroti*, ed. by Giovanni Nencioni (S.P.E.S, 1998), pp. xxiii–xlvi

Elam, Caroline, 'Lorenzo de' Medici's Sculpture Garden', *Mitteilungen des Kunsthistorischen Institutes in Florenz* 36, nos. 1–2 (1992), pp. 40–84

Elam, Caroline, 'The Site and Early Building History of Michelangelo's New Sacristy', *Mitteilungen des Kunsthistorischen Institutes in Florenz* 23, nos. 1-2 (1979), pp. 155–86

Elkins, James, 'Michelangelo and the Human Form: His Knowledge and Use of Anatomy', *Art History* 7, no. 2 (1984), pp. 176–86

Evan, Yael, 'The Heroine as Hero in Michelangelo's Art', *Woman's Art Journal* 11, no. 1 (1990), pp. 29–33

Falletti, Franca and Jonathan Katz Nelson (eds), *Venere e amore: Michelangelo e la nuova bellezza ideale* (Giunti, 2002)

Feldman, Martha, *City Culture and the Madrigal at Venice* (University of California Press, 1995)

Ferguson, Gary, *Same-sex Marriage in Renaissance Rome: Sexuality, Identity, and Community in Early Modern Europe* (Cornell University Press, 2016)

Ferino-Pagden, Sylvia (ed.), *Vittoria Colonna: Dichterin und Muse Michelangelos* (Skira Editore, 1997)

Filedt Kok, Jan Piet and Marjolein Leesberg, *The New Hollstein: Dutch & Flemish Etchings, Engravings and Woodcuts 1450–1700. The De Gheyn Family*, 2 vols (Sound & Vision, 2000)

Finlay, Michael, *Western Writing Implements in the Age of the Quill Pen* (Plains, 1990)

Forlani Tempesti, Anna, 'Studiare dal nature nella Firenze di fine '400', in *Florentine Drawing at the Time of Lorenzo the Magnificent*, ed. by Elizabeth Cropper (Nuova Alfa, 1994), pp. 1–15

Franklin, David (ed.), *From Raphael to Carracci. The Art of Papal Rome* (National Gallery of Canada, 2009)

Franklin, David (ed.), *Leonardo da Vinci, Michelangelo and the Renaissance in Florence* (Yale University Press, 2005)

Freedberg, David, *The Power of Images: Studies in the History and Theory of Response* (University of Chicago Press, 1989)

Frommel, Christoph Luitpold, *Michelangelo und Tommaso dei Cavalieri* (Castrum Peregrini, 1979)

Frommel, Christoph Luitpold, 'Michelangelos Handschrift und die Chronologie seiner frühen Zeichnungen', in *Michelangelo als Zeichner. Akten des Internationalen Kolloquiums Wien, Albertina-Museum, 19.–20. November 2010*, ed. by Claudia Echinger-Maurach, Achim Gnann and Joachim Poeschke (Rhema, 2013), pp. 117–44

Frommel, Christoph Luitpold and Maria Forcellino, *Michelangelo's Tomb for Julius II: Genesis and Genius* (J. Paul Getty Museum, 2016)

Fusco, Laurie, 'The Nude as Protagonist: Pollaiuolo's Figural Style Explicated by Leonardo's Study of Static Anatomy, Movement, and Functional Anatomy' (unpublished dissertation, New York University, 1978)

Fusco, Laurie and Gino Corti, *Lorenzo de' Medici: Collector and Antiquarian* (Cambridge University Press, 2006)

Gamberini, Diletta, *New Apelleses and New Apollos: Poet-Artists Around the Court of Florence (1537–1587)* (De Gruyter, 2022)

Garrard, Mary D., *Artemisia Gentileschi: The Hero in Italian Baroque Art* (Princeton University, 1989)

Garrard, Mary D., 'The Cloister and the Square. Gender Dynamics in Renaissance Florence', *Early Modern Women* 11, no. 1 (2016), pp. 5–44

Gayford, Martin, *Michelangelo: His Epic Life* (Fig Tree, 2013)

Gerbino, Giuseppe, 'Florentine *Petrarchismo* and the Early Madrigal: Reflections on the Theory of Origins', *Journal of Medieval and Early Modern Studies* 35, no. 3 (2005), pp. 607–28

Gnann, Achim, *Michelangelo: The Drawings of a Genius* (Hatje Cantz, 2010)

Gnann, Achim, 'Naked in the Sistine Chapel', in *Michelangelo and Beyond*, ed. by Eva Michel and Klaus Albrecht Schröder (Prestel, 2023), pp. 56–63

Gnann, Achim and Michiel Plomp, *Raphael and His School* (Waanders, 2012)

Golzio, Vincenzo, *Raffaello nei documenti, nelle testimonianze dei contemporanei e nella letteratura del suo secolo* (Arti grafiche Panetto & Petrelli, 1936)

Gould, Cecil, *Michelangelo: Battle of Cascina* (University of Newcastle upon Tyne, 1966)

Gramaccini, Norberto and Hans Jakob Meier, *Die Kunst der Interpretation. Italienische Reproduktionsgrafik 1485–1600* (Deutscher Kunstverlag, 2009)

Gramatzki, Susanne, *Zur lyrischen Subjektivität in den Rime Michelangelo Buonarrotis* (Winter Verlag, 2004)

Grassi, Umberto, *L'Offizio sopra l'Onestà: Il controllo della sodomia nella Lucca del Cinquecento* (Mimesis, 2014)

Greenblatt, Stephen, *Renaissance Self-Fashioning: From More to Shakespeare* (University of Chicago Press, 1980)

Harprath, Richard, *Italienische Zeichnungen des 16. Jahrhunderts aus eigenem Besitz* (Staatliche Graphische Sammlung München, 1977)

Hartt, Frederick, *Michelangelo Drawings* (Abrams, 1970)

Haseth Möller, Titia de, 'Anatomical Study Models from the Studio of Johan Gregor van der Schardt', *Simiolus* 41, no. 3 (2019), pp. 153–76

Haskell, Francis and Nicholas Penny, *Taste and the Antique: The Lure of Classical Sculpture 1500–1900* (Yale University Press, 1981)

Hatfield, Rab, *The Wealth of Michelangelo* (Edizioni di storia e letteratura, 2002)

Hibbard, Howard, *Michelangelo: Painter, Sculptor, Architect* (Vendome, 1978)

Hickson, Sally, 'Gian Cristoforo Romano in Rome: With Some Thoughts on the Mausoleum of Halicarnassus and the Tomb of Julius II', *Renaissance and Reformation/Renaissance et Réforme* 33, no. 1 (2010), pp. 3–30

Hillard, Caroline S., 'Michelangelo and Realdo Colombo: A Dialogue on Art and Anatomy', in *Italian Art, Society, and Politics: A Festschrift in Honor of Rob Hatfield*, ed. by Barbara Deimling, Jonathan K. Nelson and Gary M. Radke (Syracuse University in Florence, 2007), pp. 163–77

Hirst, Michael, *Michelangelo. Volume I: The Achievement of Fame, 1475–1534* (Yale University Press, 2011)

Hirst, Michael, *Michelangelo and his Drawings* (Yale University Press, 1988)

Hirst, Michael, *Michelangelo Draftsman* (Olivetti, 1988)

Hirst, Michael, 'Michelangelo in Florence: "David" in 1503 and "Hercules" in 1506', *The Burlington Magazine* 142, no. 1169 (2000), pp. 487–92

Hirst, Michael, *Sebastiano del Piombo* (Clarendon, 1981)

Hirst, Michael and Jill Dunkerton, *Making and Meaning: The Young Michelangelo* (National Gallery London, 1994)

Hollstein, F.W.H., *Dutch and Flemish Etchings, Engravings and Woodcuts, ca. 1450–1700. Volume III: Boekhorst-Brueghel* (Menno Hertzberger, 1949)

Hollstein, F.W.H., *Dutch and Flemish Etchings, Engravings and Woodcuts, ca. 1450–1700. Volume VII: Fouceel-Gole* (Menno Hertzberger, 1949)

Hughes, Anthony, *Michelangelo* (Phaidon, 1997)

Hupe, Eric R., 'Michelangelo's Strozzi Tondi? Securing Status with Art', in *Michelangelo in the New Millennium: Conversations about Artistic Practice, Patronage and Christianity*, ed. by Tamara Smithers (Brill, 2016), pp. 47–75

Jacobs, Fredrika, 'Aretino and Michelangelo, Dolce and Titian: "Femmina, Masculo, Grazia"', *The Art Bulletin* 82, no. 1 (2000), pp. 51–67

Jacobs, Fredrika, '(Dis)assembling: Marsyas, Michelangelo, and the Accademia del Disegno', *The Art Bulletin* 84, no. 3 (2002), pp. 426–48

Joannides, Paul, *The Drawings of Michelangelo and His Followers in the Ashmolean Museum* (Cambridge University Press, 2007)

Joannides, Paul, *The Drawings of Raphael* (Phaidon, 1983)

Joannides, Paul, 'Leonardo da Vinci, Peter-Paul Rubens, Pierre-Nolasque Bergeret and "The Fight for the Standard"', *Achademia Leonardi Vinci* 1 (1988), pp. 76–86

Joannides, Paul, *Michel-Ange, élèves et copistes*, Musée du Louvre, Cabinet des dessins, Inventaire général des dessins italiens, 6 (Réunion des musées nationaux, 2003)

Joannides, Paul, *Michelangelo and His Influence. Drawings from Windsor Castle* (Lund Humphries Publishers, 1996)

Joannides, Paul, 'Michelangelo to 1501', in *Triumph of the Body: Michelangelo and Sixteenth-Century Italian Draughtsmanship*, ed. by Zoltán Kárpáti (Museum of Fine Arts Budapest, 2019), pp. 23–48

Joannides, Paul, 'A New Drawing by Sebastiano del Piombo for the Semi-dome of the Borgherini Chapel', in *Michelangelo and Sebastiano* ed. by Matthias Wivel (National Gallery Company, 2017), pp. 189–96

Joannides, Paul, '"Primitivism" in the Late Drawings of Michelangelo: The Master's Construction of an Old-Age Style', *Studies in the History of Art* 33 (1992), pp. 245–61

Joannides, Paul with the assistance of Michael Clifford, 'On a War-Horse at Cascina', in *Michelangelo als Zeichner. Akten des Internationalen Kolloquiums Wien, Albertina-Museum, 19.–20. November 2010*, ed. by Claudia Echinger-Maurach, Achim Gnann and Joachim Poeschke (Rhema, 2013), pp. 237–52

Johnson, Geraldine A., 'Idol or Ideal: The Power and Potency of Female Public Sculpture', in *Picturing Women in Renaissance and Baroque Italy*, ed. by Geraldine A. Johnson and Sara F. Matthews Grieco (Cambridge University Press, 1997), pp. 222–45

Jones, Jonathan, *The Lost Battles. Leonardo, Michelangelo, and the Artistic Duel That Defined the Renaissance* (Kopf Doubleday, 2010)

Jurdjevic, Mark, *Guardians of Republicanism. The Valori Family and the Florentine Renaissance* (Oxford University Press, 2008)

Kárpáti, Zoltán (ed.), *Triumph of the Body. Michelangelo and Sixteenth-Century Italian Draughtsmanship* (Budapest Museum of Fine Arts, 2019)

Keizer, Joost, 'History, Origins, Recovery. Michelangelo and the Politics of Art' (unpublished dissertation, Leiden University, 2008)

Keizer, Joost, 'Michelangelo, Drawing, and the Subject of Art', *The Art Bulletin* 93, no. 3 (2011), pp. 304–24

Kemp, Martin, '"Il Concetto dell'Anima" in Leonardo's Early Skull Studies', *Journal of the Warburg and Courtauld Institutes* 34 (1971), pp. 115–34

Kemp, Martin and Juliana Barone, *I disegni di Leonardo da Vinci e della sua cerchia nelle collezioni della Gran Bretagna* (Giunti, 2010)

Kent, Dale, *Friendship, Love, and Trust in Renaissance Florence* (Harvard University Press, 2009)

Kirkendale, Warren, *Emilio de' Cavalieri 'Gentiluomo romano': His Life and Letters, His Role as Superintendent of All the Arts at the Medici Court, and His Musical Compositions* (Olschki, 2001)

Kleinbub, Christian K., *Michelangelo's Inner Anatomies* (Pennsylvania State University Press, 2020)

Knab, Eckhart, Erwin Mitsch, Konrad Oberhuber, Sylvia Ferino-Pagden and Paolo Dal Poggetto, *Raffaello, I disegni* (Nardini, 1983)

Kornell, Monique, 'Artists and the Study of Anatomy in Sixteenth-Century Italy', 2 vols (unpublished dissertation, University of London, Warburg Institute, 1992)

Kren, Thomas (ed.), *The Renaissance Nude* (J. Paul Getty Museum, 2018)

Kristeller, Paul Oskar, 'Francesco da Diacceto and Florentine Platonism in the Sixteenth Century', in *Miscellania Giovanni Mercati IV*, 124 (Biblioteca Apostolica Vaticana, 1946), pp. 260–304

Kruszynski, Anette, *Der Ganymed-Mythos in Emblematik und mythographischer Literatur des 16. Jahrhunderts* (Wernersche Verlagsgesellschaft Worms, 1985)

Kwakkelstein, Michael W., *Rubens: Study Heads and Anatomical Studies – Anatomical Studies. Corpus Rubenianum Ludwig Burchard XX, no. 1* (Harvey Miller Publishers, 2021)

Landwehr, John, *French, Italian, Spanish and Portuguese Books of Devices and Emblems 1534–1827: A Bibliography* (Haentjens Dekker & Gumbert, 1976)

Langer, Ullrich, 'Friendship, Renaissance Understanding of', in *Encyclopedia of Renaissance Philosophy*, ed. by Marco Sgarbi (Cham, 2020)

Laurenza, Domenico, 'Art and Anatomy in Renaissance Italy: Images from a Scientific Revolution', *The Metropolitan Museum of Art Bulletin* 69, no. 3 (2012), pp. 4–48

Lazzarini, Elena, 'The Nude in Central Italian Painting and Sculpture (1500–1600): Definition, Perception and Representation' (unpublished dissertation, University of Leicester, 2005)

Leontsini, Eleni, 'The Motive of Society: Aristotle on Civic Friendship, Justice, and Concord', *Res Publica. A Journal of Moral, Legal and Social Philosophy* 19, no. 1 (2013), pp. 21–35

Levine, Saul, 'Michelangelo's David: The Continuing Mythology', *Notes in the History of Art* 4, no. 4 (1985), pp. 15–20

Liebert, Robert S., *Michelangelo: A Psychoanalytic Study of his Life and Images* (Yale University Press, 1983)

Lo Re, Salvatore, 'Varchi e Michelangelo', *Annali della Scuola Normale Superiore di Pisa. Classe di Lettere e Filosofia* 4, no. 2 (2012), pp. 485–516

Low, Merry E., 'Receiving "Vittoria". Reformed Gift-Relations in Vittoria Colonna's and Marguerite de Navarre's Epistolary Correspondence', *Incontri* 34, no. 2 (2019), pp. 8–20

Malcolm, Noel, *Forbidden Desire in Early Modern Europe: Male-Male Sexual Relations, 1400–1750* (Oxford University Press, 2024)

Mancini, Elena, *Magnus Hirschfeld and the Quest for Sexual Freedom: A History of the First International Sexual Freedom Movement* (Palgrave Macmillan, 2010)

Mangone, Carolina, 'Generation and Ruination in the Display of Michelangelo's "Non-finito"', in *Contamination and Purity in Early Modern Art and Architecture*, ed. by Lauren Jacobi and Daniel Zolli (Amsterdam University Press, 2021), pp. 63–98

Maratos, Jessica, 'Michelangelo, Vittoria Colonna, and the Afterlife of Intimacy', *The Art Bulletin* 99, no. 4 (2017), pp. 69–101

Marongiu, Marcella, 'Michelangelo e la "maniera di figure piccole"', in *Michelangelo e la 'maniera di figure piccole'*, ed. by Marcella Marongiu (Edifir, 2019), pp. 13–73

Marongiu, Marcella, '"... perché egli imparassi a disegnare gli fece molte carte stupendissime...": I disegni di Michelangelo per Tommaso de' Cavalieri', *Horti Hesperidum: Studi di storia del collezionismo e della storiografia artistica* 4, no. 1 (2014), pp. 11–55

Marongiu, Marcella, 'Tommaso de' Cavalieri nella Roma di Clemente VII e Paolo III', *Horti Hesperidum: Studi di storia del collezionismo e della storiografia artistica* 3, no. 1 (2013), pp. 257–319

Marongiu, Marcella, 'Le tre versioni della *Caduta di Fetonte*', in *Michelangelo als Zeichner*, Akten des Internationalen Kolloquiums Wien, Albertina-Museum, 19.–20. November 2010, ed. by Claudia Echinger-Maurach, Achim Gnann and Joachim Poeschke (Rhema-Verlag, 2013), pp. 329–44

Marongiu, Marcella (ed.), *Il mito di Ganimede prima e dopo Michelangelo* (Mandragora, 2002)

Mazzotta, Antonio and Claudio Salsi (eds), *Vesperbild. Alle origini delle Pietà di Michelangelo* (Officina Libraria, 2018)

McCahill, Elizabeth May, 'Finding a Job as a Humanist: The Epistolary Collection of Lapo da Castiglionchio the Younger', *Renaissance Quarterly* 57, no. 4 (2004), pp. 1308–45

Mendelsohn, Leatrice, *Paragoni: Benedetto Varchi's Due Lezzioni and Cinquecento Art Theory* (UMI Research Press, 1982)

Michel, Eva and Klaus Albrecht Schröder (eds), *Michelangelo and Beyond* (Prestel, 2023)

Morozzi, Luisa, 'La "Battaglia di Cascina" di Michelangelo: nuova ipotesi sulla data di commissione', *Prospettiva* 53–56 (1988–1989), pp. 320–24

Mussolin, Mauro, 'I disegni di Michelangelo per le "Allegorie del Tempo" nella Sagrestia Nuova: materialità, medialità, ricomposizione dei fogli', *L'Idea* 1, no. 2 (2024), pp. 53–97

Nagel, Alexander, *Michelangelo and the Reform of Art* (Cambridge University Press, 2000)

Nagel, Alexander, 'Gifts for Michelangelo and Vittoria Colonna', *The Art Bulletin* 79, no. 4 (1997), pp. 647–68

Nagel, Alexander, 'Observations on Michelangelo's Late Pietà Drawings and Sculptures', *Zeitschrift für Kunstgeschichte* 59, no. 4 (1996), pp. 548–72

Nancy, Jean-Luc, *The Pleasure in Drawing*, trans. by Philip Armstrong (Fordham University Press, 2013)

Natali, Antonio (ed.), *L'officina della maniera: varietà e fierezza nell'arte fiorentina del Cinquecento fra le due repubbliche 1494–1530* (Marsilio, 1996)

O'Grody, Jeannine, '"Un semplice modello": Michelangelo and His Three-Dimensional Preparatory Works' (unpublished dissertation, Case Western Reserve University, 1999)

Olszewski, Edward J., 'Michelangelo's David: Full Frontal Nudity in the Age of Savonarola', *Notes in the History of Art* 35, nos. 1–2 (2016), pp. 118–25

Österberg, Eva, *Friendship and Love, Ethics and Politics* (Central European University Press, 2010)

Østermark-Johansen, Lene, *Sweetness and Strength: The Reception of Michelangelo in Late Victorian England* (Ashgate, 1998)

Ott, Christine, *Cambiare pelle: Soggettività e creatività nella poesia di Michelangelo* (Carocci Editore, 2024)

Palmer, Ada, *Inventing the Renaissance. Myths of a Golden Age* (University of Chicago Press, 2025)

Panofsky, Erwin, *Studies in Iconology: Humanistic Themes in the Art of the Renaissance* (Oxford University Press, 1939)

Papini, Giovanni, *Vita di Michelangiolo nella vita del suo tempo* (Garzanti, 1950)

Park, Katherine, 'The Criminal and the Saintly Body: Autopsy in Renaissance Italy', *Renaissance Quarterly* 47, no. 1 (1994), pp. 1–33

Park, Katherine, *Doctors and Medicine in Early Renaissance Florence* (Princeton University Press, 1985)

Park, Katherine, 'Masaccio's Skeleton: Art and Anatomy in Early Renaissance Florence', in *Masaccio's Trinity*, ed. by Rona Goffen (Cambridge University Press, 1998), pp. 119–57

Parker, Deborah, *Michelangelo and the Art of Letter Writing* (Cambridge University Press, 2010)

Parker, Deborah, 'Ovidian Influences and Figural Obsessions in Michelangelo's "Fall of Phaethon" Drawings', *I Tatti Studies* 24, no. 2 (2021), pp. 401–26

Parker, Karl T., *Catalogue of the Collection of Drawings in the Ashmolean Museum. Volume II: Italian Schools* (Clarendon, 1956)

Perrig, Alexander, *Michelangelo's Drawings: The Science of Attribution*, trans. by Michael Joyce (Yale University Press, 1991)

Perrig, Alexander, 'Über eine verkannte Michelangelo-Zeichnung', *Zeitschrift für Kunstgeschichte* 23, no. 1 (1960), pp. 19–41

Peters, Emily J. and Julian Brooks, *Michelangelo: Mind of the Master* (Cleveland Museum of Art, 2019)

Petrucci, Armando *Scrivere lettere: una storia plurimillenaria* (Laterza, 2008)

Plaisance, Michel, *L'accademia e il suo principe: cultura e politica a Firenze al tempo di Cosimo I e di Francesco de' Medici* (Vecchiarelli, 2004)

Pope-Hennessy, John, 'The Gherardini Collection of Italian Sculpture', *Victoria and Albert Museum Yearbook* 2 (1970), pp. 7–26

Pope-Hennessy, John, *Introduction to Italian Sculpture, Volume III: Italian High Renaissance and Baroque Sculpture* (Phaidon, 1963)

Popham, Arthur E., *The Drawings of Leonardo da Vinci* (Cape, 1946)

Popham, Arthur E. and Philip Pouncey, *Italian Drawings in the Department of Prints and Drawings of the British Museum. The Fourteenth and Fifteenth Centuries,* 2 vols (Trustees of the British Museum, 1950)

Popham, Arthur E. and Johannes Wilde, *The Italian Drawings of the XV and XVI Centuries in the Collections of His Majesty the King at Windsor Castle* (Phaidon Press, 1949)

Prodan, Sarah Rolfe, *Michelangelo's Christian Mysticism. Spirituality, Poetry and Art in Sixteenth-Century Italy* (Cambridge University Press, 2014)

Quaintance, Courtney, *Textual Masculinity and the Exchange of Women in Renaissance Venice* (University of Toronto Press, 2015)

Quondam, Amedeo (ed.), *Le 'carte messaggiere': Retorica e modelli di comunicazione epistolare. Per un indice dei libri di lettere del Cinquecento* (Bulzoni, 1981)

Ragionieri, Pina (ed.), *I bozzetti michelangioleschi della Casa Buonarroti* (Madragora, 2000)

Ragionieri, Pina (ed.), *Michelangelo. Drawings and Other Treasures from the Casa Buonarroti* (High Museum of Art, 2001)

Ragionieri, Pina (ed.), *Michelangelo, il piccolo crocifisso della Casa Buonarroti* (Silvana, 2010)

Rebecchini, Guido, *Un altro Lorenzo: Ippolito de' Medici tra Firenze e Roma (1511–1535)* (Marsilio, 2010)

Reeser, Todd W., *Setting Plato Straight: Translating Ancient Sexuality in the Renaissance* (University of Chicago Press, 2016)

Regteren Altena, I.Q. van, 'Rubens as a Draughtsman. I: Relations to Italian Art, *The Burlington Magazine* 76, no. 447 (1940), pp. 194–200

Reti, Ladislao, 'The Two Unpublished Manuscripts of Leonardo da Vinci in the Biblioteca Nacional of Madrid – II', *The Burlington Magazine* 110, no. 779 (1968), pp. 81–82, 85–86, 89, 91

Ridolfi, Roberto, *Studi Savonaroliani* (Olschki, 1935)

Rinaldi, Furio, 'Looking at Masaccio: A Rediscovered Drawing by the Young Michelangelo', *The Burlington Magazine* 164, no. 1431 (2022), pp. 536–45

Rocke, Michael J., *Forbidden Friendships: Homosexuality and Male Culture in Renaissance Florence* (Oxford University Press, 1996)

Rocke, Michael, 'Gender and Sexual Culture in Renaissance Italy', in *Gender and Society in Renaissance Italy*, ed. by Judith C. Brown and Robert C. Davis (Longman, 1998), pp. 150–70

Rocke, Michael J., '"Whoorish boyes": Male Prostitution in Early Modern Italy and the Spurious "Second Part" of Antonio Vignali's *La Cazzaria*', in *Power, Gender, and Ritual in Europe and the Americas: Essays in Memory of Richard C. Trexler*, ed. by Peter Arnade and Michael Rocke (Centre for Reformation and Renaissance Studies, 2008), pp. 113–33

Romani, Vittoria, *Daniele da Volterra: amico di Michelangelo* (Mandragora, 2003)

Roskill, M.W., *Dolce's 'Aretino' and the Venetian Art Theory of the Cinquecento* (New York University Press, 1968)

Rovetta, Alessandro (ed.), *L'ultimo Michelangelo. Disegni e rime attorno alla 'Pietà Rondanini'* (Silvana Editoriale, 2011)

Rubin, Patricia L., *Seen from Behind: Perspectives on the Male Body and Renaissance Art* (Yale University Press, 2018)

Rubinstein, Nicolai, *The Palazzo Vecchio 1298–1532* (Clarendon, 1995)

Ruggiero, Guido, *The Boundaries of Eros: Sex Crime and Sexuality in Renaissance Venice* (Oxford University Press, 1985)

Rumberg, Per and Scott Nethersole, *Michelangelo, Leonardo, Raphael: Florence c. 1504* (Royal Academy of Arts, 2024)

Ruston, Julia C. and Peter H. Abrahams, 'An Anatomical "Whodunnit"', in *Michelangelo: Sculptor in Bronze*, ed. by Victoria Avery (Philip Wilson, 2018), pp. 149–59

Ruvoldt, Maria, 'Gossip and Reputation in Sixteenth-Century Rome: Tommaso de' Cavalieri and Lavinia della Valle', *Renaissance Studies* 34, no. 3 (2019/2020), pp. 374–91

Ruvoldt, Maria, *The Italian Renaissance Imagery of Inspiration: Metaphors of Sex, Sleep, and Dreams* (Cambridge University Press, 2004)

Ruvoldt, Maria, 'Michelangelo's Dream', *The Art Bulletin* 85, no. 1 (2003), pp. 83–113

Ruvoldt, Maria, 'Michelangelo's Open Secrets', in *Visual Cultures of Secrecy in Early Modern Europe*, ed. by Timothy McCall, Sean Roberts and Giancarlo Fiorenza (Truman State University Press, 2013), pp. 105–25

Ruvoldt, Maria, 'Michelangelo's "Slaves" and the Gift of Liberty', Renaissance Quarterly 65, no. 4 (2012), pp. 1029–1059

Ruvoldt, Maria, 'Tommaso de' Cavalieri, Formerly Orsini: Michelangelo's Muse and Medici Cousin', *The Burlington Magazine* 157, no. 1349 (2015), pp. 530–32

Saslow, James M., *Ganymede in the Renaissance: Homosexuality in Art and Society* (Yale University Press, 1986)

Saslow, James M., 'Homosexuality in the Renaissance: Behavior, Identity, and Artistic Expression', in *Hidden from History: Reclaiming the Gay and Lesbian Past,* ed. by Martin Duberman, Martha Vicinus and George Chauncy Jr. (New American Library, 1989), pp. 90–105

Saslow, James M., 'Inventing Michelangelo: The Historical Construction of the Creative Homosexual', in *Medusa's Gaze: Essays on Gender, Literature, and Aesthetics in the Italian Renaissance, in Honor of Robert J. Rodini*, ed. by Paul A. Ferrara, Eugenio Giusti and Jane Tylus (Bordighiera, 2004), pp. 65–90

Saslow, James M., '"A Veil of Ice Between My Heart and the Fire": Michelangelo's Sexual Identity and Early Modern Constructs of Homosexuality', *Genders* 2 (1988), pp. 77–90

Schlitt, Melinda, 'Painting, Criticism, and Michelangelo's Last Judgment in the Age of Counter-Reformation' in *Michelangelo's Last Judgment*, ed. by Marcia B. Hall (Cambridge University Press, 2004), pp. 113–49

Schlitt, Melinda, '"...viri studiosi et scientifici...": Pietro Antonio Cecchini, Michelangelo, and the Nobility of Sculptors in Rome', in *Gifts in Return: Essays in Honour of Charles Dempsey*, ed. by Melinda Schlitt (Centre for Renaissance and Reformation Studies, 2012), pp. 233–61

Schoch, Rainer, Matthias Mende and Anna Scherbaum, *Albrecht Dürer: Das druckgraphische Werk*, 3 vols (Prestel, 2001)

Schultz, Bernard, *Art and Anatomy in Renaissance Italy* (UMI Research Press, 1985)

Schütze, Sebastian, '"Anchora inparo": sulla fortuna critica nell'arte e nella letteratura artistica della prima età moderna di una massima filosofica attribuita a Michelangelo', in *Ricerche sull'arte a Napoli in età moderna. Scritti in onore di Giuseppe De Vito*, ed. by Nadia Batogi (Artem, 2014), pp. 18–29

Schwartz, Daniel, *Aquinas on Friendship* (Oxford University Press, 2007)

Serra, Roberta, *Dessins bolonais du XVIème siècle,* Musée du Louvre, Département des Arts graphiques, Inventaire général des Dessins Italiens, 11 (Louvre Éditions, 2022)

Sickel, Lothar, 'Die Sammlung des Tommaso de' Cavalieri und die Provenienz der Zeichnungen Michelangelos. Mit einem Exkurs über Filippo Cicciaporci', *Römisches Jahrbuch der Bibliotheca Hertziana* 37 (2006), pp. 163–221

Smith, R.R.R., *Hellenistic Sculpture* (Thames & Hudson, 1991)

Smithers, Tamara, 'Michelangelo's Suicidal Stone', in *Michelangelo in the New Millennium: Conversations about Artistic Practice, Patronage and Christianity*, ed. by Tamara Smithers (Brill, 2016)

Soussloff, Catherine M., 'Imitatio Buonarroti', *The Sixteenth Century Journal* 20, no. 4 (1989), pp. 581–602

Steinberg, Leo, 'Michelangelo and the Doctors', *Bulletin of the History of Medicine* 56, no. 4 (1982), pp. 543–53

Steinberg, Leo, 'Michelangelo's Florentine Pietà: The Missing Leg', *The Art Bulletin* 50, no. 4 (1968), pp. 343–53

Stewart, Alan, 'The Singing Boy and the Scholar: The Various Deaths of Politian', in *Eros et Priapus: Erotisme et obscénité dans la littérature néo-latine*, ed. by Ingrid A.R. de Smet and Philip Ford (Librairie Droz, 1997), pp. 45–63

Stollhans, Cynthia, 'Michelangelo's Nude Saint Catherine of Alexandria', *Woman's Art Journal* 19, no. 1 (1998), pp. 26–30

Stone, Irving, *The Agony and the Ecstasy* (Doubleday, 1961)

Summers, David, *Michelangelo and the Language of Art* (Princeton University Press, 1981)

Sutherland Minter, Erin, 'Discarded Deity: The Rejection of Michelangelo's Bacchus and the Artist's Response', *Renaissance Studies* 28, no. 3 (2013), pp. 443–58

Symonds, John Addington, *The Letters of John Addington Symonds*, ed. by Herbert M. Schueller and Robert L. Peters, 3 vols (Wayne State University Press, 1967–1969)

Symonds, John Addington, *The Life of Michelangelo Buonarroti: Based on Studies in the Archives of the Buonarroti Family at Florence*, 3rd ed., 2 vols (John C. Nimmo, 1899)

Symonds, John Addington, *The Sonnets of Michael Angelo Buonarroti and Tommaso Campanella* (Smith Elder, 1878)

Turner, Nicholas, *Florentine Drawings of the Sixteenth Century* (British Museum Press, 1986)

Tuyll van Serooskerken, Carel van, *The Italian Drawings of the Fifteenth and Sixteenth Centuries in the Teyler Museum* (Snoeck-Ducaju, 2000)

Verdon, Timothy, 'The Infancy, Passion and Resurrection of Christ in Michelangelo', in *Michelangelo and Sebastiano*, ed. by Matthias Wivel (National Gallery Company/Yale University Press, 2017), pp. 53–63

Vollmer, Matthias, 'The Vices in Michelangelo's Dream', in *Michelangelo's Dream*, ed. by Stephanie Buck and Tatiana Bissolati (Paul Holberton, 2010), pp. 27–37

Vowles, Sarah and Grant Lewis, *Michelangelo: The Last Decades* (The British Museum Press, 2024)

Wadell, Paul J., 'Charity: How Friendship with God Unfolds in Love for Others', in *Virtues and Their Vices*, ed. by Kevin Timpe and Craig A. Boyd (Oxford University Press, 2014), pp. 369–90

Wallace, William E., 'Drawing Limits: Michelangelo Grows Old', *The Art Bulletin* 103, no. 1 (2021), pp. 37–64

Wallace, William E., *Michelangelo at San Lorenzo: The Genius as Entrepreneur* (Cambridge University Press, 1994)

Wallace, William E., 'Michelangelo at Work: Bernardino Basso, Friend, Scoundrel and Capomaestro', *I Tatti Studies* 3 (1989), pp. 235–77

Wallace, William E., *Michelangelo: The Artist, the Man, and his Times* (Cambridge University Press, 2010).

Wallace, William E., 'Michelangelo's Baby', *Master Drawings* 44, no. 3 (2006), pp. 358–61

Wallace, William E., 'Michelangelo's Late Drawings', in *Triumph of the Body: Michelangelo and Sixteenth-Century Italian Draughtsmanship*, ed. by Zoltán Kárpáti (Museum of Fine Arts Budapest, 2019), pp. 89–110

Wallace, William E., 'Michelangelo's *Leda*: The Diplomatic Context', *Renaissance Studies* 15, no. 4 (2001), pp. 473–99

Wallace, William E., 'A Week in the Life of Michelangelo', in *Looking at Italian Renaissance Sculpture*, ed. by Sarah Blake McHam (Cambridge University Press, 1998), pp. 203–22

Wasserman, Jack, *Michelangelo's Florence Pietà* (Princeton University Press, 2003)

Wilde, Johannes, 'The Hall of the Great Council of Florence', *Journal of the Warburg and Courtauld Institutes* 7, no. 1 (1944), pp. 65–81

Wilde, Johannes, *Italian Drawings in the Department of Prints and Drawings in the British Museum: Michelangelo and His Studio* (Trustees of the British Museum, 1953)

Wilde, Johannes, 'Michelangelo and Leonardo', *The Burlington Magazine* 95 (1953), pp. 65–77

Wilde, Johannes, *Michelangelo: The Group of Victory* (Oxford University Press, 1954)

Wilde, Johannes, 'Notes on the Genesis of Michelangelo's *Leda*', in *Fritz Saxl 1890–1948: A Volume of Memorial Essays from His Friends in England*, ed. by Donald James Gordon (Nelson, 1957), pp. 270–80

Wilde, Johannes, 'Eine Studie Michelangelos nach der Antike', *Mitteilungen des Kunsthistorischen Institutes in Florenz* 4 (1932), pp. 41–64

Winner, Matthias, 'Michelangelo's *Il Sogno* as an Example of an Artist's Visual Reflection in His Drawings', in *Michelangelo's Drawings*, ed. by Craig Hugh Smyth (National Gallery of Art, 1992), pp. 227–42

Wivel, Matthias (ed.), *Michelangelo and Sebastiano* (National Gallery Company/Yale University Press, 2017)

Wood, Christopher S., 'Indoor-Outdoor: The Studio Around 1500', in *Inventions of the Studio: Renaissance to Romanticism*, ed. by Michael Cole and Mary Pardo (University of North Carolina Press, 2005), pp. 36–72

Wood, Jeremy, *Copies and Adaptations from Renaissance and Later Artist, 2. Italian Artists III, Artists Working in Central Italy and France*, in *Corpus Rubenianum Ludwig Burchard,* ed. by Ludwig Burchard, Herbert W. Rott, Gregory Martin and Koenraad Brosens, XXVI, no. 2 (Brepols, 2011)

Zöllner, Frank, '"La Battaglia di Anghiari" di Leonardo da Vinci tra mitologia e politica', *Lettura Vinciana* 37 (1997), pp. 7–39

Index of names, and works by Michelangelo (excluding drawings)

Alberti, Leon Battista (1404–1472) 125, 126, 130
Albertinelli, Mariotto (1474–1515) 211
Alcibiades (c. 450–404 BCE) 42
Aldrovandi, Ulisse (1522–1605) 93, 94
Alexander the Great (356–323 BCE) 94
Allori, Alessandro (1535–1607) 168–170
Angelini, Bartolomeo (d. 1540) 60–62
Angoulême, Marguerite of, see Navarre, Marguerite de
Aquinas, Thomas (c. 1225–1274) 233, 238, 241
Aretino, Pietro (1492–1556) 42, 236, 239, 241
Aristotle (384–322 BCE) 157, 233, 238, 239
Baccio di Puccione (doc. 1525) 117, 121
Baldassare da Milano (doc. 1480–1502) 82
Baldinucci, Filippo (1625–1696) 246
Bandinelli, Baccio (1488–1560) 90, 239
Barberino, Luigi da (c. 1444–after 1520) 77
Bartolommeo, Fra (Baccio della Porta) (1472–1517) 211
Bernini, Domenico (1657–1723) 246
Bertoldo di Giovanni (c. 1440–1491) 76, 77, 80, 211, 218
Bettini, Bartolomeo (d. 1551/52) 60
Biagio da Cesena (1463–1544) 153, 168, 239
Bilhères-Lagraulas, Jean de (1434/39–1499) 173, 176, 236
Borgia, Cesare (1475–1507) 82
Bracci, Cecchino (1528–1544) 42
Bramante, Donato (1444–1514) 93
Bregno, Andrea (1418–1503) 93
Bruegel the Elder, Pieter (c. 1525/30–1569) 226
Buonarroti, Buonarroto (1477–1528) 236
Buonarroti, Lionardo (1519–1599) 192, 241
Buonarroti, Michelangelo (1475–1564)
    Architecture
        Facade of San Lorenzo (Florence) 14, 236
        Laurentian Library 14, 66, 236
    Painting
        Battle of Cascina 14, 17, 94, 100, 123, 124, 131,
            132, 141, 203–205, 208–211, 218, 220, 226,
            230, 239
        Cappella Paolina frescoes 15, 231
        Ceiling of the Sistine Chapel 14, 20, 24, 28, 42,
            74, 76, 78, 93–96, 103–110, 115–117, 121,
            125, 130, 131, 141, 220, 236, 238, 239, 242,
            243, 246–248
        Doni Tondo 14, 76, 77, 90
        The Entombment (National Gallery) 28, 173,
            175–177, 186, 187, 218
        The Last Judgement 15, 17, 42, 93, 107, 132,
            133, 141–143, 153, 154, 168, 170, 190, 192,
            218, 226, 238, 239
        Leda and the Swan 15, 58, 60
        Venus and Cupid 59, 60
    Sculpture
        Apollo-David 14, 88–90, 94
        Bacchus 14, 82, 84, 85, 88, 94
        Battle of the Centaurs 14, 38, 80, 81, 209
        Crucifix (Santo Spirito, Florence) 14, 88, 187
        David (bronze; lost) 14
        David (marble) 14, 17, 18, 88, 153, 208, 239, 246
        Day (Medici Chapel) 64, 65, 95, 108, 111–113,
            133, 138, 139
        Dying Captive 14, 76, 133, 137, 141, 147, 238
        Genius of Victory 235, 236
        Moses 14, 94, 143, 147
        Night (Medici Chapel) 114, 115, 120, 126, 133,
            238
        Rebellious Captive 14, 75, 76, 238
        Risen Christ (Santa Maria sopra Minerva) 14,
            88, 92, 192, 193–195
        Sleeping Cupid 82
        Young Archer 88, 90
Buonarroti the Younger, Michelangelo (1568–1646) 35,
    45, 246
Calcagni, Tiberio (1532–1565) 42, 186
Cappello, Bianca (1548–1587) 168, 170
Castiglione, Baldassare (1478–1529) 49
Cattani da Diacceto, Francesco (1466–1522) 155, 167
Cavalieri, Tommaso de' (c. 1512/19–1587) 15, 17, 28,
    41–43, 46, 49–53, 55, 60, 61, 64, 67, 115, 158, 162, 233
Cecchini, Pier Antonio (doc. 1524–1540) 50
Cellini, Benvenuto (1500–1571) 90, 203, 239
Charles V, Holy Roman Emperor (1500–1558) 238
Cicero, Marcus Tullius (106 BCE–43 BCE) 233
Clement VII, Pope, see Medici, Giulio de'
Colombo, Realdo (c. 1510–1559) 125, 126
Colonna, Vittoria (1490–1547) 15, 28, 190, 195, 233, 241
Condivi, Ascanio (1525–1574) 15, 38, 42, 73, 76, 80, 82, 85,
    121, 123–127, 133, 143, 155, 187, 233, 236
Conseil, Jean (1498–1535) 64
Corsi, Giovanni (1472–1547) 155
Daniele da Volterra (Daniele Ricciarelli) (c. 1509–1566) 15,
    153, 237, 238, 241
Dante Alighieri (1265–1321) 60, 239
della Rovere, Giuliano (Pope Julius II) (1443–1513) 14, 15,
    76, 88, 92, 94, 133, 203, 236
della Valle, Lavinia (c. 1527/30–1553) 50
Dolce, Lodovico (1508–1568) 239
Donatello (Donato Bardi) (1386–1466) 17, 19, 100, 218
Doni, Anton Francesco (1513–1574) 93, 236
Dürer, Albrecht (1471–1528) 125–127, 160, 162
Epigonus (3rd century BCE) 94
Erasmus of Rotterdam, Desiderius (c. 1466–1536) 55

Este, Alfonso I d' (1476–1534) 15, 60, 236
Este, Isabella d' (1474–1539) 76, 82
Fabrini, Giovanni Francesco (1516–1580) 239
Farnese, Alessandro (Pope Paul III) (1468–1549) 73, 93, 153, 239
Fattucci, Giovan Francesco (doc. 1521–1553) 241
Febo di Poggio (doc. 1534/35) 41, 50
Festa, Costanzo (c. 1480–1545) 64
Ficino, Marsilio (1433–1499) 28, 38, 153, 155–157, 162, 167, 168, 170, 176
Fludd, Robert (1574–1637) 161, 162
Franciabigio (Francesco di Cristofano) (1482–1525) 204
Francis I, King of France (1494–1547) 15, 236, 238
Fréart de Chantelou, Paul (1609–1694) 246
Gallo, Jacopo (d. 1505) 85
Gheyn II, Jacques de (c. 1565–1629) 161, 162
Ghiberti, Lorenzo (1378–1455) 124
Ghirlandaio, Domenico (1449–1494) 14, 73, 99, 100, 103, 117, 155, 209
Gilio, Giovanni Andrea (d. 1584) 123
Giotto di Bondone (1267–1337) 19
Giovanni da Viterbo (d. 1496) 176
Giovio, Paolo (1483–1552) 233
Gonzaga, Ercole (1505–1563) 76, 239
Guasti, Cesare (1822–1889) 35
Holanda, Francisco de (1517–1584) 132, 158, 162, 166
Iamblichus (c. 245–c. 325) 153
Julius II, Pope, see della Rovere, Giuliano
Leighton, Frederic, Lord (1830–1896) 203
Leo X, Pope, see Medici, Giovanni de'
Leonardo da Vinci (1452–1519) 45, 125, 203, 204, 208, 209, 239
Lippi, Filippino (c. 1457–1504) 100, 110, 205, 208
Lomazzo, Giovanni Paolo (1538–1600) 45, 46, 158
Lucian of Samosata (c. 125–after 180) 45
Lysippus (4th century BCE) 94
Mantegna, Andrea (1431–1506) 76
Masaccio (Tommaso di Ser Giovanni Casai) (1401–1428) 19, 100, 101
Medici, Alessandro de' (1510–1537) 238
Medici, Cosimo (the Elder) de' (1389–1464) 153
Medici, Cosimo I de' (1519–1574) 90, 236
Medici, Francesco I de' (1541–1587) 170
Medici, Giovanni de' (Pope Leo X) (1475–1521) 14, 155, 236
Medici, Giovanni Angelo de' (Pope Pius IV) (1499–1565) 241
Medici, Giulio de' (Pope Clemens VII) (1478–1534) 14, 15, 64, 88, 90, 93, 94
Medici, Ippolito de' (1511–1535) 55
Medici, Lorenzo de' ('il Magnifico') (1449–1492) 14, 38, 76, 88, 92, 236

Medici, Lorenzo di Pierfrancesco de' (1463–1503) 82
Medici, Piero de' (1472-1503) 14, 121
Mini, Antonio (1506–1533) 117
Navarre, Marguerite de (1492–1549) 241
Passarotti, Bartolomeo (1529–1592) 123, 124, 130
Paul III, Pope, see Farnese, Alessandro
Perini, Gherardo (b. 1504) 28, 39, 41, 42
Petrarch (Francesco Petrarca) (1304–1374) 55, 60
Phidias (5th century BCE) 45
Pius IV, Pope, see Medici, Giovanni Angelo de'
Plato (c. 427–c. 347 BCE) 42, 153, 155–157, 167
Pliny the Elder (Gaius Plinius Secundus) (23/24–79) 82, 85, 88, 92, 93
Plotinus (c. 204–270) 153
Poliziano, Angelo (1454–1494) 38, 60, 85, 88
Pollaiuolo, Antonio (c. 1432–1498) 17, 20, 211
Pontormo, Jacopo (Jacopo de' Carucci) (1494–1557) 204, 233
Praxiteles (4th century BCE) 82, 88
Proclus (412–485) 153
Quaratesi, Andrea (1512–1585) 17, 37, 39, 41, 50, 117, 233
Raphael (Raffaello Sanzio) (1483–1520) 123, 132, 158, 203, 204, 207, 211, 233, 238, 239
Raimondi, Marcantonio (c. 1480–c. 1534) 21, 211
Riario, Raffaele (1460–1521) 82, 85, 88, 236
Ridolfi, Niccolò (1501–1550) 125, 238
Ripa, Cesare (c. 1560–c. 1645) 161, 162
Rocco, Antonio (1586–1653) 45
Romano, Gian Cristoforo (1456–1512) 76, 92
Rubens, Peter Paul (1577–1640) 203, 204, 208
Salai (Gian Giacomo Caprotti da Oreno) (1480–1524) 45, 46
Salviati, Alamanno (1459–1510) 236
Salviati, Francesco (c. 1509–1563) 211, 226, 236
Sangallo, Francesco da (1494–1576) 92, 205, 211
Sangallo, Giuliano da (1445–1516) 92
Sangallo, Bastiano (Aristotile) da (1481–1551) 236
Sansovino, Andrea (1460–1529) 205
Sansovino, Jacopo (1486–1570) 90
Sarto, Andrea del (1486–1530) 204
Savonarola, Girolamo (1452–1498) 14, 38, 187, 204, 211
Sebastiano del Piombo (Sebastiano Luciani) (1485/86–1547) 60, 64, 88, 195, 238
Sellaio, Leonardo (d. 1526?) 39
Sernini, Nino (d. 1543) 239
Sforza, Francesco (1401–1466) 239
Socrates (c. 470–399 BCE) 42, 167
Soderini, Piero (1452–1522) 17, 125, 204, 205, 208, 209
Strozzi, Roberto (1515–1566) 236, 238
Symonds, John Addington (1840–1893) 35, 42
Synesius (c. 373–c. 414) 153
Tibaldi, Pellegrino (1527–1596) 226

Titian (Tiziano Vecellio) (c. 1488/90–1576) 203, 204, 206, 239

Trivulzio, Cesare (doc. 1506) 92, 93

Uccello, Paolo (1397–1475) 220

Vaenius, Otto (Otto van Veen) (1556–1629) 167, 168

Valori, Baccio (1477–1537) 88, 90

Valori, Francesco (1439–1498) 17

Varchi, Benedetto (1503–1565) 49, 50, 53, 241

Vasari, Giorgio (1511–1574) 15, 30, 39, 50, 53, 55, 73, 76, 88, 93, 99, 100, 107, 117, 123, 126, 127, 132, 133, 141, 143, 147, 153, 180, 192, 195, 203, 204, 211, 218, 233, 236, 239, 241

Venusti, Marcello (1512–1579) 238

Vesalius, Andreas (1514–1564) 123

Vitruvius (c. 80–c. 15 BCE) 125, 127

Explanatory Notes

This book is intended for a broad readership. It does not engage in discussions about the dating and/or attribution of works for which there is no scholarly consensus. The aim is to examine Michelangelo's art from a different perspective – the role of the male body – and to situate his work and relationships in a wider context. Accordingly, the book does not include an extensive catalogue section, simply a list of basic information, nor does it attempt an in-depth exploration of the works' provenance or the literature around them.

The quotations that open each section are drawn from Michelangelo's writings and can be found in: Buonarroti, Michelangelo, *The Poetry of Michelangelo. An Annotated Translation*, translated and edited by James M. Saslow (Yale University Press, 1991), nos. A3, 89, 46, 260 and 85.

The Florentines had yet to adopt the Gregorian calendar, which begins on 1 January, and continued to observe their New Year on 25 March, the Feast of the Annunciation, until 1751. The years stated in the main text of this book have been adjusted to our modern calendar system. A double notation is provided for quotations from specific documents dating from the period 1 January to 25 March.

About the Authors

Eric Boot is an art historian and researcher at Teylers Museum, Haarlem.

Klazina Botke is Lecturer in Art History at the Vrije Universiteit Amsterdam and guest curator at Teylers Museum, Haarlem.

Raymond Carlson is Research Assistant and Manager of Student Engagement at the Yale University Art Gallery, and former fellow of Magdalen College, Oxford.

Marieke van den Doel is Assistant Professor in the History of Humanism at the University of Humanistic Studies, Utrecht.

Terry van Druten is Head of Art Collections at Teylers Museum, Haarlem.

Martin Gayford is a critic, author of books on Michelangelo, Van Gogh and Lucian Freud, and guest curator at Teylers Museum, Haarlem.

Paul Joannides is Emeritus Professor of Art History at the University of Cambridge.

Michael Rocke is Nicky Mariano Librarian and Director of the Biblioteca Berenson at Villa I Tatti, The Harvard University Center for Italian Renaissance Studies, Florence.

Jennifer Sliwka is Keeper of Western Art at the Ashmolean Museum and Professorial Fellow at Balliol College at the University of Oxford.

Acknowledgements

We owe our knowledge of Michelangelo Buonarroti and his art to the impressive work of the many scholars who have gone before us. The research performed by our fellow historians laid the foundations for our own ideas and we are much indebted to them. We are also sincerely grateful to everyone who loaned items from their collections for this project. Our gratitude is similarly due to the authors who have shared their knowledge in this publication and to the teams at Hannibal Books and Teylers Museum for their friendly collaboration.

We would especially like to thank the following people for the part they have played in bringing the exhibition and this book to fruition: Cristina Acidini, Stijn Alsteens, Carmen Bambach, Paul Barolsky, Machtelt Brüggen Israëls, Alessandro Cecchi, Hugo Chapman, Ilaria Ciseri, Martin Clayton, Paola D'Agostino, Laura Donati, Willem van Ee, Bas Ernst, Maria Forcellino, Ketty Gottardo, Gert-Jan Kleinrensink, Michael W. Kwakkelstein, Grant Lewis, Elena Lombardi, Marcella Marongiu, Benedetta Matucci, Jonathan Nelson, Scott Nethersole, Patricia Rubin, Per Rumberg, Frits Scholten, Gert Jan van der Sman, Ilona van Tuinen, Xavier Salmon, Carel van Tuyll van Serooskerken, Sarah Vowles, William Wallace and Catherine Whistler.

We are likewise very grateful to the individuals and institutions who have loaned works from their collections: Rijksmuseum, Amsterdam; RKD – Netherlands Institute of Art History, The Hague; Casa Buonarroti, Florence; Gallerie degli Uffizi, Florence; Museo Nazionale del Bargello, Florence; The British Museum, London; The Courtauld, London; Maastricht Institute of Arts, Maastricht; The Metropolitan Museum of Art, New York; The Earl of Leicester, Holkham Hall, Norfolk; Ashmolean Museum, Oxford; Musée du Louvre, Paris; His Majesty King Charles III, Windsor; and a private collector.

We greatly appreciate the support of the Ministry of Education, Culture and Science, the VriendenLoterij, the Teylers Museum Friends Fund, the Mondriaan Fund, the Turing Foundation, Fonds 21, the Culture Fund, the Municipality of Haarlem and NIKI Florence.

Photo Credits

Amsterdam, © Rijksmuseum: figs 3, 22, 102, 103, 109, 134
Bayonne, © Musée Bonnat-Helleu / photo A. Vaquero: fig. 15
Berlin, © Staatliche Museen zu Berlin, Kupferstichkabinett / photo
    Dietmar Katz: fig. 41
Cambridge, © Trinity College Library, Master and Fellows of Trinity College,
    Cambridge: fig. 47
Chicago, © The Art Institute of Chicago, Anonymous loan: fig. 39
Florence, © Archivio di Stato di Firenze / Ministero della Cultura / photo
    Donato Pineider: fig. 98
Florence, © Casa Buonarroti: figs 8, 9, 16, 17, 25, 26, 38, 53, 72, 125, 128,
    154, 162
Florence, © Gabinetto Fotografico delle Gallerie degli Uffizi / Ministero
    della Cultura: figs 24, 34, 64, 68, 87, 111, 112, 144; © Galleria
    dell'Accademia di Firenze: fig. 1; © Museo Nazionale del Bargello,
    figs 37, 40
Florence, © Museo delle Cappelle Medicee / Ministero della Cultura /
    photo Antonio Quattrone: figs 69, 89
Florence, © Museo Nazionale del Bargello / Bridgeman Images / photo
    Raffaello Bencini: fig. 44 Florence, © Museo Nazionale del Bargello /
    Scala, Florence: fig. 2
Florence, © Opera di Santa Maria del Fiore / Scala, Florence / photo
    Antonio Quattrone: fig. 120
Florence, © Scala: figs 95, 123; © Scala / Fondo Edifici di Culto - Min.
    dell'Interno: figs 50, 97
Frankfurt am Main, © Universitätsbibliothek J.C. Senckenberg: fig. 105
Haarlem, © Teylers Museum: figs 4, 5, 6, 10, 20, 27, 28, 29, 55, 59, 62, 65,
    66, 69, 78, 80, 83, 84, 85, 88, 90, 92, 94, 115, 119, 140, 141, 159, 160,
    161, 163, 164, 165
London, © The Trustees of the British Museum: figs 7, 13, 19, 43, 54, 56, 58,
    63, 116, 124, 127, 129, 131, 139, 142, 156
London, © The Courtauld Gallery: figs 21, 101
London, with kind permission of The Journal of the Warburg and Courtauld
    Institutes: fig. 135
London, © The National Gallery / Scala, Florence: fig. 114
London, © Victoria and Albert Museum: fig. 117
Milan, © Castello Sforzesco / Bridgeman Images / photo Andrea Jermolo:
    fig. 122
Munich, © Bayerische Staatsbibliothek: figs 76, 99, 110
Naples, © Museo Archeologico Nazionale di Napoli / Ministero della
    Cultura / photo Giorgio Albano: figs 32, 35
Naples, © Museo e Bosco Real Capodimonte, Napoli / Ministero della
    Cultura: fig. 23
New York, © The Metropolitan Museum of Art / Art Resource / Scala,
    Florence: fig. 70
Norfolk, © Holkham Hall & Estate, By kind permission of the Earl of
    Leicester and the Trustees of Holkham Estate / Bridgeman Images:
    fig. 133
Norman, © The University of Oklahoma Libraries: fig. 75
Oxford, © Ashmolean Museum, University of Oxford: figs 57, 67, 73, 118,
    121, 126, 136, 149, 150, 151
Paris, © GrandPalaisRmn (musée du Louvre) / photo Thierry Le Mage:
    figs 11, 52, 146, 147; photo Hervé Lewandowski: figs 33, 86; photo
    Michel Urtado: figs 74, 145
Private collections: figs 51, 132, 137, 138
Rome, © Deutsches Archäologisches Institut (DAI) / photo H. Behrens:
    fig. 30
Rotterdam, © Collection Museum Boijmans Van Beuningen, on loan from
    Stichting Museum Boijmans Van Beuningen (previously collection
    Koenigs) / photo Studio Tromp: fig. 153

San Lorenzo de El Escorial, © Royal Library of Monastery of El Escorial,
    National Heritage: figs 107, 108
The Hague, © RKD – Netherlands Institute for Art History: figs 12, 104
Vatican City, © Fabbrica di San Pietro in Vaticano / photo Mallio Falcioni:
    fig. 113
Vatican City, © Governorate of the Vatican City State – Directorate of
    the Vatican Museums: figs 31, 36, 48, 49, 60, 61, 71, 93, 96, 158; ©
    Vatican Museums / Scala, Florence: figs 42, 45, 46, 100
Vienna, © The ALBERTINA Museum: figs 81, 82, 143
Windsor, © Royal Collection Enterprises Limited 2025 / Royal Collection
    Trust: figs 14, 18, 77, 79, 91, 106, 130, 166

© Cecil Gould: fig. 148
© Luka Pajovic: fig. 157
The collages (figs 152 and 155) were made by Vannessa Timmermans

Permission has been requested from the copyright holders for the
    manipulation of the coloured detail images. The following images
    have been used: 4, 5, 10, 14, 18, 19, 27, 43, 53, 62, 65, 82, 90, 92, 101,
    106, 115, 131, 140, 141, 143, 156, 160, 165

Colophon

This book was published to accompany the exhibition *Michelangelo and Men* at Teylers Museum in Haarlem from 15 October 2025 to 25 January 2026.

Authors
Eric Boot
Klazina Botke
Raymond Carlson
Marieke van den Doel
Terry van Druten
Martin Gayford
Paul Joannides
Michael Rocke
Jennifer Sliwka

Editing
Klazina Botke
Terry van Druten
Martin Gayford
assisted by Eric Boot

Image research
Eric Boot

Image editing
Fotorama

Translation Dutch-English
Ted Alkins

Copy-editing
Derek Scoins

Project management
Hadewych Van den Bossche (Hannibal Books)
Jessica Voorwinde assisted by Eric Boot (Teylers Museum)

Design
Jef Cuypers

Printing & binding
Printer Trento, Italy

Publisher
Gautier Platteau

ISBN 978 94 6494 197 5
D/2025/11922/23
NUR 642

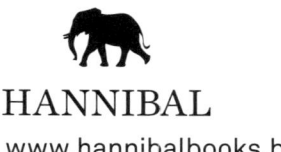

www.hannibalbooks.be

www.teylersmuseum.nl

Cover images

Michelangelo, *Seated Male Nude (ignudo) for the Sistine Chapel Ceiling*, c. 1511. Haarlem, Teylers Museum, inv. A 027

Michelangelo, *Studies for Saint Lawrence for the Last Judgement*, c. 1534–1538. Haarlem, Teylers Museum, inv. A 023

Backcover image

Michelangelo, *Studies for Haman for the Sistine Chapel Ceiling*, c. 1511. Haarlem, Teylers Museum, inv. A 016

This publication was made possible by

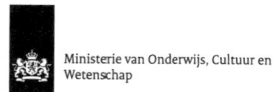
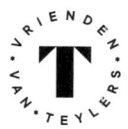

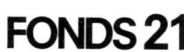
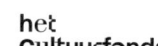
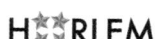
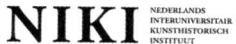

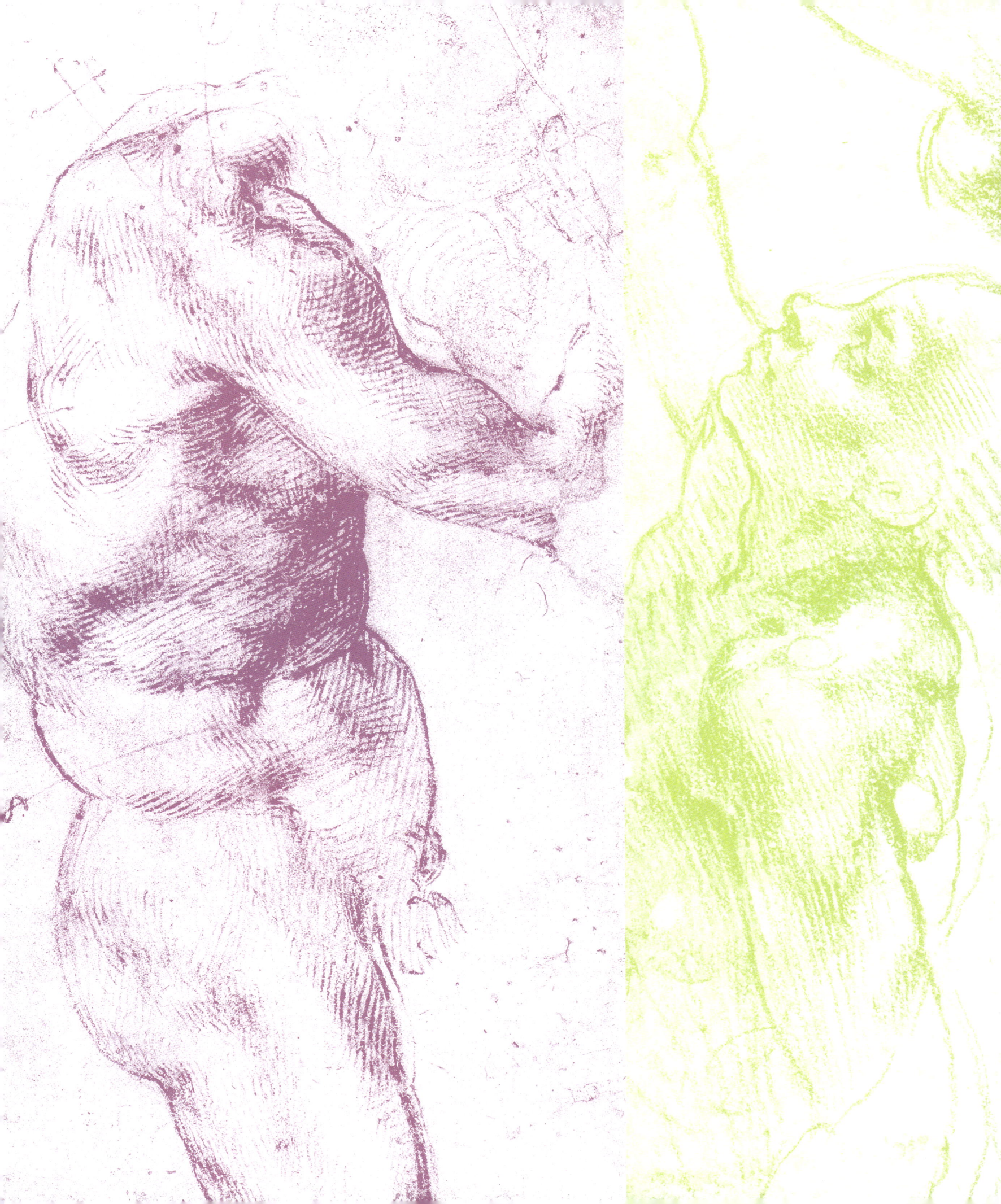

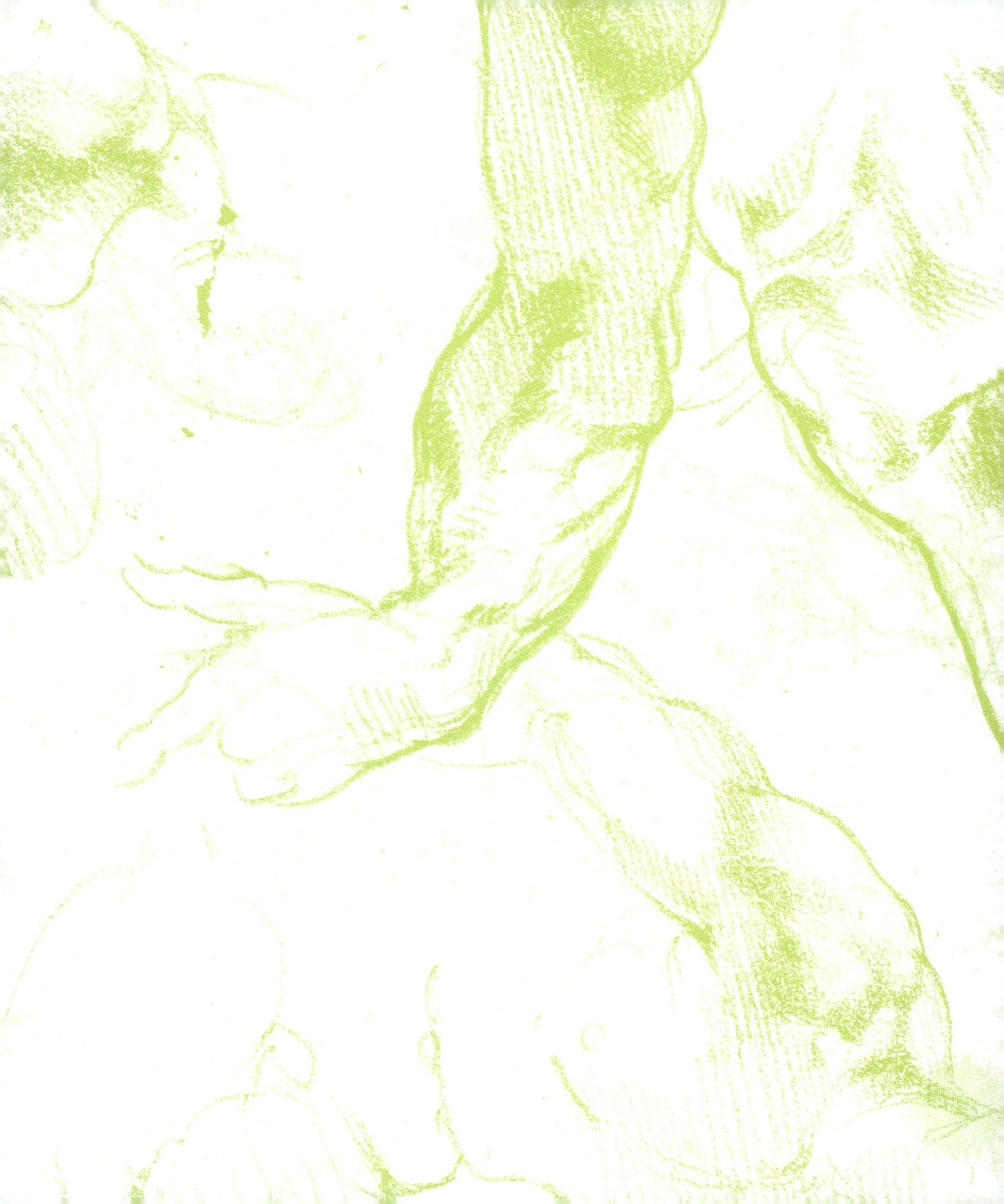

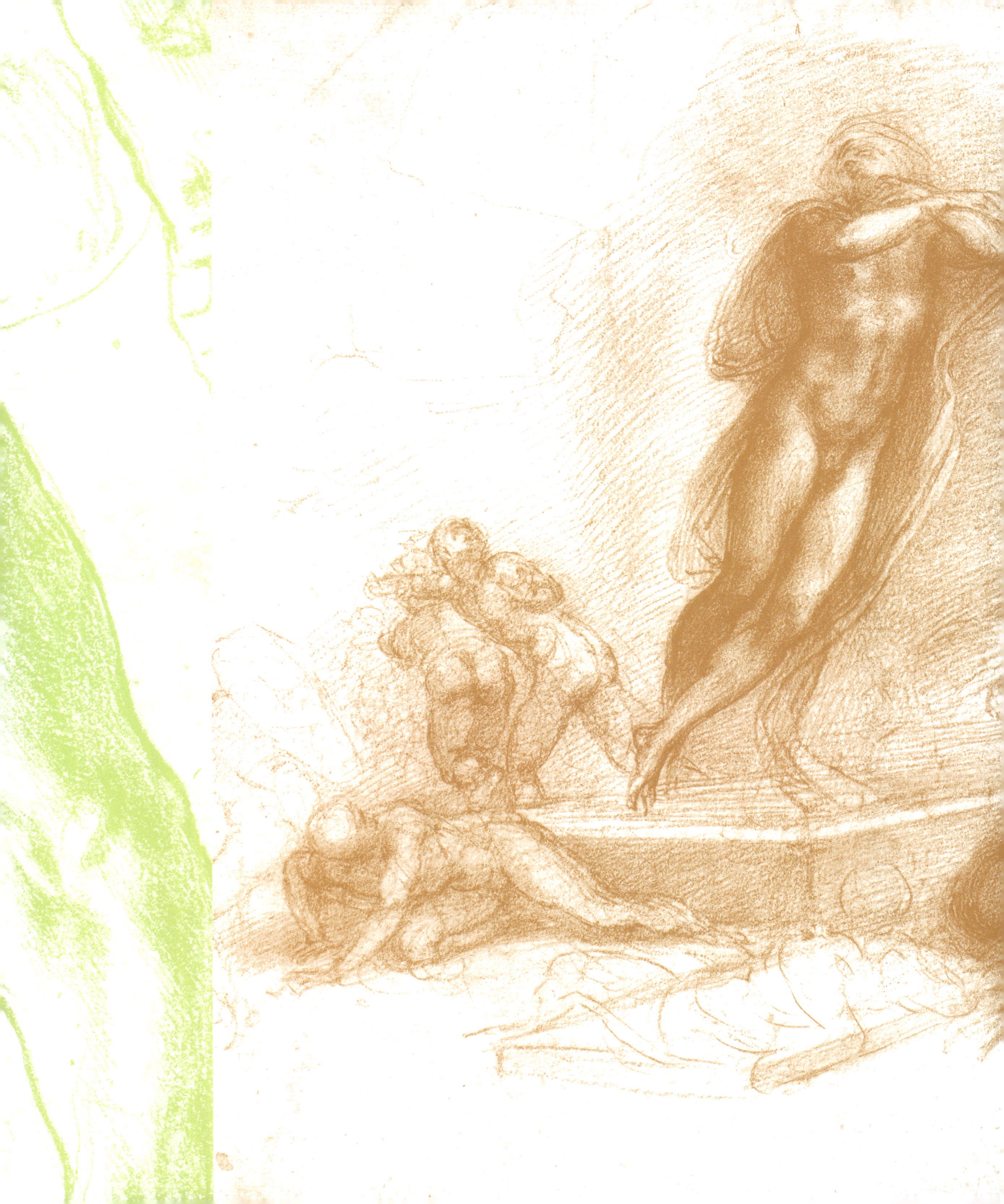

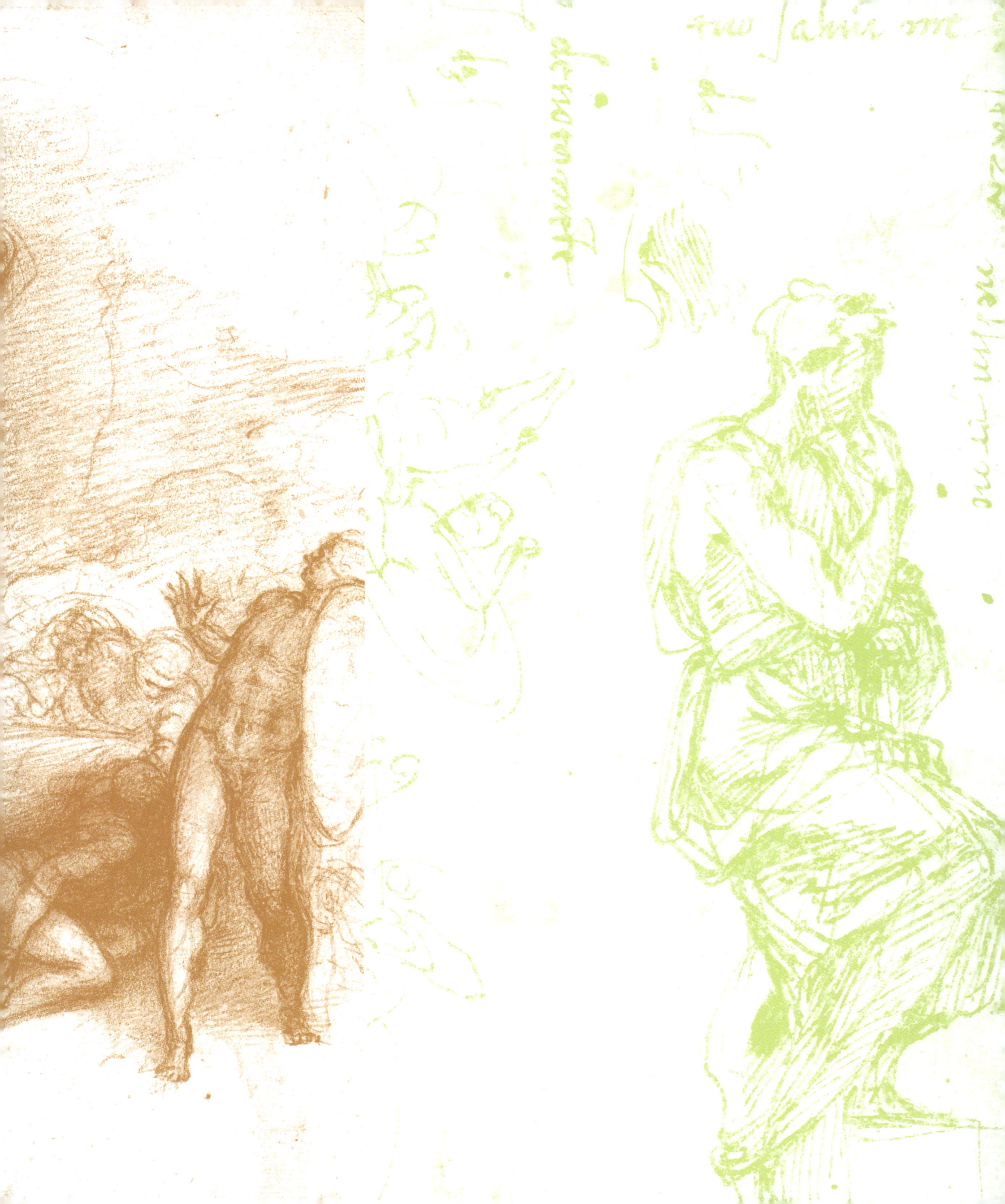

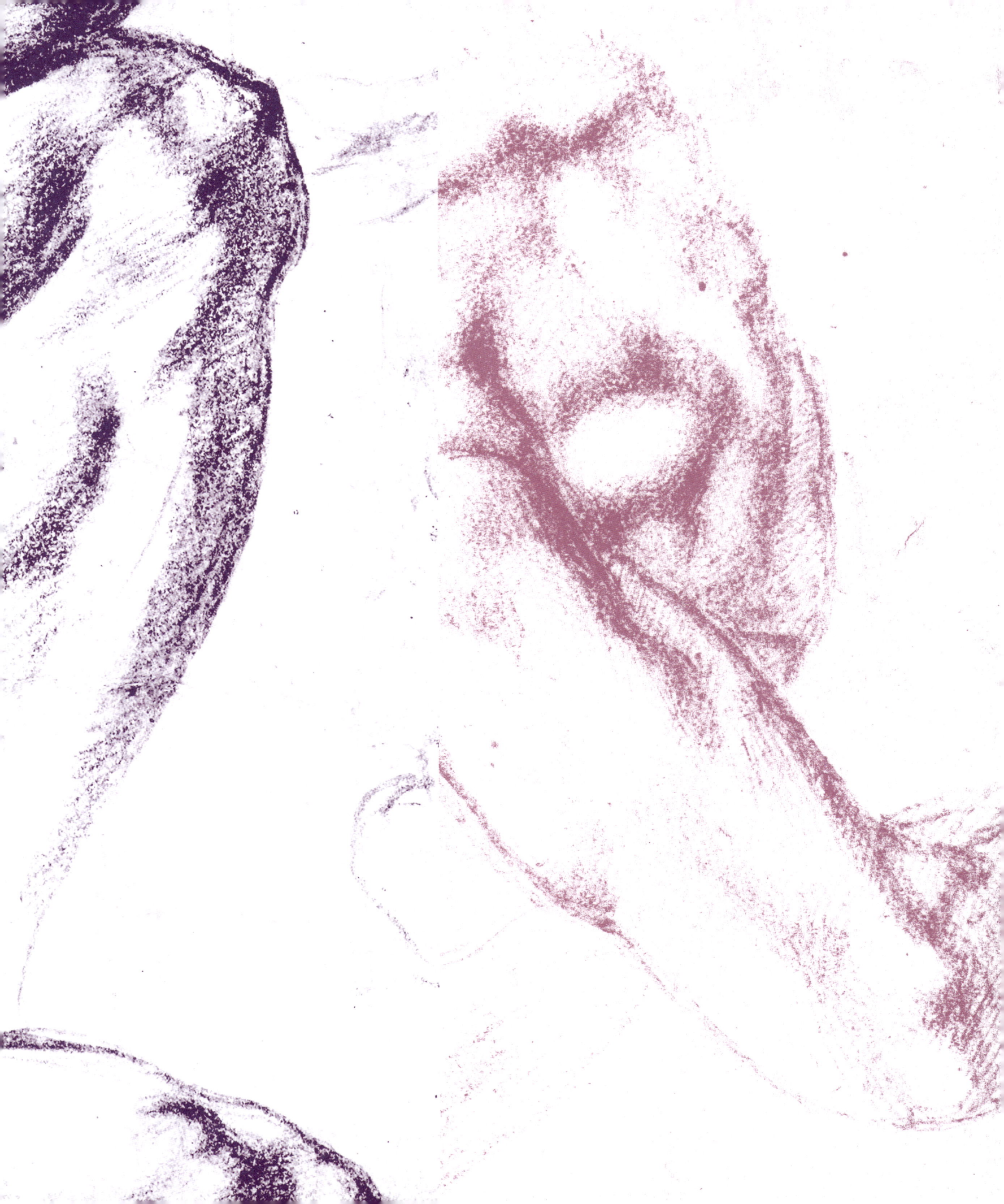

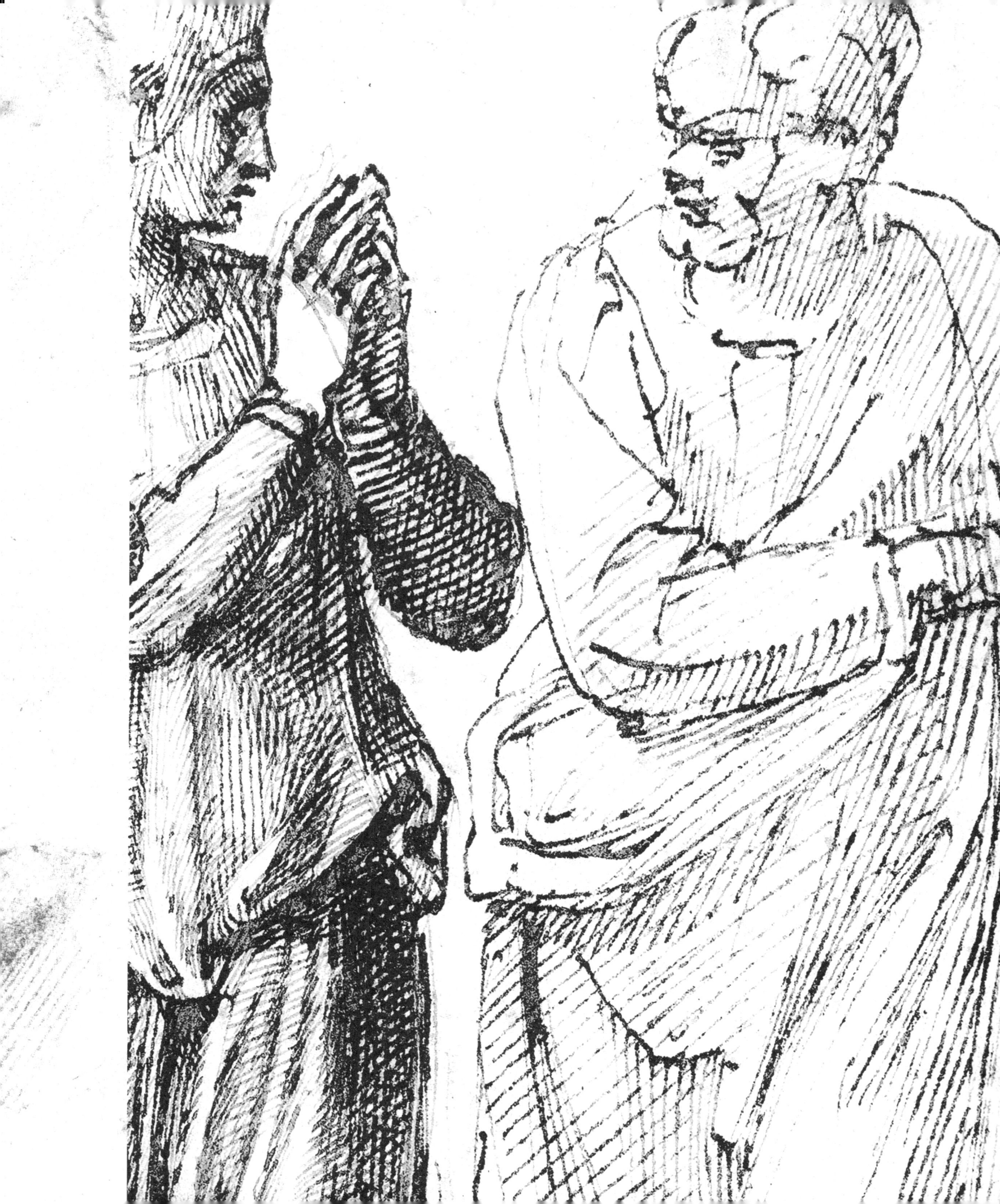